Sue Williamson

*For my children, Amanda,*
*Neil and Kate, and their children,*
*Sebastian, Wylie and Tess*

# Sue Williamson

## Life and Work

edited by Mark Gevisser

SKIRA

*Cover*
*Who is Johannes?: Johannesburg*
2009
*Other Voices, Other Cities* series
Pigment inks on archival cotton rag paper
Dimensions variable

*Art Director*
Marcello Francone

*Design*
Luigi Fiore

*Editorial Coordination*
Emma Cavazzini

*Editing*
Anna Albano

*Layout*
Barbara Galotta

First published in Italy in 2015 by
Skira Editore S.p.A.
Palazzo Casati Stampa
via Torino 61
20123 Milano
Italy
www.skira.net



The volume reproduces upon authorisation of Professor Pumla Gobodo-Madikizela the conversation held between her and Sue Williamson on April 10, 2015.

Printed and bound in Italy.
First edition

ISBN: 978-88-572-2867-9

Distributed in USA, Canada, Central & South America by Rizzoli International Publications, Inc., 300 Park Avenue South, New York, NY 10010, USA.
Distributed elsewhere in the world by Thames and Hudson Ltd., 181A High Holborn, London WC1V 7QX, United Kingdom.

*Acknowledgements*
Sue Williamson would like to thank all those who have participated in so many ways over the years in the making of the works documented in this book.

In the making of the book itself, Mark Gevisser has been a remarkable and patient editor; the editorial contributors, Chika Okeke-Agulu, Pumla Gobodo-Madikizela and Ciraj Rassool have provided illuminating essays and interviews; Liza Essers and all at the Goodman Gallery are thanked for their ongoing support; Penny Siopis gave insights and advice; my assistants Christine Cronje and latterly, Rachel Kelly have been invaluable in the preparation of the material for Skira, and the collaboration with Skira initiated by Edoardo Ghizzoni, has been a most stimulating process.

The editor and artist would like to thank the following people for permission to cite from their works: Karen Milbourne, for an extract from "Where are the bodies? Interment and the Poetics of Absence", presented at the 54th Annual Conference of the African Studies Association, November 17, 2011; Nic Dawes, for an extract from "Sue Williamson and the Trauma of History", in *Sue Williamson, Selected Work*; Donna Ruth Brenneis, Shahena Wingate-Pearse, and David Philip Publishers for an extract from *The Truth is on the Walls*, by Naz Gool-Ebrahim; Anthony Bond for an extract from *The Boundary Rider* catalogue of the 9th Biennale of Sydney; Jane Taylor, for an extract of her speech at the opening of *Truth Games* at the Dakawa Art Centre in Grahamstown in July 1999; Okwui Enwenzor, for an extract from "'Better Lives', Marginal Selves: Framing the Current Reception of Contemporary South African Art", in Sue Williamson's *South African Art Now*.

Sue Williamson is extremely grateful to the sponsors of this monograph

GOODMAN GALLERY
A4 Art Foundation
Josie Grindrod
Jennifer Morrison

# Contents

*Chika Okeke-Agulu*

# Foreword
# Sue Williamson, Art and the Ethical Imperative

Two remarkable events took place in the South African art world of 1989. The first was Albie Sachs' comments at a conference organized for an exhibition of sixteen artists from Mozambique, Angola, Zimbabwe and South Africa at the Kulturhuset in Stockholm. The second was the publication of the book, *Resistance Art in South Africa*, edited by Sue Williamson.

Sachs' comments were developed into a paper called *Preparing Ourselves for Freedom*. Controversial at the time, they have since become justifiably legendary because the author, as one of the most visible white South Africans in the leadership of the African National Congress, believed that with the dawn of freedom so near, art had to recalibrate its relationship with political doctrine and rethink its own necessity. Sachs' argument was that with the end of apartheid—contemporary South African art should chart a new direction and cease to be the instrument of a struggle that had successfully run its course. Rather than holding on to the functional imperative of 1980s art, it should recover the lost values of ambiguity, complexity and beauty for its own sake. Artistic imagination, said Sachs, now needed to be called up to counter apartheid's ugliness, by making the world anew.

Sue Williamson's book was a survey of work done over the previous decade. There are enough examples in it to appreciate why Sachs saw an urgent need for change. Two years previously, in 1987, there had been a "Culture in Another South Africa" conference in Amsterdam, where participants had ramped up the call for the international cultural boycott of the apartheid state, and for a more engaged contemporary art scene. And yet *Resistance Art in South Africa* shows us that, for the many works which confront directly the racist and oppressive machinery of apartheid, there are others that offer more complicated views of both the human condition and the dramatic formal gesture. While Paul Stopforth's plaster sculpture *George Botha* (1977) and Manfred p. 8
Zylla's participatory *Before and After* drawings (1982) set the tone of hard-hitting resistance art, others are indicative of the vastly different range of thematic and stylistic preoccupations of artists presented in Williamson's survey: Johannes Maswanganyi's funny, frank wood portraits of white and black leaders, for example, or Andries Botha's woven enigmatic sculptures.

Given its title, one might mistake Williamson's book as a collection of work produced in response to the Amsterdam declaration or, before that, to the resolutions of the "Culture and Resistance" festival in Botswana in 1982: that is, the very kind of work that Sachs declared unwelcome in a soon-to-be-free South Africa. However, the book is as much an account of resistance art in the 1980s as it is a manifesto on Williamson's part for an expanded horizon of formal possibilities within late twentieth-century South African art. It is, moreover, and crucially, a testimony to Williamson's understanding of the artistic life as an imaginative journey propelled by an ethical imperative and faith in art's signifying power.

The call for art to participate in the work of progressive social and political movements relies on a fundamental perception of the work of artists as much more than the production of things that justify themselves solely by their formal affect and aesthetic condition. If the primary task of the anti-apartheid movement was the attainment of a better society shorn of the terrors of a morally bankrupt regime, then artists who shared in this conviction imagined their works as valuable principally to the extent that they were ethical gestures: catalysts for the common good. Clearly this contradicts and rejects the twentieth-century modernist preoccupation with the implication of Immanuel Kant's notion of aesthetic autonomy: the understanding of aesthetic experience as self-referential, without any value beyond itself. We might call this counter-trend "aesth-ethics": a fundamental and synergistic fusion of aesthetics and ethics that reflects the widespread African (and equally worldwide) insistence on the pursuit of the beautiful (aesthetics) and the good (ethics) as a unitary endeavor. This principle can be best illustrated in the Igbo word and idea, *mma*, which simultaneously means beautiful/pretty, and good in the ethical sense. Thus although the desire to seek sensorial beauty (*ichọmma*) implies a preoccupation with physical appearance and optical impression, with absolute form, to be good (*idi mma*) also connotes the condition of being good *and* beautiful. This understanding of the deep connection between formal quality or condition and moral/ethical state is not unique to the Igbo. For the Yoruba have also argued for this relationship between aesthetics and ethics even more emphatically with the aphorism: "Iwalewa"—character *is* beauty.

Behind this lexical conflation and philosophical layering, I want to suggest, is the same principle that has always driven those artists who see their work—concerned as it may be with the problems of aesthetics and style—as expressive acts tasked with examining, prognosticating, commenting, or meditating on the human condition, all in the hope that such gestures can contribute in some meaningful way to the making or at the very least the imagining of a better world. Such contemporary artists would include Obiora Udechukwu in Nigeria, Ibrahim El Salahi in the Sudan, Inji Efflatoon in Egypt, Mozambique's Malangatana Ngwenya and, beyond Africa, artists such as Leon Golub, Dread Scott and Hans Haacke. This simultaneous engagement with aesthetics and ethics has, in fact, given us some of the most profound reasons why contemporary art matters; why art in the hands of artists of substance attains both dimensions of *mma*—the aesthetic and the ethical—as it reaches for full elaboration, and its ultimate condition.

Sue Williamson is one such artist, and this idea of aesth-ethics is crucial to an understanding of her work. She has, from the beginning of her career, assiduously sought the most compelling formal language with which to articulate and express ideas that in many ways exposed the moral bankruptcy of apartheid political culture and racist ideology. This has earned her a place at the leading edge of contemporary South African art. Compared to her contemporaries, she is a master of subtle

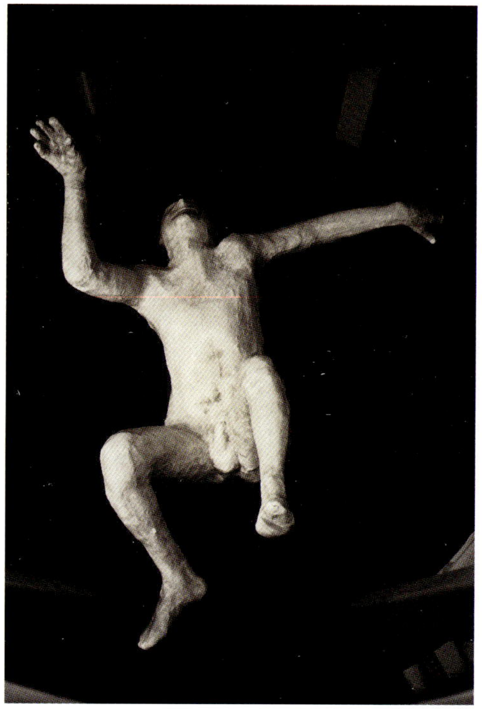

Paul Stopforth
*George Botha*, 1977
Plaster of Paris, wax
Life size

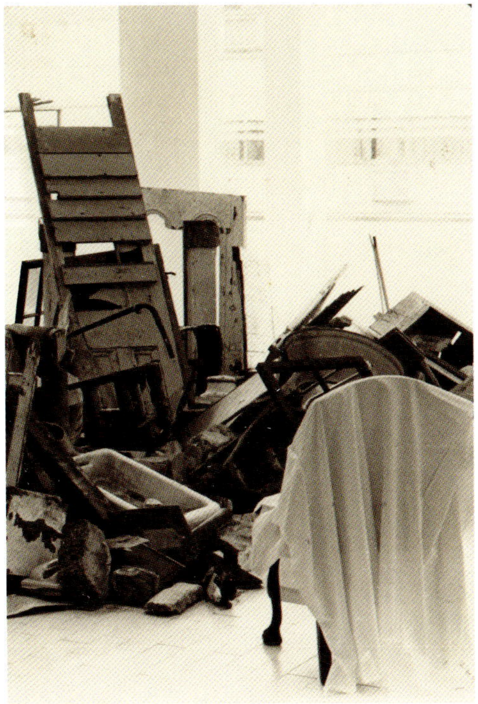

*The Last Supper*
1981
Found objects, sound, photographs
Installation view (detail)
The Gowlett Gallery, Cape Town

outrage: her work simultaneously excites us for its exploration of medium and process, and moves us to contemplate the meaning of community, citizenship and subjectivity in South Africa and other societies scarred by extreme imbalances of power.
This is evident in the series of works for which she gained early critical attention in apartheid-era South Africa; works that although they were included in *Resistance Art in South Africa* stretched the horizons of "resistance art", invariably extending the meaning and imaginative possibilities of the "culture as a weapon of struggle" mandate.

Consider for instance the structural ordinariness and conceptual power of her first major work, *The Last Supper* (1981), a gallery installation of rubble gathered from the demolition sites of Cape Town's District Six and surrounded by six chairs draped in white borrowed from Manley Villa, the home of the Ebrahim family in District Six, that had been marked for destruction as part of the racist government's promulgation of its Group Areas Act. Three photographs on the wall of the Gowlett Gallery showed the Ebrahims celebrating Eid in their home. At a time when South African photographers and journalists testified to apartheid's systemic violence by depicting District Six homes turned to rubble, or the traumatised inhabitants menaced by demolition crews—powerful testimonials no doubt—Williamson chose instead to show a family celebrating the Eid in the shadow of eviction and pending destruction of their home. Using the art gallery space, Williamson staged a confrontation between the detritus of an anxious state's terror, and a family's untarnished dignity. In this meditation on the apartheid regime's violence, and a community's quiet gestures of resistance to it, the artist gave us the first insight into her gift for works of tremendous poetic power, using relatively simple methods, found object and images. In *A Few South Africans* (1983–7), perhaps her best-known work, she produced photo-etched portraits of women at the frontline of the anti-apartheid movement; each picture shown in screenprinted decorated frames and symbolically rich matting inspired by aspects of black visual cultures. And in a major work that memorialized the crumbling of apartheid's walls, *For Thirty Years Next to his Heart* (1990), she colour-copied and displayed, in forty-nine artist-designed frames, the complete pages of a black man's passbook, perhaps the most infamous document produced by apartheid. In these landmarks of anti-apartheid art, she used the photographic image or politically charged document to insist on the dignity, substance and courage of both the oppressed black South Africans and their white allies.

pp. 10, 31-9

pp. 81-7

Williamson has continued to explore, untangle and lay bare moral knots and ethical complexes in today's world, just as she had during the decade of "resistance art". This clearly suggests that she did not quite heed Sachs' call for a radical change in post- apartheid art. She did not believe, I suggest, that the work of engaged contemporary art is ever done simply because a particular political ideology and system had expired in her homeland and in the human society.

In any case, if Williamson responded to Sachs' call in 1989, it took the form of reimagining her community as the human family, not just the post-apartheid South African world still scarred by its traumatic past and new challenges. One outcome of the racist regime's siege mentality and its vigorous control of the physical borders of South Africa and the psyche of its peoples, is that even the white artists who had opportunities to train and travel overseas tended to focus their work on South Africa's dire political and social conditions, while keeping to the normative formal genres of sculpture, painting, and documentary photography. Williamson's formal and technical procedures are as sophisticated and rigorous as that of leading contemporary artists elsewhere in the world: what she brings, additionally, is her commitment to living life in the shadow of apartheid, and to trying to grapple with this through her art. In this way, her work is similar to that of William Kentridge, Penny Siopis, David Koloane, Jane Alexander, Manfred Zylla, Paul Stopforth, and other prominent South African artists.

But with the arrival of the post-apartheid Rainbow Nation, and the ongoing difficult work of building a multiracial, just society from the ashes of apartheid, Williamson's work tracked the dense contours of this process, even as she expanded the boundary of her community and sphere of interest. In so doing, she has vigorously kept to the "aesth-ethics" principles on which her early work was founded. She continues to make compelling images that derive their formal and conceptual power from their ability to raise fundamental questions about our world today. We see this in work that excavates the archives of South
pp. 105, Africa's slave trade (*Messages from the Moat*, 1997),
107-9 or examines the apartheid-era moral quagmires exposed during the Truth and Reconciliation Commission (*Truth Games*, 2001), or documents
pp. 129, African immigrants' experience in a time of growing
135, 137, xenophobia especially among poor black South
139, 141-5 Africans (*Better Lives*, 2003). We see it, too, in work that maps fraught boundaries of ethnic nationalist claims and patriarchal political power (*Pass the* pp. 176-7
*Parcel, Jacob*, 2007), or catalyses articulations of popular resistance to globalisation and dictatorial power in Cairo, Havana and elsewhere (*What About* pp. 184-191
*El Max?*, 2005; *The Havana Series*, 2011; and *Other* pp. 193-7
*Voices, Other Cities*, since 2009). Williamson's pp. 199-221
commitment to the ethical imperative and formal rigour, these works show, remains inalienable.

In these recent works, Williamson reaffirms her unique ability to call up visually impressive sculptural and multimedia installations, and to exploit the affective power of mass-mediated images and texts in order to convey thoughts and ideas of profound social significance. With confident formal eloquence her mature work takes sides with and champions the cause of marginalised communities in democratic South Africa and in her imagined global community. It leaves us in no doubt about her enduring commitment to the rhetoric of the image, and the ethical grounds of the creative imagination.

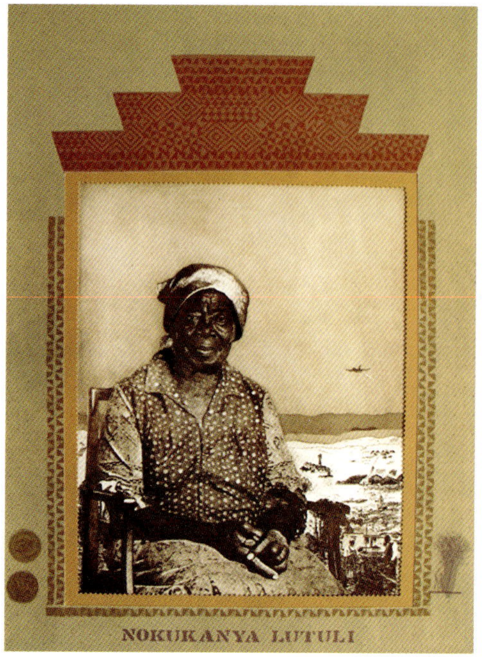


*Nokukanya Lutuli*
1983
*A Few South Africans* series
Photo etching / screenprint
collage
100 x 70 cm

*Cynthia Gabriel*
2003
*Better Lives* series
Pigment inks on cotton rag paper
144 x 112 cm

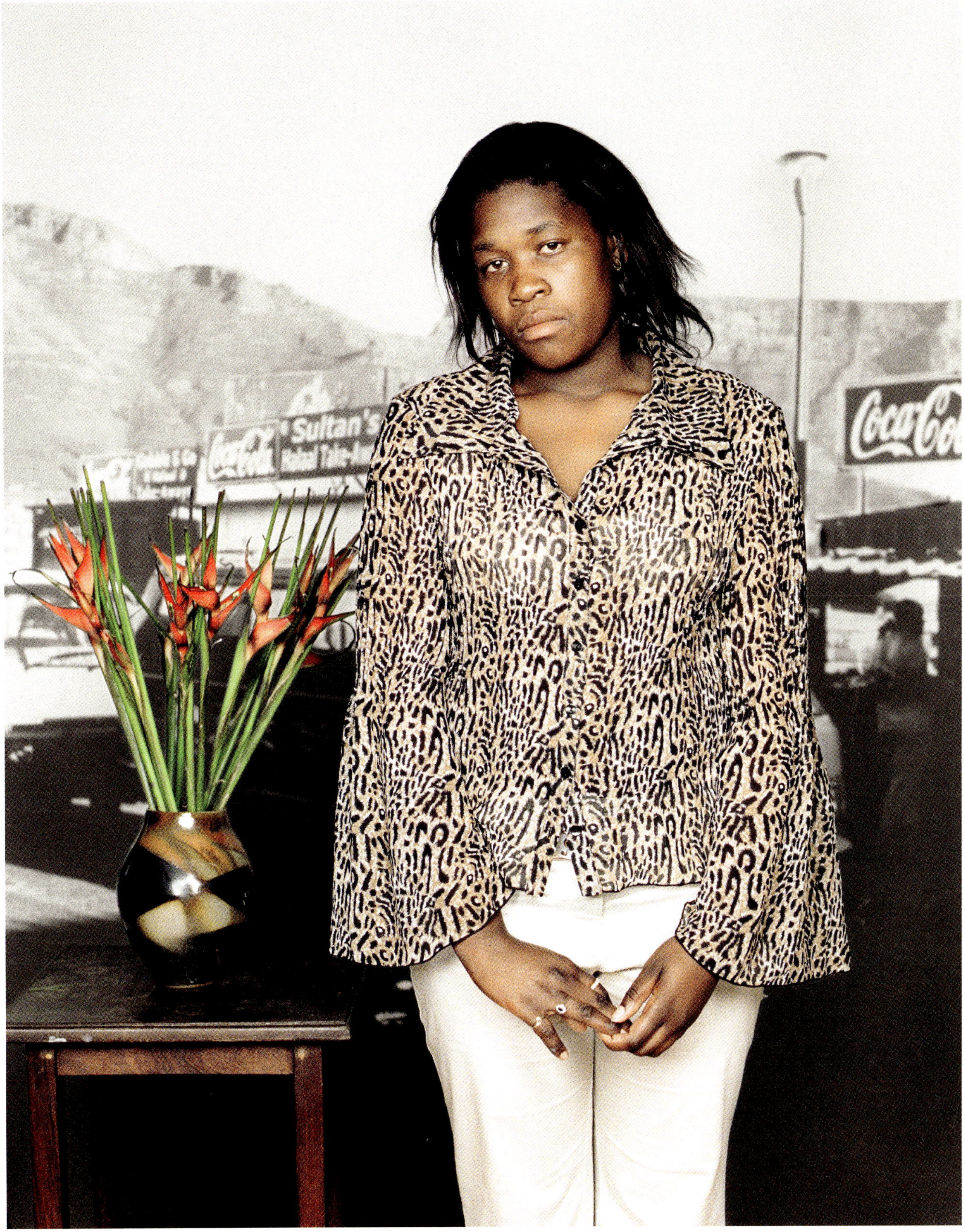

*Mark Gevisser*

# Sue Williamson: An Introduction to her Life and her Work

*A jagged fault line cuts through recent South African history. It is a year, 1976, the year the children of Soweto decided to resist their oppression. Peaceful protest was met with police gunfire, and soon Soweto was aflame ... I was one of those jolted out of lethargy by Soweto, and this book concerns the way artists responded to the truths made clear by the events of 1976.*

With these words, Sue Williamson began the introduction to her path-breaking 1989 book, *Resistance Art in South Africa*, a survey of the vibrant, edgy art scene from which she herself had emerged. In the years following the 1976 Soweto uprising, Williamson became an effective activist, a leader of the newly formed multiracial Women's Movement for Peace. She also furthered her art skills by embarking on an Advanced Diploma in Printmaking at the University of Cape Town's Michaelis School of Fine
pp. 10, 31-9 Art, and made *A Few South Africans* (1983–7), her memorable series of portraits, rendered in an iconic heroic style, of South African women in struggle. She had turned 40 in 1981 but all at once, in the tumult of those years, she was thinking of herself for the first time as both an artist and an activist.

It was in this labile environment that artists such as William Kentridge and Marlene Dumas were schooled, at liberal South African universities, steeped in the preoccupations with struggle and justice that would suffuse the work of their illustrious careers. But it was also in this environment that a particularly engaged notion of culture was developed; one in which, Williamson writes, "there would be a growing realisation amongst anti-apartheid forces that cultural resistance was a tool of immense power"; in which art, in the African tradition, would have a specific function—in this instance, "of changing society." These were certainly not new concepts at the tail end of a revolutionary century. But they generated a particular energy in South Africa: because cultural expression could carry messages that would otherwise be banned by the apartheid regime, and because "cultural work" provided a bridge for encounter across such deeply inscribed racial boundaries. They created the hothouse that germinated a remarkable generation of artists that—like Williamson herself—would gain international repute once South Africa re-entered the global arena, after decades of isolation.

In *Resistance Art in South Africa,* Williamson profiled artists, and also documented the "political art" of posters, t-shirt designs and graffiti. She made some of this herself: her t-shirt of the banned Freedom Charter p. 112
remains one of the most recognisable objects of the era, and one is now in the collection of the Museum of Modern Art in New York. Because of her immersion in the moment, much of her work from this time—such as the portraits in *A Few South Africans*—functions as historical artefact, or even as historical fetish, holding within it something of the spirit and emotion of the time. But it is much more than that. Williamson

is now in her mid-seventies, and her work remains compelling. She has risen above the didacticism and temporality of propaganda while—more than most of her contemporaries—keeping to the principles of that era. These include a commitment to challenging power and injustice, and to working with people rather than simply making art about them; an engagement with society and the forces that govern it; and a belief that the transformative nature of art is in the way it raises consciousness.

Williamson has adhered to a documentarian's credo of bearing witness and serving as a moral conscience. But she also finds new forms—aesthetic and technological—to renew her commitment to the above principles, and to draw us into the narratives she forges out of text and image and object. One thinks, for example, of how she reimagines the
pp. 14, 166, 168-73 tradition of African studio portraiture in *Better Lives* (2003), with her videos about immigrants to South Africa in a time of xenophobia. Her subjects stand very still and gaze without speaking into the camera as we—and they— hear their voices talking about their lives. Williamson's work is also emotionally affecting: her own empathic connection with her subjects pulls
pp. 155-65 us into their stories, as in *From the Inside* (2000–3),
pp. 235-43 about people living with AIDS, and *There's something I must tell you* (2013), an intergenerational dialogue between grandmothers and "granddaughters". Her commitment means, too, that she returns to her subjects: several of the women she revisits in this last work she had first encountered three decades
pp. 10, 31-9 previously, in *A Few South Africans*.

Trained not primarily in the art academy but as a journalist and a copywriter, Williamson puts great stock in effective communication. Working in advertising on Madison Avenue in New York in the 1960s taught her, she says, "to listen carefully to what people say, and to find the right words to reach your audience." In her career, Williamson has worked across media: from printmaking and photography to video and sculptural installation. She has also made some of her most significant pieces working with a colour laser photocopier, and she has explored the medium of graffiti too, building on the "writing on the walls" she documented in *Resistance Art in South Africa*. In all these media, she has maintained her interest in the graphic strategies of communication she came to understand so well through working in the advertising industry. Her work must communicate effectively: "the right words". She wants us to "get it", because by so doing we become involved in the people and issues she presents, and we leave the gallery or museum space engaged ourselves, alive to the subtexts and contexts of what appears on the surface.

• • •

Sue Williamson was born in Lichfield, England, in 1941; a war baby who remembers having to scuttle into a shelter during a London air-raid. Her father, Frank Nott, was in the construction trade; her mother, Mary Hawkins, was a teacher. Frank and Mary met in Palestine, where he was building and she was teaching. They returned to England just before the war started and, like many, decided to flee the gloom after it ended: they chose South Africa because Frank's company had opened an office in Johannesburg.

Later, when Williamson decided she wanted to be a journalist, she knew that as a woman it would be difficult to get access to the newsroom, but "I always thought I could do whatever I wanted to." In this respect she was not unlike both her mother and her

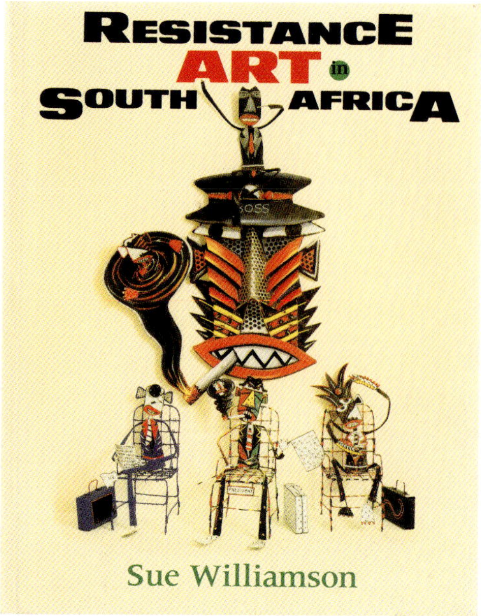


Cover of *Resistance Art in South Africa* by Sue Williamson

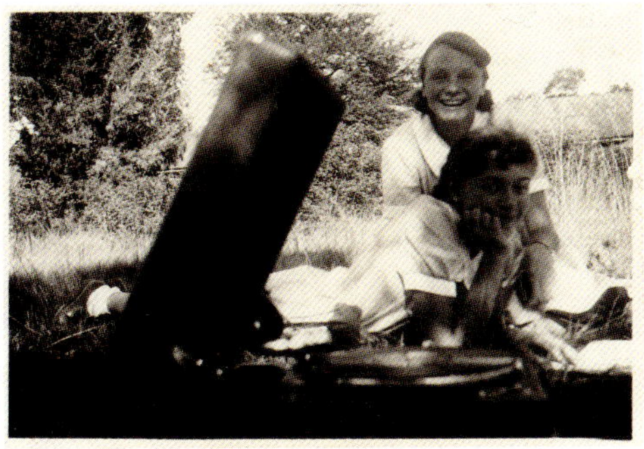

Schoolgirl friends in an early Williamson photograph

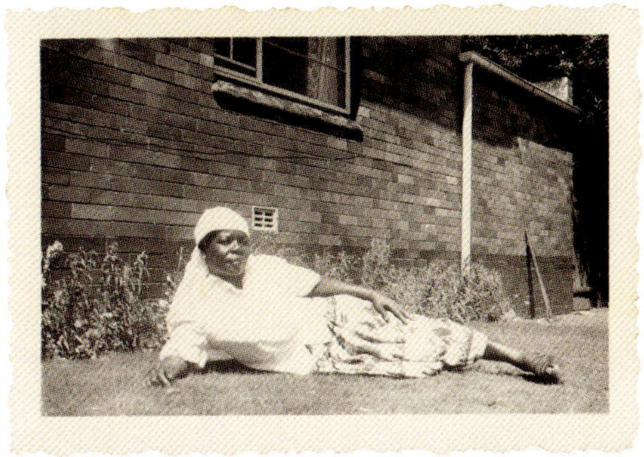

Vesta, the family's domestic worker, poses for the camera

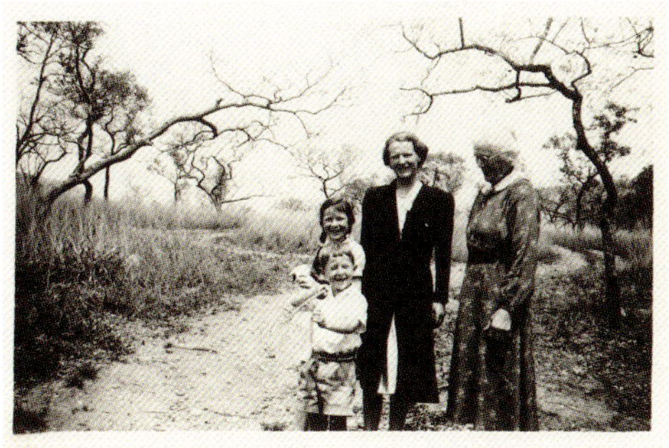

Williamson with her family in the Kruger Park

grandmother, both of whom had resisted convention. Bessie Hardy, her grandmother, had gone to America in 1902, in the job that young women of her class often found if they needed an income and an excuse to travel: a governess. Bessie married her employer, a widower; later, her daughter Mary went alone as a young woman to Palestine, after training as a teacher.

Having arrived in South Africa in June 1948, Frank and Mary Nott raised their family in Florida, a modest suburb to the west of Johannesburg, where the kids roamed free on the streets and over the *koppies*. Black people were around, Williamson remembers, but "just as part of daily life rather than, in any way, a group whom I understood as having rights denied to them." When DF Malan's Afrikaner National Party won the general election later that year on the ticket of "apartheid", what Williamson remembers most was a fear of being forced to speak Afrikaans, a language she had not yet mastered because she was an immigrant.

As a boarder at Potchefstroom Girls High in the Western Transvaal, Williamson excelled at English and loved reading; she had no noted aptitude for art. She was encouraged in photography by her father, who lent her his folding Kodak, and she started a photographic society at school. The young photographer had an eye for composition: the close-up of a portable wind-up gramophone on the lawn while school friends loll in soft focus behind; the Notts' domestic worker Vesta reclining rather awkwardly for the camera in the style of a *Drum* magazine cover girl. Most of her images capture girls in gymslips, posing on lawns or dabbling in streams: they could have been taken in the Home Counties rather than the dry Transvaal veld.

There is another photograph in the album, taken by Frank Nott of his children Sue and Stephen with their mother Mary and grandmother Bessie. In this image—from a visit to the Kruger National Park—the wintry African veld is evident. Particularly given the somewhat formal dresses the two women are wearing, one gets the sense of an English family's displacement into the African bush—and, if one knows a bit about the people being photographed, of three generations of female adventurers.

Williamson's own high school ambition was "to travel the world, meeting people and writing their stories." After completing a shorthand-typing course, she got a job at the *Natal Daily News* taking dictation from correspondents, cutting the clipping files, and doing the shipping news. It was 1959, and riots had broken out in response to forced removals in the mixed neighbourhood of Cato Manor, a symptom of these intensely troubled years and a premonition—in the police crackdown—of what would happen at Sharpeville the following year. Williamson wanted to cover the conflict, but was told it was "too dangerous for a young woman." She butted her head against this glass ceiling for a while, and eventually gave up: she did not wish to write social news for the "Women's Pages", and she chose to change careers to advertising.

Despite her interest in journalism, she did not engage with the dramatic events taking place around her: Sharpeville, the launch of the armed struggle, the political trials that culminated in the Rivonia Trial and Nelson Mandela's life imprisonment: "I felt the Nationalist Party was all powerful, and did exactly what it wanted", she says. In this she was much like the vast majority of her white compatriots. She studied at night at the University of Natal for a bachelor's degree, and even though she majored in political science, she does not recall a single lecture dealing with the South African situation. She married very young, at 21, to a young businessman named Tony Williamson, and she pushed for them to go to New York in 1964: not, like many of their contemporaries, to escape the apartheid clampdown, but rather to advance their careers in a city that she had dreamed of while reading *The New Yorker* and watching *Breakfast at Tiffany's*. And, of course, she was in the ad-industry, beckoned by the allure of Madison Avenue.

The world she found was straight out of *Mad Men*—except, unlike Peggy Olsen, she was hired not as a secretary at first but as a copywriter from the get-go, at Norman, Craig & Kummel, one of the industry's wilder outliers. She moved, after a year, to the legendary Benton & Bowles at the Tishman Building at 666 5th Ave. Her accounts included Maxwell House coffee, Stardust bleach and Post cereals. A commercial for the United Nations Children's Fund (UNICEF) won her a Hollywood award for best public service commercial, "but on the whole, we didn't take it terribly seriously", she recalls. "Copy ideas were sometimes explored by rearranging the texts from fortune cookies served after lunch and ginseng cocktails at the Arirang House. Everyone was doing something else on the side." One of her colleagues was Israel Horowitz, who was writing *The Indian Wants the Bronx* in between generating ad copy for breakfast cereal.

Her "something else on the side" came to be art classes, on a whim more than anything else, when she met a Japanese *sumi* teacher through neighbours. Impatient, after a while, with the limits of expression allowed by the soft grey and black ink washes of *sumi*, she found her way to night classes at the venerable Art Students League of New York, and to a life drawing class with John Groth, who—like her—believed that artists should be in the world: he was a sporting artist, and had been at the frontline of the Spanish Civil War with Hemingway. He sent her onto the streets of the city, demanding at least fifty sketches a week.

Writing copy by day and drawing at night, Williamson began exploring New York's museums and galleries. She could slip from a side-door at the Tishman building right into the Museum of Modern Art opposite, and lose herself during lunch break, in Claude Monet's water lilies or, later, the soaked canvases of the colour field painters. She hung out in 1st Avenue diners, on Christopher Street and at the Village Gate listening to jazz. When she thought of South Africa at all it was as her childhood home, beautiful but horribly damaged. When she took maternity leave in 1969 to give birth to her first child, her daughter Amanda, she surprised herself by choosing not to go back to work, even though Benton & Bowles had kept her place for her: she wanted to focus on mothering—and on making art. And so she put a promising Madison Avenue career on hold for what was she thought might be her true vocation.

After Amanda turned one, she and Tony decided to return home: they wanted to raise their children around grandparents, and he managed to get a transfer to Johannesburg. They had two more children—Neil, and then Kate—and Williamson got a gig writing a column for the *Sunday Tribune*. It was satirical, and she provided both the words and a sketch: the one she remembers most vividly featured the prime minister, John Vorster, in a domestic

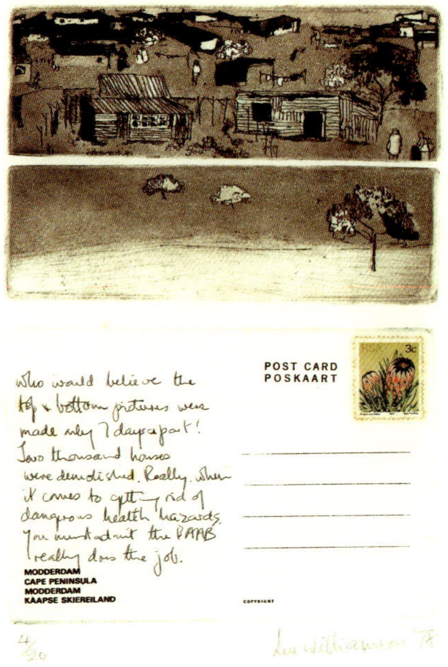


*Before and After*
1978
*The Modderdam Postcards*
Etching on paper, postage stamp, handwriting
38 x 32 cm

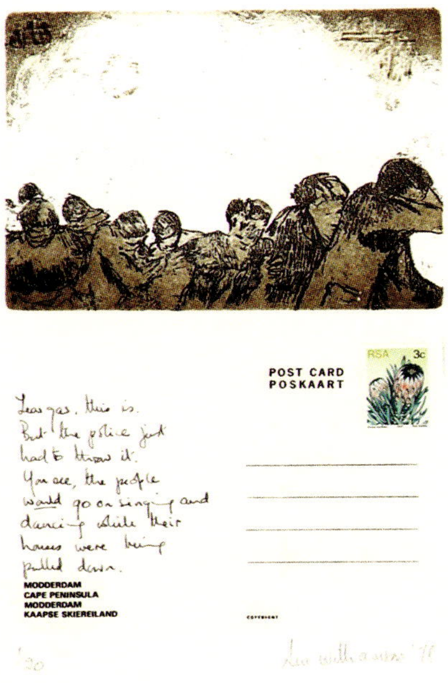


*Teargas*
1978
*The Modderdam Postcards*
Etching on paper, postage stamp, handwriting
38 x 32 cm

worker's pinafore, unsuccessfully applying for a passbook as "Vorsterina", and being summarily sent back to the homelands. As with so many liberal white South African women, her point of entry into the iniquities of apartheid was through the employment conditions of her own domestic staff. She was horrified at the bureaucratic hell involved in getting a valid passbook for her children's nanny, and then in keeping it in order. She began to feel that the subject of race was "the elephant in the room" in her white world. But it would take the Soweto uprising seven years after her return—with the townships on fire, with hundreds of schoolchildren dead and thousands more detained—to "jolt" her out of her "lethargy."

• • •

Sue Williamson recalls hearing word of a mass meeting at Cape Town's City Hall in the winter of 1976, once the uprising and violence had spread to the Cape from Soweto after the student revolt there. She tagged along, not expecting much. But the meeting was electric: chaired by the leftwing city councillor Eulalie Stott and featuring the writer Sindiwe Magona, it called for a non-racial women's movement, and Williamson found herself swept up by the idea. What had been bothering her most about her life back in South Africa was her lack of knowledge about how the majority lived: although she had done some voluntary art teaching in the township of Langa when she and Tony relocated to Cape Town in 1970, nothing much had come of it. Now she became a founder member of the Women's Movement for Peace (WMP), and what appealed to her most about it was its "encounter" aspect: she was working on a common project alongside black women who were her equals, rather than her employees or the beneficiaries of her good works.

Much of what they did was social, and took the form of a mini-defiance campaign: the women gathered in whites-only restaurants together to try to get served, share meals and talk, and argued with the management until they were thrown out. They broke the law by taking their children together to white beaches or parks. But their main objective was to change the existing system through action, and they focused primarily on the forced removal of "squatters", often the wives and children of male workers, who had "illegally" moved to the city from the Eastern Cape to be with their men, and to seek work themselves.

In August 1977, the authorities announced they were going to bulldoze a small informal settlement on Modderdam Road near the airport, and the WMP activists decided to join the protest: "I spent seven days watching the total demolition by state employees in bulldozers backed up by police of the 2000 houses of Modderdam", writes Williamson in *Resistance Art.* "Witnessing the cold brutality of this operation had a profound effect on my life."

Out of habit more than anything else, Williamson bore witness with her sketchpad. She had begun studying etching at the Art Students League of New York, and was now working with fellow printmakers at a well-equipped studio called the Graphic Workshop. Months later, struck by a solution of how to work with her sketches, she transferred some of her drawings onto etching plates and came up with a series she called *The Modderdam Postcards* (1978), a double image of the front and back of a postcard, placed one above the other. The "front" showed etched scenes of the destruction of Modderdam. On the "back" she stuck a three-cent stamp and printed "Modderdam,

Cape Peninsula", then hand wrote a message "sent" from a Bantu Affairs Administration Board official to a loved one or colleague. Thus, below an image of p. 17 a group of people running from a cloud of teargas, the "official" wrote: "Teargas, this is. But the police just had to throw it. You see, the people *would* go on singing and dancing while their houses were being pulled down."

Here was Williamson opposing her sensibilities, her ethics, to those of the white mainstream, as represented by the official whose voice she was ventriloquising. And so, for the first time in her life, she found herself swimming out of that mainstream. She no longer felt she belonged in the society from which she came. But she found her voice, and she found her subject.

Shortly after Modderdam was demolished, the state announced that it would bulldoze Crossroads, a larger and more settled community. At one of the large regular meetings held to protest the demolition, it was decided to mass-print one of Williamson's postcards and use it to raise consciousness about the settlement's impending plight. Within a week the card had been banned for distribution. Williamson laughs about the letter she received from the authorities in Pretoria: "'Although it is not without artistic merit, it fails to tell the whole story—that the people are there illegally.'"

*The Modderdam Postcards* was, in fact, the strongest work she had done to date. She had been etching landscapes up to this point, and had also been drawn to Carlos Castaneda's mystical books, very much in vogue at the time, and was making composite drawings out of symbols, harvested largely from Latin American iconography, representing dreamscapes. Her Castaneda prints are striking, but they are pastiche: in her own words, "inauthentic, not directly rooted in my experience." In transforming her Modderdam sketches into a series of etchings, though, she had discovered what she identified as "authenticity": "Because I was there, watching these houses being knocked down, taking things out for people, giving them lifts, little things you tried to do to alleviate very slightly what they were going through, I could make the *Modderdam Postcards* and not feel that I was doing so as an outside observer." One hears the voice of a white South African straining to find her place—her relevance—in her home country and in the struggle for its liberation. Out of this personal struggle emerged what was to become her life's work.

In the months to come, Williamson found herself spending most of her days in Crossroads: meeting and talking to people, planning protests, drawing, and looking. She began taking postcard-sized etching plates with her on these visits. Needling an image directly onto a plate, she would bite it in acid and print it back in the studio. In *Rev. Kani* (1981) she etched a Crossroads priest's makeshift church and screen-printed his own handwritten plea against the demolitions beneath it. Williamson gave the image a screen-printed frame of patterned orange, reminiscent of *shweshwe* wax print. She clearly saw style in Crossroads: in the aesthetic way the priest had papered the walls of his church with cat food labels, in the wrought iron fencing made from scrap, in the way people framed their own photographs with whatever was at hand, like gift-wrap or newspaper. More than anything, the *Rev. Kani* print suggests rootedness, the dense patterning of years. Once more, she was looking at the world differently to the white authorities

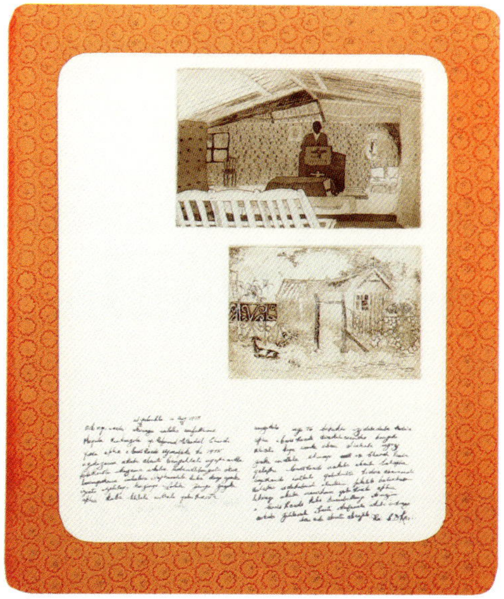

*Rev. Kani*
1981
Etching, screenprint and embossing on paper
65 x 50 cm

and the mainstream they represented. They saw Crossroads as a slum, populated by rootless transients who needed to go "home"; Williamson saw it as a place of innovation and even beauty, a community she admired.

In 1982, when Williamson went back to art school at Michaelis, her print-making tutor Jules van der Vijver urged her to delve deeper into Crossroads, and to "be bolder" in her work. Out of this—and the need to find out more, for herself, about the history of the
pp. 10, liberation struggle—came *A Few South Africans*,
31-9 which she would later print onto postcards and distribute not only through South Africa, but also the US and England.

Williamson had noticed the family photographs Crossroads residents put on their walls, and also the way they framed them out of cut-out gift-wrap and other cheap materials. At the same time, she had become aware that in the white daily newspapers, women considered worthy of a photograph were always white: wives of government ministers, or socialites or entertainment personalities. Black women seemed invisible.

This was brought home to her most forcefully one day when she picked up the *Christian Science Monitor*, an American publication, in the library of the University of Cape Town and saw the image of a dignified, serene black woman. The caption told her that the woman was Winnie Mandela.
p. 33 Williamson realised this was the first time she had ever seen a photograph of the wife of the imprisoned leader. She decided to remedy these deficiencies, in seventeen pieces, which she made over four years between 1983 and 1987: from an unknown domestic worker to Winnie Mandela herself. The process began with a photograph: if possible she took this portrait herself, but if not, she would use a found image. From this image she made a photo-etching on to a metal plate, and added more visual information by hand. She extended the narrative with silkscreened frames, into which she added biographical images of the women's lives, and zig-zagged inner borders cut with pinking shears in the manner of the handmade frames she had seen at Crossroads. The result was an elaborate collage. Williamson had also been looking at Renaissance portraiture, and drew on the tradition of putting elements of the subject's life into the background. The narrative density of these images, and way the artist frames them, gives the series a sense of "lives of the saints".

By 1978, Williamson had become the chair of the WMP. A few years later, her marriage to Tony Williamson broke down and she married Bruce Gordon in 1992, a journalist she had met while he was covering the demolition of District Six, the fabled mixed-race quarter in the very centre of the city (she and Gordon are now divorced). Alongside her work in Crossroads, District Six was Williamson's major political preoccupation during the late 1970s and early 1980s. Her response as an artist to demolitions and forced removals led to a series of very different works, made over a long period of years. At the height of the forced removals, she made *The Last Supper,* pp. 55-6
an installation of the raw rubble taken from the demolition sites and "dumped" into the pristine white space of a city gallery, the Gowlett. Twelve years later, revisiting the un-redeveloped site, she collected relics from the ruins, to make *The Last Supper Revisited* pp. 59-61
and *Mementoes of District Six* (both 1993). Later in pp. 63-5

the 1990s she made, an on-site installation on the pp. 67-9 bare slopes of the destroyed area—*Viewsites: District Six* (1997)—and a series of photographic prints, pp. 71-3, 75 *Last Supper at Manley Villa* (1981 and 2008). Through her District Six work, Williamson developed the theme that was to preoccupy her over the next two decades: how one engages with the trauma of history when the easier thing would be to erase it.

• • •

In late 1990, just months after FW de Klerk had announced the unbanning of the liberation movements and the release of all political prisoners, Sue Williamson was asked to design a cover for a collection of stories pp. 79, 228 by Ellen Kuzwayo. She decided to use a passbook in the design, but she struggled to find one—although it was just three years since the *dompas* system had been phased out, and black South Africans no longer had to carry the hated passbook everywhere they went. The negotiations towards democracy had begun, and the country had been plunged into an interregnum that was terrifying in its violence but exhilarating in its possibilities. For Williamson, the difficulty she had in finding a passbook was a sign of the risk of amnesia, and she now committed herself to a "lest we forget" agenda.

She eventually found a passbook, handed to her out of his breast pocket by an old man named Ngithando John Ngesi, who still kept it "next to his heart" out of habit and some form of comfort, although he no longer needed to. She used Mr Ngesi's passbook for the Kuzwayo cover, and also for a work that would become pp. 81-7 one of her most celebrated: *For Thirty Years Next to his Heart* (1990). The work's power lies in its laying bare of the banality of apartheid bureaucracy: a grid of the 49 double pages of one man's passbook, with long lists of smudged signatures and purple stamps, and an occasional hand appearing as if to examine the page. But it is also an exercise in the empathic humanism, elicited through narrative, which is at the root of Williamson's practice: the work simultaneously lays out a brutal system and commemorates an individual, the passbook's owner.

Williamson used a new technique for this work: the making of an image by laying objects onto a screen of a colour photocopier. The idea had come to her when, in October 1990, she was asked to be an artist in residence at the South African National Gallery. Transporting all her printmaking equipment over to the gallery was clearly impractical, and so she began thinking about an article she had read, which described prints David Hockney had made using a standard Canon photocopier equipped with interchangeable cartridges of red, yellow, black and blue toner. Hockney would make his prints by feeding the sheet of paper through several times, using different originals for the machine to copy, so the colours and images would be built up in layers, almost like making a screen-print. The idea was immensely appealing to Williamson, and so she approached Canon, who offered to loan her such a machine for the residency, but also asked if she would like to try out their brand new full-colour copier. To test it out, she went to the Canon offices armed with the material she had planned to use for the Kuzwayo cover, including Mr Ngesi's passbook, some beads, a satin evening glove, and some *shweshwe* fabric. She arranged the objects face down on the glass of the copier and covered them with the fabric. The image which slid out of the tray astonished her, she says: "In an era in which pre-dated digital photography, and in which any image which needed scanning had to be taken to a

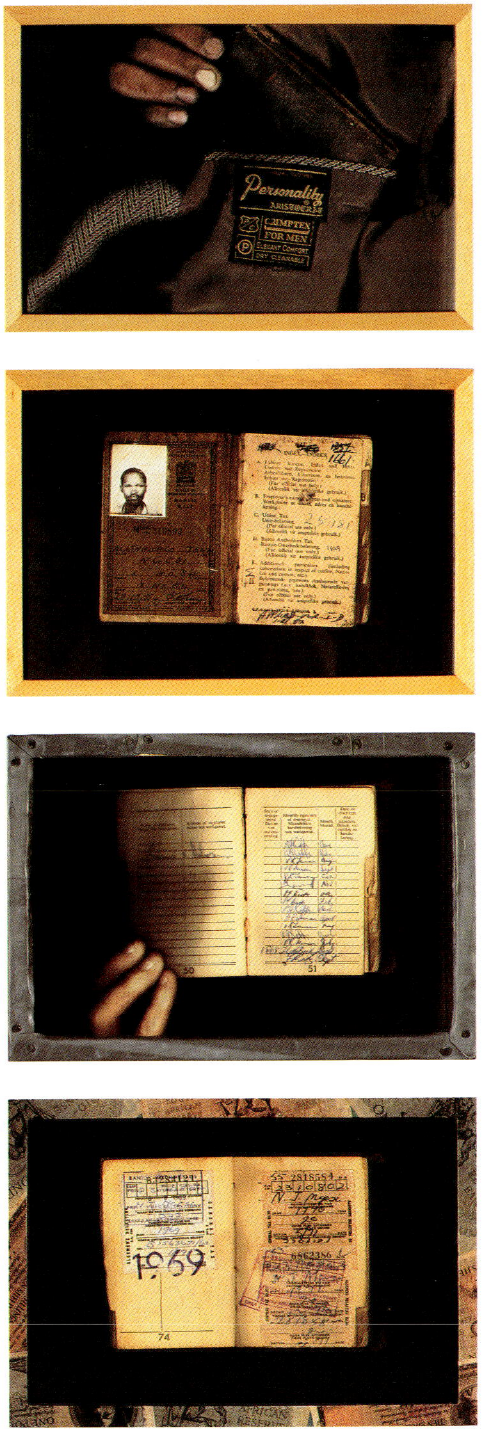


*For Thirty Years Next to his Heart* (detail)
1990
Colour laser copies, hand covered frames,
22 x 31 cm each

professional repro house, this image had a richness, a depth and an immediacy. Because of the shallow depth of field of the copier, there's a sense of three-dimensionality that you never get in a photograph: you can actually *see* Mr Ngesi's hand, almost in relief, as he holds his passbook against the glass."

Williamson decided to buy one of these copiers—there were only three others in Cape Town—and set herself up as a Canon agent, out of her studio in Observatory. Here, while providing copying services to others, she made most of her work over the next decade, often using other printed material, such pp. 101-3 as tourist brochures in *Pages from a Government* pp. 89-93 *Brochure* (1992) and *A Tale of Two Cradocks* (1994), and even a children's colouring book of the Boer War pp. 94-9 in *Colouring In* (1992). In all these works, she used this technique to comment on the way traces of history showed through, in defiance of amnesia, even when rubbed out.

pp. 10, 31-9 *A Few South Africans* had travelled abroad before the end of apartheid, to a group exhibition of Southern African artists at the Kulturhuset in Stockholm in 1989, approved by the African National Congress despite the cultural boycott. Now, in the early 1990s, Williamson became one of the first South African pp. 81-7 artists to gain international exposure. *For Thirty Years Next to his Heart* was exhibited on the 4th Havana Biennale in 1991 and the 9th Sydney Biennale in 1992. She began to work on a larger scale, and to broaden pp. 105, 107-9 her own methodologies. *Messages from the Moat* (1987), for example, used sculptural form to explore, further, her "lest we forget" agenda: a monumental installation featuring glass bottles inscribed with the names and prices of more than 1400 slaves transported to the Cape from 1657 to 1702.

This notion of reckoning with the past had now become primary in her work, and found fertile ground once Archbishop Desmond Tutu's Truth and Reconciliation Commission was established in 1997. Through the press and the nightly television broadcasts, Williamson found herself swept up in the tide of revelations of callous brutality and dehumanisation—some of which involved people she knew personally, or had met. She processed this, in her art, through the means by which she received it: the media.

She began experimenting with interactive technology. In *Can't forget, can't remember* (1999), the viewer pp. 149-151 manipulated a cursor to unlock audio recordings of two particularly dramatic direct encounters between victims and perpetrators. And in *Truth Games* (1998), pp. 129, 135, 137, 139, 141-5 Williamson set images of victim and perpetrator against each other in triptychs, with the "scene of the crime" between them: she then printed text fragments of each side's testimony onto coloured transparent sliding panels which the viewer had to manipulate to get to the "truth" of what had actually happened, and why.

Williamson's interest in presenting the printed word as a component of a visual work has its roots in her training as a journalist and copywriter, and in her commitment to the artwork as a mode of efficient communication. It is also, of course, informed by the international contemporary traditions of textual art exemplified by artists such as Robert Rauschenberg and Jasper Johns. But text written on public walls has a particular significance for Williamson, as a form of "resistance art". The "writing on the wall" that had influenced her most profoundly was that which had been at the root of her District Six work: the act of rage her friend Naz Gool-Ebrahim—a District Six community leader—had perpetrated on the walls of her own home, Manley Villa, when she received her eviction notice in 1981. Gool-Ebrahim covered her walls with expressions of her anger in black marker pen, and invited neighbours and friends to cover the house similarly in graffiti: words of memory about the district and the house, and words of protest about its impending demolition.

Williamson wrote on the walls of Manley Villa herself, and documented this act of protest, using the photographs of Gool-Ebrahim's act of protest in much of her District Six work. Writing on public walls would be a strategy she would employ, repeatedly,
pp. 155-165 in future projects. In *From the Inside* (2000–3), she referred directly back to the tradition of graffiti by collaborating with people living with HIV/AIDS to paint statements about their situation on public walls. Later, she was invited to El Max, a fishing community in Alexandria, Egypt, where she collaborated with fishermen whose homes were threatened with dispossession, and she worked with them to write statements of protest on the outside of their houses. In a nod to Naz Gool-
pp. 184-191 Ebrahim, she presented the result, *What About El*
pp. 71-3, 75 *Max?* (2002-03), together with *The Last Supper at Manley Villa* series (1981 and 2008) at the 10th Havana Biennale in Cuba in 2009, and initiated a "writing on the walls" project in the Cuban capital too. Because of state repression in Cuba, however, she decided to use cardboard cut-outs of letters in *The Havana*
pp. 193-7 *Series* (2009), to inscribe the urban landscape more ephemerally, with statements made by Cubans reflecting on their society. This was the genesis
pp. 199-221 of *Other Voices, Other Cities* (2009–), her ongoing series, in which she sets up workshops with groups of young people to come up with and finally vote on the statement which best describes their home-cities.

• • •

When I asked Sue Williamson whether she experienced fear once she had been "jolted" out of her lethargy and become an activist in the Women's Movement for Peace, she reminded me of something Ilse Fischer had said to her, and which she used in *There's something I must tell you*. Ilse was the daughter of the South African Communist Party Leader Bram Fischer: in the 1960s she would have to deal with the detention and arrest of both her parents, the death of her mother in a car-crash and the sentencing of her father to life imprisonment. But the 1950s, that decade of defiance, "were very exciting years", Ilse says. "One knew one was part of something bigger… One felt part of something, even as a child."

Feeling "part of something bigger", Williamson told me, was far more significant than any feelings of fear she might have felt. Any appreciation of her life and work must hold this in account: her understanding of social groups, and her skills at working within them—both in her art-making and in her role, more broadly, within the South African art scene. She is keenly involved in organisations, associations, informal groupings of artists and collective art projects, and often takes a leadership role within them.

In the 1980s, she came to lead not only the WMP, but a cultural activists' organisation too, the Visual Arts Group, which was responsible for acting as a pressure group, organising exhibitions in the black townships, painting banners and murals, helping black artists become more visible in the art world and liaising with the exiled African National Congress

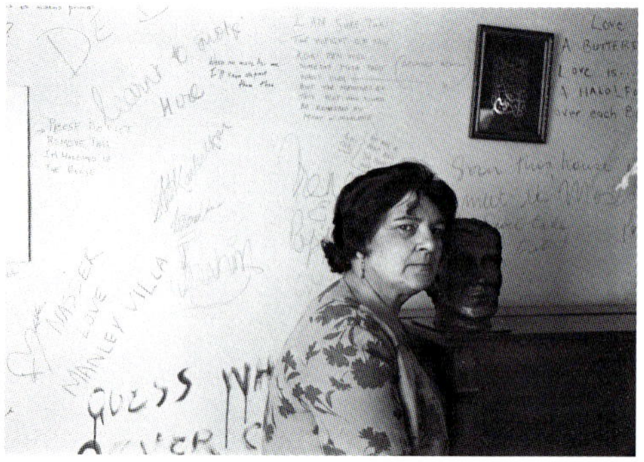

*Naz Ebrahim at piano*
pp. 235-243 *Last Supper at Manley Villa*
1981
Archival print on cotton rag
50 x 67.5 cm

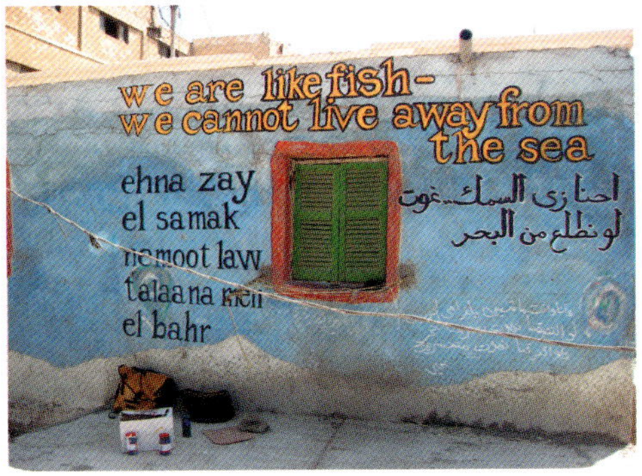


*We are like fish I*, 2002–3
*What about El Max?* series
Pigment inks on Hahnemühle paper
Image size: 38.5 x 52 cm

about how to manage the cultural boycott. Her decision to write *Resistance Art in South Africa* came out of an assessment that the work of South African artists needed to be more broadly known. Her later publishing ventures arose out of a similar impulse: *Art in South Africa: the Future Present* (1996), co-authored by Ashraf Jamal), *South African Art Now* (2009), and *ArtThrob*, launched in 1997, a path-breaking website, on which she still holds the position of "founding editor". She is often the oldest and most experienced person around, providing space—and mentorship—to younger artists.

Perhaps because she was a white South African artist, Williamson was particularly sensitive to the ethos of working collaboratively: she tried to find a way to give back not only her skills, but her artworks themselves, to the people whose lives she was documenting. Her ongoing engagement with the Silinga family is
p. 38 notable in this respect: when Annie Silinga died, two years after Williamson did her portrait for *A Few South Africans*, Williamson provided clothing screen-printed with Silinga's portrait for the funeral at Langa cemetery. Then, a decade later, when she received a commission to revisit a work for the first Johannesburg Biennale, she used her commission to make a memorial for Silinga—a steel cradle commemorating her and inscribed with the epitaph "I will never carry a pass"—once she discovered that nothing but a wooden cross marked her gravesite. She exhibited the memorial
p. 44 cradle at the Biennale as *R.I.P. Annie Silinga* (1997) before arranging a ceremony, attended by Winnie Mandela and others, to consecrate it at the gravesite.

Her later work is suffused with these notions of partnership. In *From the Inside* and *What About El Max?* her objective was to work with people she now described as "collaborators" rather than "subjects", and to help them figure out what *they* wanted to tell the world and to provide them with the platform to do so. The physical artwork, in the end—that which she signs and for which she takes credit—is the photographic evidence of this process of collaboration. She does not abdicate authorship: perhaps because she understands that it is her status as an artist, and the worth of the artworks as commodities, which enables her to do the work in the first place.

In *Other Voices, Other Cities*, she stretches the notion of collaboration into new territory. She travels to cities she does not know and convenes a somewhat random collective of young people, leading them through a workshop process to determine a statement which best represents their city. The very method of selecting a "statement" suggests a branding exercise and comes from Williamson's background in advertising, but it also comes from her work as an activist: going to Crossroads or District Six, for example, and asking people, "what do *you* want to happen?". And so while these works might present one-liners about the cities in which they are made, they are the subject of intensive preparation and research, and are informed by Williamson's engagement with the locals. Williamson has no say in what the statement will be, and she is compelled to work with whatever the group gives her. When her Johannesburg collective came
up with "Who is Johannes?" for example—no-one pp. 200-1
knows whom the city is named after—she read it as a wry statement about its mongrel nature and its chaotic development, and she posed her collaborators in the throng of one of its densest downtown cityscapes.

There is a grammar to these pieces that is inescapable. The individual, each suggesting a different statement in the workshop process, and each ultimately holding up just a single letter of a word from this slogan, only has meaning as part of a collective: you cannot make a sentence without words, and you cannot make a word without letters. So too does a city only exist because it is a collection of the individuals within it. The converse applies too: a city is a string of individuals, each holding his or her own letter, playing his or her own part in the urban narrative. Once more, though, the artist does not submerge her role in editing this prose—and publishing it. She signs the prints.

• • •

*Who am I in this new South Africa?*
*How do the prejudices or privileges which came about because my family was black, white, coloured, mixed, Indian, other or Afrikaans affect me now?*
*How can I reflect these cross-cultural influences in my work?*

In "South African Art in the 1990s", an essay Sue Williamson published in the online journal *ArtThrob,* she wrote that these questions animated a new wave of post-apartheid artists, for whom "the new subject" became "identity." Perhaps because such questions were "often hard and painful" in a country "so deeply dependent on the complexities of heritage for one's received identity", Williamson found that "the work that has emerged from this soul-searching and perusing of family archives has often been sharp, honest and conceptually strong".

Still, Williamson herself eschewed this identitarian trend in her own practice, and has not, since her Carlos Castaneda prints, worked in a way that is self-consciously introspective. She has taken some flak for this, in a South Africa hyper-sensitive to issues of exploitation and representation. In a 1993 review in *The Cape Argus* of *The Last Supper Revisited*, the artist Stanley Hermans called her "our very own conscience crazed cultural bag lady" for picking up rubble from District Six and making an installation out of it. And the artist Thembinkosi Goniwe criticized her, at a conference in 2009, for always making work about "the other", rather than herself. She responded, unapologetically, that she was a "reporter" and a "recorder", and that it was her job to reveal things about our society that we do not, or cannot, or will not, see.

pp. 59-61

Williamson thus places herself not only in the tradition of South African political art, but the very particular one of South African documentary photography too. This has been acknowledged: she was included by Okwui Enwezor and Rory Bester in their magisterial 2012 exhibition, *The Rise and Fall of Apartheid: Photography and the Bureaucracy of Everyday Life*, curated for the Institute of Contemporary Photography in New York.

The curators chose to include one of Williamson's most conceptually accomplished works, *A Tale of Two Cradocks* (1994), although it seems out of place, formally, in what is largely a survey of documentary photography. The work takes the form of a long accordion of framed prints set along a passage. Walk one way down the passage and you read the tale of this small Eastern Cape town as told through an official tourist brochure in the 1980s, in which black people are invisible. Walk the other way, and you traverse a narrative of black life in the town, focused on the murder of the "Cradock Four", activists murdered by security police in 1985. Here Williamson uses her photocopying technique to layer her own photographs with newspaper clippings, and with

pp. 89-93

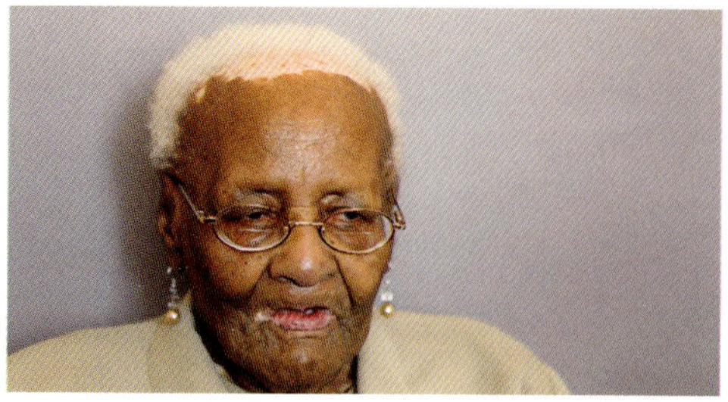

*There's something I must tell you*
2013
Rebecca and Nompumelelo Kotane
Video still (detail)

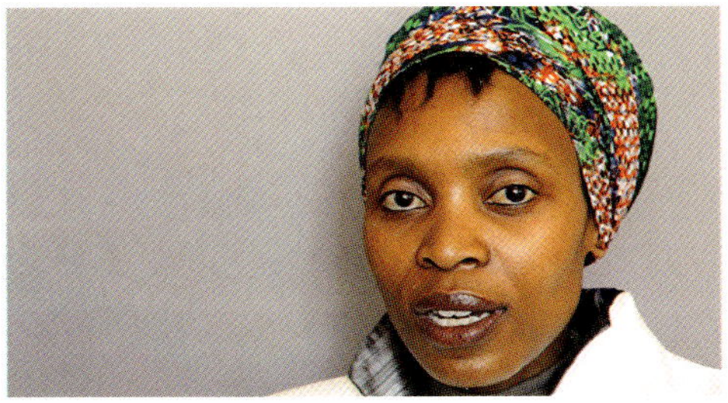

*There's something I must tell you*
2013
Rebecca and Nompumelelo Kotane
Video still (detail)

the transcript of the testimony of Nyameka Goniwe, the widow of Matthew Goniwe.

Looking at this work alongside the several photographs of the funeral of the Cradock Four included in *The Rise and Fall of Apartheid*, one is struck by how Williamson pushes the conventions of South African documentary photography, one of the world's great canons of the genre. First, there is her use of collage, and her technique of arranging materials onto the glass screen of the copier; of taking artefacts from the world—and representations of the world, as seen through her own camera—and making something new of them, rather than making her composition within the lens of the camera. Then there is her use of text and insistence that images "speak". It is not enough to see Nyameka Goniwe, the artist says: we need to hear her too, and we need to hear her within the context that denied her existence.

Because of her abiding interests in narrative and voice, Williamson found her way, inevitably, to video. As I write this introduction, one of her most recent works in
pp. 235-43 this medium, *There's something I must tell you* (2013), is playing as part of mini-retrospective at the Iziko
pp. 72-3 South African Museum's Slave Lodge in Cape Town. The exhibition begins with a full set of *A Few South Africans*, and passes through a series of photographic
pp. 71-3, 75 prints from District Six (*Last Supper at Manley Villa)*
pp. 227-33 and "straight" photographic portraits of women (*All Our Mothers*, 1983–) before culminating in *There's something I must tell you*. The sense of continuity, and of time passing, is compelling, as you encounter, sometimes repeatedly, the women with whom Williamson developed such strong relationships, and who provided her not only with the subjects for her artworks, but with an entrée into—and deeper understanding of—her country and its transition over the past three decades. Although Williamson resists turning her gaze inwards, in her work, you begin to understand her own journey through this work.

When she was making *A Few South Africans* she was a daughter herself, looking for mothers in the struggle. pp. 55-6
When she was making *The Last Supper*, in District Six, she was connecting with her friend Naz Gool-Ebrahim, as a fellow mother. Then, later in life, while making *There's something I must tell you,* Williamson was—in fact—a grandmother herself. Through these portraits of older women and the feisty young women who are their granddaughters, she is looking back over the landscape of the past three decades herself, and the journey she has traversed towards her own self-discovery as a South African and as an artist. But characteristically, while she honours the women of her generation, she does not privilege them: she has no truck with nostalgia. She wants to hear what the young ones have to say, and it is they who light up the work.

Cape Town, June 2015

# The Women

A Few South Africans
R.I.P. Annie Silinga

pp. 10, 31-9 *Sue Williamson's first major body of work was* A Few South Africans (1983–7), *a series of 17 portraits of iconic women in the liberation struggle. The experiences of South African women, before, during and after the South African transition to democracy has been one of the most consistent themes of her work.*

**Mark Gevisser**: Sue, what was the trigger for your interest in making art about South African women?
**Sue Williamson**: When we came back from New York in 1969, my first brush with the apartheid system was the depressing and utterly useless attempt of trying to get a pass book for Mary, our new domestic worker, so she could legally live in the city. She used to run away to hide if she saw a policeman on the street in case she was arrested.
Mary was born in this country, but because she came from a rural area, under the apartheid government, she had no right to live in the city! Of course, black men were also deeply affected by the pass laws, but somehow I felt that black women really were at the bottom of the heap.
Things seemed to have got even worse during my five years in New York. But apart from writing a satirical column for the *Sunday Tribune* making angry fun of the absurdities of apartheid, I didn't know how to intervene. The Black Sash women were playing a very important role in protesting abusive legislation, but it was an all white organisation and that wasn't really what I wanted. So in 1976 when Soweto blew up, and the police reacted to the peaceful protest of the school children by opening fire, and that set off a countrywide reaction, I felt, finally, that it was no longer possible to go on doing nothing, so I went to a mass meeting of women in the Cape Town City Hall. A number of black women spoke, very powerfully, and it just suddenly felt like, "Okay, I can get involved in this…"

**MG**: What happened next?
**SW**: Finally, I had access to that other section of the South African community from which I had been so cut off. One of the first actions the new Women's Movement for Peace undertook, working alongside other human rights organisations, was to try to prevent the demolition of the Modderdam squatter camp, a community of 20 000 people. On the day demolitions were to begin, we stood in the path of the bulldozers, but they simply waited till late afternoon to begin their work, once protesters had started to leave.
It was devastating watching those carefully built homes being flattened while the owners stood helplessly by, trying to save their possessions. But at least you felt you were bearing witness, and visibly giving support.

**MG**: You were bearing witness, as an activist, but you were also inspired to make art…
**SW**: Yes, I had my sketchbook with me at Modderdam, and the sketches I made eventually became a series of small etchings known as *The*

pp. 16, 17 *Modderdam Postcards* (1978). Those were really my breakthrough work into finding a way to make art which addressed social issues.

After Modderdam, the next squatter camp in the line of fire was Crossroads, a much larger community. Lessons of unpreparedness learned through the Modderdam experience meant that this time around, the human rights organisations were much more organised, and regular twice weekly meetings were held to plan strategy.

I found myself spending a lot of time out in Crossroads. I was taking postcard-sized etching plates already covered with a wax hard ground with me, and I would start a new etching by drawing directly onto the plate, to finish it later in the studio. I was sharing printmaking facilities with a group, in an old Victorian house we called The Graphic Workshop.

When I started an Advanced Diploma in Printmaking at the Michaelis School of Fine Art in 1982, I showed all my previous work to my tutor, Jules van der Vijver, including the Crossroads ones. He said I should work bigger and bolder. I also showed him some photos I had taken in Crossroads of the kinds of pictures people had on the walls of their shacks.

Favourite subjects for these pictures were biblical texts, family photos and certificates, all beautifully framed with coloured gift wraps, often with layers of edging trimmed into zigzags with pinking shears. And bound with raffia. Jules told me to take a hundred more photos. So I did. I still have them. Interestingly, I found that the same photo turned up in a number of houses. Differently framed, but the same photo—a woman in a long white dress. I found out she was a faith healer named Elizabeth Paul. If she was important to so many people, I decided I would make the first of my new prints about her. That was
pp. 10, 31-9 the beginning of my *A Few South Africans* series.

**MG**: When you found the portrait of Elizabeth Paul you knew nothing about her. The act of making the artwork required you to learn about her. Was making all the work that followed a form of political education for you as well?

**SW**: Very much so. Doing picture research, I found those famous photographs of the 20 000 strong Women's March to Pretoria in 1957, to protest against black women having to carry a passbook. So I set about educating myself about the four women who led the march—Lilian Ngoyi, Helen Joseph, Rahima Moosa and Sophie Williams. And about other leading lights of the Federation of South African Women, like Amina Cachalia and Caroline Motsoaledi. Ma Lilian was dead already, but I found a photograph of her and included her in *A Few South Africans*. Amina and Helen were very much alive, and through photographing them for the series, they became good friends and important mentors.

**MG**: What did you learn from them?

**SW**: Courage. They did what they wanted to do.

**MG**: What was the next work you did, after Elizabeth Paul the faith-healer?

**SW**: Maggie Magaba, a domestic worker, just an ordinary person. But representative of an enormous group of black women who had very little opportunity to take any other kind of employment. I learned of her through a woman she had raised, the film-maker Betty Wolpert, who set up a trust to fund self-help groups in her name.

Soon after that I thought I'd do Annie Silinga. She was a member of the Women's Movement for Peace, and I had met her at meetings.

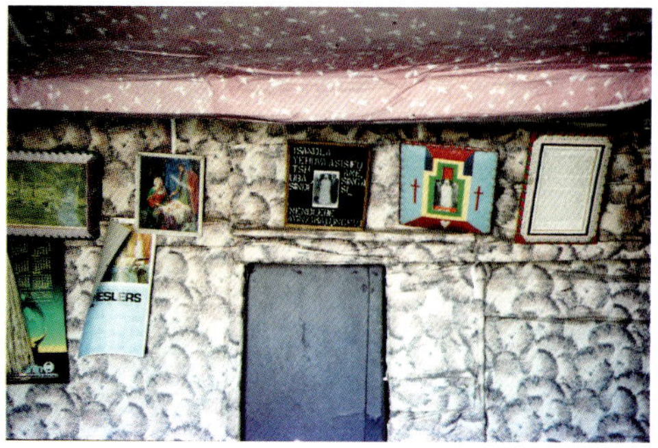

The interior of a Crossroads home, with photographs of Elizabeth Paul on the wall

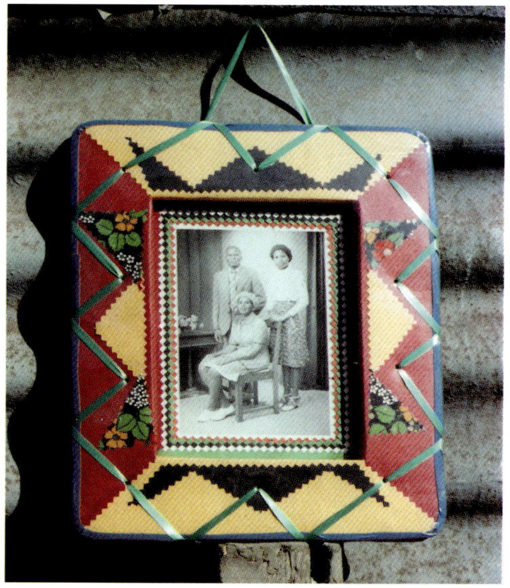

An example of a Crossroads framed family photo

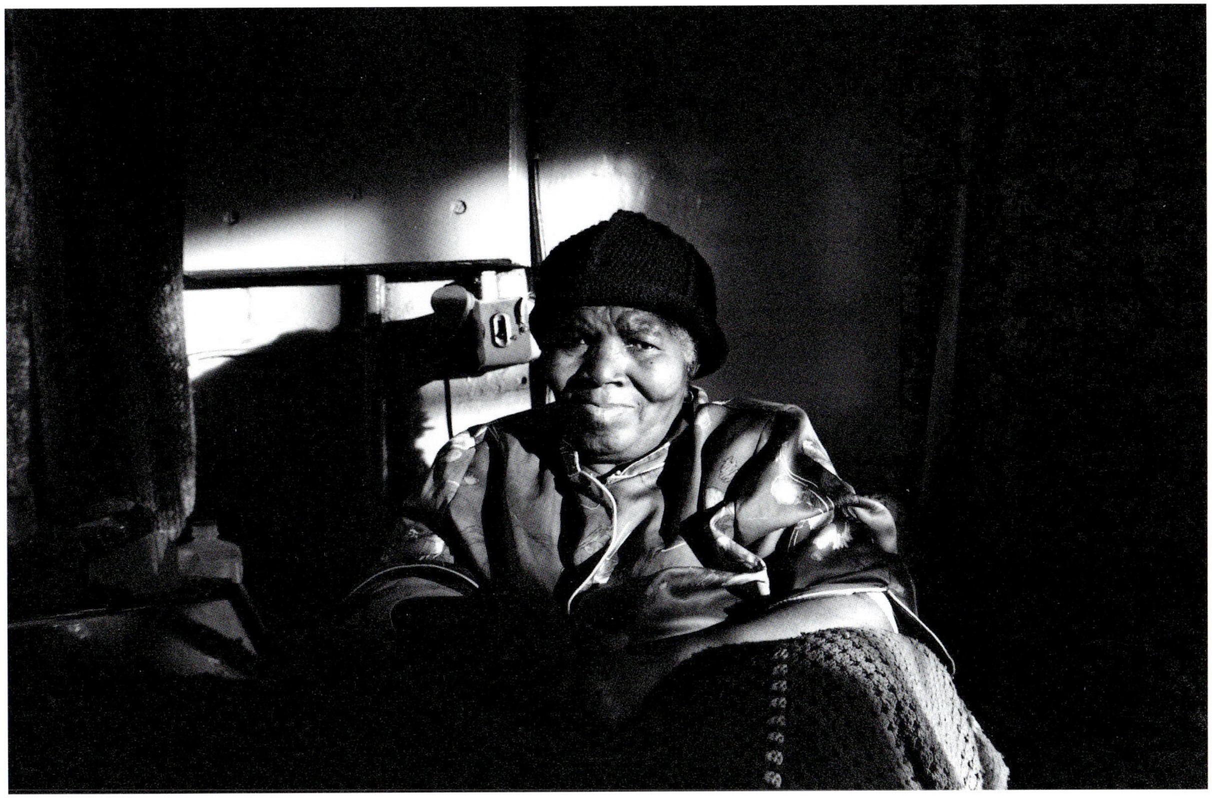

*Annie Silinga 1*
1983
*All Our Mothers* series
Pigment inks on archival paper
39 x 59 cm

**MG**: Why Annie?
**SW**: The short answer is, because she was there, I'd already met her, and I admired her story and wanted to tell it.
Annie was famous, in struggle circles, from the Defiance Campaign of the 1950s when people decided to defy unjust laws—black women sat on benches at railway stations marked for whites only. That kind of thing. Annie had announced at a large mass meeting outside the Cape Town City Hall that she would not carry a pass until the prime minister's wife carried one. She never in her whole life accepted a subservient position. But few white people had ever heard of her.
Anyway, Annie agreed to participate in my *A Few South Africans* series and I went to take her portrait p. 38 in her home in Jungle Walk, Langa.
The first photo I took was in her kitchen, but I didn't think it was appropriate. Too intimate, too domestic. So I asked if I could come again. Next time, she was fully dressed in the regalia of the Federation of South African Women, with robes and a special hat. She was confined to a wheelchair, which almost becomes a throne on which she sat.

**MG**: Why didn't you want it intimate and domestic?
**SW**: She deserved recognition of her public persona and for the stand which she took in refusing a pass, a stand which led to her being sent back to the Transkei.

**MG**: You mainly chose women who had public lives.
**SW**: And also some who were unknown. And although I've made a lot of work around men's stories too, that series was to begin a lifelong and particular focus on women.

# A Few South Africans

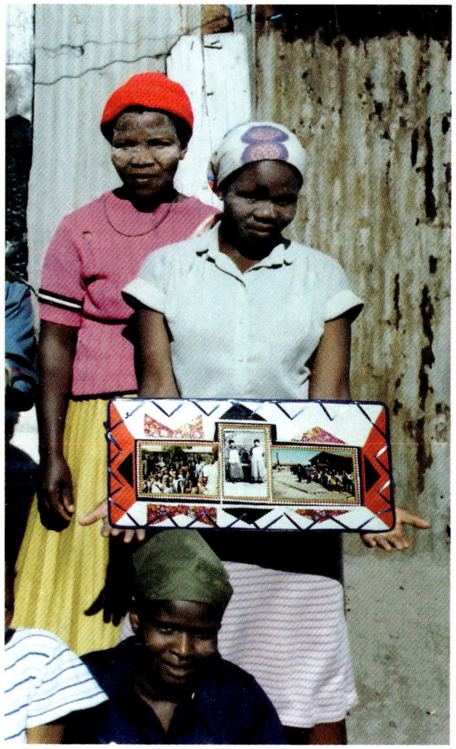

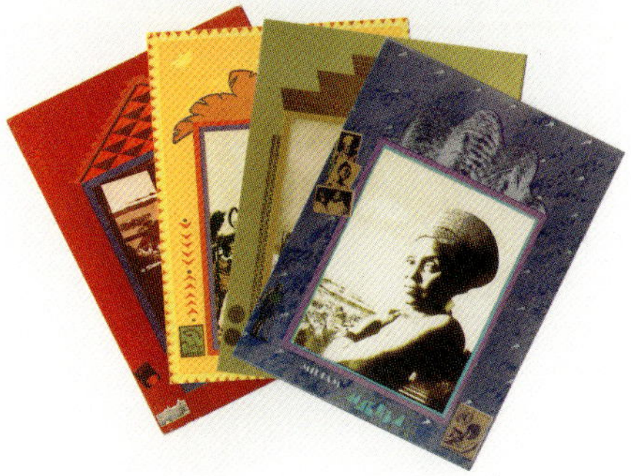

Crossroads residents hold up a triptych of photographs framed in the local style

Postcards of the *A Few South Africans* portraits

Sue Williamson began making this series of portraits of remarkable South African women in 1982. While visiting homes in Crossroads, a Cape Town squatter community designated for clearance, she had noticed several portraits of the same woman, and was told she was a Xhosa faith-healer named Elizabeth Paul. The artist began thinking about women who were important in the black community and as Elizabeth Paul had a fascinating story, she decided to make her the first in the new series.

It was the year Williamson had gone back to the Michaelis School of Fine Art to learn new printmaking skills, and the complex darkroom technique of photo etching lent itself perfectly to her new series. More portraits followed, telling the stories of women who had fought against or struggled under apartheid. By having been banned and placed under house arrest, women like Helen Joseph, Winnie Mandela and Mamphela Ramphele had, literally, been removed from society and placed out of view.

Opening the first public viewing of these works at the Gallery International in Cape Town in 1984, Helen Joseph said: "You have taken our history out of the cupboard and hung it on the wall."

In a radical era where there was much critique of the elitism of art, Williamson was not content with these portraits remaining in galleries. Following an earlier project, where she had made postcards of the forced removals of illegal squatters in Modderdam, she made a series of postcards of *A Few South Africans* too.

These could be easily distributed, and used to publicise the women and their stories. The postcards themselves are artworks, and the artist attributes her openness to the mass production of her work to her previous career in journalism and advertising copywriting, both of which define communication as an efficient relationship between medium and message. The postcards became iconic artefacts, themselves, of the era of anti-apartheid resistance. Williamson demonstrated a similarly demotic—and eclectic—approach to materials. In squatters' shacks, she admired the frames that women made with recycled material such as coloured raffia and shiny wrapping paper. At the same time, she was researching Renaissance portraiture, and was struck by the way a landscape behind a portrait—such as in Piero della Francesca's *Duke and Duchess of Urbino*—provided a narrative frame for the subject's life.

She etches such landscapes into the background of her portraits, extending them thematically even into the Renaissance-shaped silkscreened frames, some decorated to look like African waxprints. Thus we see the Johannesburg landscape that Virginia Mngoma had to traverse on foot when she led the famous Alexandra Bus Boycott of 1957; the "frame" itself is of Renaissance form, but made in African waxprint style, depicting the bicycles that boycotters rode to work, and the coins they were expected to pay in the fare-increase which provoked the boycott.

Virginia Thokozile Mngoma (1919–95) was born in Alexandra, a township bordering Johannesburg. At the age of 14, she had to leave school and go into domestic work. She joined the African National Congress when the call came in 1950 to take action against the government. Though the youngest person in her area, Mngoma was elected local chairperson. In 1952 she was jailed for defying the pass laws, and in 1955 was an organizer for the mass meeting of the Congress of the People where the Freedom Charter was drawn up, but she is best remembered for organizing a renowned bus boycott in 1957. The increased fares were seen as exploitative, so the entire township walked for hours to and from work. The protest continued for three months until the bus company withdrew the increases.

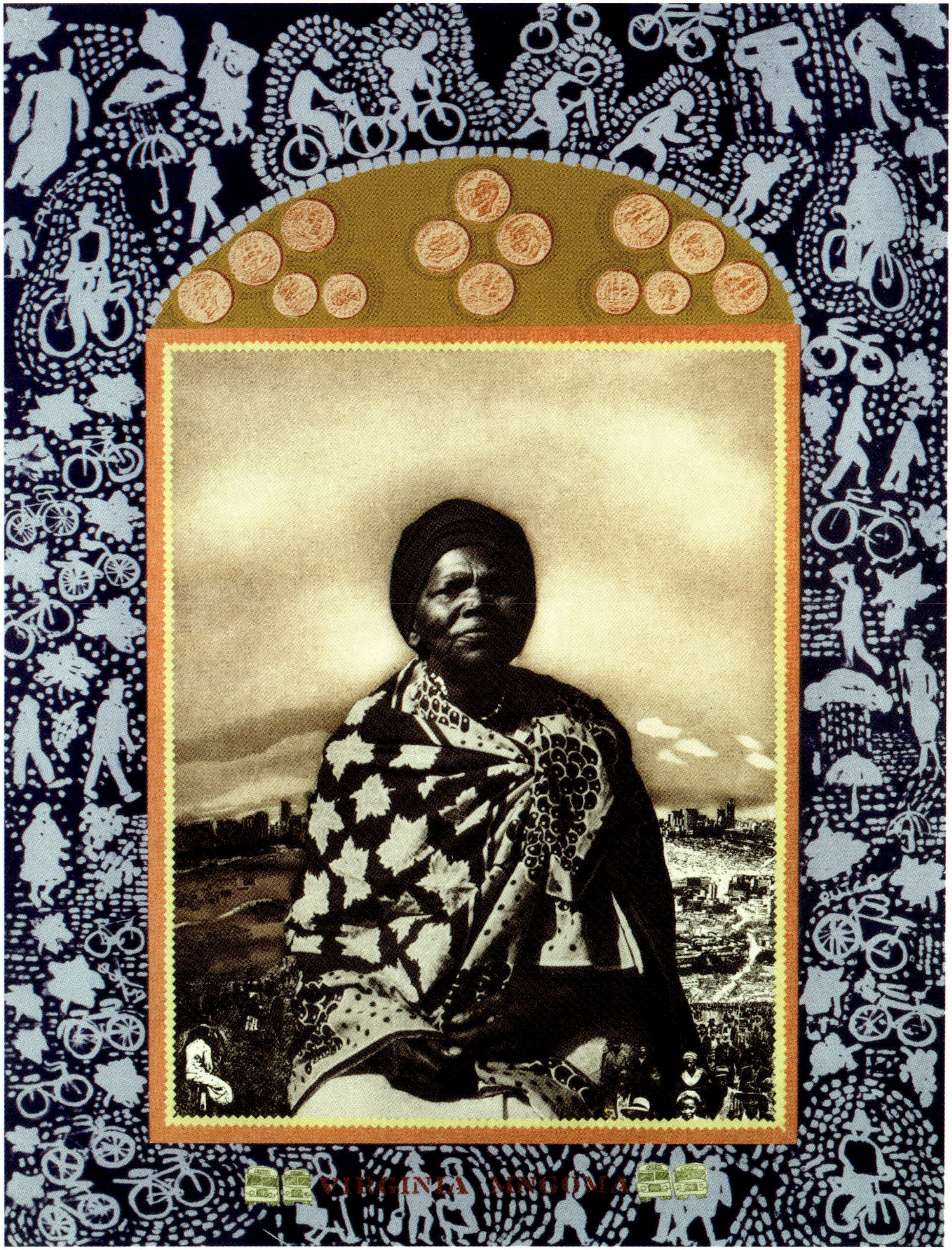


*Virginia Mngoma*
1984
*A Few South Africans* series
Photo etching / screenprint collage
100 x 70 cm

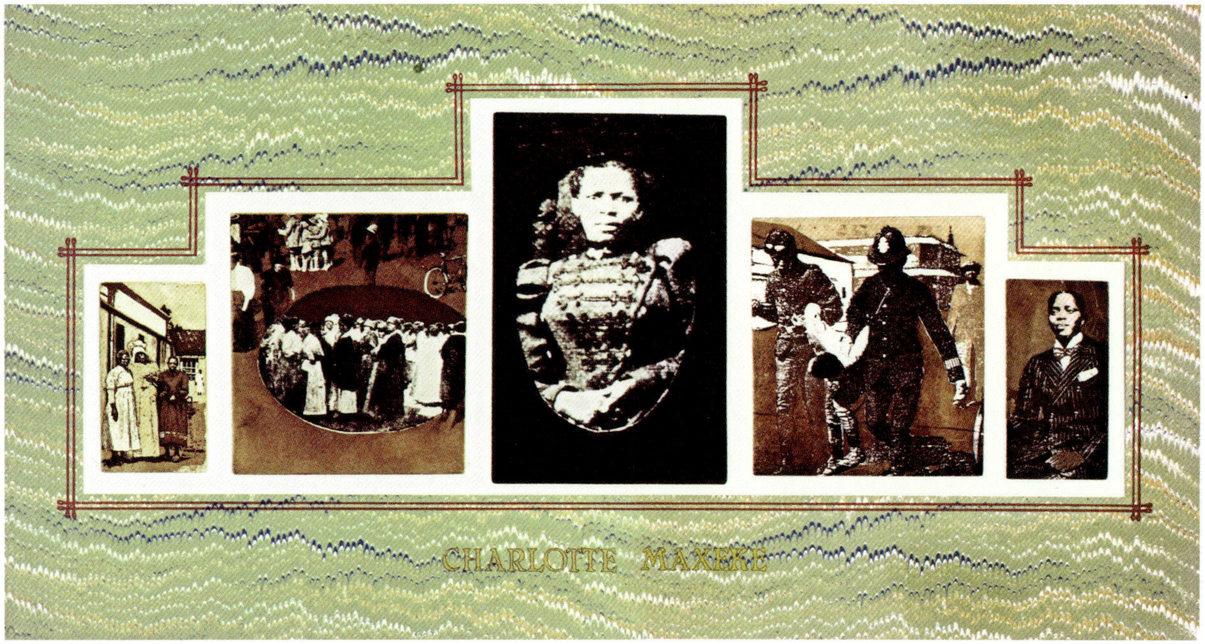


Charlotte Manye (1874–1939) was born in the Karoo and educated in Kimberley. As a young woman she joined an African choir and toured England—where she became a supporter of the suffragette movement—and North America. Here, she attended Wilberforce College and graduated with a Bachelor of Science, the first black South African woman to obtain a university degree. In 1901 Charlotte returned to South Africa with her husband, the Rev M. Maxeke, and together they founded the Wilberforce Institute at Evaton, South Africa's first college for Africans. Charlotte could be seen as a forerunner of Black Consciousness thinking, declaring in a 1935 speech: "The Non-Europeans, while thanking their European friends for their support, had to go ahead themselves. The Natives were not a peculiar people who had to be carried on the backs of others for ever."

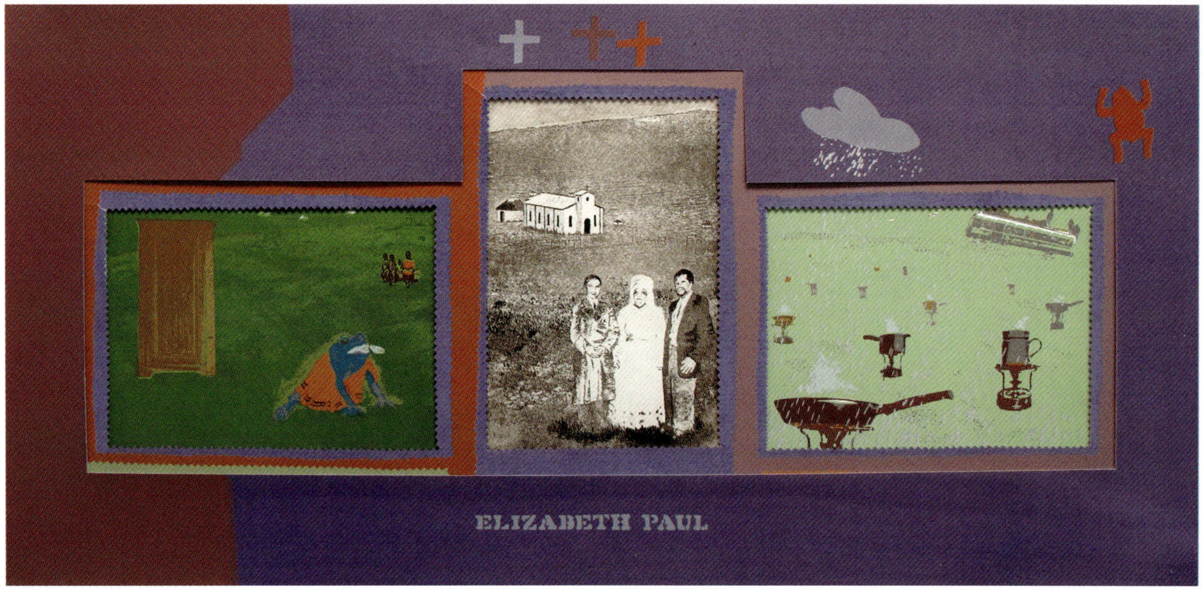


Elizabeth Paul was a faith healer, with a large following of believers. Her photo hangs in many Crossroads homes, and to this day, buses come from all over the country to Tsolo, in the Eastern Cape to celebrate the anniversary of the vision of healing she received on the 14th of May, 1950. "I heard a voice speaking. The voice spoke in tongues Xhosa and English. I was filled with joy and fear", she has written.

She started preaching and healing. One day, she was called to the bedside of Chief Sabatha, who was so ill that doctors could not heal him. Elizabeth Paul prayed by his bedside for two days, then the cupboard in the room opened, and a giant frog dressed in the robes of a Xhosa chief jumped out. The frog was not real, but was found to contain a spell. It was killed. Chief Sabatha recovered.

*Charlotte Maxeke*
1984
*A Few South Africans* series
Photo etching / screenprint collage
70 x 100 cm

*Elizabeth Paul*
1983
*A Few South Africans* series
Photo etching / screenprint collage
70 x 100 cm

In 1983, at the time this portrait was made, social worker Nomzamo Winnie Madikizela-Mandela was regarded as one of the heroines of the struggle. Her husband, the great political leader Nelson Mandela, had been in jail for many years, and Winnie herself had undergone detention, house arrest and solitary confinement in prison. In 1977 Winnie was banished from her home in Soweto to the small, dusty Afrikaner *dorp* of Brandfort in the Orange Free State, and perpetual harassment extended even to the confiscation of a bedspread in the colours of the African National Congress. In post-apartheid South Africa, she is still politically powerful in spite of the deep controversies caused by her behaviour.

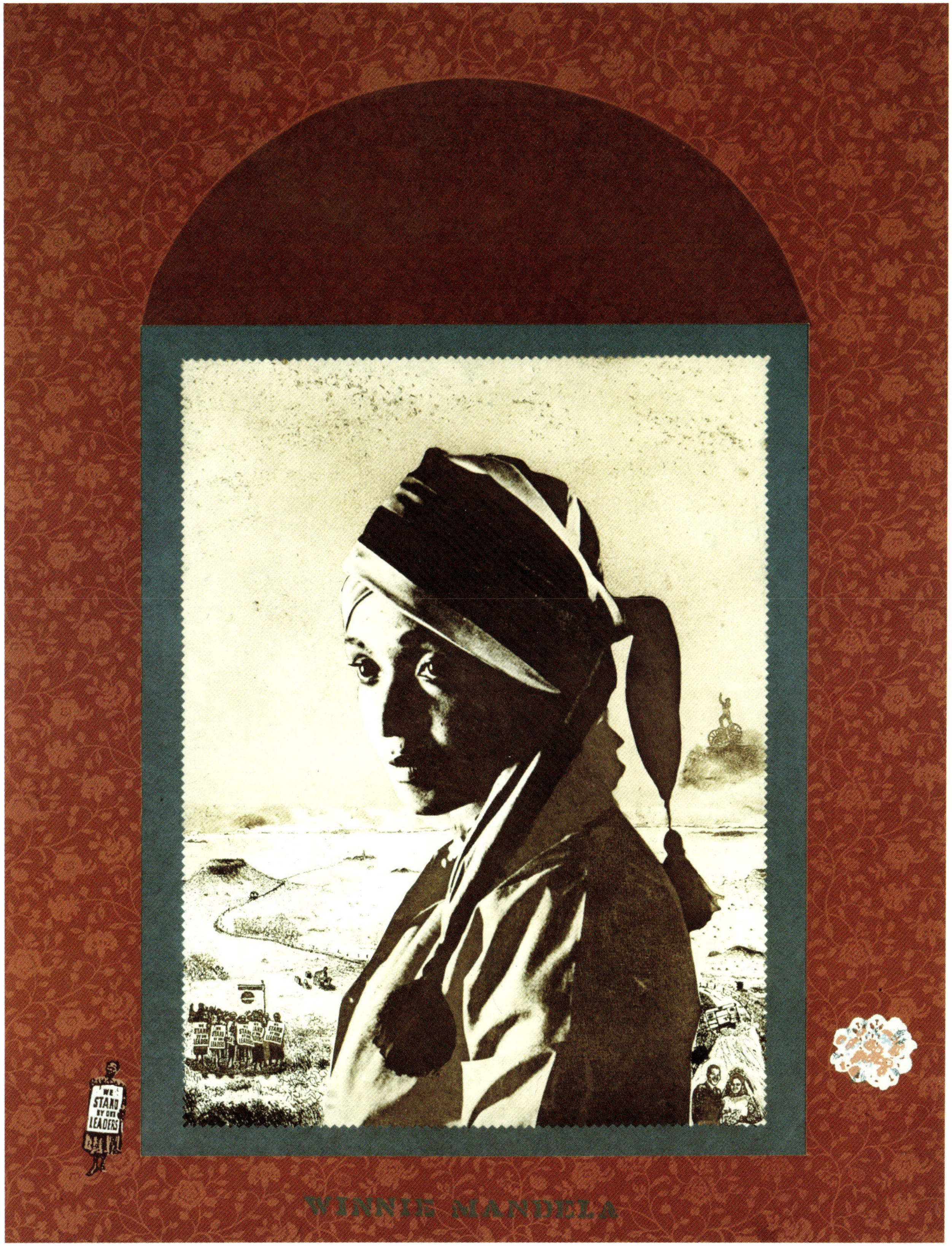


*Winnie Mandela*
1983
*A Few South Africans* series
Photo etching / screenprint collage
100 x 70 cm

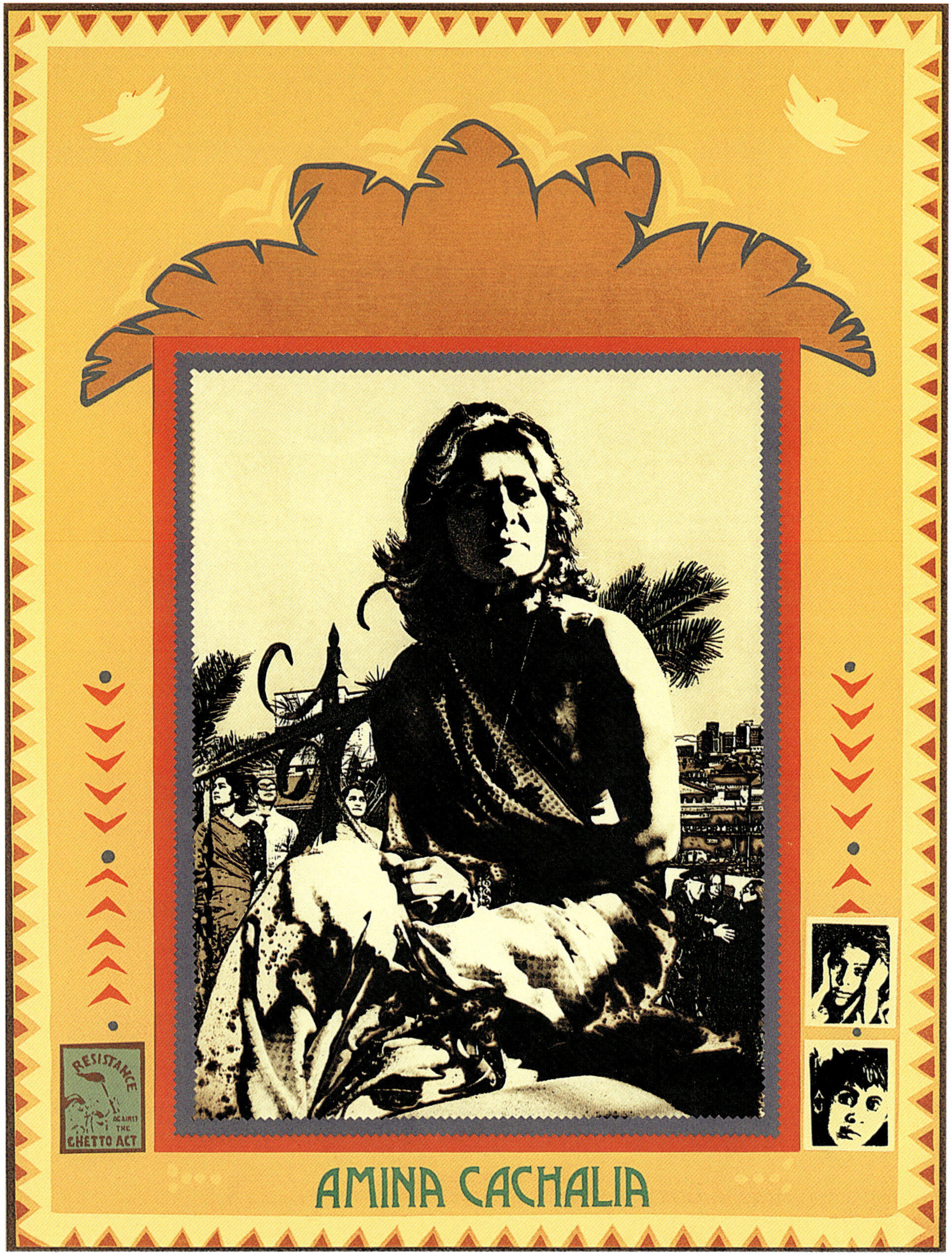


In her high school years, Amina Cachalia (1930–2013) joined the Indian Youth Congress and in 1952 she was one of a group of women of all races who went into the Boksburg African location without permits as part of the Defiance Campaign. She was arrested with 28 others and served a 14-day sentence. She and her husband Yusuf were long time friends and political allies of Nelson Mandela. In 1956, Amina took part in the Women's March on Pretoria, to protest the carrying of passes by women, and spent fifteen years under house arrest in the 1950s and 1960s. In 1962 Amina and Helen Joseph went on a countrywide trip to visit activists banished to remote areas, to take them food parcels and offer assistance. Amina died in 2013, shortly before the publication of her autobiography, *When Hope and History Rhyme*.

*Amina Cachalia*
1984
*A Few South Africans* series
Photo etching / screenprint collage
100 x 70 cm

Albertina Sisulu (1918–2011) was one of Soweto's most important community leaders. After the life imprisonment of her husband, Walter, following the Rivonia Trial of 1964, she was frequently detained and spent ten years under house arrest. Despite this, she brought up and educated five of her own children and two of her deceased sister's, and continued working as a nurse and midwife. She was one of the founding members of the Federation of South African Women, and in 1983, became a founder of the United Democratic Front. In 1989 Albertina managed to get a passport and led a delegation of the UDF overseas, meeting British prime minister Margaret Thatcher and US president George Bush. After the first democratic election in 1994, she was elected a Member of Parliament.

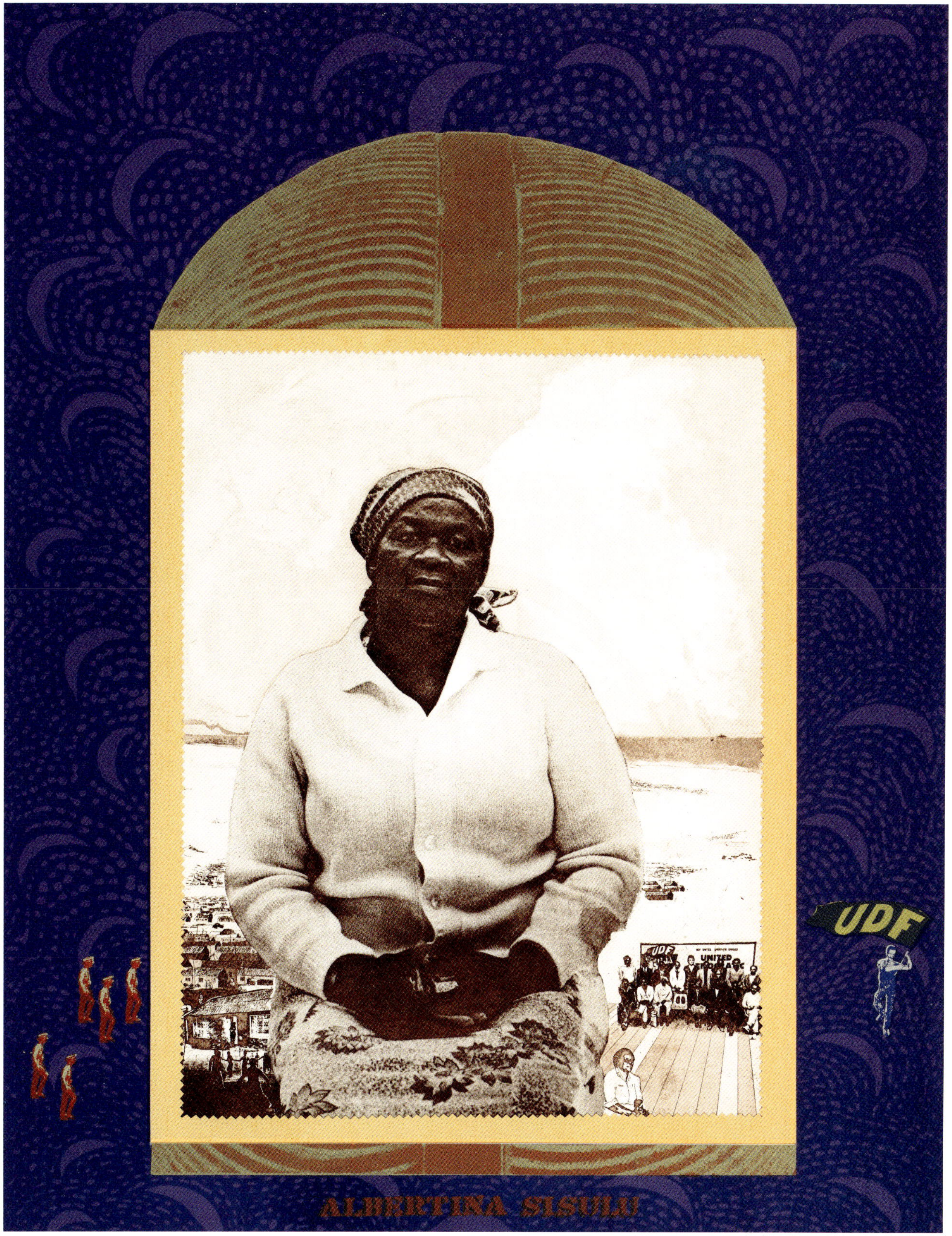


*Albertina Sisulu*
1983
*A Few South Africans* series
Photo etching / screenprint collage
100 x 70 cm

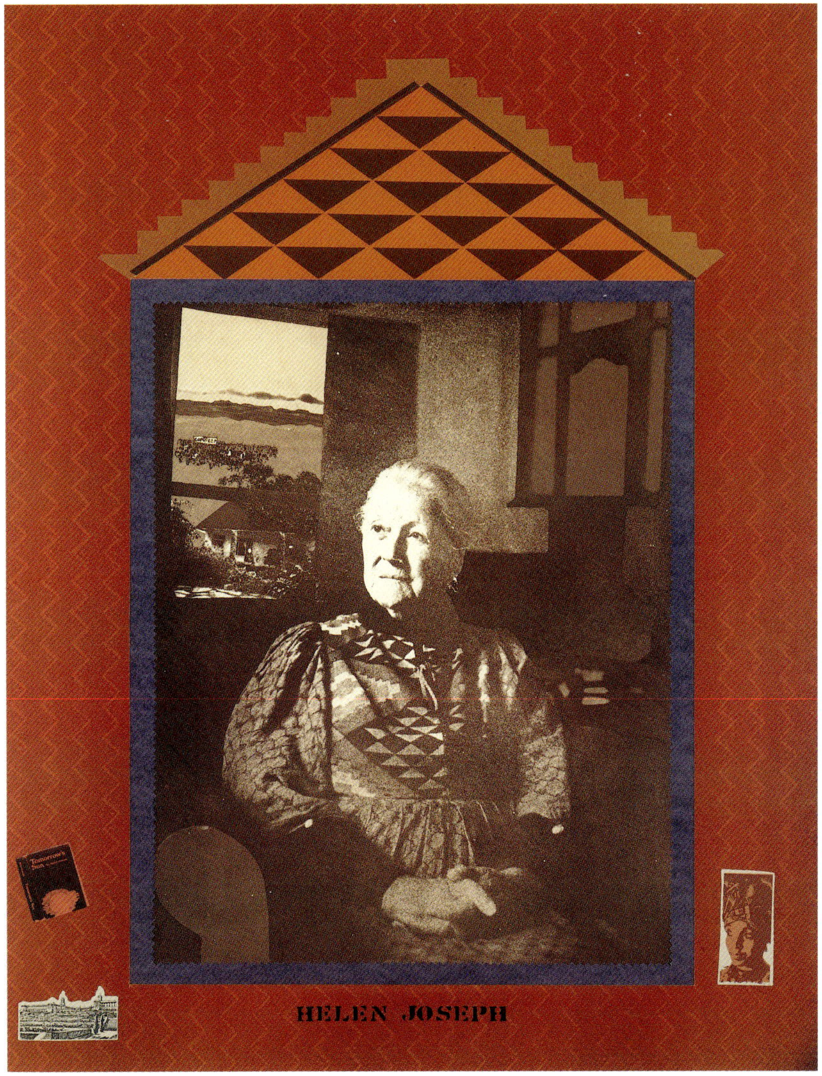


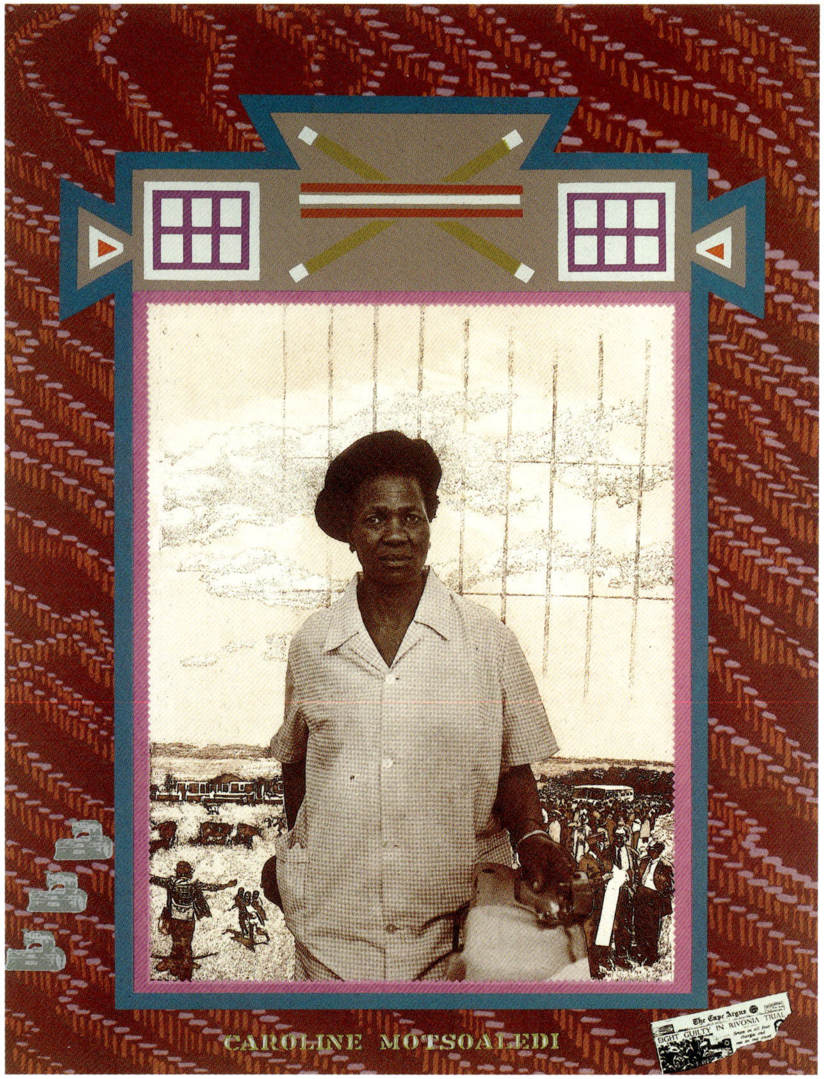


Helen Joseph (1905–92) was an anti-apartheid activist who came to national prominence when she read out the clauses of the new Freedom Charter at the Congress of the People at Kliptown in 1955. In 1956, she was one of four women who led 20 000 to Pretoria to protest against the carrying of passes by African women. Helen was one of the 156 defendants in the Treason Trial in 1956, and was finally acquitted in 1961. However, her activities led to her house arrest in 1962, the first person to receive this restriction, which lasted for ten years. Bullets were shot through her bedroom window late at night and a bomb was wired to her front gate .

Caroline Motsoaledi (1927–2014) was the wife of Elias Motsoaledi, one of the Rivonia trialists. When he was imprisoned on Robben Island, she was left to bring up her large family by herself. Caroline had been one of the women who had marched to Pretoria in 1956 to protest against women carrying passes, and after her husband was arrested she herself was detained for 180 days. Her baby was 5 months old at the time. As a prison widow, she worked at a clothing factory to support her family, and was able to travel to Cape Town to visit Elias for thirty minutes only once or twice a year.

*Helen Joseph*
1983
*A Few South Africans* series
Photo etching / screenprint collage
100 x 70 cm

*Caroline Motsoaledi*
1984
*A Few South Africans* series
Photo etching / screenprint collage
100 x 70 cm

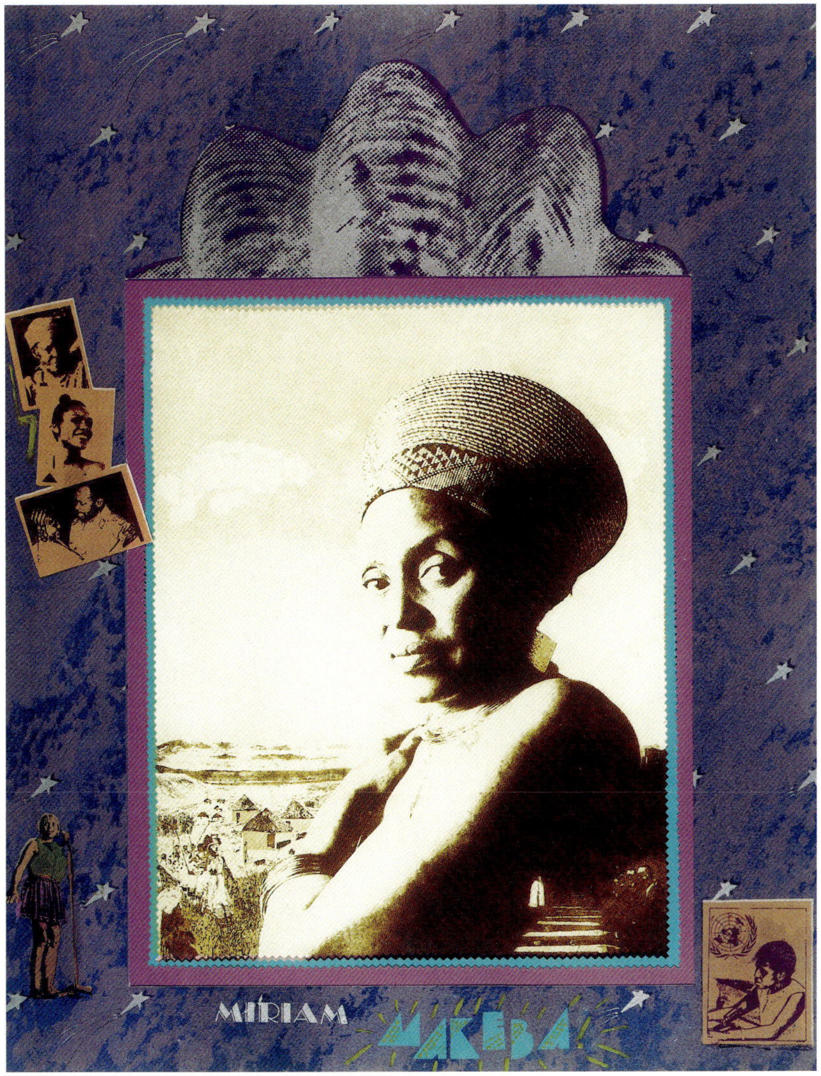


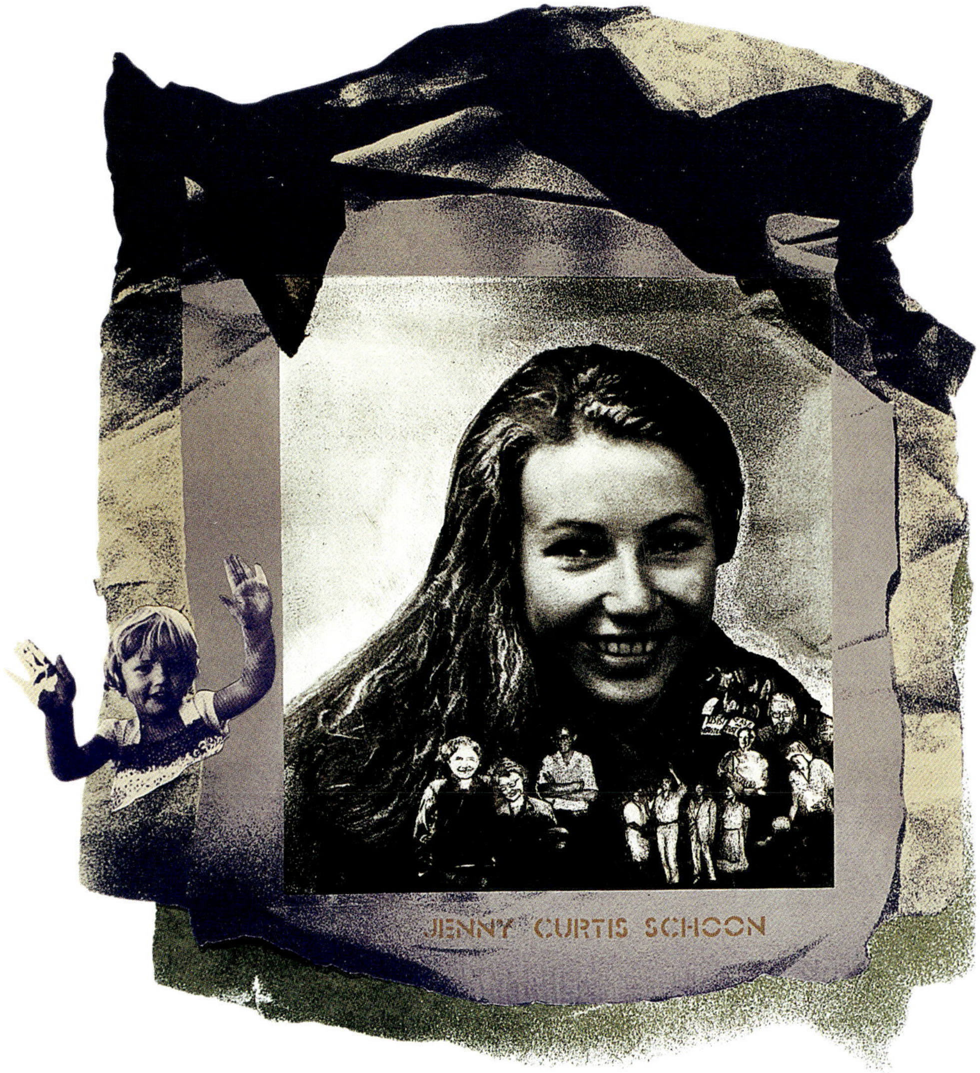


*Miriam Makeba*
1987
*A Few South Africans* series
Photo etching / screenprint collage
100 x 70 cm

*Jenny Curtis Schoon*
1985
*A Few South Africans* series
Photo etching / screenprint collage
100 x 70 cm

Miriam Makeba (1932–2008), internationally acclaimed as a singer, first left South Africa for London in the late 1950s with the cast of *King Kong*, a musical. After giving evidence at the United Nations in New York against the apartheid state, Makeba had her South African passport withdrawn. She was not allowed to return to the country even for the funeral of her mother. "Mama Africa", as she was known, was one of the first singers to popularize African music globally, and her song *Pata Pata* has been viewed on YouTube more than 9 million times.

Jeanette Curtis (1948–84) was a young Johannesburg academic who as a student played an active role in the National Union of South African Students (NUSAS), and was instrumental in the establishment of the Wages Commissions on various campuses. Helen Joseph was her mentor. She was harassed by the State and left the country. Together with her husband, Marius Schoon, also an exile, she set up a base in Angola where the two worked for the ANC. In 1984, Jenny and her young daughter Katryn were blown up when she opened a parcel bomb sent by the South African security police and addressed to her husband.

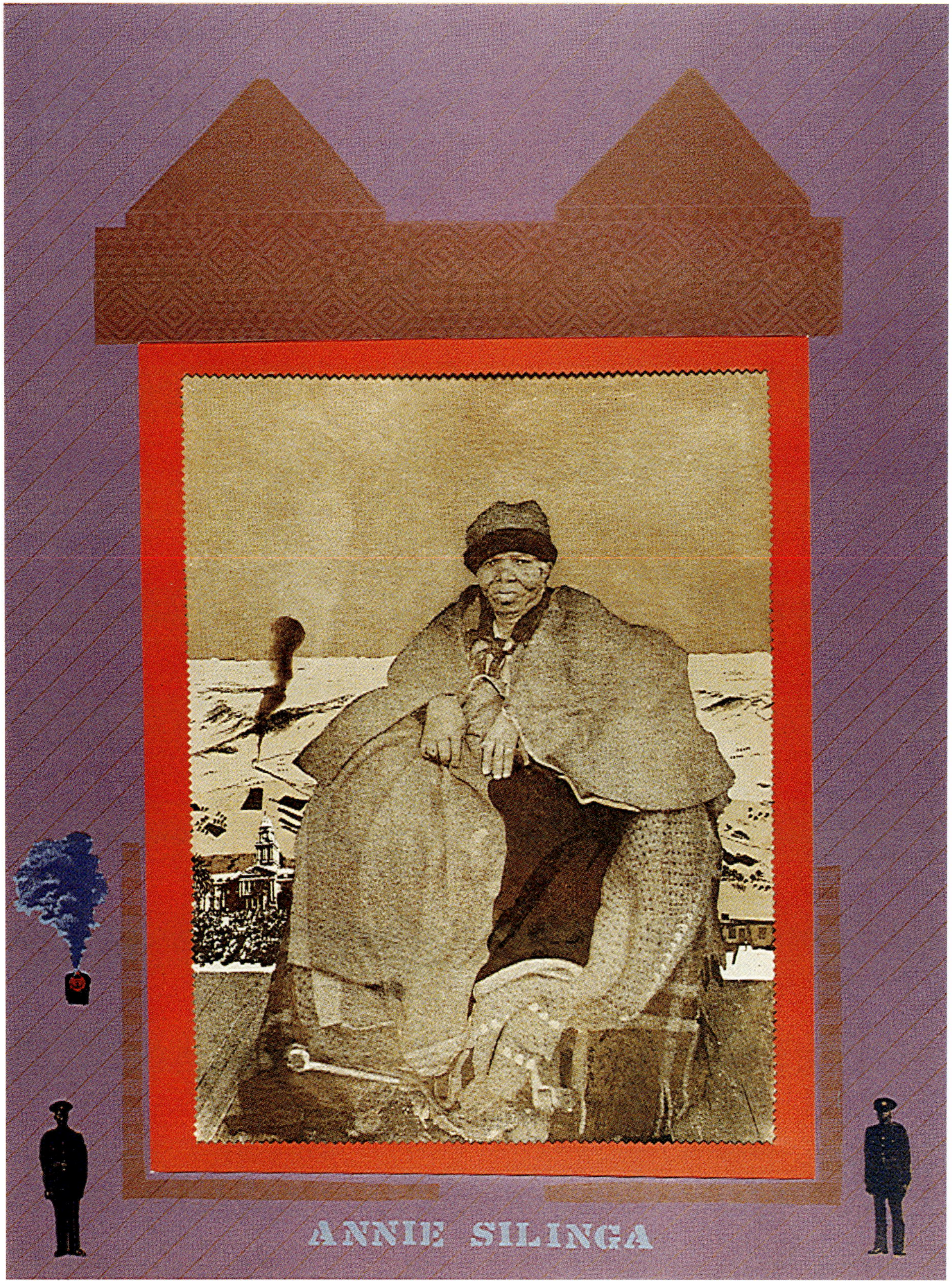


Annie Silinga was born in 1910 at Nqamakwe in the Butterworth district of the Transkei, where she completed only a few years of primary school. In 1937 she moved to Cape Town, where her husband was employed. She was an active participant of the Defiance Campaign of the 1950s, sitting on benches in railway stations marked WHITES ONLY, and in 1952, announcing to a large public meeting in central Cape Town that "I will carry a pass the day the Prime Minister's wife carries a pass." For refusing to submit to pass legislation, Annie was arrested and sent back to the Transkei, declaring, "My children are orphans though their mother still lives, and my husband is a widower though his wife is alive." Annie returned to Cape Town and in December 1956 was again arrested in a pre-dawn roundup, becoming one of the 156 defendants of the five year long Treason Trial. She was a proud executive member of the Federation of South African Women and is wearing those robes in this portrait.

*Annie Silinga*
1983
*A Few South Africans* series
Photo etching / screenprint collage
100 x 70 cm

This mother of two was born in the Transkei, but came to Cape Town eleven years before this photo was taken to be with her husband, a contract worker on a construction site. Under the apartheid laws, she had no legal right to live in the area, and was constantly harassed, finally finding lodging in the Crossroads Squatter Camp. As "Case no. 6831/21", she was swept up in a police raid, appearing before the court in Langa as an illegal resident of Cape Town, and sent back to the Transkei. But she returned, and found new lodging at Crossroads, where Sue Williamson encountered her.

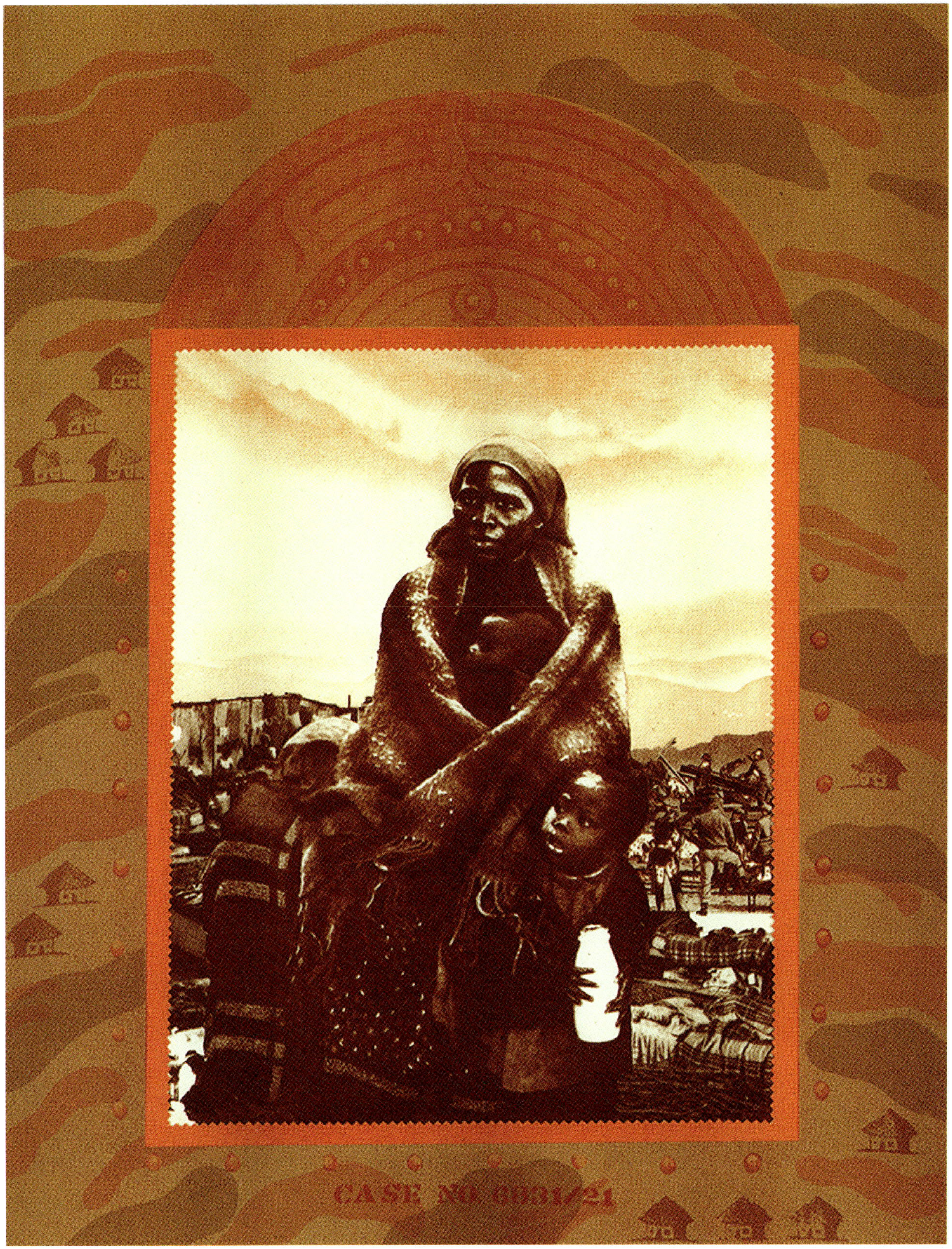


*Case no. 6831/21*
1984
*A Few South Africans* series
Photo etching / screenprint collage
100 x 70 cm

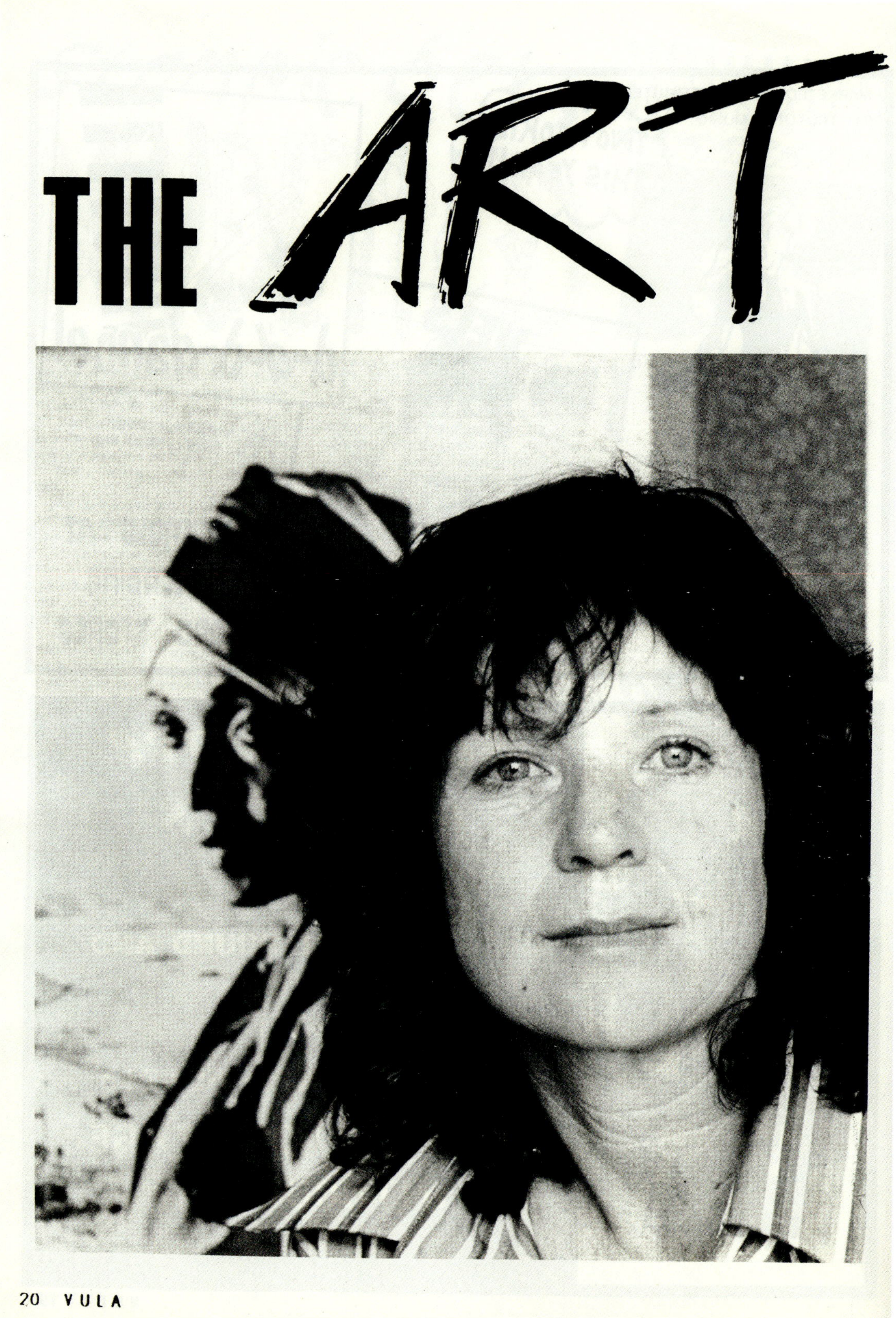
THE ART

20 VULA

"The Art of Activism", *Vula*, February 1985

# OF ACTIVISM

**SUE WILLIAMSON** has produced a series of powerful portraits of some outstanding South African women MARCELLE KATZ put away her paint by numbers set to interview the artist at her studio in Observatory.

STRIJDOM - YOU HAVE TAMPERED WITH THE WOMEN
YOU HAVE STRUCK AGAINST ROCK...

SUE WILLIAMSON, artist and social activist has put together a fierce and compelling portfolio of women who have been tampered with - South Africans who have kicked against a repressive system and left their mark.

She aimed to document chunks of history that had previously been curtained off. The result is provocative and politically disturbing. No compromises. It's a powerful combination of emotion, strength and pride.

The stories behind the women and the visual translation punches you in the head, makes you want to bleed a bit, and sigh. It also jabs at the murky part of your conscience which comes from living in a strange, strange land.

Look at the portrait of Winnie Mandela. It will haunt you for a thousand years. The dignity and intense beauty says it all without need for words.

Time spent in America during the 1960's changed Sue's relative indifference to political rumbles. "To come back to South Africa and find the extent to which apartheid still prevailed was a cultural shock. There's this awful barrier of fear between black and white people, like getting to know each other might be awkward and embarrassing." The system's made sure of that.

When the Soweto riots in '76 erupted, Sue joined the Women's Movement for Peace. A new door hinged open. Her involvement was sealed when the Government demolished Modderdam. "They just knocked it down. Bang!," she says, still somewhat perplexed.

The women got up early in the morning. They stood in front of the bulldozers. The bulldozers waited. The women eventually had to go pick up kids and finish chores so the bullies gnashed teeth and went ahead.

Back to Sue's studio and the landscapes she'd been working on seemed irrelevant. And she wanted to do something more serious than political cartooning. She made postcards of Modderdam, before and after the demolition.

It was her start. "I didn't think they were that radical," she says. The cards were banned within a week of being sent out.

"It's always interesting to see how quickly something can get hit on the head when the government thinks it's necessary. Also, that things are considered 'safe' as long as they're on the hallowed walls of the art gallery."

Sue is an optimist, dressed in jeans and running shoes. She's not naive and she's not scared. "I don't see any hope in the government. The only time there's ever any change is when they're absolutely forced into it. They never work from a basis of humanity or common sense. They'll never get Crossroads down."

There's a man selling timber to build houses right next to the Administration Board's offices. She believes that with a spirit like that, the government will only make fools of themselves.

"They'd better just leave it alone. Really."

At her exhibition someone asks, "Isn't having to carry a pass similar to carrying a driver's license?" Sue has calm blue eyes. They can become brittle. "I don't think that's a good analogy," she answers thinly.

There is a lot of explaining to do. In her dual role of artist and educator, Sue Williamson has to wrangle with enemies like ignorance and prejudice.

It took her over three years to complete the fourteen images presented in her portfolio. And she's still not finished. Her task is ongoing, researching and hunting out the brave ones who refuse to be crushed by propoganda and law.

She puts her faith in the women of this country. They are less egocentric and aggressive. "When it comes down to it," she says simply, "they are just better people."

She manifests the same qualities as the women in her series - an indefinable solitude and strength. It was sung about in the 1956 protest march: "Strijdom, you have tampered with the women ... You have struck against rock."

## A FEW SOUTH AFRICANS IN PORTRAIT

CHARLOTTE MAXEKE - Dubbed the Mother of African freedom in this country. A forerunner of Black Consciousness thinking, she declared in a speech in 1935: "The Non-Europeans, while thanking their European friends for their support, had to go ahead themselves. The Natives were not a peculiar people who had to be carried on the backs of others forever."

LILIAN NGOYI - President of the Federation of South African Women in the 50's. "I started feeling some changes in this whole matter of race. It was so exciting, I felt like writing with all my fingers." A treason trialist in 1956, she was placed under heavy banning orders in 1961 and lived almost the last third of her life as a "non-Person".

ANNIE SALINGA - "I will carry a pass the day the Prime Minister's wife carries a pass," Annie Salinga told the huge crowd gathered outside the Cape Town City Hall during the defiance campaign in 1952. And to this day neither of them do. Now, old and bedridden, officials have urged her to take a pass so that she may qualify for a pension. She laughs them away. "After all these years? No thank you."

WINNIE MANDELA - Key person in many black organisations now banned, Winnie has been repeatedly subject to detention, house-arrest and imprisonment. Banished to a small, dusty Afrikaner dorp, she is still perpetually harassed but nothing has prevented her from speaking out fearlessly when able to. She remains a powerful symbol of the African struggle.

HELEN JOSEPH - Determined activist against apartheid and leader over the years of powerful protests. In 1962, became the first person put under house arrest in South Africa. One of the patrons of the United Democratic Front, and the affectionate name with which she was introduced at the launch rally in Cape Town -"the mother of the struggle" - is no more than her due.

VULA 21

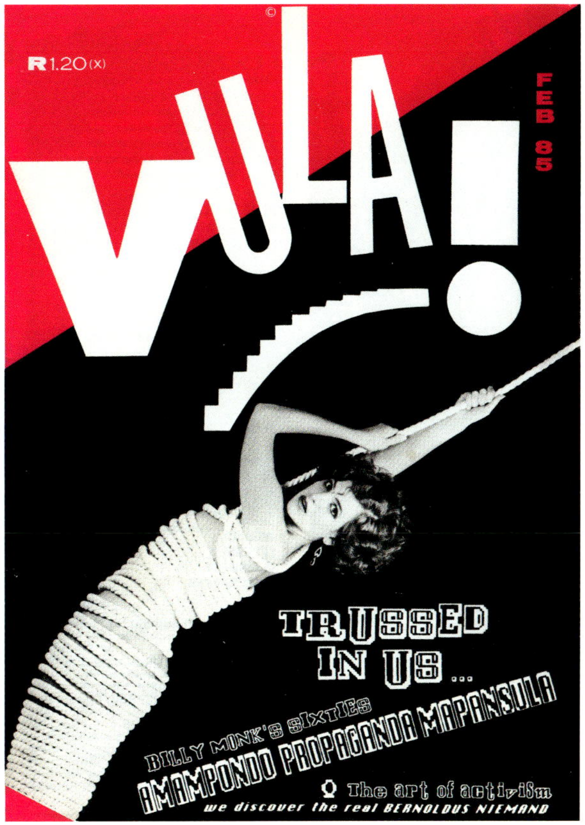


*Vula* magazine first appeared in December 1984, a product of the first wave of desktop publishing which allowed small groups to enter the magazine market. *Vula*'s subject was art, music, fashion and popular culture, and it quickly became one of the country's top alternative publications, before disappearing sometime in 1987.

*Vula* cover, February 1985

# R.I.P. Annie Silinga

Annie Silinga was a veteran anti-apartheid activist who was prominent in the Defiance Campaign of the 1950s and who was an accused alongside Nelson Mandela in the 1957 Treason Trial. She famously refused to carry a passbook until the wife of the Prime Minister did so herself. In 1982, Sue Williamson photographed her at her home in Langa, a Cape Town township, dressed in the green and black robes and hat of the South African Federation of Women. Annie died in 1984, and at the family's request, the artist designed T-shirts screenprinted with her portrait of the deceased, to be worn at the funeral.

A decade later, in 1995, after South Africa's first democratic elections, the artist was invited to participate in the First Johannesburg Biennale in a show entitled *Objects of Defiance, Spaces of Contemplation.* The curator, Emma Bedford, asked participants to revisit an old work and make a new one.

Williamson considered making a portrait of Annie's daughter, Eslina, but when she and Eslina visited Silinga's grave, in the Langa cemetery, the artist was shocked to see that only a wooden cross decorated the grave. She decided to make a funereal work, in the "cradle" style popular among black South Africans, and to install it on red earth at MuseuMAfrica in Johannesburg for the Biennale. The cradle was made of cut steel plates and inlaid with circles of glass silkscreened with Williamson's portraits of Silinga and events from her life. It bore the epigraph, "I will never carry a pass." On the piled red earth were plastic spheres purchased from a funeral florist. To fill them, Williamson made flowers from photocopies of photographs of the 1956 Women's March to Pretoria to protest against the carrying of passes for women. Annie had been one of the marchers.

After the exhibition, the steel cradle was moved permanently to Silinga's actual gravesite in Langa, where it was cemented into the ground and consecrated in a ceremony attended by Winnie Mandela, Adelaide Tambo, and other struggle veterans following a memorial event at the Silinga home. President Mandela sent his regrets at being unable to attend.

In Langa, the work was a collaborative effort with the family—which elected, for example, to lay stones inside the cradle spraypainted in the green, black and yellow colours of the African National Congress. A decade or so later, the gravesite was vandalised and the stolen metal probably sold as scrap.

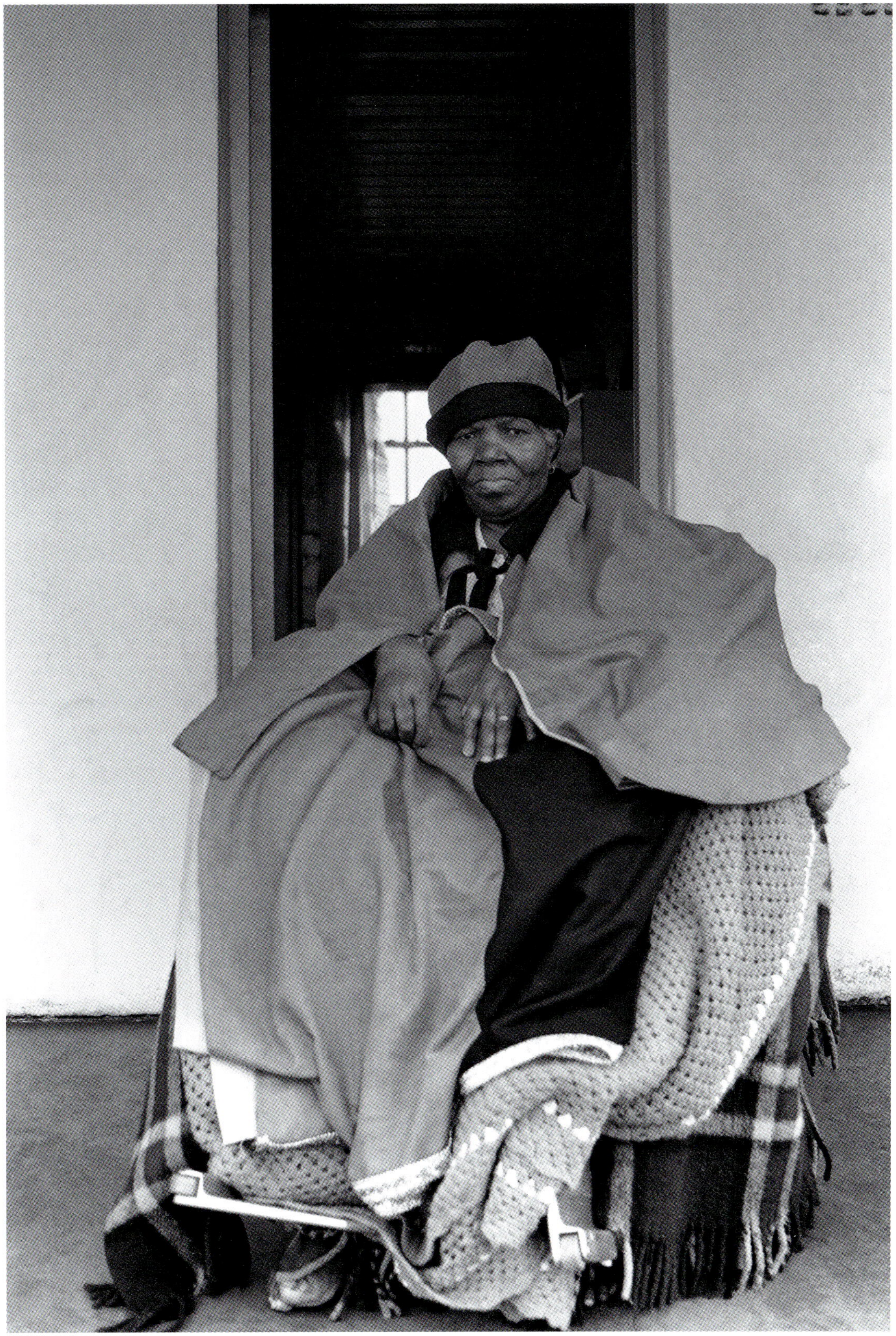

*Annie Silinga II*
1983
*All Our Mothers* series
Pigment inks on archival paper
59 x 39 cm

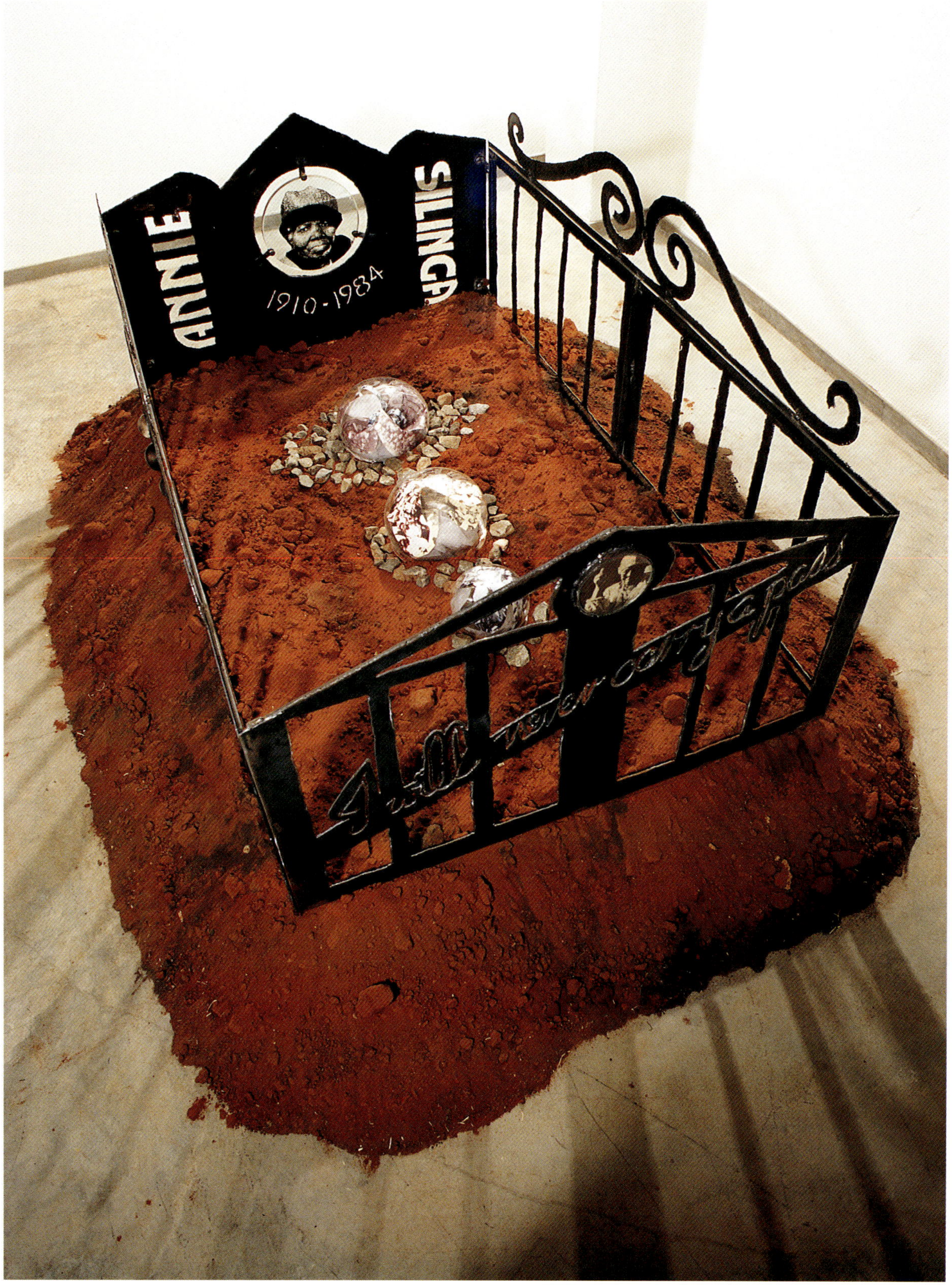


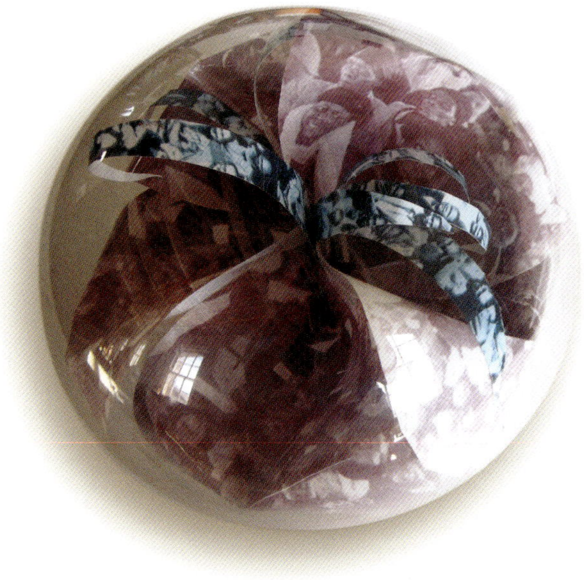

*R.I.P. Annie Silinga*
1997
Steel, glass, etching, cast resin, plastic domes,
laminated colour photocopies, earth
Dimensions variable
Installation view, MuseuMAfrica, Johannesburg

"*R.I.P. Annie Silinga* … provides an interesting inversion of landscape, that "desperately confused" medium as James Elkins once described it, in which humans frame relationships to memory, place, and a host of other deeply held personal and cultural ideals and values. Sue Williamson neither conceives nature—as Kenneth Clark so formatively defined the transition of landscape into art —nor does she manipulate the landscape directly in the fashion of Robert Smithson or her fellow countryman, Strijdom van der Merwe. She enacts it …

Through its form and its destined use, this work of art allowed one individual and her family to sustain a physical presence for a body absent from the landscape … [It] is the integration of a body lying beneath the landscape yet made readily apparent by a work of art that I find so compelling. *R.I.P. Annie Silinga* provides an easily accessible vision of a landscape as vertical. In its fragmented attention to the site of burial, our focus is drawn neither to the scenic, horizontal vistas of the earth's surface nor to the specific features of Annie Silinga's person, but to a subterranean connection where land and being meet."

*From "Where are the bodies? Interment and the Poetics of Absence" Karen Milbourne, presented at the 54th Annual Conference of the African Studies Association, November 17, 2011*

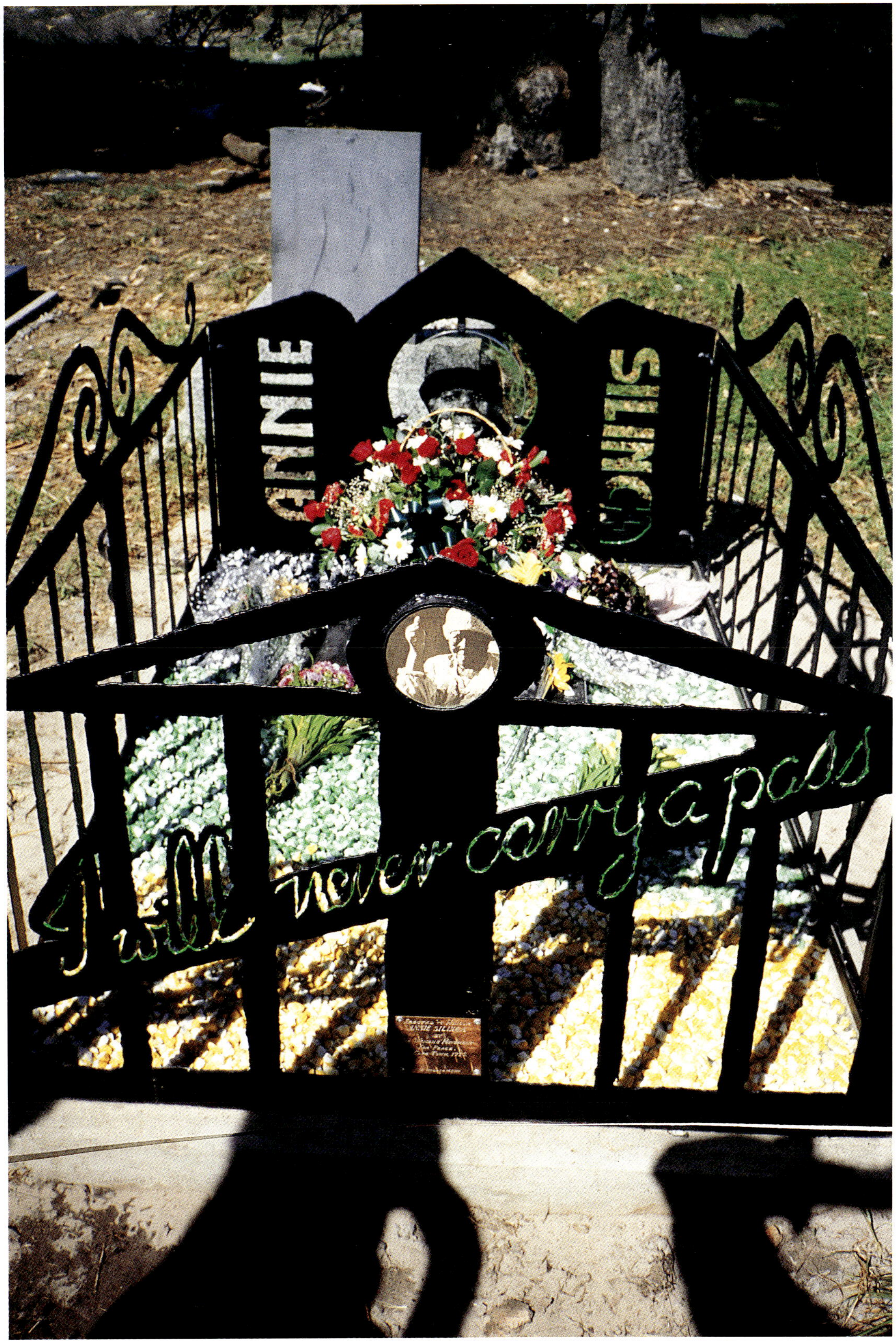


Annie Silinga's grave, installed in Langa Cemetery, Cape Town

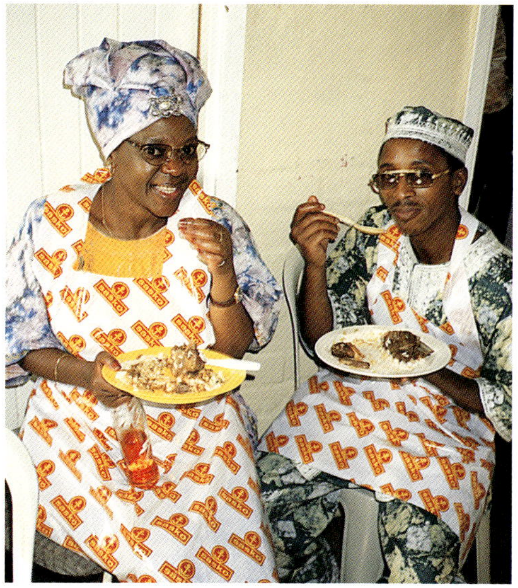

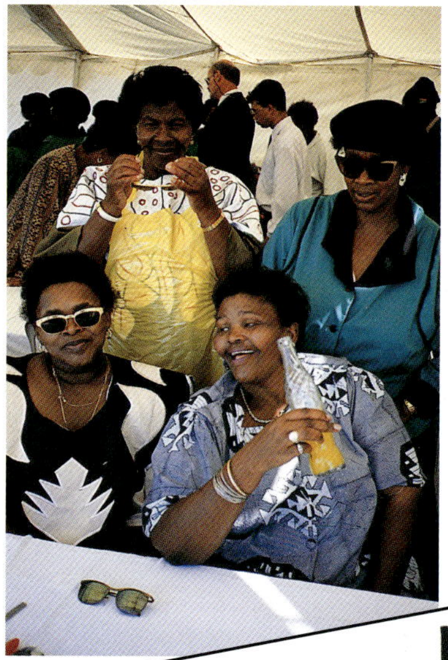

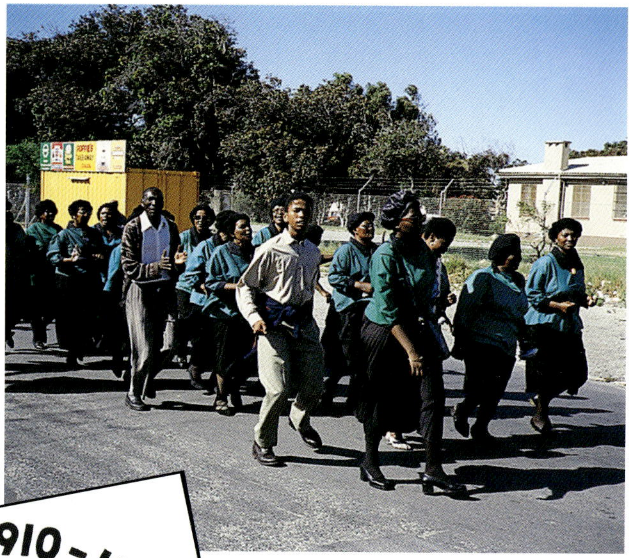

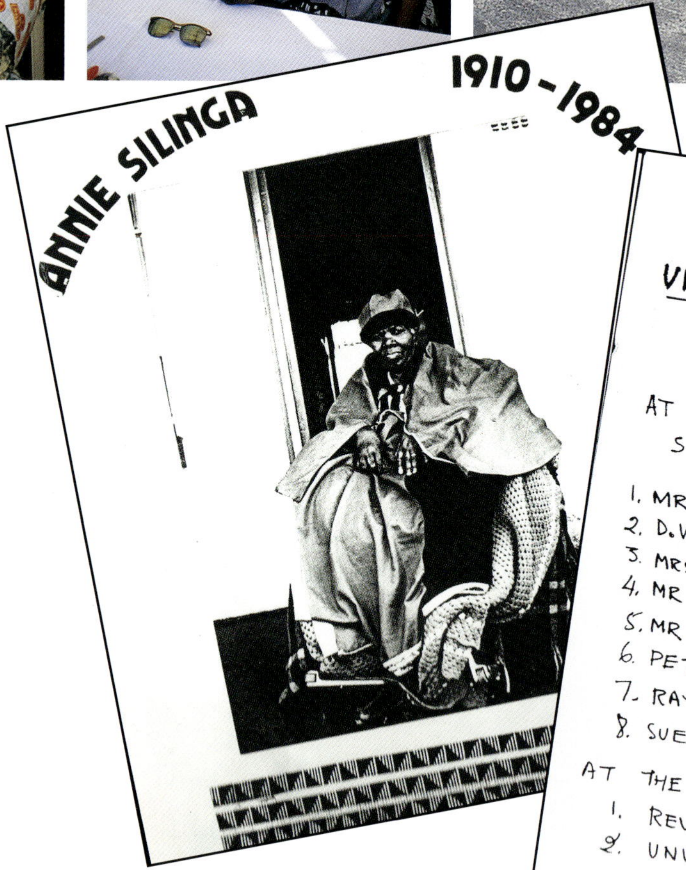

ANNIE SILINGA 1910-1984

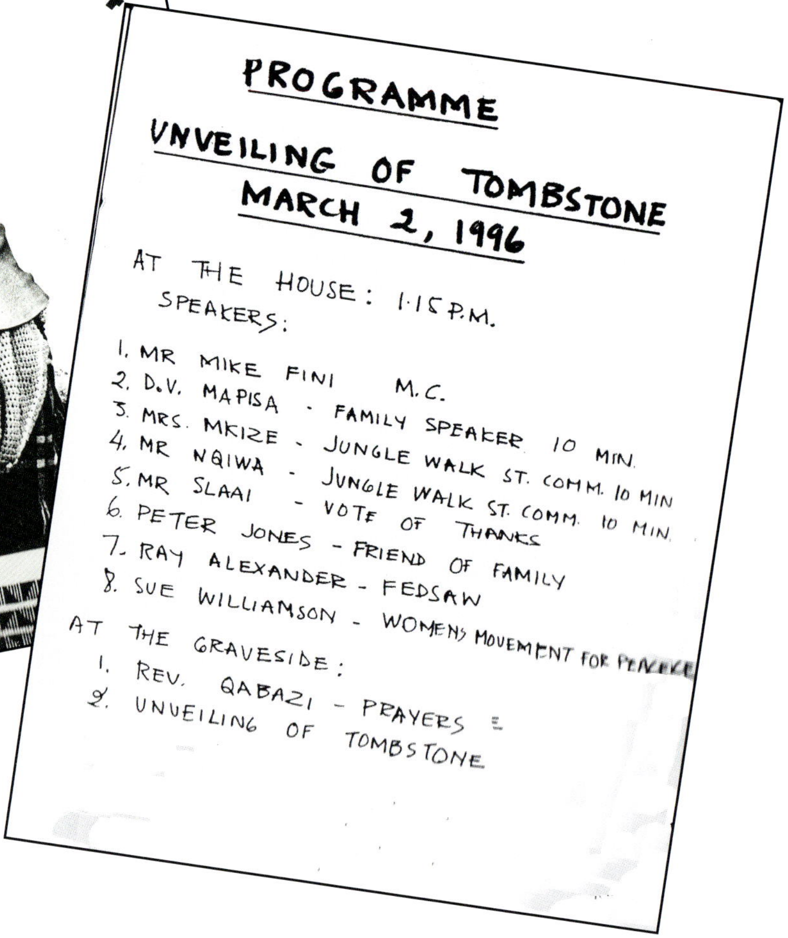

PROGRAMME

UNVEILING OF TOMBSTONE
MARCH 2, 1996

AT THE HOUSE: 1.15 P.M.
SPEAKERS:

1. MR MIKE FINI M.C.
2. D.V. MAPISA - FAMILY SPEAKER 10 MIN.
3. MRS. MKIZE - JUNGLE WALK ST. COMM. 10 MIN
4. MR NQIWA - JUNGLE WALK ST. COMM. 10 MIN.
5. MR SLAAI - VOTE OF THANKS
6. PETER JONES - FRIEND OF FAMILY
7. RAY ALEXANDER - FEDSAW
8. SUE WILLIAMSON - WOMENS MOVEMENT FOR PEACE

AT THE GRAVESIDE:
1. REV. QABAZI - PRAYERS
2. UNVEILING OF TOMBSTONE

Before the grave dedication ceremony, guests attended a memorial meal in the Silinga home

As above

The guests on their way from the Silinga home to the Langa cemetery for the dedication service

Williamson made and photocopied a leaflet giving the order of events

As above

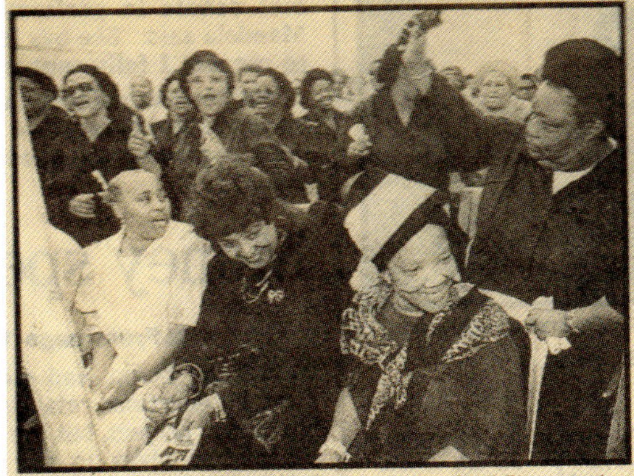

Pictures: ROY WIGLEY, Staff Photographer.

☐ **EXCITED CROWDS:** The arrival of Winnie Mandela, above, who now goes by the name of Nomzamo Winnie Madikizela-Mandela, caused excitement at the ceremony in Langa.

☐ **DEFIED PASS LAWS:** Veteran activists, including Ray Alexander, right, gathered at the graveyard to unveil the tombstone for Annie Silinga, who died in 1984.

# Langa honours former activist

CAPE ARGUS 2/3/96

**GLYNNIS UNDERHILL**
Staff Reporter

WINNIE Mandela was swamped by tourists trying to snap her photograph when she attended a ceremony to unveil a tombstone for veteran African National Congress activist Annie Silinga.

Tourists travelling through Langa in two buses yesterday chanced upon the house where speeches and prayers were dedicated to Mrs Silinga, who became famous during the apartheid years for refusing to carry a pass.

The presence of Mrs Mandela at the ceremony caused a buzz of excitement and the tourists rushed over with cameras at the ready as she left the house to travel in convoy to the graveyard.

Mrs Silinga, who died in 1984, was deported to the Transkei twice but defiantly re-entered the country on both occasions.

Her tombstone, surrounded by stones in the ANC colours, was unveiled at the Langa graveyard near her house. The words "She died, never carrying a pass" were a fitting tribute to a woman who defied the odds under apartheid.

Her daughter, Eslina Silinga, said her mother had been brave "until the last."

"We cannot forget her. She might have died but her spirit is still here," she said.

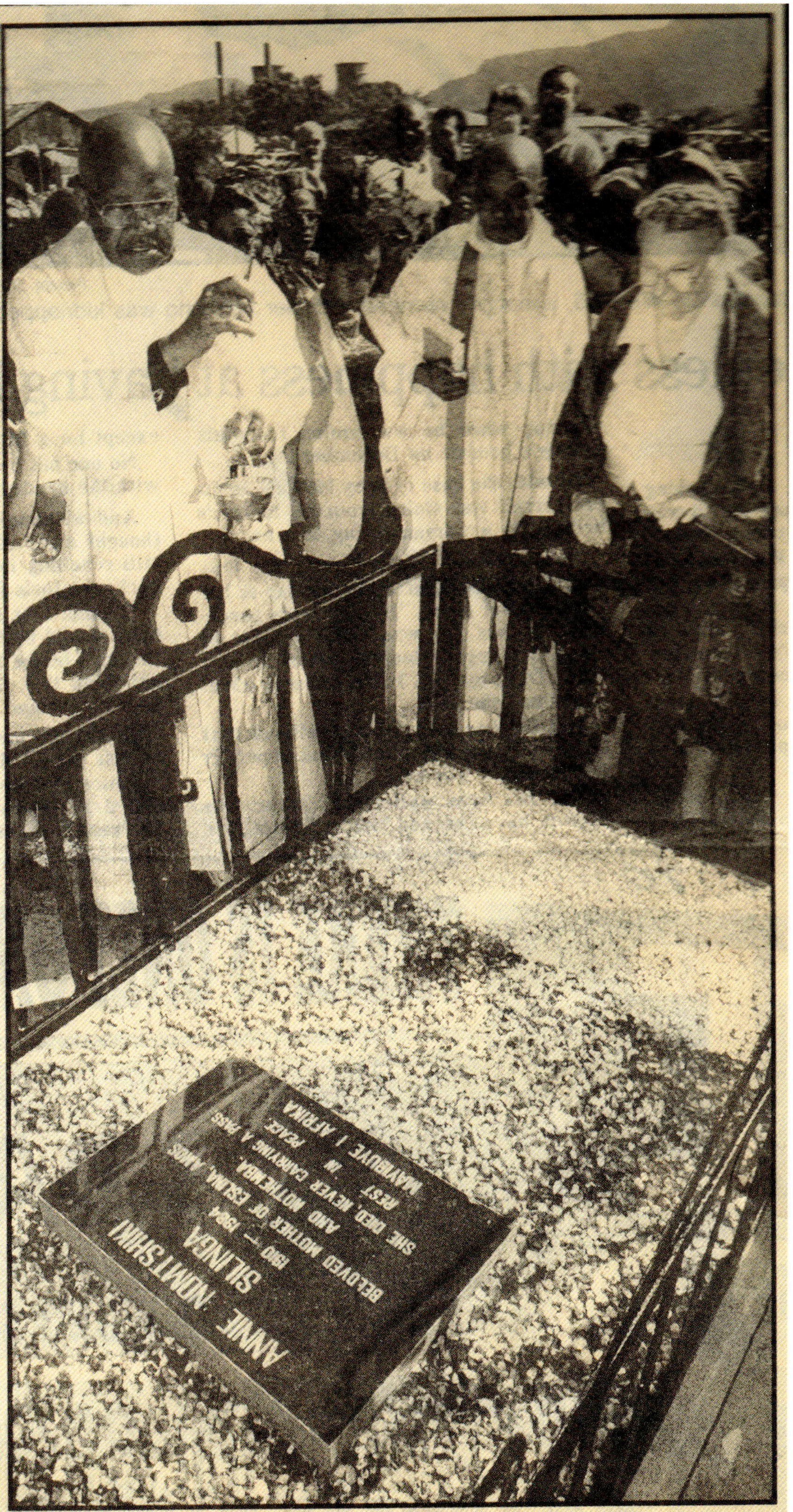


A press cutting of the event

# District Six

## Sue Williamson in conversation with Ciraj Rassool



*When Sue Williamson lived in Cape Town in 1964, working in an advertising agency, her downtown office overlooked the fabled, vibrant, racially mixed District Six. Plans were already afoot to declare this very desirable inner-city neighbourhood, on the slopes of Devils Peak and overlooking the docks, into a white Group Area, and to remove its 60 000 residents to the distant Cape Flats. By the time Williamson returned to live in Cape Town in 1971, the eviction process was just beginning; later in the decade she began to mobilise against it as an activist with the Women's Movement for Peace and the Friends of District Six. The district was renamed Zonnebloem, "Sunflower", but it was never substantially resettled. The works which follow were all made in response to the destruction of District Six, and of the home of one family in particular: the Ebrahims of Manley Villa on Rochester Road. She had met Naz Gool-Ebrahim, a community leader, through the Women's Movement for Peace. They became fellow activists and good friends. In May 2015, Williamson went to the site of Manley Villa with Ciraj Rassool, writer, cultural historian, and a professor at the University of the Western Cape. Rassool was born in District Six and went to school there; he is a close relative of the Ebrahims and knew the house well. The two stood at the site of Manley Villa and spoke about the district, its legacy, Manley Villa and their work.*

**Sue Williamson**: The view from here hits me every time.
**Ciraj Rassool**: The people of District Six lived between the mountain and the sea, but also in the middle of the city. This was their vista. You could be a whole human being here…

**SW**: I know your family is from District Six, Ciraj. Tell me about them.
**CR**: My father moved from District Six to Woodstock in 1954, but I was born in the maternity home in District Six, and much of my family lived here. That's my preparatory school down there, it still stands. In fact I had two aunties who lived here on Rochester Road. Aunty Didja and Aunty Naz. I have such rich memories of this landscape. Uncle Ozzie, my dad's friend, lived lower down on Rochester Road, and then there was the man who always slept in his motor vehicle. I don't know if he had been kicked out or what. You'd make your way past him, and past Aunty Didja's house, where there was always ice-cream waiting for you, because Uncle Ganief worked for an ice-cream company, and then on to Naz's house. That's where you wanted to be! The cousins were there…
**SW**: Someone might be playing guitar, and if you were lucky, Naz would be in the kitchen making *roeties*, or something delicious. She was always so pleased to see everyone. She loved company, and she'd always welcome you. And she was always busy sorting out people's business for them, going and looking at their eviction notices, and saying she would phone or *do* something.

CR: She was a powerful personality. A magnet. She had been a teacher, and she was persecuted for her beliefs. She came from one of the Western Cape's most important political families: her aunt and mentor was Cissy Gool, and so she grew up with the politics of mobilisation of the 1950s all around her. When her own community was threatened in the 1970s, she took up the cudgels.

SW: I started hanging out here in the late 1970s. Every time I stepped out of the house you'd have this beautiful view over the bay. There was still a row of houses just below here. But by then one was aware of these holes in the fabric of the "District". They took the houses out bit by bit. And look at it now.
CR: It's such a complex and contested landscape. As we stand here we can see the Zonnebloem homes, into which white people were moved after the removals, but there weren't many; it was only policemen and the like who moved in. We can see the old mosques and churches that remained. At least they were spared the bulldozers by the activism of people like Naz. Over there, we can see the homes of returnees from Phase Two of the land restitution programme, which has taken an unacceptably long time. And slightly to its left, you see a building of absolute shame. This is the new residential complex of the Cape Peninsula University of Technology, built on top of the remains of old Hanover Street, a District Six memorial site where ex-residents had built a cairn of stones and where they went to remember their lives in the District for decades after their removal.

SW: One of our biggest struggles, as Friends of District Six, was to prevent the building of the Cape Technikon, as it was then called. We failed.
CR: Yes, and its presence was the most arrogant assertion of whiteness. But for the most part, District Six did not become a lived-in white area, because by the time they came to finish the removals, in the early 1980s, apartheid itself was changing. It had become, much more, a project by which the state was trying to win over the black middle classes. So alongside the repression of the apartheid state there was a kind of an odd reformist agenda. And the result is that District Six was never developed much… Of course the activism that Naz's group and people like you did was highly significant. It gave solace to the last remaining residents, and mobilised public opinion in quite a significant way.
SW: We went to prominent people and got signatures. When Shell announced they were going to build a garage we went and told them we'd consider organising a national boycott. We learned from our victory in Crossroads. By that time it was too late of course. They picked out houses here and there. They'd take this little street and that little street…

*As they are talking, an elderly man in a knitted prayer-cap picks his way down the track that used to be Rochester Road.*

CR: I know that man! I went to school with his kids. He comes walking down here as if he's walking down District Six. It's fantastic!
SW: It reminds me of elephants who know their ancient pathways. You can dam a river and they'll swim through the dam! What would you like to see here in ten years time, Ciraj?
CR: The land restitution process is very complex. I'd like to see returnees move back into homes, and to see them living their lives with a historical understanding of how people used to live here. We don't have to romanticise it, but this was the area where everybody lived, and everybody had a home. And it is possible to remake such a community, and to do so requires the cultural work of community building. What's significant about it is that it's going to be one of the only cases in South Africa where

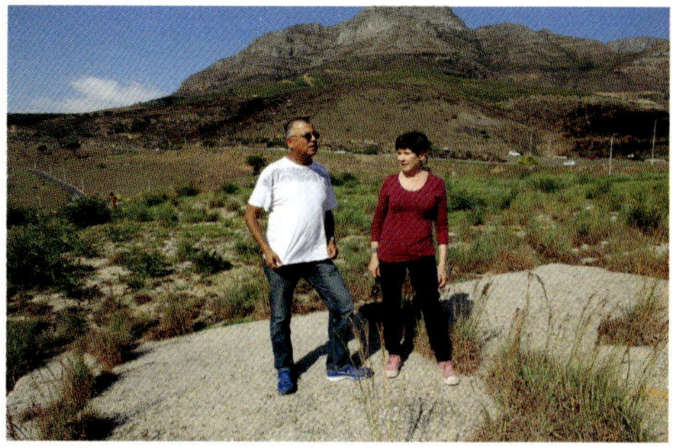

Ciraj Rassool and Sue Williamson in Rochester Road, District Six, April 2015

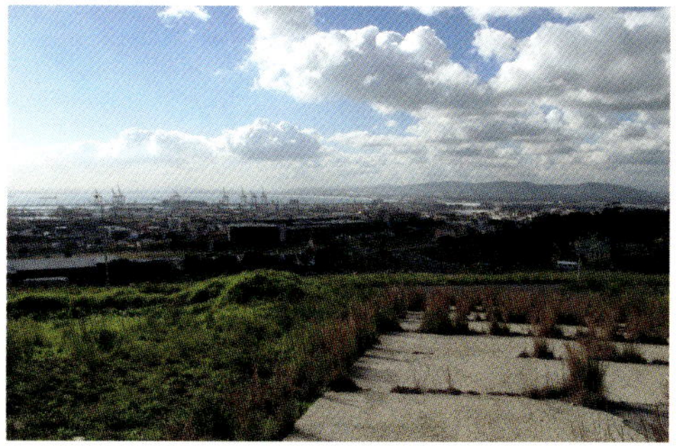

View down to the sea from the remains of Rochester Road

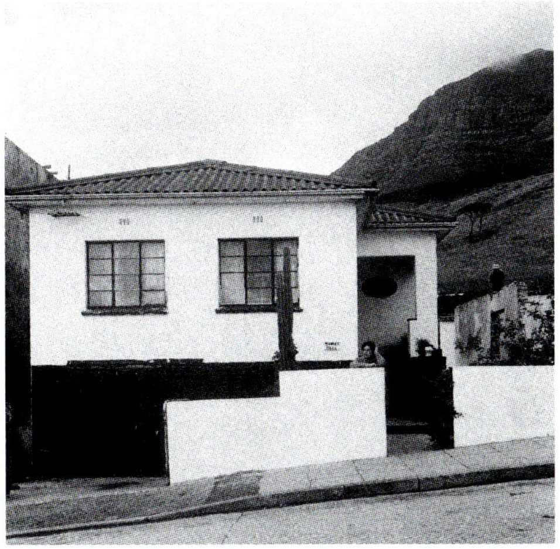

*Manley Villa*, 1981
*Last Supper at Manley Villa* series
Archival print on cotton rag
50 x 67.5 cm

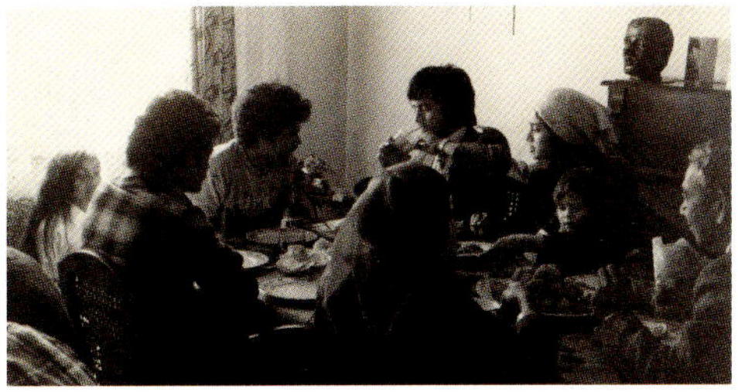

A family photograph of the Ebrahim family celebrating *Eid al Fitr* in their home for the last time, 1981

the poor are returned *to* the city centre. All over the country, you have the reverse: the poor on the periphery.

SW: That's exactly what one would wish to see. I hope it happens. But I have very little confidence in the city council and the various groups which seem to be fighting for control over these issues…
CR: It remains in flux. Look, you can see those quantity surveyors over there, hinting at the possibility of redevelopment. But you also have informal settlements…
SW: Yes, there's someone having his morning wash over there. Homeless people live here. Particularly down there, under the bridge…

CR: Sue, I want to talk to you about your work on District Six, all of which springs from that cataclysmic experience in 1981, of being inside Naz's home, inside Manley Villa, right here, with removals happening all around it, and bulldozers doing their demolitions right next door. It was at Ramadan, and Naz had just received her eviction order, and you came in with camera and your tape recorder!
SW: I was always interested in being here. On the day of Eid everyone who came was made to sign the wall next to the piano. I brought my whole family—my kids, and my brother. Naz had decided to cover her walls with graffiti, in defiance of the eviction, and she invited everyone to join her—with memories, with words of protest. Someone wrote on the walls, "Welcome to the Last Supper! The Truth is on the Walls!"
CR: She was turning her house into an artwork. Later, she would serve on the founding committee of the District Six Museum, where I would do work as a member of its board. At the museum, we would use methodologies of inscription, asking former residents to write on cloth, on a map on the floor, etc. I think we can say, then, that the District Six Museum began with Naz's "Last Supper".

SW: As for me, I was taking photos as background documentation for an installation I was planning for September at the Gowlett Gallery around the destruction of District Six. I'd been learning how to screenprint, and early in the year, the idea came to me to take pieces of rubble and screenprint addresses on to them to make an installation. But I decided in the end that the rubble was evocative enough, without having anything on it. I wanted to have a voice track with background sounds to accompany the rubble, so that through Naz and others I could make the District come alive. I'd interviewed Naz a lot already, and she steered me in the direction of others.

CR: I only became aware of your work later, when you exhibited *The Last Supper Revisited* at the Irma Stern Museum in 1993. I read the review by Stanley Hermans and the response. The debate was about who had the right to depict experiences of trauma. pp. 59-61
SW: "Who owns the story? Shouldn't it be left to the people of District Six to tell their own story?"

CR: There's a much more interesting set of questions that emerges out of the relationship between the process of documentation and the creative process. You were doing both. You were doing the work of history. You were witness to an unfolding history, and at the same time, while the blood was still wet, you were taking it into the gallery! This was at a time when you couldn't speak about these events without attracting state attention.
SW: It was a challenge. With the first exhibition, *The Last Supper*, I wanted to say to Capetonians, "as people interested in art, you have come to the gallery to look at this installation of rubble from District Six. But actually, you're passing it on a much larger scale every single day of your lives as you drive in and out of Cape Town. Have you thought about that?"

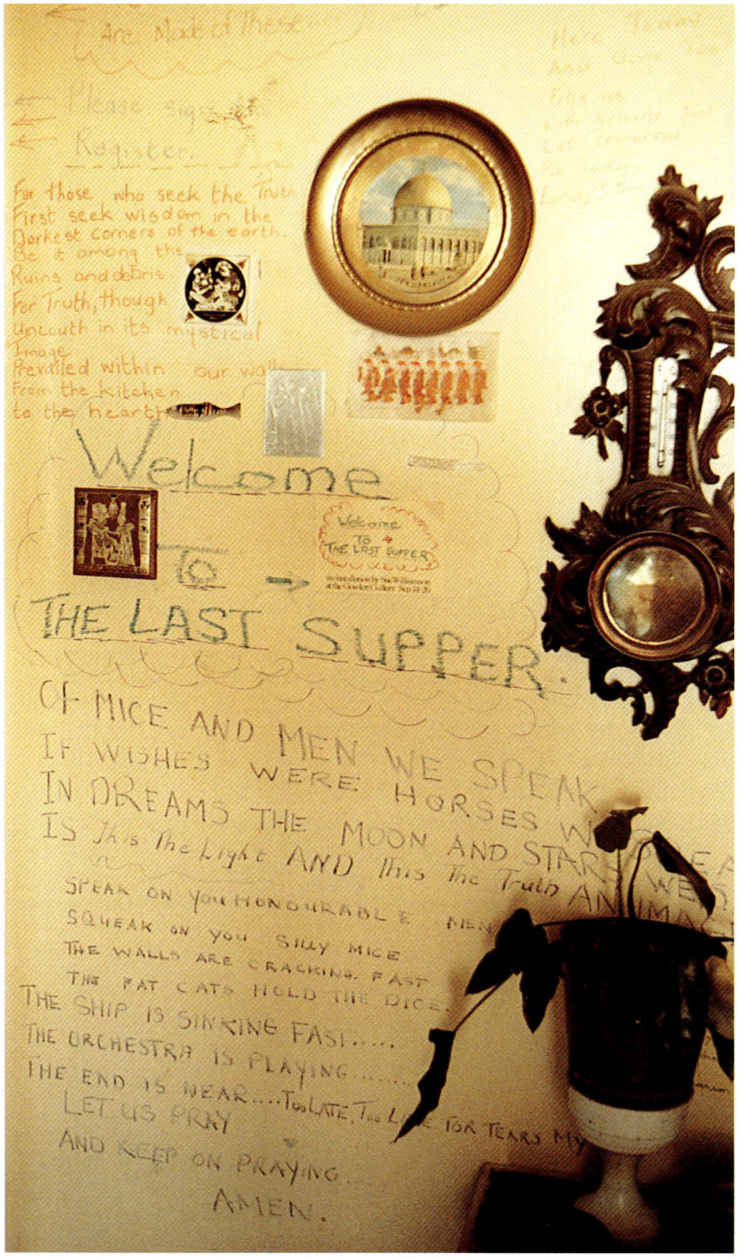


A wall in the entrance hall of Manley Villa

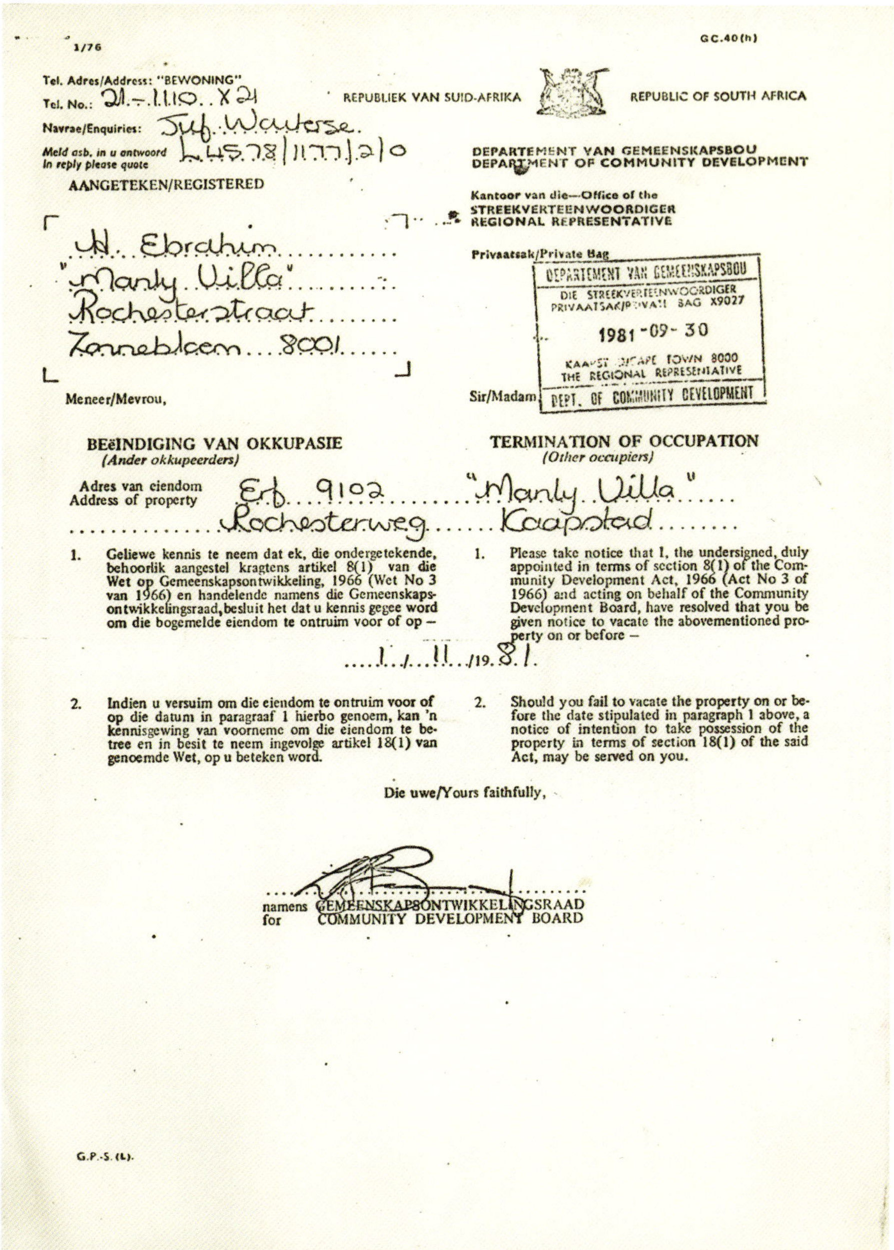

1/76 GC.40(h)

Tel. Adres/Address: "BEWONING"
Tel. No.: 21-1110 X21
Navrae/Enquiries: Juf. Wauterse.
Meld asb. in u antwoord / In reply please quote L4578/11771210

REPUBLIEK VAN SUID-AFRIKA — REPUBLIC OF SOUTH AFRICA

DEPARTEMENT VAN GEMEENSKAPSBOU
DEPARTMENT OF COMMUNITY DEVELOPMENT

AANGETEKEN/REGISTERED

Kantoor van die—Office of the
STREEKVERTEENWOORDIGER
REGIONAL REPRESENTATIVE

H. Ebrahim
"Manly Villa"
Rochesterstraat
Zonnebloem 8001

Privaatsak/Private Bag

DEPARTEMENT VAN GEMEENSKAPSBOU
DIE STREEKVERTEENWOORDIGER
PRIVAATSAK/PRIVATE BAG X9027
1981-09-30
KAAPSTAD/CAPE TOWN 8000
THE REGIONAL REPRESENTATIVE
DEPT. OF COMMUNITY DEVELOPMENT

Meneer/Mevrou, — Sir/Madam

**BEëINDIGING VAN OKKUPASIE**
*(Ander okkupeerders)*

**TERMINATION OF OCCUPATION**
*(Other occupiers)*

Adres van eiendom / Address of property: Erf 9102 "Manly Villa" Rochesterweg Kaapstad

1. Geliewe kennis te neem dat ek, die ondergetekende, behoorlik aangestel kragtens artikel 8(1) van die Wet op Gemeenskapsontwikkeling, 1966 (Wet No 3 van 1966) en handelende namens die Gemeenskapsontwikkelingsraad, besluit het dat u kennis gegee word om die bogemelde eiendom te ontruim voor of op –

1. Please take notice that I, the undersigned, duly appointed in terms of section 8(1) of the Community Development Act, 1966 (Act No 3 of 1966) and acting on behalf of the Community Development Board, have resolved that you be given notice to vacate the abovementioned property on or before –

1/11/1981.

2. Indien u versuim om die eiendom te ontruim voor of op die datum in paragraaf 1 hierbo genoem, kan 'n kennisgewing van voorneme om die eiendom te betree en in besit te neem ingevolge artikel 18(1) van genoemde Wet, op u beteken word.

2. Should you fail to vacate the property on or before the date stipulated in paragraph 1 above, a notice of intention to take possession of the property in terms of section 18(1) of the said Act, may be served on you.

Die uwe/Yours faithfully,

namens GEMEENSKAPSONTWIKKELINGSRAAD
for COMMUNITY DEVELOPMENT BOARD

G.P.-S. (L).

A copy of the eviction notice received by the Ebrahim family

**CR**: For me, that is the most profoundly activist of all your work. It was in the moment of removal. It was done at a time when it was dangerous to do such work. There was a very direct relationship between the documentation you were doing and the way these were becoming artworks. You actually used Naz's chairs!
**SW**: Yes, she had to make do without them for a while. She was very much part of the process. She came and opened the exhibition.

**CR**: Later, you brought Naz back to District Six.
**SW**: What do you mean?
**CR**: (Pointing) That highway, now called the Nelson Mandela Boulevard, was built in 1967. It cut District Six in two. Forced removals only took place in the upper section.

**SW**: Yes, so my gallery, the Goodman Gallery, in the Fairweather Building down below the highway, is actually in District Six.
pp. 71-3, 75 **CR**: Exactly! And you exhibited *Last Supper at Manley Villa* there, in 2008.
**SW**: Did you see it there?
**CR**: Yes I did, and it gave me pause to think about the journey you've come with this work, from the documentation of an artist at work in the midst of a traumatic situation where people were trying to cope with the sound of bulldozing all around, to the photographs of *Last Supper At Manley Villa* nearly thirty years later, photographs of the same event, but now printed on Hannemuhle paper in an edition of 20 of which a certain amount are available as special portfolio copies.
The status of the work has changed, inevitably.
And there's something unresolved about this.
**SW**: It's always difficult. I make work about social issues because that is my deep interest, and I want to raise awareness, but it is still art.

**CR**: I thought about it again when I was part of a related event a few years later: the launch of this book with the same name, *The Truth is on the Walls*, a posthumously-published memoir by Naz. You were there…
**SW**: Yes. It was at the District Six Museum.
**CR**: I think the photograph on the cover must be yours, because you are thanked in the acknowledgements.

**SW**: I'm glad about that…
**CR**: I can hear in the way you say those words that there's an unresolved element in all this...
**SW**: I had lost touch with the family over the years…
**CR**: So after the launch of this book, you invited Naz's daughters, Shahena and Drizzie, to your studio. Shahena came out especially for the book launch. She had left in the 1980s because she married a white man, and they had gotten sanctuary in the US. I was privileged to be present in your studio, and what I saw there was a kind of "truth and reconciliation" event between you, the artist, and Naz's daughters. I took photographs. Very few words were spoken, but the mood was profound.

**SW**: I was so pleased to have them in the studio. I had never met Shahena. Drizzie I'd known. But as I said, I'd lost touch with her, and didn't know how to find her. I was relieved.
**CR**: You had laid everything out. All of your clippings, all of your prints, photographs, all the things you collected, and you said, "Please take whatever you want". It seemed to me an acknowledgement that the position of the artist who works with historical experience is necessarily a difficult one…

# The Last Supper

Through the Friends of District Six, Sue Williamson met and befriended Naz Gool-Ebrahim, a community leader, who lived in Manley Villa on Rochester Road. By 1981, the house was one of the last standing in the once tightly packed district, and the Ebrahims, along with the other few remaining families, called themselves "The Last Supper."

Gool-Ebrahim received her eviction notice on the eve of Eid Al Fitr, the feast at the end of the Ramadan fast. She channelled her rage by writing her anger all over the walls of the house, and when her visitors arrived for the feast, she asked them to join her in inscribing their feelings and memories onto the walls of Manley Villa too. One of her lodgers wrote outside the front door: "The truth is on the walls inside this house. The truth that is denied". In the front hall, visitors were greeted with, "Welcome to the Last Supper."

Williamson had been working for months collecting rubble smashed down by the bulldozers, and picking up objects left behind by departed families. She was planning an art installation which would focus on the merciless state destruction of the district. Now, having attended Naz Gool-Ebrahim's Eid Al Fitr feast, she decided to reference this act of commemoration by calling her exhibition *The Last Supper*.

In September that year, Williamson piled the debris she had collected from District Six in the centre of the pristine white space of the Gowlett Gallery in central Cape Town. On the floor at the base were small remnants of domesticity: broken cups, stained school exercise books, half a basin, a decorative plaster column, which had once stood in a garden, chunks of brickwork with six layers of paint discernible, an elaborate wrought iron grille, half a door with a peace symbol.

The artist borrowed six chairs from the Manley Villa dining room and shrouded them in white cloth. She set them around the rubble, symbolizing the people who had been forced to leave. She had also made a soundscape for the exhibition, recording the ear-piercing sounds of the bulldozers knocking down buildings and the muezzin's call, and interspersing these with the voices of residents from District Six recalling the good old days, or expressing anger at the apartheid state. Miriam, the wedding singer, sang her classic song.

Naz Gool-Ebrahim opened the exhibition.

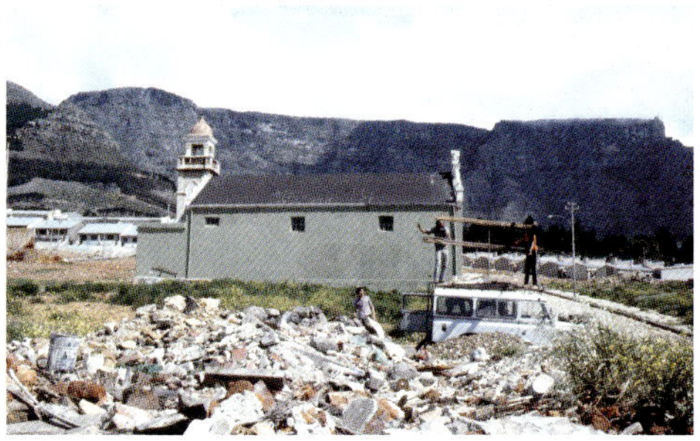

Williamson and friends from District Six load up rubble from a demolition site

*The Last Supper*
1981
Found objects, sound, photographs
Installation view
The Gowlett Gallery, Cape Town

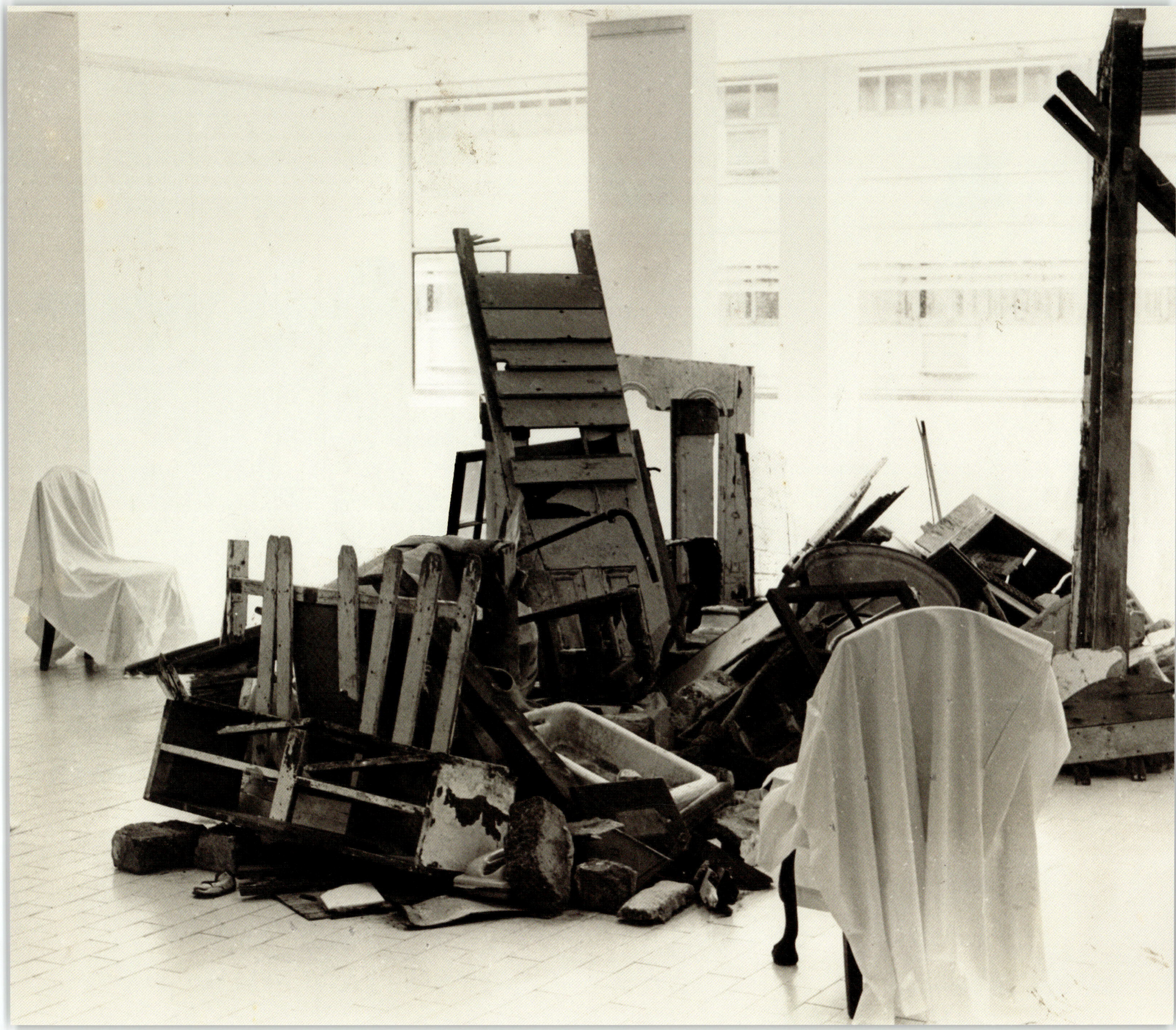

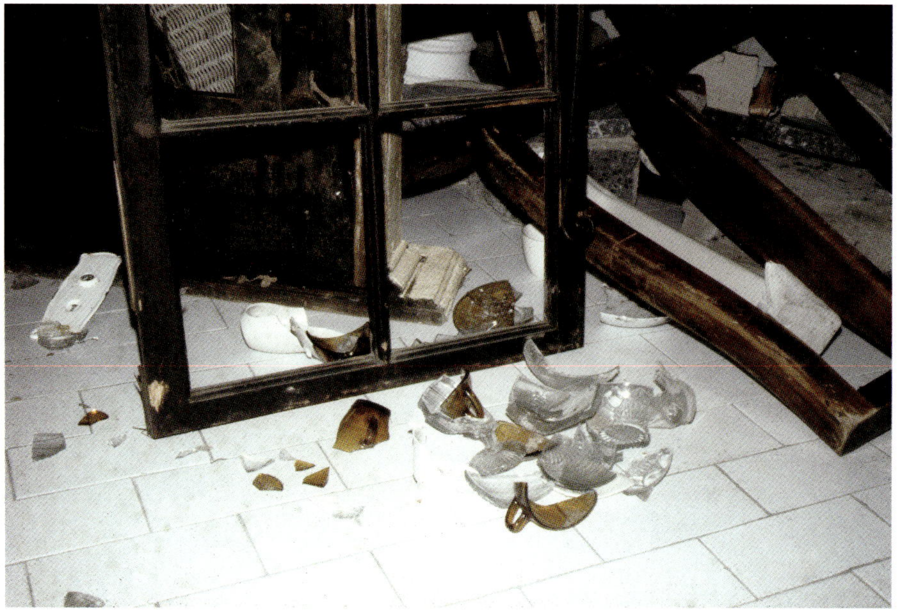

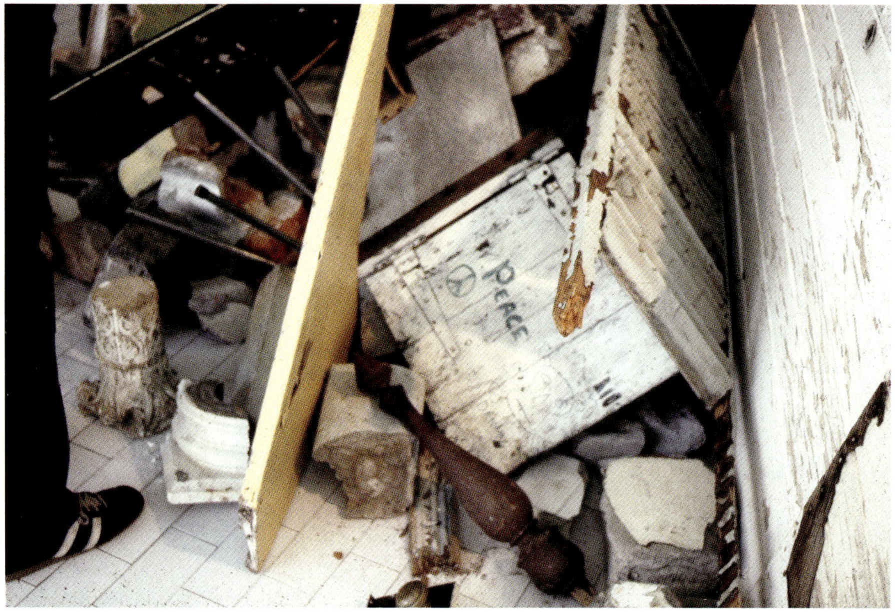


*The Last Supper* (detail)
1981
Found objects, sound
The Gowlett Gallery, Cape Town

*The Last Supper* (detail)
1981
Found objects, sound
The Gowlett Gallery, Cape Town

"[The Group Areas official] said "Whether you like it or not, this is not District Six any more. This is Zonnebloem."
I said, "Fine, Zonnebloem, so where you gonna put us?"
He said, "Mitchells Plain."
I said, "I'm not going to Mitchells Plain."
He said, "Well if that's your attitude, *hoekom trou jy nie a witman en gaan woon in Sea Point?* [Why don't you marry a white man and go and live in Sea Point?]
And I said, "I don't need to marry a white man to live in Sea Point. I'm quite satisfied where I am, and I don't want to move.""

Drizzie Ebrahim, Naz's daughter
From the soundtrack for *The Last Supper*, 1981

"1981 is actually my golden jubilee year in District Six. I came here in 1931 during the depression. And fifty years is a damn long time. I've been sitting and wondering how was District Six when I came here? It was a bustling metropolis with people in every shape and form, with humour and all the love in their hearts. We were like one family. And today, this family's been broken up. Very sad indeed. Why would all this happen to a community so closely knitted together? I ask myself, "has Man gone insane?"
The people itself, with their cultures, diverse cultures and traditions made District Six one of the most colourful nooks in this world. It was known throughout the world as District Six. Some people call it Fairyland, others call it Peyton Place, others just called it Crazy Corner. But call it what you may, I think that District Six, it was a legend."

Naz Ebrahim
From the soundtrack for *The Last Supper*, 1981

SUNDAY TRIBUNE, SEPTEMBER 20, 1981

HOW A CAPE ART EXHIBITION SLAMS HOME THE MESSAGE OF GROUP AREAS CRUELTY . . .

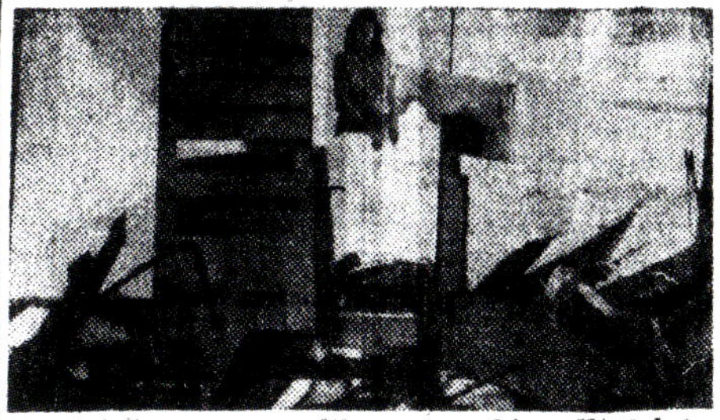

Sue Williamson with some of her District Six junk

# Junk tells tragedy of District Six

EVERYONE agrees — the exhibition at a Cape Town art gallery is a pile of junk.

by TONY SPENCER-SMITH

Cape Town artist Sue Williamson is currently holding one of the most unusual exhibitions ever seen in this country — and it is all to bring home to people the tragedy of the destruction of District Six under the Group Areas Act.

It comes at an appropriate time, with the recommendation of the President's Council this week that the area be given back to the coloured people.

The Government still has to consider the recommendation.

People who enter the spacious, gleaming, white-walled gallery in Long Street are confronted by a heap of rubble and broken bric-a-brac in the centre of the white-tiled floor.

And some even buy some bits.

Said Derek Gowlett, owner of the gallery: "Some people think we're doing building alterations and ask when the exhibition's starting.

"And one or two have been moved to tears by what they saw."

Sue Williamson — a graphic artist with a distinguished record who has exhibited her work at a number of centres, including Durban, London and Bologna — said she and friends had picked up all the bits and pieces in District Six since July in the wake of the bulldozers which turned the area into an urban desert.

Originally she intended to do a series of silkscreen prints about the destruction of the area. "But when I started looking at the rubble, it seemed so incredibly touching that I felt it would make a stronger statement than anything I could do."

So her home began to fill up with junk, which was eventually transported to the gallery and arranged with the help of boys from District Six.

There, viewers can stare at the heap while they [illegible] to tape recordings of growling bulldozers calling [illegible], and interviews with present and former residents — all made by Mrs Williamson.

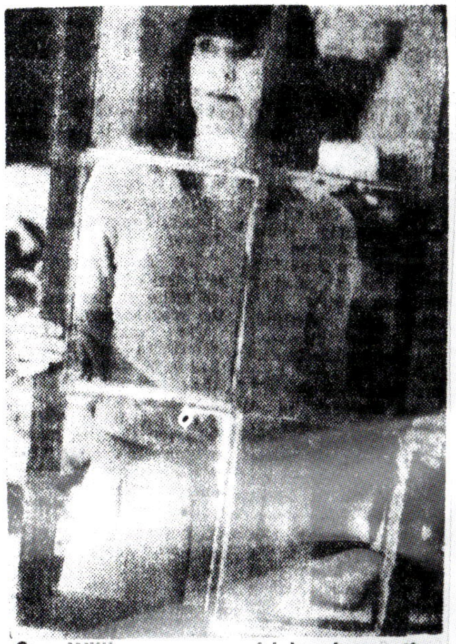

Sue Williamson . . . driving home the cruelty of the Group Areas Act

"To smash up community is bad, this one had such a s[…] of belonging and m[…] co-operation.

"Even the skoll[…] were gentlemen skoll[…] who would help little [...] ladies home with th[…] shopping.

"The destruction [...] District Six is a sym[…] of white greed — th[…] wanted it because it [...] close to the centre [...] town.

"The exhibition is n[…] just about District Six [...] it is about power and t[…] abuse of power, and t[…] kind of total devastati[…] that can occur whe[…] those who have absolu[…] power use it again[…] those who have none," says Mrs Williamson.

She has long bee[…] involved in District Si[…] and other communitie[…] like the Modderdam squatter camp.

Mrs Williamson is [...] senior member of Cap[…] Town's Women'[…] Movement for Peace an[…] as such she was ver[…] active in the Nyanga squatter crisis.

She said that if the Government did give the area back to the coloured people it would be better than keeping it for whites, but it would, in a sense, be rubbing salt in the wound.

"The real District Six is gone forever, and such a move could never cancel out all the bitterness caused.

"And the Government would only be doing it because they couldn't get whites to build in the area and it was just standing empty."

The exhibition is called The Last Supper, a reference to the last time the Muslim festival of Eid — the breaking of the fast Ramadan — was celebrated there last month.

It is also the name the few remaining families in District Six, who are holding out pending eviction, have given themselves.

Items on show, besides pure rubble, include a battered old cast-iron fireplace, a tin kettle, a yellow window frame with every pane broken, shoes, used school exercise books, including one with a drawing of a skeleton and smashed cups.

Everything is for sale "for any price a buyer cares to name".

The proceeds will go.

"Junk tells tragedy of District Six", *Sunday Tribune*, September 20, 1981

# The Last Supper Revisited

After the demolition of District Six, the area was never redeveloped, and remained a scar on the landscape of Cape Town, a vacuum in the middle of the city. Slowly the piles of rubble were covered by grass, and the slopes took on the appearance of an old bomb site.

In 1993, ten years after the last houses in District Six were demolished, the long-planned District Six Museum became a reality. This prompted Sue Williamson to return to the ruins of the district, to look for traces of the old community. Many of the old streets had been demolished, and the building of the new Cape Technikon had permanently altered the topography of the area. But the remains of the community were still there, just below the surface.

The process of collection began again. Scraps of building materials, china, books, the plastic wheel of a toy car. Some objects had their own charm and character, while others were just chunks of matter, unidentifiable except as the remains of something. Reprising the idea first explored in *The Last Supper* of rubble representing a bitter and indigestible meal, Williamson cast these scraps in resin blocks and laid them out on a circular glass table. At the Cape Town's Irma Stern Museum, they were illuminated from below so that they glowed, like precious objects set in amber.

Williamson has said that she quite deliberately gave all the remains she found "an equality of value, because they are all part of the fabric of District Six: a shard of porcelain that must have come from a quite-precious tea-pot, the shoe of a child's Barbie doll, or a bit of plastic packet which once held rice."

Three photographs of Naz Gool-Ebrahim and her family taken in Manley Villa covered the windows of the museum, and were in turn, partially covered by yellow plastic blinds, pulled down because the family had left. The original soundscape made in 1981, of the voices and sounds of District Six, accompanied the installation.

The work is now in the collection of the Museum of African Art at the Smithsonian Institution in Washington DC.

*The Last Supper Revisited* (detail)
1993
Glass, steel, found objects in casting resin,
digital images, plastic lighting, sound

Pages 60-1
*The Last Supper Revisited*
1993
Glass, steel, found objects in casting resin,
digital images, plastic, lighting, sound
Dimensions variable
Installation view
National Museum of African Art, Smithsonian
Institution, Washington D.C.

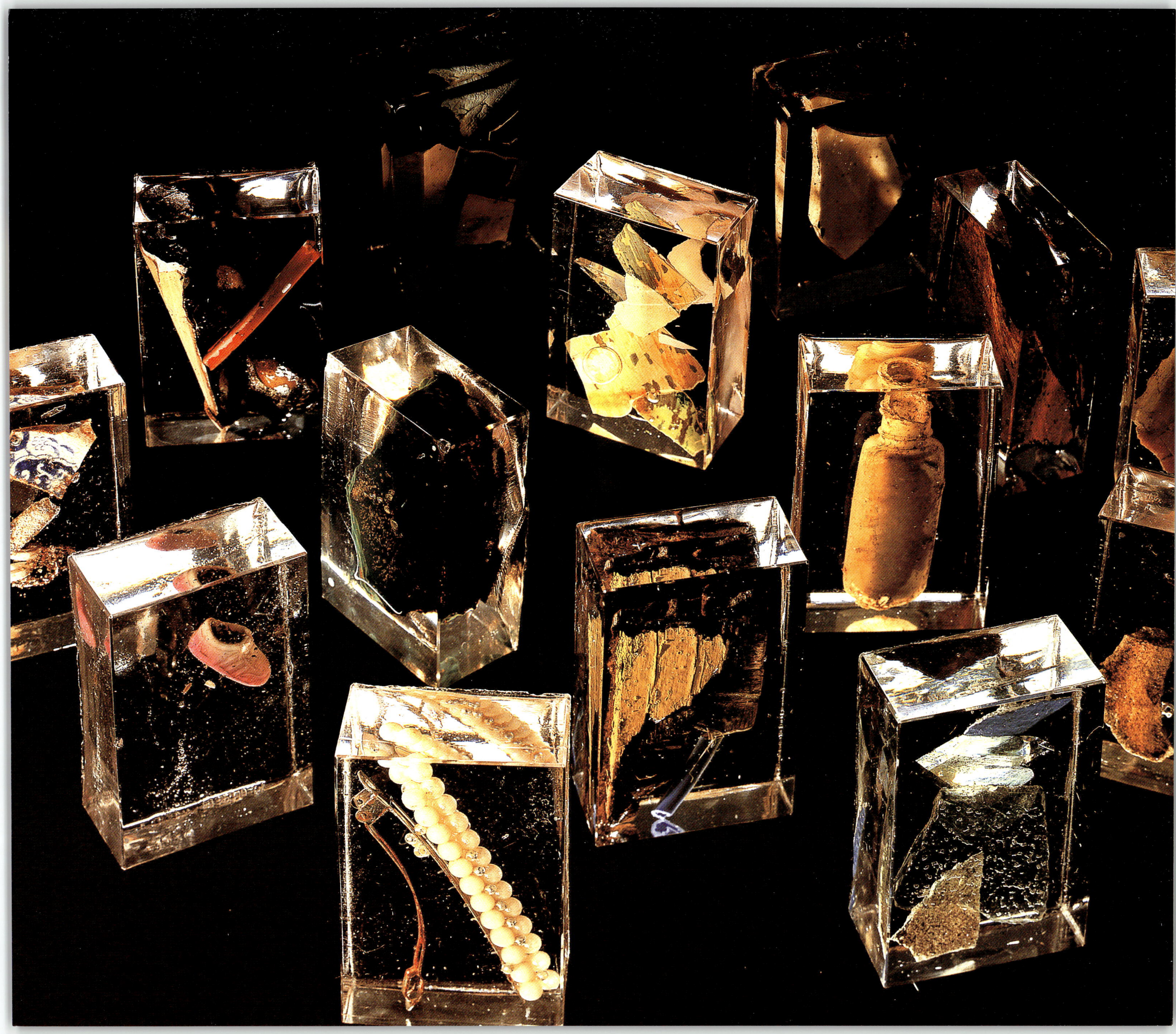

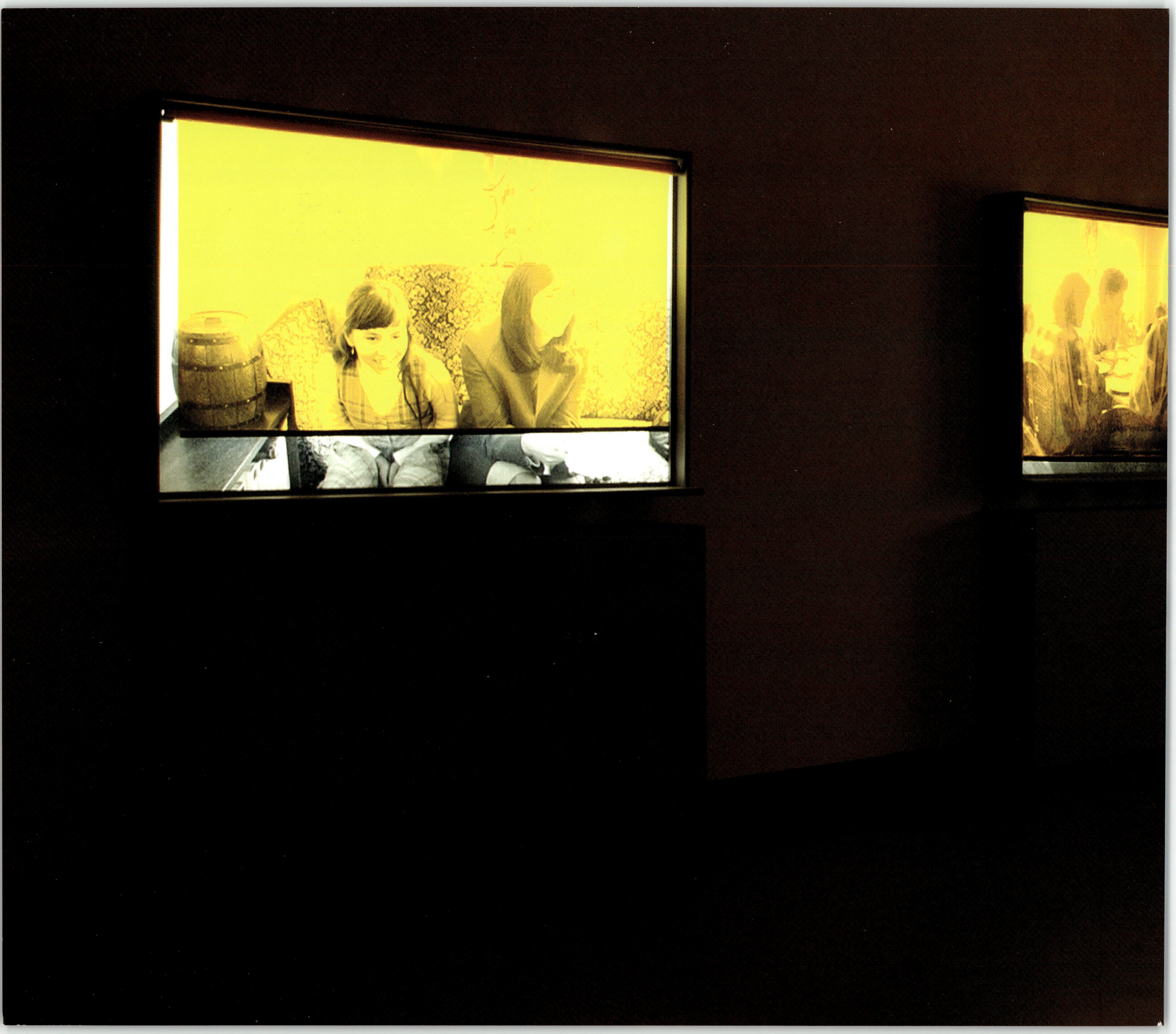

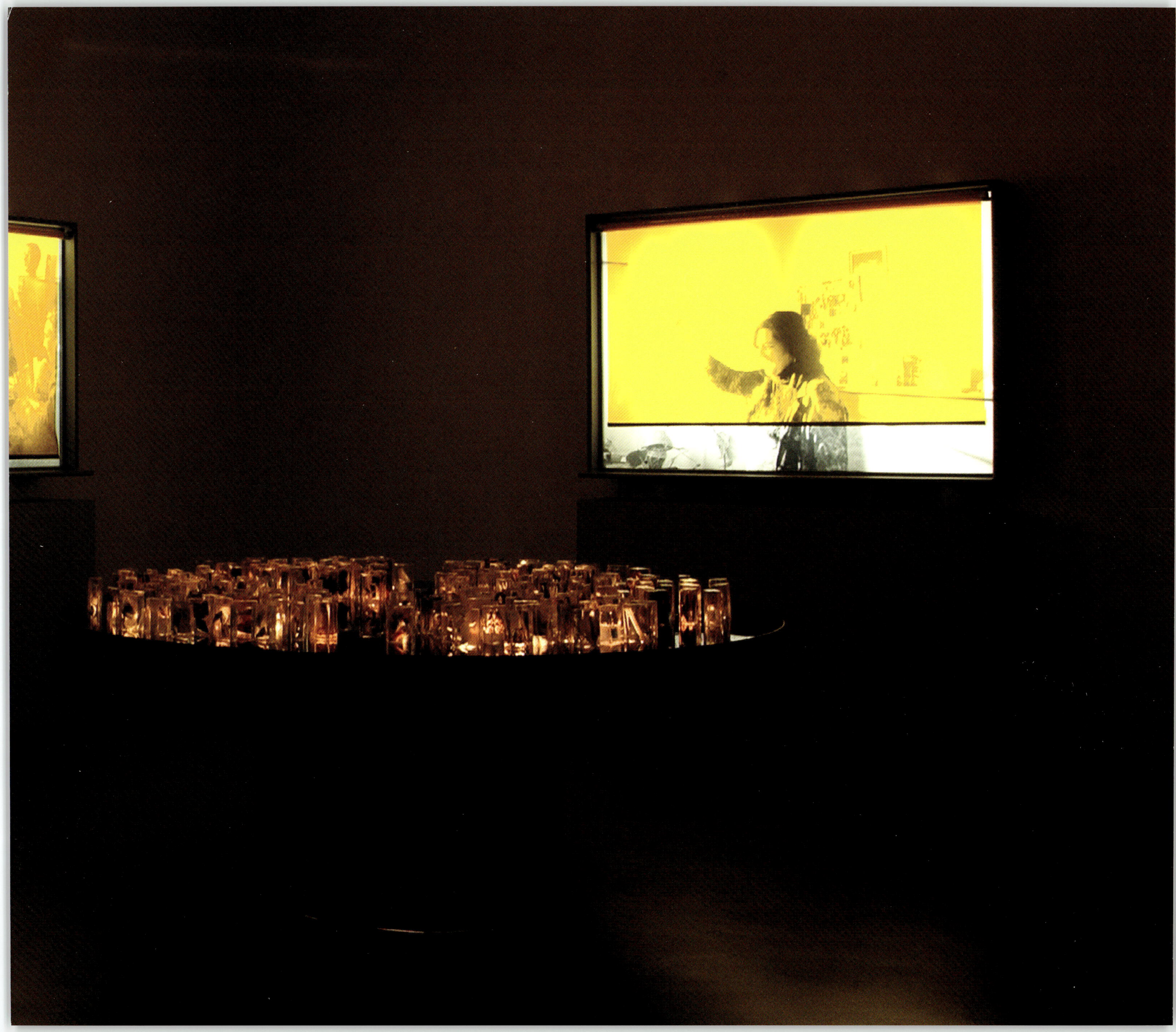

# Mementoes of District Six

pp. 59-62 At the same moment that *The Last Supper Revisited* was about to open at the Irma Stern Museum in Cape Town, Sue Williamson was invited to be one of the first group of South African artists to participate in the Venice Biennale of 1993. The country was in transition to democracy following Nelson Mandela's release from prison, and the cultural boycott of the apartheid state had been lifted.

Williamson conceptualised a new piece using small resin blocks containing fragments she picked up from the old demolition sites at District Six. This time she laid the blocks, like bricks, along bars of a steel "house" she had designed, and set the whole structure onto a pile of red earth brought from District Six. The front panels of the framework were lit from the sides.

It was an act of reconstitution of the homes that had been demolished; "somewhere between a museum display and a commemorative chapel", Williamson says. Visitors enter the house, and are able to examine, closely, the linoleum scraps, bits of torn curtain, paint flakes and china chips that are set into the resin blocks. Williamson's 1981 tape of the voices and sounds of District Six allows visitors to listen to the long-departed residents.

Williamson made the resin blocks for these works from the kind of set one normally buys in a craft shop to cast butterflies, or souvenirs. This was a considered irony, as was her choice of title, as if to say that these "mementoes" are all that is left, materially, of the thriving, rich urban culture that existed for over a century along Hanover, Constitution and Horstley Streets.

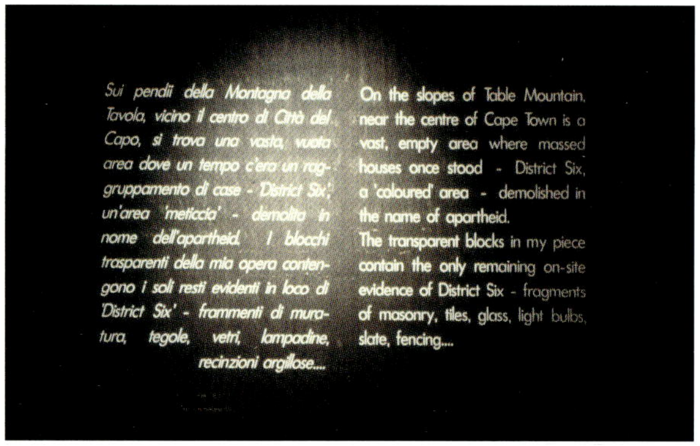


The wall text accompanying *Mementoes of District Six*, Palazzo Giustinian Lolin, XLV Venice Biennale, 1993

*Mementoes of District Six*
1993
Steel, perspex, found objects in casting resin, lighting, sound, earth
220 x 260 x 260 cm
Installation view
Sala Uno, Rome

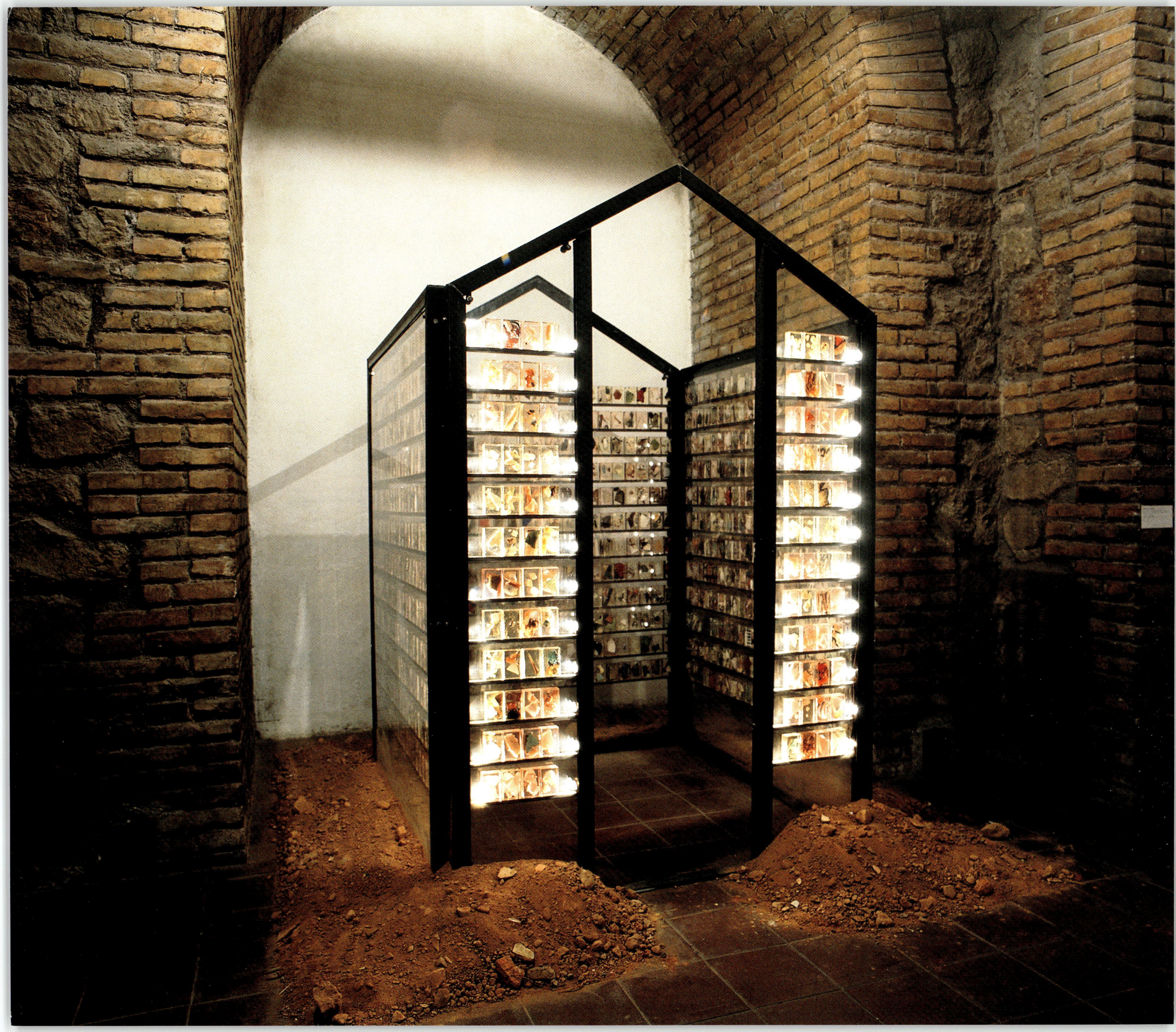

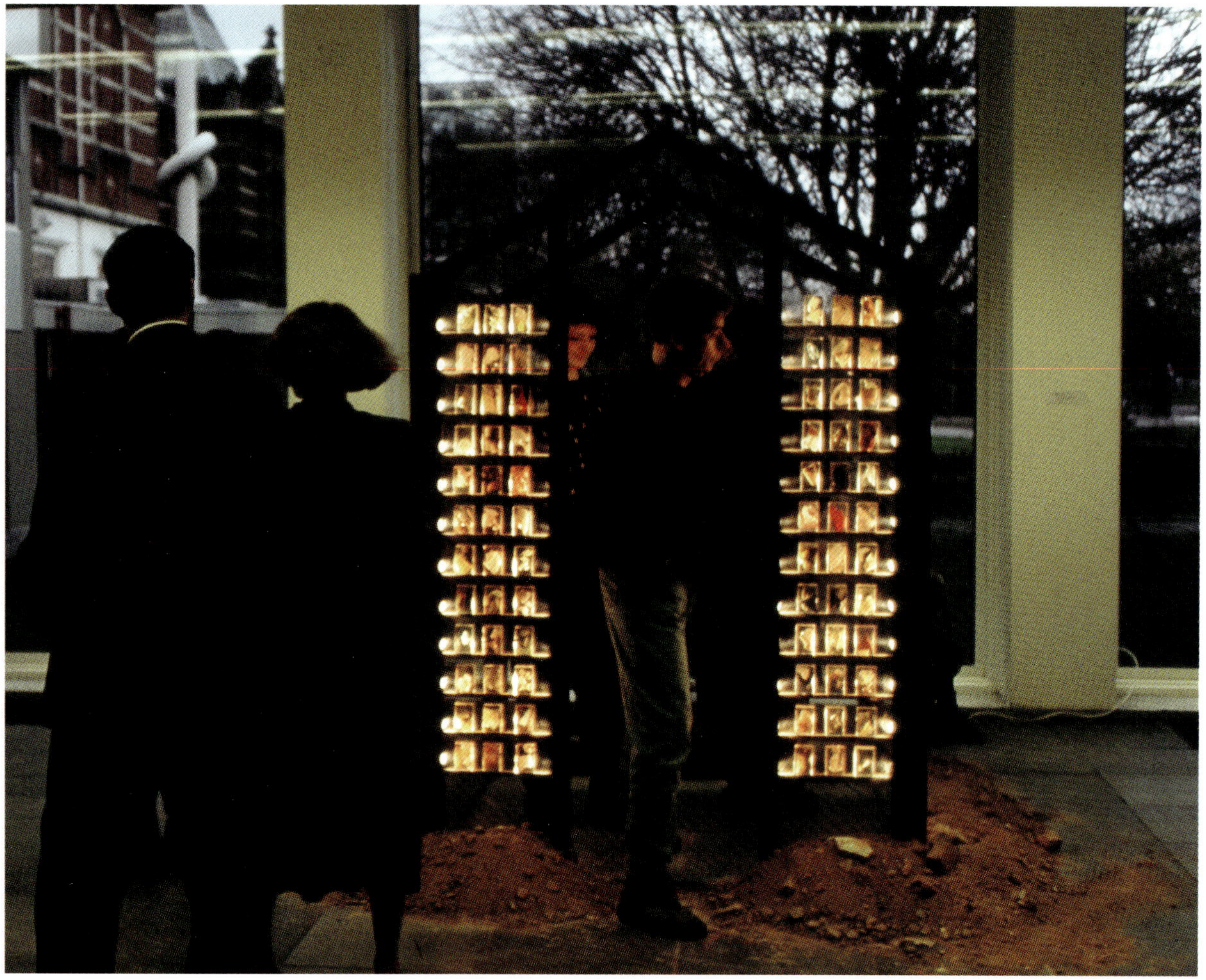

*Mementoes of District Six*
1993
Steel, perspex, found objects in casting resin, lighting, sound, earth
220 x 260 x 260 cm
Installation view
Stedelijk Museum, Amsterdam

pp. 55-6 "*The Last Supper* was a votive work, and an act of mourning, but it also transported to the interior of the gallery the massive, shattering fact of what was happening outside, and the art-historical aspect of its polemic was unmistakable.

In *Mementoes of District Six* ... the soundtrack from *The Last Supper* is still playing, and piles of earth excavated from District Six are scattered around. The basic impetus of the earlier work is still present, as is its sense of an appalling event, but in this cooler, more ironic memorial, awkward questions about nostalgia, the nature of monuments, and the specific force of historical objects begin to raise themselves."

From Nic Dawes, "Sue Williamson and the Trauma of History", in Sue Williamson, *Selected Work*, p. 7

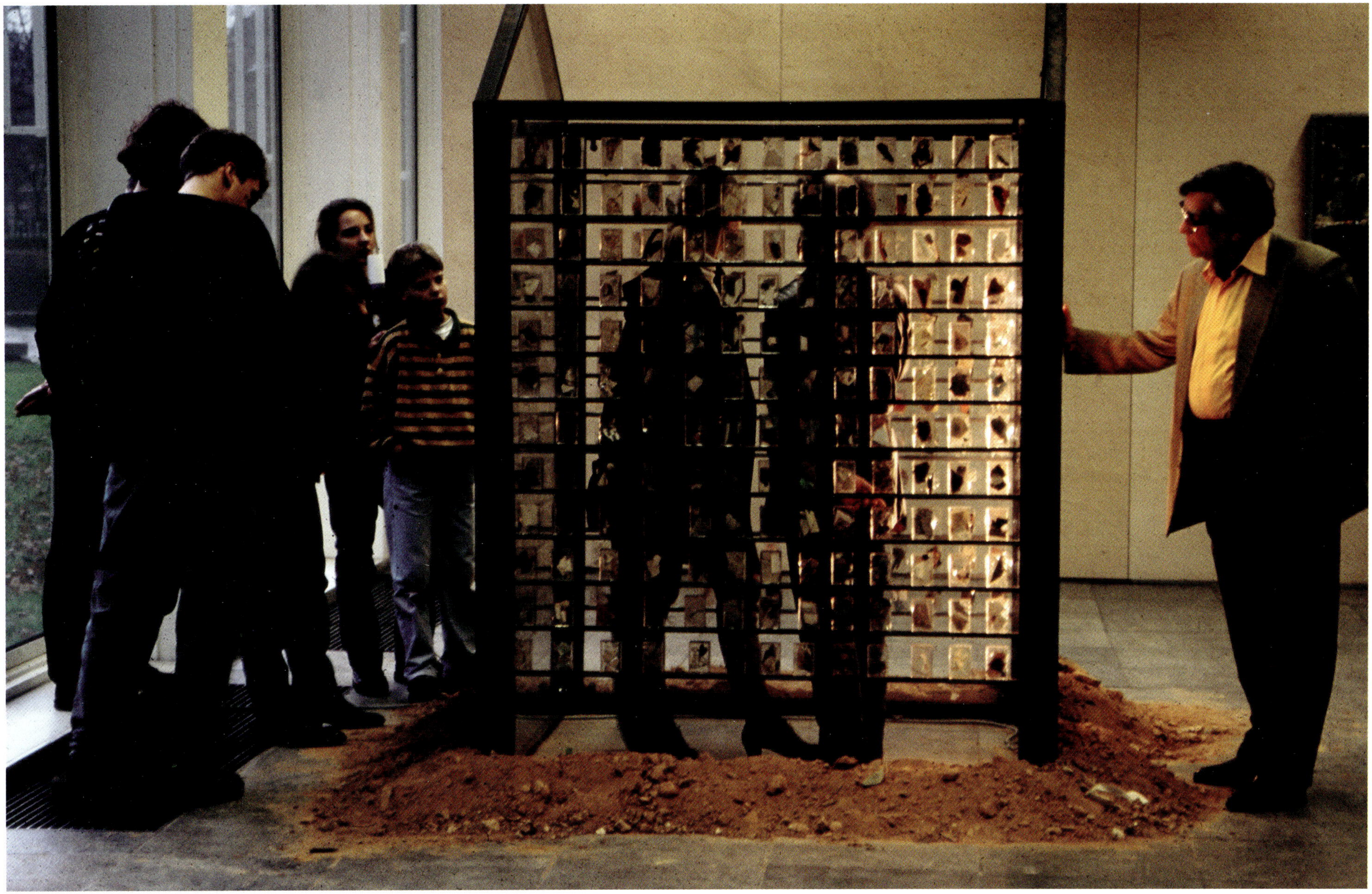

*Mementoes of District Six*
1993
Steel, perspex, found objects in casting resin,
lighting, sound, earth
220 x 260 x 260 cm
Installation view
Stedelijk Museum, Amsterdam

# Viewsites District Six

Three structures, taking their form from the steel drawing
pp. 63-5 of a house Sue Williamson used in *Mementoes in District Six*, appeared again for her 1997 work, *Viewsites: District Six*. The house in *Mementoes* had no roof. These three houses were reduced even further. Only the front façade remained, propped up by diagonal steel supports. Each had an old window set into the front of the façade.

The *Viewsites* were part of the District Six Sculpture Festival, organised by the District Six Museum, to commemorate the demolished neighborhood. Over seventy artists took part, making site-specific work along the deserted roads and in the fields where the houses once stood. The timing of the exhibition was chosen to coincide with the 2nd Johannesburg Biennale which, under the directorship of Okwui Enwezor, was also taking place in Cape Town.

The title was ironic. The "view" visitors could see as they stood within the shell of a house and looked through the window was of the demolished slopes. But Williamson hand-engraved into the glass the scene that would have been apparent when District Six was in its heyday. Spidery houses, or the figure of a woman who once had walked down the street, interrupted the vision of the viewer.

And so, as you stood at *Viewsites: Muir Street*, you looked pp. 68-9
at the Muir Street Mosque, now standing alone, without the houses and shopfronts which once surrounded it. The mosque was spared only because of its religious character.

Similarly, at *Viewsites: Horstley Street*, you looked at the etched view of the houses tumbling down the hillside along the cobbled street, superimposed onto the grasslands now standing there. These ephemeral works created a delicate palimpsest that evoked the ghost-like presence of the past upon the deserted land where District Six once was.

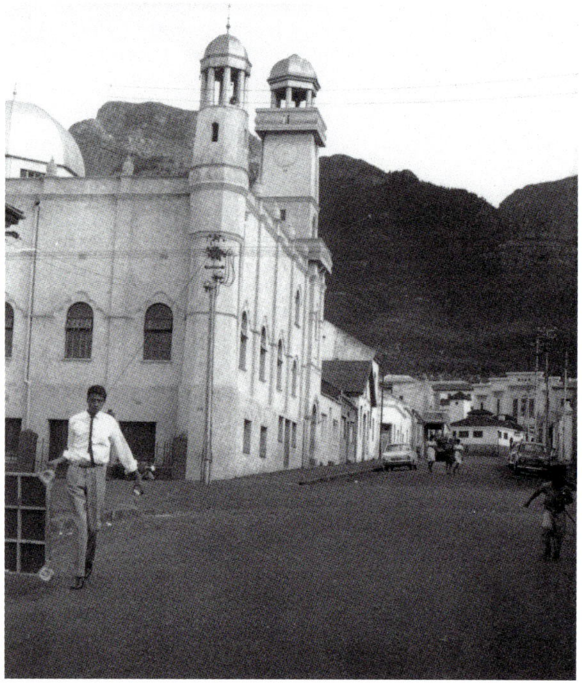

Muir Street Mosque, District Six, Cape Town, December 1965

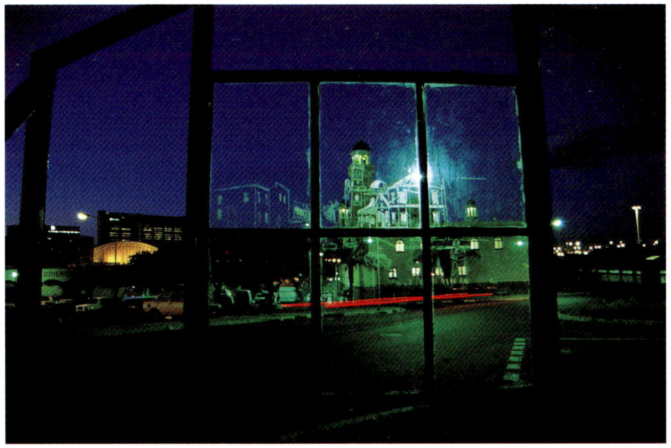

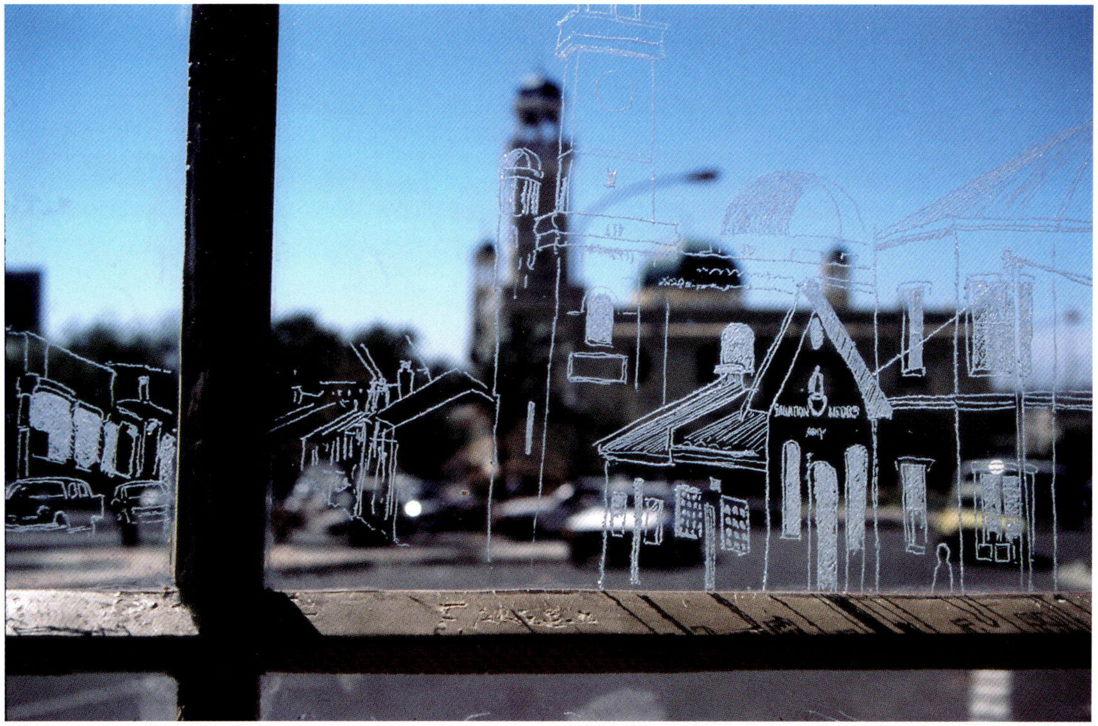

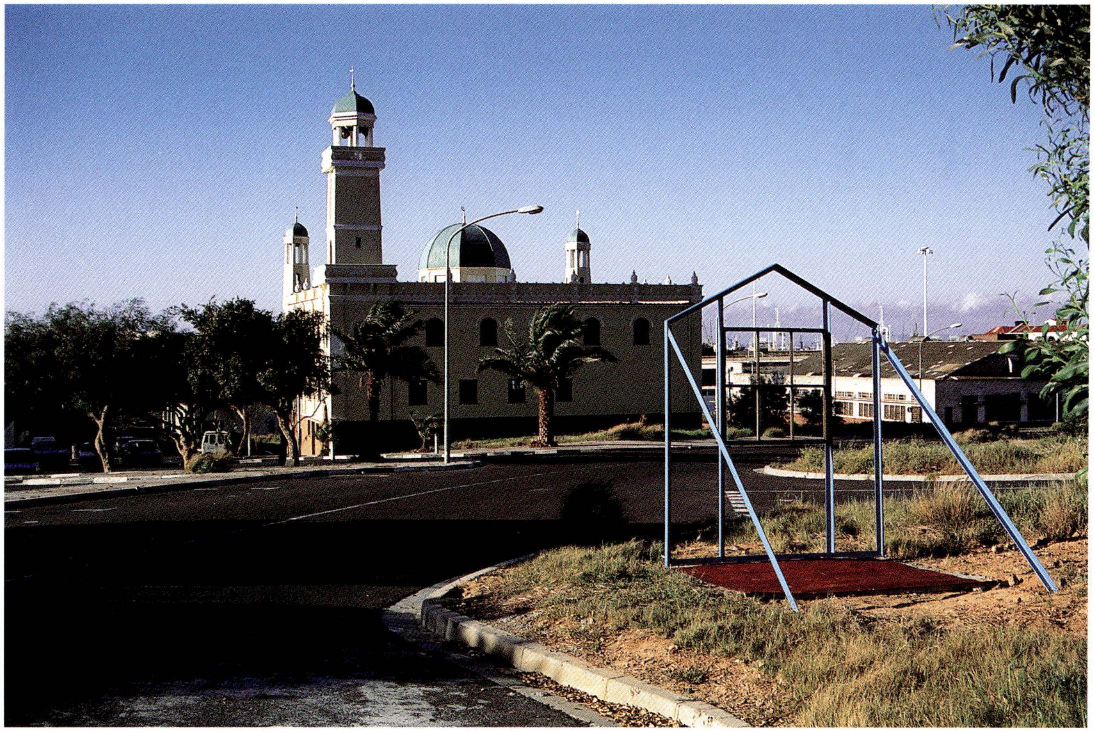

*Viewsites District Six: Muir Street* (detail)
1997
Painted steel, found window
250 x 200 x 227 cm

*Viewsites District Six: Muir Street* (detail)
1997
Painted steel, found window
250 x 200 x 227 cm

*Viewsites District Six: Muir Street*
1997
Painted steel, found window
250 x 200 x 227 cm

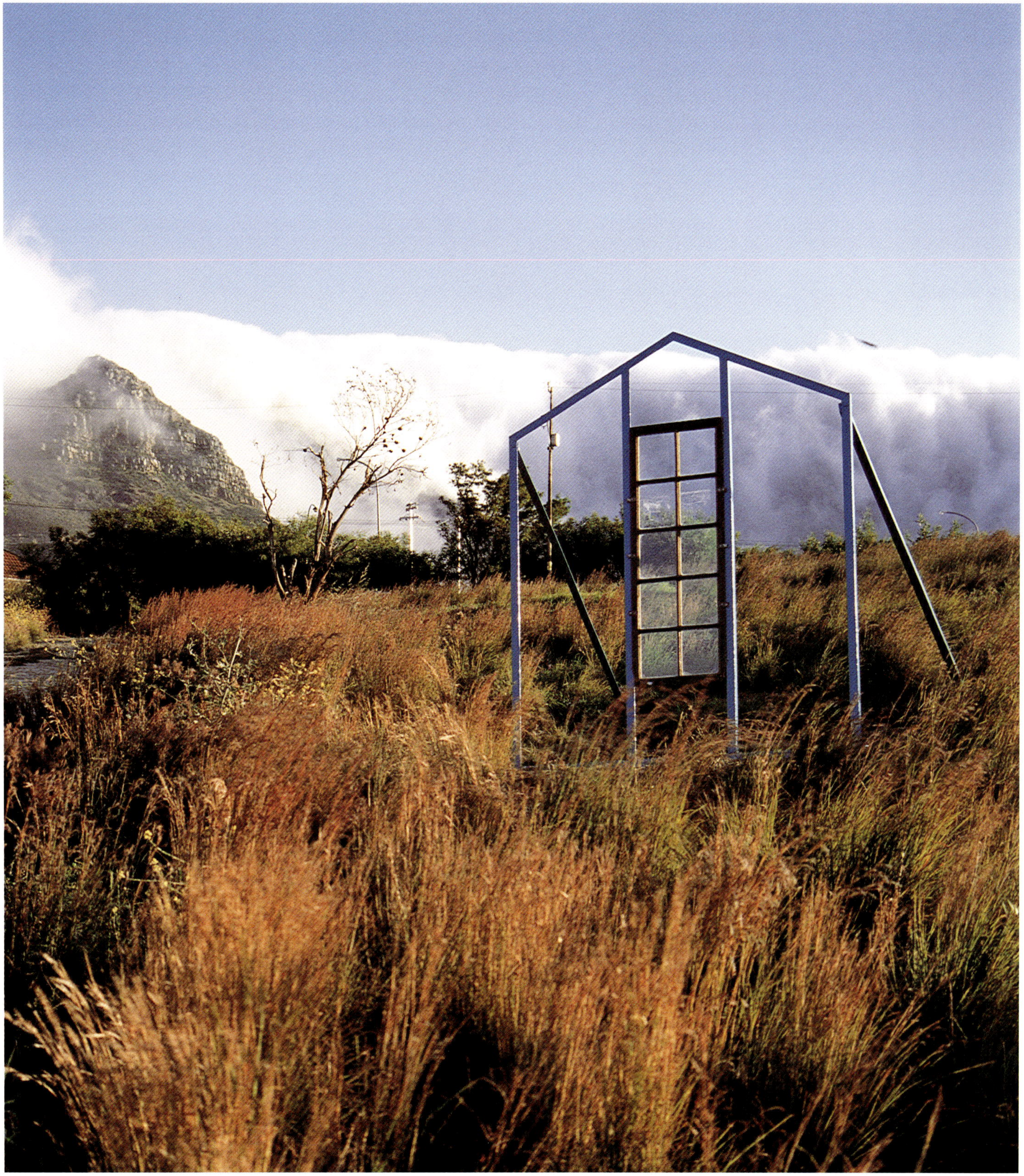

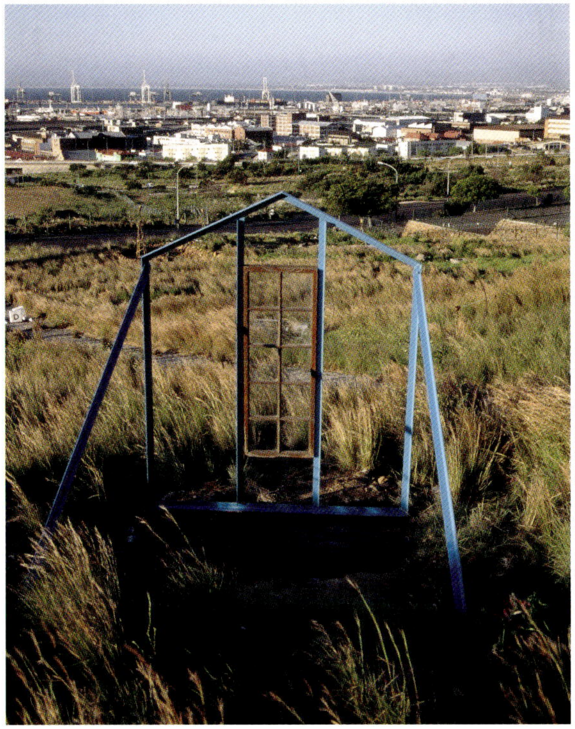

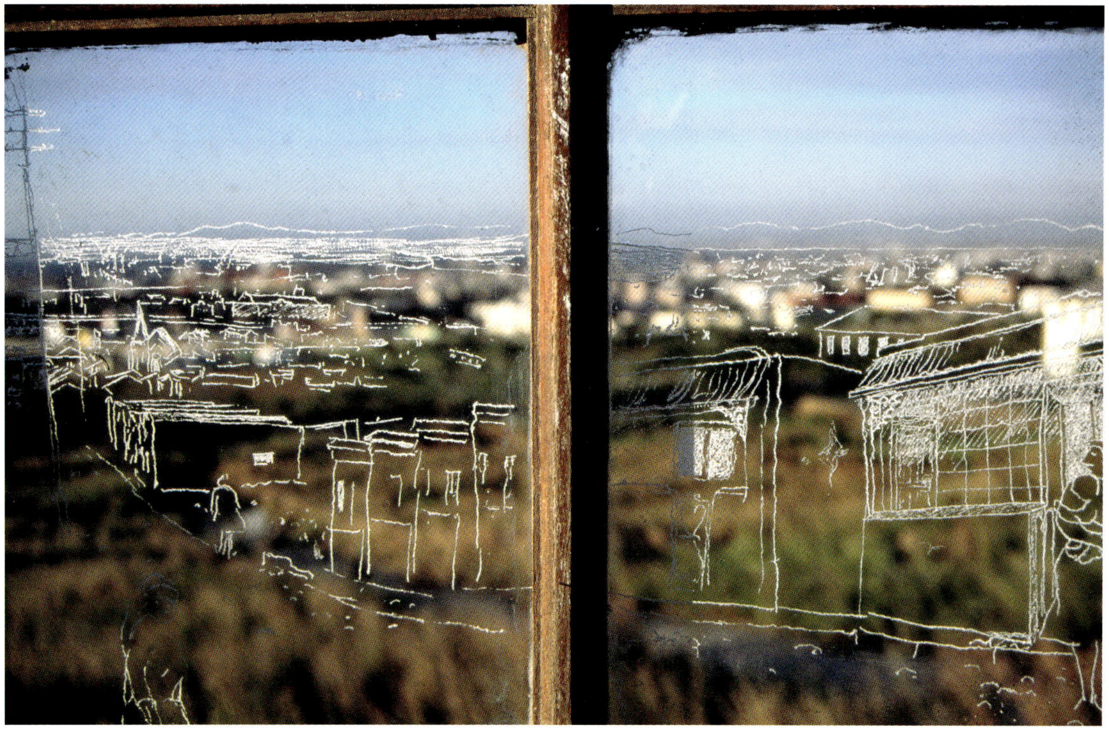

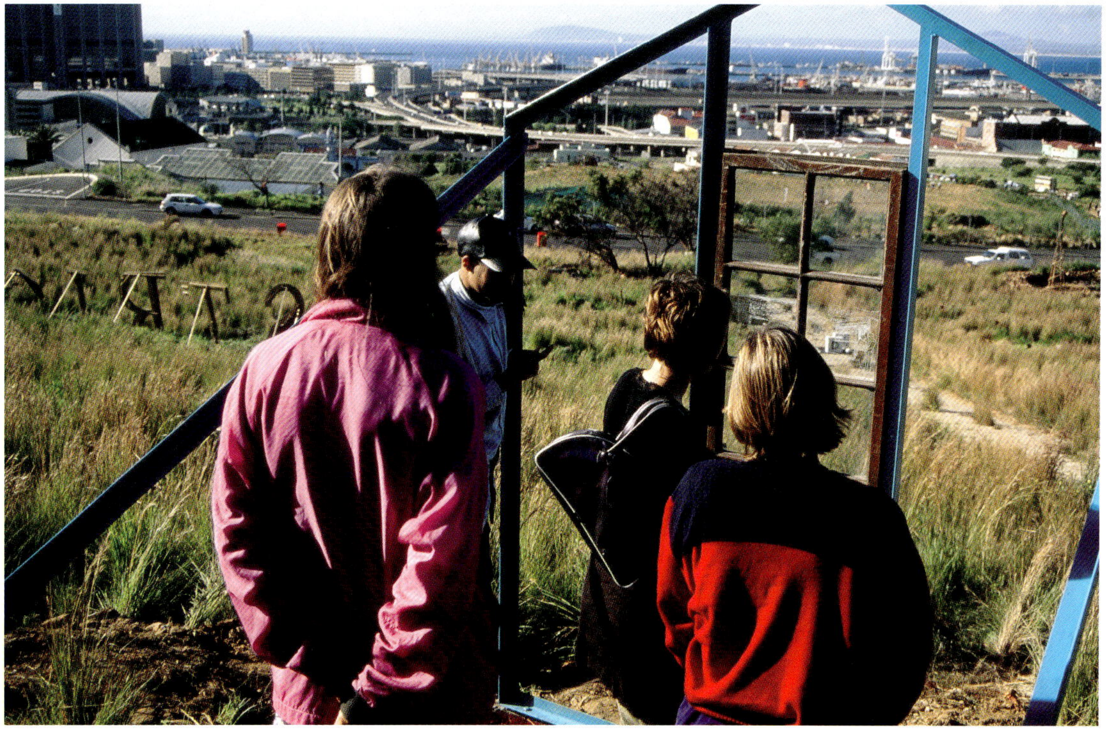

*Viewsites District Six: Horstley Street*
1997
Painted steel, found window
250 x 200 x 227 cm

*Viewsites District Six: Horstley Street* (detail)
1997
Painted steel, found window
250 x 200 x 227 cm

*Viewsites District Six: Horstley Street* (detail)
1997
Painted steel, found window
250 x 200 x 227 cm

## Last Supper at Manley Villa

Naz Gool-Ebrahim, the symbol of the resistance of District Six's last residents, died in 2005, in the home of her son in Belhar, a township of the Cape Flats, a few years after her husband Hari. After her eviction from Manley Villa, she and Hari had been moved to a small flat in Gatesville, the Indian "Group Area" on the Cape Flats, but she never settled in. In Sue Williamson's 1981 photograph, she leans on the garden wall of her Rochester Road home, her face turned away from the partially demolished house next door, her gaze steely and determined.

pp. 55-6 In 2008, Sue Williamson revisited *The Last Supper* one final time, by printing ten photographs taken in Manley Villa in1981, many of which she had looked at before only on old black and white contact sheet. There is the house, Manley Villa, solid and substantial, with Naz leaning on the wall. There are the smiling children passing the house on their way to the school which has not yet been knocked down. There is the message, written outside the front door: "The Truth is on the Walls of this House, the Truth that is Denied." There are the visitors who have come to celebrate Eid, and the young girl, signing her name on the wall. There is the homeless man who has received a plastic container of food from Naz's bountiful table, as he does every year at Eid al Fitr. Cigarette smoke drifts upwards as Naz bends to greet a friend.

Amongst these poignant images, is a facsimile of the eviction notice, received by Naz on September 30, giving the family thirty days to move. Referring to District Six by its new official name Zonnebloem (Sunflower) the round handwriting of a Juffrou (Miss) Waterse gives the family its final notice.

In 2005, Sue Williamson went back to Rochester Road, to see if she could find where Manley Villa once stood. There was still nothing but grass. The final shot in the series shows the hill, and is printed in reduced colour, to mark the passage of the seventeen years since the first photographs.

*Last Supper at Manley Villa* was part of the work the artist exhibited at the Havana Biennale of 2009, alongside *What About El Max?*, her work about a threatened pp. 184-9 fishing community in Alexandria, Egypt. For this series, Williamson invited the residents of El Max to write statements about why they should not be moved out of their homes on the walls of their houses.

By juxtaposing the two series, Williamson was tracing the influence, on her work, of the graffiti she had encountered during the anti-apartheid struggle, when, as she wrote in *Resistance Art in South Africa,* "the walls of our cities" had become "the noticeboards of the people." The appeal of graffiti was "its directness. It is a message sent at personal risk. Here is a cry from the heart or a call..."

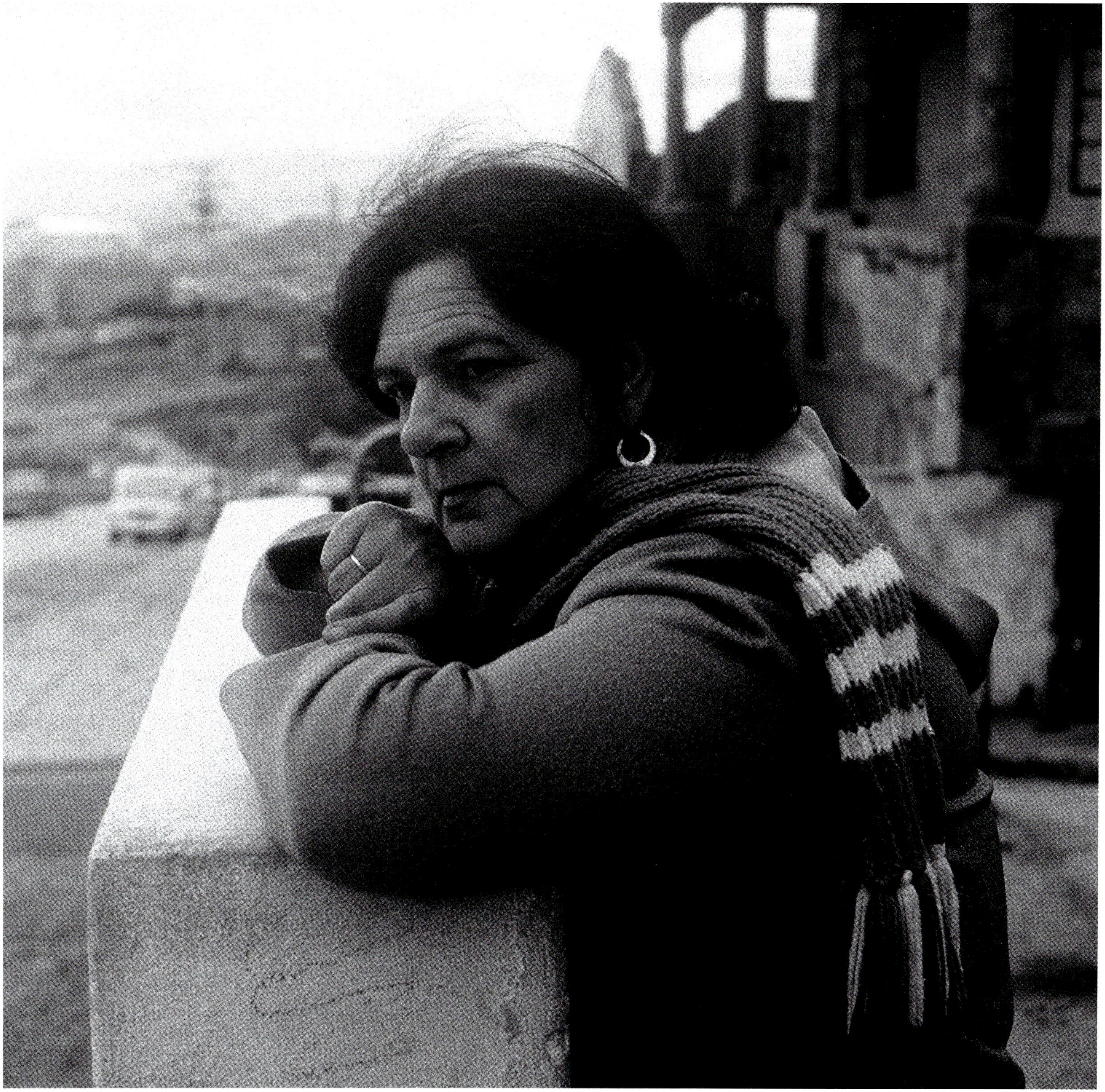

*Naz Ebrahim*
*Last Supper at Manley Villa*
1981
Archival print on cotton rag
50 x 67.5 cm

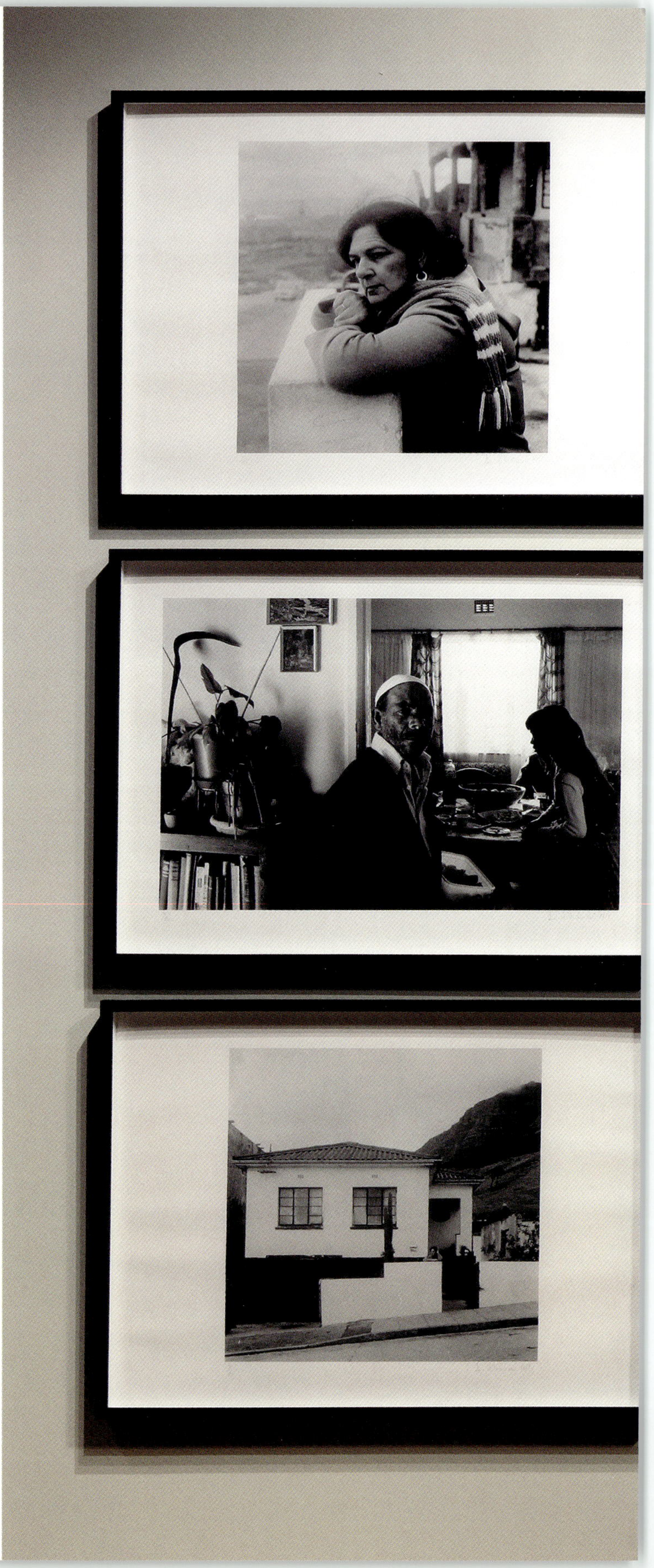

*Last Supper at Manley Villa* portfolio
1981
Archival prints on cotton rag
50 x 67.5 cm each
Installation view
Iziko Slave Lodge, Cape Town

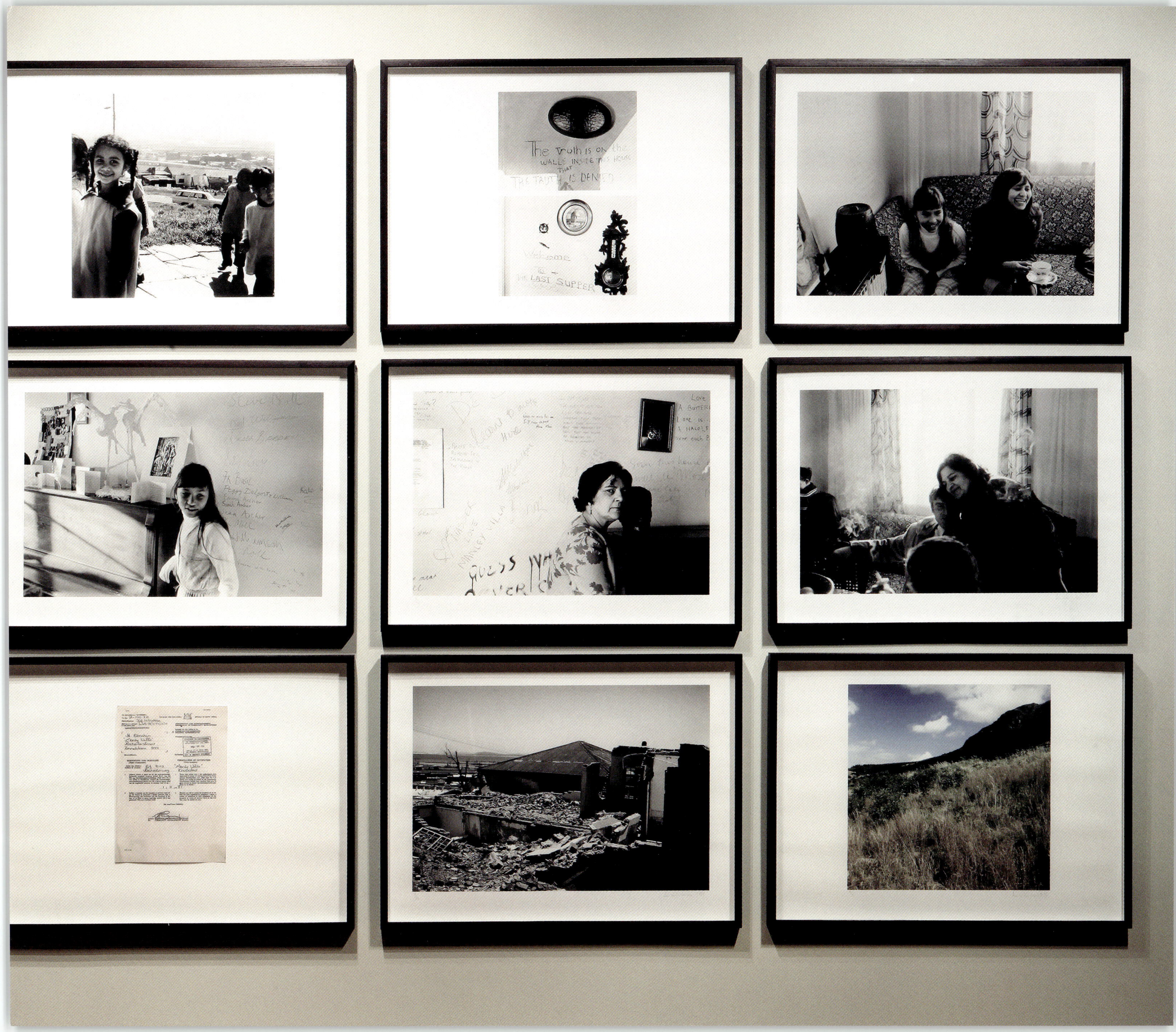
The truth is on the
WALLS INSIDE THIS HOUSE
THAT
THE TRUTH IS DENIED
Welcome
THE LAST SUPPER
GUESS WHO

"My family's eviction from the once-harmonious District was imminent, but I was determined to stay as long as possible. When my home was among the last to be bulldozed, all I could do was stall the outcome. Any form of resistance was a victory over apartheid and symbolised a family tradition.

2 August 1981 was a joyous yet sad day. Joyous, because the few remaining District Six families were celebrating the end of the month long fast, Eid al Fitr—a Muslim feast day. Sad, because we could hear the bulldozers. Even Eid-al-Fitr did not deter the Maliki Moud (Angels of Death) from carrying out their merciless duties…

At 10 am I was busy in the kitchen, cooking the celebration meal, when there was a loud knock on my door. I froze at the sight of Maliki Moud.

[She recounts how an official asked for her husband's identity card and, on viewing it, tells her that she has been evicted to the Indian 'Group Area' of Gatesville.]

'From one hell-hole to another!' I exclaimed. As he walked out, I slammed the door behind him. My hand clung to the knob for strength … Guests were arriving at one o'clock. I regained my composure. The walls of Manley Villa began to vibrate as the bulldozer ploughed through the home behind us. I stared at my walls and fury seized me. [We] were viewed as less than subhuman by the Government. We had no choices … Suddenly graffiti madness seized me. I grabbed my *koki* [marker] and began to scrawl my outrage and frustration on the walls with reckless abandon, which was another criminal offence. I poured out 15 years of bottled-up emotion. They could take my home, but they weren't going to break my spirit. I wrote all the things I dared not say out loud, but which burned within me. Messages, epigrams, poetry, prose, the names of friends who had frequented Manley Villa covered every available bit of wall space…

By the time the men returned from Mosque, several walls were covered with my graffiti. When Hari saw it he was stunned and exclaimed, 'My dear Naz, what in the world have you done?... Have you gone mad?'

'No', I assured him. 'I haven't. Our guests will be arriving at one o'clock. They can all read the writing on the walls and add whatever they want. Everyone should see what our real feelings are about this whole ordeal before the walls are torn down.'"

From *The Truth is On The Walls*, published posthumously.
Naz Gool-Ebrahim, with Donna Ruth Brenneis and Shahena Wingate-Pearse, 2011 (David Phillip: Cape Town)

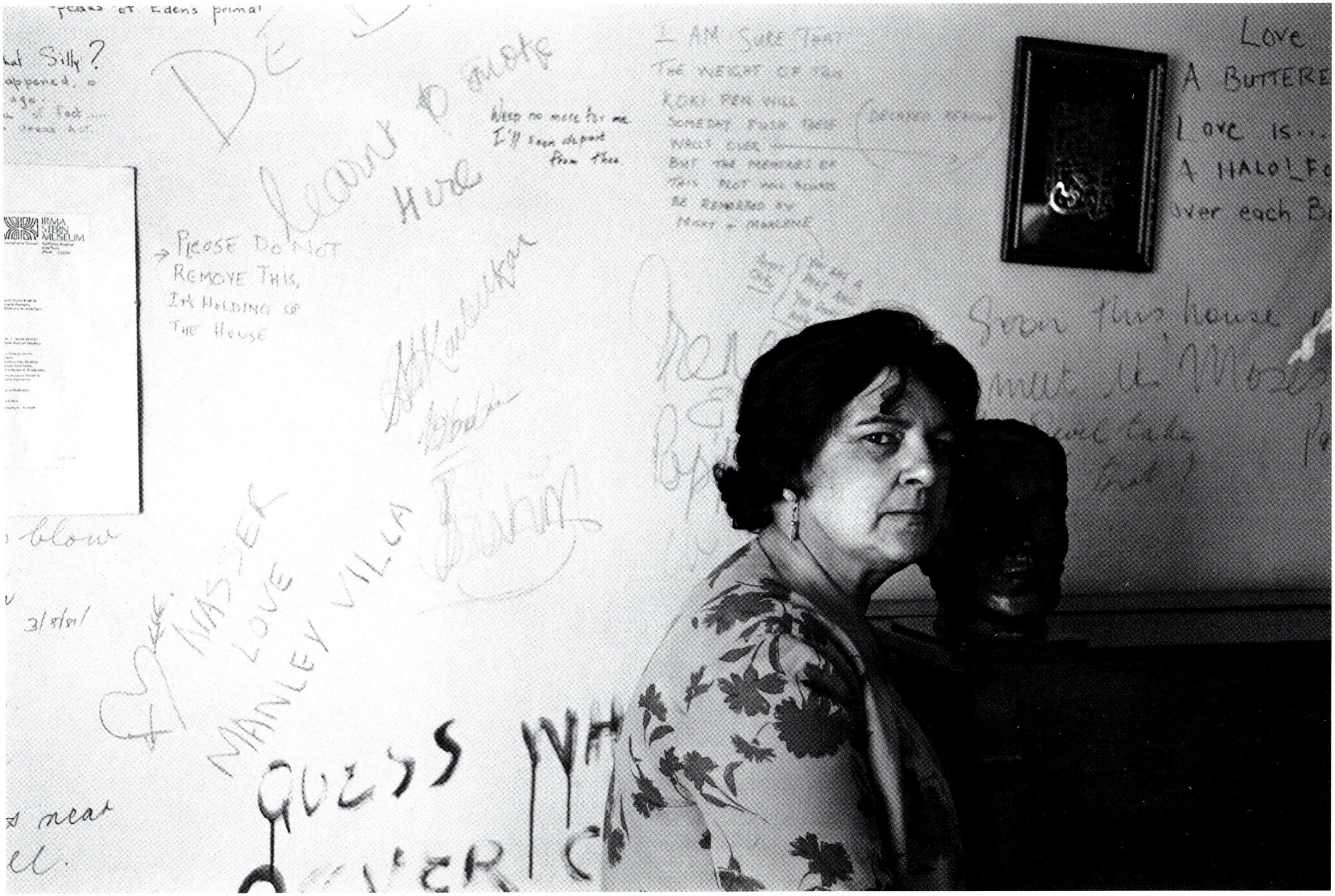


*Naz Ebrahim at piano*
*Last Supper at Manley Villa*
1981
Archival print on cotton rag
50 x 67.5 cm

# Measures of Control

For Thirty Years Next to his Heart
A Tale of Two Cradocks
Colouring In
Pages from a Government Tourist Brochure
Messages from the Moat

*On February 2 1990, the South African president FW de Klerk announced that he would unban the liberation movements, release all political prisoners—including Nelson Mandela—and begin the negotiated transition towards democracy. The ensuing interregnum was euphoric, but also, at times, frightening. Parts of the country were thrown into civil war between supporters of the African National Congress and those of the Zulu nationalist Inkatha Freedom Party; rightwing Afrikaner separatists also mobilised for war. Sue Williamson's work in these years reflected her sense that the future was far from certain: in the works represented in this section, she looks back at the "Measures of Control" which were put into place during the preceding eras of apartheid and colonialism.*

Mark Gevisser: The works in this section were all made after 1990, once Nelson Mandela had been released and we were looking forward to democracy…
Sue Williamson: Mandela had been released, but there was no guarantee that the country was going to work. It was a time of great uncertainty, really. Already, by 1987, the need to carry a passbook had been repealed. If there was one icon which represented the injustice of apartheid, it was the passbook. All black South Africans had to carry it ready for inspection at all times, and if it was not in order, they could be immediately arrested. In 1990 I was commissioned to design a book cover for a
pp. 79, 228 book of short stories by Ellen Kuzwayo entitled *Sit Down and Listen*. I wanted to use an image of the passbook on the cover, but I struggled to find one. It was as if the "dompas"—and all it represented—had been erased already. I went down to the Black Sash's Legal Advice Bureau and asked around, and eventually an old man stood up and gave me his book, which he still carried with him. I would go on to make *For Thirty Years Next* pp. 81-7 *to his Heart* about Mr Ngesi and his passbook. Now, as I paged through it, and looked at all bureaucratic detail it contained, I thought, "these things are going to be forgotten…"

MG: Your impulse was, "We're in this interregnum. Let's not forget!"
SW: Exactly, let's not forget. Particularly since we don't know, yet, what the future will bring. All my work in the early 1990s was driven by this impulse. I wanted to remember the measures of control which were in place, throughout the three centuries of colonialism and apartheid, as we were thinking about our new society.

MG: Why were you working with documents in this series of works?
SW: I am a hoarder of old documents. The subtexts and language are always so revealing. But it also had to do with the means of production I suddenly had at my disposal! I was given a residency at the South African National Gallery, and because I couldn't move all my printmaking equipment into their Annexe, I searched around for something else to do. The new Canon colour copier had just arrived in the country, and Canon invited me to test one out. I was sceptical at first, but when I played around on one, trying out different objects and

images to copy, I was enthralled. Especially if you left the lid up, making a "sky" copy as the technician called it.

There was such a shallow depth of field. Whatever was directly on the glass was incredibly sharp, and everything else just faded into a wonderful obscurity. I loved it. It was so immediate! Like an instant A3-sized camera. This was before the age of the digital camera, of course, though no camera replicates the look of the scan.

I had made the Ellen Kuzwayo cover just by laying various things on the glass of the copier, and now I persuaded Canon to loan me a copier for my residency at SANG. By the time my residency was over, I was in love with the copier and couldn't let go of it, so I did a deal with Canon: I would buy one over a period of years, paying for it month by month by running a copy business out of my studio in Observatory, the Graphic Workshop. At first, there were only three Canon copiers in the city. It cost me a fortune! Three times the price of the house we'd bought as our studio, but it sustained my work for years.
pp. 81-7, *For Thirty Years*, *A Tale of Two Cradocks*, *Colouring In*,
89-93, 94-9 were all made on the copier.

**MG**: What happened to the copier?
**SW**: I bought a second one in 1994, which was stolen at gunpoint. One day, two young men came in to have copies made, and said they were so impressed with the quality that they'd be back. And a few days later, they were. This time, there were four of them. One had a gun. He hit me on the back of my head with it. The artist Willie Bester was visiting us, and there was also my assistant Tanya and two other studio artists. The men made us all lie down on floor and tied us up then moved us into a back room. They said they would not hurt us, although if we made any trouble they would kill us. We heard "bang crash bang" from the next room, for a long time, and then silence.

When we untied ourselves and got up, we saw they had taken the copier. Then, about six months later, a Canon techie told me he had been called to service a machine in Gugulethu, and it was mine. He told the police, and the police went to stake it out and caught the guys. It turned out they were copying money! I had kept my bloody shirt from the attack. Later I copied the shirt.

**MG**: Were you traumatised by the robbery?
**SW**: Not all that much. I was hurt. The crack on the back of my head bled a bit. I walked out into the street afterwards, and I thought, "another day in South Africa." I did become hypervigilant afterwards though: if I was driving and a beggar came up to me at the traffic lights, for example, I found that my tolerance was shortened.

**MG**: Did your attack become to you a symptom of turmoil of interregnum?
**SW**: No. It was just a criminal thing. They wanted a copier.

**MG**: Did your idea to do *For Thirty Years* actually *come* from having the copier?
**SW**: Yes. It was such a direct way of capturing an image instantly. And yet, by shifting the object during the copying process, one could produce a sense of movement. The result was somewhere between a still and a moving image. So I treated the passbook piece like a series of film strips, reading downward, with different hands coming in from time to time as if to examine the book on various occasions, with the passbook moving and blurring.

**MG**: Measures of control. The apartheid machine. You were using a machine yourself. Were you relating form and content in any way?

**SW**: Absolutely. *For Thirty Years* is a riff on the information that the government was holding on its citizens. All the files that were endlessly being copied. I was doing the same thing. I was copying detailed information in the way the government copies. But with a very different end in mind.

And in a way, I guess I was following the same
methodology in *Messages from the Moat*, the installation pp. 105,
I made in 1997 for the 2nd Johannesburg Biennale. For 107-9
that work, I took the information from the old slave deeds of sale from dating from the seventeenth century, and kept in the Cape Town deeds office, and engraved that information onto bottles.

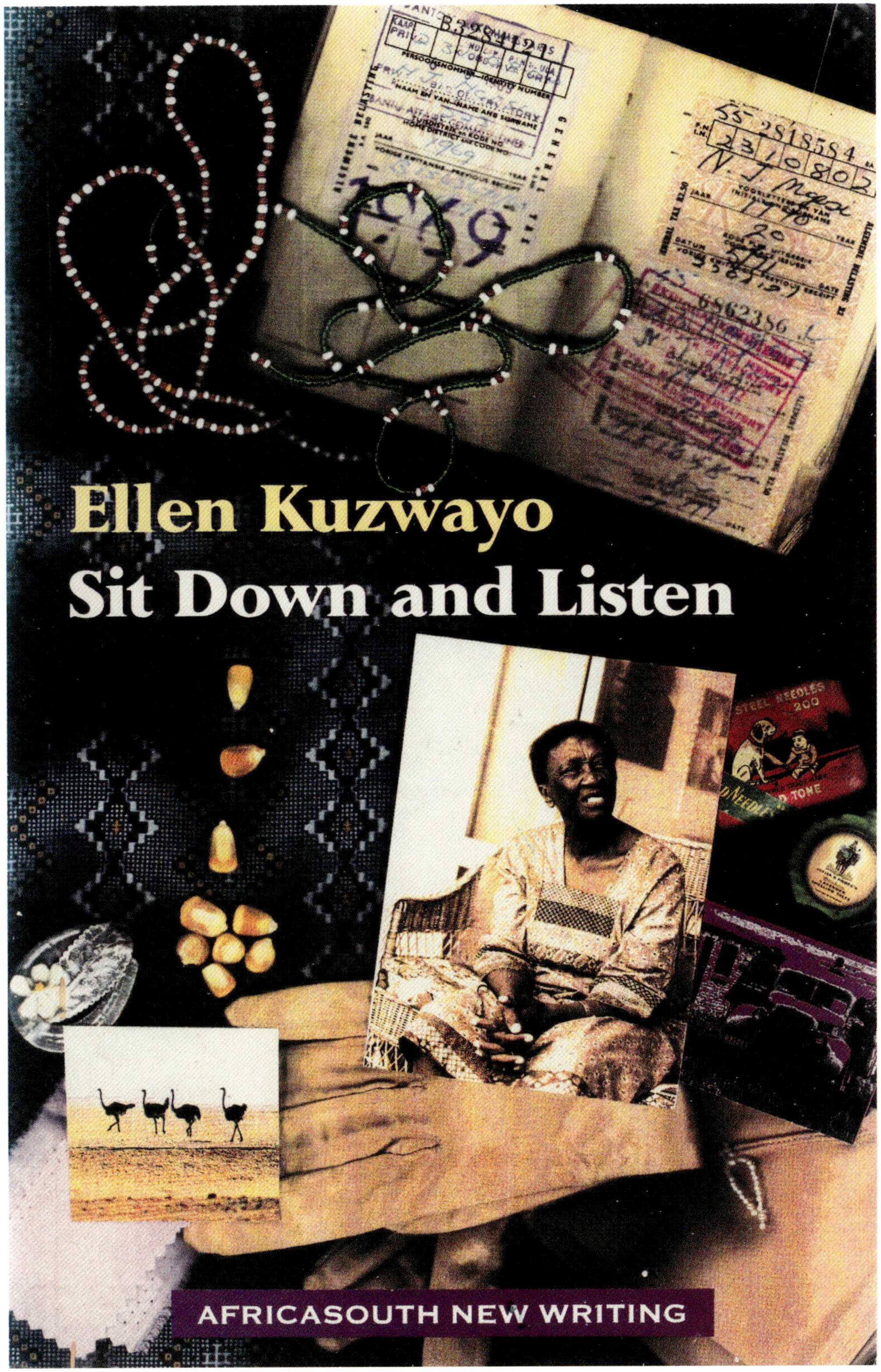


Cover of *Sit Down and Listen*, by Ellen Kuzwayo.
Cover design by Sue Williamson

## For Thirty Years Next to his Heart

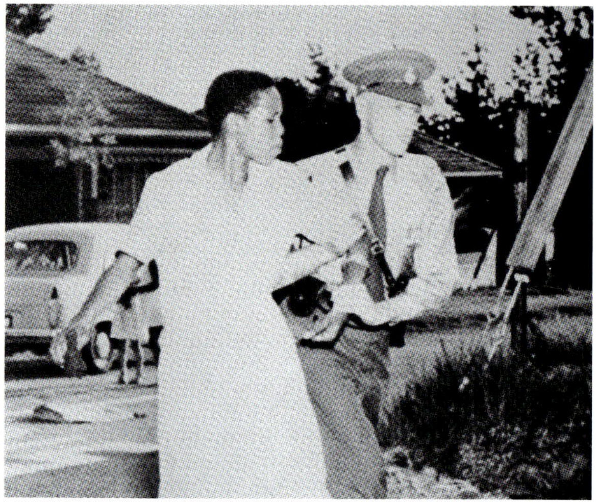

Woman being arrested
Photo: Eli Weinberg
Courtesy Mayibuye Centre UWC

Like all white South Africans who employed black workers, Sue Williamson had signed a passbook each month for years in order to make sure her one-day-a-week gardener, Lennox Cengani, could legally live in Cape Town. In 1987, the passbook law was repealed. So when Williamson needed a passbook in 1990 for a book design cover, Lennox no longer had one.

She had to find one elsewhere. And after having borrowed the passbook belonging to Ngithando John Ngesi, Williamson began to wonder why the elderly man still carried it, day in and day out, though the law had changed.

"I realised that although it was a hated instrument of control", she says, "it was also his security, and the habit of years". Williamson went to see Ngesi and asked if he would like to collaborate with her to make an artwork about the book. He agreed, and came into the Annexe of the South African National Gallery where Williamson was undertaking an artist's residency, using a Canon Colour Laser Photocopier as her printmaking equipment.

The piece reads downwards, like film strips. For the first frame, Williamson arranged Ngesi's jacket on the copier glass, with his own hand pulling the passbook out of the pocket, almost as it had done on dozens of occasions over the years.

The next frame is the open page with his photo. Another 47 images follow, with sections about where Ngesi was allowed to live, who was employing him (the employer's signature was necessary every month), whether he had paid his taxes, and a last section for any other information. Sometimes a random hand appears, as if inspecting the pages.

The frames in the first section are handcovered in old documents, copies of the ones Williamson had filled in for her gardener, and kept. The employment sections reflect the nature of Ngesi's employment: his first job was for a café, then he worked for shipping companies. Copies of old currency framed the tax section.

*For Thirty Years Next to his Heart* remains one of the artist's most widely-travelled pieces. One edition of the work is in the collection of the MuseuMAfrica, in downtown Johannesburg: "The museum has a number of actual passbooks too", Williamson says, "but when one sees a shabby little brown book, sitting on a shelf, it looks innocuous. Displayed like this, a big wall full of pages, each one with a signature or a stamp, the heartless bureaucracy of the apartheid state is fully exposed.

*For Thirty Years Next to his Heart*
1990
Colour laser prints, hand covered frames
196 x 262 cm
Installation view
Museum of Modern Art, New York

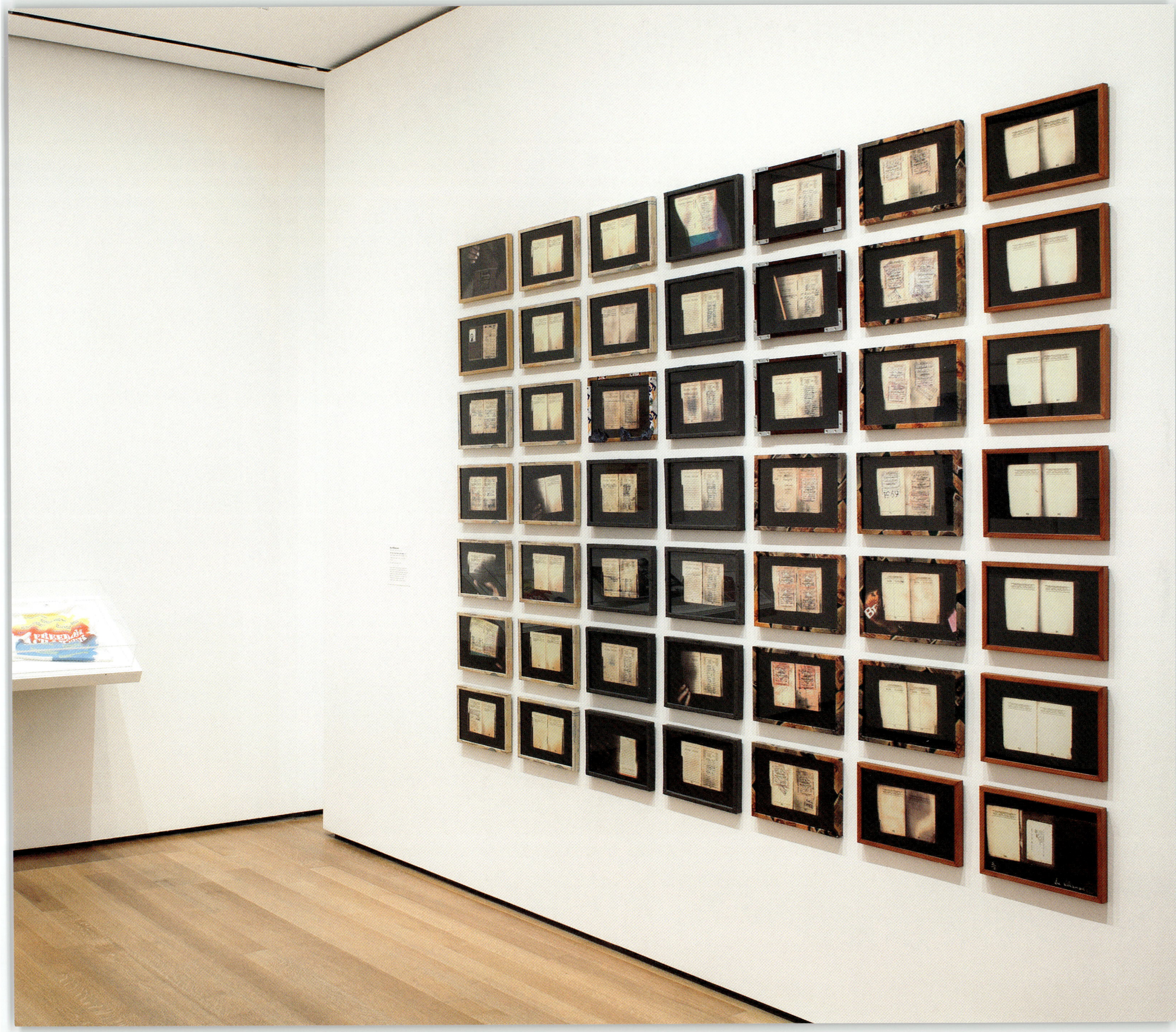

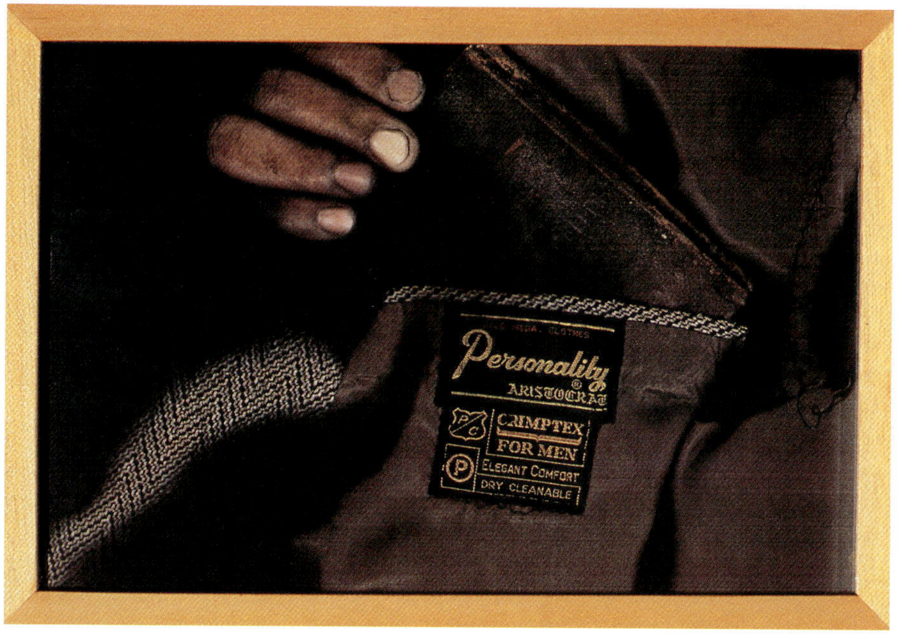


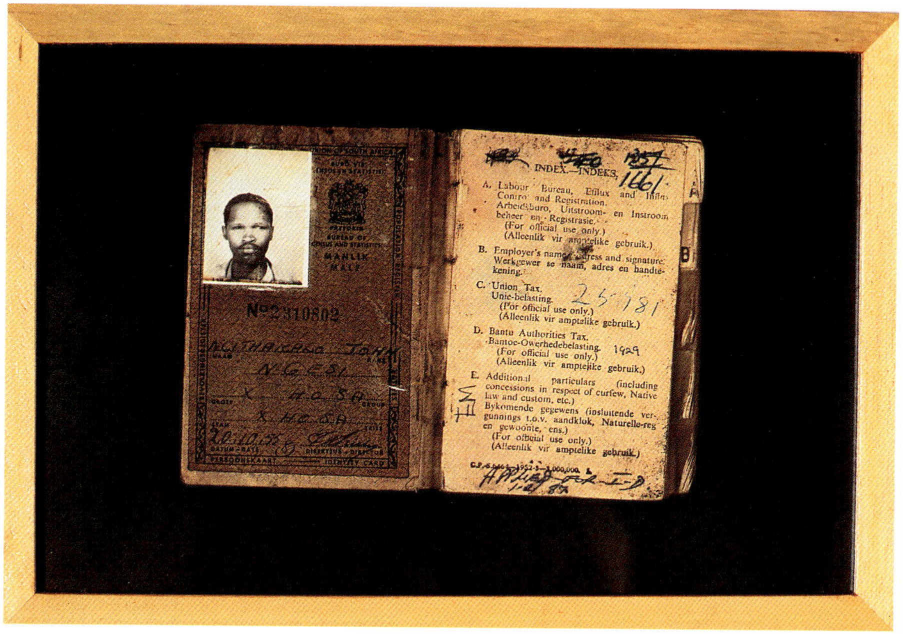


*For Thirty Years Next to his Heart* (detail)
1990
Colour laser print
22 x 31 cm

*For Thirty Years Next to his Heart* (detail)
1990
Colour laser print
22 x 31 cm

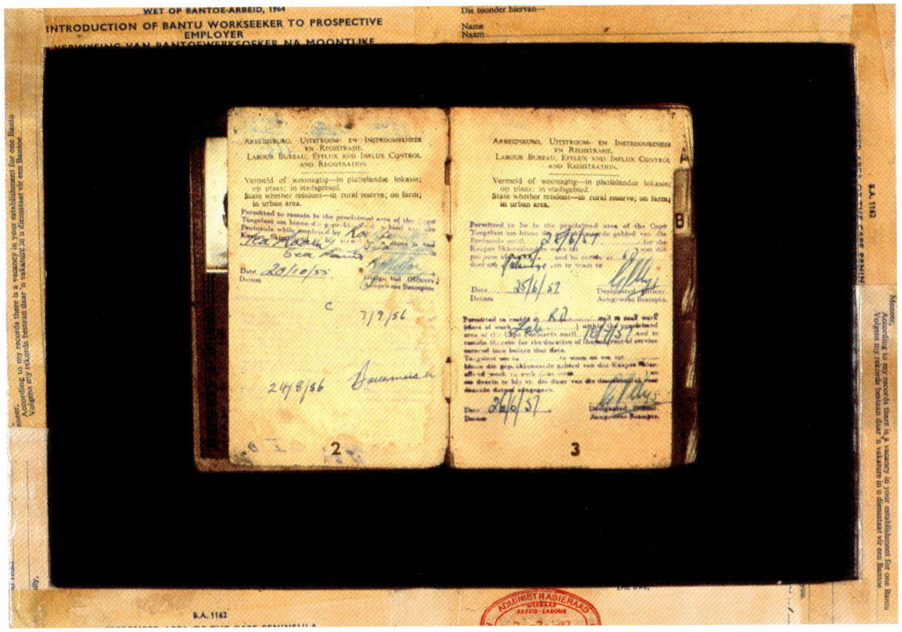


*For Thirty Years Next to his Heart* (detail)
1990
Colour laser print, hand covered frame
22 x 31 cm

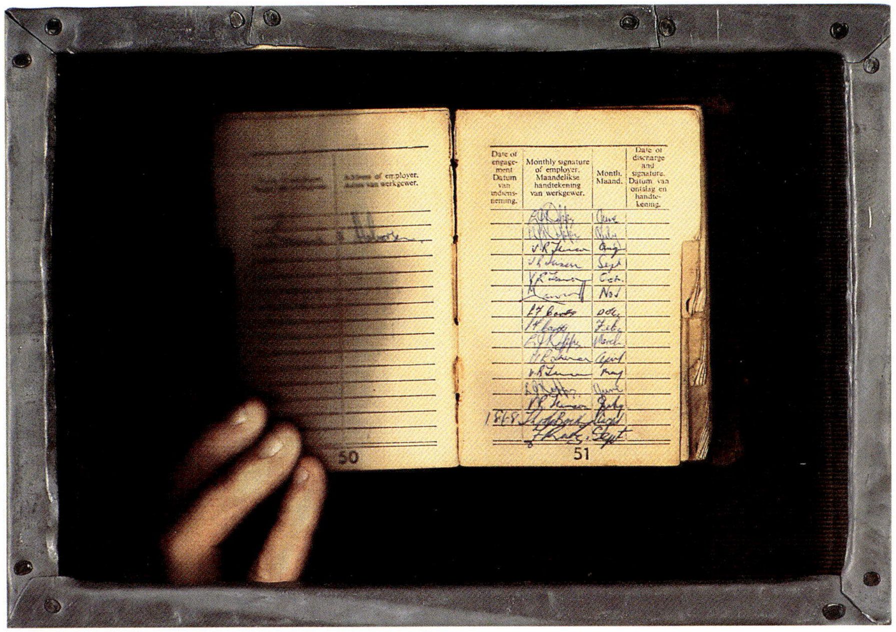

*For Thirty Years Next to his Heart* (detail)
1990
Colour laser print, hand covered frame
22 x 31 cm

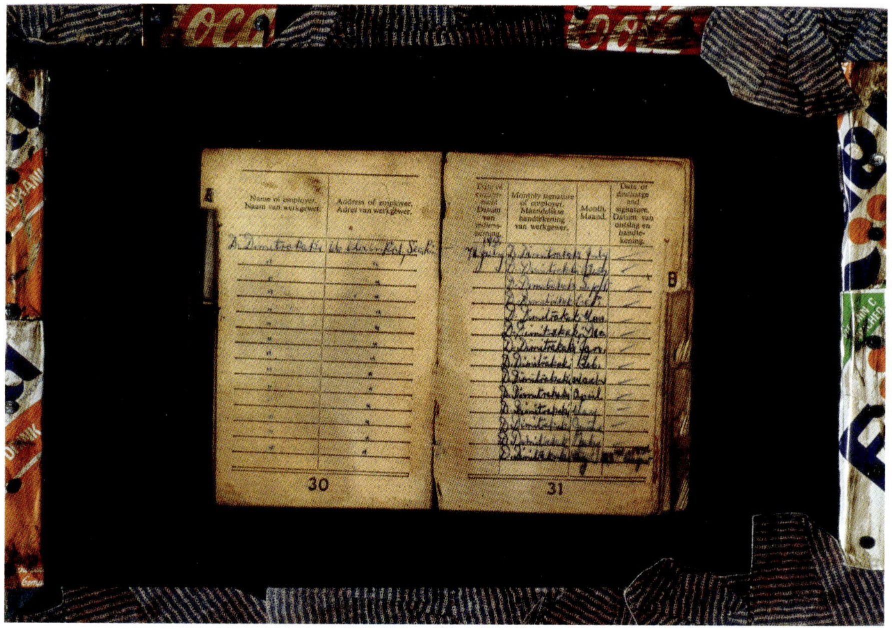

*For Thirty Years Next to his Heart* (detail)
1990
Colour laser print, hand covered frame
22 x 31 cm

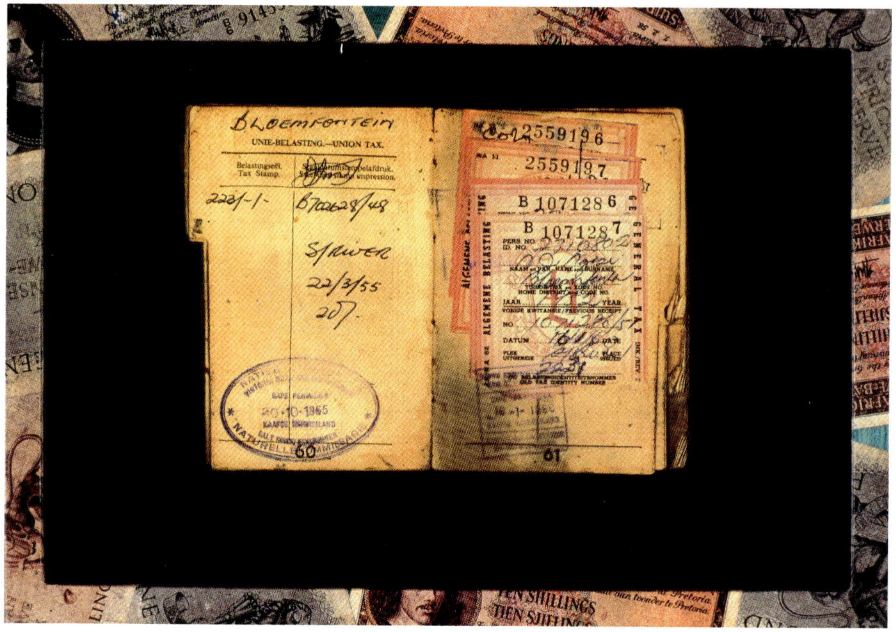

*For Thirty Years Next to his Heart* (detail)
1990
Colour laser print, hand covered frame
22 x 31 cm

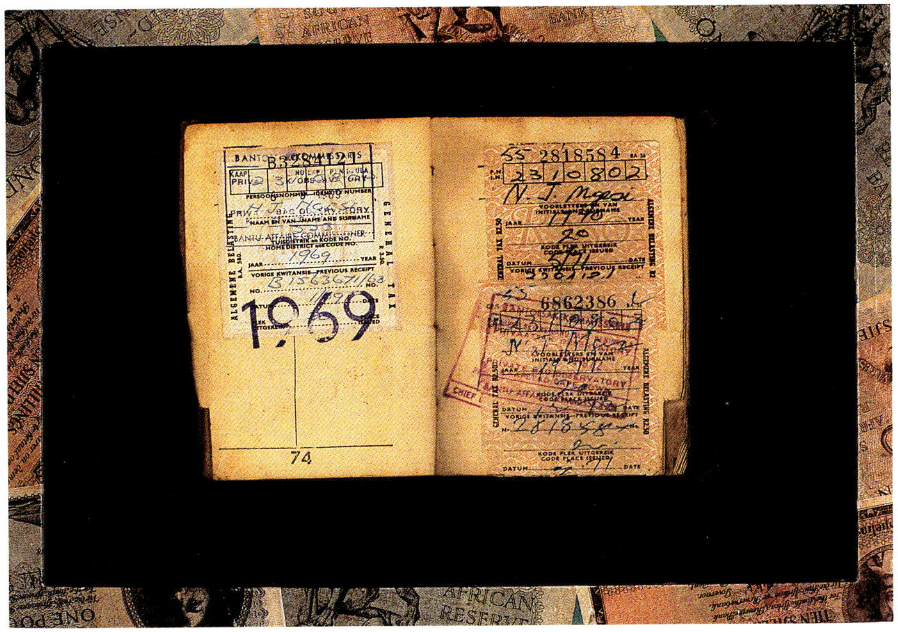


*For Thirty Years Next to his Heart* (detail)
1990
Colour laser print, hand covered frame
22 x 31 cm

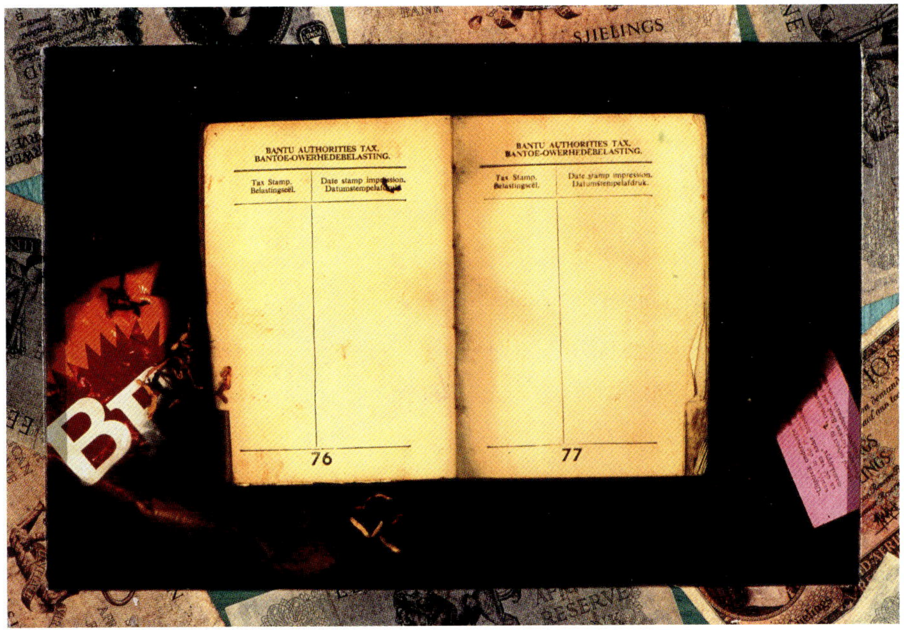


*For Thirty Years Next to his Heart* (detail)
1990
Colour laser print, hand covered frame
22 x 31 cm

"Sue Williamson has chosen to present her work as a modernist grid. The associations of a grid are usually rational process and logical order. However, by its reference to the window, it may suggest a symbolist view of the world beyond—the utopian dream. These apparently opposed readings are, in effect, the poles between which most modernist work vacillates.

Looking closely at the separate rectangles in Williamson's grid, we find that each one is a framed page from a black man's passbook, issued under apartheid regulations in South Africa. The content of these pages sustains attention for the sheer disgust such invasive material induces in those unfamiliar with this bureaucracy gone mad.

The passbook format is familiar, setting out categories, times and places like a census form or tax document, but the details requested deny the most fundamental human privacy and dignity.

In a way, the lunacy of its content placed in the order of such a document, reiterates the language of the grid. The stark truth is that utopia is denied, and the window is that of a barred cell…"

Anthony Bond
Director of the 9th Biennale of Sydney, 2003
*The Boundary Rider* catalogue, p. 248

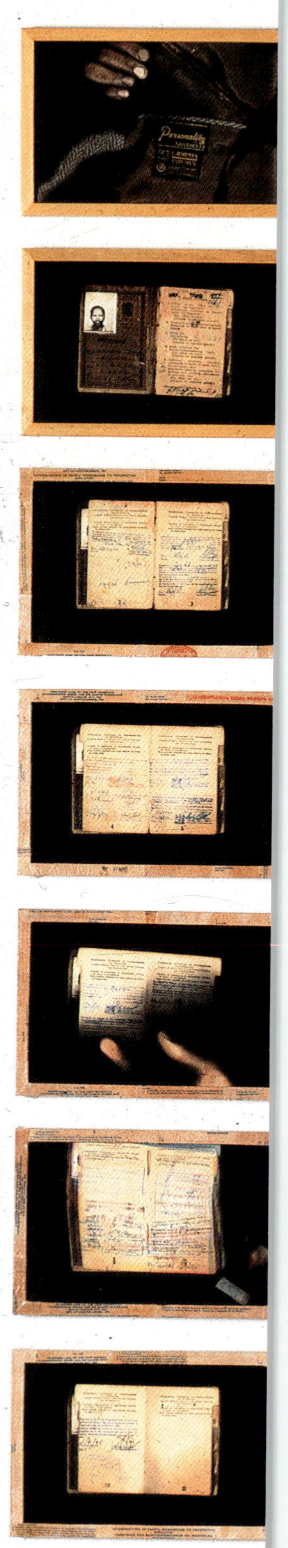

*For Thirty Years Next to his Heart*
1990
Colour laser prints, hand covered frames
196 x 262 cm

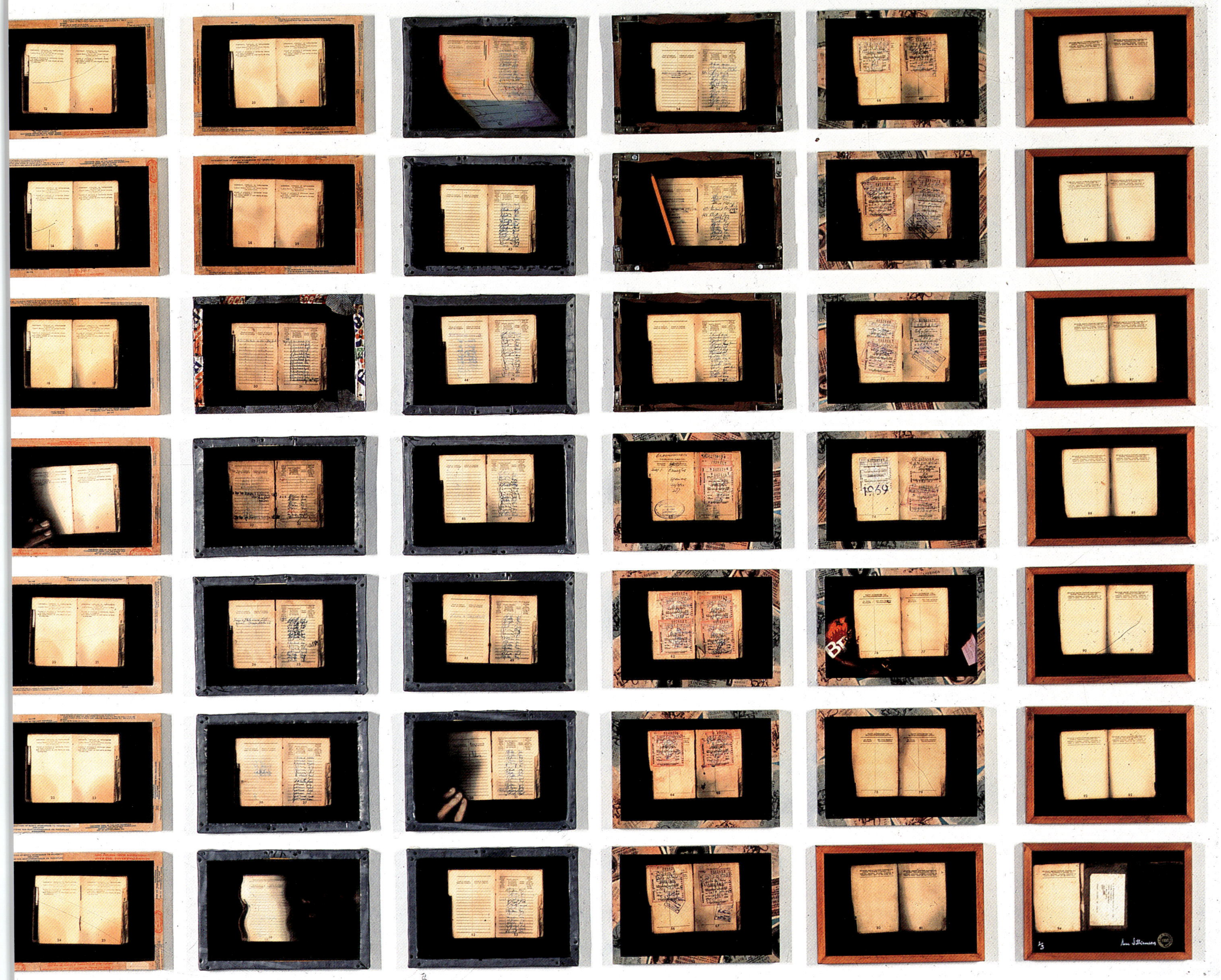

# A Tale of Two Cradocks

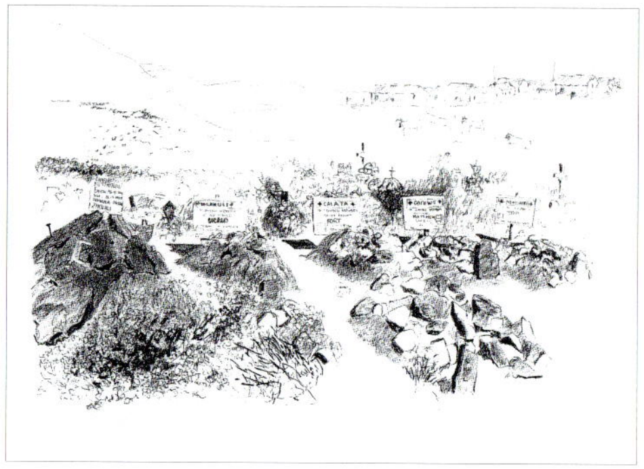

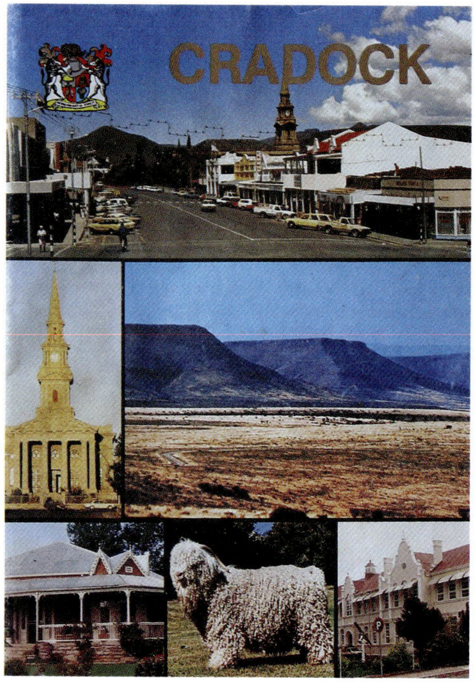


*Graves of the Cradock Four*
1989
Print from a lost drawing made in situ
in Cradock in 1989
83 x 60.5 cm

The cover of the Cradock guide book, 1989

In 1989, Sue Williamson travelled to the small town of Cradock, in the Eastern Cape, to meet Nyameka, the widow of the charismatic schoolteacher and community leader Matthew Goniwe. Driving through the town on her way to Lingelihle, the black township adjoining Cradock, Williamson stopped to pick up the guide to the town at the local tourist centre.

She was struck by the fact that while the brochure gave details of schools, hotels, churches and recreational facilities, only white people appeared in the photos. The only mention made of the presence of black people in the town was a note that businesses could rely on a large "labour reserve".

This was despite the fact that the town had become notorious after the 1985 police murder of Goniwe and three of his comrades: Fort Calata, Sparrow Mkhonto and Sicelo Mhlauli. The funeral of the four was a national rallying-point for the burgeoning popular movement against apartheid, and a turning-point in the struggle. On the day of the funeral, 5 March 1985, the South African president, PW Botha, declared the first of the States of Emergency that would last the next five years, until his successor, FW de Klerk, released Nelson Mandela and unbanned the liberation movements in 1990.

In her artwork, Williamson alternates pages of the guidebook with the story of Matthew and Nyameka Goniwe and, specifically, the killing of the Cradock Four. As she had been doing since pp. 10, 31-9 *A Few South Africans* (1983–7), the artist endeavoured to tell those stories erased from the official history, and to use the research in an artwork to educate herself, and her viewers, about her country's real history.

Williamson's own practice is an act of restitution. If white Cradock is "received" through official channels and presented, flat and official, without the artist's intervention, then the black Cradock we view is seen through her own camera and found documentation, sketched by her own hand, and understood through the words of Nyameka Goniwe.

In *Selected Work* the artist writes that "the concertina form of the piece relates to the effects of apartheid: depending on where you stand, only one side of the tale can be seen."

After many years away from Cradock, Nyameka Goniwe returned to the town and was elected its first female mayor in 2011.

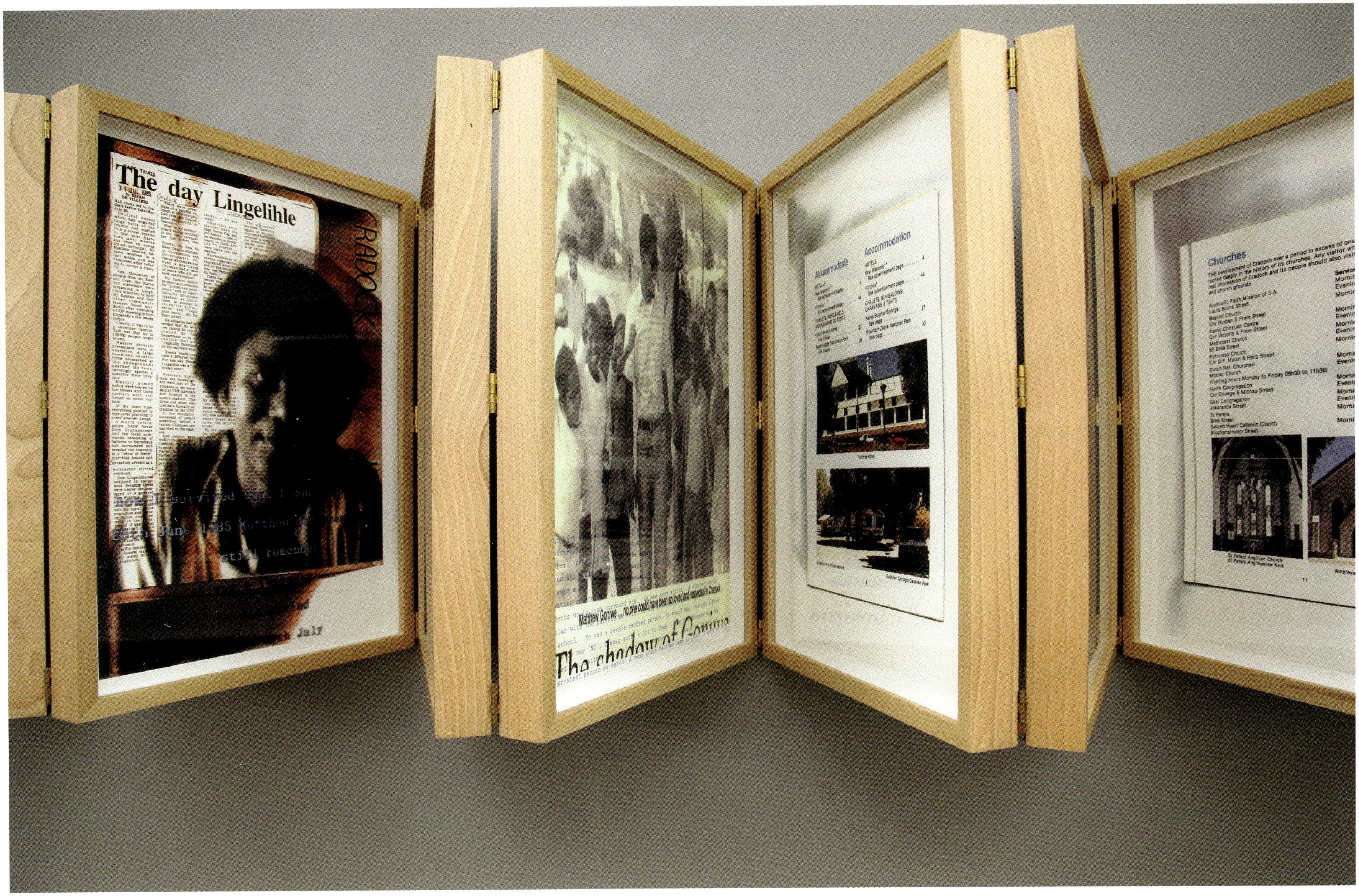


*A Tale of Two Cradocks* (detail)
1994
Colour laser prints, wood, extruded acetate
43 x 500 x 25 cm

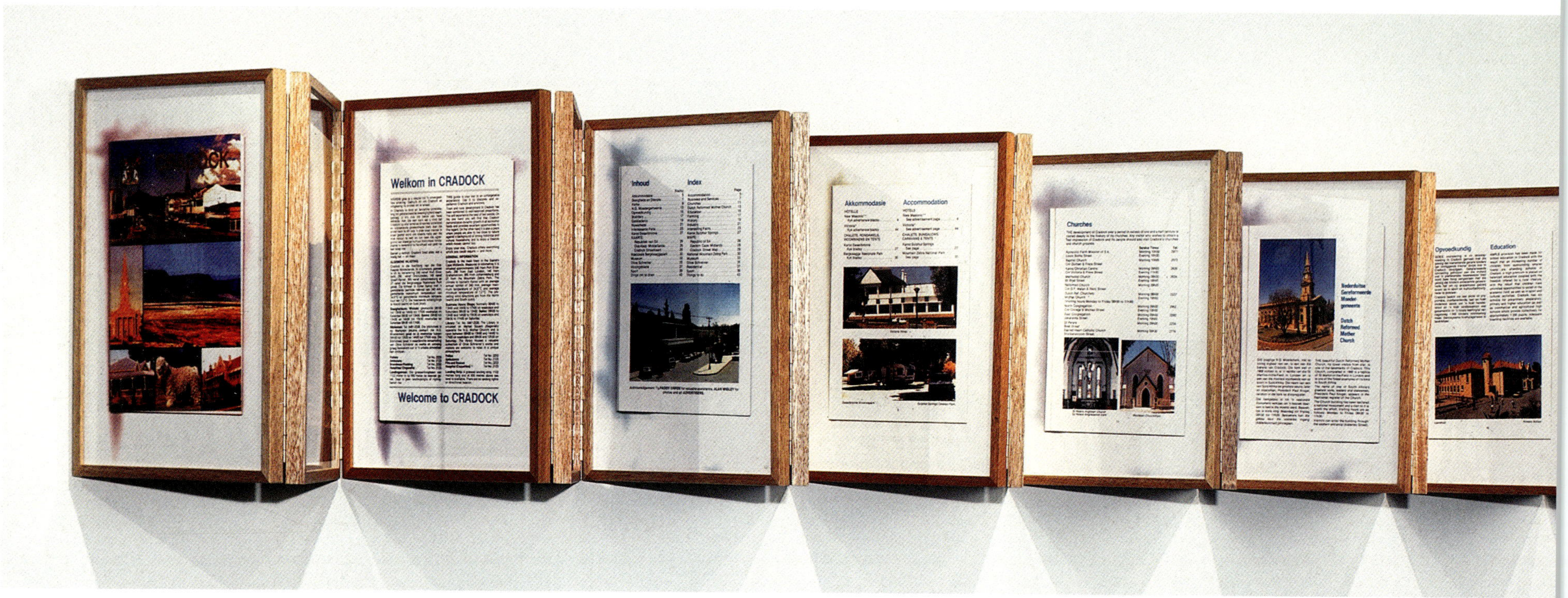


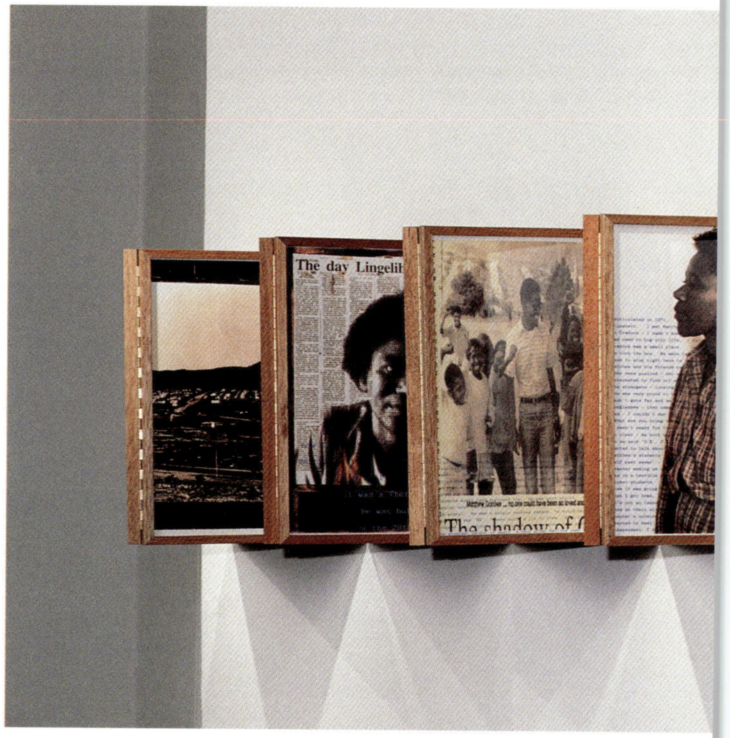

*A Tale of Two Cradocks*
1994
Colour laser prints, wood, extruded acetate
43 x 500 x 25 cm

*A Tale of Two Cradocks*
1994
Colour laser prints, wood, extruded acetate
43 x 500 x 25 cm

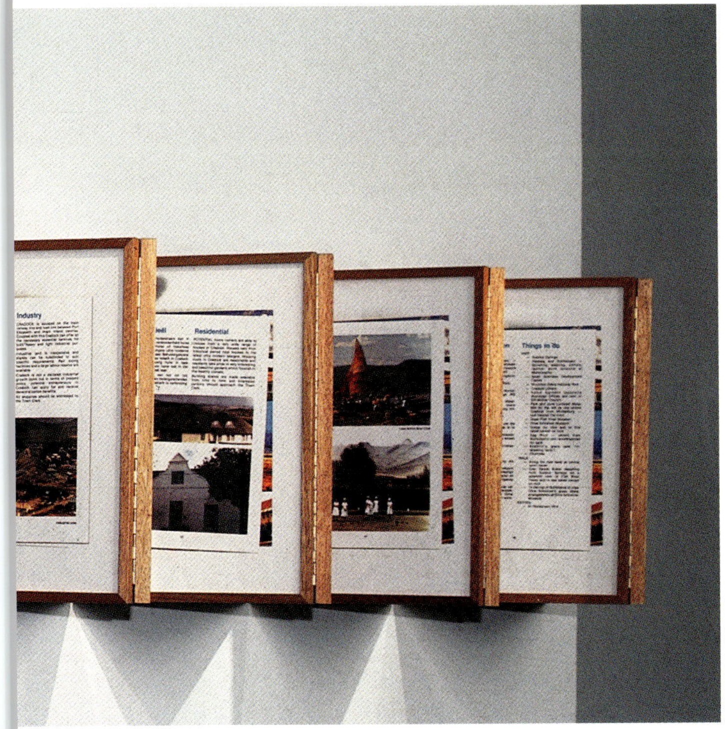
Industry
Residential
Things to do

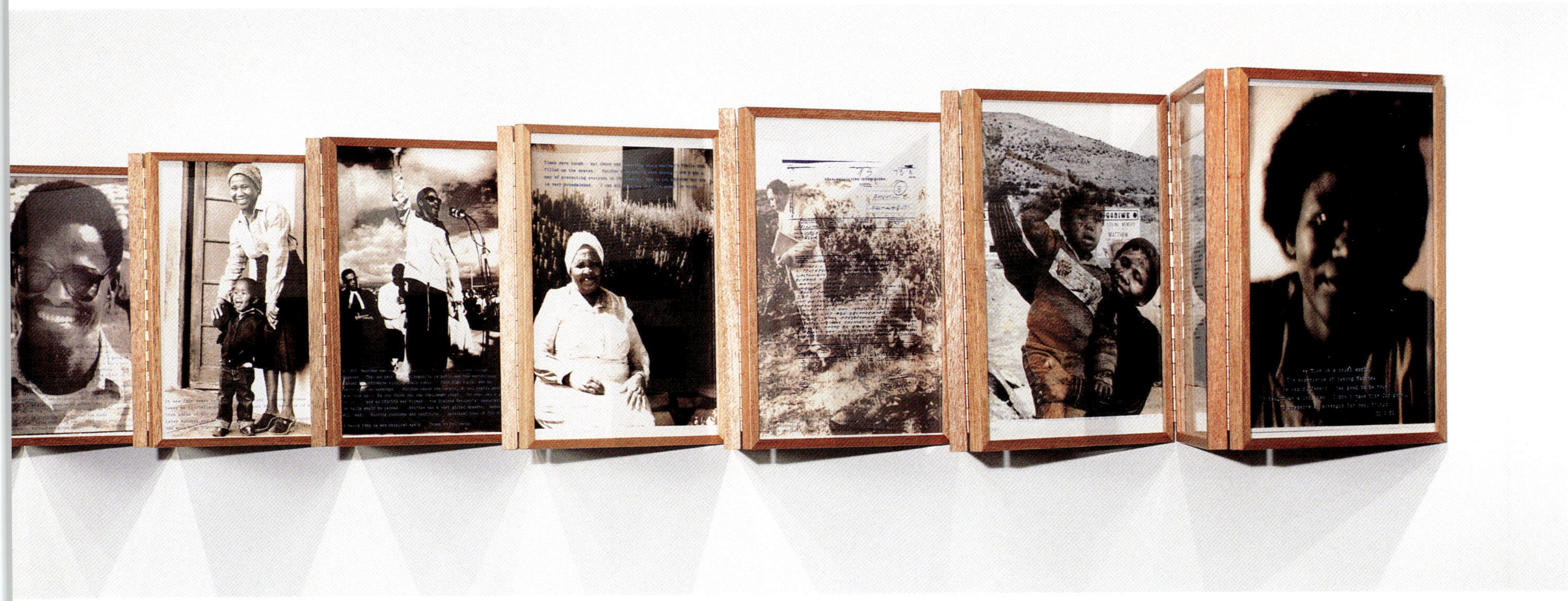

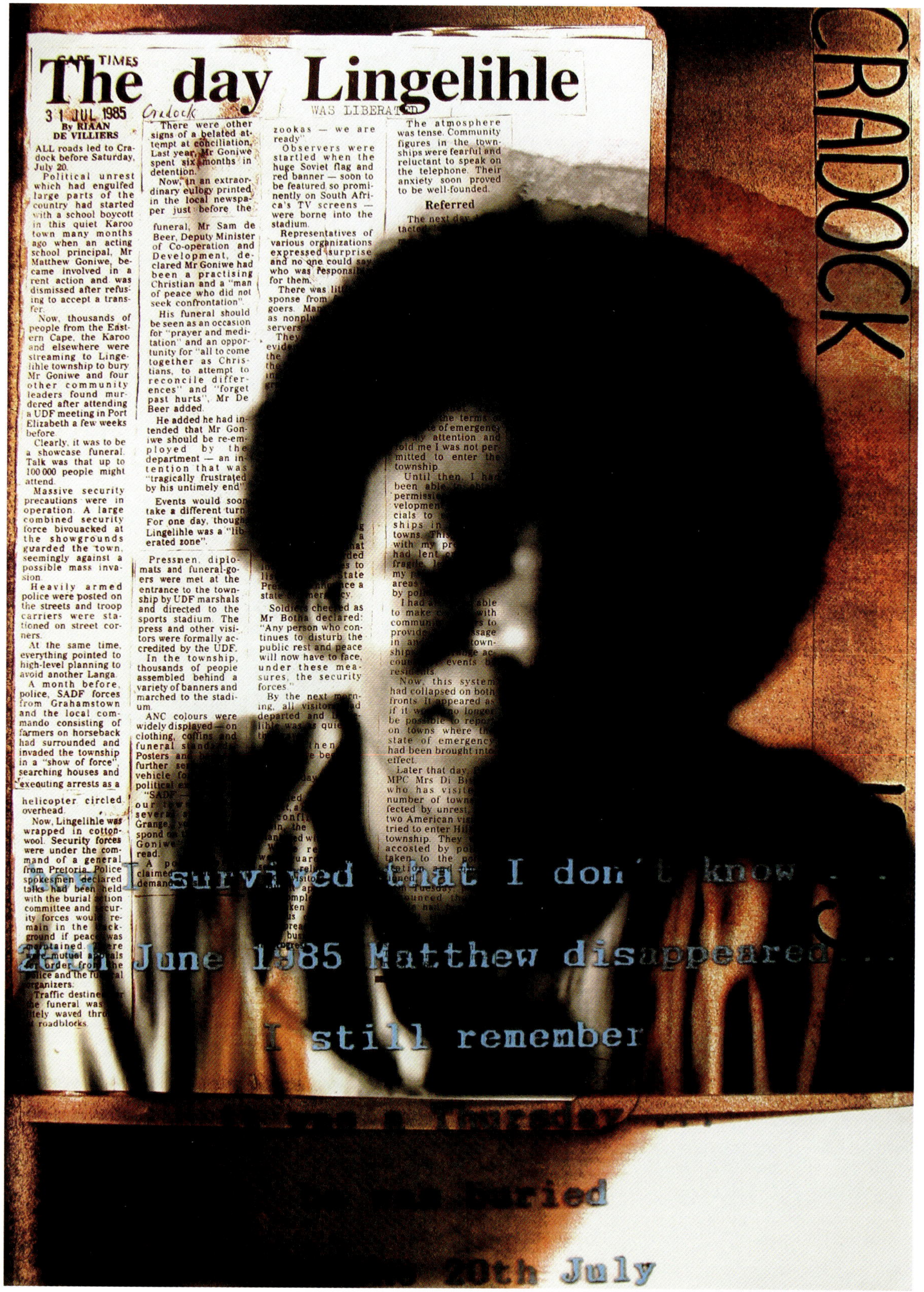


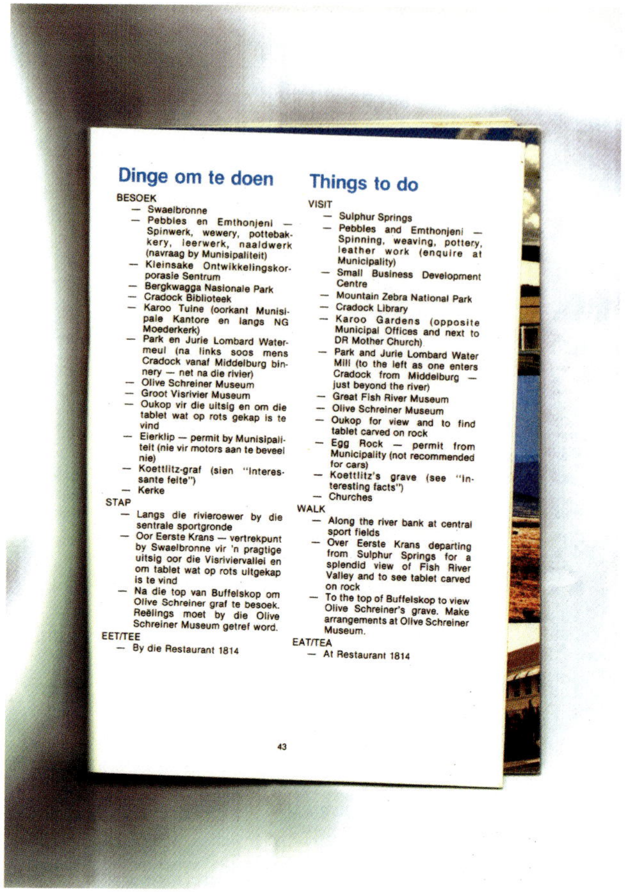


*A Tale of Two Cradocks* (detail)
1994
Colour laser prints, wood, extruded acetate

*A Tale of Two Cradocks* (detail)
1994
Colour laser prints, wood, extruded acetate

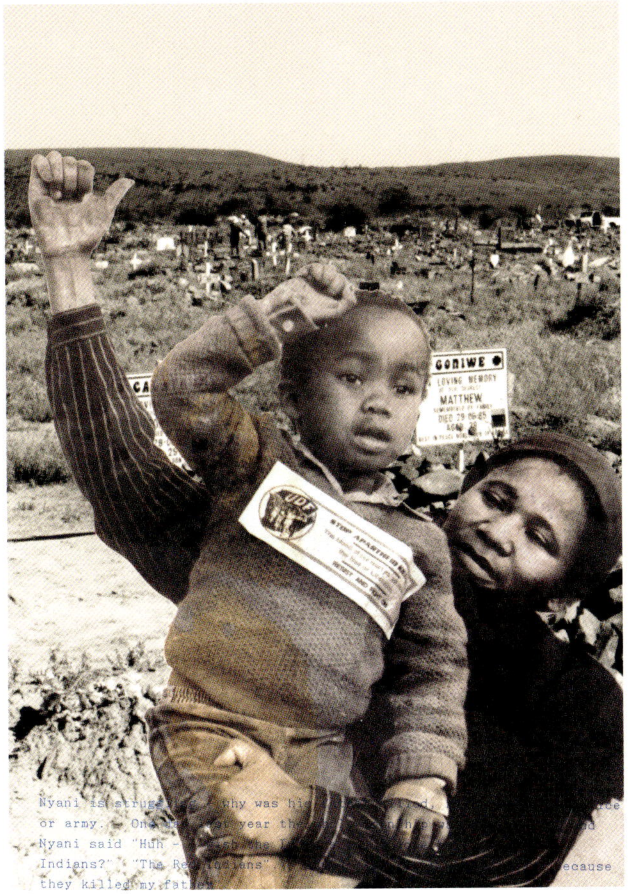


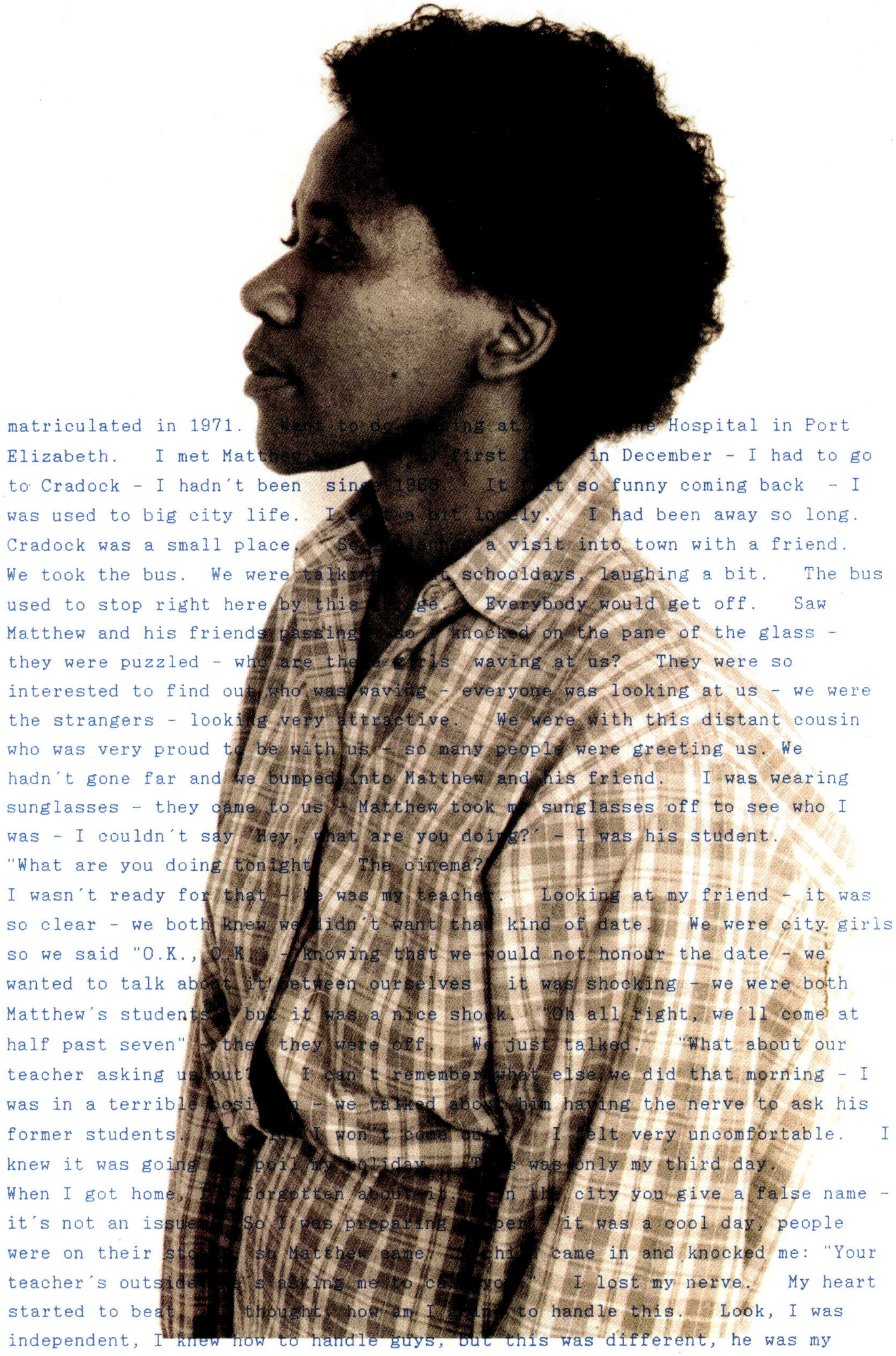


*A Tale of Two Cradocks* (detail)
1994
Colour laser prints, wood, extruded acetate

*A Tale of Two Cradocks* (detail)
1994
Colour laser prints, wood, extruded acetate

# Colouring In

"History is often circular: the same patterns repeat themselves, and only the casts of characters change." Sue Williamson made this observation when she visited the Boer War Museum in Bloemfontein in the early 1990s, and bought a children's colouring book at the gift shop.

The Anglo-Boer War was fought in South Africa between 1899 and 1902, as Britain fought to subjugate the independent Boer republics in the British colony. Williamson noted how the colouring book, designed for Afrikaans children, told the story of the destruction and burning of Boer farms, the deportation of the menfolk to concentration camps in St Helena, India and Ceylon and the placing of their women and children in camps within the country where 26 000 would die of malnutrition and sickness: "Seventy years later", she writes in *Selected Work*, "the now powerful Afrikaans nation behaved in much the same way towards black people. The abused child became an abusing parent."

To depict this historical irony, Williamson made an artwork which superimposes photographs of the Boer War era over the crudely drawn illustrations of the colouring book. She then introduces matching images of the destruction of Cape Town's squatter camps in the 1970s. We see, for example, a Boer farmhouse on fire, next to a squatter's homestead on fire, or Boer commandoes being sent into exile, next to images of squatter residents being taken away in police vans. We also see, poignantly, a Boer family at prayer, matched with a scene from a black church.

Always alive to how narratives are framed, Williamson returns in this artwork to the resource she used in *A Few South Africans*: popular modes pp. 10, 31
of framing in communities that must "make do". Here she uses another form of picture making she encountered as an activist in that era: religious texts in *isiXhosa* are stencilled through glass painted black and highlighted with coloured silver paper. The frames of the colouring book pages are covered with lists from *Die Bannelinge* of the names of the Boer prisoners of war who died in the British concentration camps, and the names of the diseases that killed them.

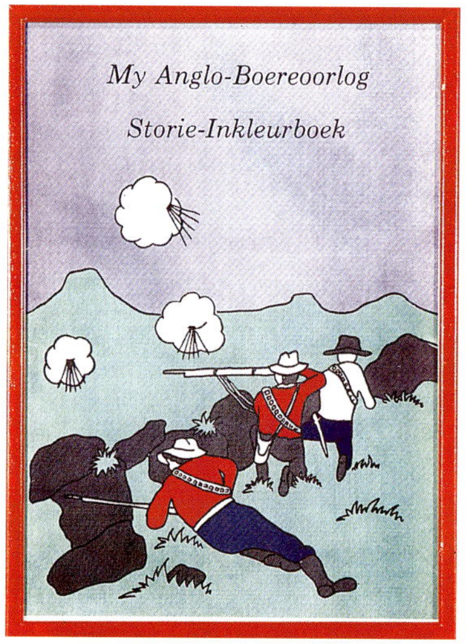


*Colouring In* (detail)
Colour laser print
43.8 x 31.8 cm

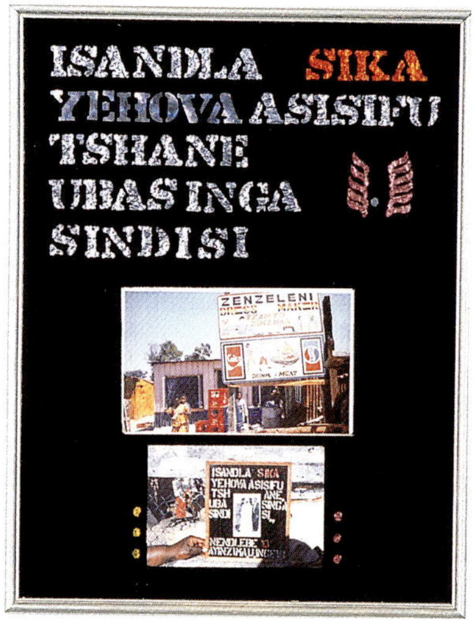


*Colouring In* (detail)
Black paint, colour laser prints, silver paper, cellophane
40 x 31.5 cm

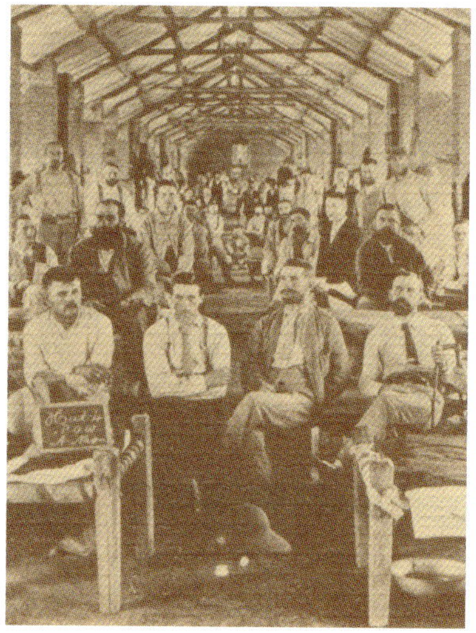

The cover of *Die Bannelinge*

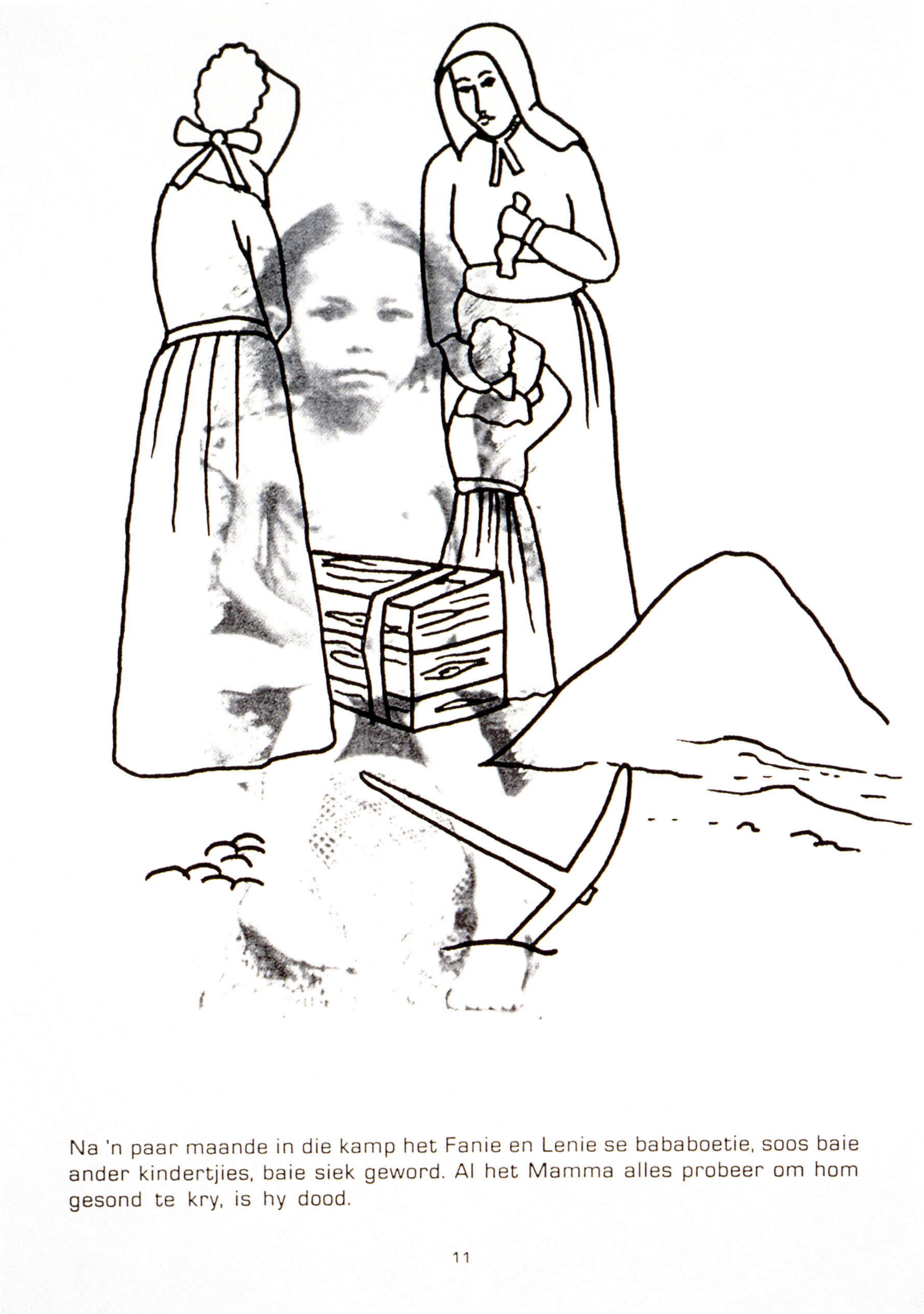


*Colouring In* (detail)
Colour laser print
43.8 x 31.8 cm

Pages 96–7
*Colouring In*
1992
Colour laser prints, découpage frames, lead, black paint, silver foil, cellophane
148 x 386 cm

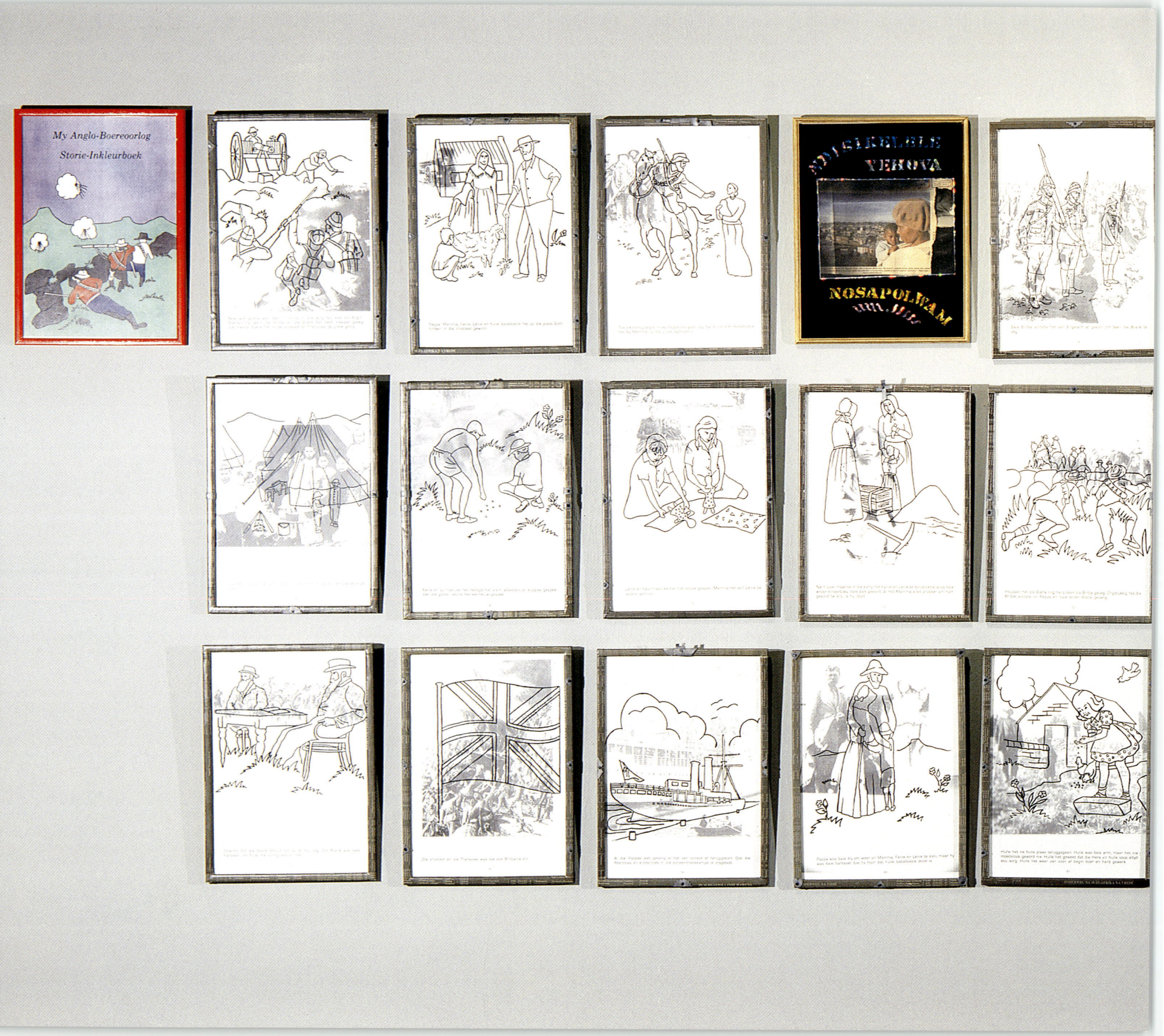
My Anglo-Boereoorlog
Storie-Inkleurboek
YEHOVA
NOSAPOLWAM

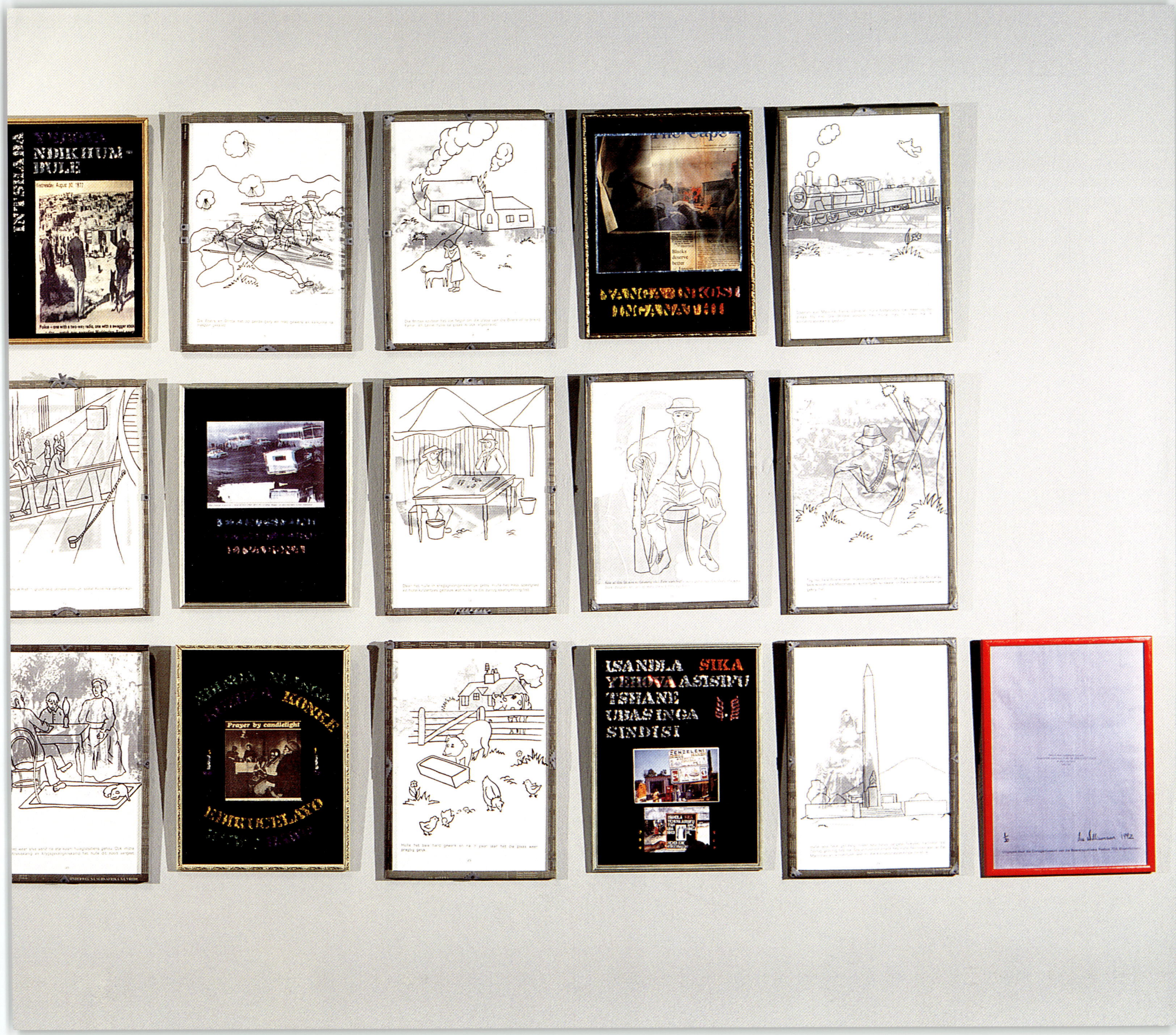
INTSIKANA
NDIKHUMBULE
Prayer by candlelight
ISANDLA SIKA
YEHOVA ASISIFU
TSHANE
UBASINGA
SINDISI

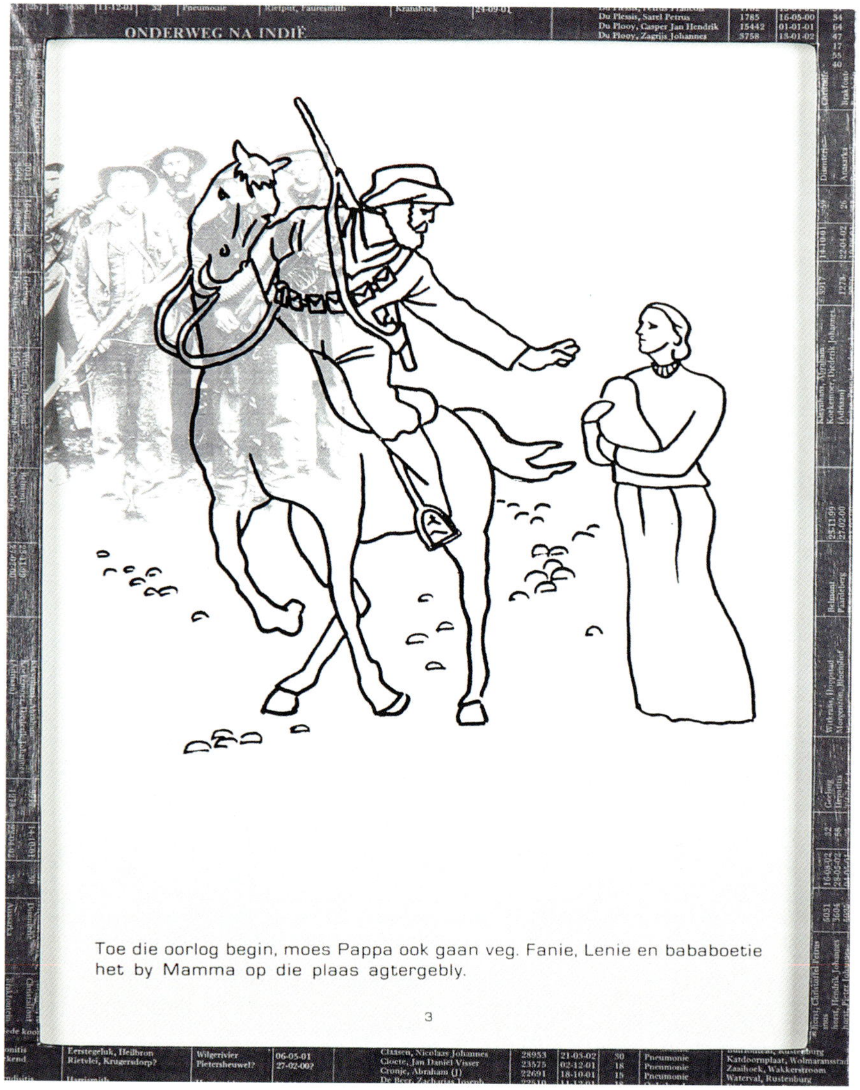


*Colouring In* (detail)
Colour laser print, decoupage
covered frame
43.8 x 31.8 cm

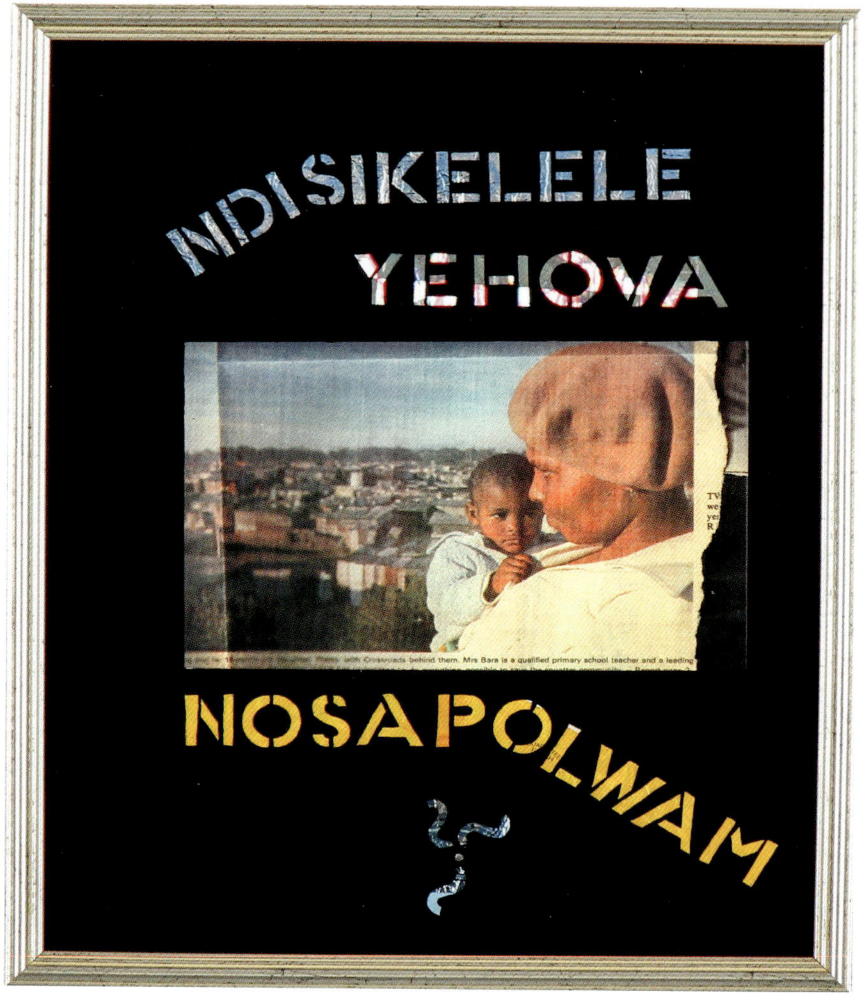


*Colouring In* (detail)
Black paint, colour laser print,
silver paper, cellophane
40 x 31.5 cm

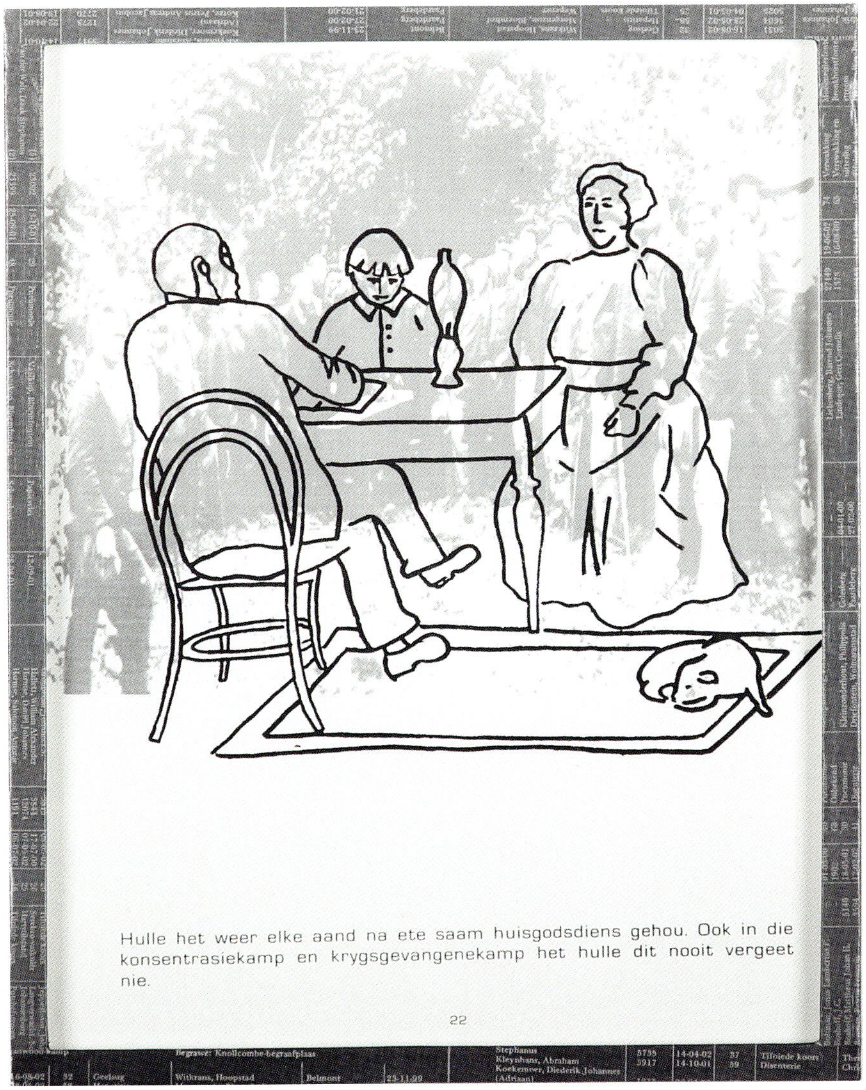


*Colouring In* (detail)
Colour laser print, decoupage
covered frame
43.8 x 31.8 cm

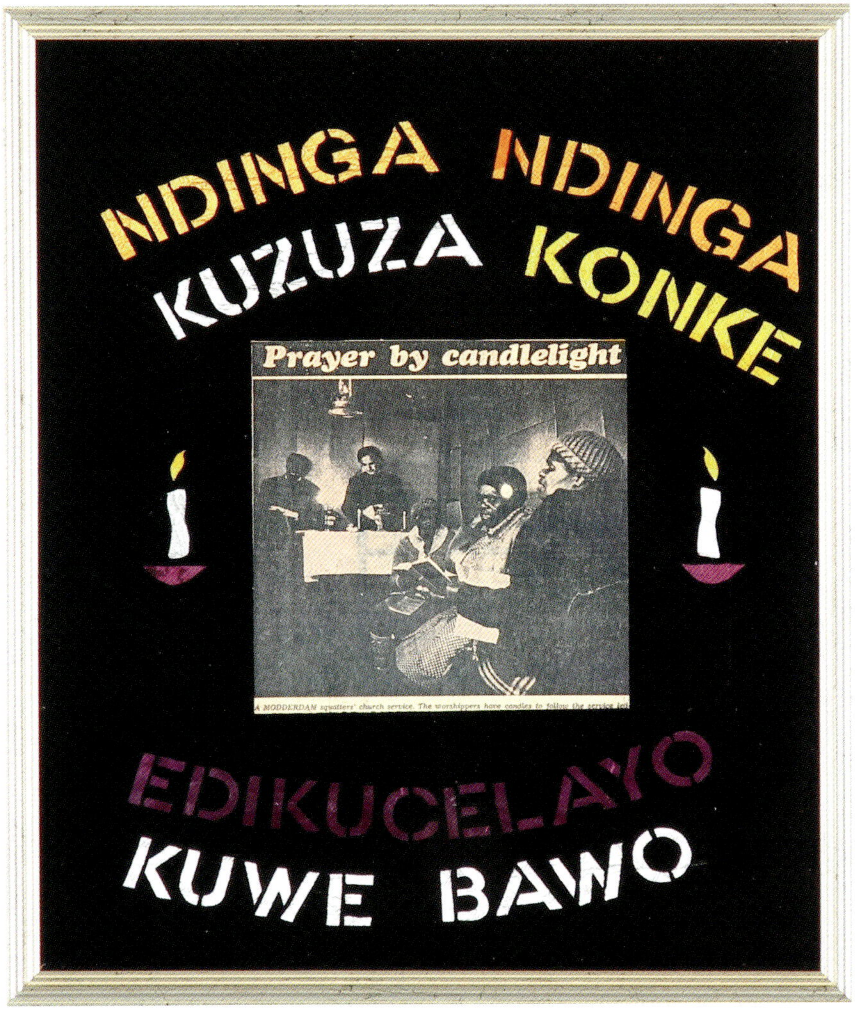


*Colouring In* (detail)
Black paint, colour laser print,
silver paper, cellophane
40 x 31.5 cm

# Pages from a Government Tourist Brochure

*Native Life in South Africa* is the title of a brochure published by the South African tourism department in 1936. In the seven works comprising *Pages from a Government Tourist Brochure*, Williamson draws out the insidious subtexts of the brochure's pseudo-ethnographic discourse, which would form the basis for the doctrine of apartheid to be implemented twelve years later.

Visitors are promised, in the brochure, that "South Africa today is a veritable tourist paradise. Here the traveller encounters a remarkable conglomerate of races, ranging from the most backward and primitive to the most virile and intelligent of the dark-skinned tribes."

The artist has framed the prints in thick steel and materials of confinement, such as chain-link and barbed wire. She writes in *Selected Work* that "the psychological barrier the brochure sets up is underlined by the rigid steel frames, and a physical barrier between subject and viewer." She notes that she used barbed wire, in particular, in *The Hottentot*, because "early settlers fenced off traditionally open lands and indigenous people who trespassed were exterminated like vermin."

Williamson's training in journalism and copywriting attracted her to the "printed matter" of this series of works. In *Pages from a Government Tourist Brochure* she pulled text out of context to evince subtext: dismembered words are etched deep into the steel frames, like warped advertising copy.

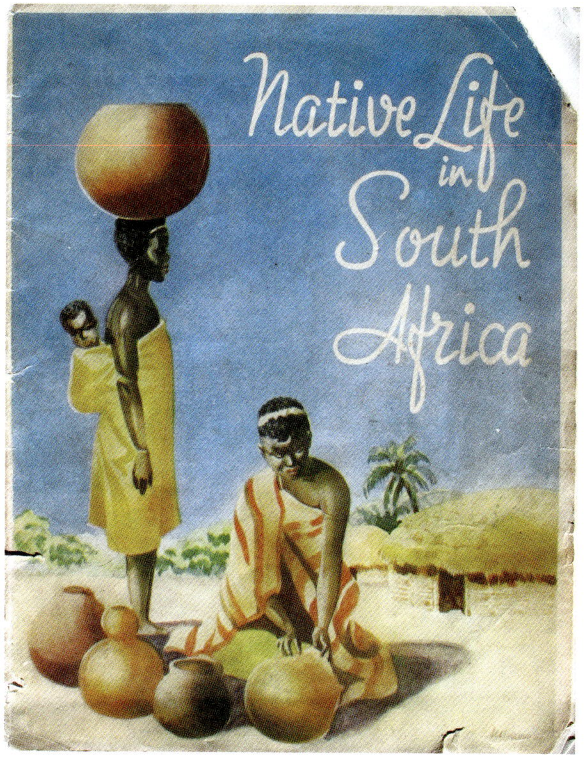


The cover of *Native Life in South Africa*, published by the State tourist department in 1936

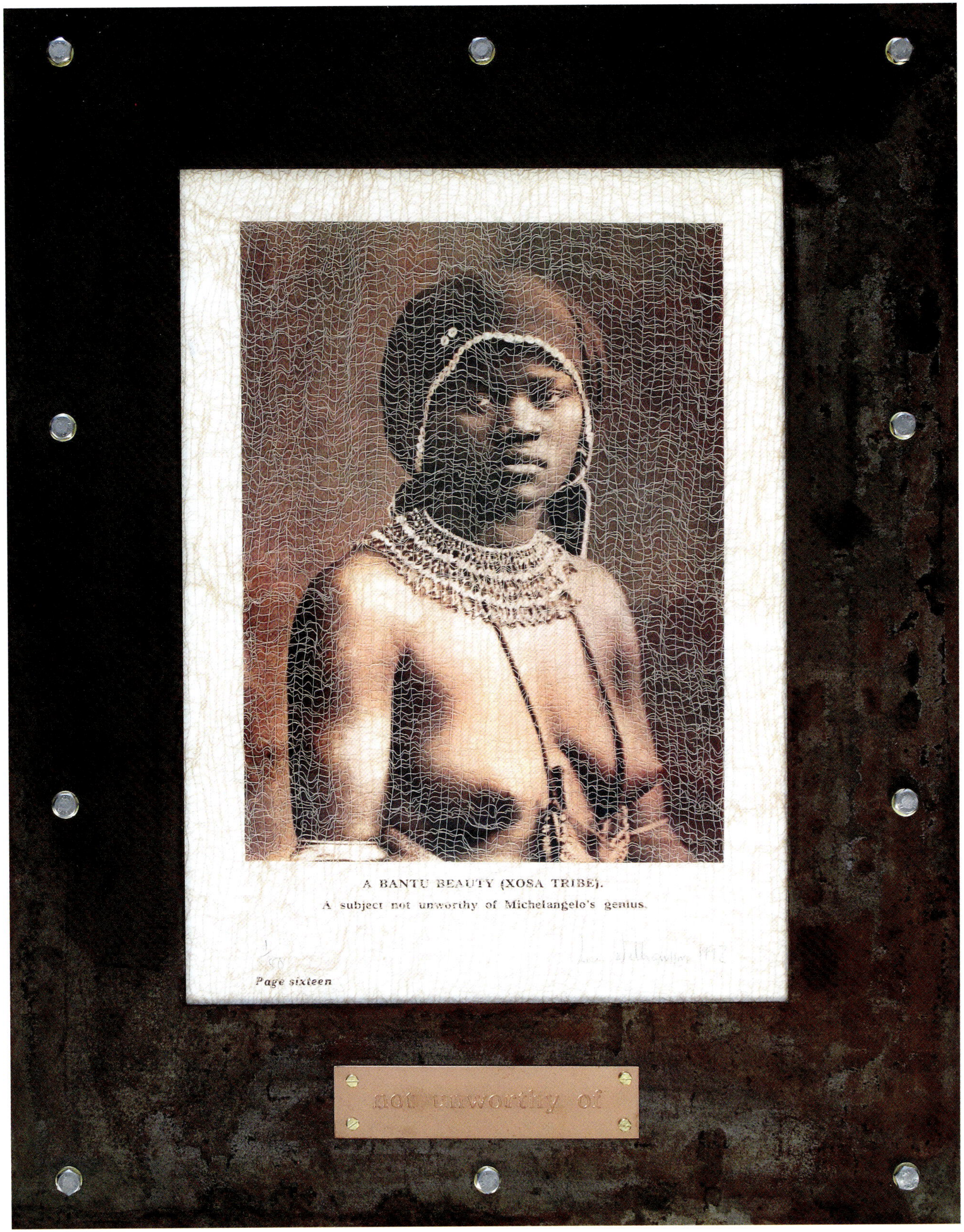


*Not Unworthy*
1992
*Pages from a Government Tourist Brochure* series
Steel, extruded acetate, archival digital print,
wood, copper
53 x 45 cm

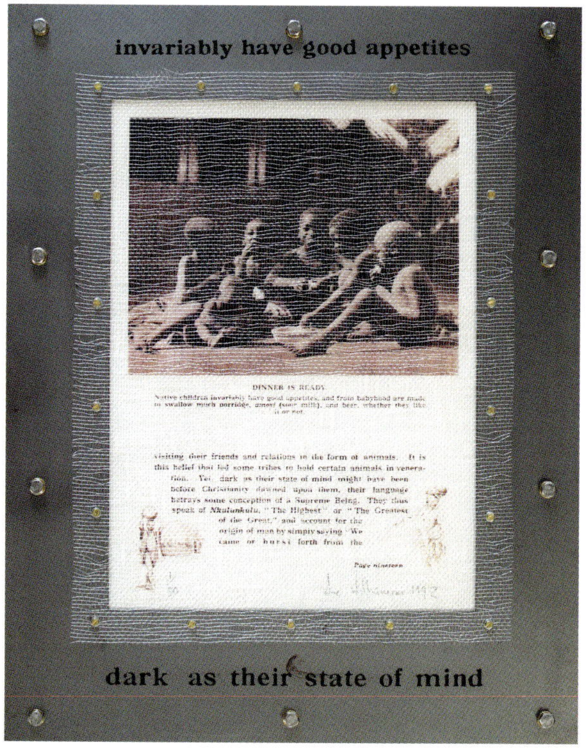


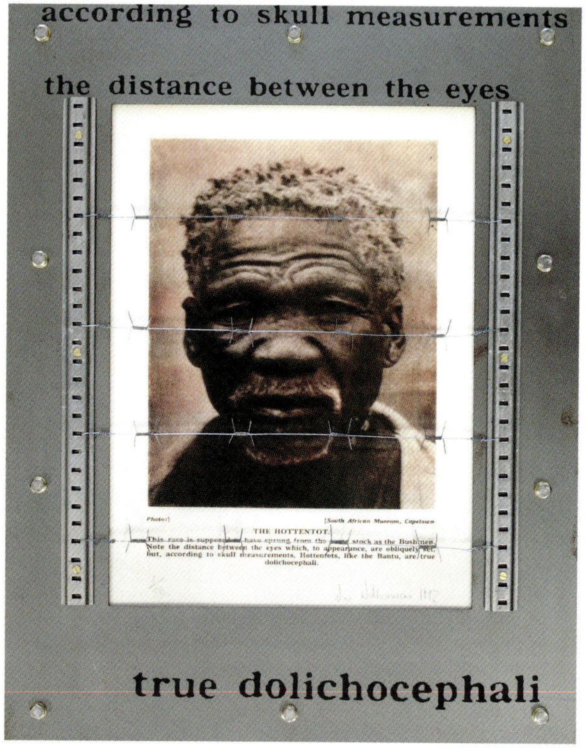


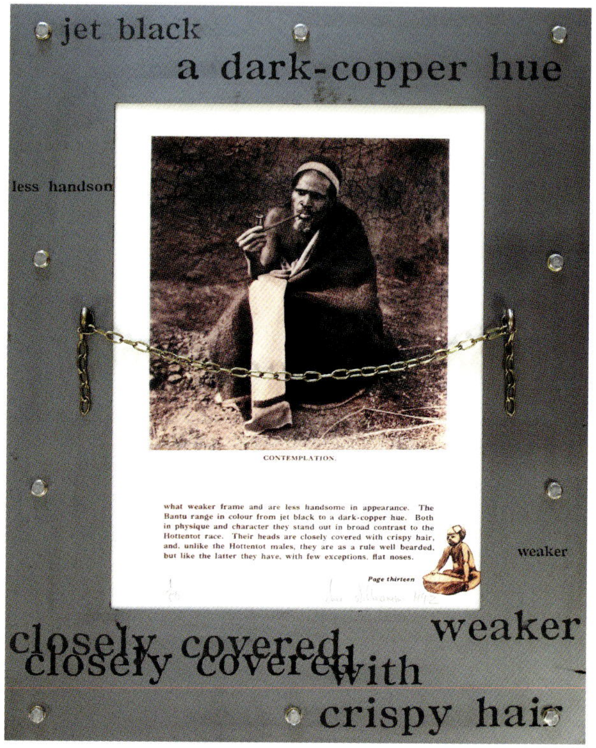


*Dinner is ready*
1992
*Pages from a Government Tourist Brochure* series
Steel, extruded acetate, archival digital print,
wood, wire mesh
53 x 45 cm

*The Hottentot*
1992
*Pages from a Government Tourist Brochure* series
Steel, extruded acetate, colour laser print,
wood, wire
53 x 45 cm

*Contemplation*
1992
*Pages from a Government Tourist Brochure* series
Steel, extruded acetate, archival digital print,
wood, brass-plated chain
53 x 45 cm

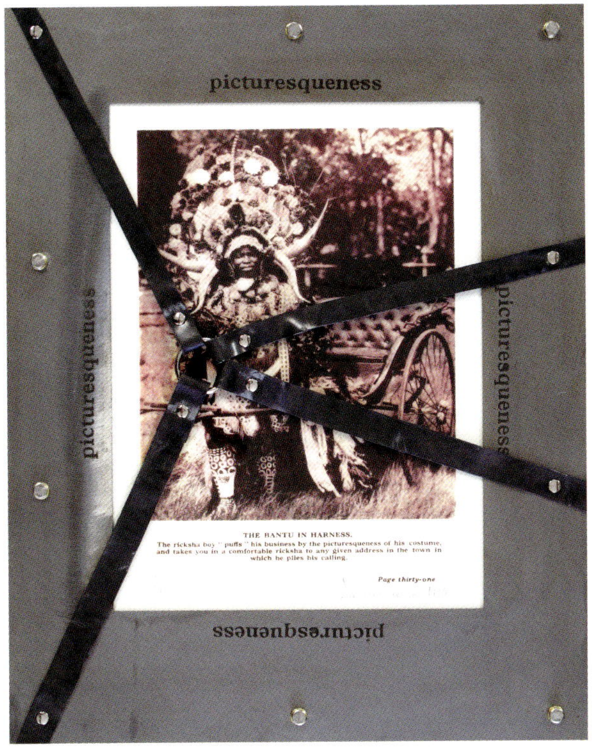


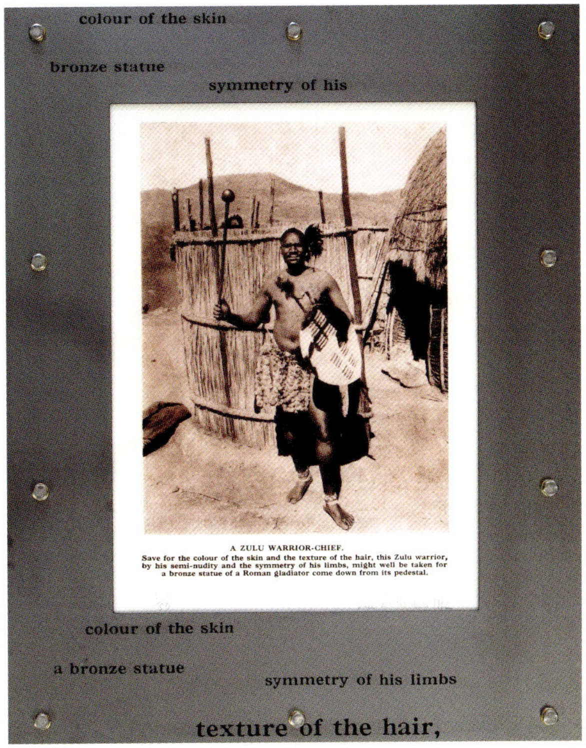


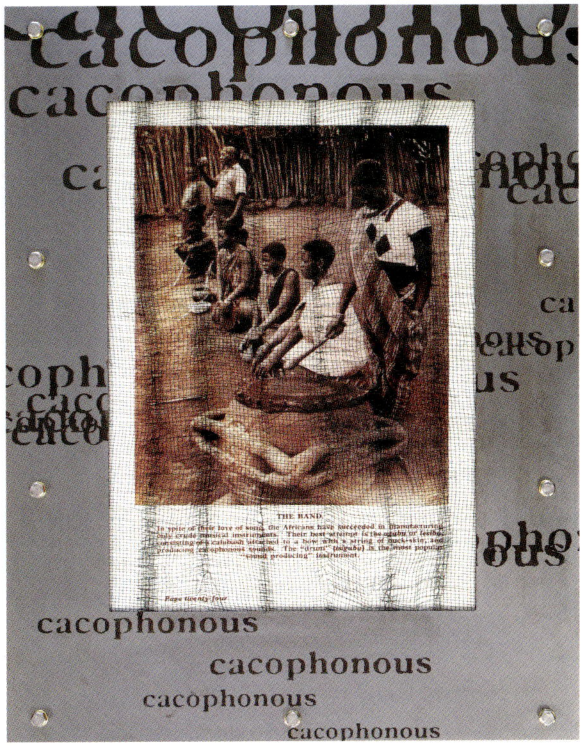


*Ricksha*
1996
*Pages from a Government Tourist Brochure* series
Steel, extruded acetate, archival digital print, wood, lead, steel ring
53 x 45 cm

*Zulu Warrior*
1992
*Pages from a Government Tourist Brochure* series
Steel, extruded acetate, archival digital print, wood
53 x 45 cm

*The band*
1996
*Pages from a Government Tourist Brochure* series
Steel, extruded acetate, archival digital print, wood, coated wire mesh
53 x 45 cm

# Messages from the Moat

Okwui Enwezor's theme for the 2nd Johannesburg Biennale in 1997 was "Trade Routes: History and Geography". When he invited Sue Williamson to participate in the Biennale, she decided to work on the early history of the Cape Town Castle—the Dutch settlement's first structure—and the Cape slave trade that was run from within it.

Slavery was introduced to the Cape by the Dutch East India Company in 1653, and legally ended as an institution only in 1838. Williamson was told by a Dutch art historian that Cape Town had the most complete slave records in the world, and in fact, the Deeds Office in Cape Town still holds the original Deeds of Sale for the period between 1658 and 1702: there are more than 1400 of them. Each deed registers the name of a slave, his or her age and birthplace, the buyer, the seller, the price paid in rixdollars, and the date. The artist decided to screenprint and engrave by hand each of these records onto a separate bottle. The slave records are thus rendered physical, so many empty vessels washed up onto the shore, like traded bodies devoid of the spirit that must once have filled them before they were transformed into bloodless commodities.

Williamson amassed the bottles in a vast net from which water dripped down onto more bottles floating in water below: a representation of the moat around the Castle. She used a soundscape of unidentifiable creaks. This work was installed first at the cavernous Electric Workshop, for the Johannesburg Biennale, then went overseas, first to Sweden and then to the Netherlands, where appropriately, it was installed in the old Archive Building in the Hague. The Hague was

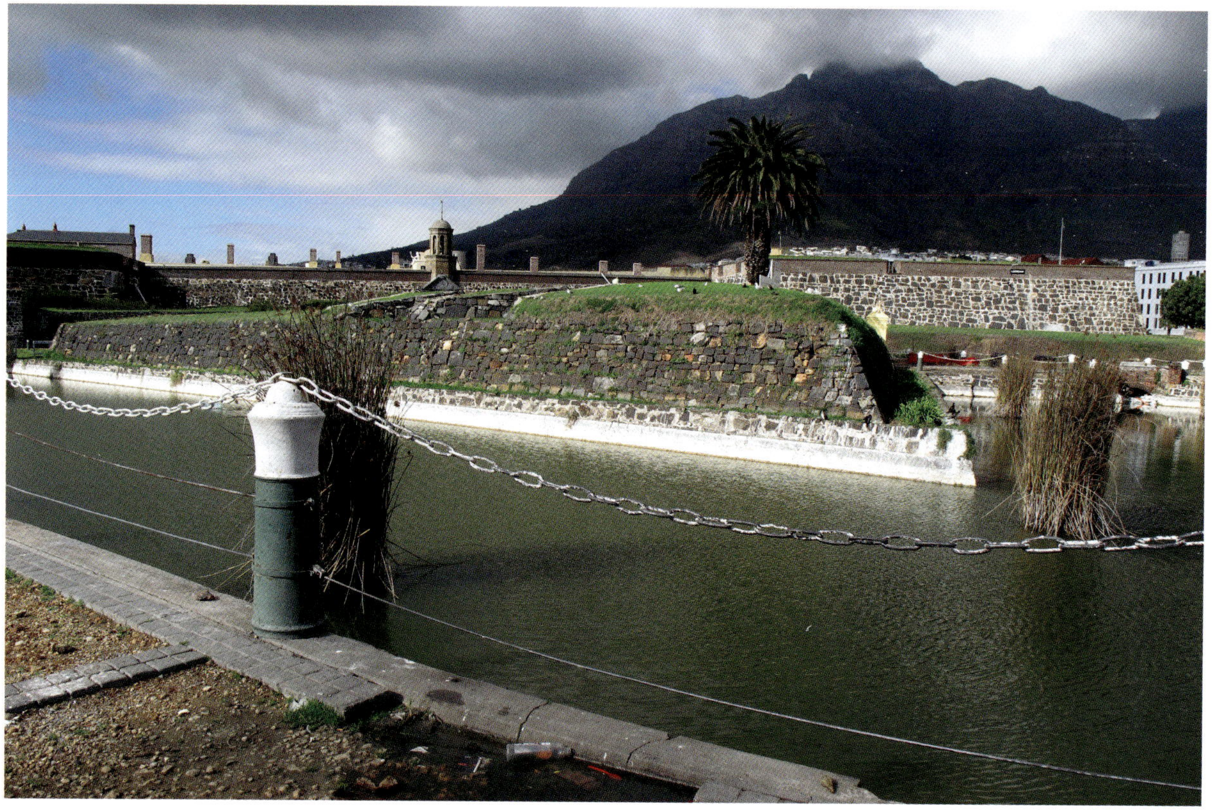

The moat surrounding the Castle of Good Hope, Cape Town

the former administrative centre of the Dutch trading empire, and when the work was shown in the Archive Building, pages listing all the slave transactions made in Cape Town were laid out on reading ledges surrounding the central installation of the bottle-filled net. "If the VOC [Dutch East India Company] was the world's first multinational company, the slaves were one of its most important commodities", the artist writes in *Selected Work*. "*Messages from the Moat* was conceived not only to recover a hidden history, but in order to consider the human price paid for amassing the fine collections of seventeenth-century paintings, glassware and china still to be found in Dutch museums and also at the Cape Town Castle."

The title refers to the mass of objects—like bottles and pieces of china—that were found in the Castle moat when it was dredged: allegedly thrown, in rage, by the slaves who worked within it.

*Messages from the Moat* is in the permanent collection of Iziko South African National Gallery, and was last seen in a dark interior room in the Cape Town Castle, where the bottles bobbed in a deep well set in the floor.

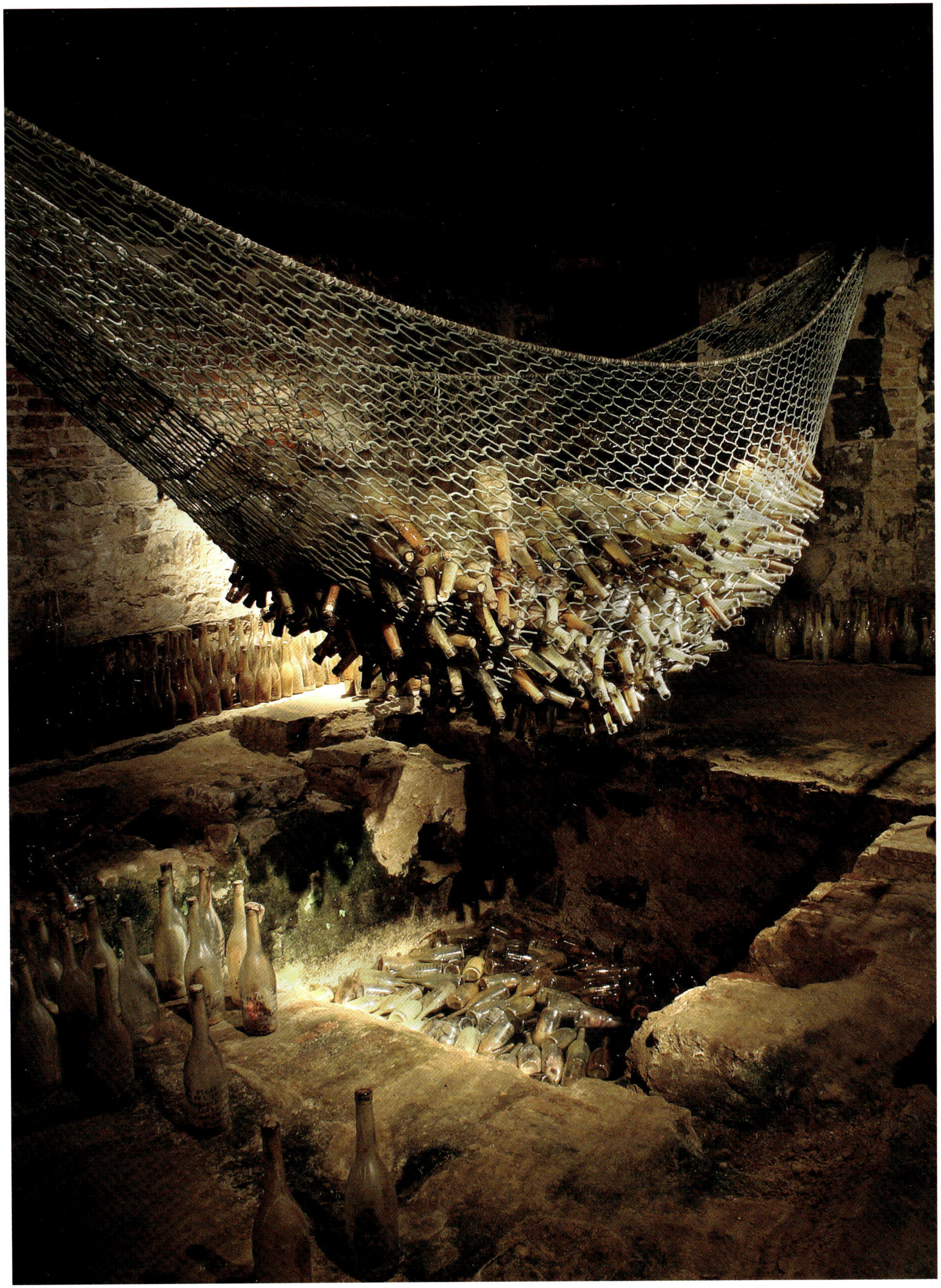

*Messages from the Moat*
1997
Engraved and stenciled glass, printed canvas,
found fishing net, water pump, soundscape
Dimensions variable
Installation view
Castle of Good Hope, Cape Town

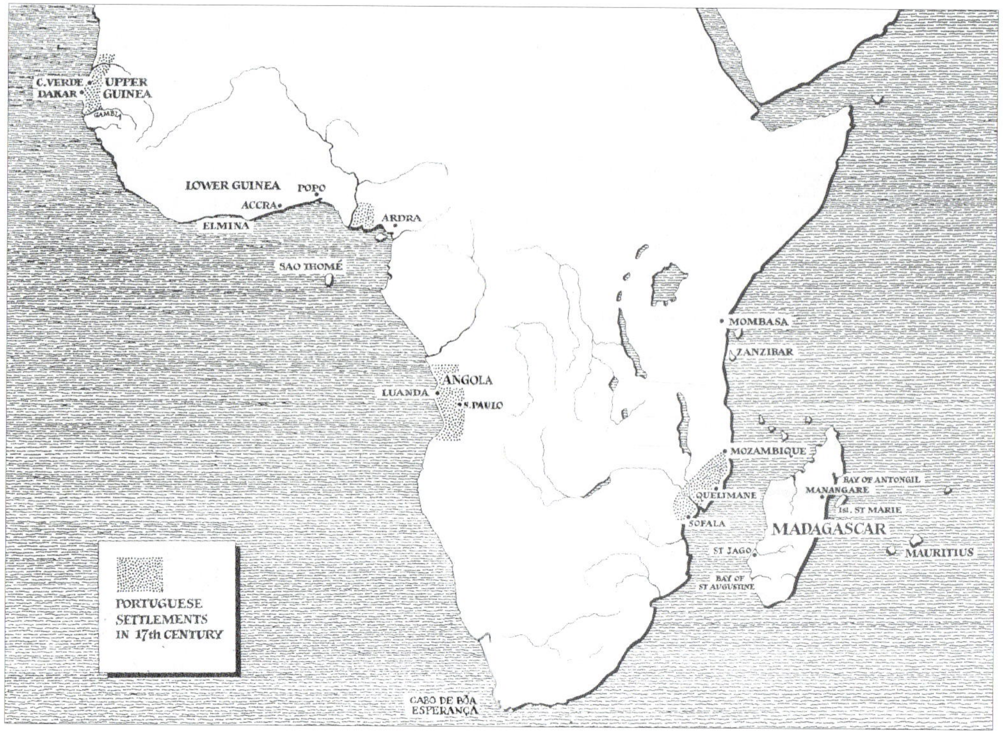


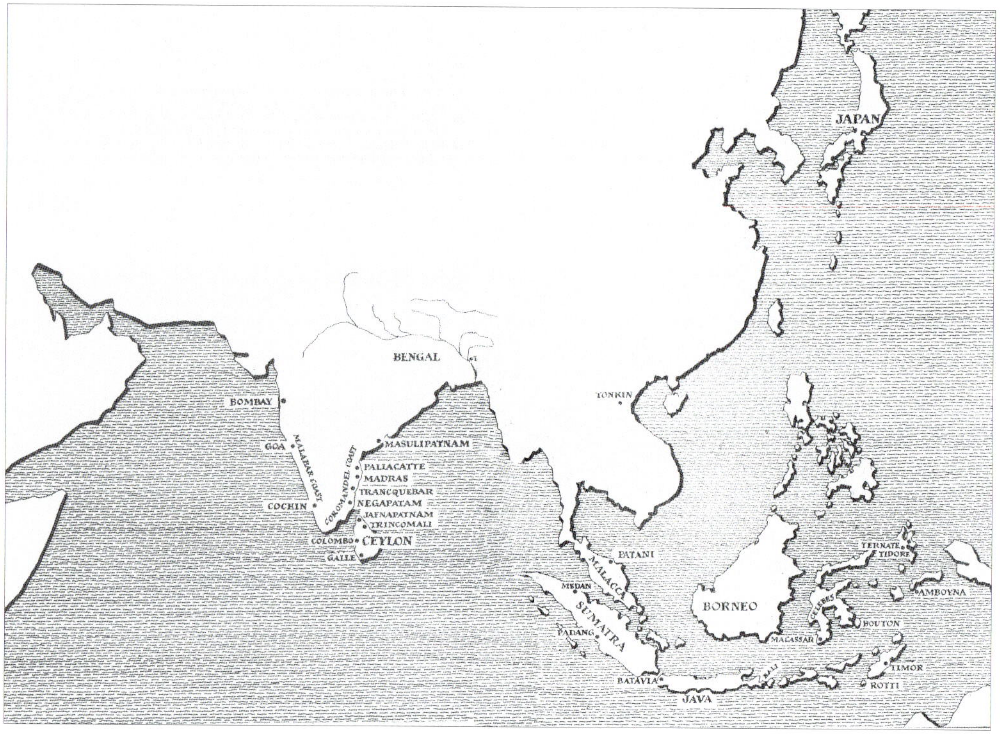


Maps indicating places where the Dutch ships picked up slaves for transport to Cape Town

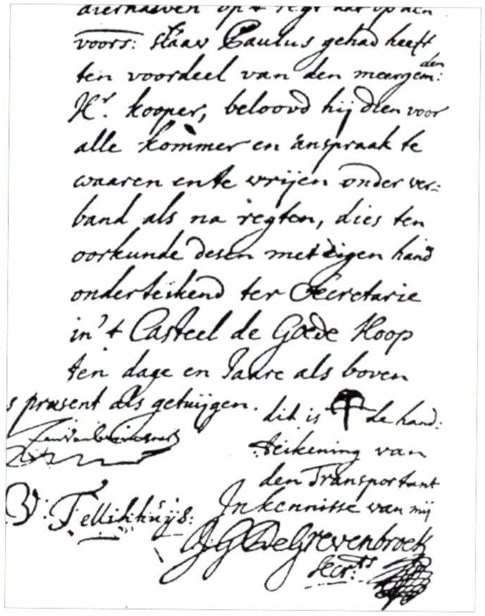
voors: slaav Paulus gehad heeft
ten voordeel van den meergem:
Hr. kooper, beloovd hij den voor
alle kommer en ansprak te
waaren ende vrijen onder ver-
band als na regten, dies ten
oorkunde desen met eigen hand
onderteikend ter Secretarie
in't Casteel de Goede Hoop
ten dage en Jaare als boven

Facsimile of a slave transaction from the Deeds Office, Cape Town (detail)

"4.9.1660 Mary from Guinea, sold by Casper Brinkman, who had bought her on the 10th of May 1658, from the Company, to Maria de la Quellerie, wife of Jan van Riebeeck. No price mentioned."

"13.8.1671: The slave Isaacq (16/18) sold by Jan Pitersz Broertje for four oxen and an old wagon."

"7.4.1687: Thobias from Madagascar (16), sold by skipper Carel Goske to Casper Willemsz for Rds.40."

"10.4.1687: Jason from Malabar (21/22), and Evert from Macassar (25/26) sold by Carel de Mervelje, skipper of the Oosterland to Jan Direx de Beer for Rds.50 each"

"28.5.1693 Paul from Porca (27) and his son Adam (aged two) born in Galen sold by Bonfacius Ingels, a junior merchant on the *Oosterland* to Jan Blesius for Rds. 70."

"8.5.1698 Martha from Bengal (14) sold by William Erle to Maria Everts, for Rds 60."

Extracts, in translation, from the records of the Deeds Office, Cape Town

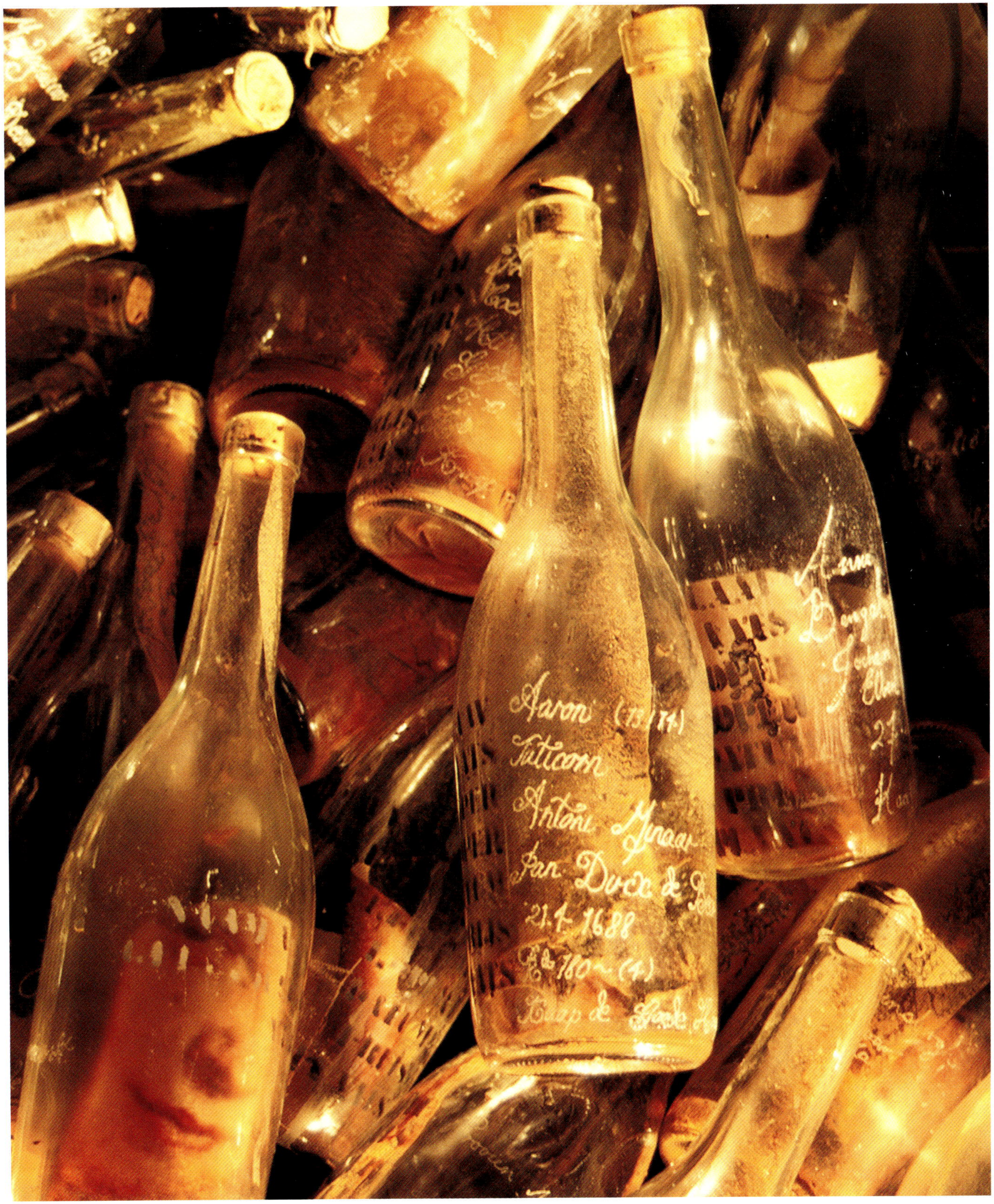

*Messages from the Moat* (detail)
1997
Engraved and stenciled glass, printed canvas
Dimensions variable

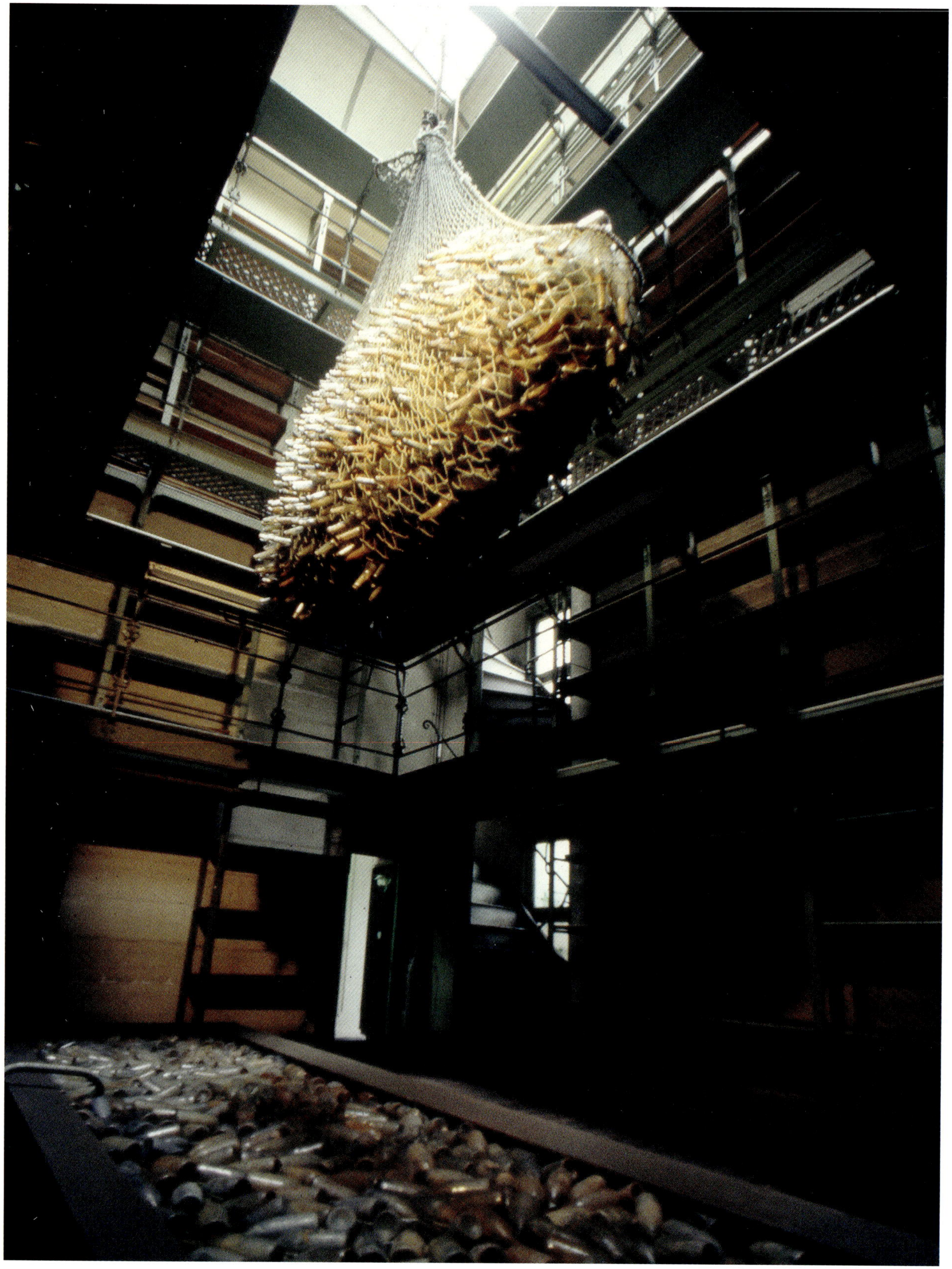

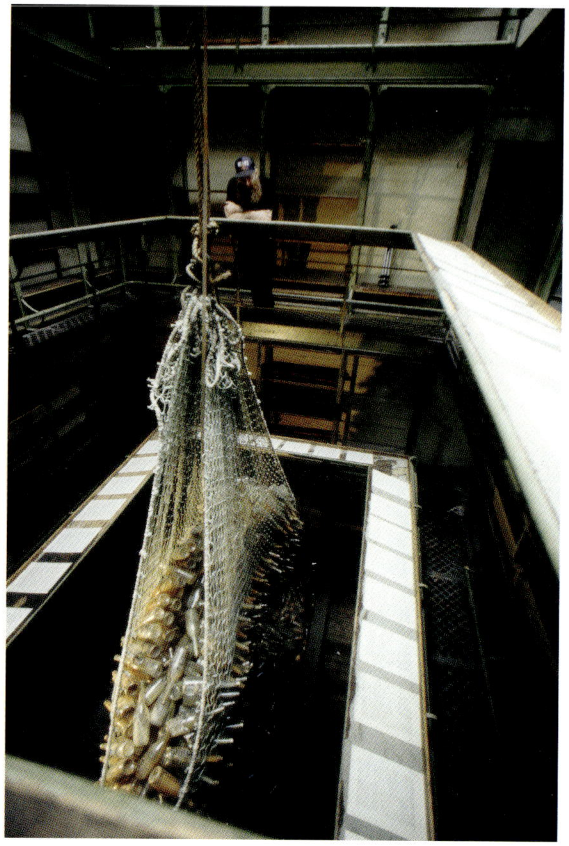

*Messages from the Moat*
1997
Engraved and stenciled glass, printed canvas
found fishing net, water pump, soundscape
Dimensions variable
Installation view
The Old Archive Building, The Hague

*Messages from the Moat*
1997
Engraved and stenciled glass, printed canvas
found fishing net, water pump, soundscape,
printed paper
Dimensions variable
Installation view
The Old Archive Building, The Hague

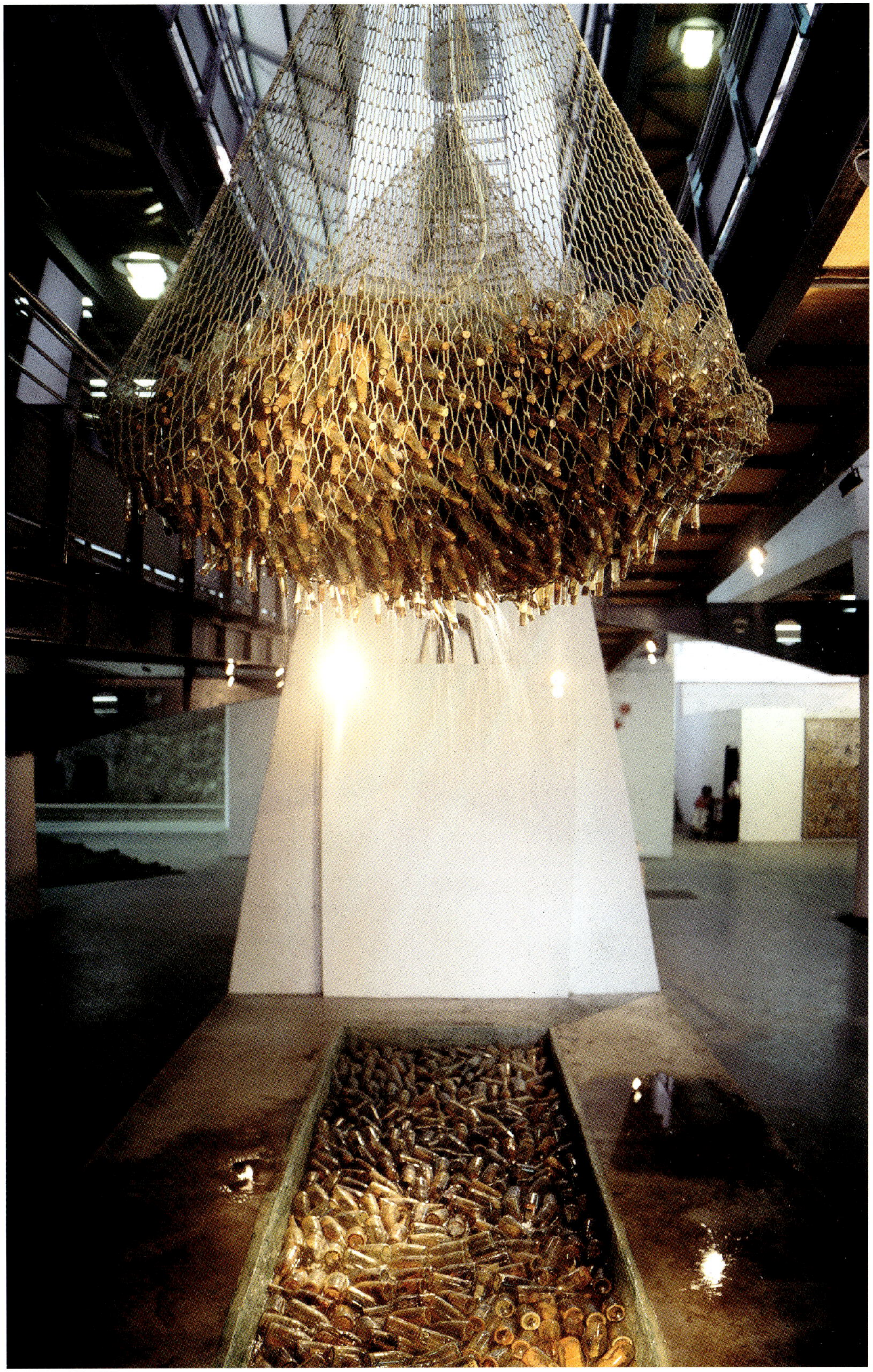

*Messages from the Moat*
1997
Engraved and stenciled glass, printed canvas
found fishing net, water pump
Dimensions variable
Installation view
The Electric Workshop, Johannesburg

# The Transforming Moment



*On April 27, 1994, South Africans went to the polls in the first democratic elections, forming the long, snaking lines outside polling stations that became iconic images of the transition. Nelson Mandela's African National Congress won, and on May 10, Mandela was inaugurated as the country's first black president. Sue Williamson shared the national exhilaration—from Cuba, where she was exhibiting at the Havana Biennale—but also the anxiety, about whether the country would settle into a stable democracy.*

**Mark Gevisser**: Was there a "transforming moment" for you, Sue, in the early 1990s, once the liberation movements were unbanned and the country started moving towards democracy?

**Sue Williamson**: In terms of my work, it all came together most powerfully in 1990, when I saw Gille de Vlieg's photograph of Nelson and Winnie Mandela doing their triumphal turn at the FNB Stadium outside Soweto just after his release.

One of his hands is holding Winnie's, and the other is turned towards the crowds, giving the power salute.

Right behind Mandela is a marshall on a walky-talky wearing a T-shirt printed with the clauses of the Freedom Charter, drawn up in 1955 and the foundation document of the liberation struggle. The first clause is "South Africa belongs to all who live in it".

p. 112 And that T-shirt was one I designed in 1985, soon after the Charter was unbanned. It was a way of getting the promises of the Charter out on the street at a time when they were still widely considered subversive. It's screenprinted using a "rainbow" pull for the background. You mix the colours on the screen so they blend when the squeegee is pulled across. I chose really bright colours.

My partner Bruce Gordon printed hundreds and they were sold all over the country, so it was such a thrill to see one of those T-shirts there, at that victorious moment.

I couldn't help thinking back to the troubled times in which the T-shirt was designed, when the possibility of change seemed so remote. And then, looking forward, one wondered whether Mandela would really be able to unify this deeply divided country. Still, in *that* moment, what I felt most was exhilaration.

**MG**: There are so many ways that the unbanning of the ANC liberated all South Africans, black and white. How so for you, as an artist?

**SW**: You have to remember that during the 1980s, when I was making *A Few South Africans* (1983–7), there was pp. 10, 31-9
very much an ethos of "Culture is a weapon of struggle". Like most of the artists I worked with and respected, I subscribed to that ethos, and believed that artists needed to be socially responsible and do their bit.

In 1989 I was exhibiting *A Few South Africans* at the Kulturhuset in Stockholm, on an exhibition of 16 artists from Southern Africa—Mozambique, Angola, Zimbabwe and South Africa—when [ANC activist and future Constitutional Court judge] Albie Sachs first made the comments which prefigured his famous speech *Preparing Ourselves for Freedom: Culture and the ANC*

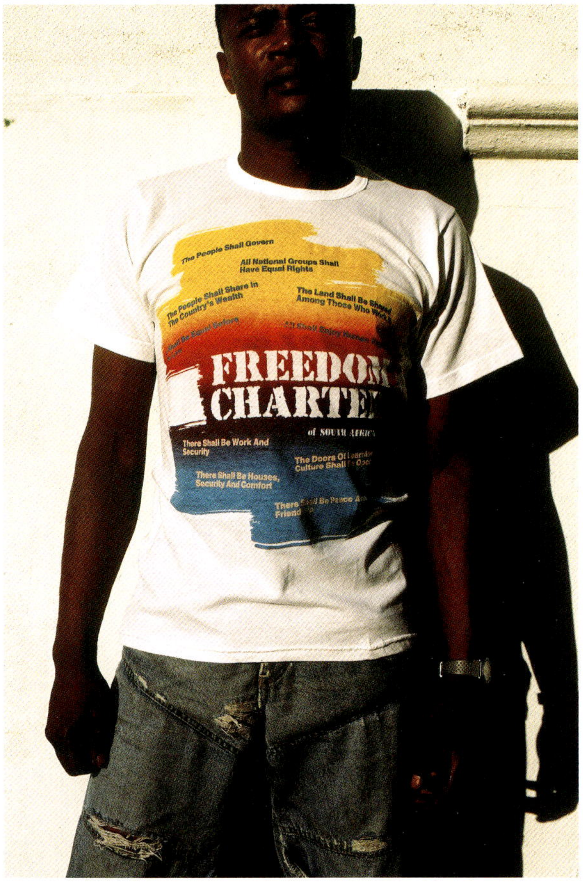


*Freedom Charter T-Shirt*, 1984–5
Screen printed t-shirt
Dimensions variable

*Constitutional Guidelines*. The essence of it was that with the advent of liberation, South African artists should no longer feel bound to make politically correct art.

**MG**: Did you feel liberated, hearing that?
**SW**: Yes. Before then, the ANC was a banned organisation and had no voice—well at least no voice that I was able to hear, living in South Africa—and so I had no idea what their position was. But I wanted to support everything that I could, for the liberation struggle to come to fruition. Now I thought "It's not as if I won't make work that in some way engages with social issues any more, because that will always interest me. But now I have a choice."

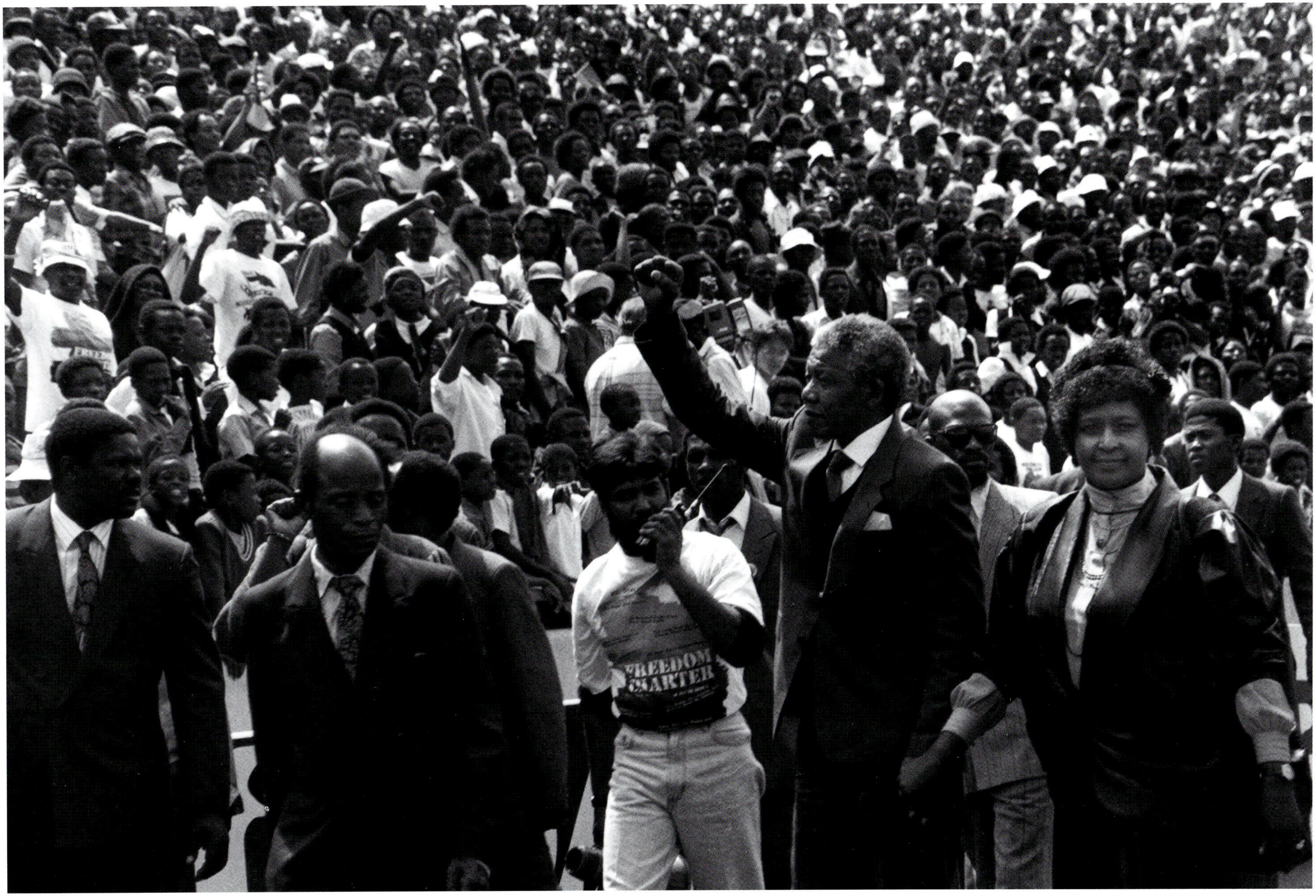

Nelson and Winnie Mandela arriving at the
Welcome Home Rally for Nelson Mandela after
his release from prison, Soweto, February 1990.
Johannesburg
Photograph: Gille de Vlieg

# Out of the Ashes

Sue Williamson was in Havana, Cuba, participating in the 5th Biennale, during South Africa's first democratic elections, on April 27 1994. Her installation, *Out of the Ashes*, was planned specifically to occupy its space in the Fortaleza de la Cabana, Havana's seventeenth-century fortress: like the Castle in Cape Town, the Fortaleza de la Cabana had a brutal history, but was now a cultural centre.

Entering the long vaulted white space at one end, the viewer walked between two low banks of ashes, punctuated with glowing coal-like forms cast from resin and lit from below, and shards of glass embedded with small torn newspaper photographs of victims of apartheid. At the far end of the gallery, five hanging towers billowed, made from translucent white organza and hovering just above the floor. Stitched to these towers were relics of the past intended to be retained and carried forward into the future: small plaques of plaster printed with more photographs and thin tablets of resin containing scraps from District Six.

In the dim space, ultraviolet lighting within two of the towers gave them a soft mauve glow; concealed electric fans caused them to sway softly where they hung. The concept of a shimmering new city was evoked, still undeveloped and ephemeral, an alluring but vulnerable vision. As one walked towards the towers, an infra-red beam at the end of the embankments of ashes triggered the powerful voice of the South African soprano Sibongile Khumalo, pouring out a song of atonement for the rivers of blood that had flowed.

Through an orchestration of different media in a resonant space, *Out of the Ashes* commemorated lives lost in the struggle and prefigured the work Williamson would later make about the Truth and Reconciliation Commission.

The installation suggests that the sadness of the past needs to be reckoned with before a new future can be embraced.

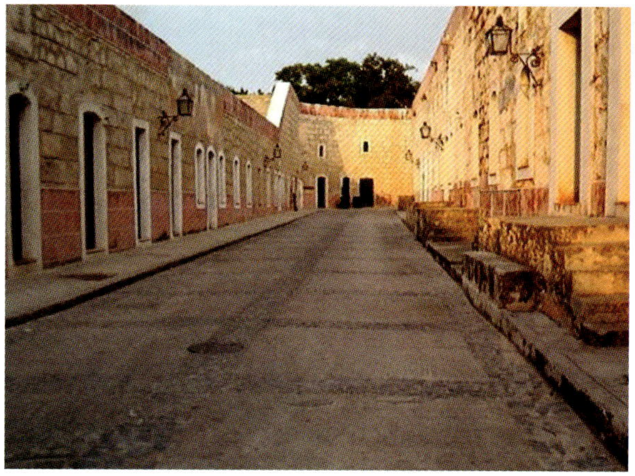

Fortaleza de la Cabaña, Havana

*Out of the Ashes*
1994
Ashes, glass, fabric, lighting, sound
and other mixed media
Dimensions variable
Installation view
Fortaleza de la Cabaña, Havana

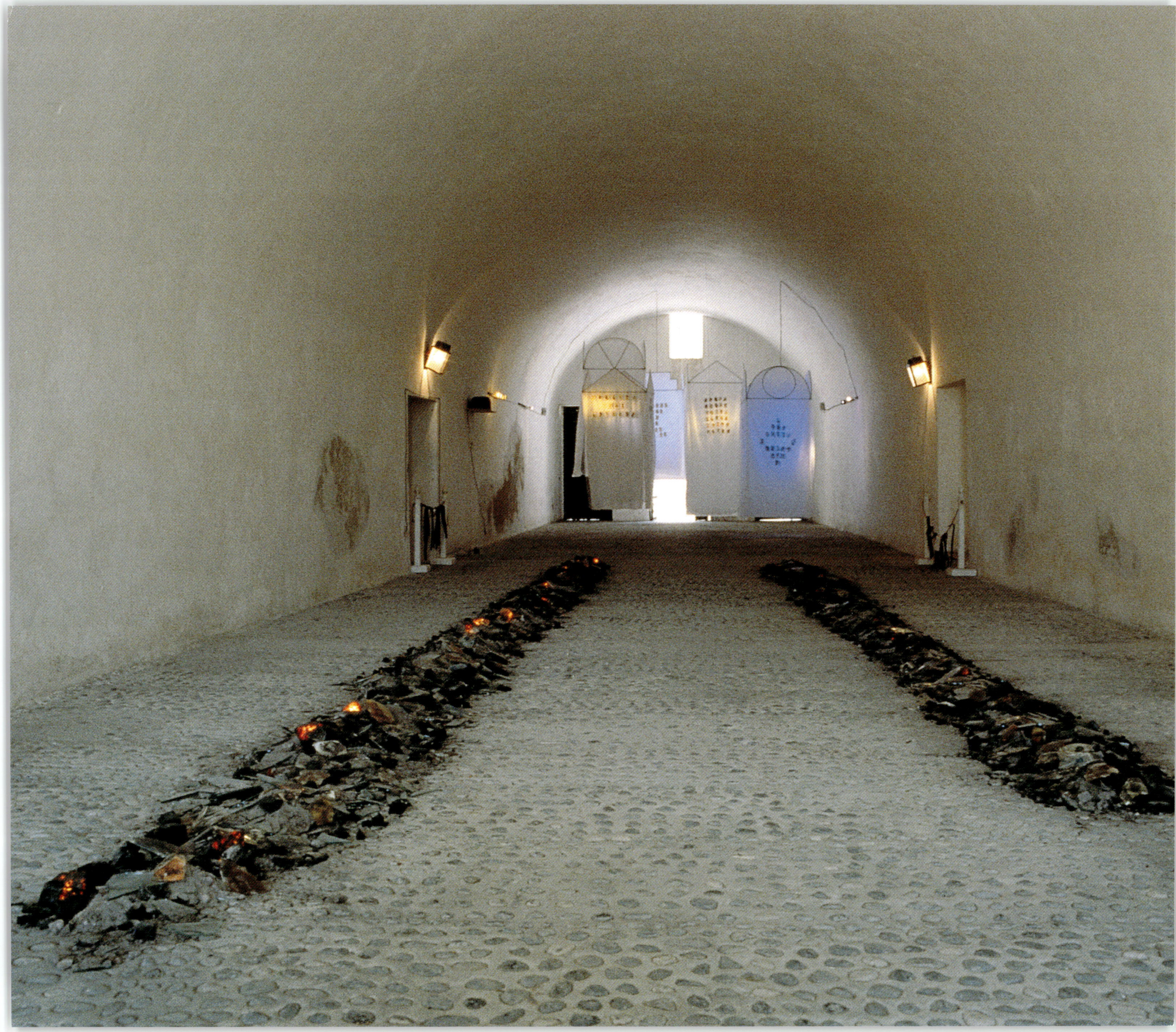

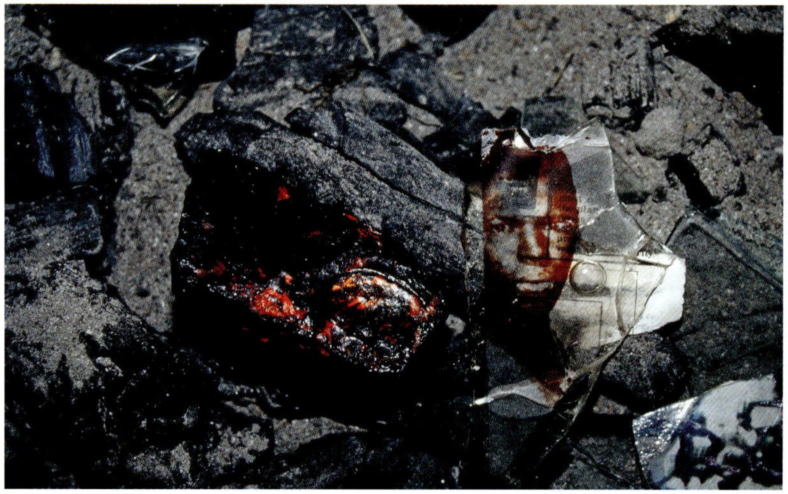

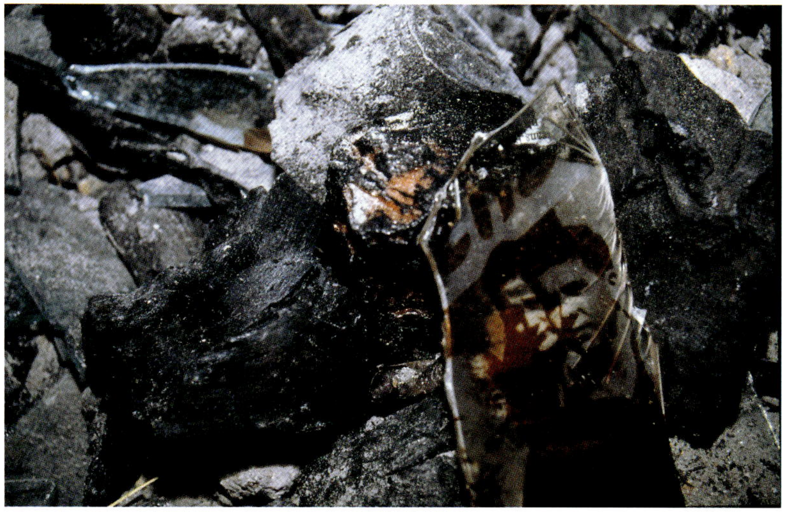

*Out of the Ashes* (detail)
1994
Ashes, glass, fabric, lighting, sound
and other mixed media
Installation view
Fortaleza de la Cabaña, Havana

*Out of the Ashes* (detail)
1994
Ashes, glass, fabric, lighting, sound
and other mixed media
Installation view
Fortaleza de la Cabaña, Havana

*Out of the Ashes*
1994
Ashes, glass, fabric, lighting, sound
and other mixed media
Installation view
Ludwig Forum, Aachen

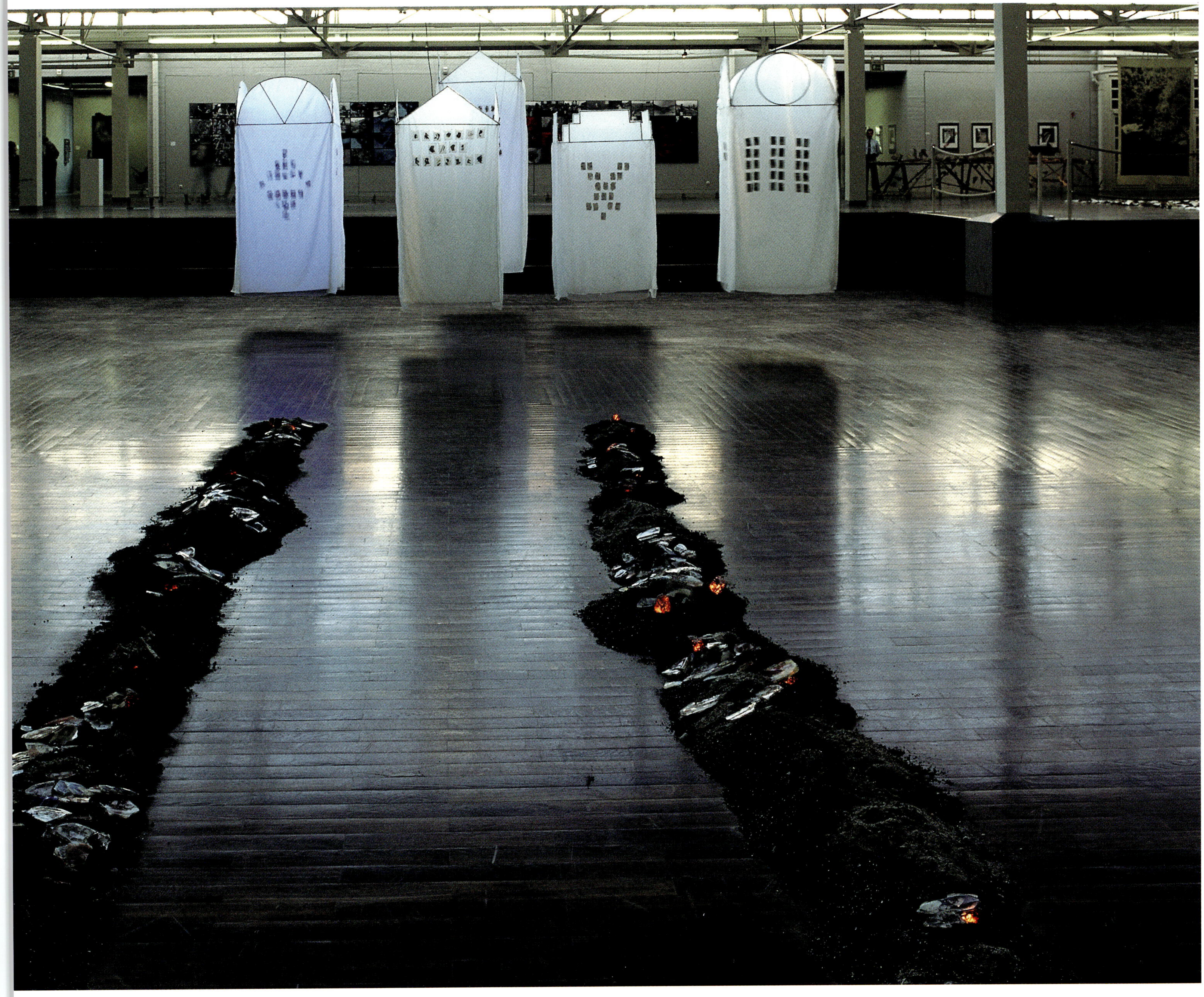

# Art Home Art

In 1994, Sue Williamson was invited to participate in Steirischer Herbst, an annual Austrian art festival in the city of Graz. The curatorial idea was that the invited artists would make work in and about their home country—thus *Kunst Heimat Kunst*—"Art Home Art".

Williamson was intrigued by the possibility of the new mobility in South African life, a country no longer regulated by apartheid; a country, too, in which (she hoped) people would now be more curious about one another. And so she conceived a travelling exhibition, and invited two fellow Cape Town artists to collaborate: Willie Bester and Andrew Putter. She persuaded Transnet, the national rail company, to loan her a luggage coach that, she proposed, would travel the country, with stories of Capetonians aboard.

It was in mid-1994, just after the first democratic elections. The three artists asked their subjects to talk about the most memorable thing that had happened to them that year—in this, a year, where the most important national event had been the African National Congress' election into power. The artists constructed wooden crates of the kind one might find in a luggage car, and turned each into a cabinet of curiosities, activated by a button or a handle, that would start the story and illuminate the scene inside the box.

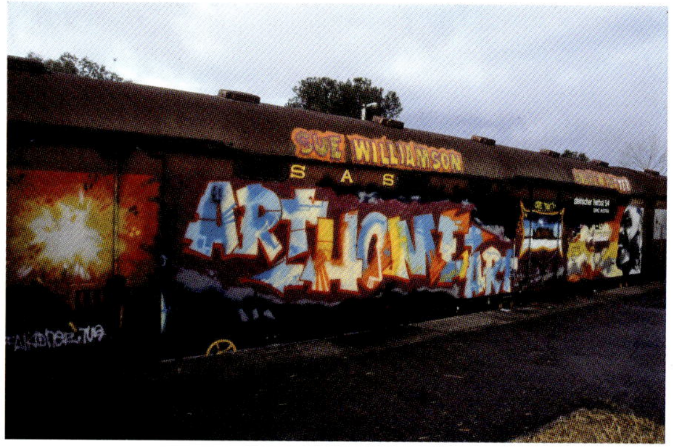


*Art Home Art* 1994
Exterior of Transnet railway luggage van

In Williamson's first box, viewers gazed down the cylinder of a brass tube—evocative of looking down the barrel of a gun—and, through headphones, heard the story of her assistant recounting the terror when four men broke into their studio, held them up at gunpoint, and stole the photocopier. In the second box, Williamson returned to District Six and its memories, and recorded the animated conversation of a young bride, with her mother, about her wedding. In the third box, the musician Josh Hawks recalled the thrill of playing with his group, *The Streaks*, at Mandela's victory rally in Cape Town after his election. And for the fourth, she interviewed a group of street-children living beneath the Eastern Boulevard in the city.

*Art Home Art* opened at the July 1994 Grahamstown Festival, and then made a stop at the first Johannesburg Biennale the following year, and did a two-week stint at the Cape Town station. A country-wide tour was, however, logistically impossible.

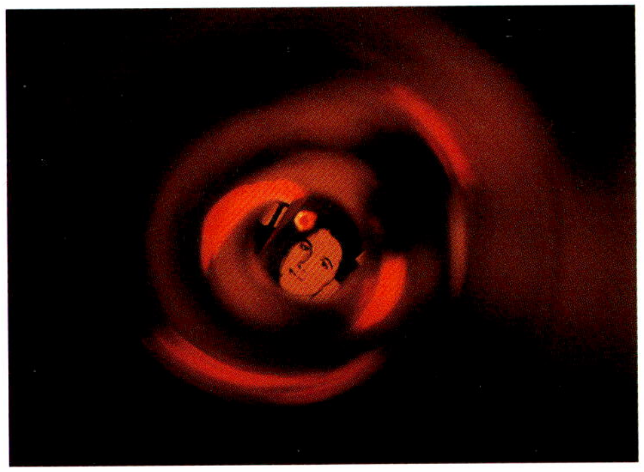

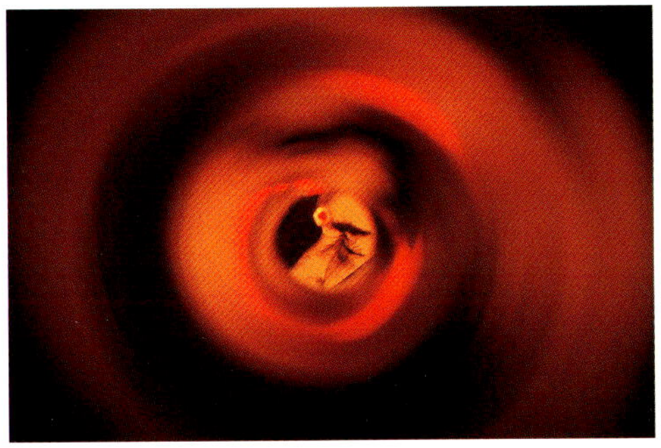

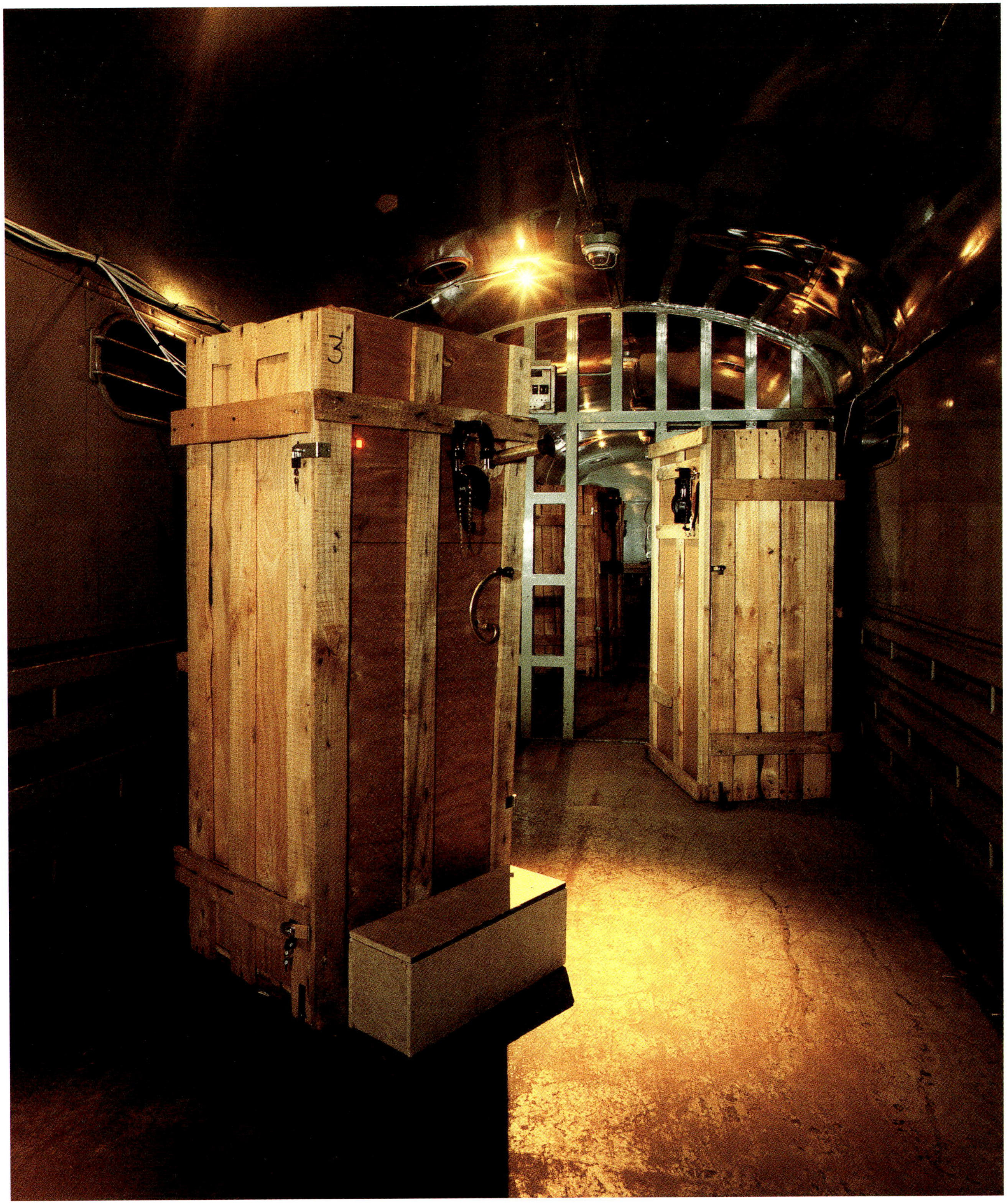


*Art Home Art* (detail)
1994
Wooden crates, mixed media, sound, lighting

*Art Home Art* (detail)
1994
Wooden crates, mixed media, sound, lighting

*Art Home Art* (detail)
1994
Wooden crates, mixed media, sound, lighting
Interior of Transnet railway luggage van,
Grahamstown station

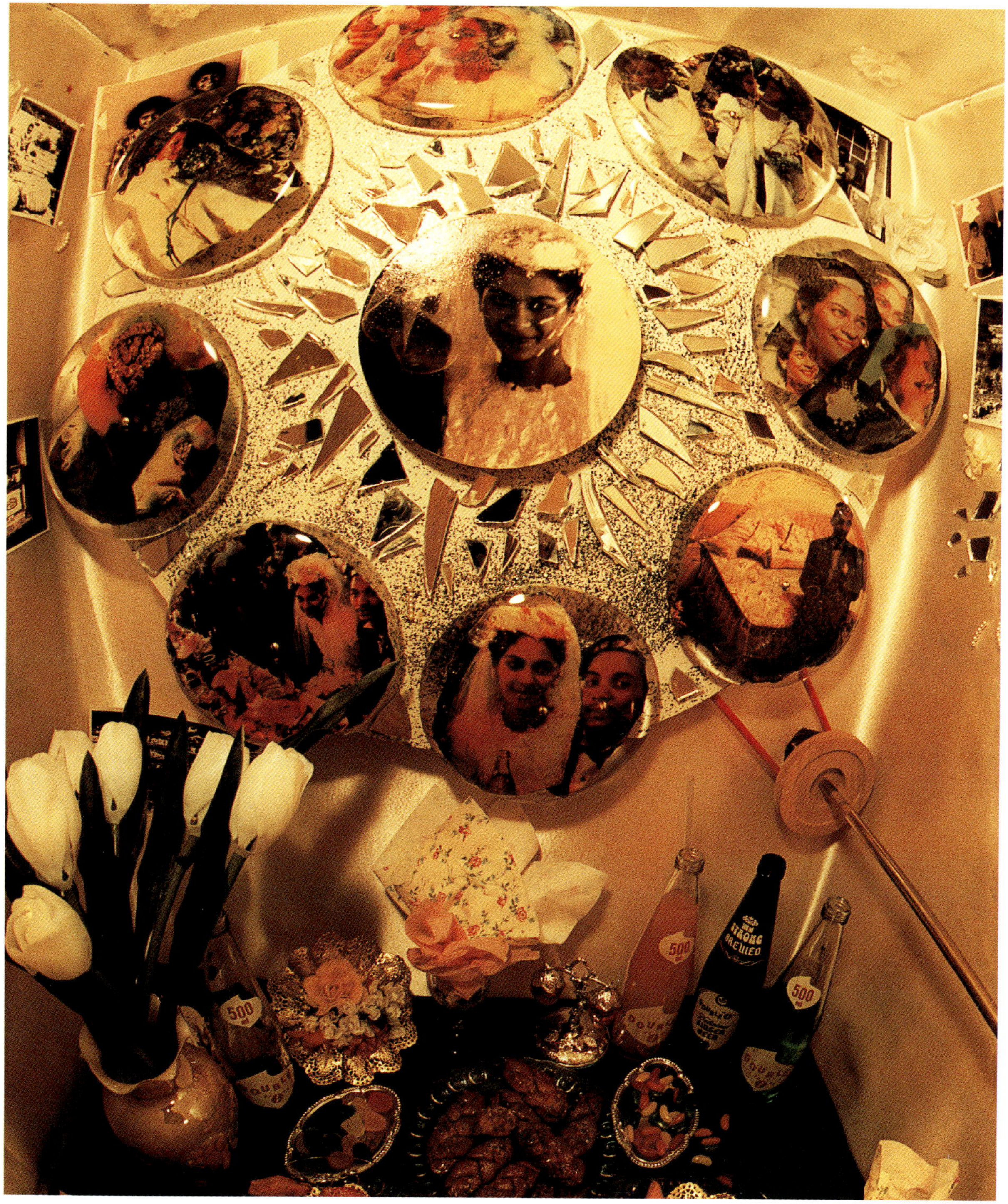

"The wedding was lovely, but I wish we could have had it in District Six, rather than so far away from there in Mitchell's Plain."

Fasiega Hendricks, from the soundtrack to *Art Home Art*

*Art Home Art* (detail)
1994
Wooden crates, mixed media, sound, lighting

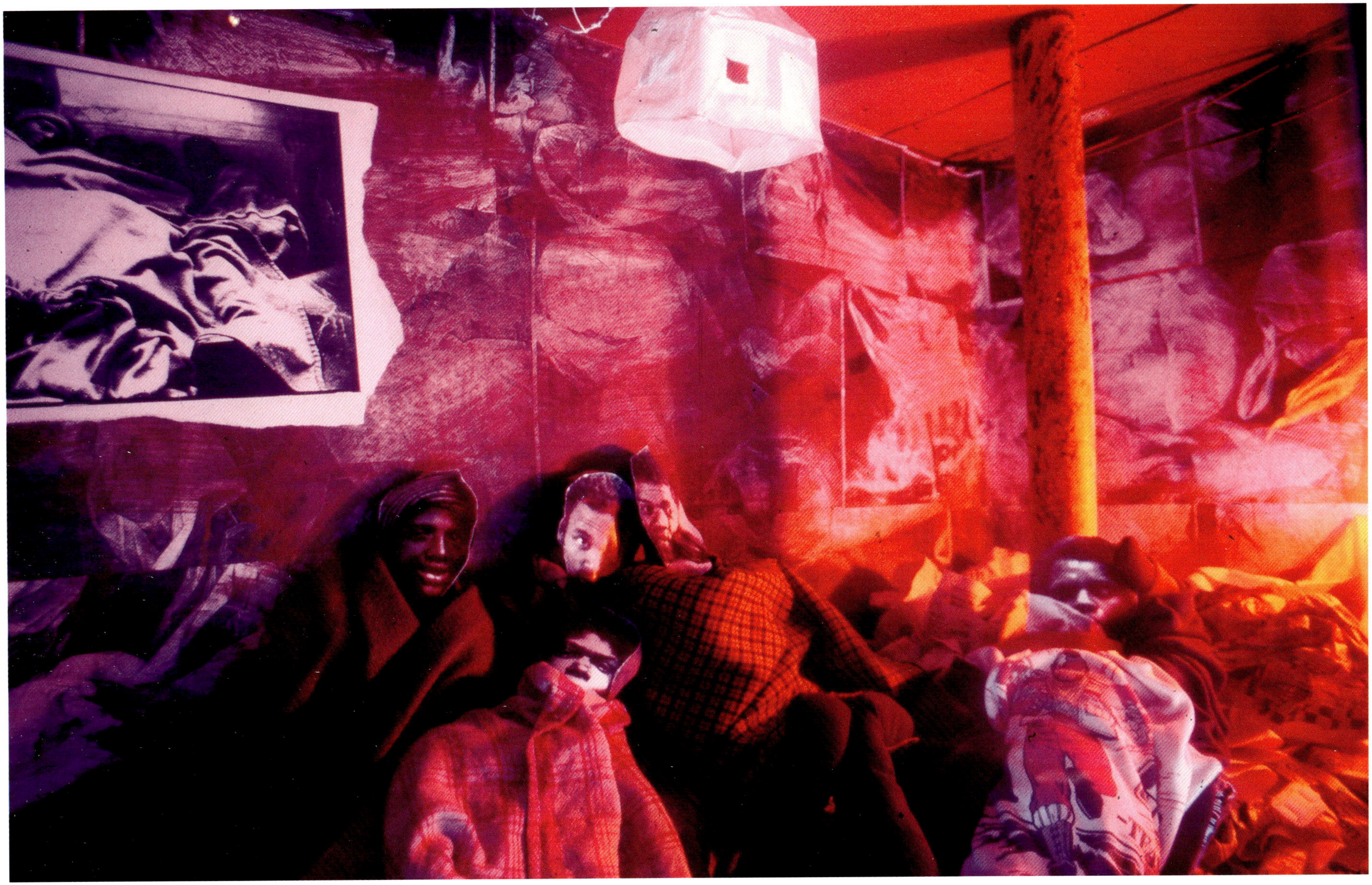

"Teenager 1: We can't go to the robots [traffic lights] today, it's raining. You'd get wet today if you go to the robots for money. But if you ask people for money, they say, "go ask Mandela" (laughter) and I don't like that word. They said Mandela is *ons* father, our *oupa*, our grandfather. *New Suid Afrika*.

Teenager 2: They must be nice now because we have a new president in our country and they say they are going to give us a nice warm house. Mandela said he is going to give us a house, a wife, husband, stove, fridge, everything, money, everything. But I don't believe it."

From the soundtrack to *Art Home Art*

*Art Home Art* (detail)
1994
Wooden crates, mixed media, sound, lighting

# Is Anybody?

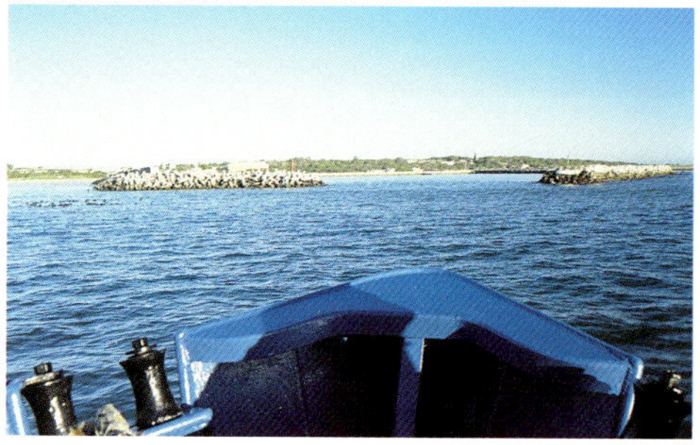

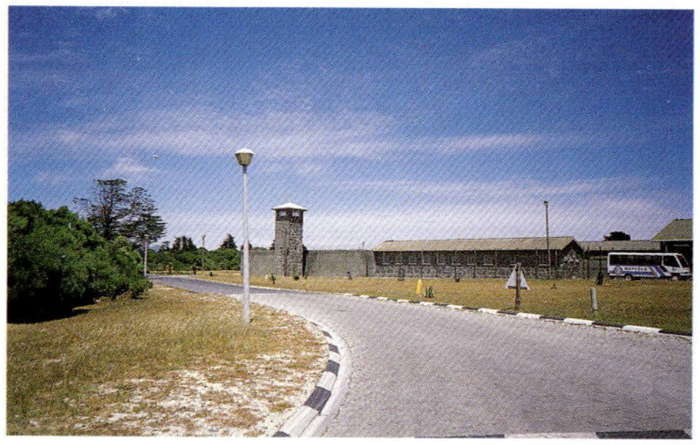

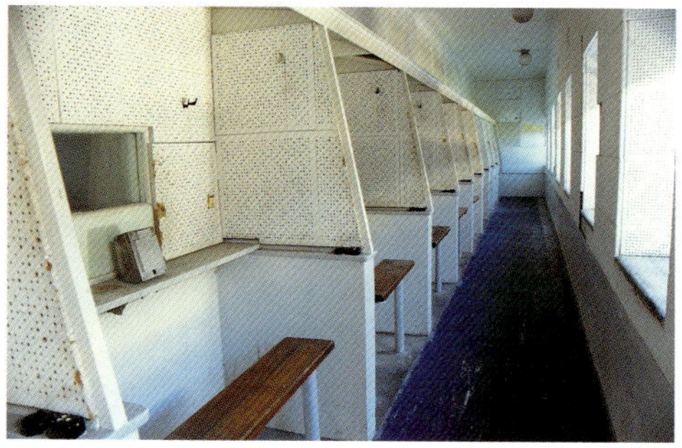

Robben Island viewed from the ferry

Jail building, Robben Island

Interior of the prisoners' visitor's block, Robben Island

Robben Island, a short ferry ride from the Cape Town docks, was turned into a museum in 1997. To commemorate its new status, the curator Zayd Minty commissioned nine artists to make site-specific installations in the former prison's Visitors' Block. The exhibition was called *Thirty Minutes*, because this was the length of time that prisoners such as Nelson Mandela and his Rivonia co-accused were allowed with visitors. Only one or two of these brief visits were permitted a year.

Each artist was given a booth in the Visitors' Block: visitors to the exhibition would sit down on the visitor's bench and peer, through the glass, at the artwork. One participant was a former long-term prisoner himself, Lionel Davis, who used text and sculpture to depict both the cacophony and the control of an experience in the Visitors' Block. Williamson took audio tiles of the kind already used in the visitors' booths to muffle sound, and used them to create a cell-within-a-cell on the other side of the glass. In this chamber was nothing but a video monitor, which played back the image of the viewer. The intercom—through which prisoners would have had to talk with their loved ones—played the scratchy sound of a tape being rewound.

In his catalogue essay, Jeremy Cronin, a former political prisoner but at another (white) jail, writes of the window at the visitor's booth as "the glass frontier": "an aquarium of sorts, where your bottled emotions release small speech bubbles that float off in the swimming bewilderment of it. How to condense everything you want to say into thirty minutes, as hopelessly as you feel the drift of those closest to you into other lives? ... Here, in the mere thickness of a double-glazing, here is the frontier between freedom and incarceration, its coldness on the palm of your hand."

Cronin also refers to the visitor's booth as a confessional of sorts, "lips to God's ear", but notes that this was "a false semblance", as all conversations were monitored. This was precisely Williamson's intention: to remind the viewer that "everyone in the country was liable to be watched under apartheid."

As Cronin writes: "The outside, beyond the walls, across the short ferry stretch, over there the mainland itself was a prison society. The prison regime in here was merely one facet of a countrywide grid of spatial controls."

*Is Anybody...?*
1997
Acoustic tiles, wood, airbrick, monitor, camera, sound
86 x 126 x 94 cm

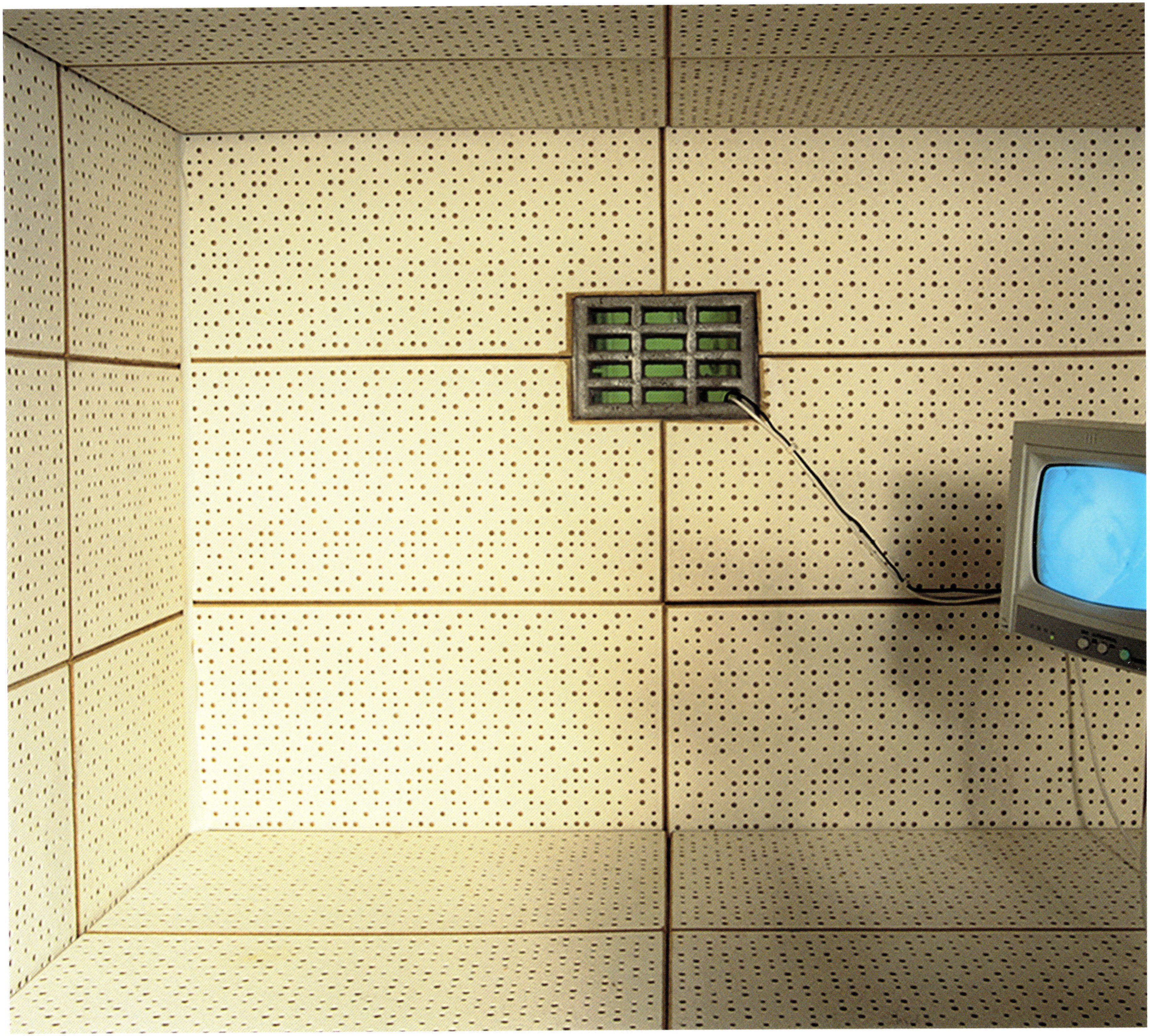

# The Reckoning

## Sue Williamson in conversation with Pumla Gobodo-Madikizela and Mark Gevisser

Cold Turkey: Stories of Truth and Reconciliation
Truth Games
Winnie Mandela and the Assassination of Dr Asvat
Can't forget, can't remember

*As part of the negotiated settlement that led to the transition to democracy in South Africa, the new government mandated the appointment of a Truth and Reconciliation Commission [TRC]. The commission was established in 1996, under Archbishop Desmond Tutu: its unique aims were to document "gross violations of human rights" from all sides in the past conflict, and to grant amnesty to those who gave full disclosure of the crimes they had committed. It was also mandated to provide reparations. It sat for two years, before its final report was tabled before parliament in 1999. Hearings were held all over the country and were public and televised, and anyone could participate: they constituted an intense national conversation which played its part in enabling the peaceful transition to democracy.*

*During the years of the TRC, Sue Williamson made a significant body of work about it and the issues of trauma and memory that it raised. As a result of this, she was asked, in 2015, to join a project run by Professor Pumla Gobodo-Madikizela, a psychologist at the University of the Free State, looking at intergenerational trauma. Gobodo-Madikizela served on the TRC and is the author of* A Human Being Died That Night, *an award-winning book about her encounters with one of the apartheid state's most notorious murderers, Eugene de Kock. In April 2015, she visited Williamson's studio to talk about the TRC and to look at the work Williamson has made about it. The conversation was moderated by Mark Gevisser.*

**Sue Williamson**: Pumla, how did you become involved in the Truth and Reconciliation Commission?
**Pumla Gobodo-Madikizela**: I was at Harvard at the time, writing my PhD in psychology, when I got a call asking me if I was interested in joining the TRC as a member of the Human Rights Violations Committee. Of course I was, having been a student activist, and worked with human rights lawyers in my early days as a clinical psychologist—it was like coming a full circle. I suspended my doctoral studies and came home. I was based at the Cape Town office of the TRC, and there were three of us who were appointed to facilitate the work of the Human Rights Violations Committee. I was appointed the head of the Human Rights Violations Committee in the Western Cape. And you, Sue?
**SW**: Because I was a member of the Women's Movement for Peace, many of the actions we were involved in landed up in front of the TRC later, like the case of Simphiwe Mthimkulu [the student activist]. When he was in hospital after having been released from detention without trial, very ill from the rat poison he had been given in jail, a call went out to, "go visit this young man in hospital", which I did. On the second visit, I made a recording of him telling me about what happened to him in police custody. His voice was very rough because of the poison. Soon after he was released from hospital he disappeared.
As in so many of these cases, we knew what had happened—that the police were responsible for his disappearance—but we didn't know the details. So when the TRC was formed, it seemed like the moment the new dispensation was going to do something about this. I

started collecting newspapers. I had a whole mountain of them, and I'd keep all those with TRC stories and photos. It came to me eventually that what I'd like to do is pick out the cases I felt were most symbolic, and work with those.

**Mark Gevisser**: What was the effect of the TRC?
**SW**: It came out better than I expected, I think. There were some people like Neville Clarence, who lost his sight in the Church Street bombing, who said that he understood it had been an act of war, and shook hands with the bomber. But there were other moments, like [the former defence minister] Magnus Malan refusing to accept responsibility of any kind for the death of [Mozambican president] Samora Machel…
**PGM**: The bigger scale of accountability was never addressed. Like FW de Klerk saying that Eugene de Kock [who ran the state's secret assassination and "dirty tricks" programme] was a bad apple, and that he [de Klerk] was not the one who gave the orders, telling the TRC that his hands were clean.

**MG**: Pumla, you have a public profile as a scholar who continues to think and write about trauma and reconciliation. You've recently begun using the phrase "empathic connection" rather than "forgiveness"…
**PGM**: I am beginning to understand "forgiveness" as the wrong word. Why do the family members want to meet the man who killed their loved one, for example? Is it to hear his contrition and forgive him, or is it to make a connection? It is as if they need to set their eyes on the person who was the last one to see their loved ones. The encounter between family members of a victim and a perpetrator becomes a kind of reconstitution of the family's loved one's final moments, recreating this moment so that in a symbolic way, they are present to witness it. By facing the perpetrator, innumerable possibilities—both destructive and restorative and all that cannot be reduced to these oversimplified categories—arise. The potential for the unexpected, unforeseen and endemic to the human condition is always present because of what each of the people encountering each other brings.

**MG**: You wrote *A Human Being Died That Night*, about your encounter with Eugene de Kock. During the process, you came to understand de Kock and establish an empathic connection with him…
**PGM**: It was a difficult realisation of a truth about what's possible in human relations, and realising that the line between evil and good is not as bright as we would like it to be. That was the greatest lesson for me. I think that Eugene de Kock's accounts of his life of violence as a decorated member of the security force police during apartheid, and what I experienced as an expression of genuine remorse, forced me to think about how so often ordinary human beings are driven to cruelty by ideology. Yet it is possible to transcend the hateful destruction, and the desire for revenge that it inspires. A perpetrator's remorse opens the door to transformative moments of change. Understanding the context of human rights crimes committed in the name of the state is an important start, it is not explaining evil away.

**SW**: The photo that's always been very interesting for me is this one by George Hallett, where de Kock is sitting with Jann Turner behind his shoulder. I think it's a remarkable photo, because of course we still don't know who killed Rick Turner, her father, but there's Jann sitting behind his shoulder.
**PGM**: And Jann there, standing behind him, in the hope that he might tell her something, because of course he became this figure that represents everything that encompasses the past. So people like Jann and others have gone to him—mothers, grandmothers and siblings

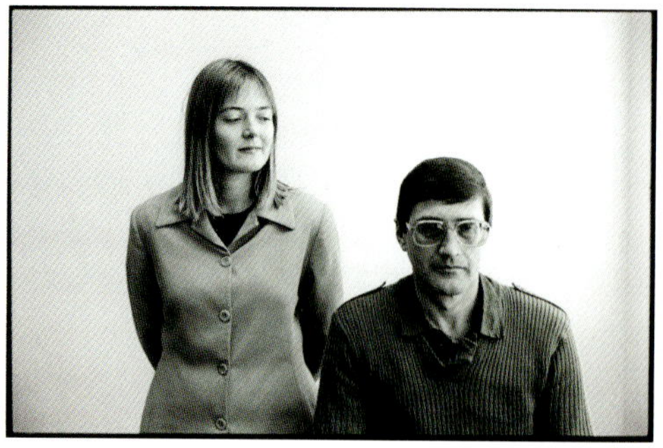

Jann Turner, daughter of slain activist Rick Turner with Vlakplaas Commanding Officer Eugene de Kock. She asked him to identify her father's killer. TRC headquarters, Cape Town, 1997
Photograph: George Hallett

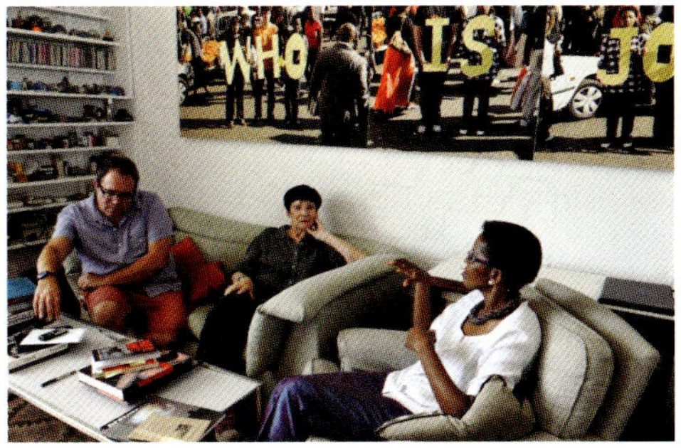

Mark Gevisser, Sue Williamson and Pumla Gobodo Madikizela in conversation in Williamson's studio, April 2015

of victims he killed have gone to prison in the hope he'll tell them what happened to their loved ones. And he has done so in some instances. He has led people to some kind of truth about their loved ones.

SW: When I read your book, Pumla, it made me feel far more sympathetic to him. You opened up that space of humanness in your own humanity to him. It was quite a moment for me, because I had always looked at him as…

PGM: Prime Evil…

SW: Yes. This very cold, crass person who would do just about anything he was told to. My first work about
p. 133 the TRC was this one, *Cold Turkey: Stories of Truth and Reconciliation*, about De Kock and the killing of Bheki Mlangeni.

PGM: De Kock *was* taking his orders from above, but this was also something he believed in.

SW: How did you feel about the response to his parole and release?

PGM: You know, I've always supported it. My sense is that this is a man who has really turned the corner. From what I've witnessed in my interviews with De Kock, and from the stories of his encounter with children of his victims, it seems clear to me that De Kock has gone through significant reflection about his past. One of the children of his victims, Candice Mama, told me about going to visit him in prison. After he told her everything concerning the killing of her father by De Kock and his men, she asked him the question, "have you forgiven yourself?" De Kock avoided answering the question, but she insisted on wanting an answer. When De Kock started to speak, his voice broke. "After all I've done, how can I ever forgive myself?" Candice explained how she was moved to tears by this moment.

SW: The empathic connection…

MG: Sue, you weren't a victim of gross human rights violations, but you'd borne witness to many of them, as an activist, and as someone documenting what happened. You've also spoken about how, in works like *Truth Games*, you tried to present each side's "best defence"—the victim and the perpetrator—and let the viewers decide for themselves.

SW: I didn't want to add my own voice in any way in *Truth Games*. So when we look at this panel from the series,
for example, we see Nomonde Calata on the left, giving p. 129
evidence before the Human Rights Violations committee, about the murder of her husband Fort Calata in 1985. We read snatches of her testimony. Then, on the right, we see Colonel Harold Snyman applying for amnesty with snatches of *his* testimony. I'm trying to reduce the encounter to its simplest essence in which I tried to represent each side in the best possible light. So that it is left to you to assess what the media is giving you and decide for yourself. You have to become complicit with the work, to get up to it and move the slats around to uncover the images beneath. If you don't move the slats, you will not get the full story.

PGM: For me, the power of your work, Sue, is that it forces engagement. The details are so real, they challenge the distancing mechanisms that so many white people had. From afar, one may separate oneself from it. But the moment a person gets closer, it may strike her or him that, "Wow, *I* was prepared to lie to avoid facing this, or, *I* was a committed Christian, yet this is the government that I supported. Standing on the right hand side of the panel, and seeing the white face, these images confront: "This is who I was too. I was in denial, pretending it's not happening. I was prepared to avoid, sit in a comfort zone". Those who are implicated in this evil past can "hear" the words, but by moving the words across these slats, they actually engage with them.

And then moving to this side, and looking at Nomonde Calata, and reading the words from her testimony, "They burnt him [her husband] … He was everything to me," the experience is bound to evoke a profound and complex set of emotions for any white person with a conscience who was complicit with apartheid. It moves the reader in a very strong way because that's the story of the victim. Even if you're white and you identified with Snyman, you are forced to visualise this human being, who comes from your own group of people, burning the husband of this woman. This evokes an empathic connection with the pain of this person, of Mrs Calata. In a way, Sue, these works restage what was happening in the TRC, through image and text.

**SW**: I'm very moved by what you've just said, Pumla. That's what it's about. It's about bearing witness, and questioning the values you might have had and how you feel. Acknowledging it. Not pushing it behind a curtain. Coming up to the work and reading these stories.

**MG**: What was the experience of making and exhibiting this work about the TRC for you, Sue?

**SW**: It was a tremendous relief to hear the endings of these stories. It was a relief that this information was coming out, but there was also a horror of the things that had gone on. For me, personally, it was very important that the TRC happened. It's like having a terrible argument with your partner, and then you pretend it didn't happen and move on. I couldn't have been enthusiastic in any way about the new dispensation without some facing up to the past. What I found so interesting was that it wasn't just black activists against white policemen. It was everyone against everyone. It was not cut and dried. There were so many people who felt they'd been wronged or violated in some way…

**MG**: As, for example, in your work about Winnie Madikizela-Mandela…

p. 33 **SW**: My first image of Winnie was for *A Few South*
pp. 10, 31-9 *Africans*, where I portray her as a heroine, beautiful and innocent. But then we come to Winnie as the person p. 167
allegedly behind the shooting of Stompie Seipei, and Dr Abu-Baker Asvat. Winnie is a larger-than-life character, forceful, but also a diva. We can't forget that she spent so many months in isolation, in Brandfort, and that she alone had to bring up a family while her husband was in jail. Of course she was not the only one. Albertina Sisulu had much the same kind of life. But Winnie is one of those people who gathers around her enormous power. People still love her. She's still the person who will come and help you when your house burns down, even today. She's still hugely popular. So you think: she should be forgiven, because after all so many things that happened in apartheid were forgiven. And yet there are these two dead people, and no disclosure, no contrition. I try to reflect that complexity in this piece
I made, *Winnie Mandela and the Assassination of Dr* p. 167
*Asvat*, by using media headlines such as "martyr or murderer?"

**PGM**: *A Few South Africans* is beautiful because the women are almost blameless, and they represent so much of that hope, that sense of motherhood, grandmotherhood, that we want to see. We *want* our grandmothers' histories to represent that kind of blamelessness. We want them to be heroines. We *need* heroines. Winnie disrupts that narrative.

**MG**: There was a line I read, from an essay by Stephanie Marlin-Curiel about "mediatized memory" in relation to your work, Sue: "The TRC manufactured a new South African-ness by saturating the public with a newly collected official history." Is that fair? And if so, was the effect positive or negative?

**PGM**: We came to be upheld as a country that has dealt with the past successfully, and that became our story, and we came to believe this story of success about ourselves. But perhaps we believed it too much, too quickly. There

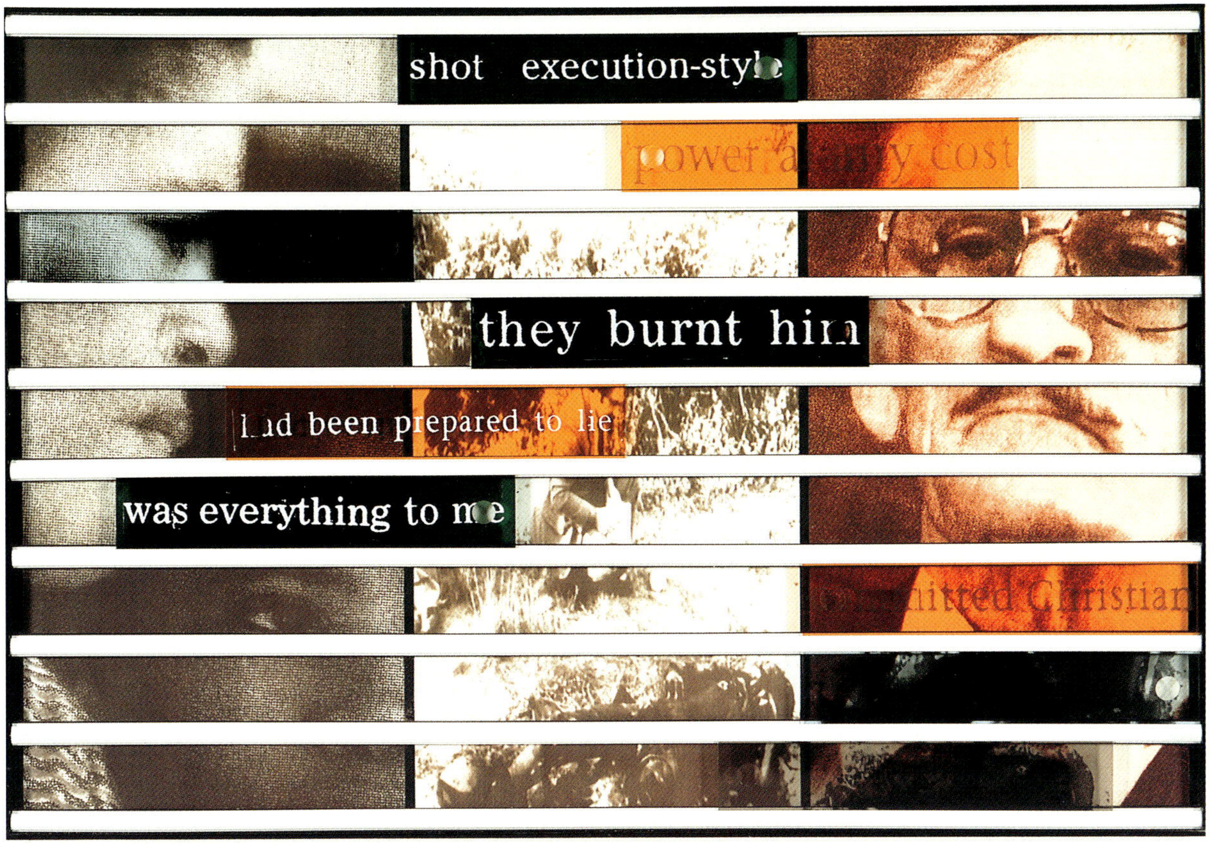


*Nomonde Calata – was everything to me – Harold Snyman*
1998
Truth Games series
Laminated colour laser prints, wood, metal, plastic, perspex
80 x 120 x 6 cm

was a euphoria in the early 1990s, but things started to turn in early 2000s with the first service-delivery protests, because now people realised that little had changed. Those leading the country and those on the ground began to relate to this story differently. The leaders were riding the wave of this success narrative, and they were not paying attention to what they had to do to make the transition meaningful for the majority of South Africans. The TRC had laid the foundation for the reparation work that had to be done, but very little of what the commission recommended was done. The winds of change did not reach the people on the ground.

SW: That's the huge problem. The birthday present that was promised and never arrived... Pumla, do you agree that without the example of Mandela who came out of jail and was able to forgive, the TRC would never have happened?

PGM: His leadership was critical. But once more, I think "forgiveness" is not quite the right word. It's much more about the willingness to cross the boundaries. And we *watched* him crossing the boundaries. He said it with his body. This is what I think is missing somehow, in conversations about reconciliation, how some of these words are embodied. And this aspect of embodiment is what I really believe Sue's TRC work is about—compelling us to engage with these narratives by making us interact with the work. If our bodies are moved, if something moves us, something shifts.

## Cold Turkey: Stories of Truth and Reconciliation

In Sue Williamson's first works on the TRC, she examined two of the more devastating revelations to emerge out of the hearings, by creating narrative sequences out of transparent photo prints illuminated by lightboxes.

Lightboxes are generally used to bring the darkened areas of a transparent image into sharper focus. Thinking back to the days when dentists used to pin up x-rays of teeth in front of the illuminated surface to search for areas of decay, Williamson drew an analogy with the processes of the TRC.

At the hearings, each case would produce its images, its hidden details, its disclosures, its darkened areas, which could then be pinned up against the lightbox for examination and discussion. The lightboxes Williamson made to highlight the chosen cases were fabricated in a clunky government-issue style. The "x-rays" were photographs and texts taken from the media, and the artist handled them as if she were designing a storyboard for a narrative. The first, *De Kock Ready to Sing* was taken from a story in the *Weekly Mail*.

Notorious security policeman Eugene de Kock is seen in medium close up, walking. The camera moves in. He turns towards the camera which pulls into a tight close up of his mouth. The camera then pulls back again. But the mouth now belongs to a pig's head De Kock had bought from a butchery in order to test out his new killing device: a bomb built into a music cassette player attached to headphones. In the test, the pigs ears were blown off, so De Kock went ahead with his plans to send the concealed bomb in a parcel addressed to Dirk Coetzee, a rogue security operative who had joined the ANC.

In the end, the parcel was opened by Coetzee's lawyer, Bheki Mlangeni in May 1990. The bomb killed him.

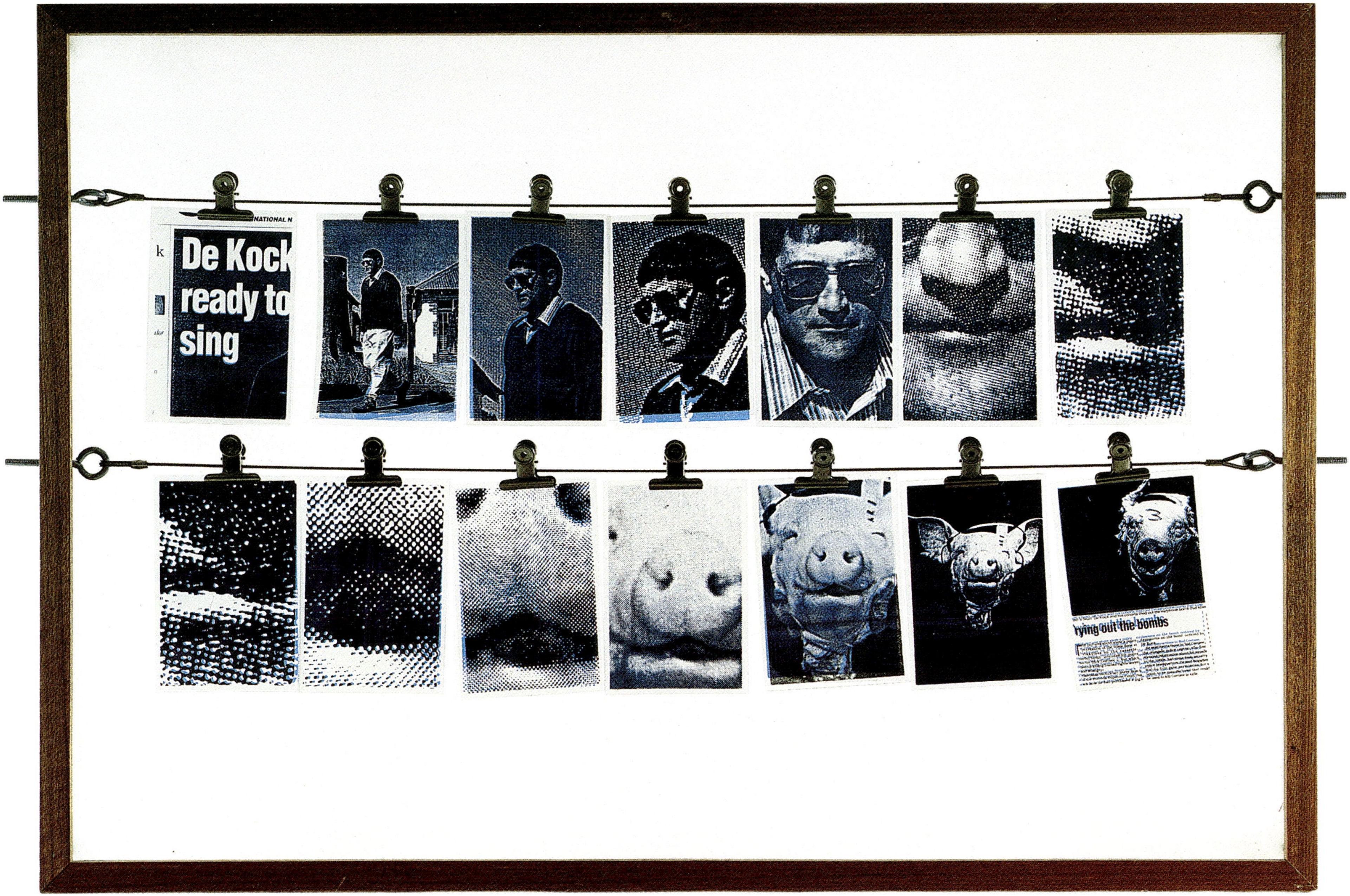


*De Kock ready to sing*
*Cold Turkey: Stories of Truth and Reconciliation*
1997
Lightbox, metal, electrostatic prints
63 x 91 x 7 cm

The second work in *Cold Turkey: Stories of Truth and Reconciliation* is titled *Poison Victim*. It concerns the case of Simphiwe Mthimkulu, the activist Sue Williamson had visited at Groote Schuur Hospital after he had been fed rat poison while in detention in the Eastern Cape. Williamson remembers that he could barely move and that his voice was raspy from the poison: he was eventually discharged, lame and wheelchair-bound. He declared his intention to sue the police, but a few months later, in April 1982, he disappeared, together with his friend Topsy Madaka. He was never seen again.

In the work, the top row of the images proclaims a limited optimism: Mthimkulu has been released from hospital in a wheelchair, but he is leaning on one arm, and looks reflective. The story reads: "Poison victim: hope in sight." The three right-hand images reflect the smile of his mother, Joyce

Moving down, Simphiwe is jubilant as he returns to his home town, Port Elizabeth. But the story is about to take a frightening turn: "Poison Victim: detainee missing." Joyce shows her anguish as she holds up his photo.

In 1997, four policemen, led by the notorious Gideon Nieuwoudt, applied to the TRC for amnesty from prosecution for having murdered Mthimkulu and Madaka. They revealed that they had abducted the two men in Port Elizabeth, taken them to Cradock, drugged them with sleeping pills, shot them, and then burned their bodies over a fire for six hours before throwing their remains into the Fish River. They were granted amnesty.

The year previously, Mthimkulu's mother Joyce had given testimony at the Human Rights Violations hearings of the TRC. She had brought a pile of hair with her, which she said had fallen off her son's head after his poisoning: "This is all I have left of him", she said.

A memorial service for Mthimkulu and Madaka finally took place, on the banks of the Fish River where their remains had been discarded, in 2009.

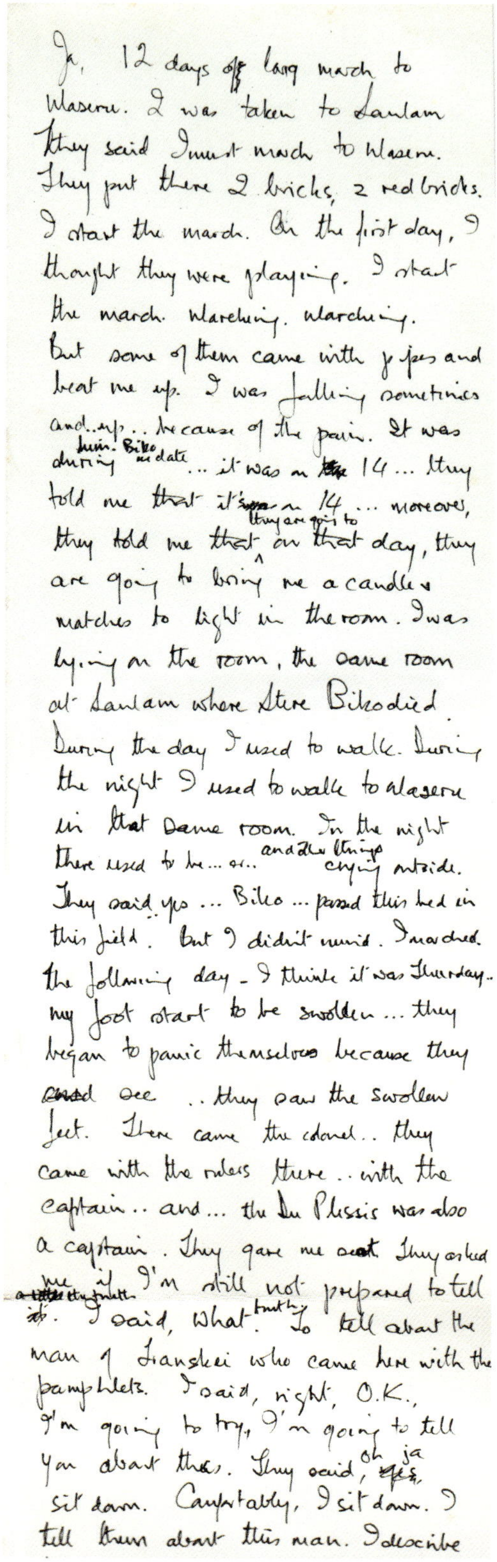
Ja, 12 days of long march to Wasemi. I was taken to Sanlam. They said I must march to Wasemi. They put there 2 bricks, 2 red bricks. I start the march. On the first day, I thought they were playing. I start the march. Marching, marching. But some of them came with pipes and beat me up. I was falling sometimes and..up.. because of the pain. It was during Biko date ... it was on 14 ... they told me that it's on 14 ... moreover, they told me that on that day, they are going to bring me a candle & matches to light in the room. I was lying on the room, the same room at Sanlam where Steve Biko died. During the day I used to walk. During the night I used to walk to Wasemi in that same room. In the night there used to be... or... and the things crying outside. They said yes ... Biko ... passed this bed in this field. But I didn't mind. I marched the following day - I think it was Thursday. My foot start to be swollen ... they began to panic themselves because they see .. they saw the swollen feet. There came the colonel .. they came with the orders there .. with the captain .. and ... the Du Plessis was also a captain. They gave me They asked me if I'm still not prepared to tell it. I said, what truth? To tell about the man of Transkei who came here with the pamphlets. I said, right, O.K., I'm going to try, I'm going to tell you about this. They said, oh ja, sit down. Comfortably, I sit down. I tell them about this man. I describe

Williamson's transcript of Mthimkulu's account of his torture in police custody

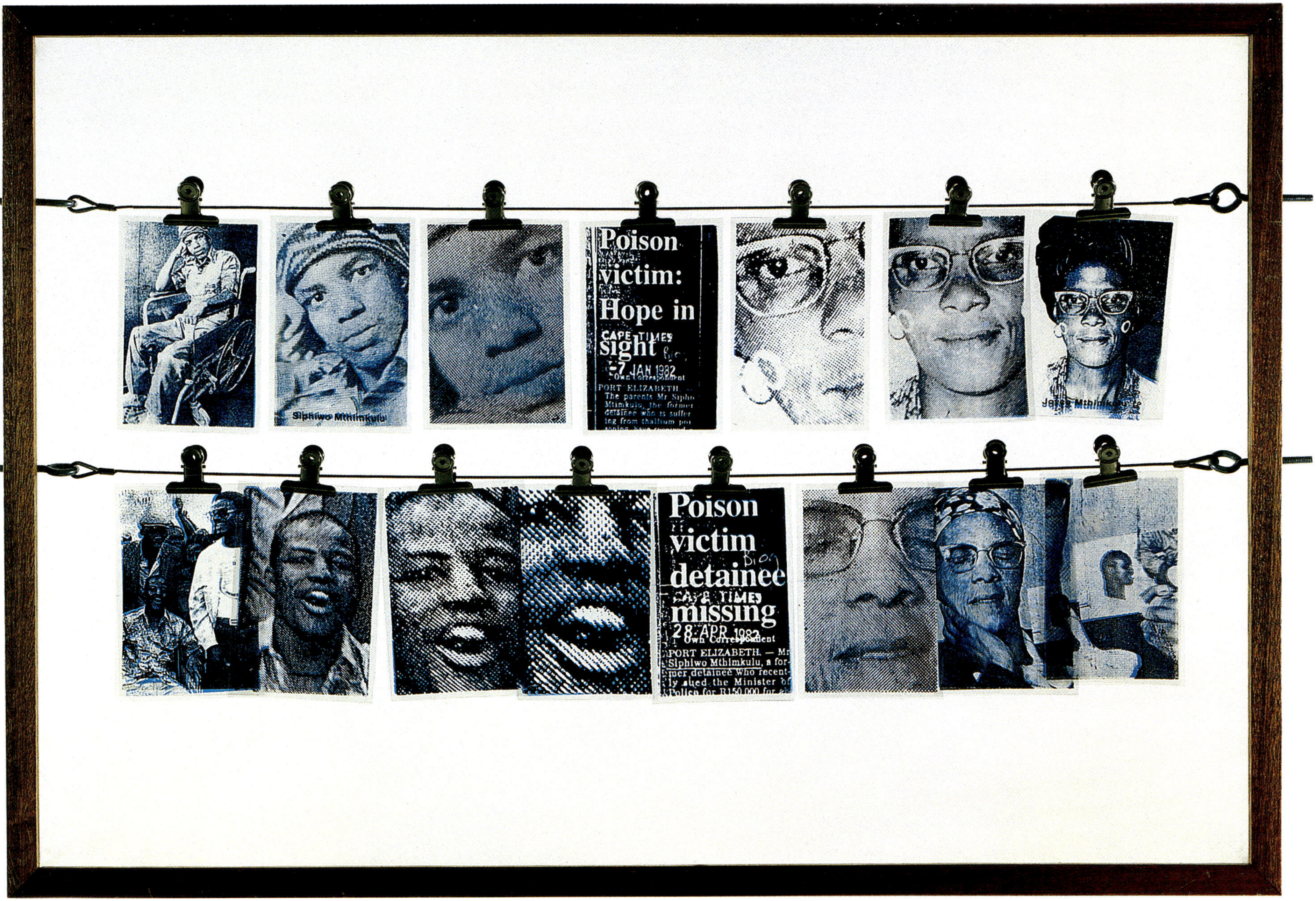


*Poison Victim*
*Cold Turkey: Stories of Truth and Reconciliation*
1997
Lightbox, metal, electrostatic prints
63 x 91 x 7 cm

# Truth Games

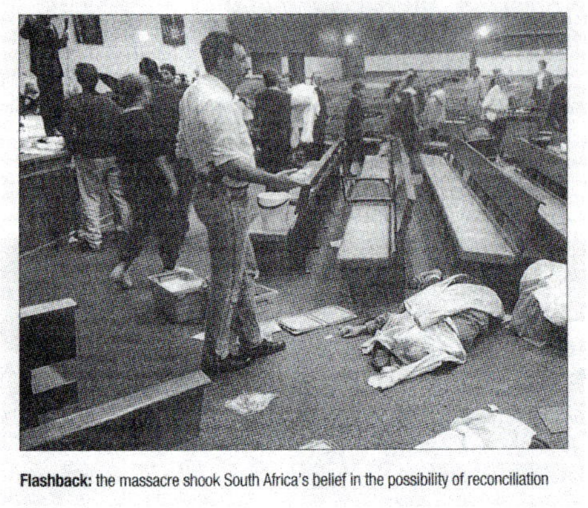


The massacre at St James Church, July, 1993
Photo: Jim McLagan
Courtesy Independent Newspapers

Sue Williamson's work on her *Truth Games* series began as a clippings-file, as she cut articles and photographs out of newspapers documenting the Truth and Reconciliation Commission. "I was interested in the exact words people used to present their case", she says. "I wanted to use those phrases. And even in the low-quality newspaper photographs, the body language of the speakers came through, the gaze either directed or averted."

In 15 large-format panels, Williamson used blow-ups of these newspaper images to tell the stories of the most high-profile cases before the TRC. Her panels follow a strict format: on the left the victim, on the right the perpetrator, and in the middle an image of the "scene of the crime".

Williamson laid white grooved plastic strips across these triptychs, inspired in part by a 1950s film in which a person standing in a dark garden sees the closed venetian blinds of a window in front of him open suddenly to reveal a dramatic confrontation taking place within. Pulling phrases out of the testimonies of both victim and perpetrator, the artist printed them on semi-transparent slats which viewers could then slide from one side to the other: "At no time is the whole picture visible", she writes in *Selected Work*. "Viewers are invited to engage with the work by moving the slats across the images, revealing a glance, a hidden detail, underlining the complex and shifting nature of the evidence."

One work was of a massacre in Kenilworth, Cape Town, in July 1993, when five young men from the Azanian People's Liberation Army burst into the Sunday services at St James Church firing AK-47s. The daughter of one of the 11 people killed, Liezl Ackerman, confronts one of the young men, Gcinikhaya Makoma. He finally says, "I'm sorry about your Mom" and she responds, "I wanted to hear that."

Williamson attended some of the TRC hearings herself, and in other works she examines the amnesty hearings for the perpetrators of the deaths of the American student Amy Biehl and the black p. 141
consciousness leader Steve Biko, as well as notorious p. 137
"unsolved" cases such as the murder of student activist Simphiwe Mthimkulu.

In restricting herself only to the material which was already in the public domain rather than interviewing any of the participants herself, the artist saw herself as a kind of editor, reducing the enormous amount of material in the popular media to an essential—but sometimes inconclusive —précis of each case.

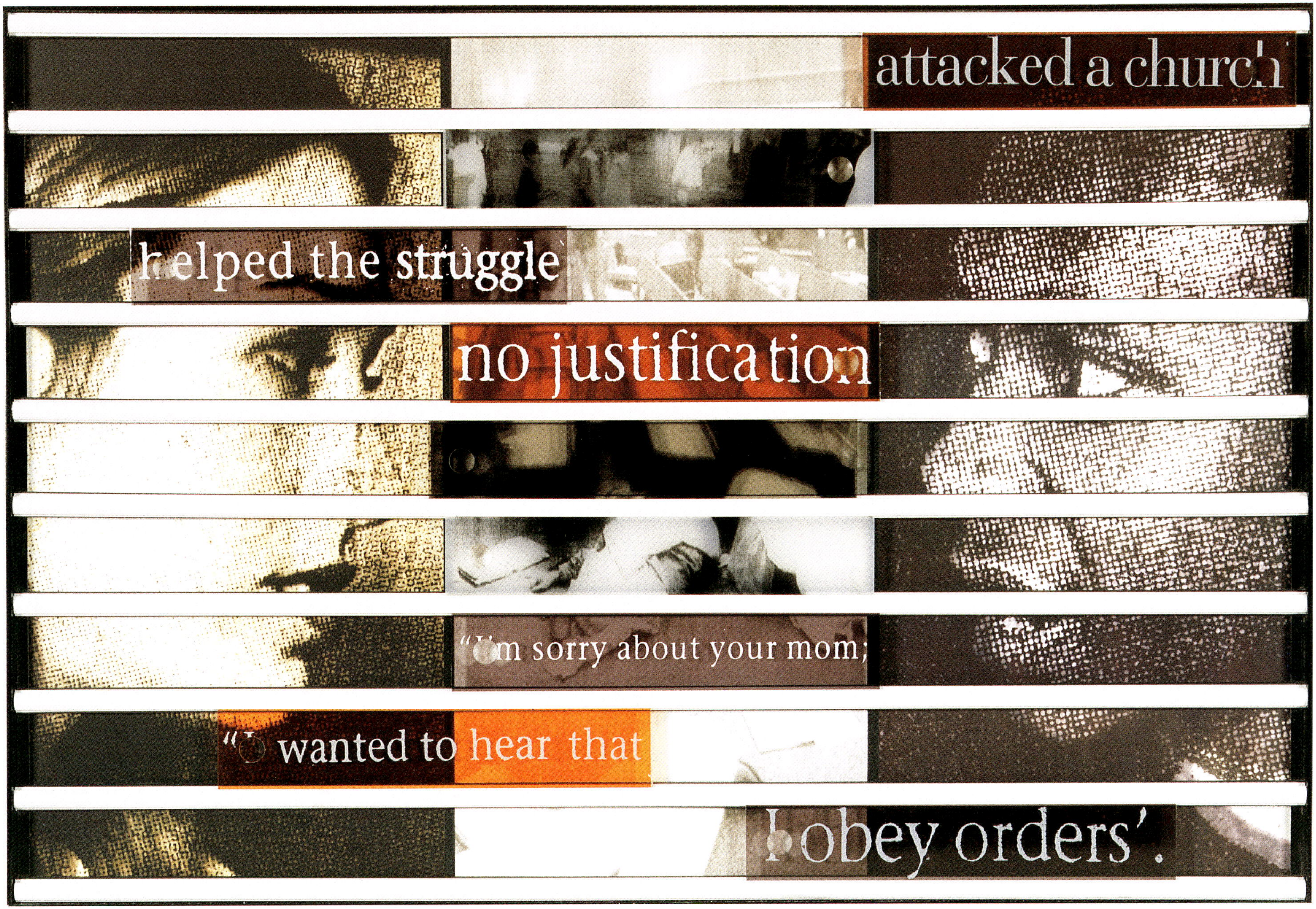


*Liezl Ackermann – not a church – Gcinikhaya Makoma*
1998
*Truth Games* series
Laminated colour laser prints, wood, metal, plastic, perspex
80 x 120 x 6 cm

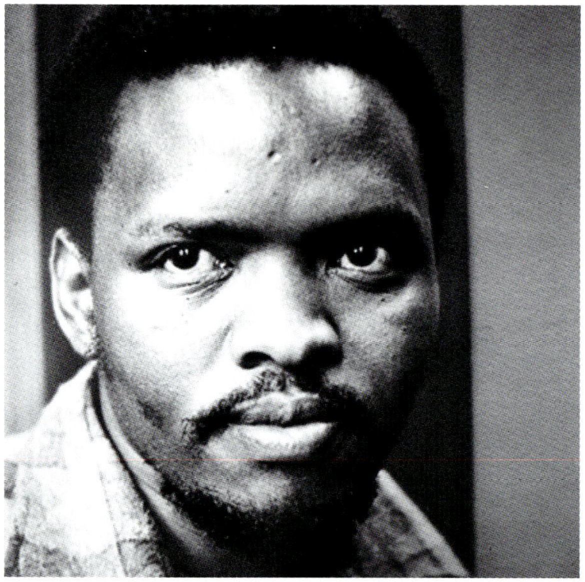
Steve Biko

One of the most shocking deaths in police detention was that of Black Consciousness leader Steve Biko at the hands of the Port Elizabeth security police in 1977. Also implicated in the killing were the medical doctors who gave Biko a clean bill of health shortly before he died of massive injuries received at the hands of the police. For his part in Biko's death, Chief District Surgeon Dr Benjamin Tucker was eventually struck off the roll in 1985.

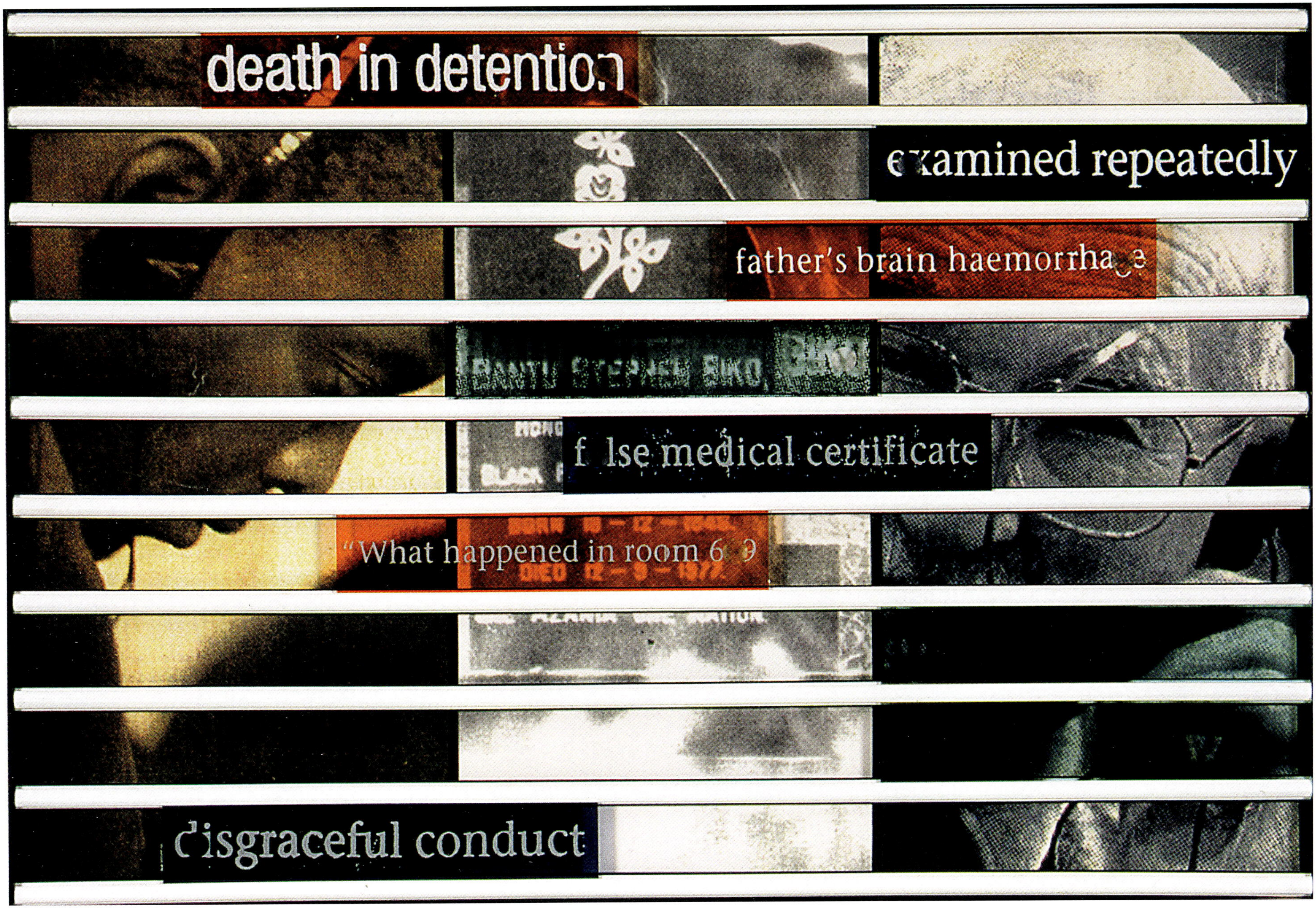


*Nkosinathi Biko – false medical certificate –*
*Dr Benjamin Tucker*
1998
*Truth Games* series
Laminated colour laser prints, wood, metal, plastic, perspex
80 x 120 x 6 cm

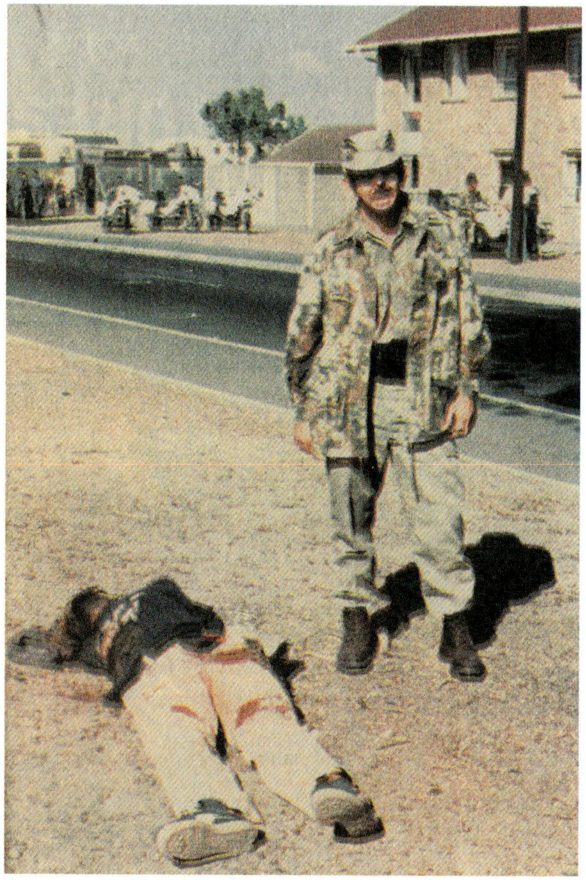

A police picture showing John Sterrenberg minutes
after he shot and killed Christopher "Rasta" Piet
Courtesy: Cape Argus

The Gugulethu Seven, as they became known, died in a shootout with the police on March 3 1986 in Gugulethu, outside Cape Town. The seven activists were Zandisile Mjobo, Zola Swelani, Mandla Mxinwa, Jabulani Miya, Themba Mlifi, Zabonke Konile and Christoper Piet. Two consecutive inquests at the time cleared the police, but relatives of the seven urged the TRC to investigate the matter further, and nine policemen were subpoened to give evidence. At the hearing, Capt. John Sterrenberg was asked why he had been "photographed smiling" next to the dead body of Christopher Piet.

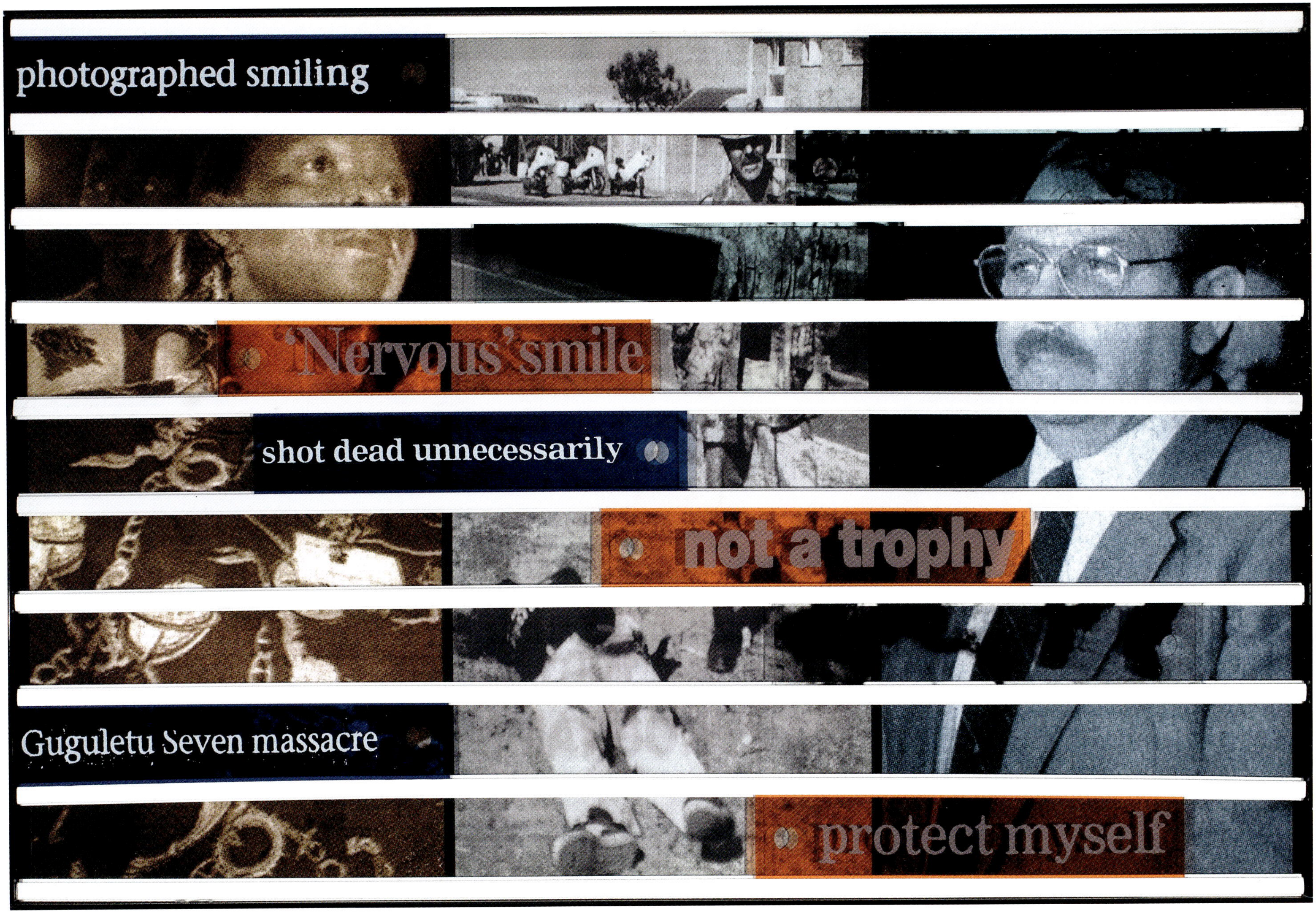


*Family of Guguletu Seven – why were you smiling –*
*Capt. John Sterrenberg*
1998
*Truth Games* series
Laminated colour laser prints, wood, metal,
plastic, perspex
80 x 120 x 6 cm

"The visual arts are not simply about "seeing" and the visual, but are also about scale, relationships of size and space. The pieces that make up *Truth Games* engage the body of the viewer in a particular relationship of scale: our bodies, we, the viewers, address these images and are addressed by them.

This is particularly important, given the subject matter of these works; which arise out of the documentation of the Truth and Reconciliation Commission hearings. Sue Williamson commented to me that she thought of herself as a repository for the stories that were emerging. Now, there are other repositories; places where the stories are recorded: there are aural records, and video-tapes; and there are books and articles… But part of what is distinctive about the documentation that Sue has produced is that it calls us up into a particular physical relationship to the material. Further, the works draw us in to actually interact with the pieces themselves…

Part of the power of the visual arts, is that they can remind us of our own physicality: we too have bodies. In this strange late-twentieth century, so marked by a sense of relativism, and the decline of absolutes, there is, we become increasingly aware, one absolute that holds fast: that is that we all, as human subjects, live within the body, and that while it is a site of pleasure, it can also become a place of terror. From Bosnia to Sierra Leone, to the Eastern Cape, the final battleground is the human body.

So the works of *Truth Games* in their scale, and their mode of physical address, call us to engage bodily. At the same time, the works explore the enormously complex terrain around culpability, blame, justification, and accusation, that the processes of confession invoke. This does not suggest in any way that Sue Williamson's work implies that there is a parity between the survivor and the perpetrator: she is not saying, in a reductive way, that the agent of violence is himself a victim, and therefore there is no way of attributing blame. Rather, I think she is making the more complicated argument, that in the processes of scrutiny and self-scrutiny, the web of material between perpetrators and victims is enormously complex and contradictory, and the relationships between those seeking forgiveness and those offering it is ambiguous at best.

By way of example, the young men responsible for the death of Amy Biehl have apparently approached her parents, asking for money to have T-shirts made for a club they have started. Those responsible for Amy's death feel, it seems, not a sense of obligation, but rather a sense of entitlement: that having once received forgiveness from the parents of the murdered woman, they now feel that the parents owe them in some extended way.

Forgiveness, like any gift, does not balance the books: there is always an unequal relationship between the giver and the receiver that sets up invisible lines of obligation that defy rational understanding."

*An extract from a speech by Jane Taylor, Wole Soyinka Chair of Drama and Theatre at the University of Leeds, at the opening of Truth Games at the Dakawa Art Centre in Grahamstown, July 1999*

Amy Biehl was a 26-year-old American Fulbright Scholar working at the University of Western Cape, near Cape Town. Dropping off friends in the black township of Gugulethu during a schools boycott in April 1993, Biehl was stoned and stabbed to death. Four men were found guilty of her murder and sent to jail the following year; in 1997 they applied for amnesty, claiming the murder to be politically motivated. Biehl's parents, Linda and Peter, supported amnesty for the killers, saying they understood the context in which she was killed. The four were granted amnesty and released.

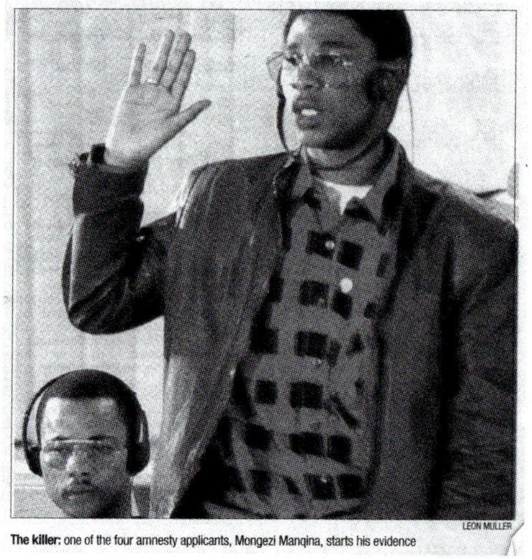


Mongezi Manqina gives evidence at the TRC hearing into the death of Amy Biehl
Photo: Leon Muller
Courtesy: Cape Argus

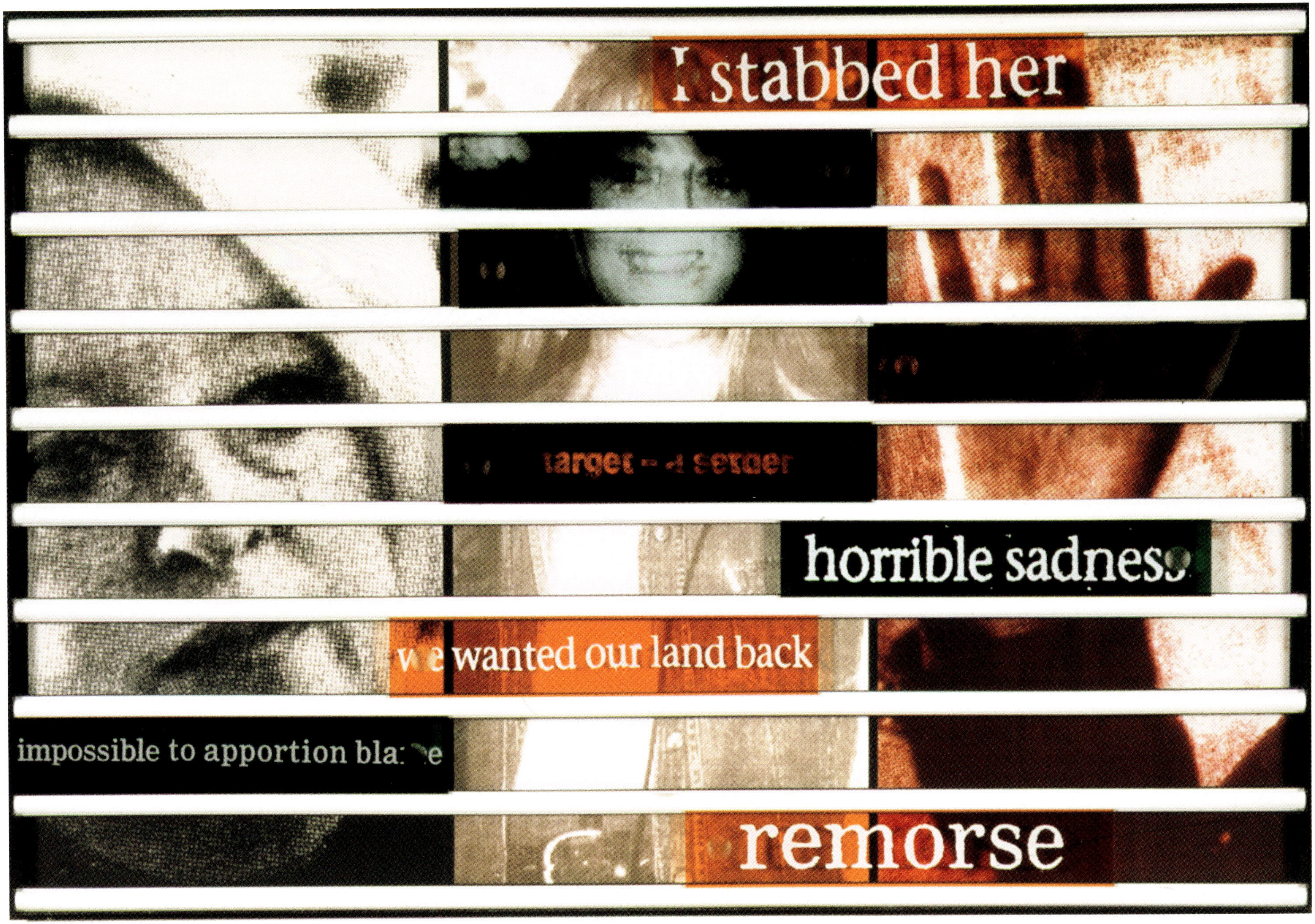


*Linda Biehl – understand the context – Mongezi Manqina*
1998
*Truth Games* series
Laminated colour laser prints, wood, metal, plastic, perspex
80 x 120 x 6 cm

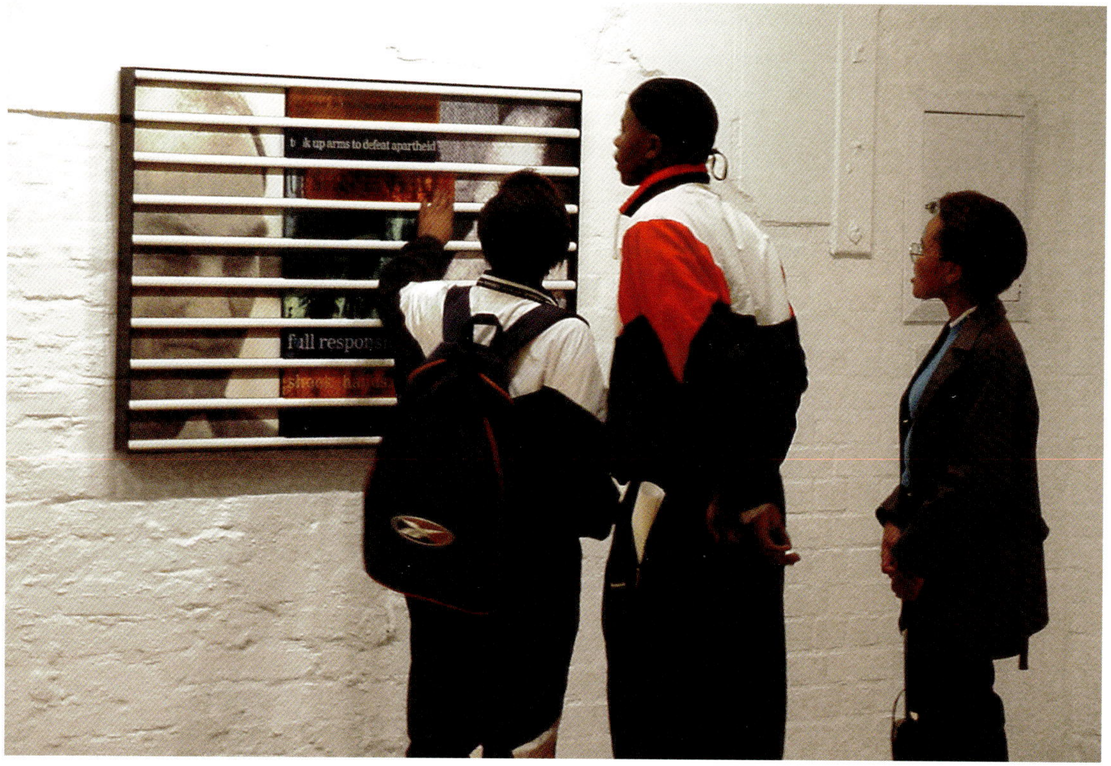

Neville Clarence was an officer of the South African Air Force when he lost his sight in a car-bomb attack on the SAAF headquarters in Church Street, Pretoria, in 1983. More than 200 people were injured in the attack and 19 died. The attack was perpetrated by Umkhonto we Sizwe, the armed wing of the ANC. At the TRC hearing in May 1998, the then Chief of Policy and Planning in the Defence Force, Aboobaker Ismail, took full responsibility for the attack. Clarence said he understood the circumstances, and the two men shook hands.

Visitors to an exhibition of the *Truth Games* series at the Dakawa Art Centre in Grahamstown, Eastern Cape, 1999

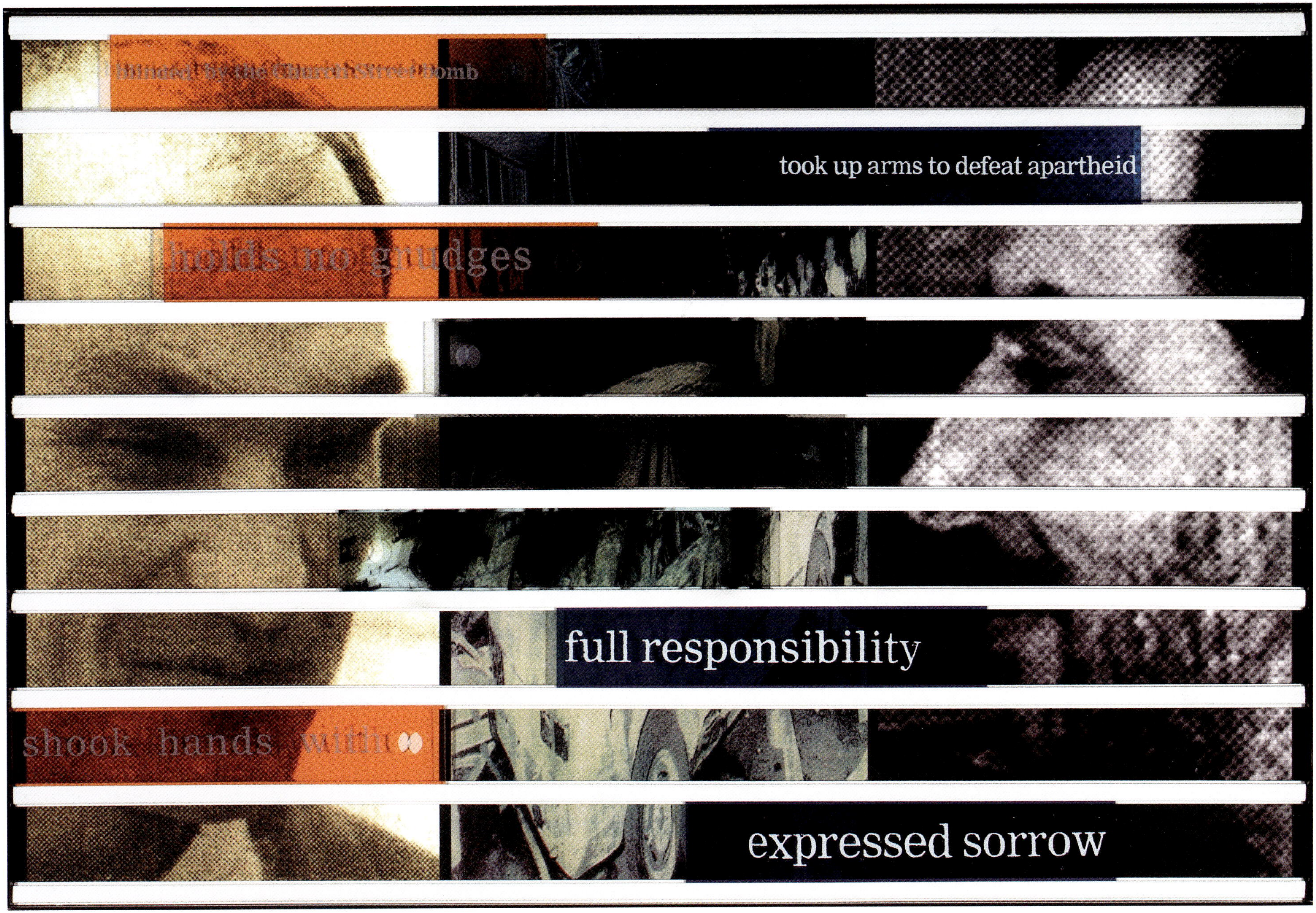


*Neville Clarence – hold no grudge – Aboobaker Ismael*
1998
*Truth Games* series
Laminated colour laser prints, wood, metal, plastic, perspex
80 x 120 x 6 cm

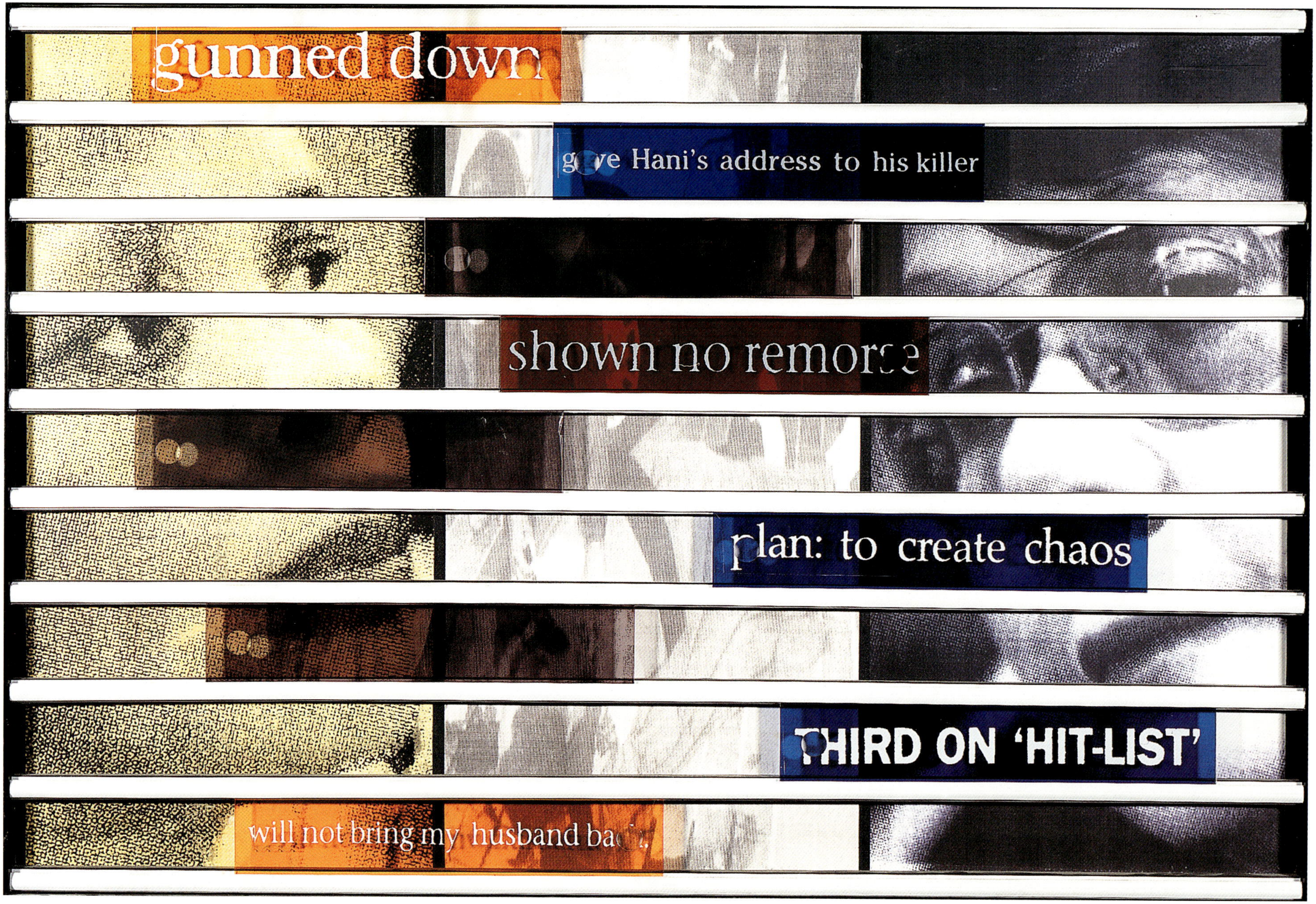


*Limpho Hani – no remorse – Gaye Derby-Lewis*
1998
*Truth Games* series
Laminated colour laser prints, wood, metal, plastic, perspex

On April 10 1993, the SA Communist Party leader Chris Hani was assassinated in the driveway of his home, east of Johannesburg. Two men who were part of a right-wing cell were caught and sentenced to life imprisonment: Janus Walusz, the hitman, and Clive Derby-Lewis, the group's leader. Gaye Derby-Lewis, the latter's wife, was the one who gave Walusz his assignment, and Hani's address. The men were denied amnesty by the TRC.

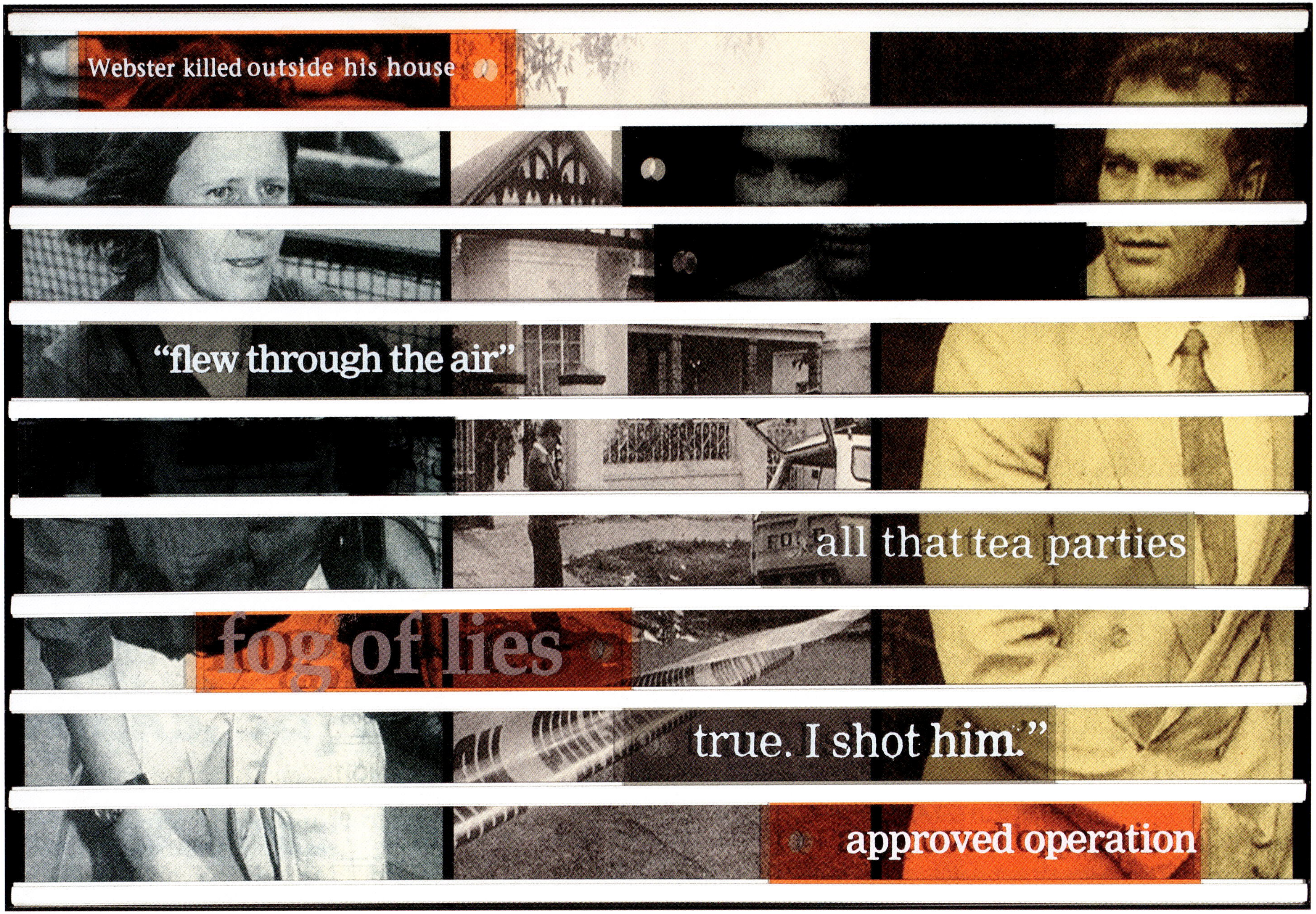


*Maggie Friedman – senseless murder – Ferdi Barnard*
1998
*Truth Games* series
Laminated colour laser prints, wood, metal, plastic, perspex
80 x 120 x 6 cm

After many denials, the state security operative Ferdi Barnard admitted shooting the University of Witwatersrand academic David Webster in 1989, firing from a car as Webster returned home from an early morning jog in the Johannesburg suburb of Troyeville. Webster had been active in the detainee support movement.

# Winnie Mandela and the Assassination of Dr Asvat

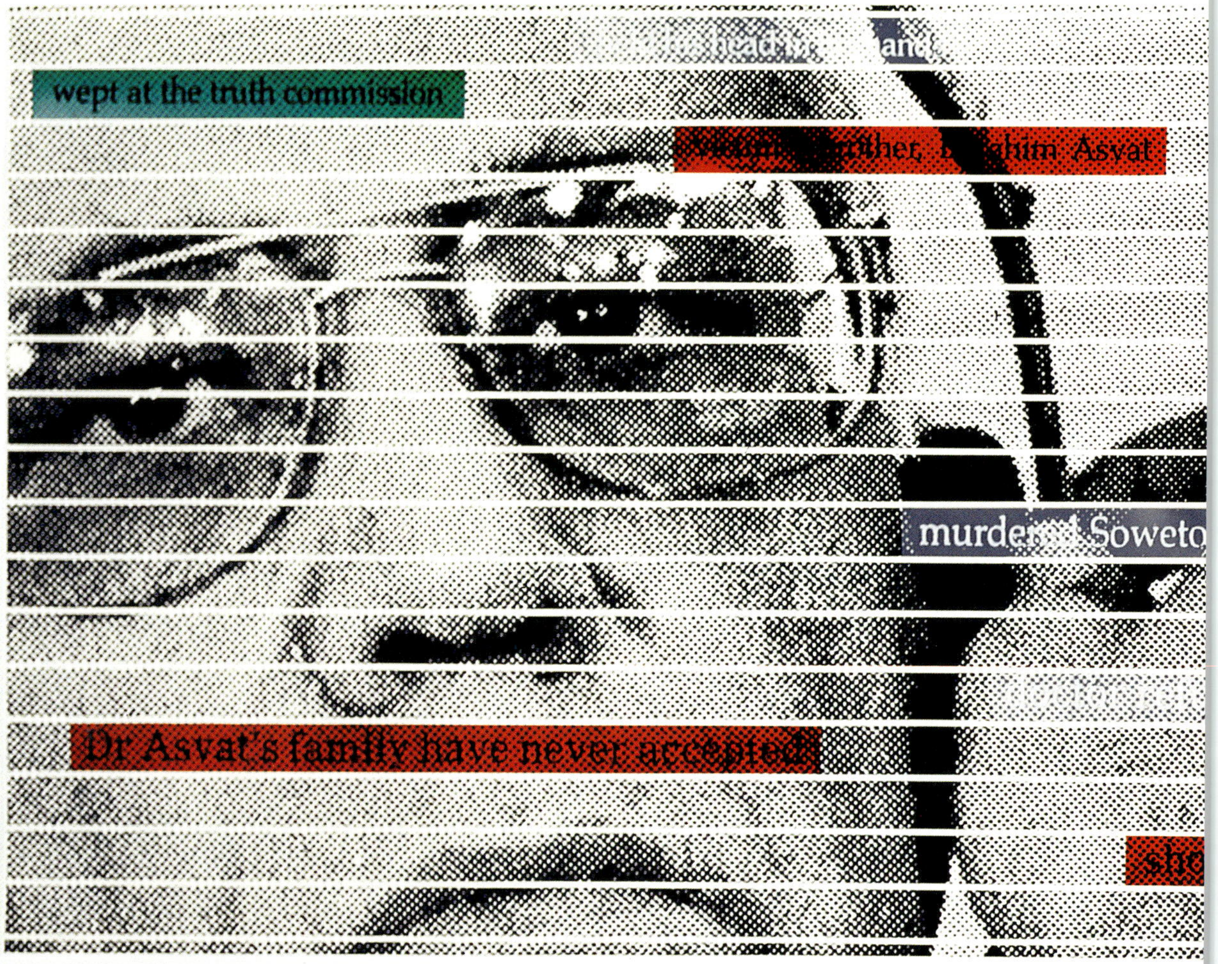


*Winnie Mandela and the Assassination of Dr Asvat*
1999
Lithograph with printed and collaged gel papers
Printed by Eileen Foti at the Rutgers Center
for Innovative Printmaking, New Jersey
55.5 x 187 cm

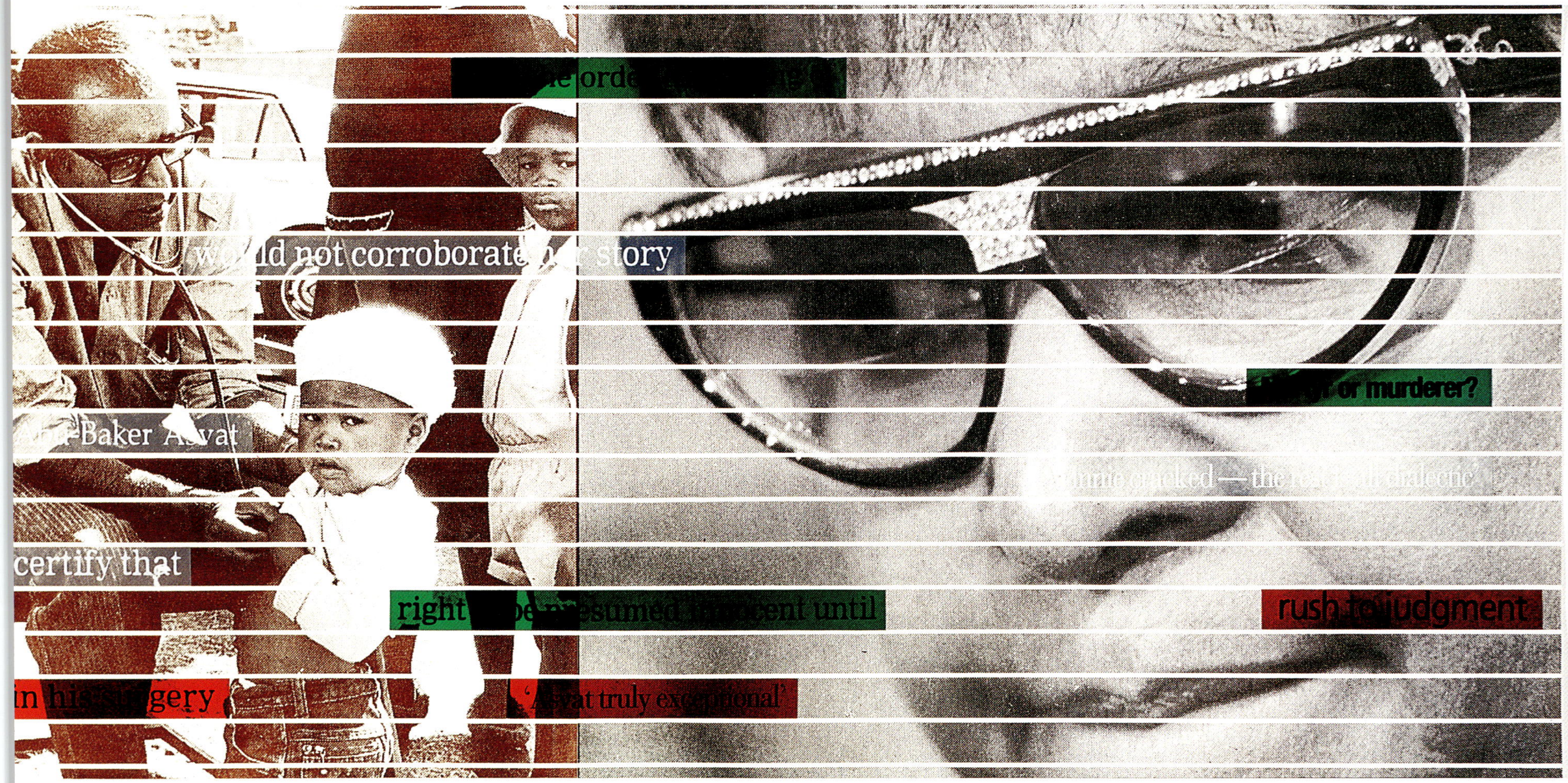


Sue Williamson made this lithograph at the Rutgers Centre for Innovative Print and Paper in 1999, in response to Winnie Madikizela-Mandela's appearance before the Truth and Reconciliation Commission over the death of Dr Abu Baker Asvat. Asvat was a beloved Soweto doctor who was assassinated in his surgery in January 1989: many believed he was killed because he refused to supply false medical records clearing Madikizela-Mandela of involvement in the death of the teenager Stompie Seipei. The lithograph shows Dr Asvat's brother Ebrahim appearing before the TRC; Dr Asvat himself; and Madikizela-Mandela. The texts, printed onto strips of coloured film inserted through the paper, are commentary from the media: the white press was judgmental, the black press more forgiving.

## Can't forget, can't remember

In July 1997, Sue Williamson was present at the amnesty hearing, before the Truth and Reconciliation Commission, of Captain Jeffery Benzien. She watched as one of his victims, the activist Ashley Forbes, questioned his former torturer. It was one of the rare occasions when there was a face-to-face confrontation between victim and perpetrator. Usually, one side would give evidence, and then the other.

It was clear that Forbes hoped the setting of the TRC hearing would elicit truthful answers from the policeman. "Do you remember saying to me that … you are able to treat me like an *animal* or like a human being?", Forbes asked accusingly, barely able to conceal his emotion. Benzien's flat response was: "I wouldn't remember, sir, but I would concede that I may have said it."

The power of such voices and the gap between the memory of the victim and that of the perpetrator led Williamson to produce the work *Can't forget, can't remember*. In this interactive installation, the viewer is invited to stand at a lectern facing a projected screen and navigate, with a mouse and a cursor, over images and texts from two TRC hearings. By clicking on the texts scrolling down the screen the viewer activates audio-recordings of these hearings. The silence is broken by the voices of victim or perpetrator.

"The viewer is cast as a kind of judge", Williamson writes in *Selected Work*, "attempting to read between the lines of what is being uttered—sentences can be repeated, cut short or layered over each other." What becomes apparent is the gap between the recollection of victim and perpetrator, and the flawed nature of memory.

In the second sequence, the viewer engages with the story of the St James Massacre in Cape Town, in 1993, when five operatives from the Azanian People's Liberation Army opened fire on the church and killed eleven people. Only one man had been convicted, Gcinikhaya Makoma. Dawie Ackermann asks whether Makoma can remember shooting his wife, seated right by the door. "She was wearing a blue coat". Makoma replies that he does not remember. He just fired his gun.

Both Makoma and Benzien were granted amnesty.

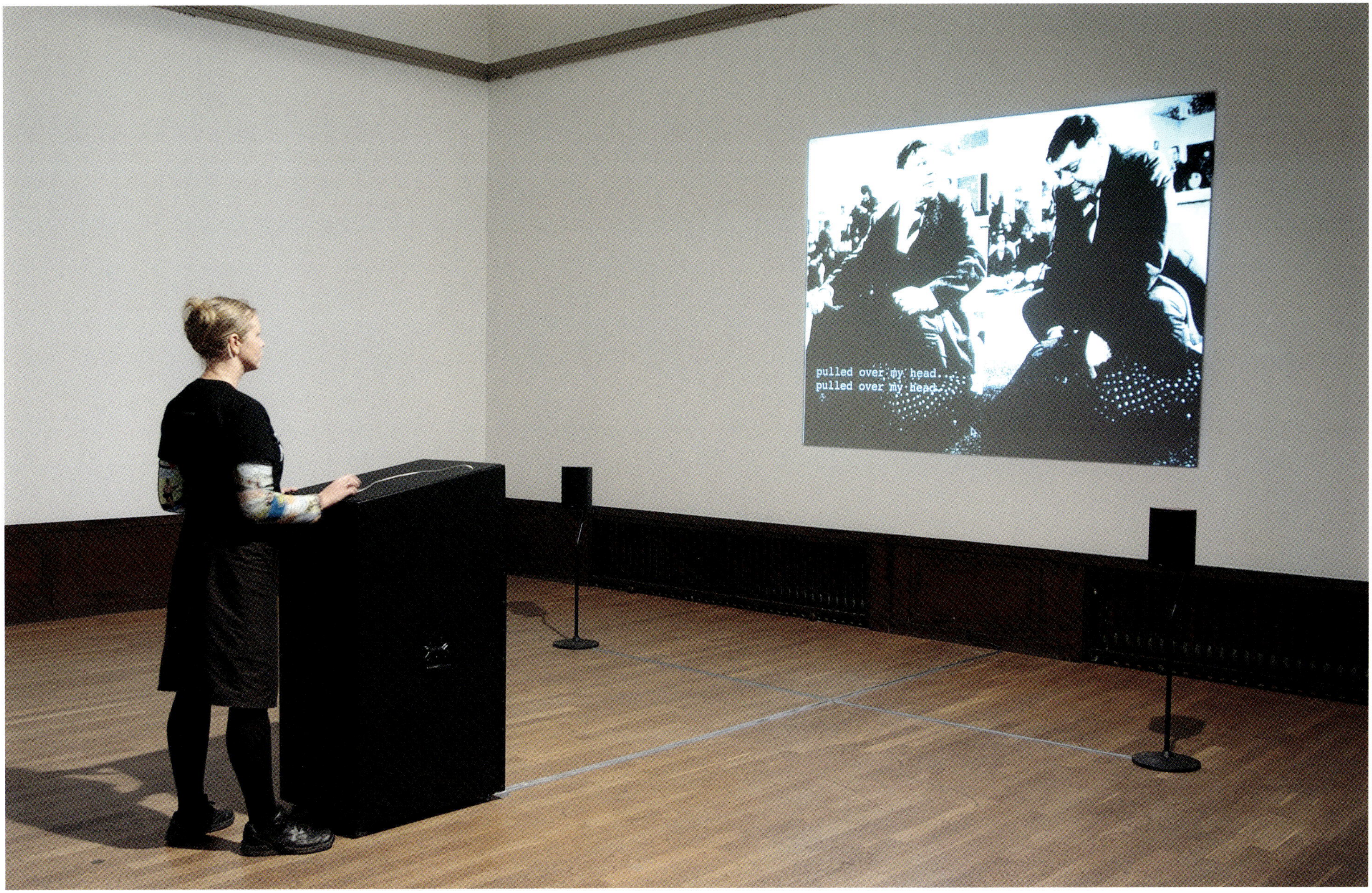


*Can't forget, can't remember*
1999
Interactive video projection
Graphic designer: Tracy Gander
Soundtrack: Arnold Erasmus
Installation view, Liljevalchs Konsthal, Stockholm
55.5 x 187 cm

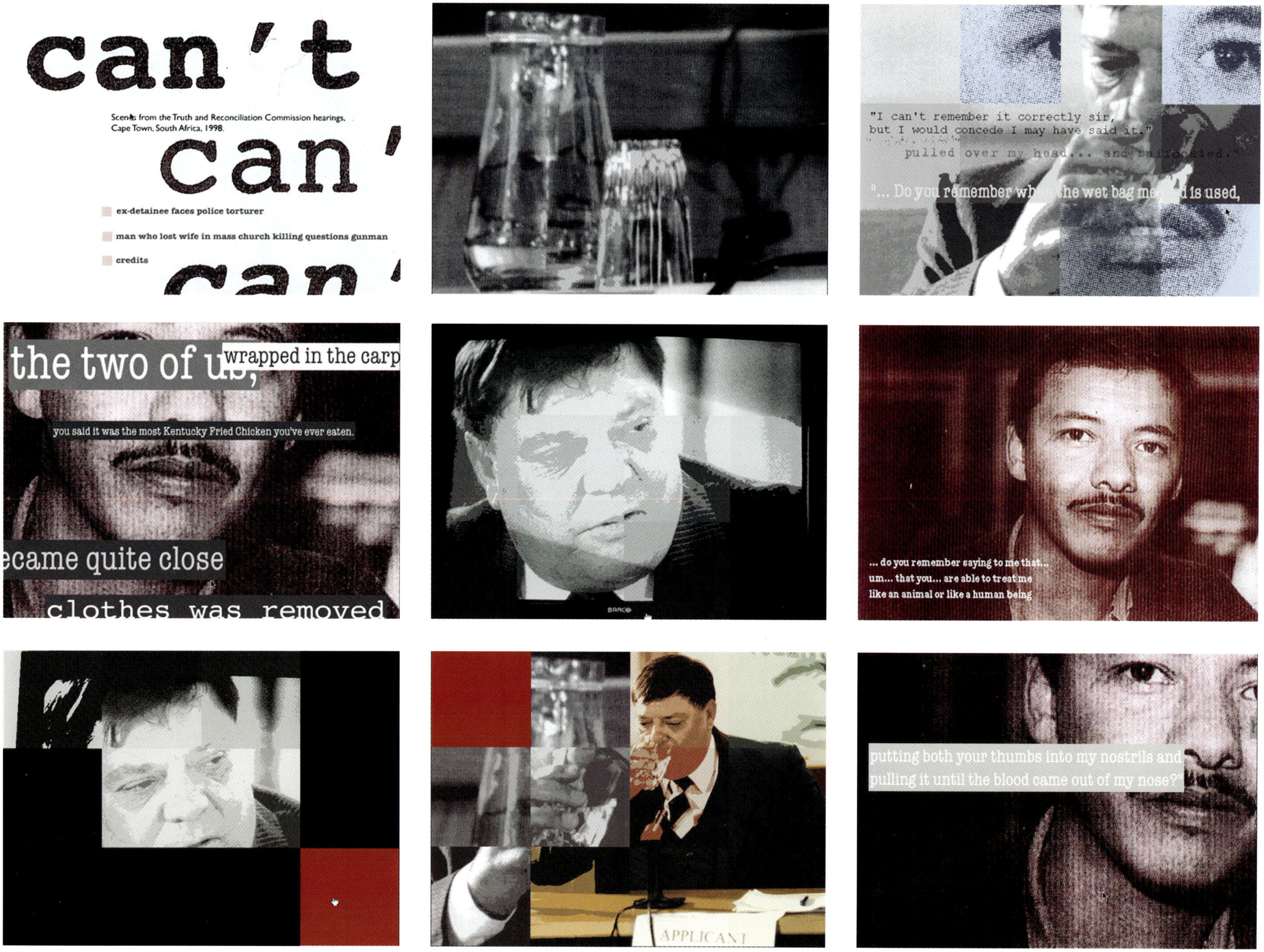


*Can't forget, can't remember*
1999
Interactive video projection
Video stills

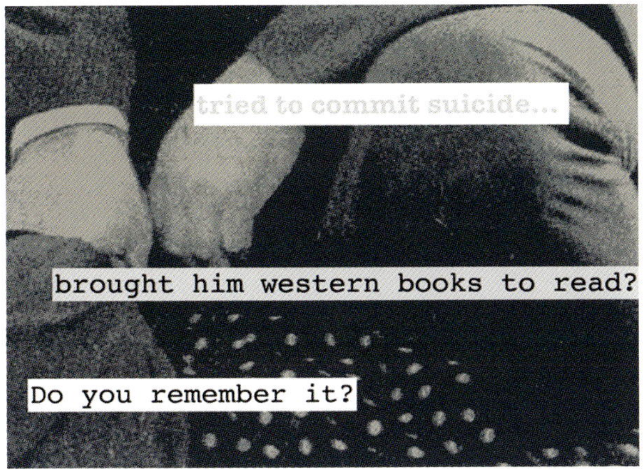
tried to commit suicide...
brought him western books to read?
Do you remember it?

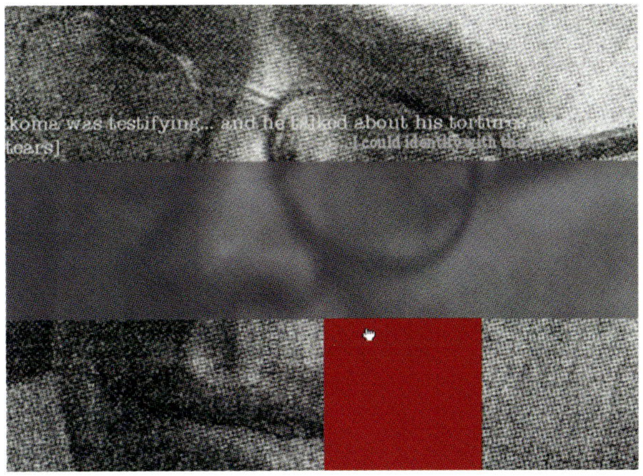

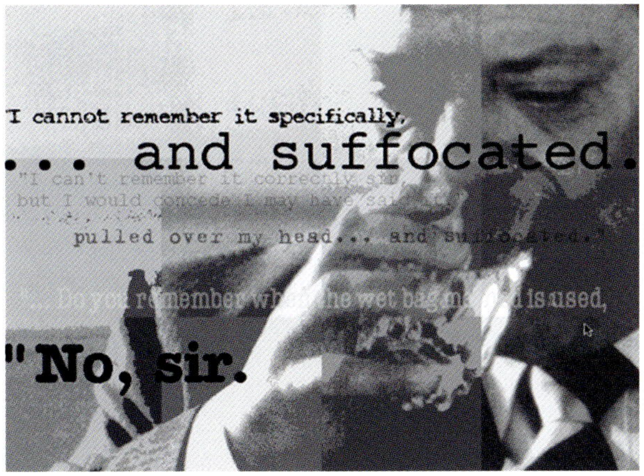
"I cannot remember it specifically,
... and suffocated.
pulled over my head... and suffocated."
"No, sir.

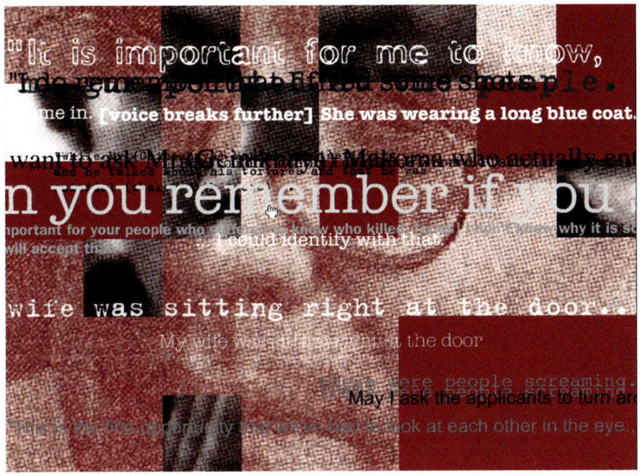
"It is important for me to know,
[voice breaks further] She was wearing a long blue coat.
I could identify with that.
wife was sitting right at the door...

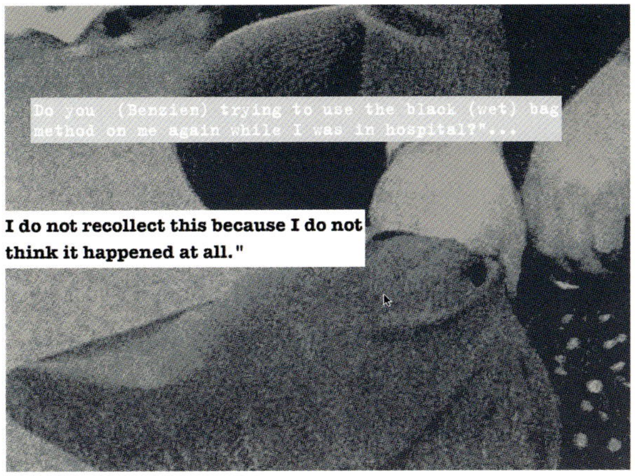
Do you (Benzien) trying to use the black (wet) bag method on me again while I was in hospital?"...
I do not recollect this because I do not think it happened at all."

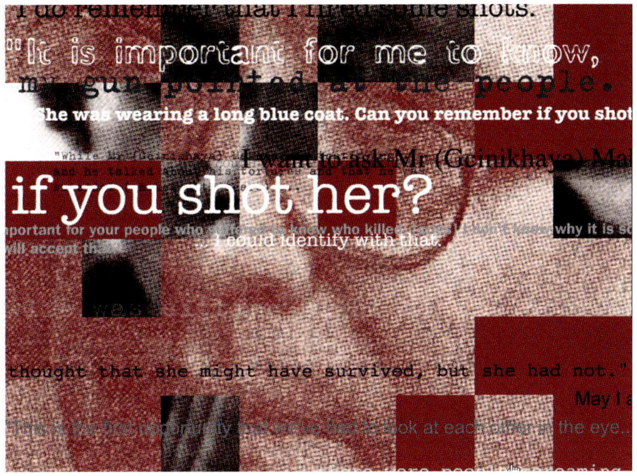
"It is important for me to know,
She was wearing a long blue coat. Can you remember if you shot
if you shot her?
I could identify with that.
thought that she might have survived, but she had not."

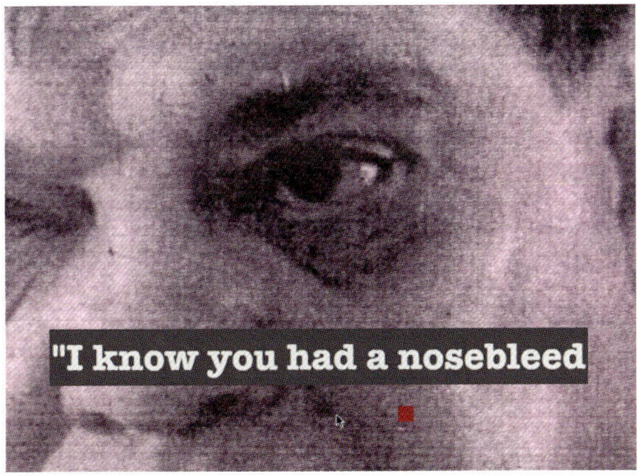
"I know you had a nosebleed

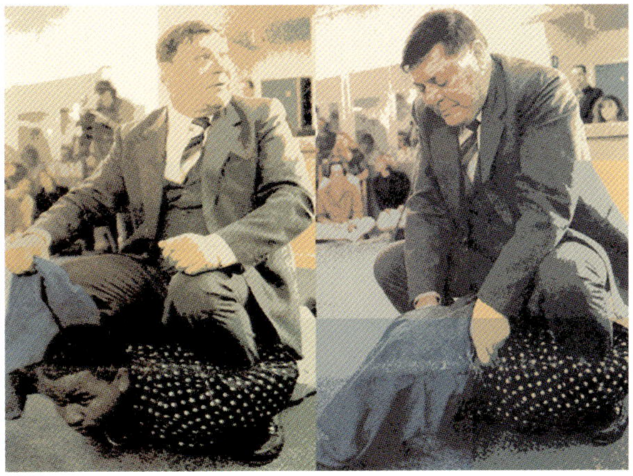

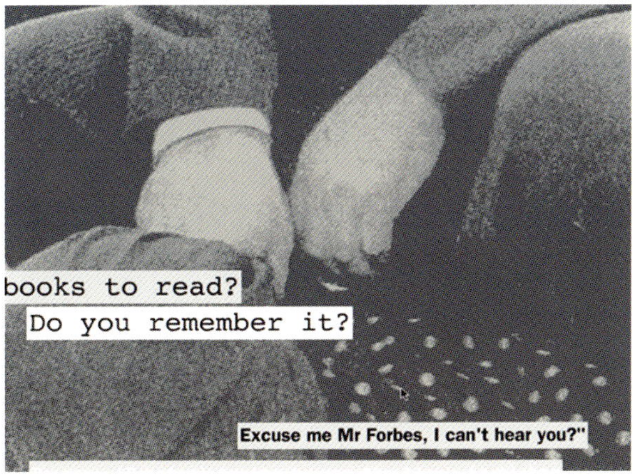
books to read?
Do you remember it?
Excuse me Mr Forbes, I can't hear you?"

# The New Struggles

From the Inside
Better Lives
Pass the Parcel, Jacob

*Once in power, the African National Congress was faced with the formidable task of meeting the expectations of the country's black majority in terms of provision of services and redistribution of resources. Nelson Mandela retired in 1999, making way for Thabo Mbeki. Although the economy grew, and services such as welfare and electrification were dramatically extended to the black majority, unemployment figures rose too—and the Mbeki era was plagued by a number of scandals, including the president's refusal to acknowledge the link between HIV and AIDS, and to implement a national antiretroviral programme. The murderous xenophobic violence that wracked the country in 2008 was a signal of deep discontent among the urban poor, and the ascent of Mbeki's successor, Jacob Zuma, was marred by corruption and rape charges. By 2007, the euphoria of the Mandela era was a distant memory, and politically engaged artists such as Sue Williamson had reoriented themselves towards the "new struggles" of the post-apartheid era.*

Mark Gevisser: In the first years of the twenty-first century, you made art about people living with HIV/AIDS, about new immigrants to South Africa, and about the gender politics surrounding Jacob Zuma's 2005 rape trial…
Sue Williamson: Yes, it was obviously a very different terrain now. We finally had an equal society in terms of rights under rule of law. And that was wonderful. It was such a relief after all the years of living in a society of discrimination. But of course there was still a hierarchy of "haves" and "have nots". There were still those sections of society who were being ostracised, for one reason or another.

In the very years of transition, the AIDS pandemic was becoming more prevalent and virulent. In South Africa, AIDS was seen as a shameful thing, a result of sexual promiscuity. The government would not give free anti-retrovirals, because the president, Thabo Mbeki, did not believe that HIV caused AIDS, and people were getting ill and dying by the thousands.

So severe was the stigma of AIDS, that the cause of these deaths was seldom acknowledged by family members. It was not until 2005, when Nelson Mandela publicly reported that the death of his son Makgatho was as a result of AIDS, that it was clear that the subject had become less taboo.

MG: What was the role of the artists in raising awareness around AIDS?
SW: There were a number of initiatives that arose in response to this national crisis. One was by Marilyn Martin, who was then director of the South African National Gallery. For an international AIDS conference to be held in Durban in mid 2000, Marilyn commissioned artists to make a special work, and I was one of them.

**MG**: You have always used your art-making as a way of finding out more about the world. How so with these projects?
**SW**: It was quite revelatory to me. Quite often when something life-threatening happens to people, it changes them in a way they don't expect. Some of the people I met even took their HIV status as an unanticipated blessing. There was a young girl who told me she had been sleeping around and stealing on the streets. Then when she found she was HIV positive she went back to school and changed her life around completely.

I called the project *From the Inside* [2000–04]. It became about writing a statement on a public wall—a statement about what the person had learned from living with HIV. One of the other participants, Peter Busse—a leader of the AIDS movement—wrote on a concrete wall on Harrow Road, Johannesburg, "Being diagnosed HIV+ can be a new beginning. You reassess what is important."
I keep on learning, through my work, about the human spirit—about what people will produce for themselves in difficult times.

**MG**: Similarly with the immigrants from other African
pp. 166, countries you interviewed and documented for *Better*
168-9 *Lives*?
**SW**: Yes, I could not believe the stories people told me. The extent of the trauma they had undergone in their home countries was extreme, followed by an epic journey to what they believed would be a safe haven: South Africa. And then the xenophobic jealousy and resentment they encountered from South Africans—so ironic, after other African countries were so welcoming to our exiles during the struggle. In *Better Lives* I set out to show the dignity and humanity of the participants, and their value as new citizens in the way I presented them.

**MG**: I assume you supported the African National Congress in 1994.
**SW**: Yes, completely.

**MG**: When did disillusion begin to set in?
**SW**: Well, I never thought it was going to be easy. But when Jacob Zuma became president of the African National Congress in 2007, I was appalled. He had all these corruption charges against him. One kept on thinking, "He cannot possibly survive this". But he did.

**MG**: There is real anger in *Pass the Parcel, Jacob*, pp. 176-7
with the impression one has of the artist ripping through layers of lies, represented by wrappings with news-clips printed onto them, to get to the "truth" of the matter in the Jacob Zuma rape trial.
**SW**: Yes, I suppose there is…

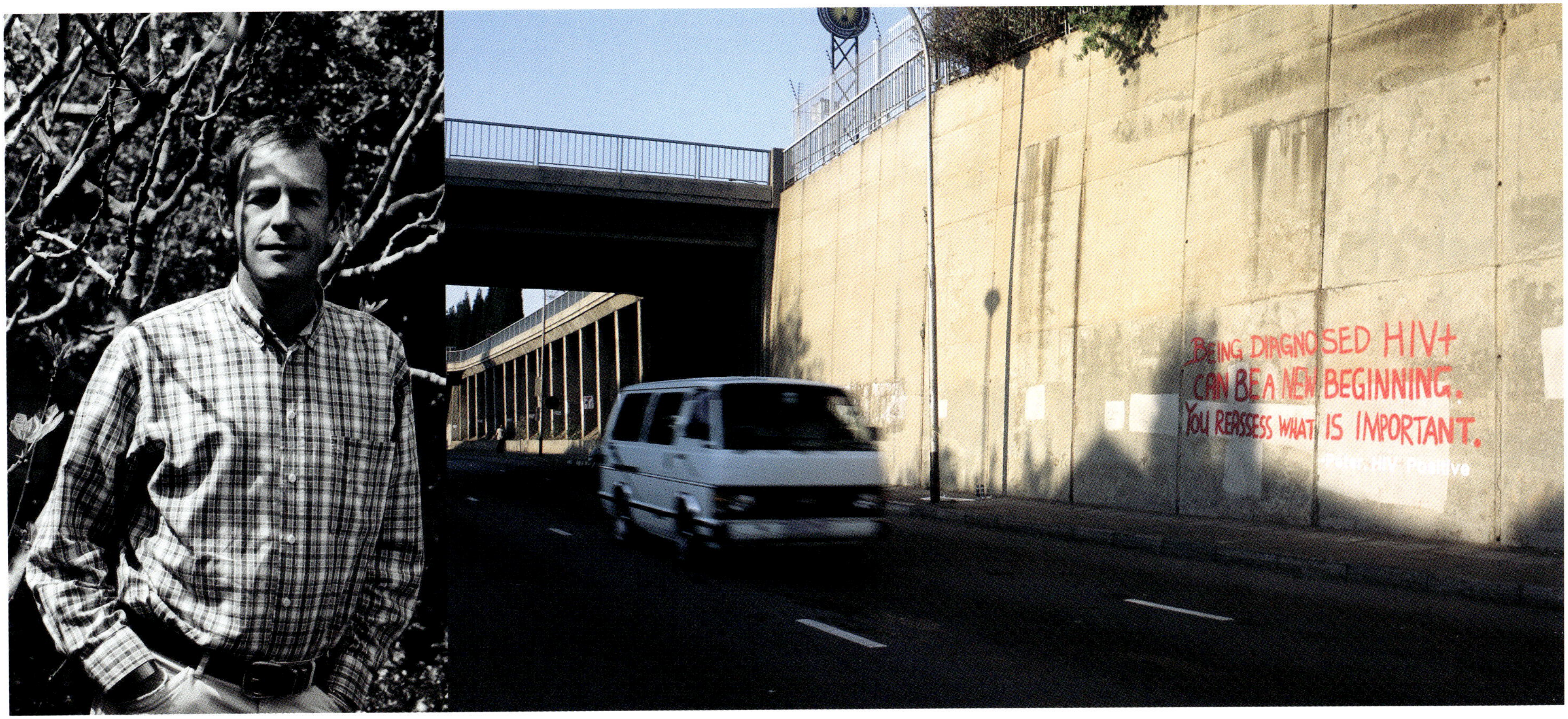


*Peter Busse*
2002
*From the Inside* series
Pigment inks on archival paper
90 x 200 cm

# From the Inside

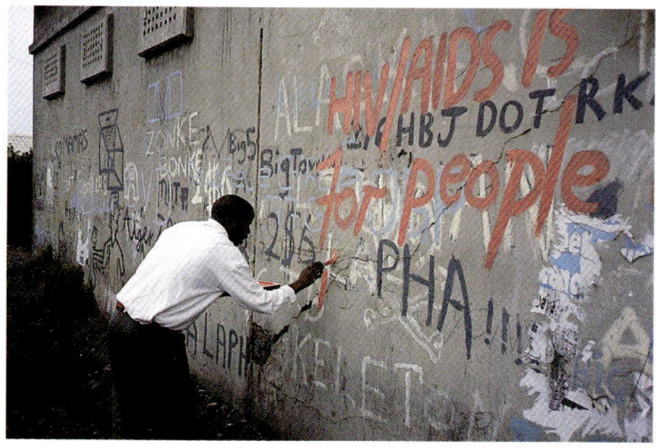

In 2000, Sue Williamson was commissioned to make an artwork about HIV and AIDS in South Africa, for that year's World Conference on AIDS in Durban. At this conference, the South African president Thabo Mbeki repeated his scepticism about the link between HIV and AIDS. In this era of denial, Williamson decided to make a series of collaborative pieces with people living with HIV/AIDS in which the truth about the epidemic would be written large on city walls.

Each work began with an interview with someone who was HIV-positive. The participant then decided on a message, or a statement which he or she wanted to be made public, so that it could enter the community discourse. Often, the person would paint this message up him or herself onto a public wall. In Johannesburg, a team of volunteers helped too. As someone who had studied South African resistance art during the apartheid era, Williamson was familiar with the power of unsigned graffiti as a medium of protest, but in *From the Inside* she printed the participant's name and HIV status in vinyl or painted letters beneath each statement, thus moving her work beyond the anonymity of graffiti: "The willingness to be named is important in a society where shame and silence over the illness prevail", she has written in an artist's statement accompanying the work.

Williamson took portraits of each of her participants and paired these with photographs of the walls. These double images were the gallery works, a documentation of the public project. One of them was also selected for a public art project in downtown Johannesburg, and an enormous blowup of the work was hung on the Turbine Building in Newtown for the Johannesburg Art City project in 2002. The work shows the statement that Johannes Bukhali painted on an already graffiti-spattered wall in his home township of Daveyton, together with the portrait the artist took of him with his parents. His quote reads: "HIV/AIDS is no longer only for people who are infected[,] it's everyone's task to help!" Bukhali asked to be photographed with his parents because unusually for the time, they had fully accepted his HIV status.

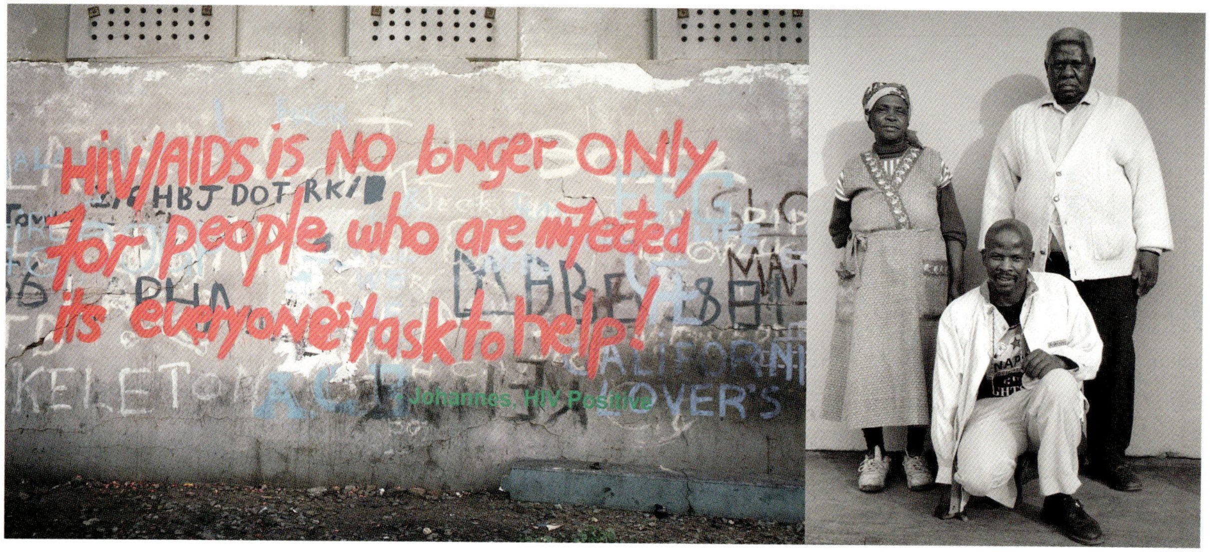


Johannes Bukhali paints his message on a wall in Daveyton, near Johannesburg

*Johannes Bukhali, with parents*
2002
*From the Inside* series
Pigment inks on archival paper
90 x 200 cm

*Johannes Bukhali, with parents*
2002
*From the Inside* series
Blown up to banner size on the Turbine Building as part of the Art City Project in Johannesburg

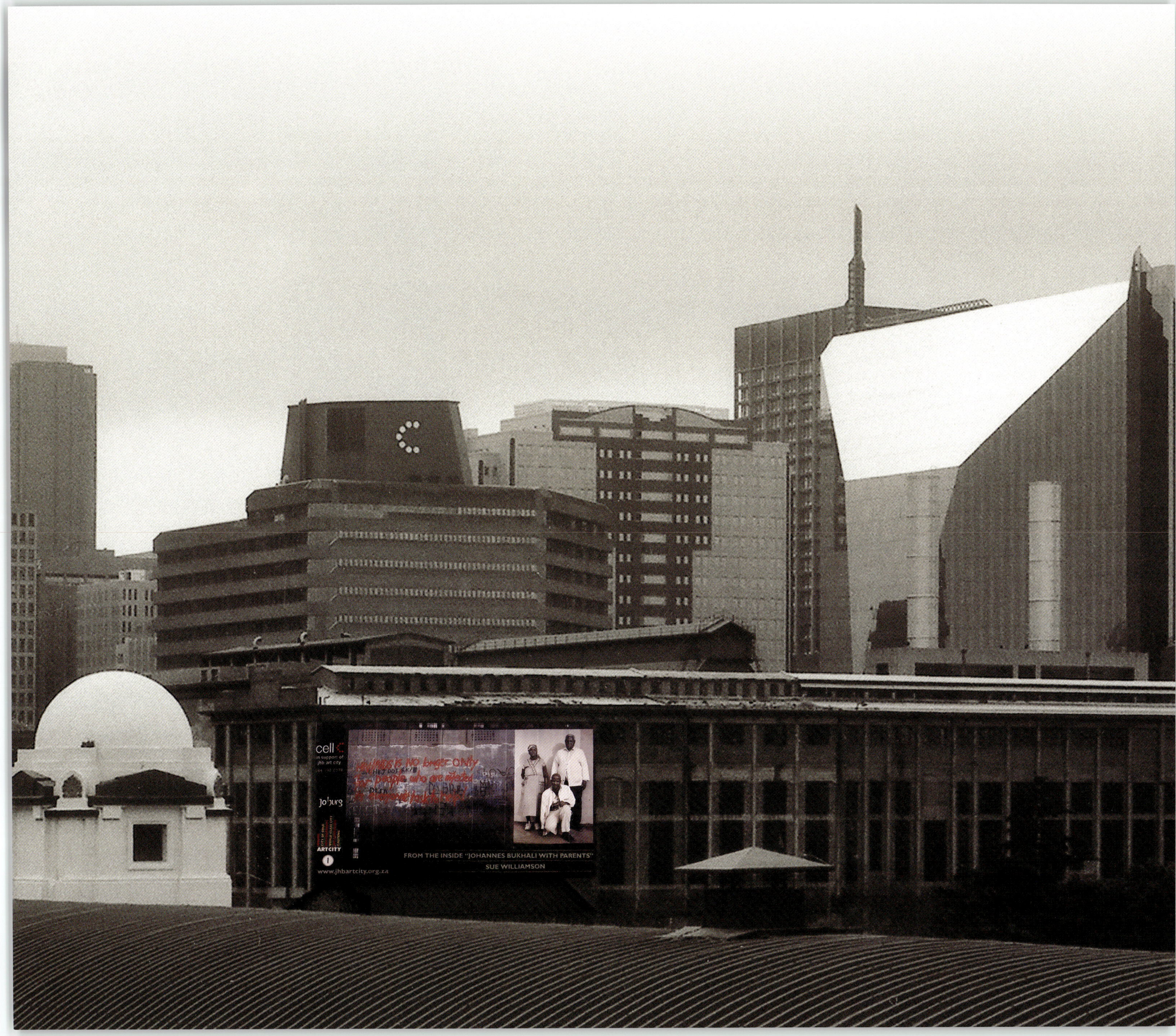
cell C
in support of
jhb art city
jo'burg
ARTCITY
www.jhbartcity.org.za
FROM THE INSIDE "JOHANNES BUKHALI WITH PARENTS"
SUE WILLIAMSON

For the first work in the *From the Inside* series, made for the 2000 AIDS conference in Durban, Williamson worked with Mitchells Plain graffiti artist Falko to install young AIDS activist Busi Maqungo's message next to a railway bridge in Cape Town. The wall they chose already displayed graffiti of the Sexy Boys gang, setting up a resonance with Busi's message: "It should be taken as a crime if someone doesn't wear a condom and he makes you go to bed." Initiation rites for new members of the Sexy Boys gang included raping a virgin.

Busi had contracted the AIDS virus from her boyfriend, who would not wear a condom. After their baby was diagnosed HIV positive but was refused treatment at Conradie Hospital, Busi was one of a group of women who marched on parliament in early 2000 to demand treatment for AIDS patients.

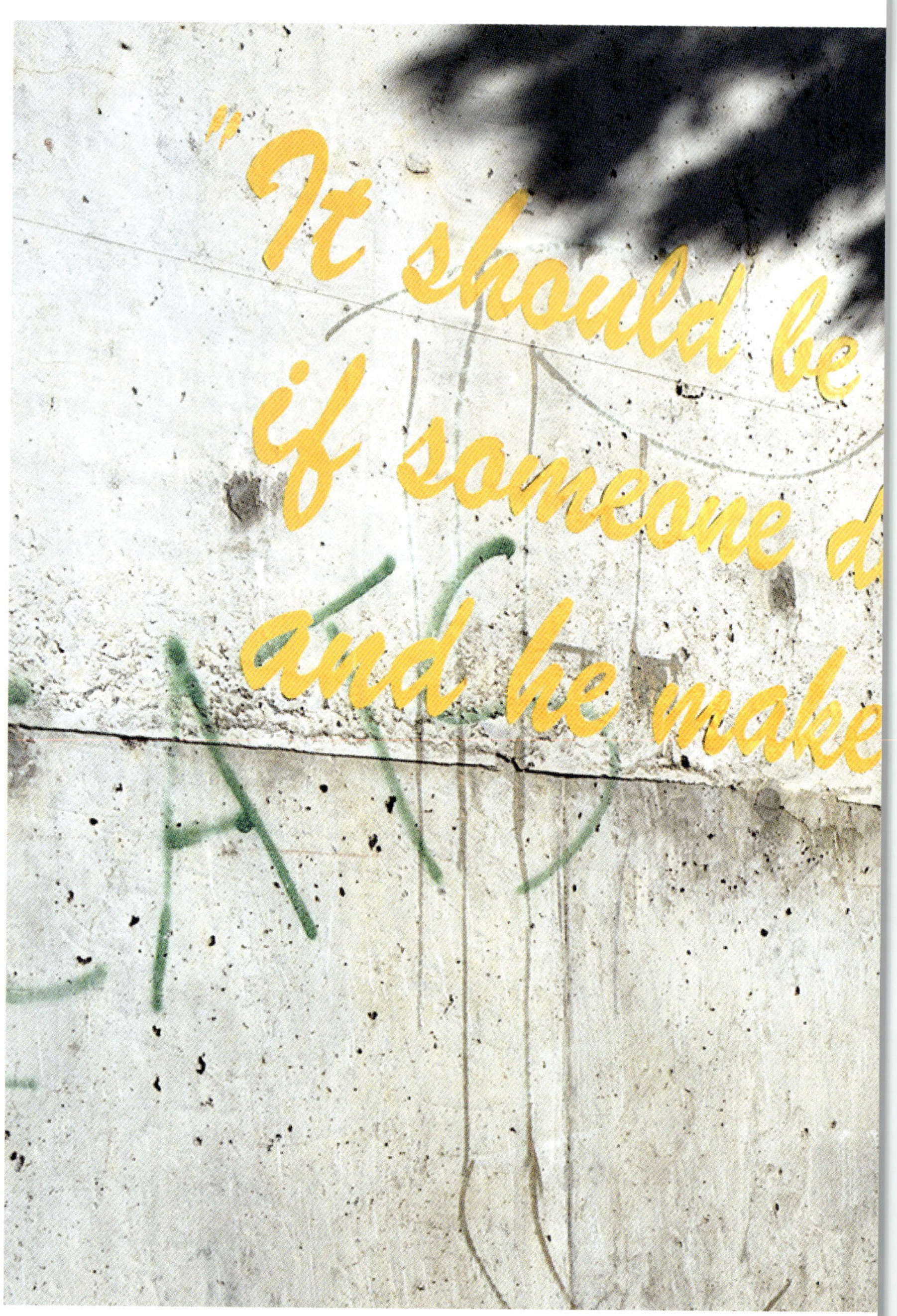

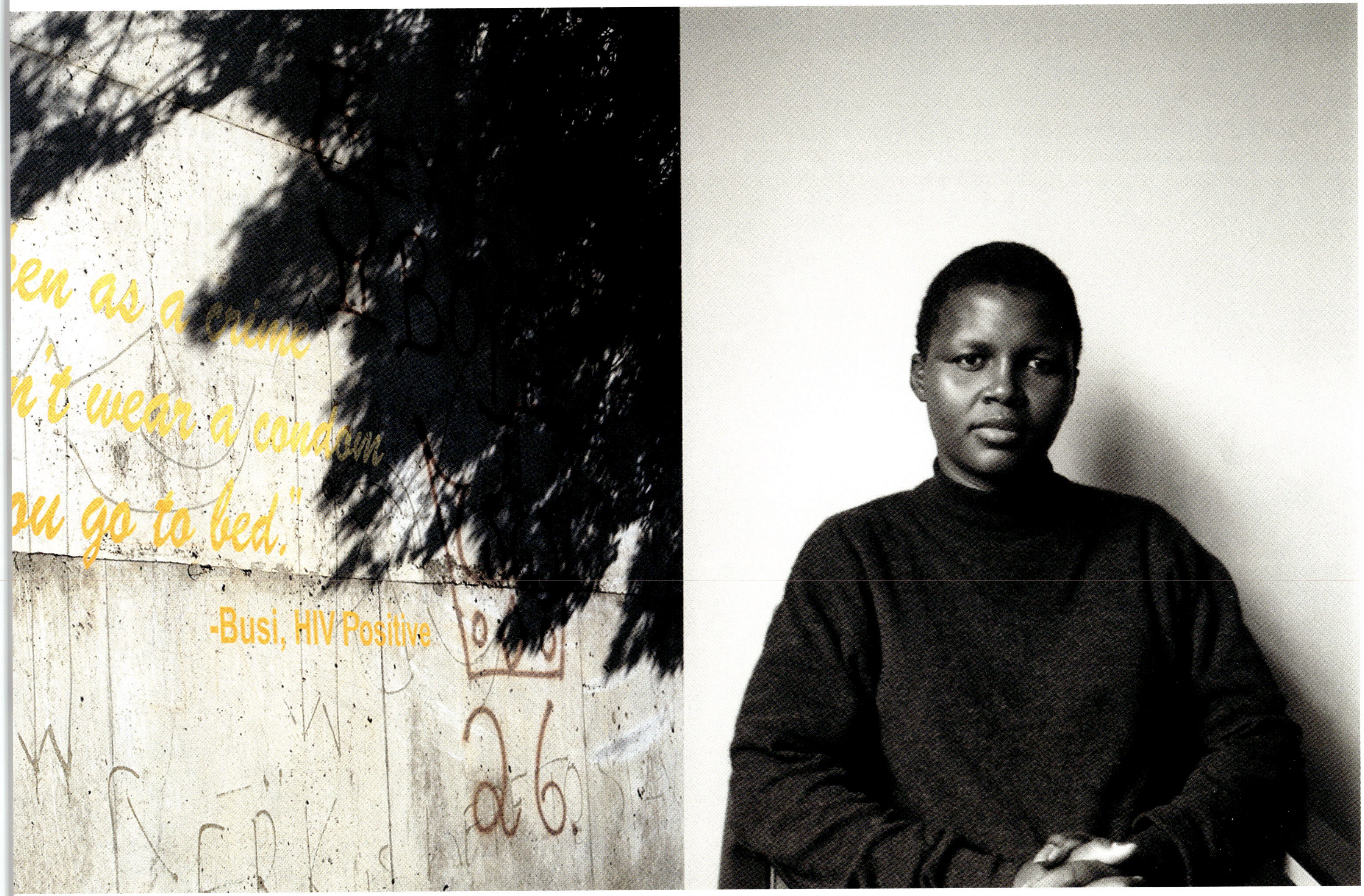


*Busi Maqungo*
2000
*From the Inside* series
Pigment inks on archival paper
90 x 200 cm

In a response to President Mbeki's AIDS-denialism, and his consequent refusal to make anti retroviral medication available, through the state, to people with AIDS, 42-year old disc jockey Benjamin Borrageiro came up with a telling statement: "I'm sick of Mbeki saying HIV doesn't cause AIDS". Williamson painted up this message above a colourful mural beneath a busy bridge near the Gardens Centre in central Cape Town.

Borrageiro died two weeks later, but the statement remained for more than two years, albeit altered by a counter-graffitist who had unsuccessfully attempted to paint out the name "Mbeki".

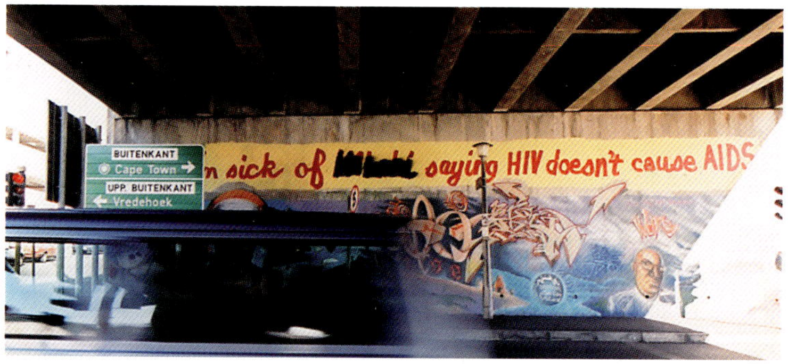


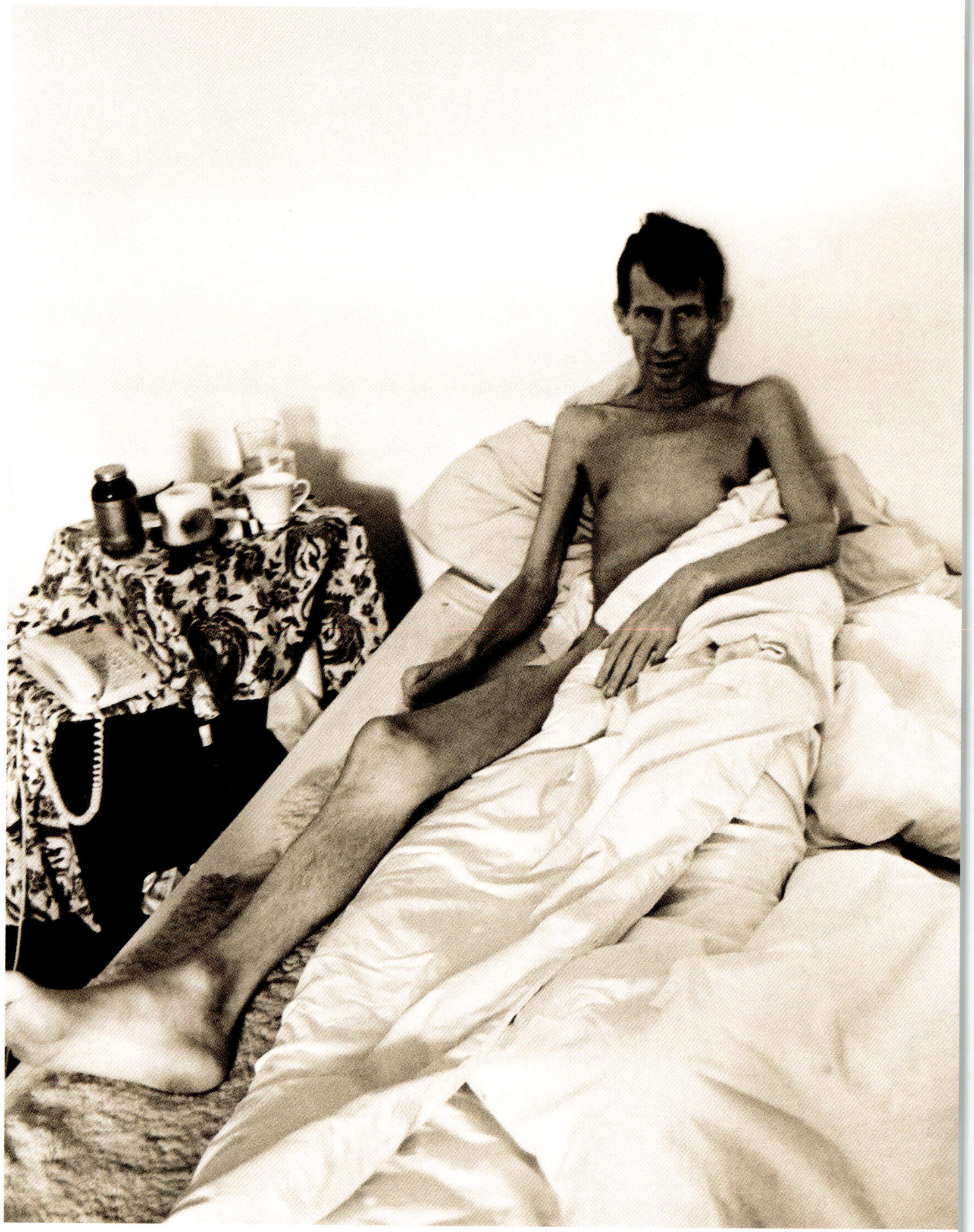

Underpass wall with Mbeki's name painted out

*Benjamin Borrageiro*
2000
*From the Inside* series
Pigment inks on archival paper
90 x 200 cm

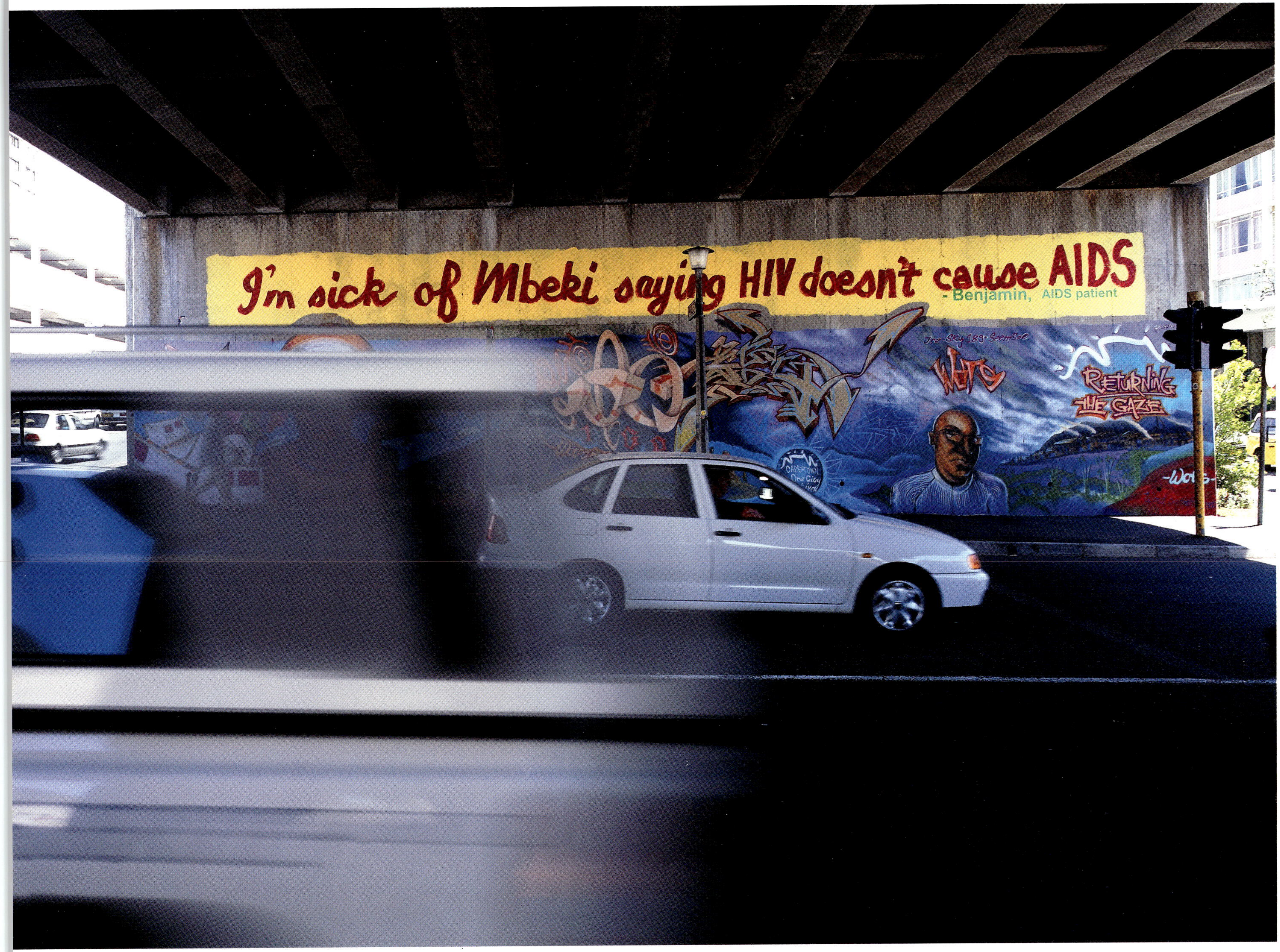
I'm sick of Mbeki saying HIV doesn't cause AIDS
- Benjamin, AIDS patient
RETURNING THE GAZE

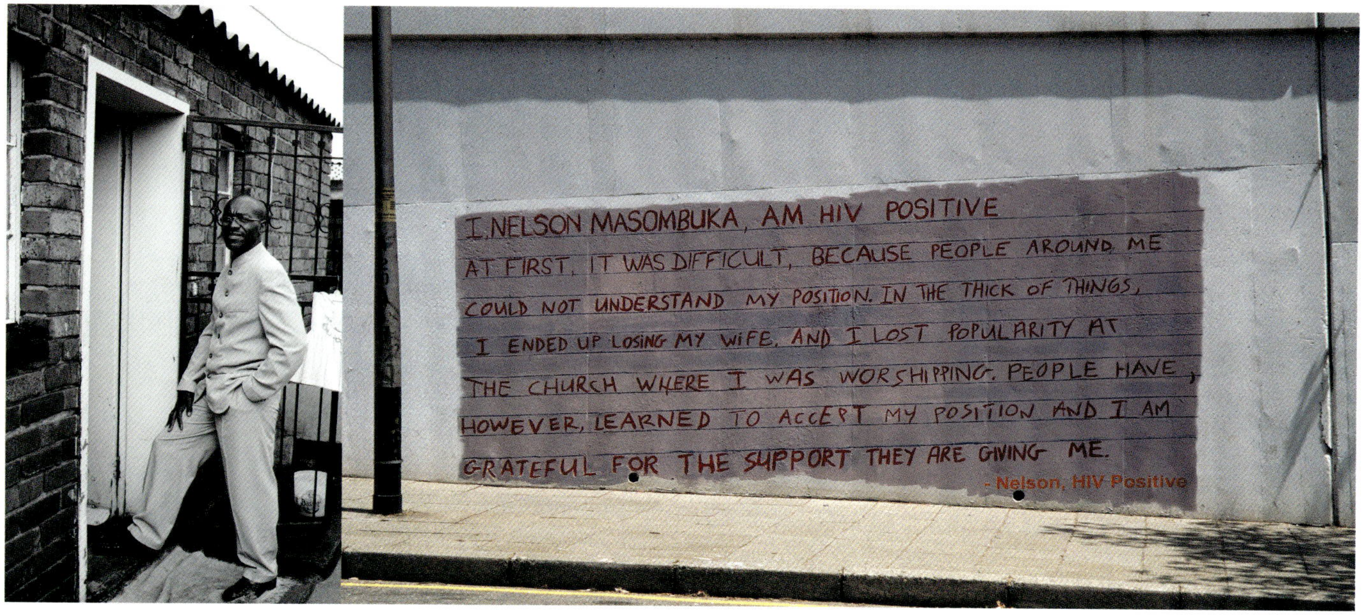


*Nelson Masombuku*
2002
*From the Inside* series
Pigment inks on archival paper
90 x 200 cm

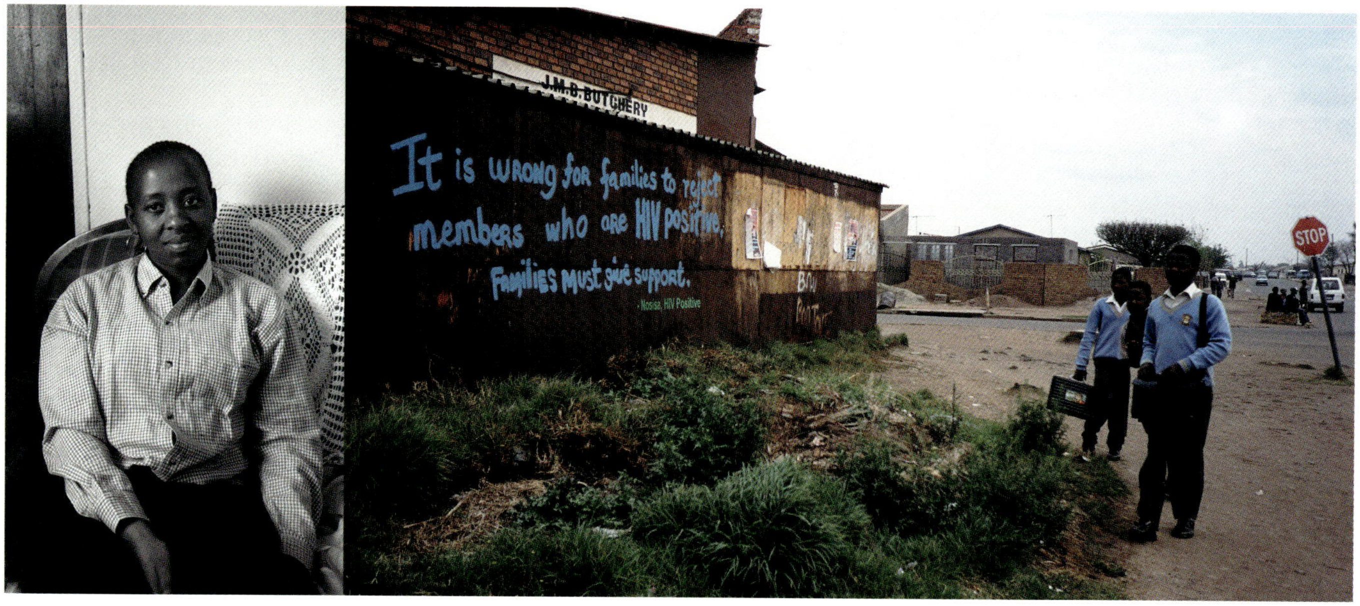


*Nosisa Ndlela*
2002
*From the Inside* series
Pigment inks on archival paper
90 x 200 cm

*John Masuku*
2002
*From the Inside* series
Pigment inks on archival paper
90 x 200 cm

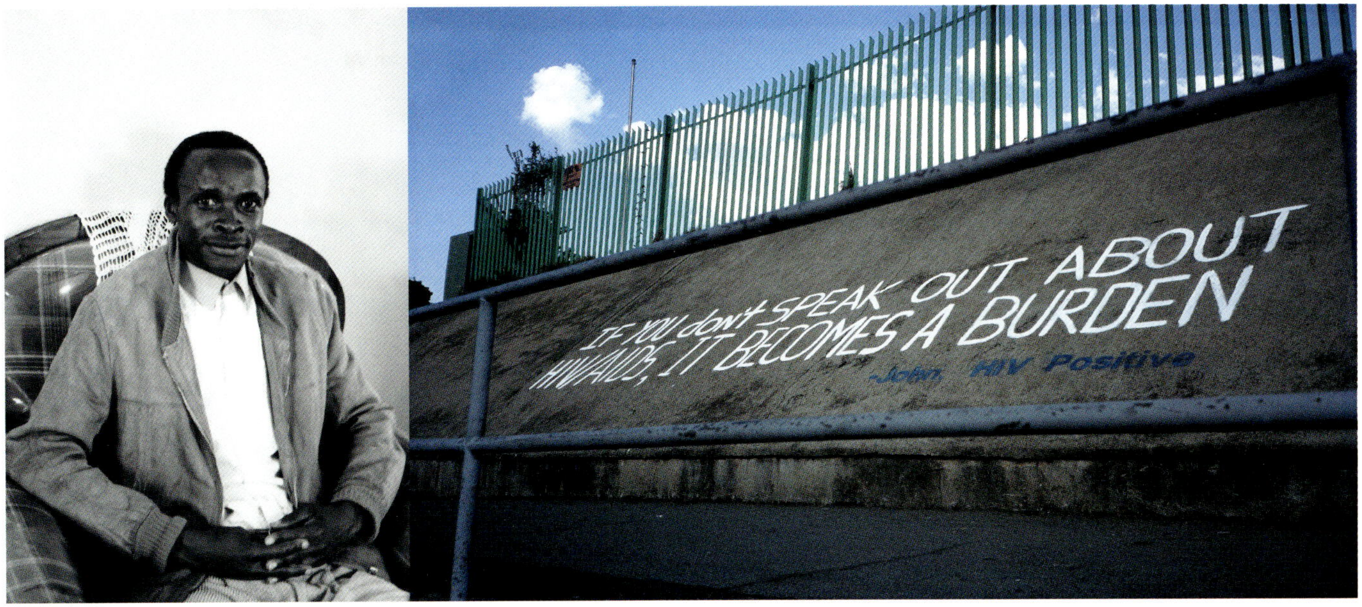


*Judy Seidman*
2002
*From the Inside* series
Pigment inks on archival paper
90 x 200 cm

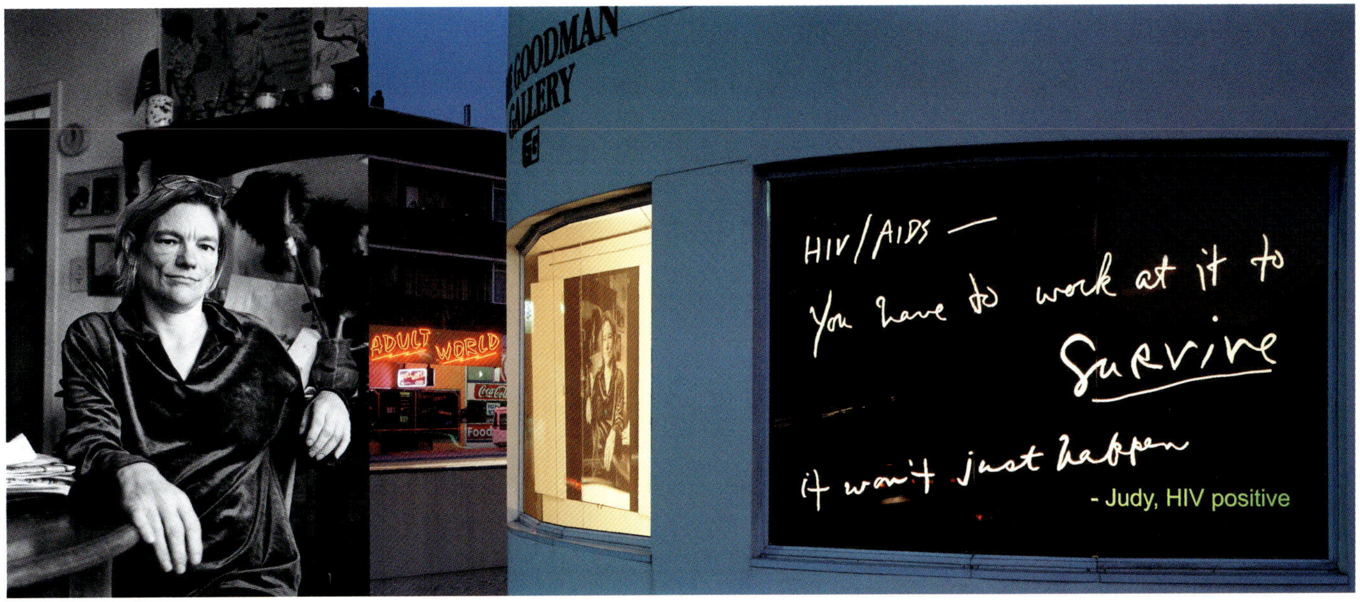

Given the global reach of the AIDS epidemic, Sue Williamson attempted to contact AIDS organisations in Cuba and Egypt, while working there, to see if the *From the Inside* project could be extended to those countries. In Havana, she was told that there was no one suffering from AIDS, and in Egypt, that she would have to approach the Minister of Health with her request. Her time in those countries was too short to bypass these stone walls, but in Berlin in 2005, she had more success.

After a discussion and a photographic session with Latin American AIDS activist Pablo Fernandes, he wrote on a Kreuzberg wall. "Being HIV positive gives me the chance for more humanity".

Although the wall had been selected for the project because it was already heavily covered in graffiti, someone reported the new activity to the police, who arrived on the scene as Pablo finished writing. Williamson was told to clean up the message by 5 p.m. that day, but pragmatically, the police neglected to ask her for any contact details. Perhaps the statement still stands, a message of hope and courage.

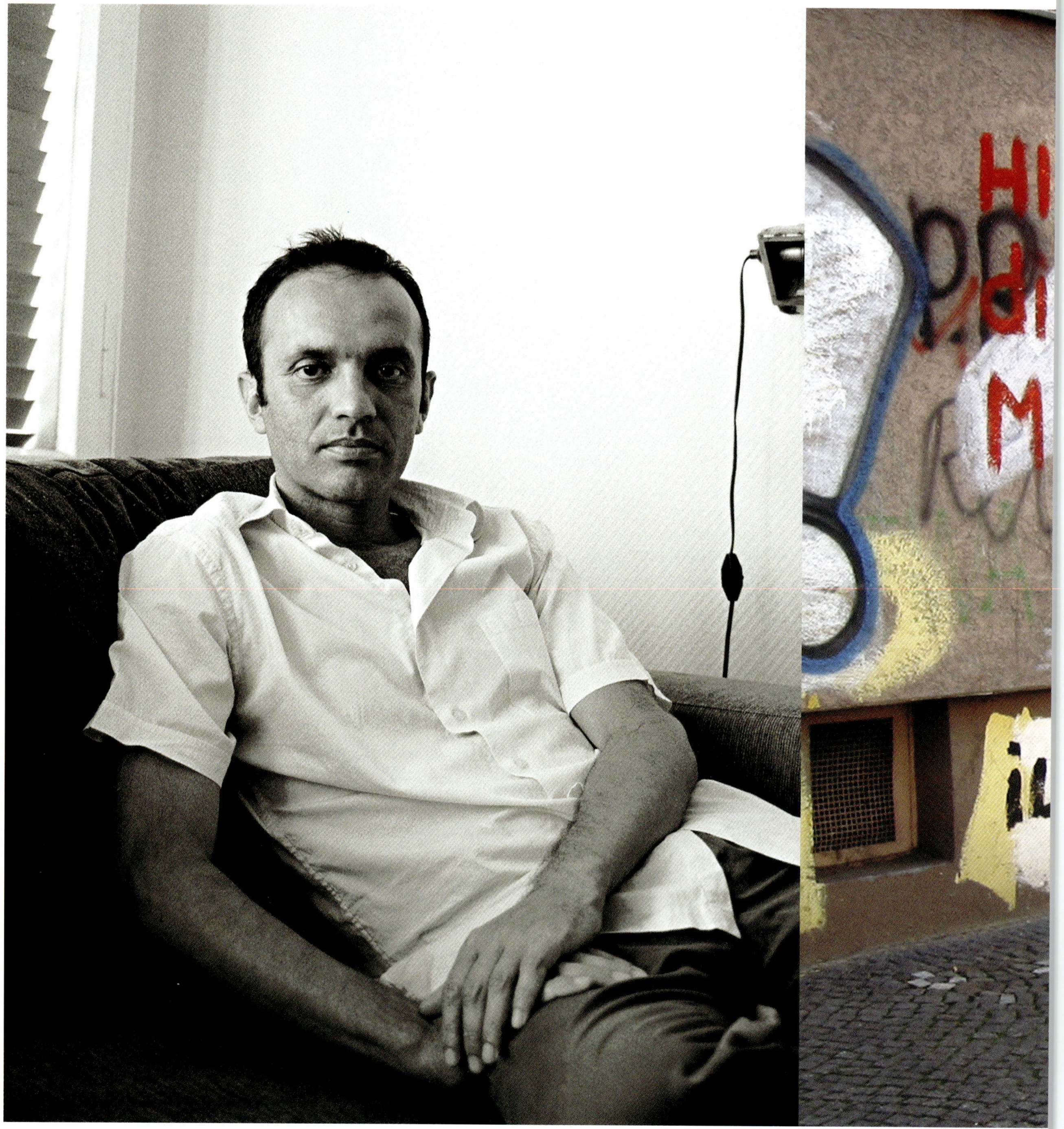

*Pablo Fernandes*
2004
*From the Inside* series
Pigment inks on archival paper
90 x 200 cm

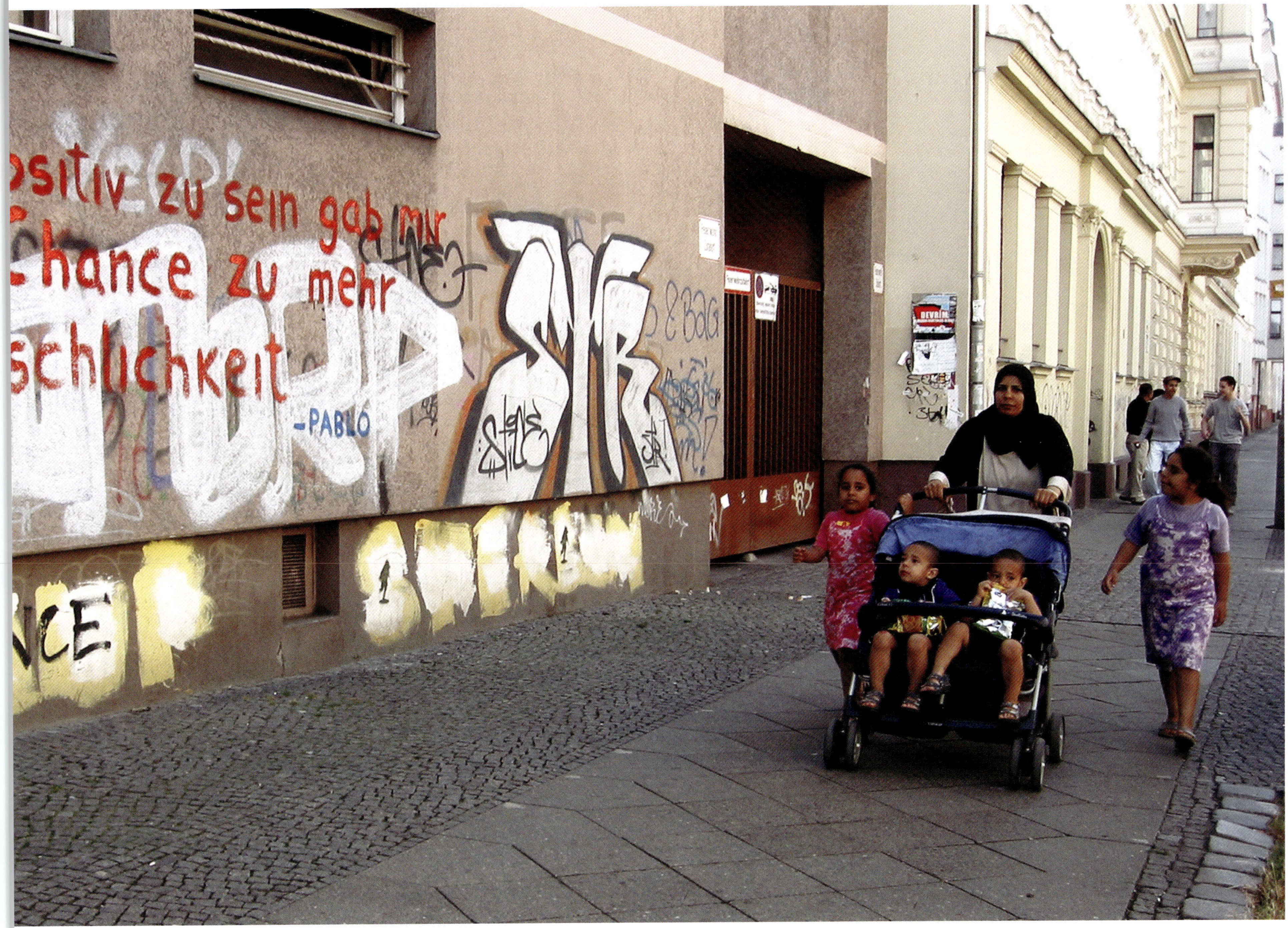
ositiv zu sein gab mir
hance zu mehr
schluchkeit
-PABLO

## Better Lives

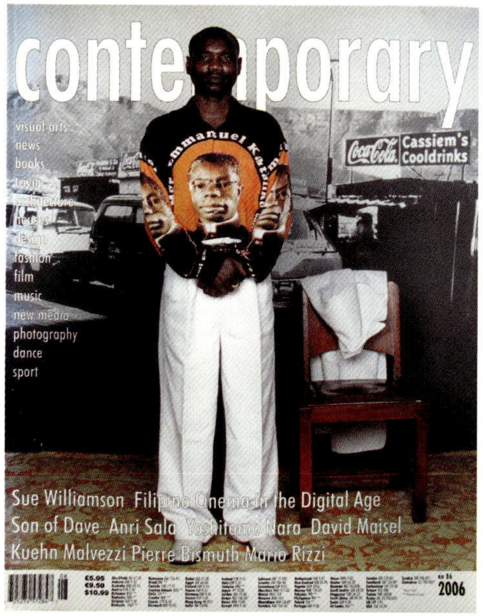


In the six videos which make up Sue Williamson's *Better Lives* series, the subjects of her portraits gaze into the camera, keeping silent as they listen to a tape of their own voices telling the story of how they came to South Africa from their home countries.

Isabelle Ngandu's stillness, for example, is broken only by the nervous tapping of her hand as she hears herself describing her four-year separation from her husband.

Albert Ngandu left the DRC for political reasons, in 1992. He fled to Johannesburg with two of their four children, then came to Cape Town, where he found a job in a bakery. His wife Isabelle joined him with the other two children four years later, and gradually they built up a business selling curios.

Behind the couple is a blowup of a black and white photograph taken by the artist from the taxi rank on the roof of Cape Town station—often the point of entry into the city for immigrants. Table Mountain looms in the background, thus identifying the city where the photo is taken.

Williamson made the series as a direct response to the xenophobia against other Africans that was beginning to take root in the country by 2003: in the post-apartheid era of heightened expectations, these new immigrants from countries all over Africa were perceived to be taking the scarce resources away from indigenous South Africans. As we hear in the six stories, their journeys to the country have been arduous, and their experiences in their new home country have been very mixed.

*Better Lives* is also an investigation into the practice of studio portraiture in the age of the moving image. Originally filmed on 35mm film stock before being transferred to video, single frames from each film have also been printed as large scale portraits and in this medium are presented as "film stills".

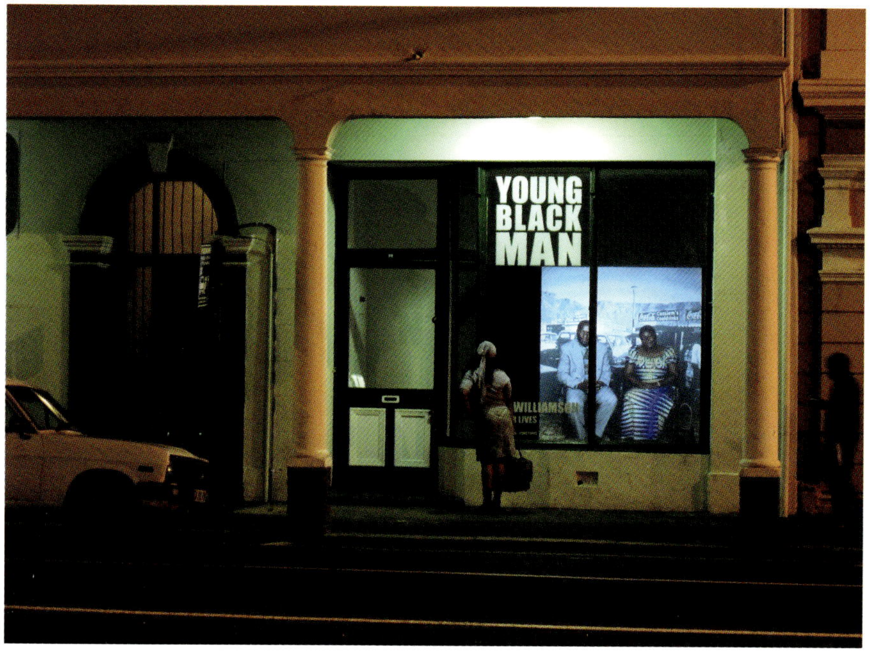


Cover of *contemporary* magazine #86, 2006

*Albert and Isabelle Ngandu*
2003
*Better Lives* series
Video projection
Installation view
Young Blackman, Cape Town

**Albert Ngandu**: Before I move from Congo to South Africa, the death was waiting for me. The leadership, which was Mobutu in power at that time, divided the people that at one stage were chased to get out of Congo.

**Isabelle Ngandu**: They push everyone, they get you out in the house. You leave everything, even the clothes…

**AN**: For four years we couldn't communicate, there was no communication between me and my family. You end up in a situation where they think you are having the good life and you don't think about them. It's like you dump them, while you are struggling the other side. So it was quite, very tough.

**IN**: Almost four years, we didn't even speak.

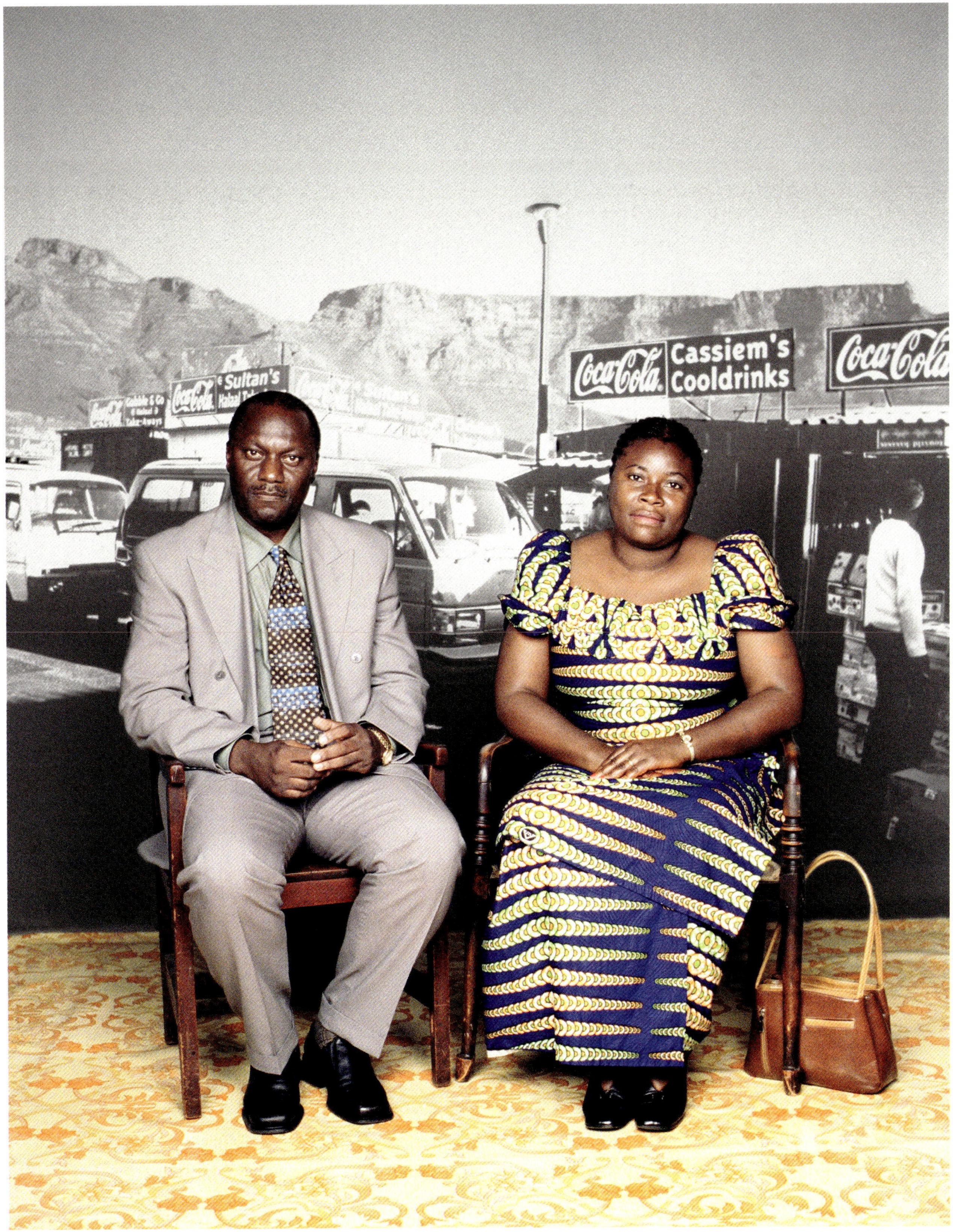


*Albert and Isabelle Ngandu*
2003
*Better Lives* series
Pigment inks on cotton rag paper
144 x 112 cm

"*Better Lives* is concerned with the post-apartheid moment. A video studio portrait project, it is one of the few collaborative projects by artists in South Africa to examine the corrosive effect of mounting xenophobia and rising racism in the country… By focusing on these marginal lives and the contingent circumstances in which migrants live, [Williamson] also illuminates the dark contours in which black subjects exist in the globalizing processes of which South Africa and her artists have become an integral part.

This work, to my mind, serves as reminder that though the post-apartheid moment has been justifiably seen as triumphant, the work of art surrounding it has been, to a surprising extent, far more ambivalent toward such an assessment. In thinking about the state of contemporary South African art today, the challenge of all critical reflection on its many evident successes is how to think historically ... about the present state of South Africa and the ambiguity of its cultural landscape toward those who live on the margins."

From Okwui Enwenzor, "'Better Lives', Marginal Selves: Framing the Current Reception of Contemporary South African Art", in *South African Art Now*, by Sue Williamson

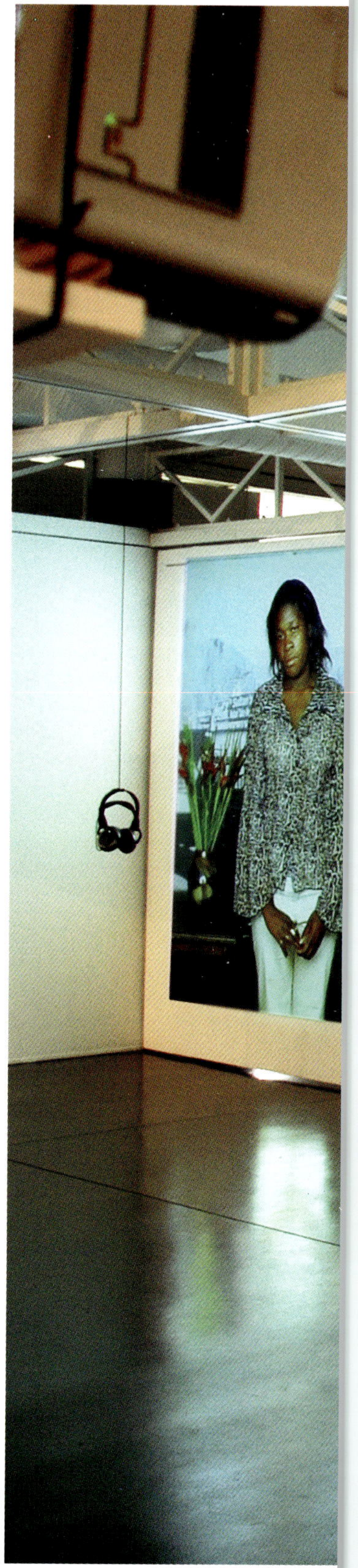

*Better Lives*
2003
Video projection
Installation view
Goodman Gallery, Johannesburg

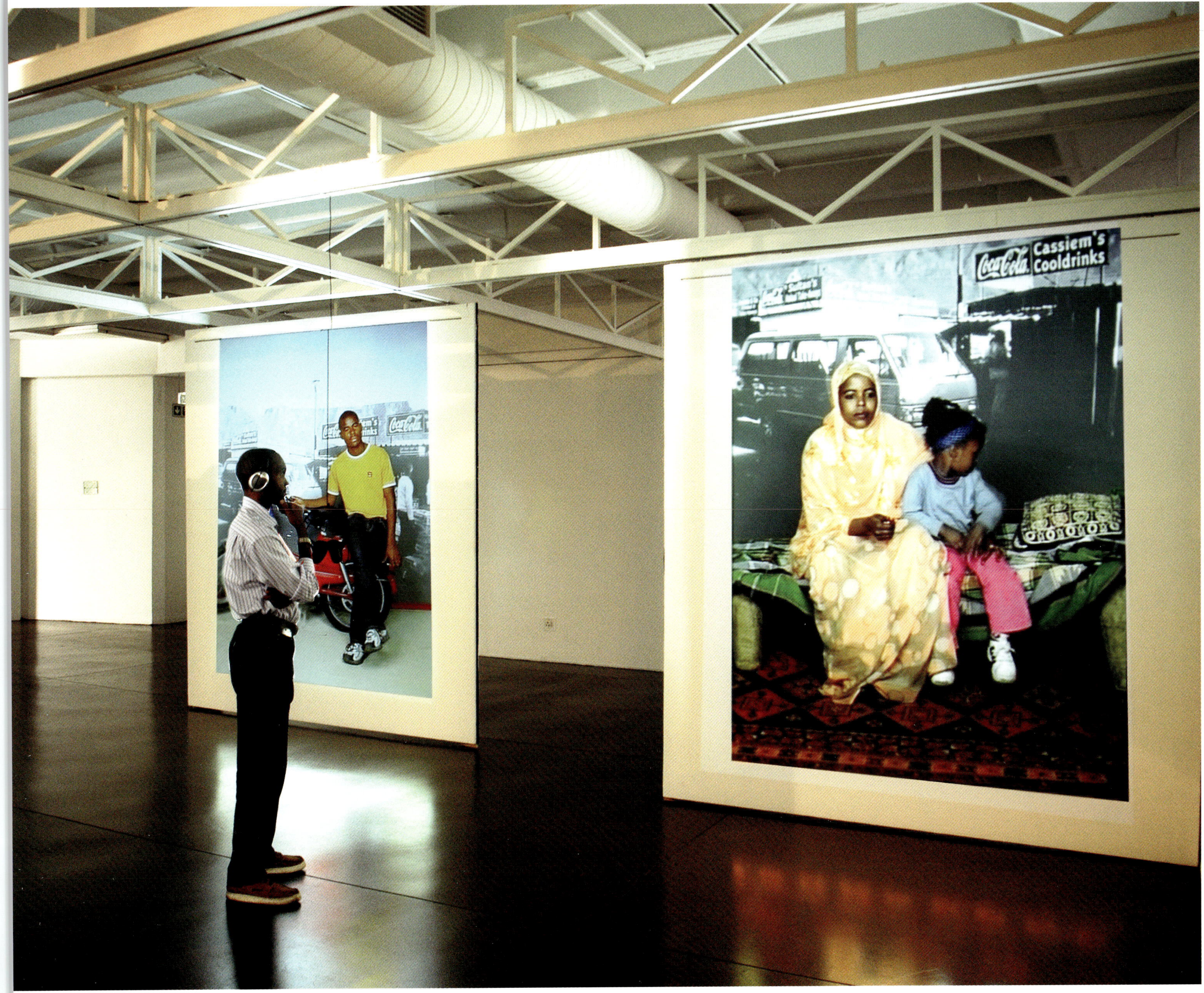
Coca-Cola
Cassiem's
Cooldrinks

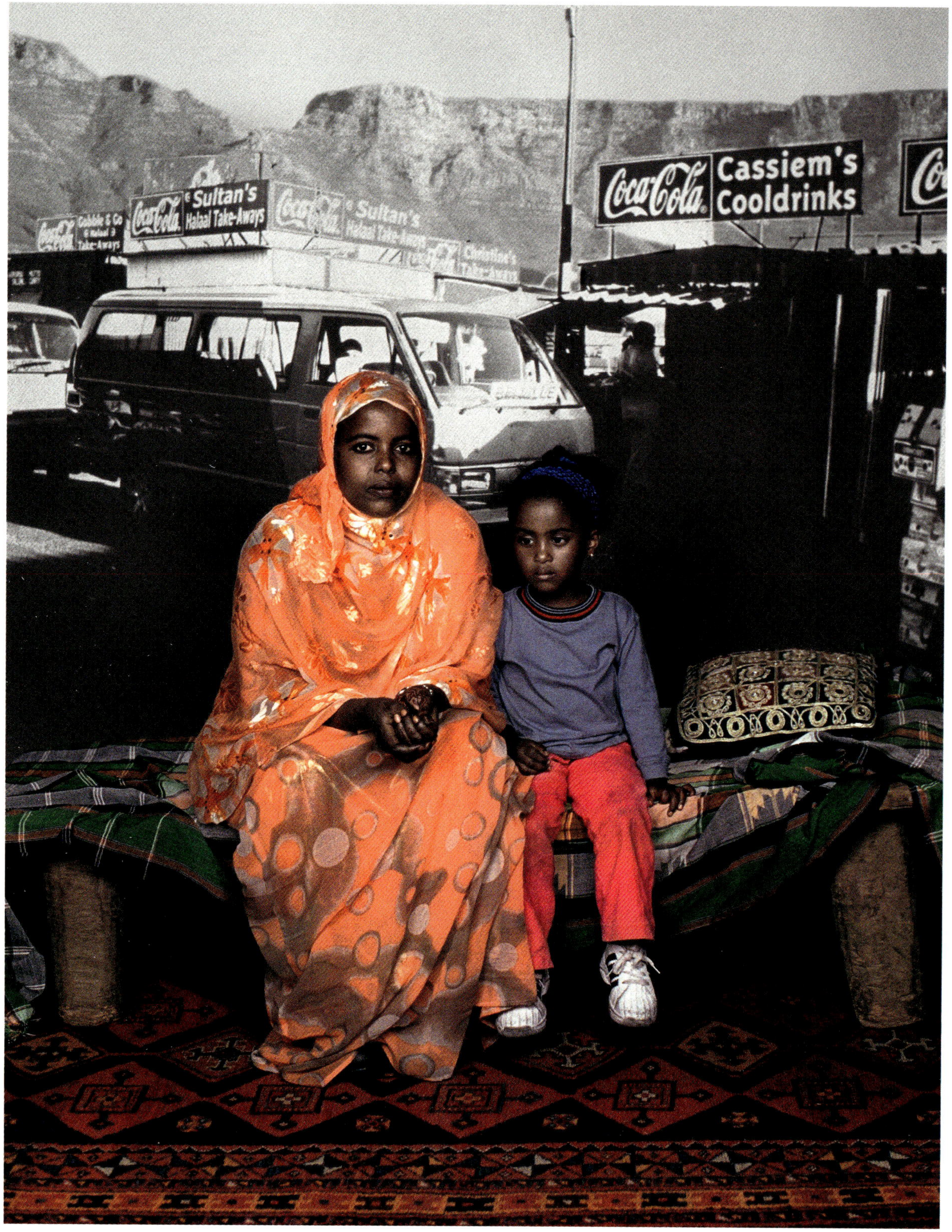


Six months pregnant, Deka Farrh was arrested on the Namibian border when she tried to slip into South Africa after she fled overland from Somalia following her father's murder. She spent six months in jail where she gave birth to her daughter, Nisa. Her mother sent her money to bribe officials and get to Cape Town. At the time she was interviewed she was running a little cigarette stand on the street, and had lost all contact with her mother.

*Deka Yusuf Farrh and Nisa*
2003
*Better Lives* series
Pigment inks on cotton rag paper
144 x 112 cm

Francois Bangurambona was a deputy minister in the Burundi's Hutu-led government, when Tutsi soldiers came in to his office in 1993. They asked for the minister, who was absent, and as they left, they threw a grenade into his office. It knocked him unconscious, but his driver was on the street below and rescued him and put him on a plane to Kenya. At the time he was interviewed, he ran a car repair business in Nyanga, outside Cape Town.

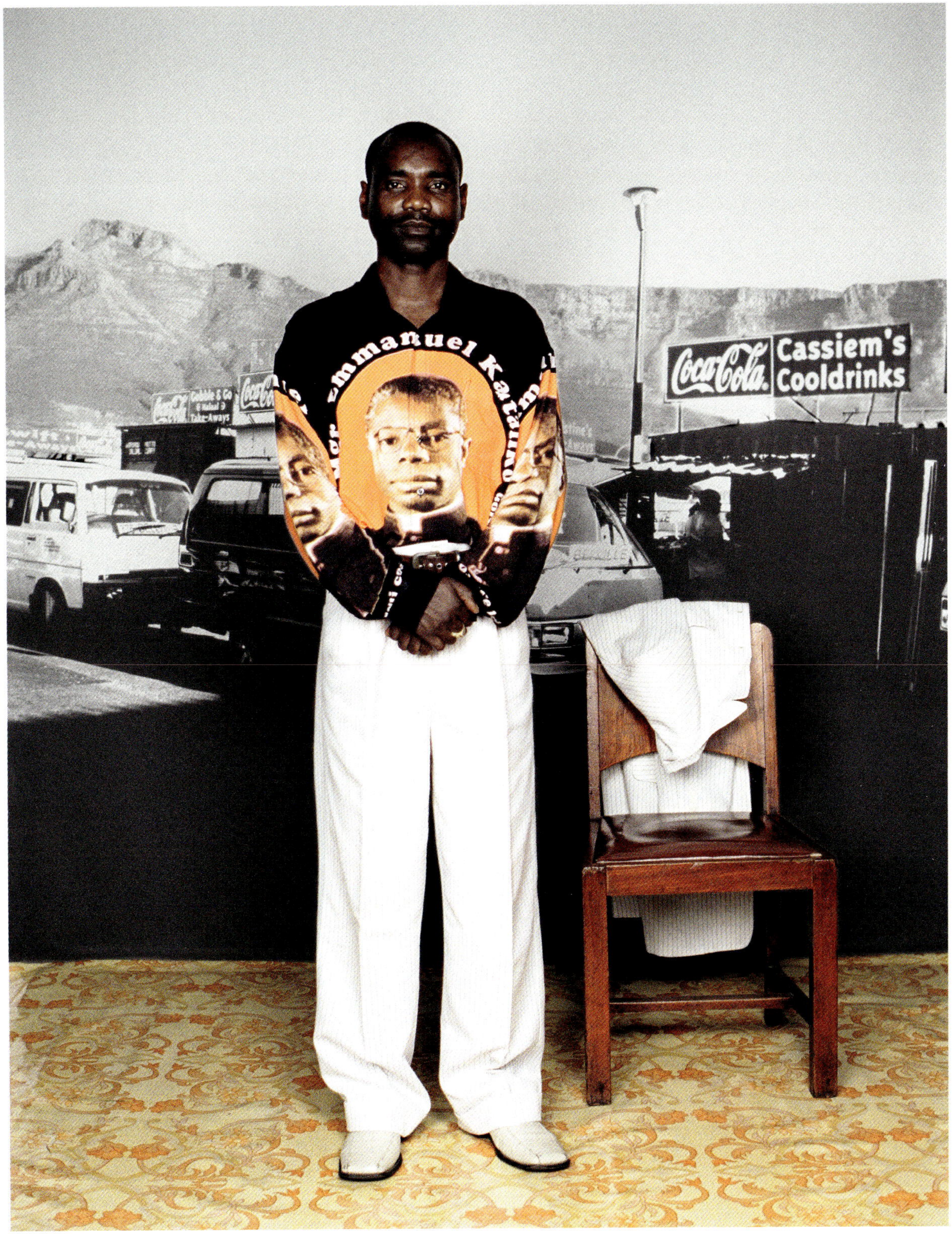


*Francois Bangurambona*
2003
*Better Lives* series
Pigment inks on cotton rag paper
144 x 112 cm

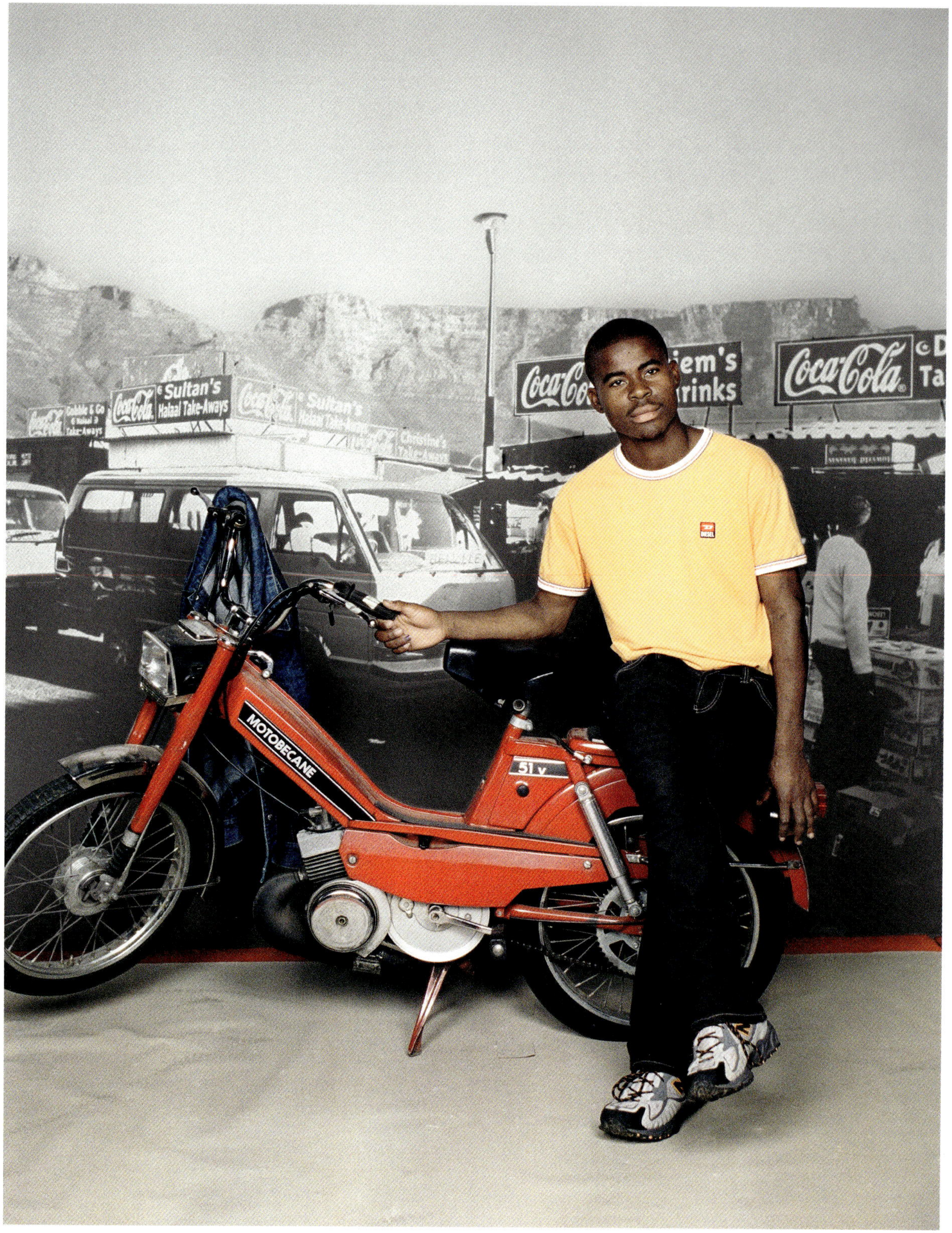


In his early twenties at the time he was interviewed, Nelson Manuel was sent from Angola by his father to avoid conscription. He was working as a car guard in Cape Town, and although he had already been threatened once by gunmen wishing to steal a car, he had no choice but to continue, as his girlfriend was pregnant and he needed to support her.

*Nelson Manuel*
2003
*Better Lives* series
Pigment inks on cotton rag paper
144 x 112 cm

Richard Belalufu is an electro-mechanical engineer. He fled a big job in Zaire, as it was then known, in 1994, when he was revealed as a double agent. At the time of his interview he worked on a construction site in Cape Town.

**Richard Belalufu**: Xenophobia, it's a serious problem here for us black foreigners in South Africa. Just the way that you are dressing, the way that you are living, your style of life… They can't understand. They're jealous. They are shouting at you, insulting you, they are calling you by the funny names… South Africa, it's a nice country. Big country. But for the black foreigners it's a calvary and not [the] road to paradise.

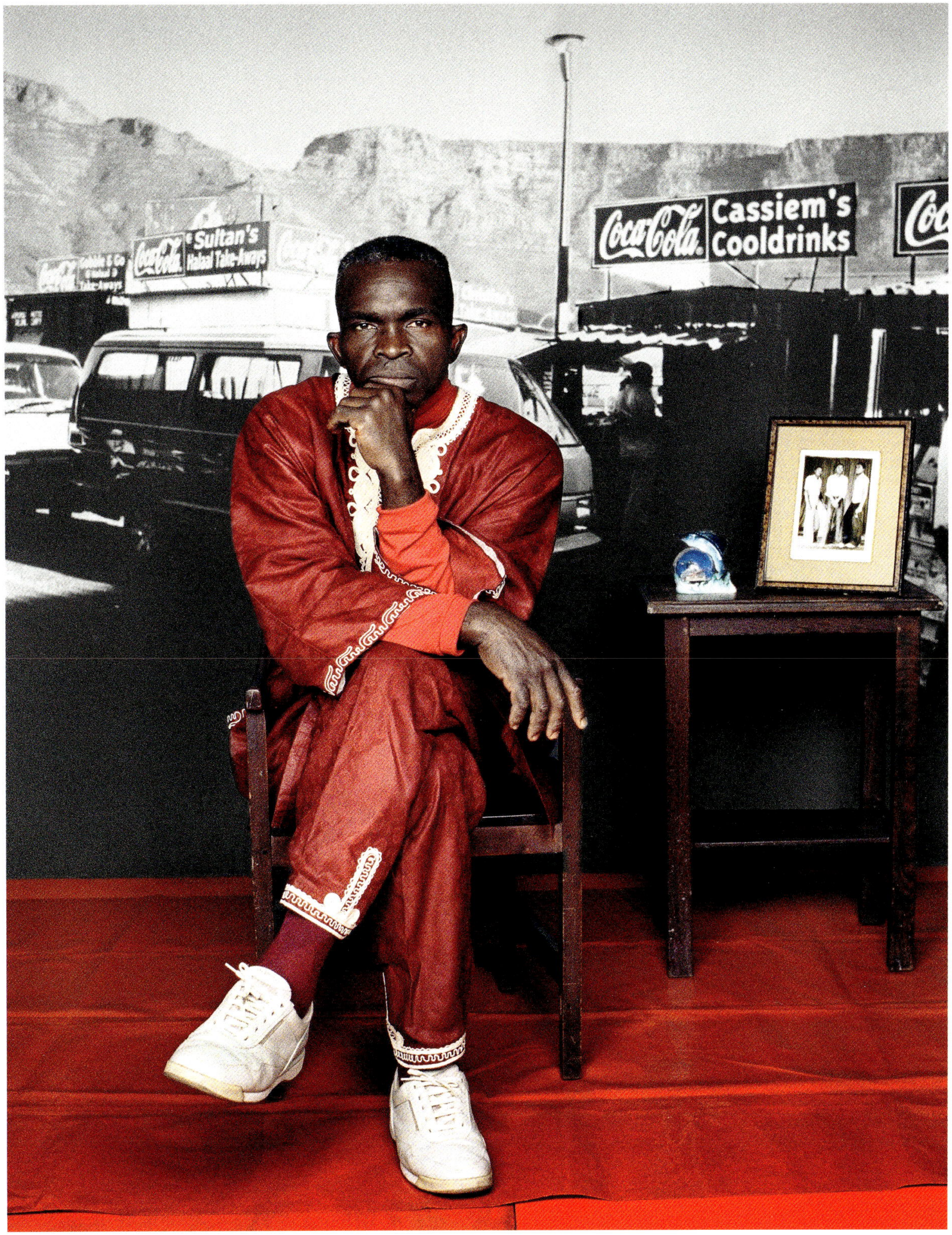


*Richard Belalufu*
2003
*Better Lives* series
Pigment inks on cotton rag paper
144 x 112 cm

# Pass the Parcel, Jacob

In *Pass the Parcel, Jacob*, Sue Williamson focuses on the 2005 rape trial of Jacob Zuma. Zuma had just been fired as deputy president (on the basis of corruption allegations), and was charged with raping a young female friend of the family, who had come to his house to ask his advice.

Williamson's project was initially in response to a commission for a site-specific work at Shibuya Station, in Tokyo, where artists were asked to make small works which would fit into lockers at the station. The rape trial was happening at the time, and Williamson left a layered parcel in the locker, to be "passed" from visitor to visitor, as in the game "Pass the parcel", until the last "player" received the "gift" at the centre.

Each layer carried a dated and attributed press cutting of the court proceedings, and each visitor could keep one layer, or one aspect of the story. The "gift" at the centre, to be "won" once all the layers of meaning had been torn off, was a small black box containing a printed kanga, the traditional cloth that women wrap around their bodies. In his evidence, Zuma had said that as the woman was wearing a kanga when she came to say goodnight to him, he assumed she wanted sex. This assumption was vociferously disputed by women protesters outside the court.

Williamson was struck by the way the Zuma rape trial became something of a lightening rod for debates around male abuse of power in South Africa, and she made the work to explore this issue.

For the second version of the work, the artist framed each layer of the parcel and hung the story as a grid. Each layer still retains the folds of having been used as wrapping-paper, and the piece of string is also included in the frame.

She was particularly affected by an open letter to Zuma, written by his former comrade Nomboniso Gasa, which forms one of the outer layers of the parcel. In the letter Gasa wrote how she watched closely for a sign of regret on Zuma's part—and pointed to the chivalrous rituals of Nguni stick fighting. Here, young men may engage in battle for hours without bloodshed, and the victor lays down his stick first, as a guide to the appropriate behaviour for a victor. "Supposing you are acquitted of the rape charge, will you have won?", Gasa asked.

Gasa continued: "Watching the unfolding court saga, my eyes remained fixed on you. My ears have been pinned to the radio and I have scanned the papers for a sign that you are aware of the power you command. I have waited, in vain, for an indication that you understand the burden of that power and you will exercise it wisely and judiciously."

Zuma was acquitted in January 2006. He would go on to be elected president of the African National Congress the following year, and would assume presidency of the country in 2009. His accuser, known to her supporters as "Kwesi" ("Star"), received asylum in The Netherlands.

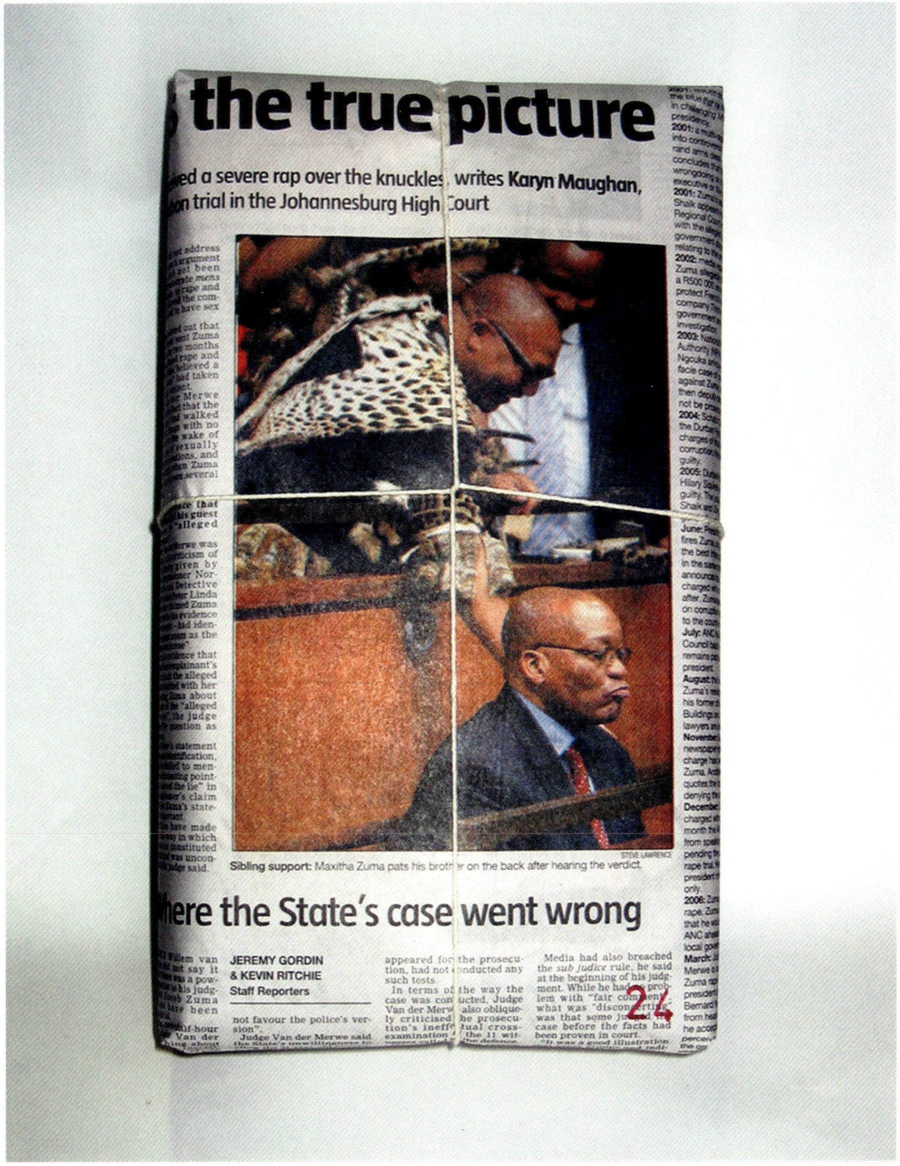


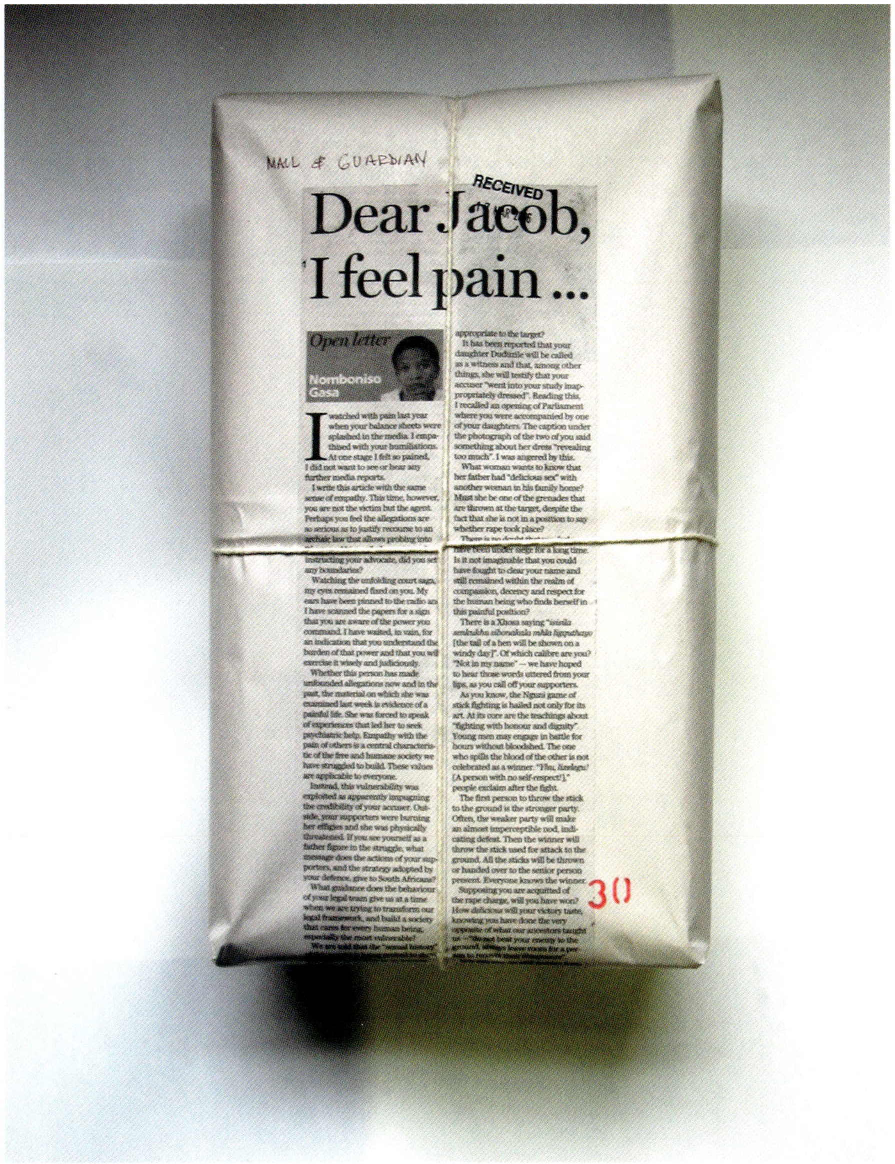


Object for "Off the Record", Shibuya Station, Tokyo
2006
Archival prints on Tyvek, string, hand stamping, found object
32.5 x 18.5 x 18 cm

Object for "Off the Record", Shibuya Station, Tokyo
2006
Archival prints on Tyvek, string, hand stamping, found object
32.5 x 18.5 x 18 cm

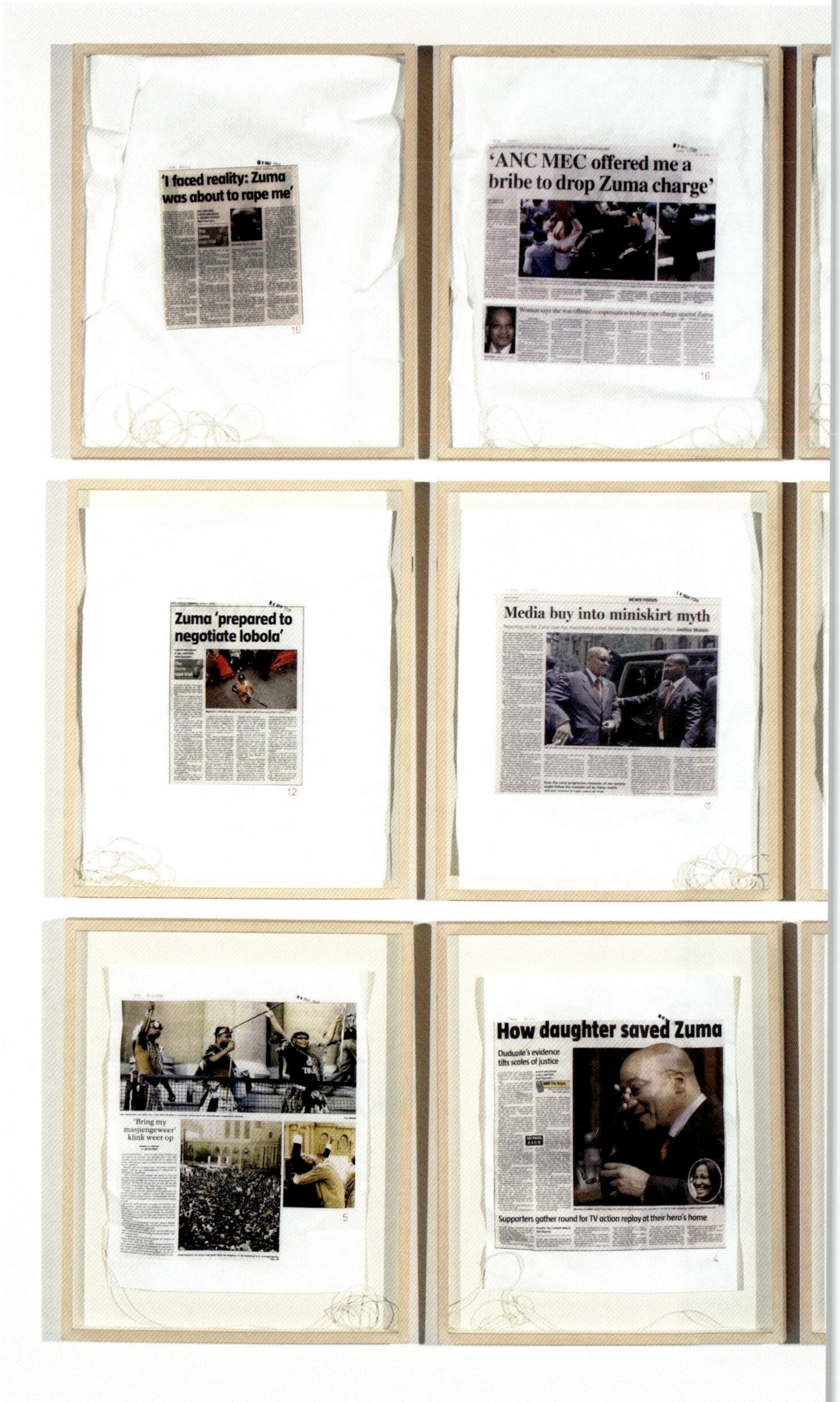


*Pass the Parcel, Jacob*
2007
Archival prints on Tyvek, string, hand stamping, found objects (installation of 21 pieces)
189.5 x 385.5 cm

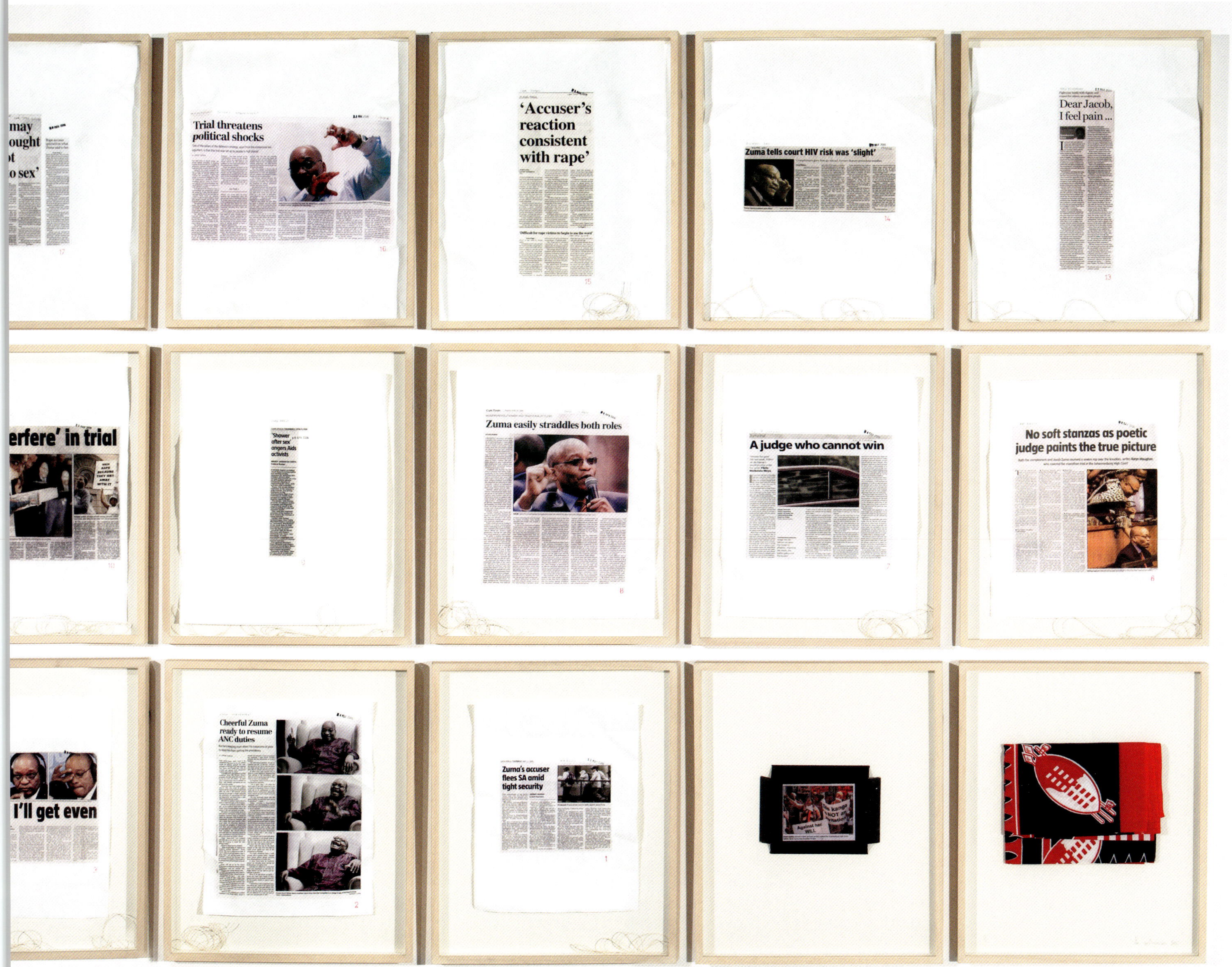
Trial threatens political shocks
'Accuser's reaction consistent with rape'
Zuma tells court HIV risk was 'slight'
Dear Jacob, I feel pain ...
'Shower after sex' angers Aids activists
Zuma easily straddles both roles
A judge who cannot win
No soft stanzas as poetic judge paints the true picture
I'll get even
Cheerful Zuma ready to resume ANC duties
Zuma's accuser flees SA amid tight security

# Outwards

W*A*S*H
What About El Max?
The Havana Series
Other Voices, Other Cities

*Starting in the 1960s, a cultural boycott was imposed on South Africa, in an attempt to force an end to apartheid. Many filmmakers, writers, musicians and artists refused to have their work presented in the country, and South African visual artists were banned from participating in international events like the Venice Biennale. Artists involved in the anti-apartheid movement accepted these restrictions as necessary. Once the country embarked on its passage to democracy in the early 1990s, the boycott was lifted. South African art experienced something of a "big moment" when the 1st and 2nd Johannesburg Biennales—the latter directed by Okwui Enwezor—brought the international art world to these events in the newly liberated country. For local artists such as Sue Williamson, the creative challenge was not only in working inside a radically changing country, but also in beginning to work and exhibit abroad, applying the methodologies which had been forged during the "resistance art" era back home.*

**Mark Gevisser**: Sue, how did you come to work outside of South Africa?
**Sue Williamson**: I was fortunate enough to be one of the first South African artists invited onto an international biennial after the release of Mandela: pp. 81-7 to Havana, in 1991. I sent *For Thirty Years Next to his Heart* (1990), but I wasn't able to go to Cuba myself. Then Anthony Bond, the director of the 1992 Sydney Biennale selected the same work for his Biennale, and this time, I did go. It was a transforming moment for me. I was impressed by the way the participating artists were treated: the respect given the work, the talks programme, the parties—but the real eye-opener was the large scale on which artists worked, and the freedom of the materials they used. I found it very empowering. It broadened my own approach. Many of my subsequent ideas were a result of this new boldness, particularly for installations like *Mementoes of District Six* and *Messages from the Moat*. pp. 63-5 pp. 105, 107-9 And it also made me eager to see more of the world, and to work in new places.

**MG**: And, perhaps, to use your art-making as a pretext for getting to know those new places better, just as through making your *A Few South Africans* pp. 10, 31-9 (1983–7) series you got to understand South Africa and the South African struggle better?
**SW**: Indeed. I wanted to work on a new project—rather than just exhibiting work I had already made—in other parts of Africa. And so when, out of the blue, an invitation came to me to work in Egypt, it was very exciting. A group of around 20 artists from around the world were to spend some weeks working with a fishing community in Alexandria who were in danger of losing their homes. The artists could do whatever seemed appropriate.

**MG**: Your work in Alexandria refers to the ideas about writing on walls that you'd first encountered at Naz Gool-Ebrahim's house in Manley Villa, District Six…
**SW**: Yes. The power of a message in a public place

which can be read by everyone who passes, is undeniable. And in this case, it seemed like a good solution to work with the householders to paint statements on their walls. But it was also about me trying to learn Arabic, communicate better. When I went to El Max, the fishing community, all the writing I saw on the streets was in Arabic. No English. And most people didn't speak much English either, so I worked with students from the University of Cairo who acted as interpreters to interview householders and help me learn about why they didn't want to move, and what they wanted to tell the world. In English and in Arabic.

**MG**: What *did* they want to tell the world?
**SW**: I particularly liked "Tell your people this place is perfect". It was a challenge to whoever read it to look past the modesty of the small dwelling and recognize it as someone's loved home.

**MG**: Like your AIDS work then: taking something "from the inside" and putting it on the outside. It also reflects your consistent understanding of yourself as a documentarian—as a medium or a recorder. That's what you've done with much of your work: you sit quietly with someone, with a recorder or your camera or your pencils, and then you take a message that they've given you and you put it on the outside of their homes for the world to see.
**SW**: Or in a video, or in a photograph…

**MG**: And through statements. Later on, when you went to Havana again for the third time, how did you come upon the idea of using cut-out letters to spell out the words?
**SW**: I was one of five artists invited to have an individual exhibition at the 2009 Havana Biennale, and in addition to showing existing work, the proposal was that I would do a special project for the Biennale. The theme that year was "Integration and Resistance in the Age of Globalisation" and the suggestion of the curators was that I should interview the fishermen of Cojimar, just outside Havana, as I had done in El Max.

But it was the 50th anniversary of the Cuban revolution and I proposed to the curators I make a work to be entitled *50 Letters to the Revolution* for which I would ask a wide range of Cubans what the revolution had meant for their families, good or bad. I imagined a grid of sheets of paper with short handwritten statements on them, not necessarily signed. Not surprisingly, this proposal was rejected by the curators as being potentially "embarrassing".

So I moved into Cojimar for a month planning to start making contacts and ask my questions and see what happened. One man said, "Before the revolution, we were treated like dogs. A man and a dog were the same." A clear statement. I decided to use letters cut out of cardboard and put them up in public spaces so the speakers would not be identified. And the letters would be ephemeral and come down at the end of the Biennale period.

I had been given three beautiful interleading rooms in the Wifredo Lam Centre in old Havana as an exhibition space, and before the Biennale opened, I used that as a studio. I had two assistants to help me cut out letters and paint them.

But generally, the Cojimar people were not very communicative. One night, a Cuban artist friend, who lived in the village, said I had to understand that it was not only that Cuba was deeply affected by the American blockade, but also that the blockade had affected the way people think, that it was embedded in the mind.

This statement made so much sense to me that I decided to make it the main text of the project, and to put the letters up in English and in Spanish on a derelict hotel, in the centre of Cojimar as a public art statement for the period of the Biennale.

Although the curators seemed to agree to this, for many reasons, this did not take place as I visualized it. In the end, one version of this was people—friends, the taxi driver, Biennale staff—standing in a banana plantation holding up the words one by one—EL
pp. 194-5 BLOQUEO ESTA TAMBIEN EN LA MENTE (2009).

**MG**: And that was the beginning of your *Other Voices, Other Cities* series.

**SW**: Yes. I came home and put together the skinny strip of photographs of people in the banana plantation spelling out the statement. I liked the way it looked. The sun was going in and out from photo to photo, so there was a sense of time passing. And it reminded me of the way we would hold up protest banners in South Africa. Except here, the same people would reappear from photo to photo, like a cast of characters. And it was a little absurd. But it also captured the zeitgeist of Havana.

So what was the zeitgeist of other cities? I became interested in thinking about that. What would New Yorkers say? Berliners? Johannesburgers? I wanted to find out.

## *W*A*S*H*

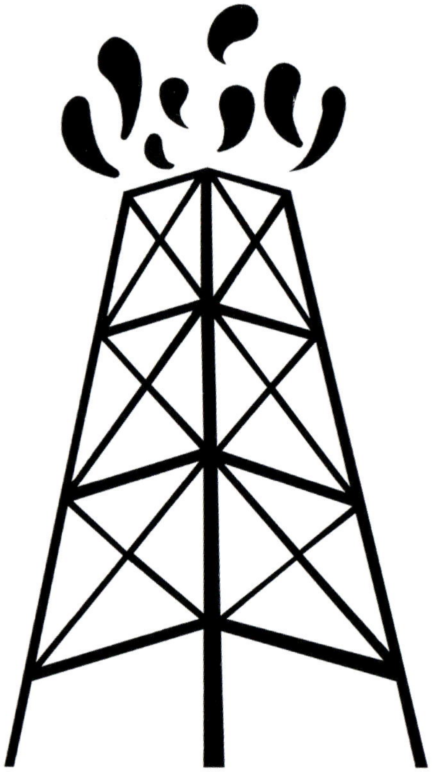

Sue Williamson went to Washington DC for two months in 2007, on a Visual Arts Research Award from the Smithsonian Institution's National Museum of African Art. She became engrossed in the museum's unique photographic collections from the African colonies, but was even more interested in what she saw on the streets. Under President George Bush, Washington seemed on full military alert. Posters glorifying the armed forces or warning against terrorism were in every bunker-like subway station, where public announcements constantly reminded commuters, "if you see something, say something".

Williamson was struck by the way the constant threat of terrorism was used to justify the continuation of the war in Iraq. She could not but recall her experiences in South Africa, a country where *swart gevaar* ("black terror") was used by the apartheid government to keep whites in a state of fear.

This led her to make the satirical short film, *W*A*S*H* (a play on the title of the Robert Altman movie about the war in Korea, *M*A*S*H*), in which three oil rigs, allegedly escaped from Iraq, have found their way to Washington. The artist was commenting on the revelations that billions of dollars in Iraqi oil had gone missing during the war, and on the allegations that the "War on Terror" was a fig leaf for the U.S.'s designs on Iraq's oil resources.

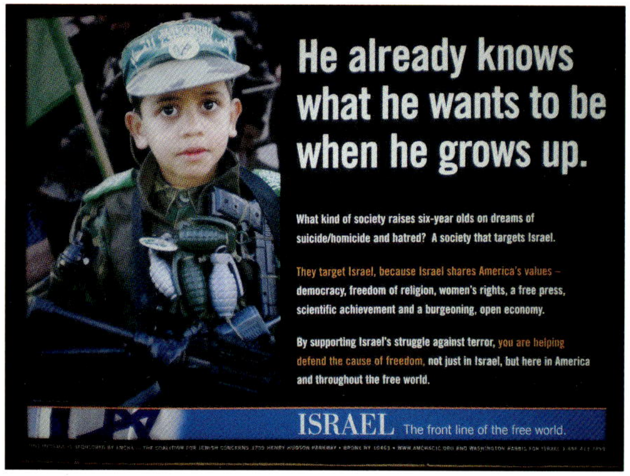


Williamson made three costumes depicting oil rigs and filmed her actors as they inserted themselves into Washington's daily life. The rigs are spotted everywhere: being buzzed by a helicopter at the Lincoln Memorial, mingling with incredulous bikers at the Vietnam War Memorial, waiting on subway stations, visiting museums, riding a merry-go-round, hanging out at an armed forces display of military materials where a little girl has been left alone to play with a machine gun. In voice-over, a radio announcer warns the citizens of Washington of the presence of the oil rigs and of the impending danger.

In the final scene, one rig is seen wandering, ghost-like, amongst the graves during a military funeral at the Arlington National Cemetery.

A clipart image of an oil rig

A poster in a Washington subway station

*W*A*S*H*, 2007
Single channel video
Playing time: 20 mins
Video stills

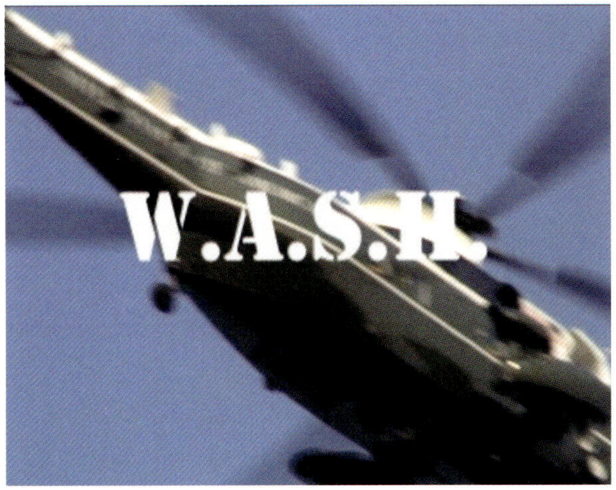
W.A.S.H.
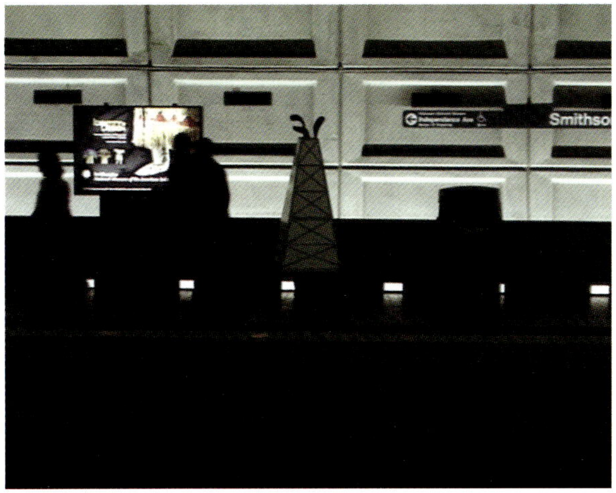
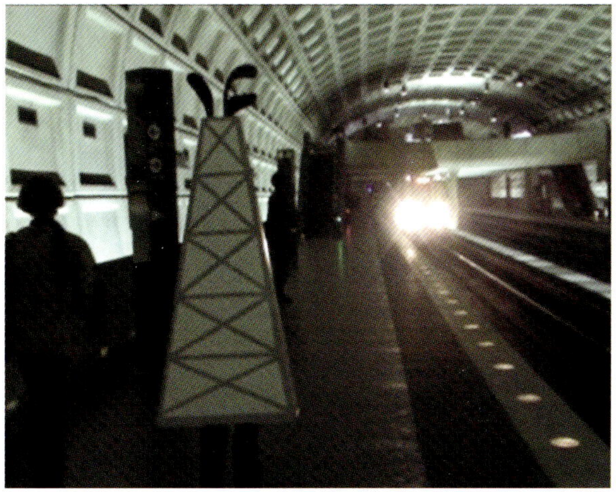
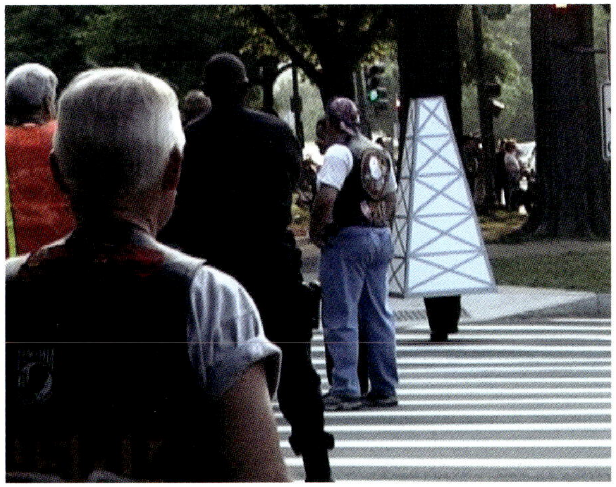
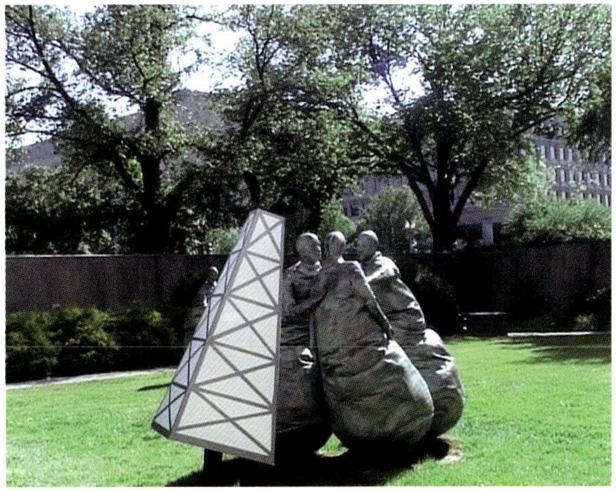
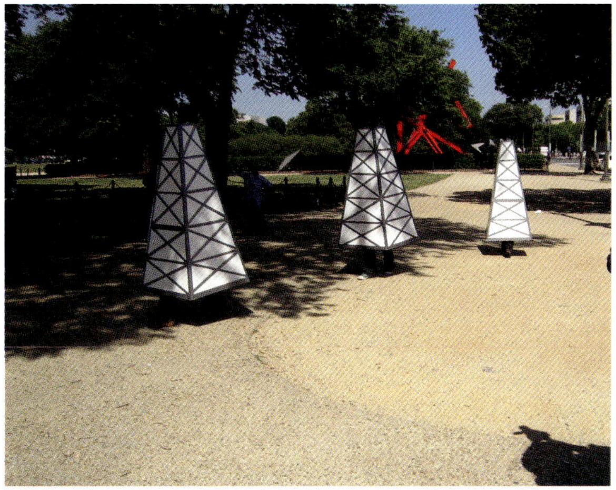
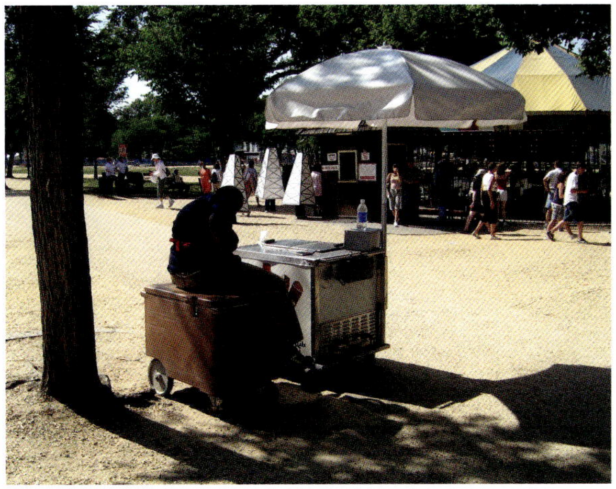
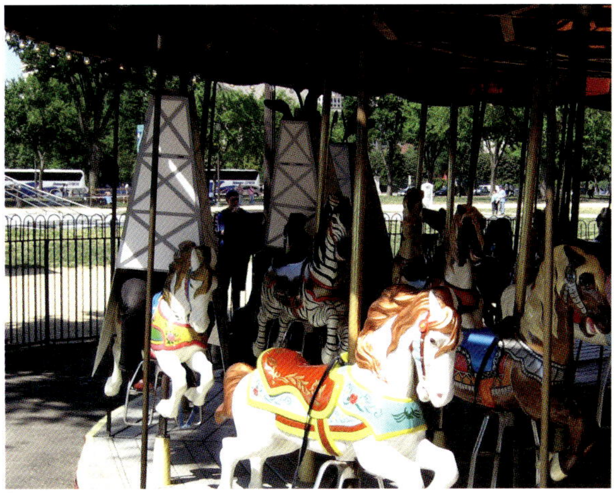
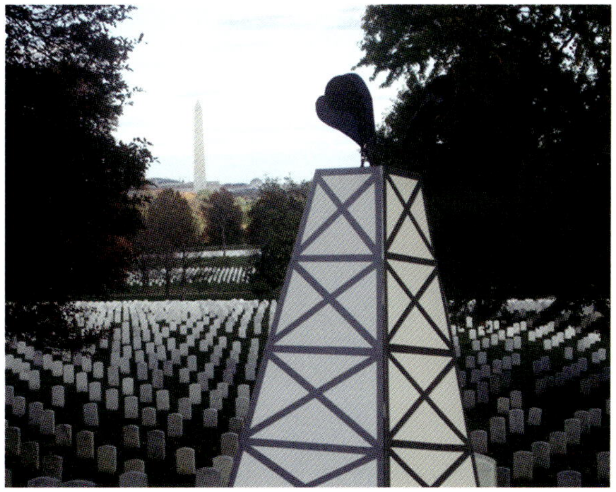

# What About El Max?

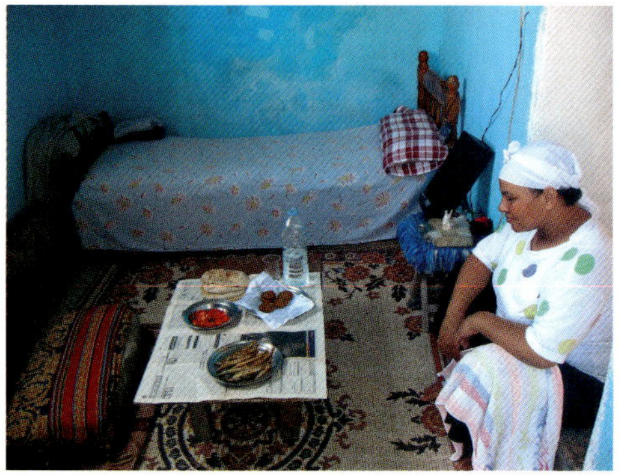

*Oza's Room*, 2002–3
*What About El Max?* series
Pigment inks on Hahnemühle paper
Image size: 38.5 x 52 cm

In 2004, Sue Williamson received an invitation to Egypt to work with a group of other artists in El Max, a fishing community in Alexandria set along a canal that runs into the sea. Each family had a boat and fished for the daily table and the market, but their livelihood was being threatened by the pollution of an upstream petrochemical company that wanted them removed, and the military, who sometimes closed the entrance of the canal to the sea for naval exercises.

The overall title of the project was *Boustashy 2004*, and each artist was invited to make their own work, helped by volunteers from Gudrun, the local art centre. Williamson started meeting residents and talking to them, and found that the first question the locals asked her was almost always, "What about El Max?", meaning, "How do you like El Max?"

The artist turned the question round, saying, "I am the stranger here. You tell me what *you* think about El Max. Wouldn't it be better to move where life is easier?" This suggestion provoked denials, and in conversations over mint tea and hibiscus juice, people expressed their love for their community. Williamson suggested the outside world would know how they felt if their statements were painted on the walls of their houses .

This was a development of the approach she had
pp. 155-165 taken in *From The Inside*, her work on AIDS, where she worked with people with HIV to develop a message which was then painted on a public wall. It also had its roots in the notion of "writing on the walls", which Williamson had encountered documenting graffiti art in South Africa in the
p. 75 1980s—and in Manley Villa in District Six.

At first, the El Max people were nervous about this idea. Other artists' projects had been halted by the police or the Muslim Judicial Council for one reason or other. But after the first message went up, requests from other residents followed, and their statements was painted on the outside wall, in English and romanised Arabic by Williamson, and in Arabic by a helper.

One householder, a woman named Oza, came up with the statement, "Everything fits to our daily needs". Williamson recalls that while she was painting these words up on the wall outside, "Oza had prepared a classic lunch which perfectly expressed the sentiment of her words: grilled fish, pita bread, falafel, tomatoes and water."

The signs were still there, several years later, and one could be viewed by cars on the main highway into Alexandria: "We are like fish. We cannot live away p. 186
from the sea".

*Everything fits to our daily needs I*, 2002–3
*What About El Max?* series
Pigment inks on Hahnemühle paper
Image size: 38.5 x 52 cm

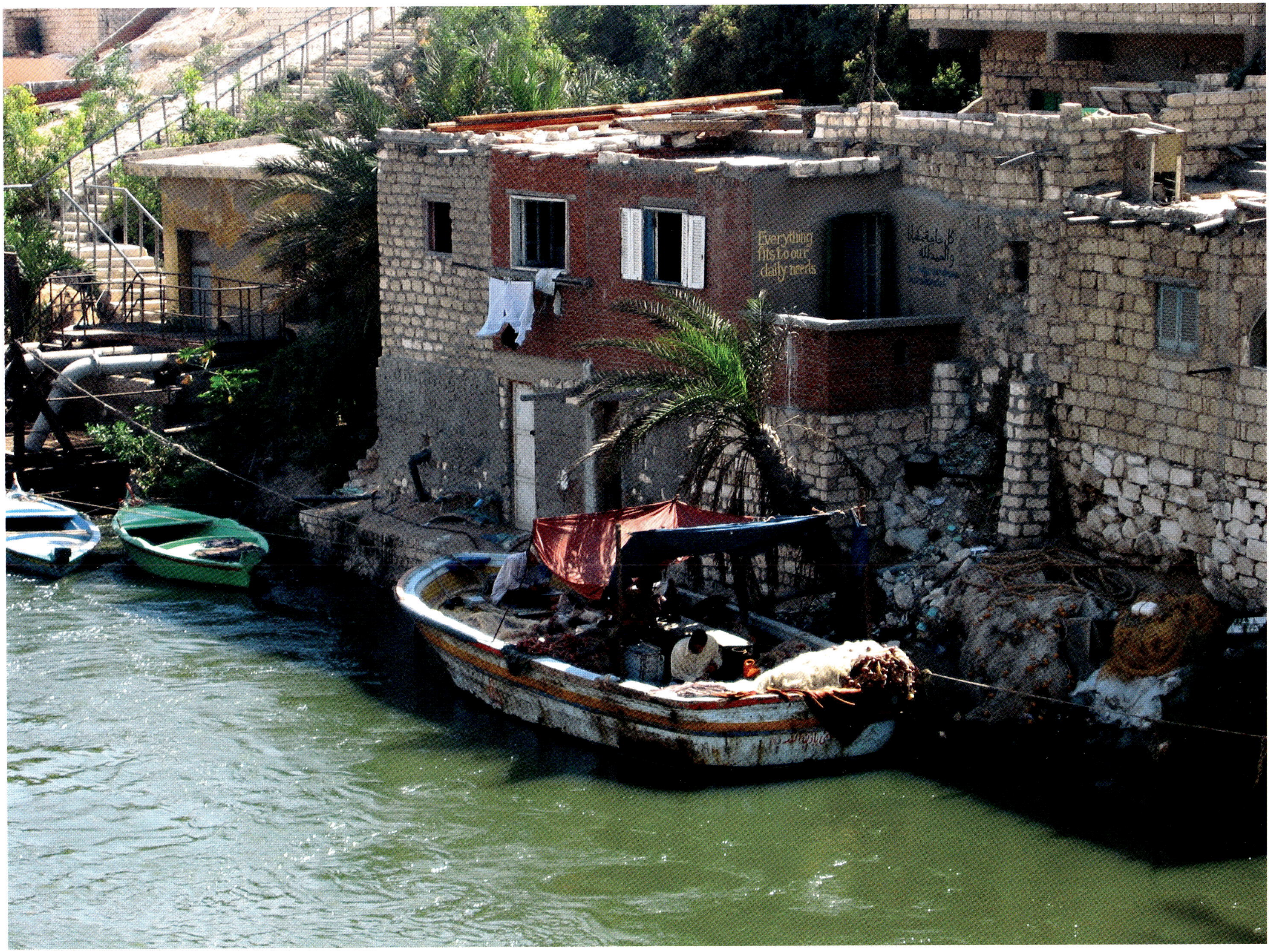
Everything
fits to our
daily needs

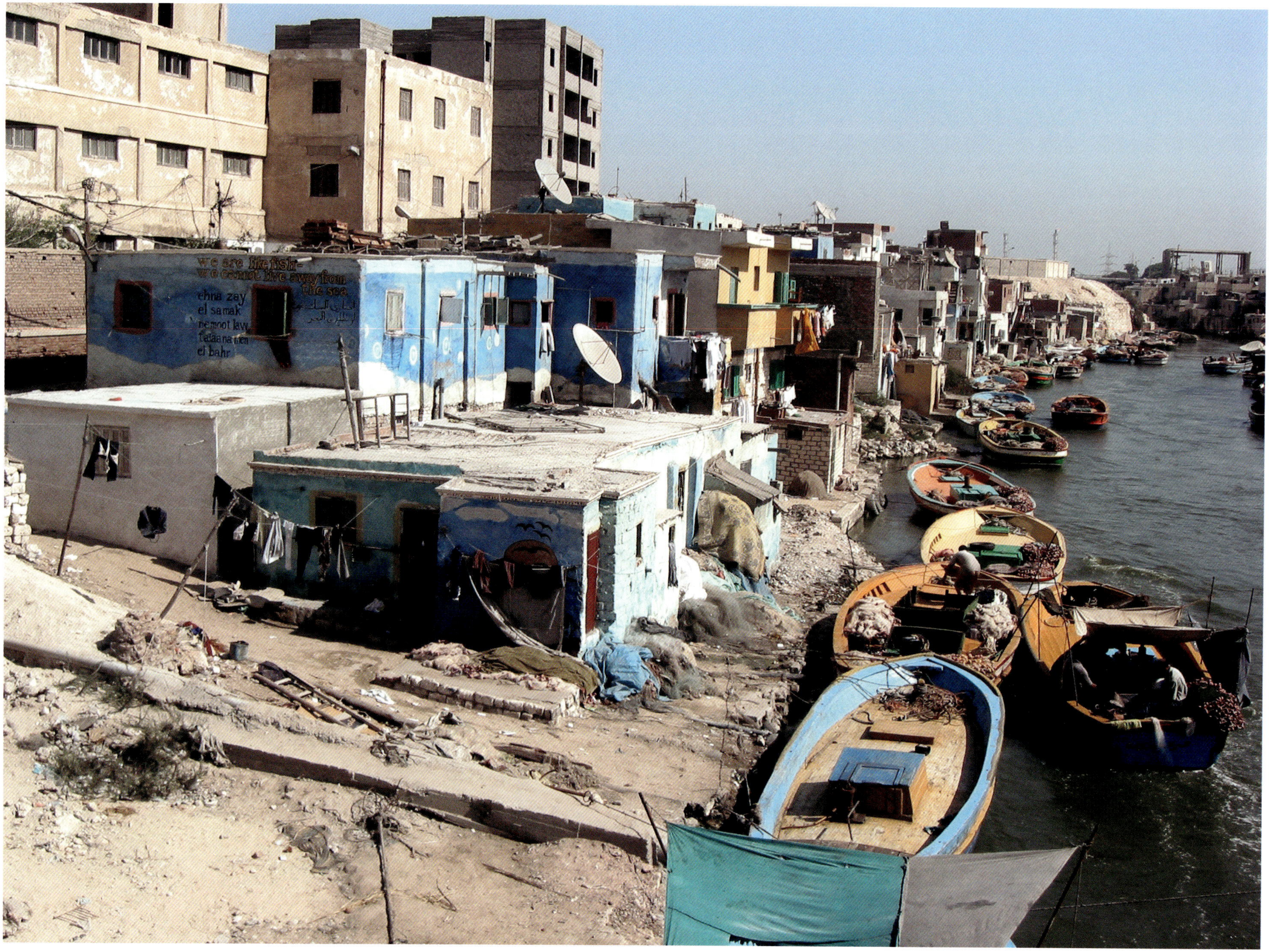


*We are like fish II*, 2002–3
*What About El Max?* series
Pigment inks on Hahnemühle paper
Image size: 38.5 x 52 cm

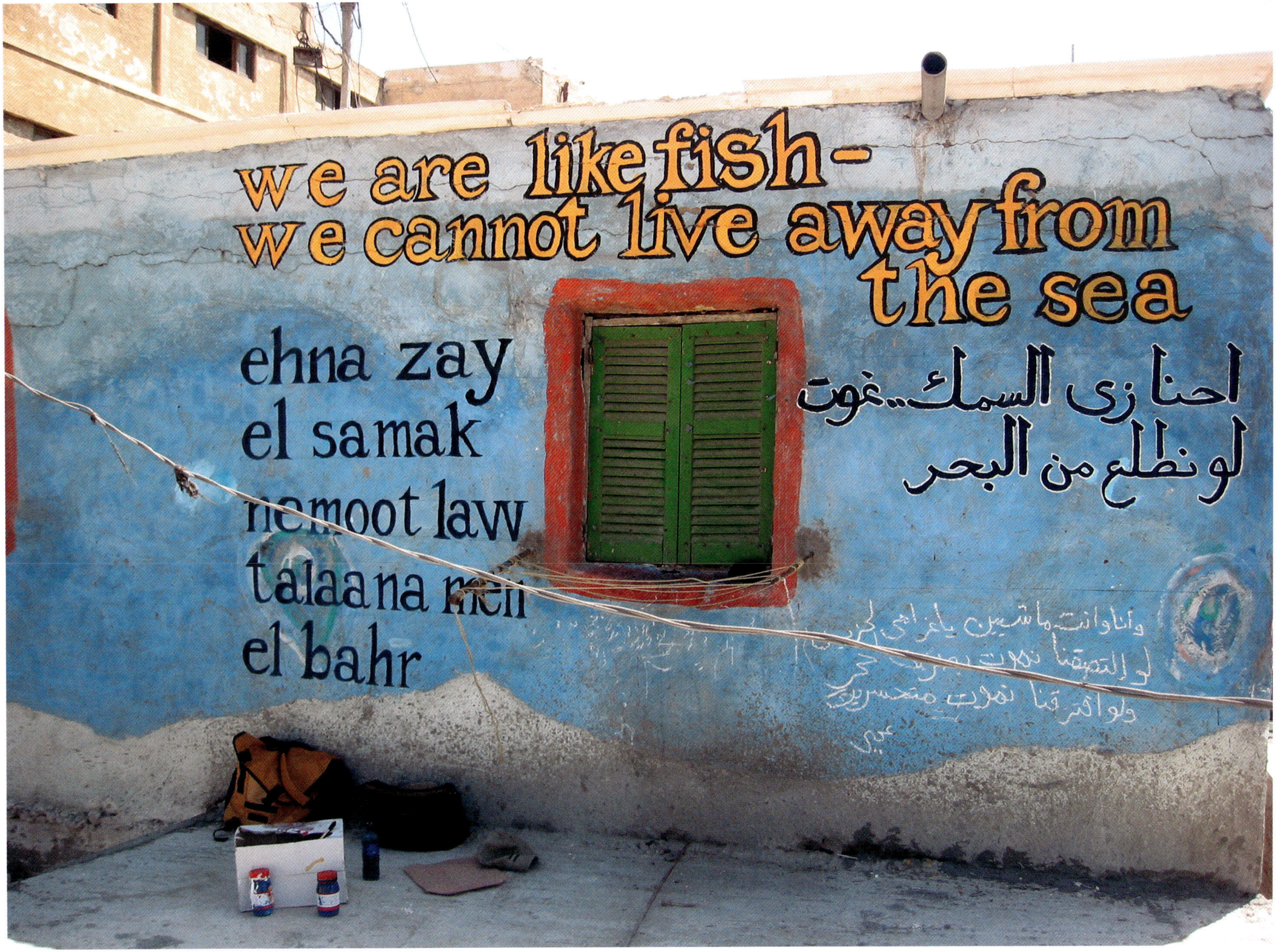


*We are like fish I*, 2002–3
*What About El Max?* series
Pigment inks on Hahnemühle paper
Image size: 38.5 x 52 cm

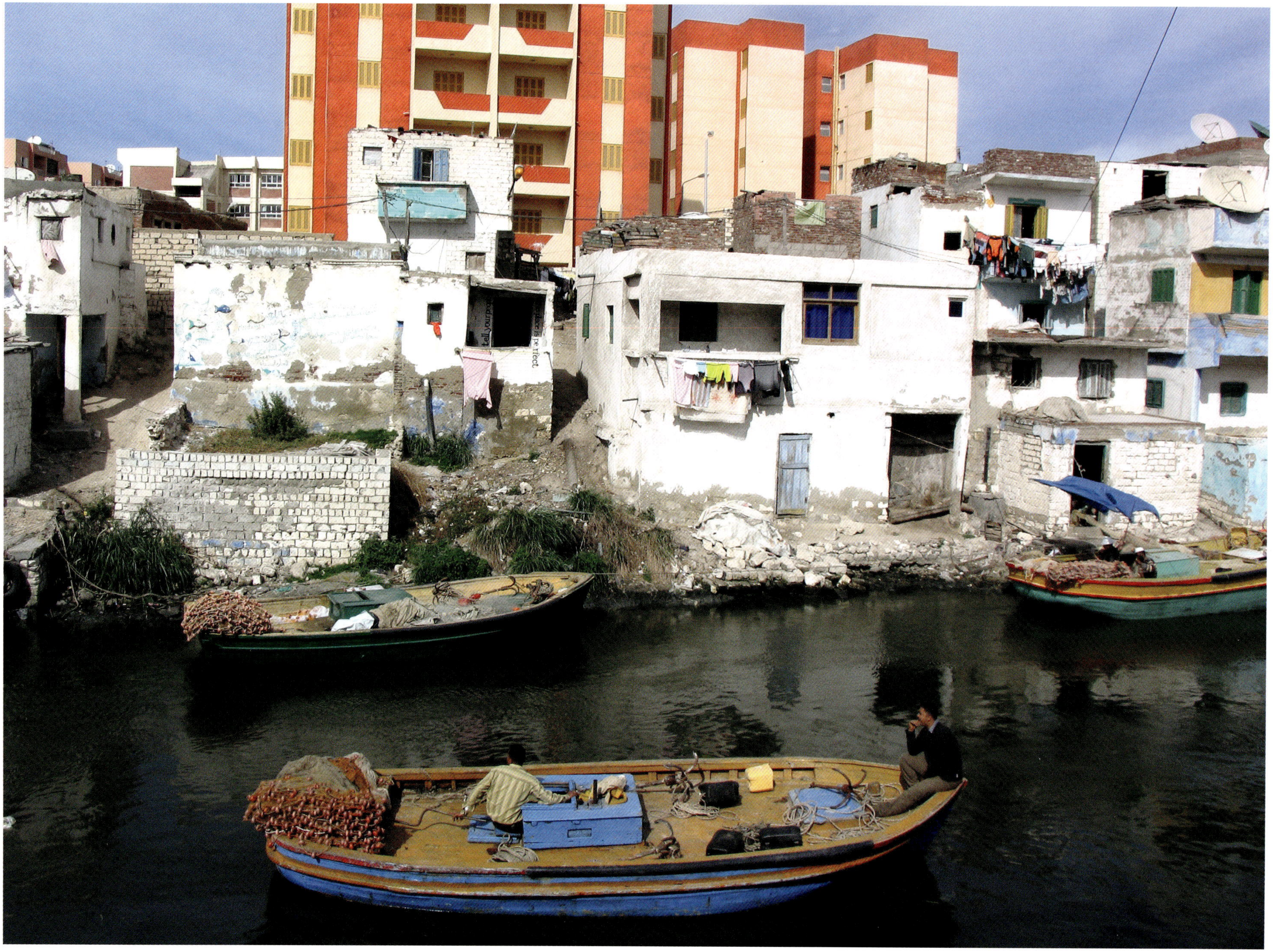

*Tell your people this place is perfect II*, 2002–3
*What About El Max?* series
Pigment inks on Hahnemühle paper
Image size: 38.5 x 52 cm

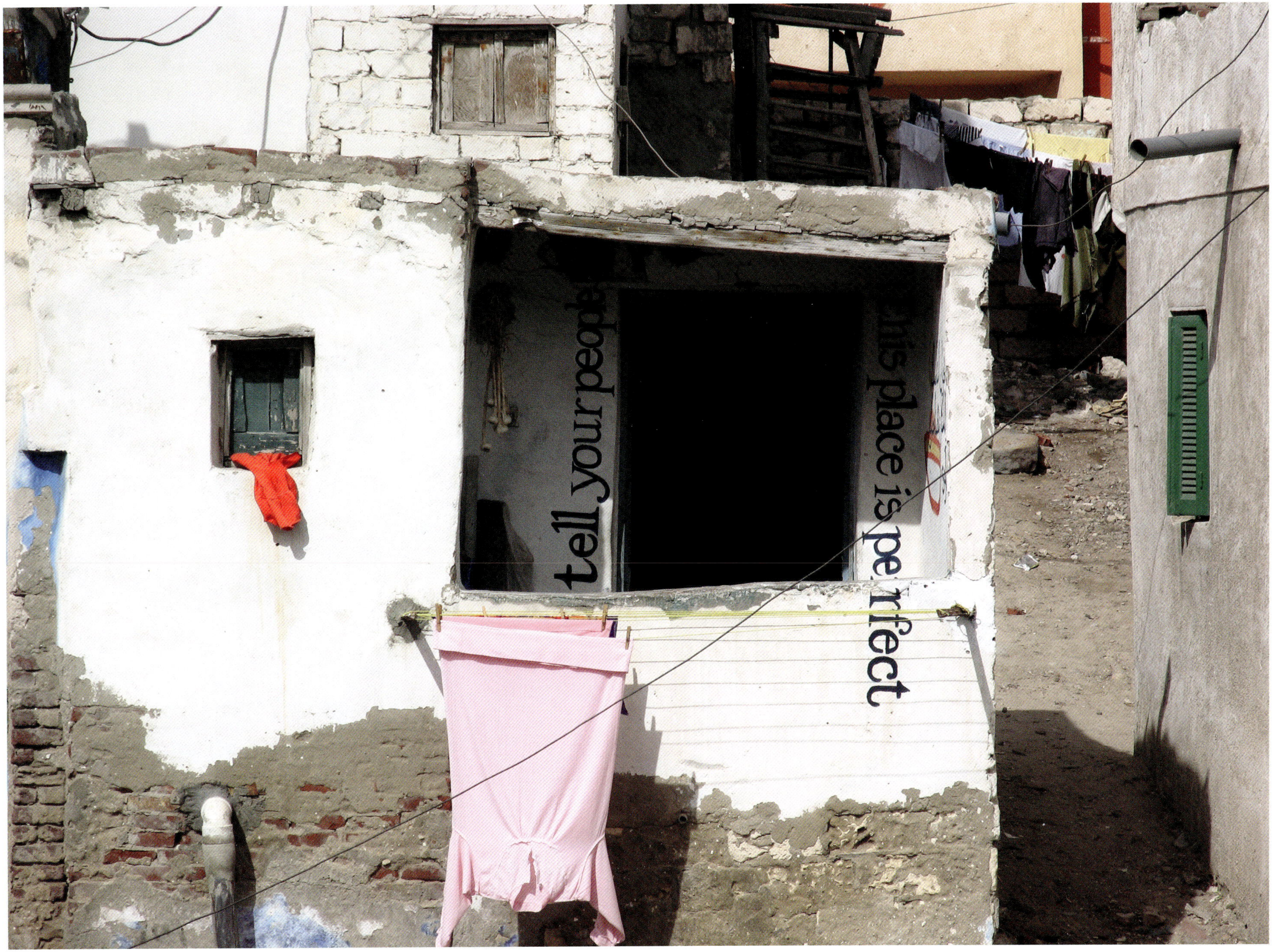


*Tell your people this place is perfect I*, 2002–3
*What About El Max?* series
Pigment inks on Hahnemühle paper
Image size: 38.5 x 52 cm

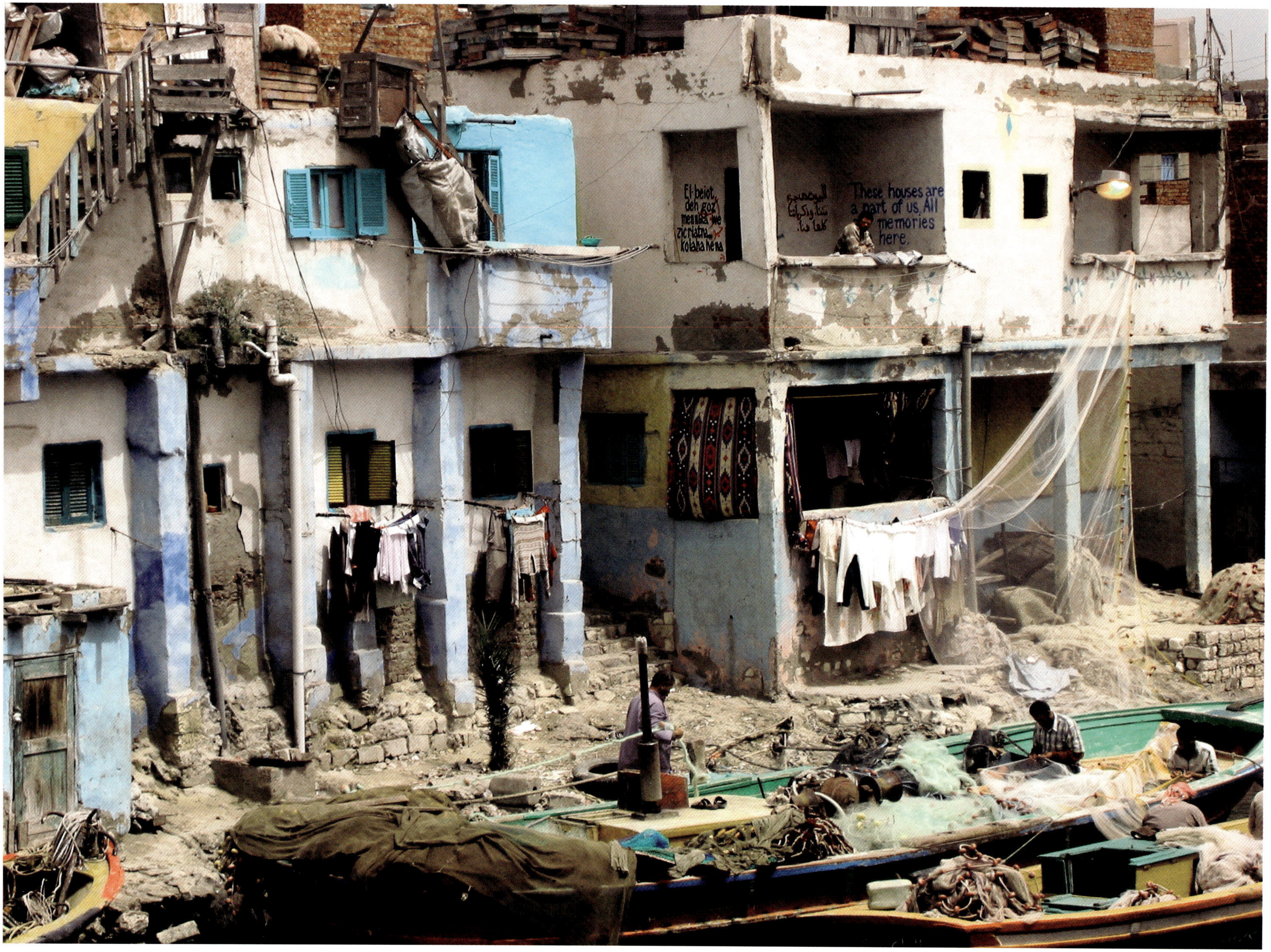


*These houses are a part of us II*, 2002–3
*What About El Max?* series
Pigment inks on Hahnemühle paper
Image size: 38.5 x 52 cm

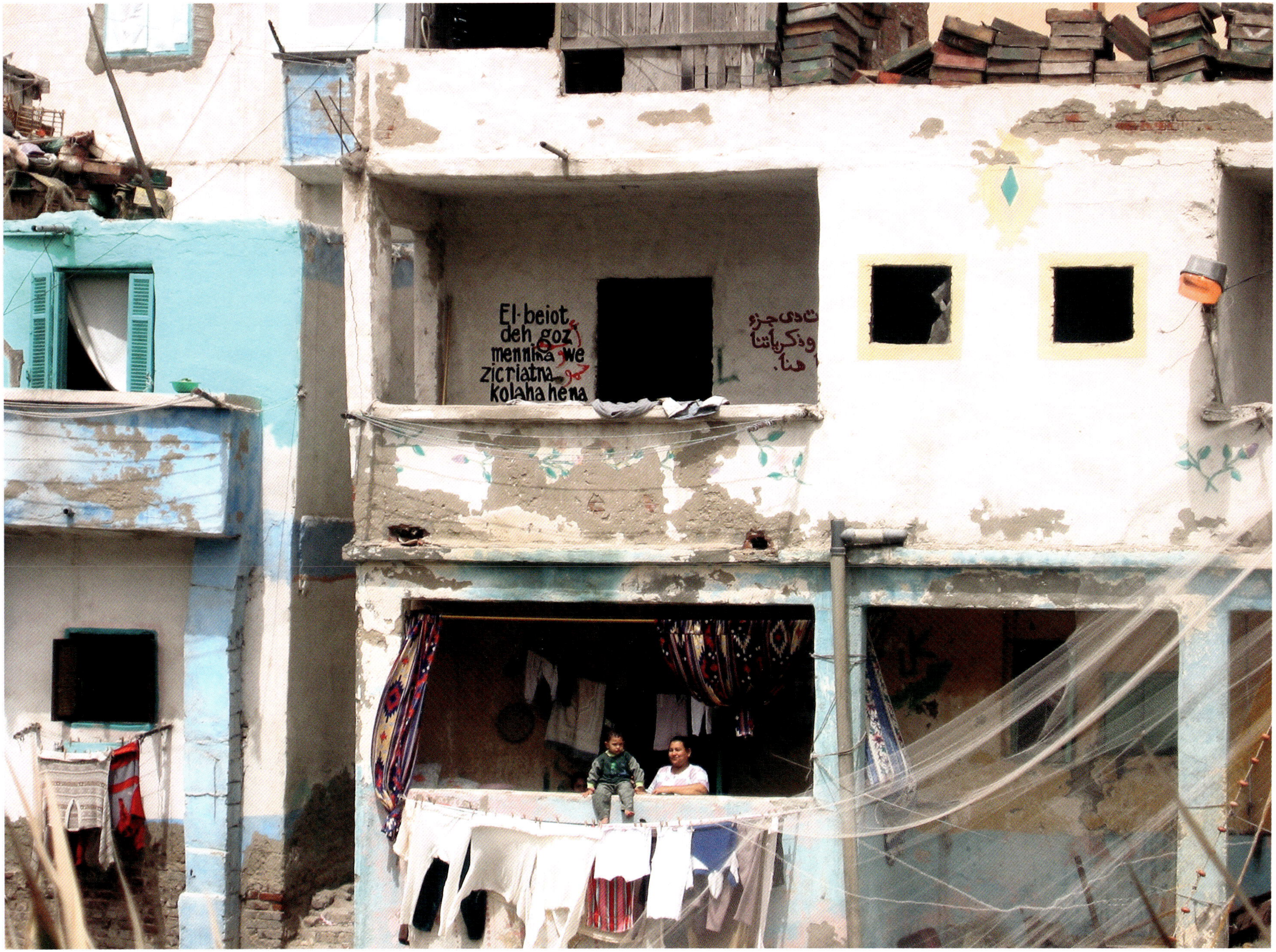


*These houses are a part of us I*, 2002–3
*What About El Max?* series
Pigment inks on Hahnemühle paper
Image size: 38.5 x 52 cm

# The Havana Series

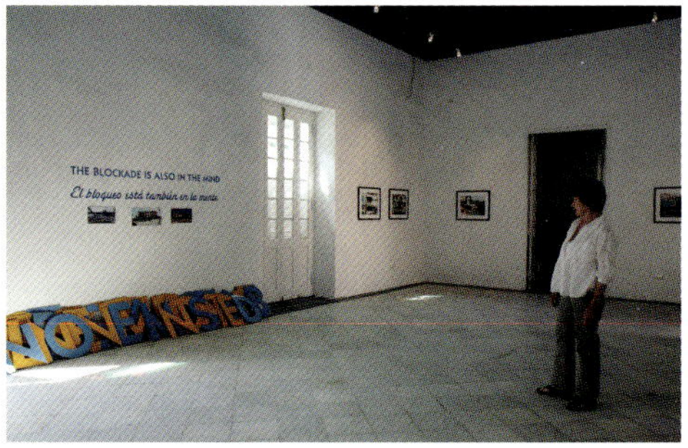

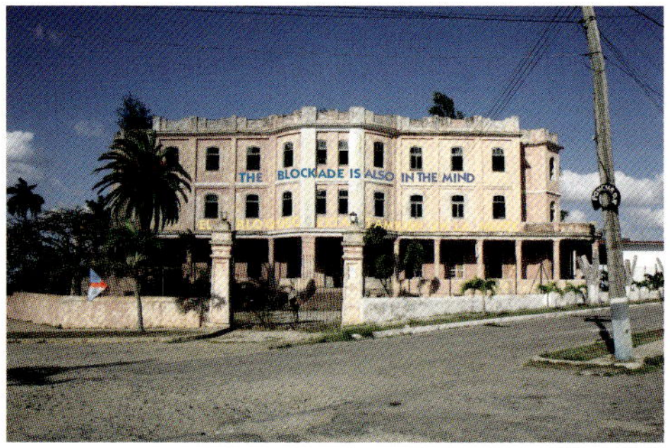



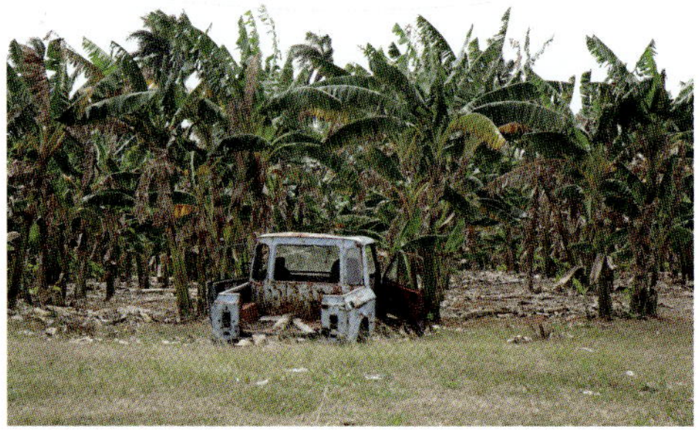

Williamson in her exhibition space at the Wifredo Lam Center, Havana

*Other Voices: The blockade is also in the mind (Refused Proposal), Hotel Campoamor, Cojimar, Cuba*
2009
Archival inks on Hahnemühle paper, lasercut letters
60 x 90 cm

Banana plantation in Havana, the location for the first work in the *Other Voices, Other Cities* series

In 2009, Sue Williamson was one of five artists invited to hold a special exhibition at the 10th Havana pp. 72-3 Biennale. She showed *Last Supper at Manley Villa*, p. 183 *What About El Max?*, and *W*A*S*H*, and undertook a special project for the Biennale.

In the month leading up to the opening, she interviewed many people in the small fishing town of Cojimar, adjacent to Havana, about their lives, and living in Cuba, and chose phrases from these interviews. She then made up these phrases in cardboard letters, to be used as temporary interventions in appropriate places. One of these phrases was *El Bloqueo Esta Tambien En La Mente*: "The Blockade is Also in the Mind". This was a response to the way that Cubans often blamed all problems on the American blockade.

The project was seemingly approved by the curators, but at the last minute Williamson was told she could not put the text up on a derelict hotel as she had planned, as local authorities would not agree. In the end, she put up a photoshopped image of the hotel with her proposed signage on the wall of her exhibition space, wrote the statement above the photos, and dumped the letters she had not been allowed to put up at the bottom of the wall.
At her exhibition opening, in front of the television cameras, Minister of Culture Abel Prieto promised he would sort it out. When this did not happen, Prieto offered his office as a venue, but Williamson refused: this was not a public place. In the end, she was given an alternative location, which turned out to be a fenced-in film location outside the city. "We had little choice", Williamson recalls," and so put the letters up on an old factory building and photographed that. The deserted spot was as far from the public arena as it possibly could be." Behind that building was a banana plantation, and Williamson asked friends and assistants to stand holding the letters, and that was photographed, word by word. This series of photos, spelling out "El Bloqueo Esta Tambien En La Mente", was the birth of the *Other Voices, Other Cities* series.

Williamson was subsequently instructed not to put up the rest of her texts anywhere, even on the grounds of the Fortaleza de la Cabana where the Biennale itself was in progress. She did not accept this ruling, and put her text up on the wall which overlooks the bay and the city of Havana with the Capitolo at the centre and left the letters there.

In other interventions, Williamson propped the letters up on the seats of baseball stadium with a large poster of Che Guevara. This text read: "The information is small. *No vemos CNN* (We don't see p. 193
CNN)." And on the beach of Cojimar, once the scene of hundreds of boats leaving Cuba for Miami, the artist arranged the statement of an old woman from the community, Amalia Rodriguez: "My son left."

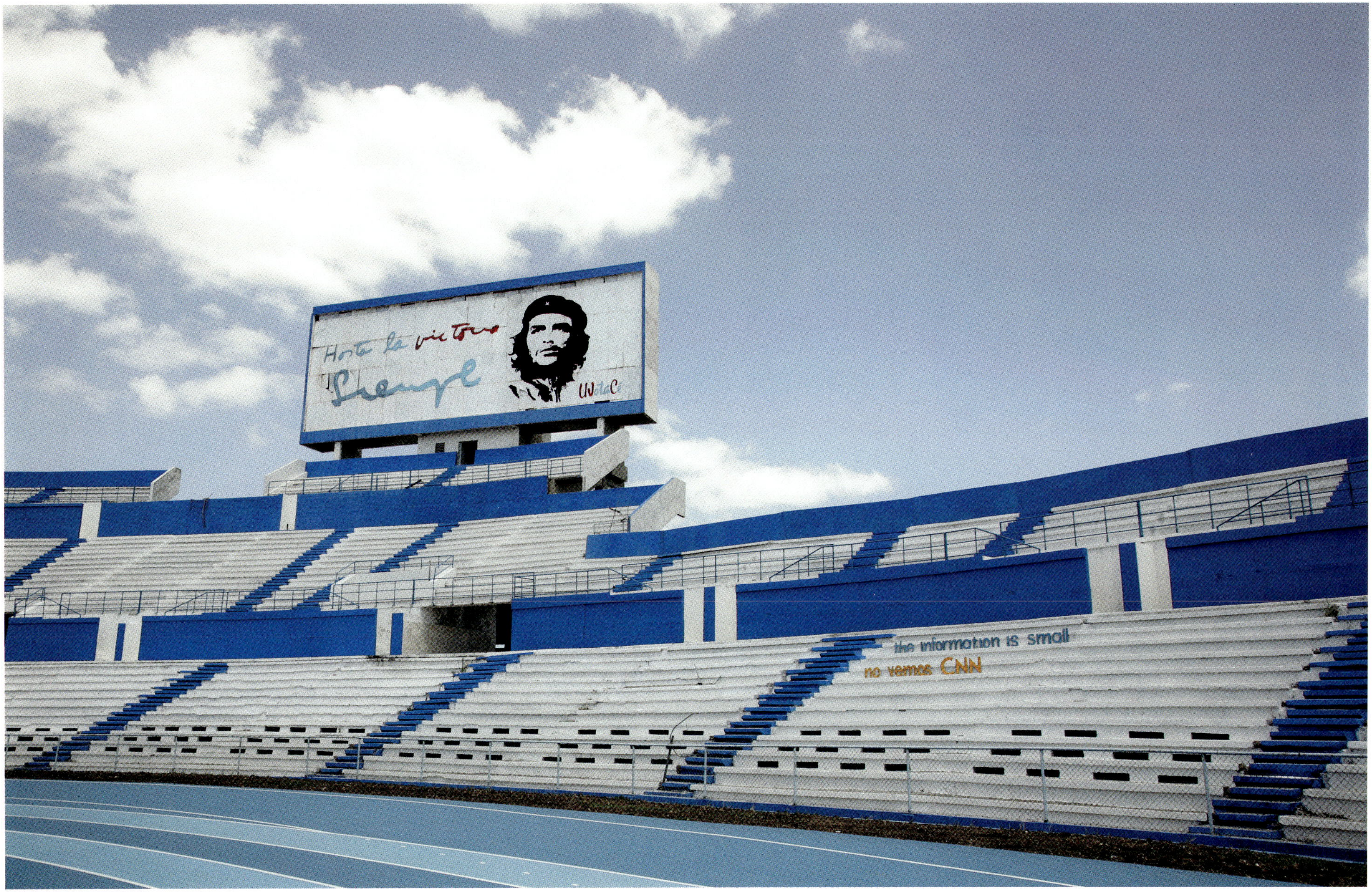


*The blockade is also in the mind*, 2009
*The Havana* series
Archival inks on Hahnemühle paper, lasercut letters
60 x 90 cm

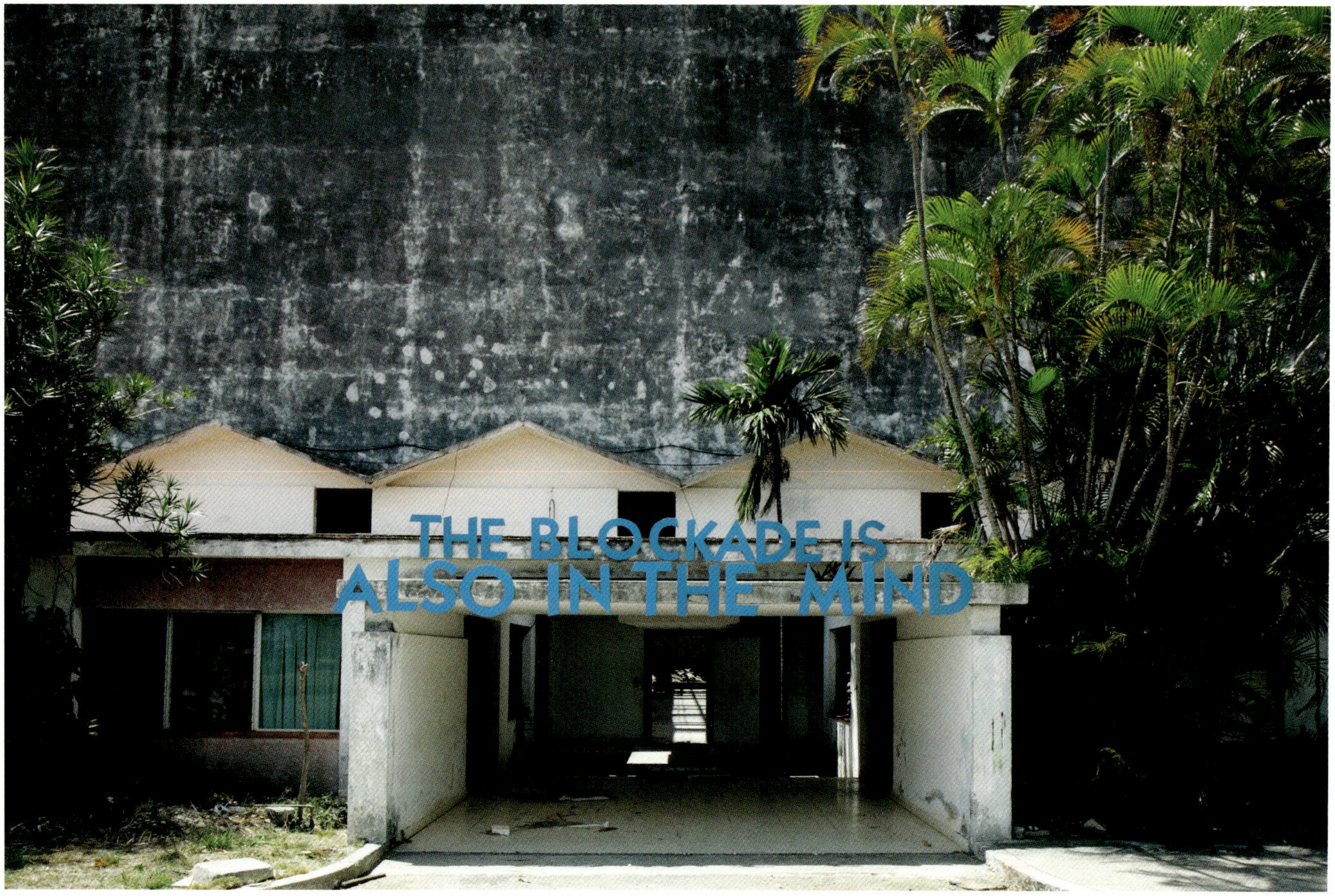


*The blockade is also in the mind*
2009
The *Havana* Series
Archival inks on Hahnemühle paper
60 x 90 cm

*El Bloqueo esta También en la Mente,*
*The Blockade is Also in the Mind*
2009
*Other Voices, Other Cities* series
Pigment inks on archival cotton rag paper
Dimensions variable

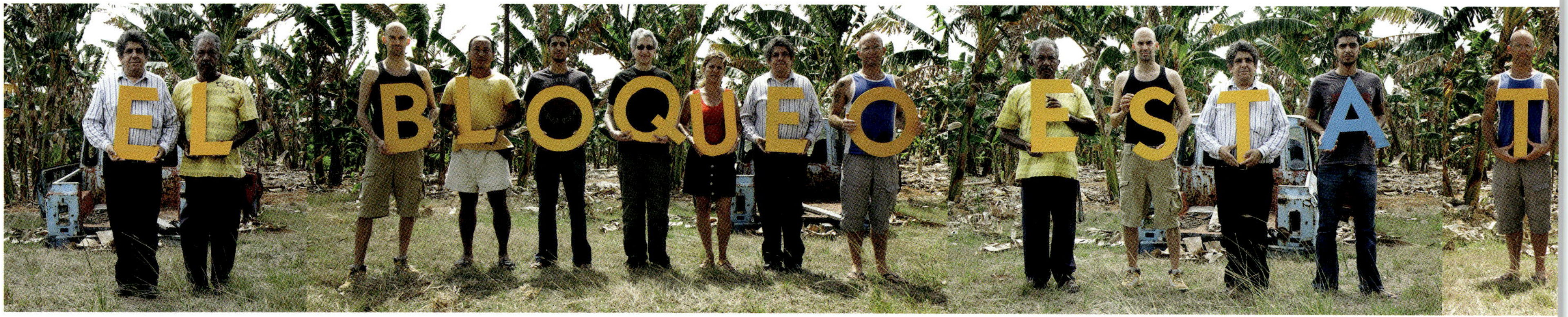

*El bloqueo esta también en la mente*, 2009
The *Havana* series
Archival inks on Hahnemühle paper
60 x 90 cm

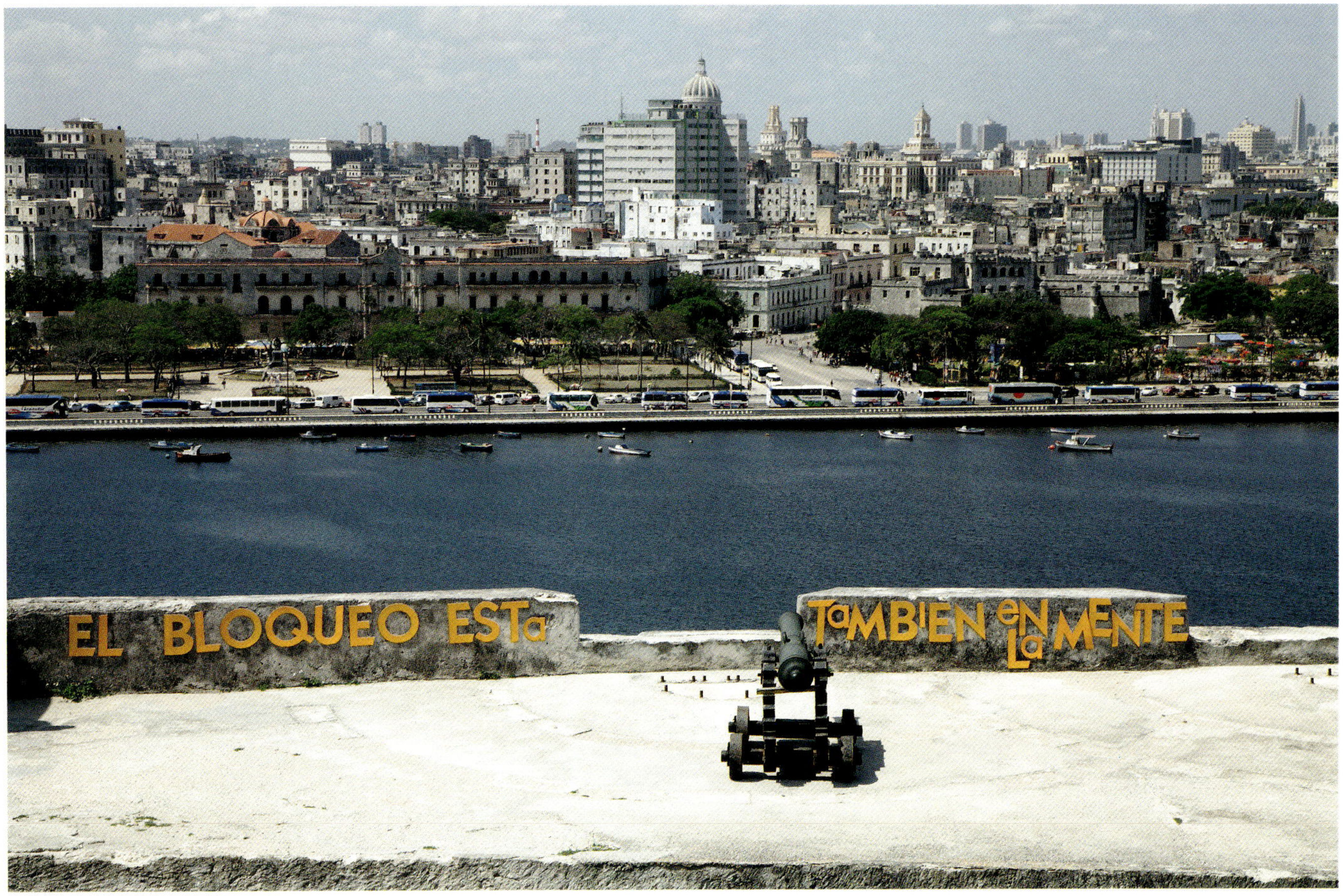


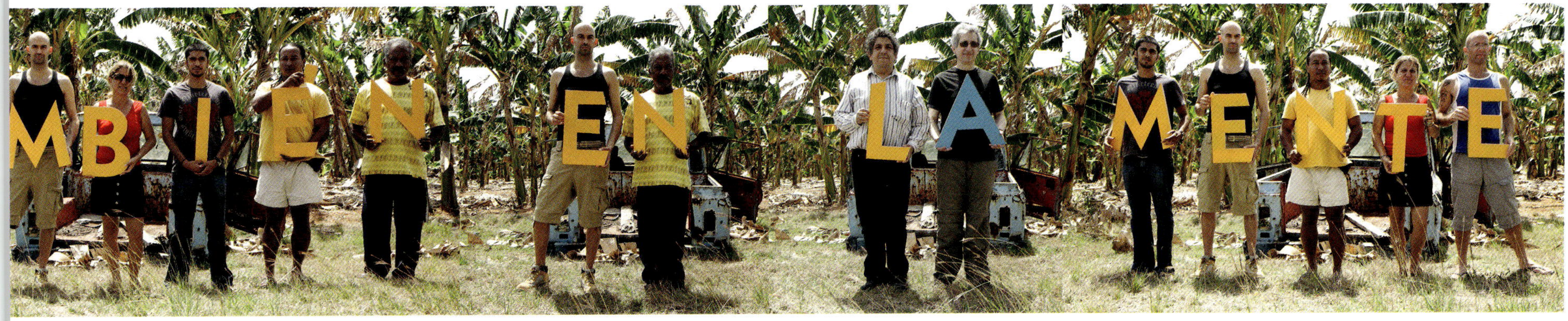

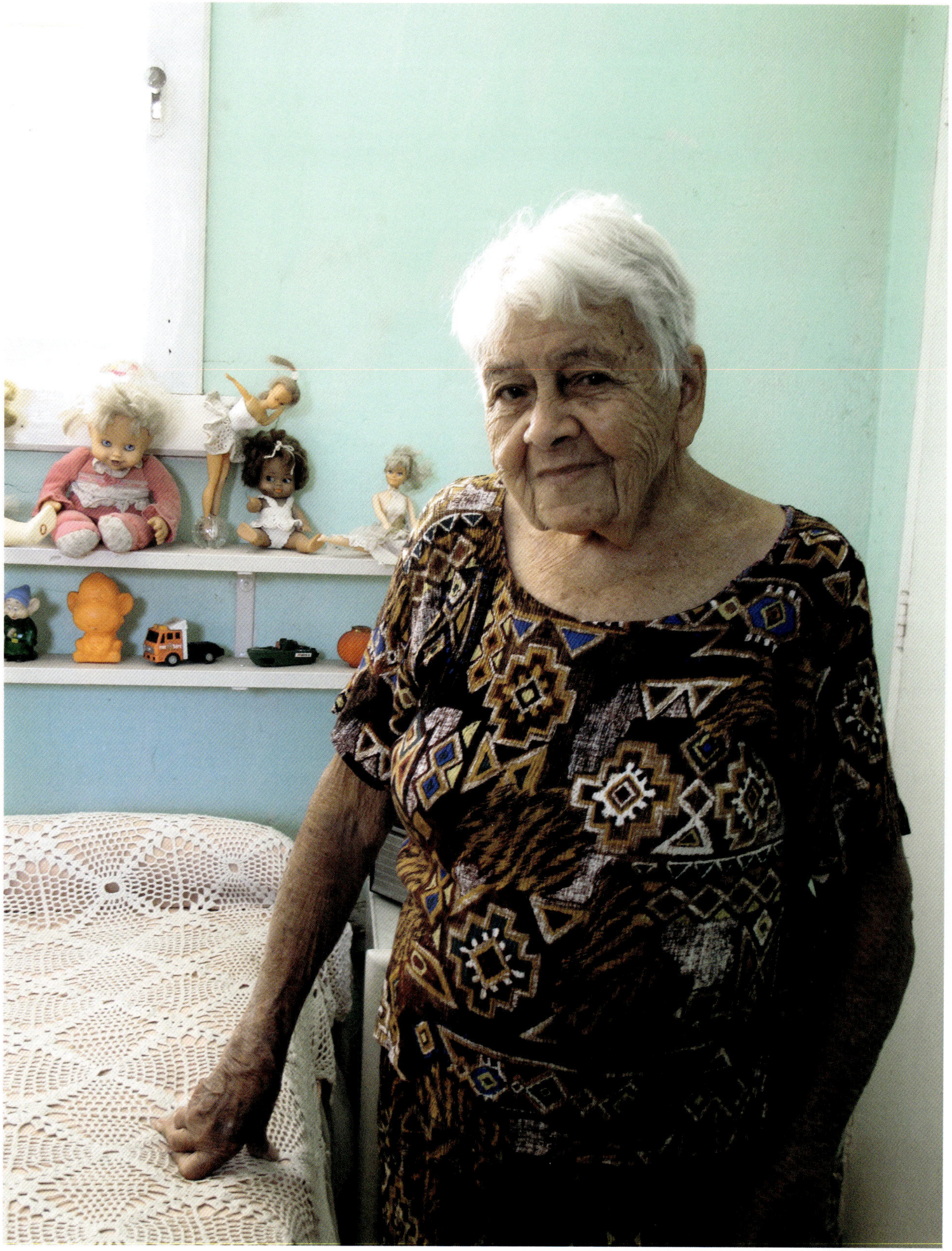

Amalia Rodriguez, Cojimar, who made the statement, "My son left"

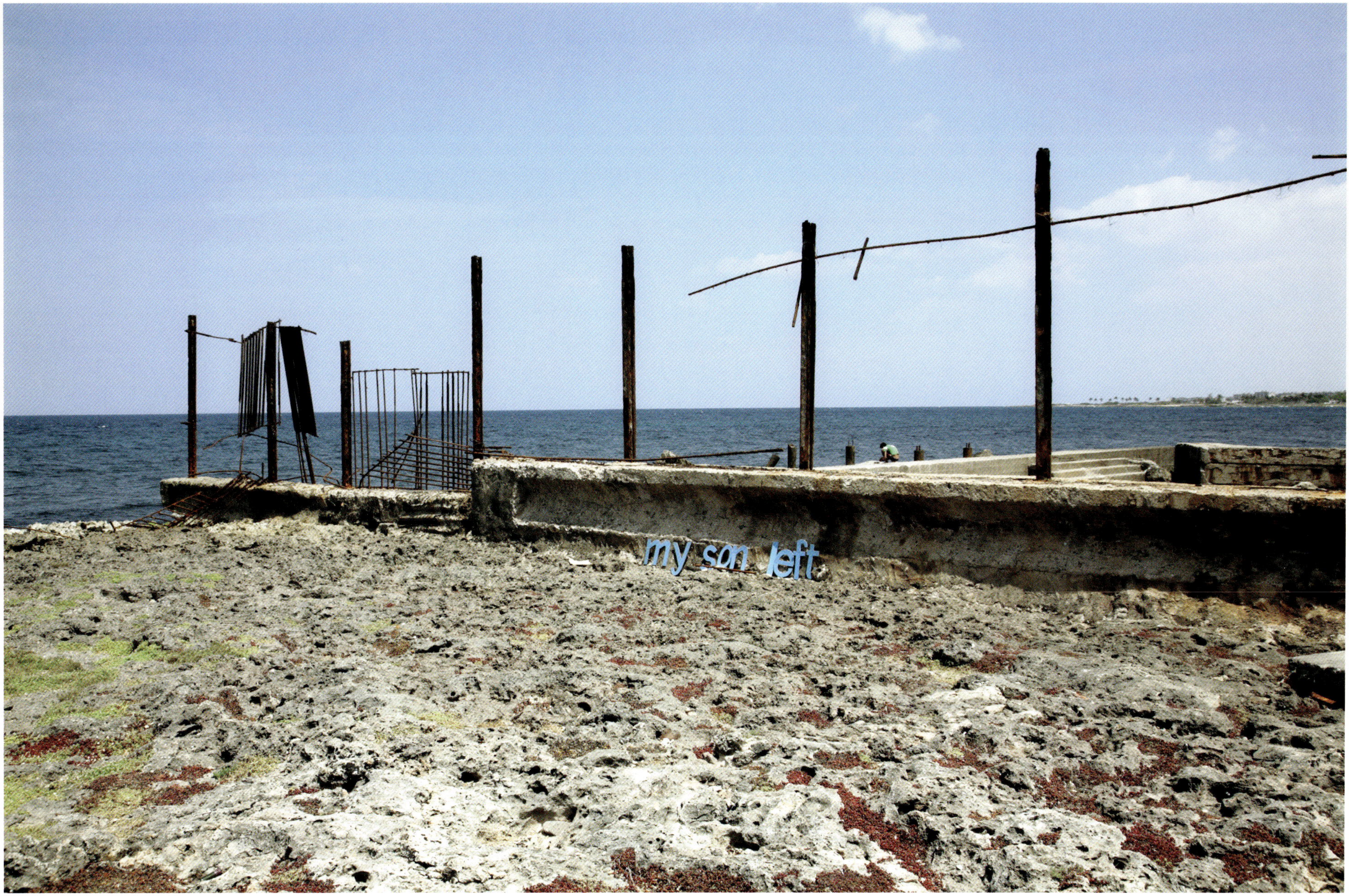


*My Son Left*
2009
Archival inks on Hahnemühle paper
60 x 90 cm

# Other Voices, Other Cities

In this age of globalisation, what does it mean to live in a particular place? Why do the residents of a city choose to live there, and if there is one message that would express the essence of that city, what would it be? These are the questions Williamson has been exploring in this ongoing series.

In each new city, Williamson works by setting up a workshop of young artists and other residents, and asking them to talk about what distinguishes their city and the people of that city from any other. What is good, what is bad, what is peculiar? If the city has an image and an attitude, what is it? At the end of the workshop, participants vote on the most popular statement.

The letters of the statement are fabricated in cheap signage material, and Williamson hunts out a location in the city appropriate to the message for a photoshoot. On the day, the workshop participants meet again and hold up the letters to spell out the message in a word-by-word series of photographs.

Cities in the series so far are Havana, Johannesburg, Harare, London, Bern, Berlin, New York, Krakow, Naples, Istanbul and Hong Kong.

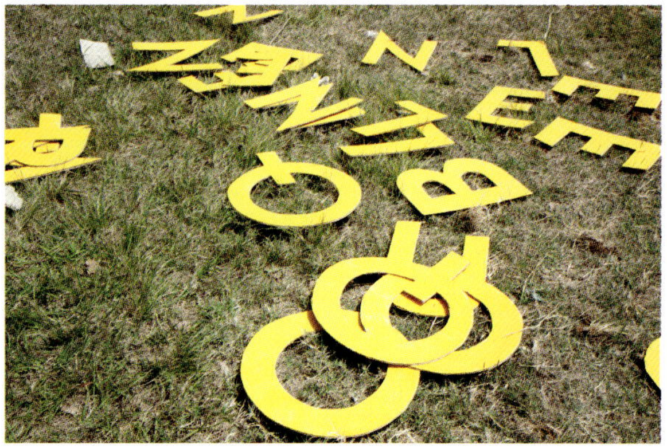

The cardboard letters for the Havana statement on the grass

Says the artist: "What is really interesting is how, each time, this somewhat random process has come up with a statement that seems to capture the ethos of the city. For instance, you won't get Londoners saying, 'I mean, where else are you gonna go?' Only New Yorkers would say that. Or 'Youth Facing History'. You could only get a serious slogan like that from a city with a weighty past, like Krakow. I don't want, in any way, to hide the arbitrary nature of this process, but each group convened produces a voice for that city, one of many voices of course."
From 2016, Williamson plans to include new cities: Beirut, Athens, Mumbai, somewhere in South America.

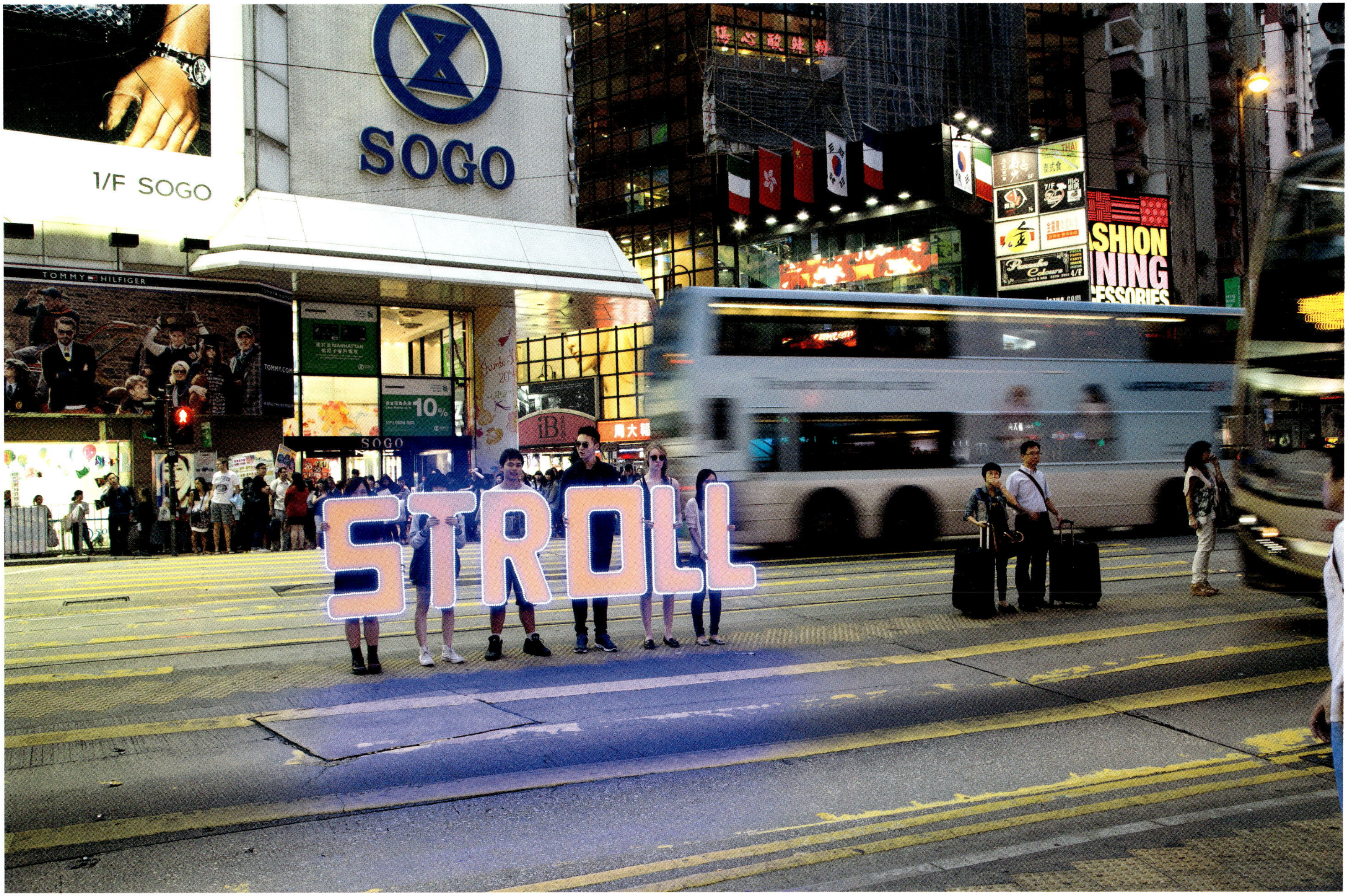


*No Time to Stroll: Hong Kong* (detail)
2013
*Other Voices, Other Cities* series
Pigment inks on archival cotton rag paper
Dimensions variable

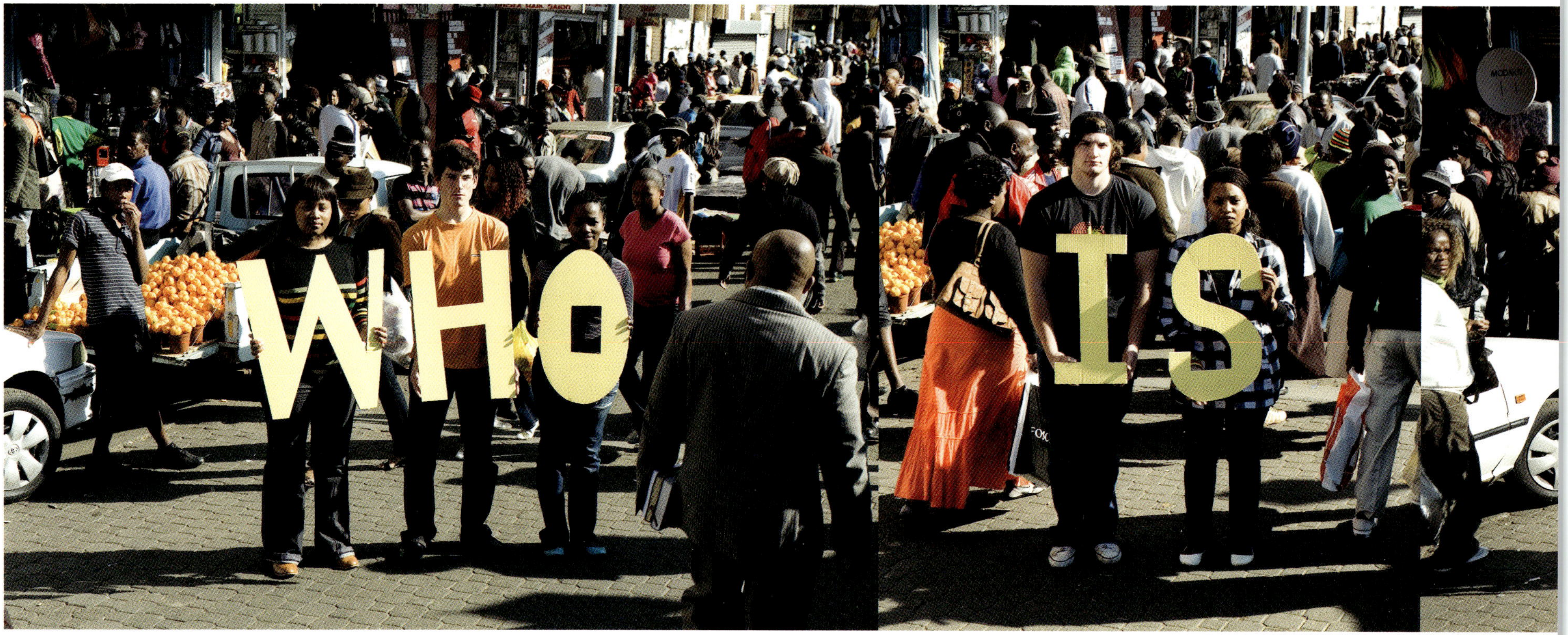


Nobody is sure who Johannesburg is named for, and the statement chosen by the workshop participants also speaks to the anonymity of the swirling city, home to thousands of immigrants. The photographs were taken in downtown Johannesburg, at the central taxi-rank, from which people commute to and from Soweto and Johannesburg's other townships.

*Who is Johannes?: Johannesburg*, 2009
*Other Voices, Other Cities* series
Pigment inks on archival cotton rag paper
Dimensions variable

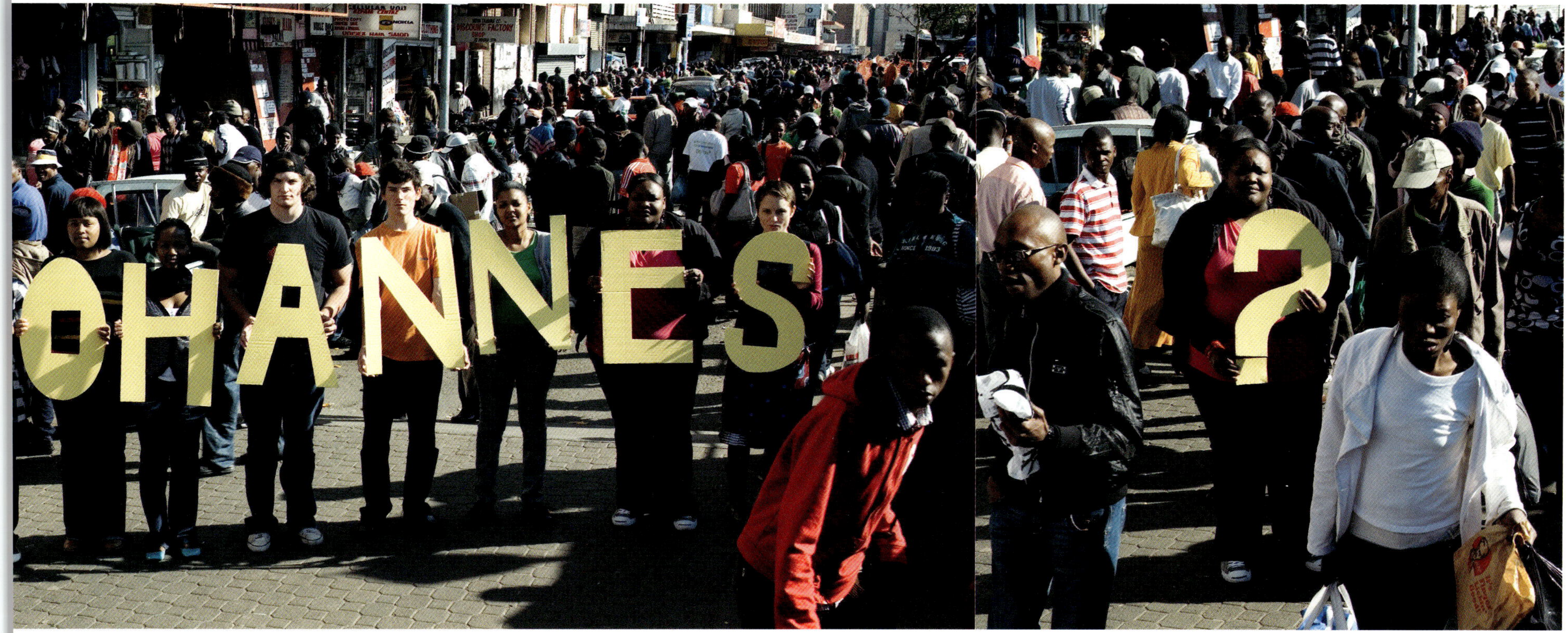
OHANNES ?

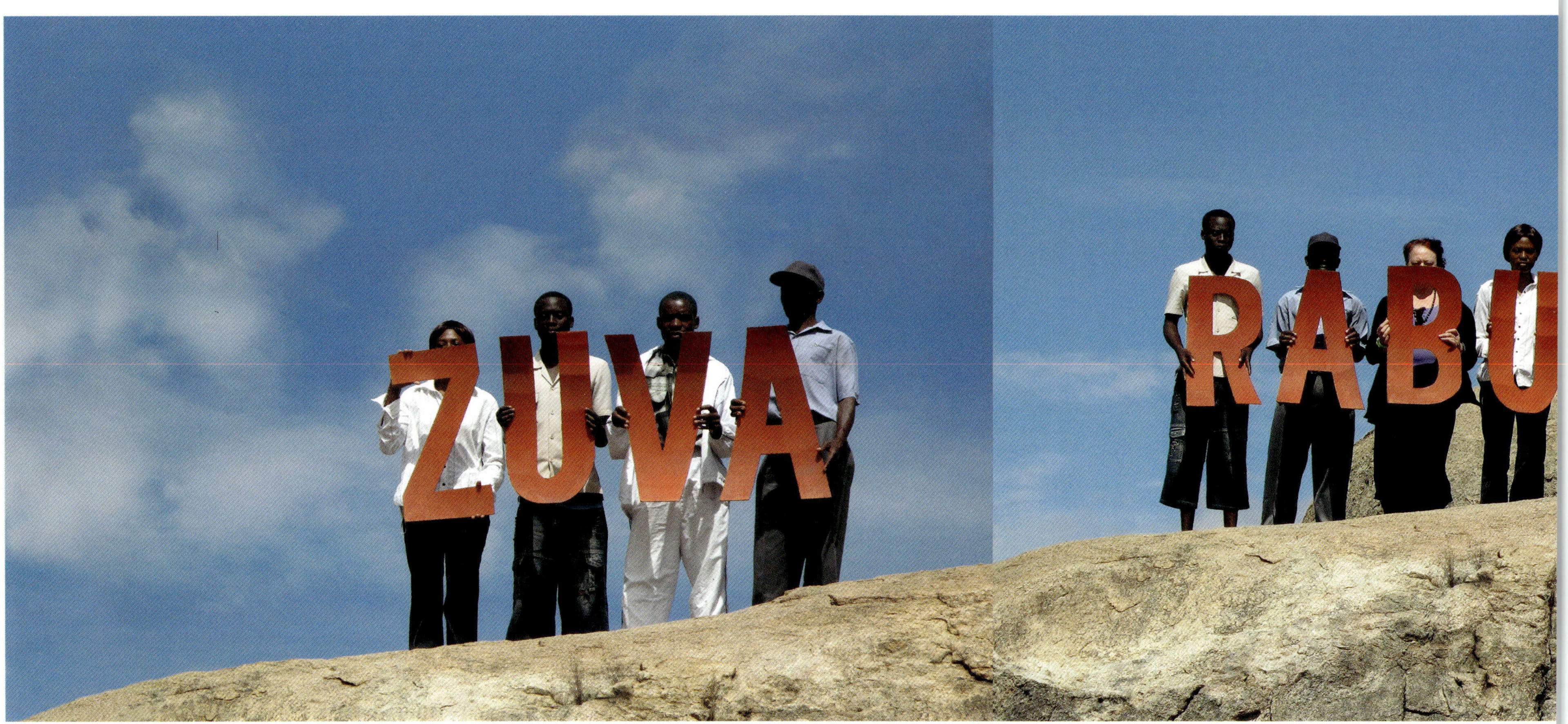


At a workshop conducted at the Zimbabwe National Gallery in Harare in 2009, young artists and photography students decided on a Shona saying which can be translated as "For whom has the sun risen?". This is a questioning of the authoritarian power of Robert Mugabe, who at the time, was the world's longest-serving ruler. It was not possible to get permission to photograph in Harare itself, so the photos were taken in Chitungwiza, a rural area nearby.

*Zuva Rabudirepi? For Whom Has the Sun Risen?: Harare, Zimbabwe*, 2009
*Other Voices, Other Cities* series
Pigment inks on archival cotton rag paper
Dimensions variable

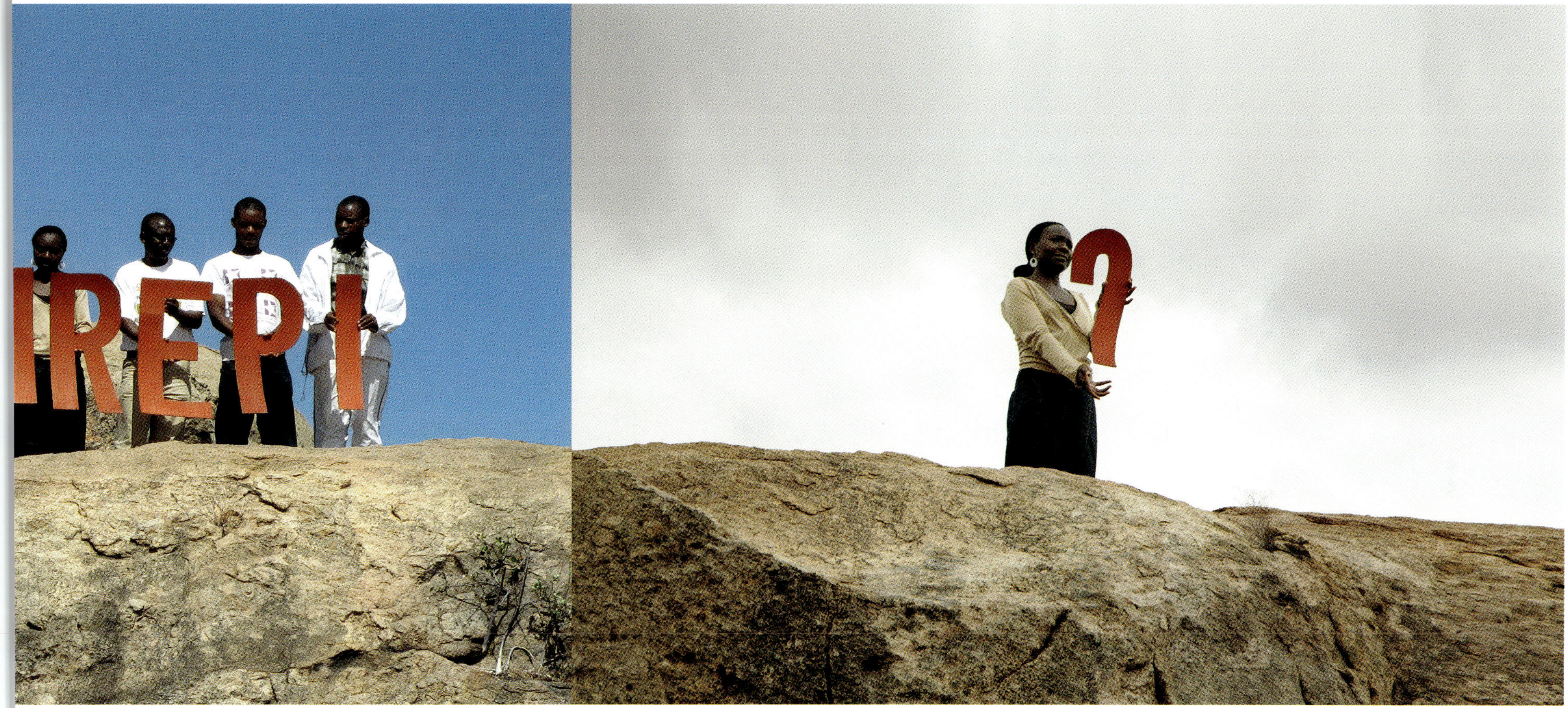
REPI
?

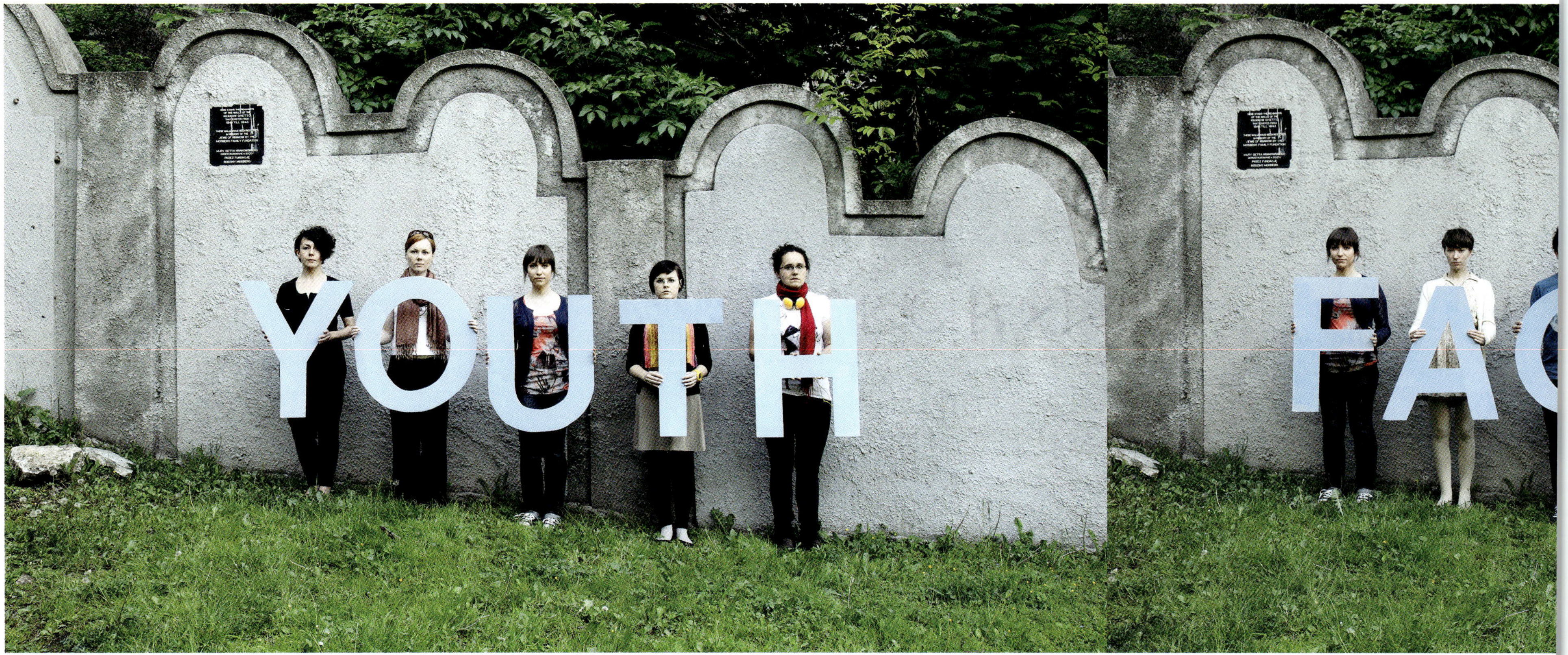


History hangs heavy in Krakow, where primary tourist attractions are the old Auschwitz concentration camp and the Schindler factory. When the workshop participants came up with the statement "Youth Facing History", Williamson chose to shoot the photographs against one of the two remaining sections of a wall built by the Nazis in 1942 to contain the city's Jewish ghetto.

*Youth Facing History: Krakow*, 2011
*Other Voices, Other Cities* series
Pigment inks on archival cotton rag paper
Dimensions variable

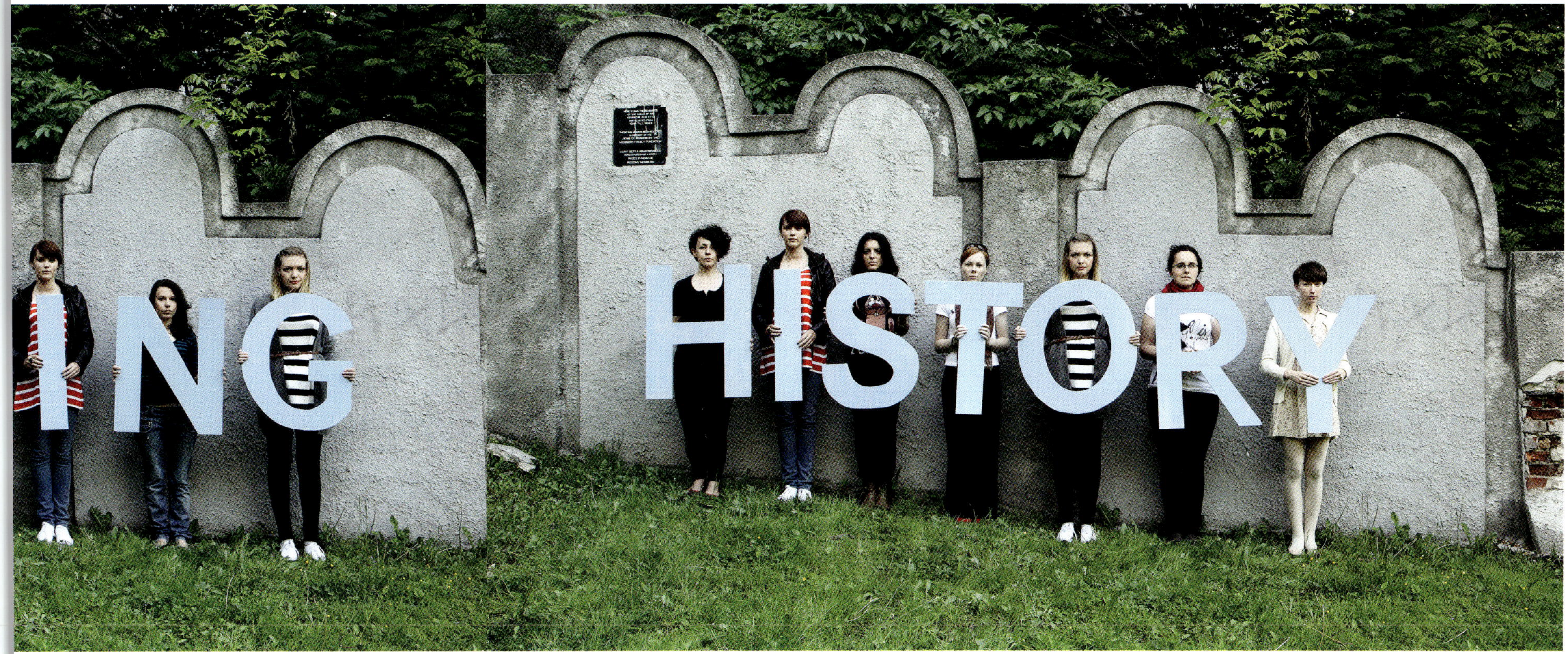
ING HISTORY

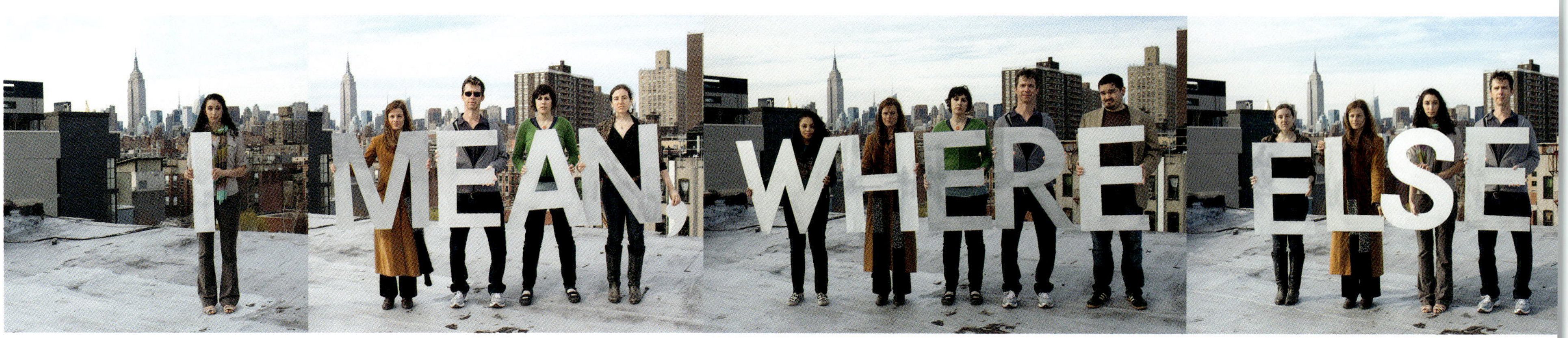


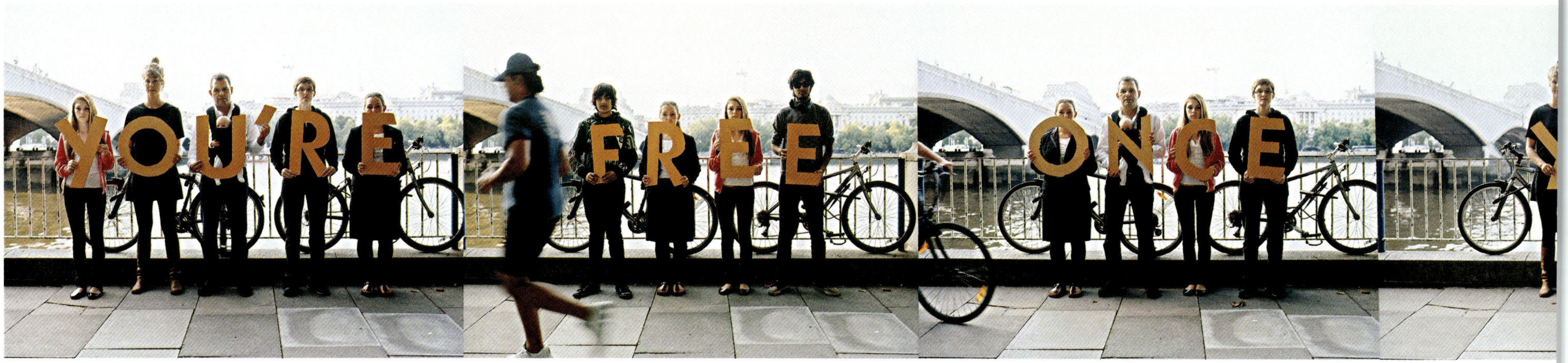


The New York workshop participants came up with a slogan expressing their essential belief that they live in the centre of the world, while their London counterparts chose one which reflected the way that their global metropolis it is still governed by class codes. Williamson shot the first on an East Village rooftop and the second in the South Bank cultural precinct along the Thames.

*I Mean. Where Else Are You Gonna Go?*:
New York, 2011
*Other Voices, Other Cities* series
Pigment inks on archival cotton rag paper
Dimensions variable

*You're Free Once You Know The Rules*: London
2009
*Other Voices, Other Cities* series
Pigment inks on archival cotton rag paper
Dimensions variable

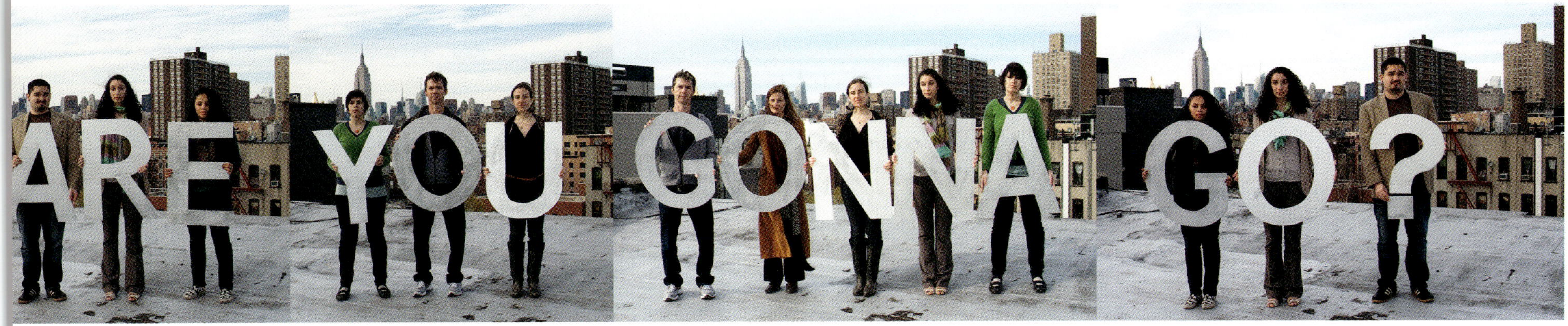
ARE YOU GONNA GO?

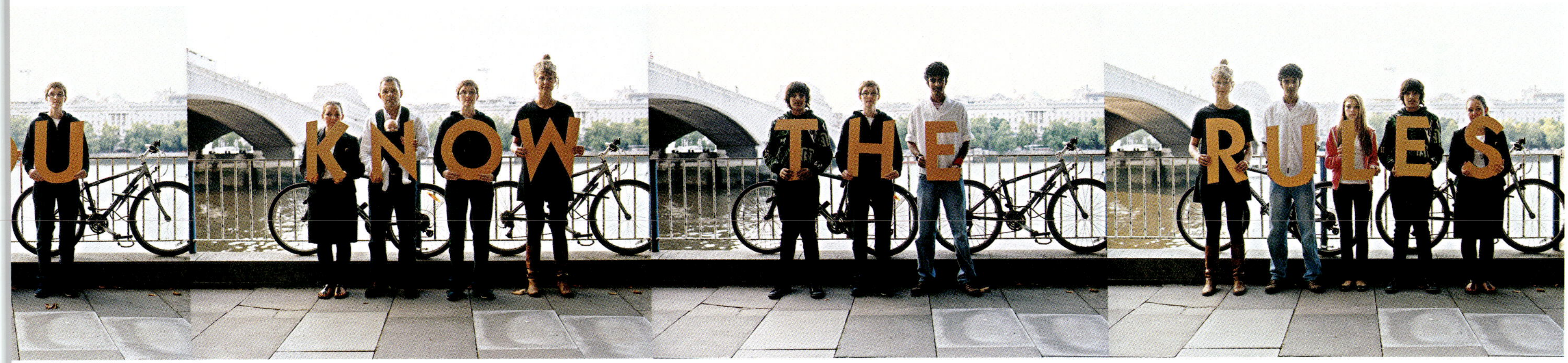
U KNOW THE RULES

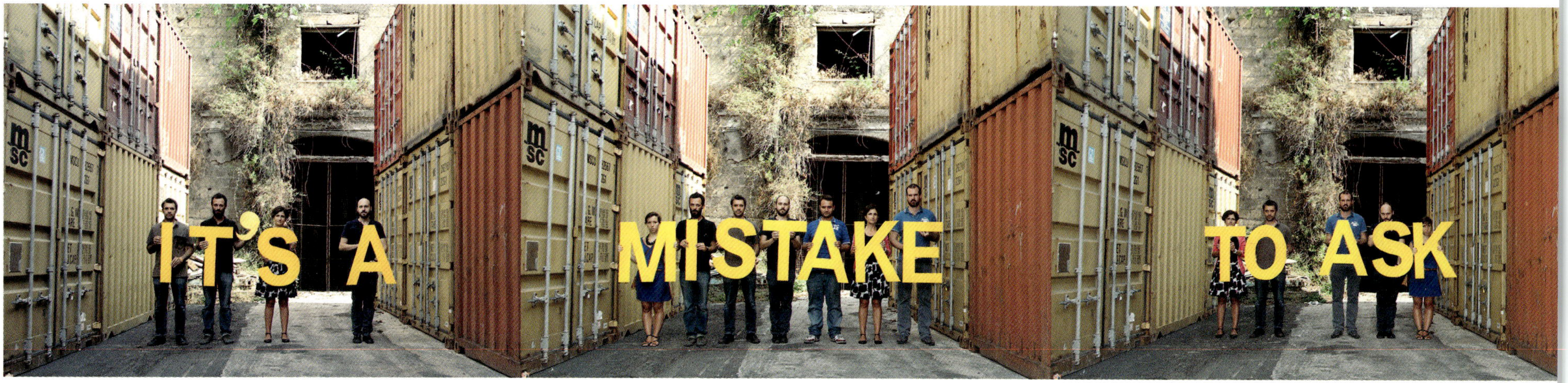


The Naples participants' statement is a reflection of the way so many of the city's social problems can be traced to the fact that the Camorra—the mafia of the city—controls so many aspects of local government. Williamson chose to shoot in a container yard at the docks: Naples is Europe's most notoriously porous port, with containers arriving and disappearing without ever being documented.

*It's a Mistake to Ask for Advice: Naples*, 2012
*Other Voices, Other Cities* series
Pigment inks on archival cotton rag paper
Dimensions variable

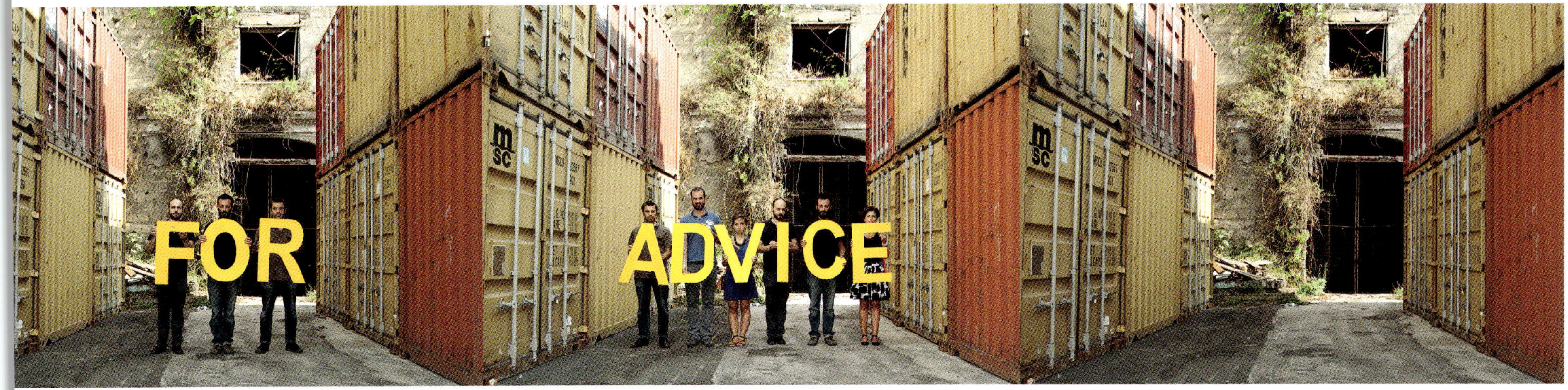
FOR
ADVICE

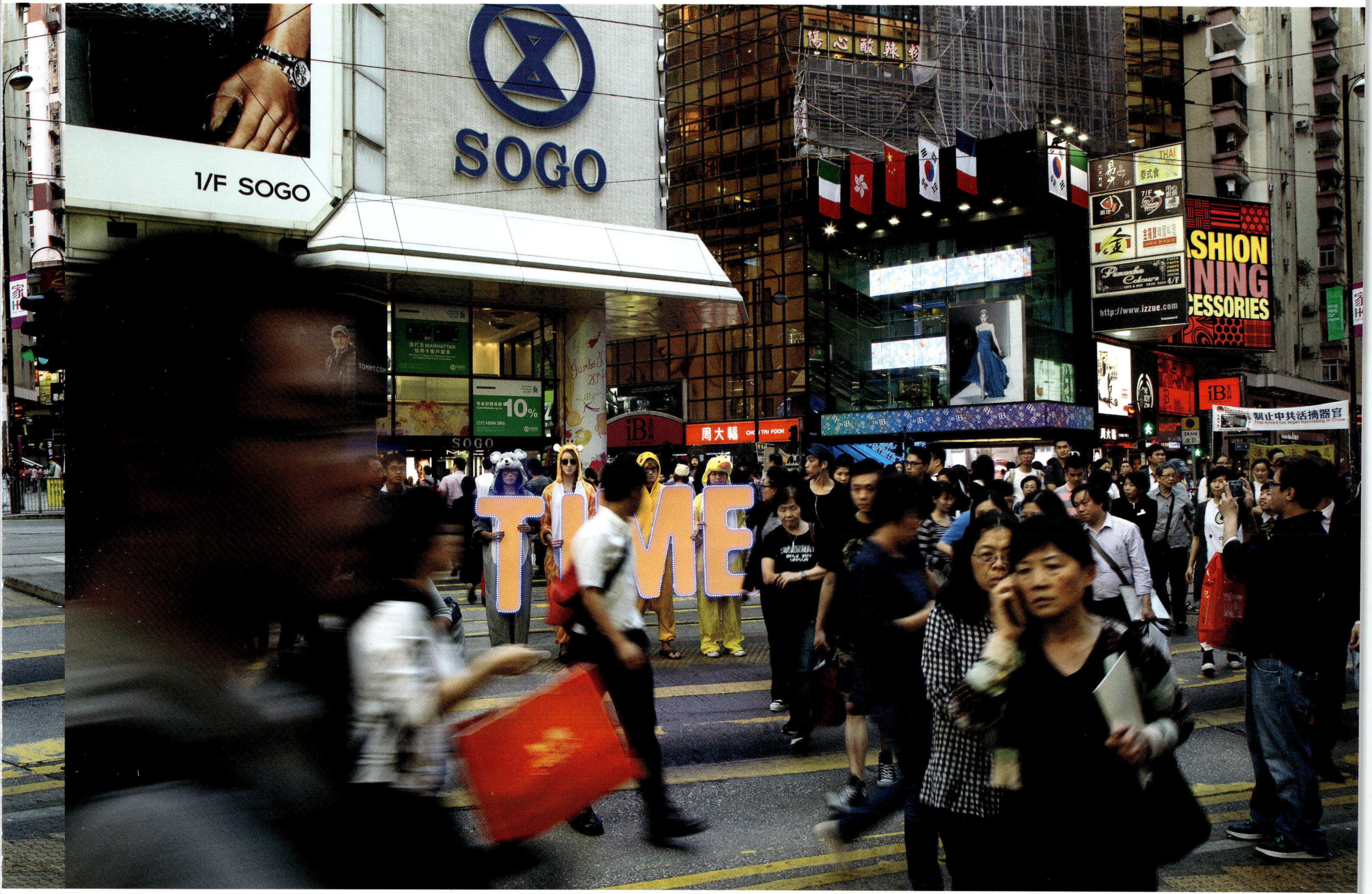


Williamson and her Hong Kong group, students at the Savannah College of Art and Design, chose to shoot at a busy intersection in Causeway Bay: as the traffic lights change to green, vast hordes of pedestrians swarm across the street. If you are strangers to the city—like the couple with large suitcases in the last frame—you can find yourself trapped between the bus lanes when the lights turn red again. Williamson tried to suit the letters to the location: in glitzy Hong Kong they were framed with blue lighting strips.

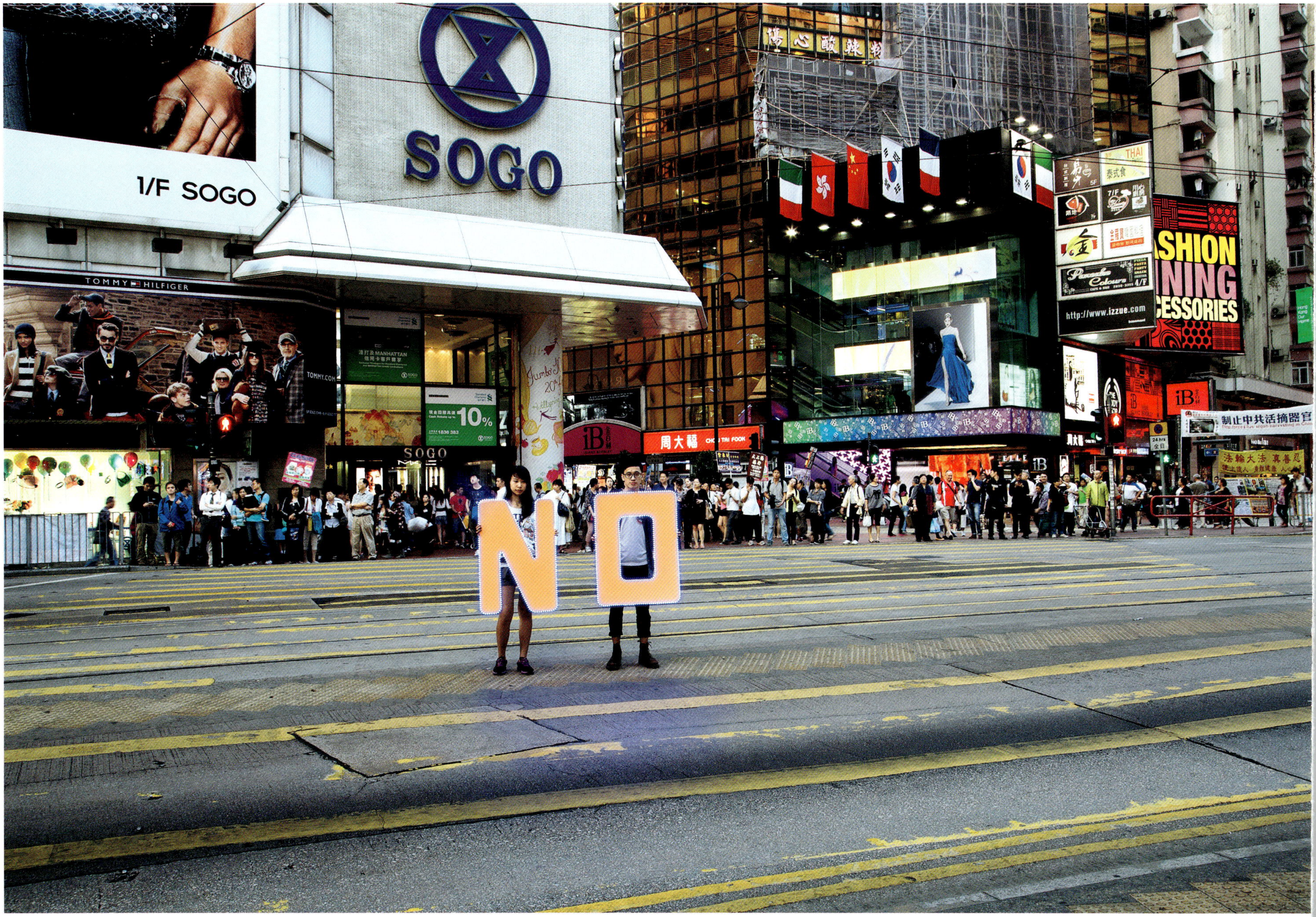


*No Time to Stroll: Hong Kong*
2013
*Other Voices, Other Cities* series
Pigment inks on archival cotton rag paper
Dimensions variable

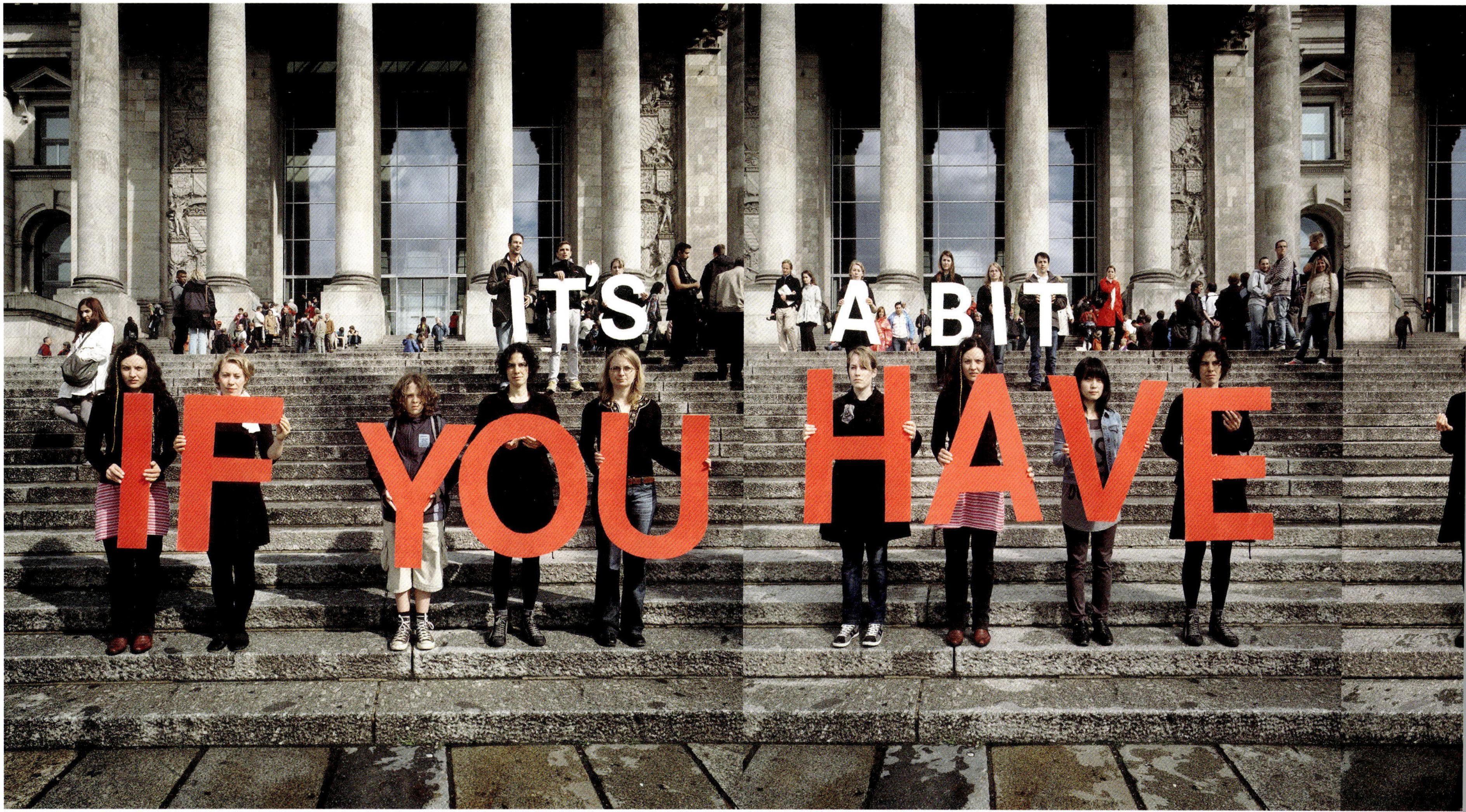


Berliners believe in a laid-back style, and in a project sponsored by the Daimler Art Collection, workshop participants came up with the statement, "It's a Bit Suspicious if You Have Too Much Money". The location selected for the shoot was the steps of the Reichstag, the meeting place of the German parliament.

Police intervened halfway through, and prevented the project from proceeding, saying the statement compromised the dignity of the building. In the end, participants were allowed to mime holding the remaining letters as long as they did not actually display them.

*It's a Bit Suspicious if You Have Too Much Money: Berlin*, 2010
*Other Voices, Other Cities* series
Pigment inks on archival cotton rag paper
Dimensions variable

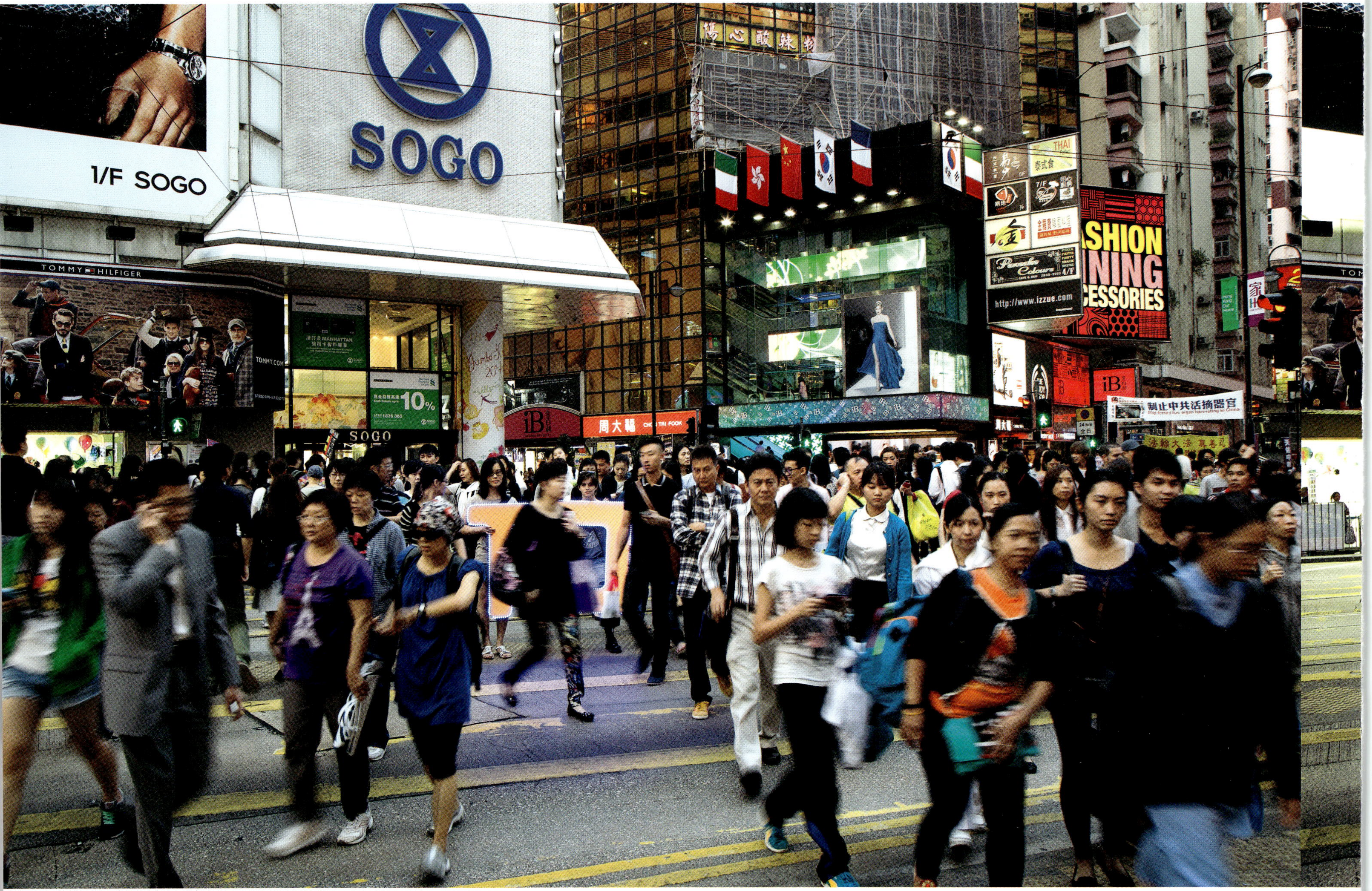
SOGO
1/F SOGO
TOMMY HILFIGER
SOGO
周大福
http://www.izzue.com
ASHION
NING
CESSORIES
THAI

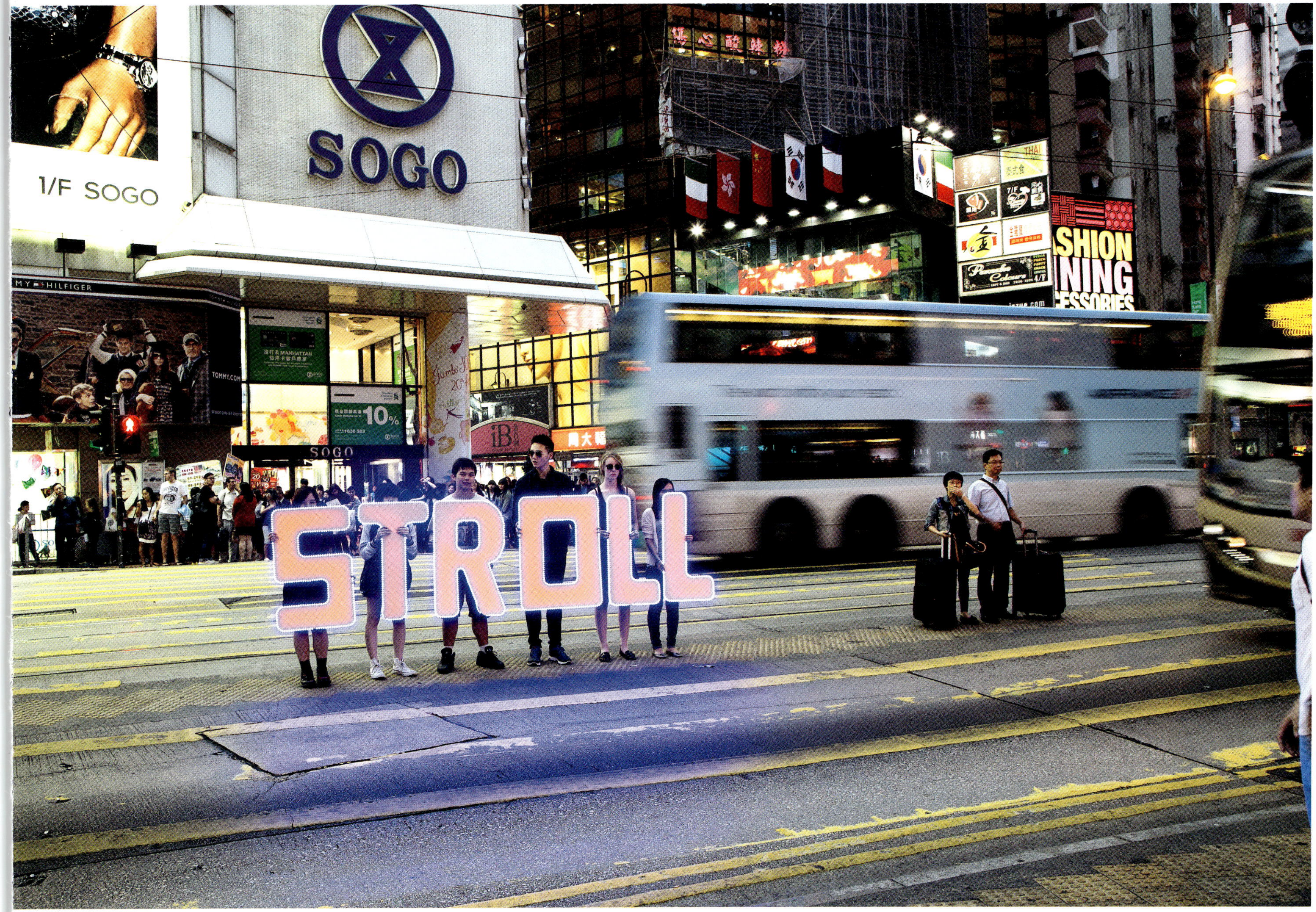

SOGO
1/F SOGO
STROLL

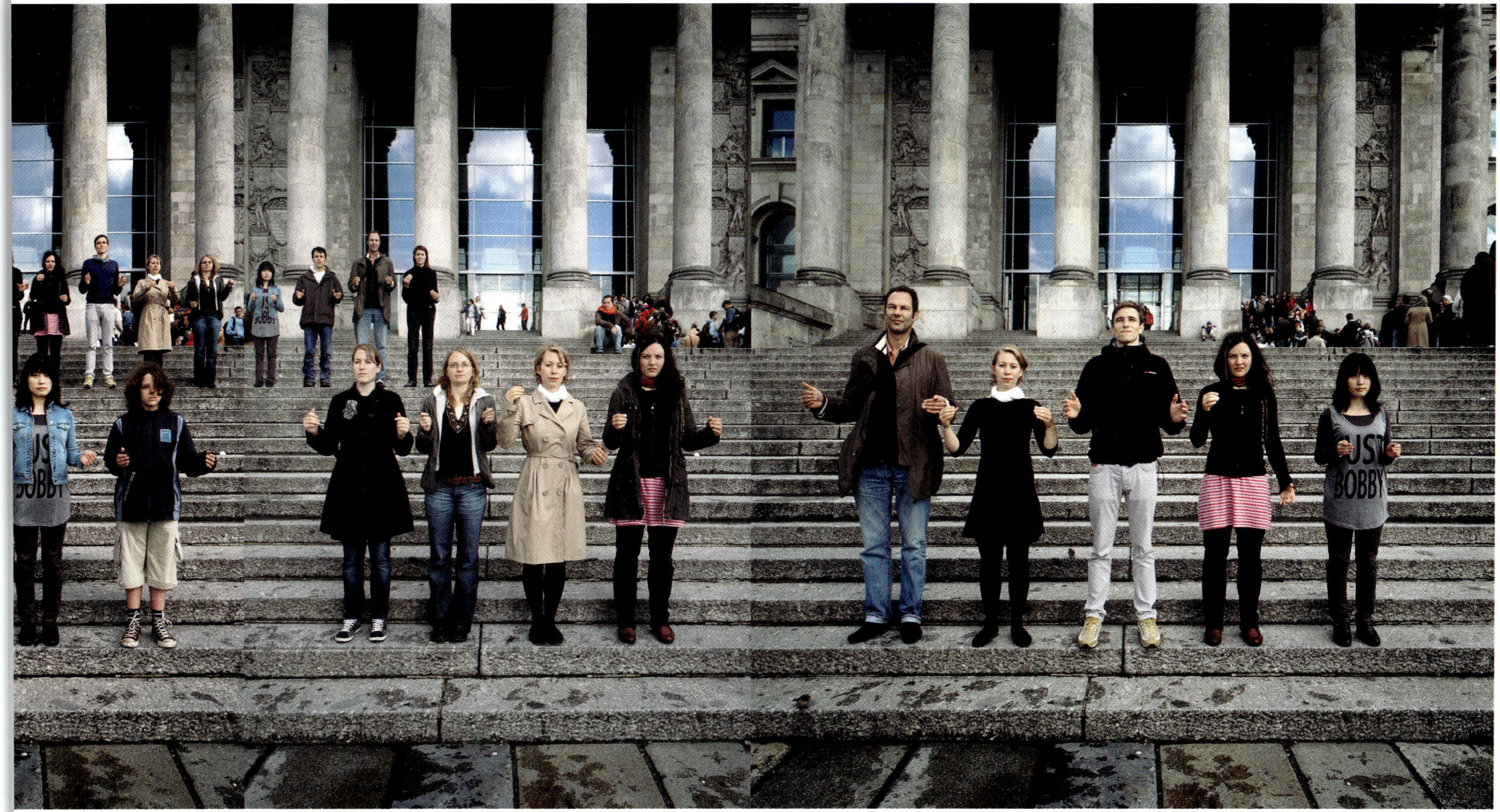

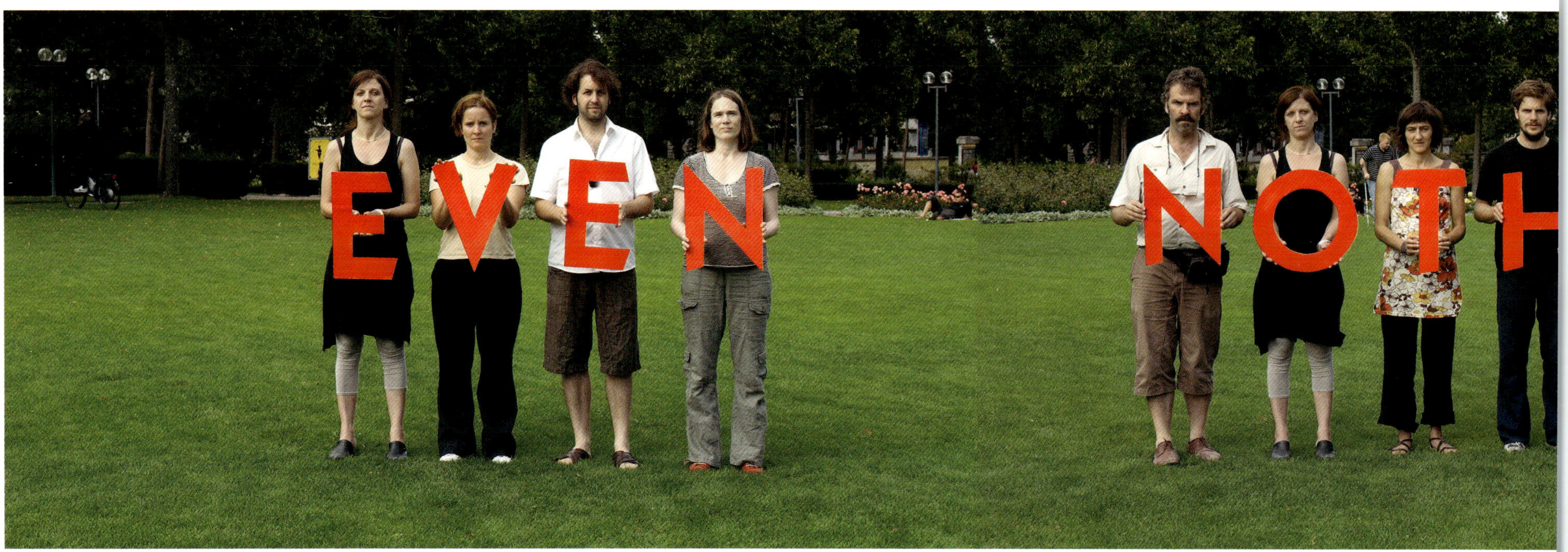


The statement of the artists in Williamson's Bern workshop is a Swiss existential joke: everything works perfectly in this well ordered country, so even if you do nothing you will still be supported by the excellent social security system. The work was shot in the placid Bern Rosengarten.

*Even Nothing Works: Bern*, 2009
*Other Voices, Other Cities* series
Pigment inks on archival cotton rag paper
Dimensions variable

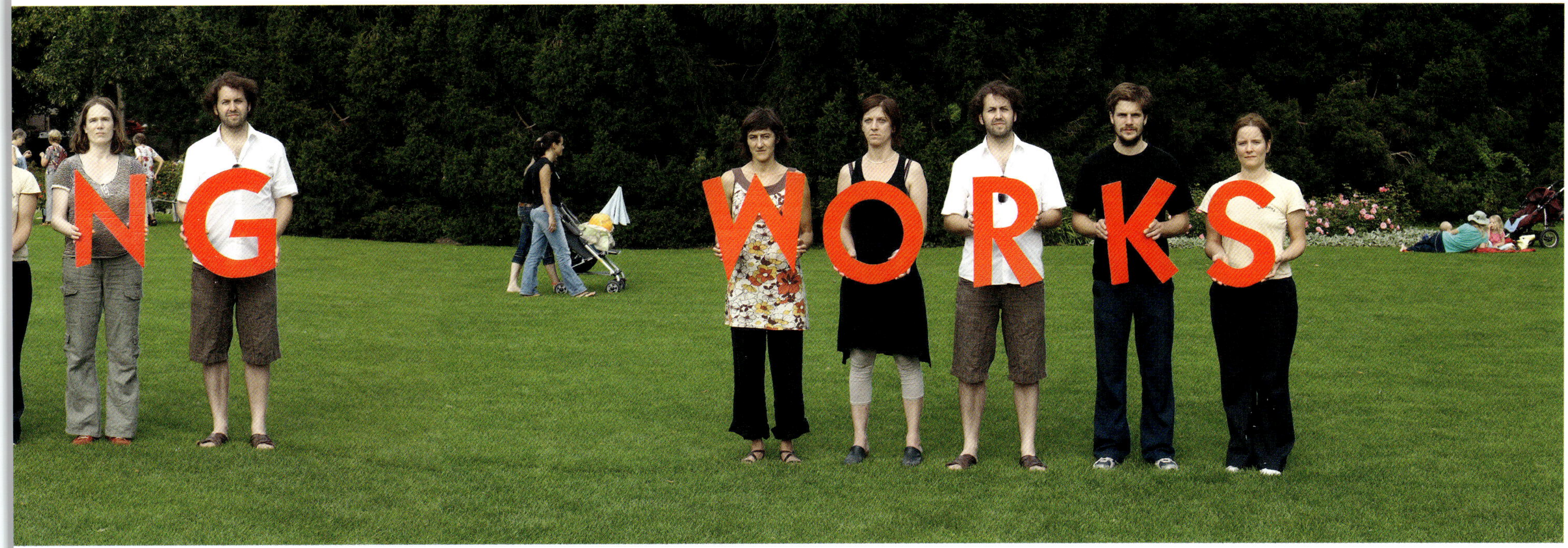
NG WORKS

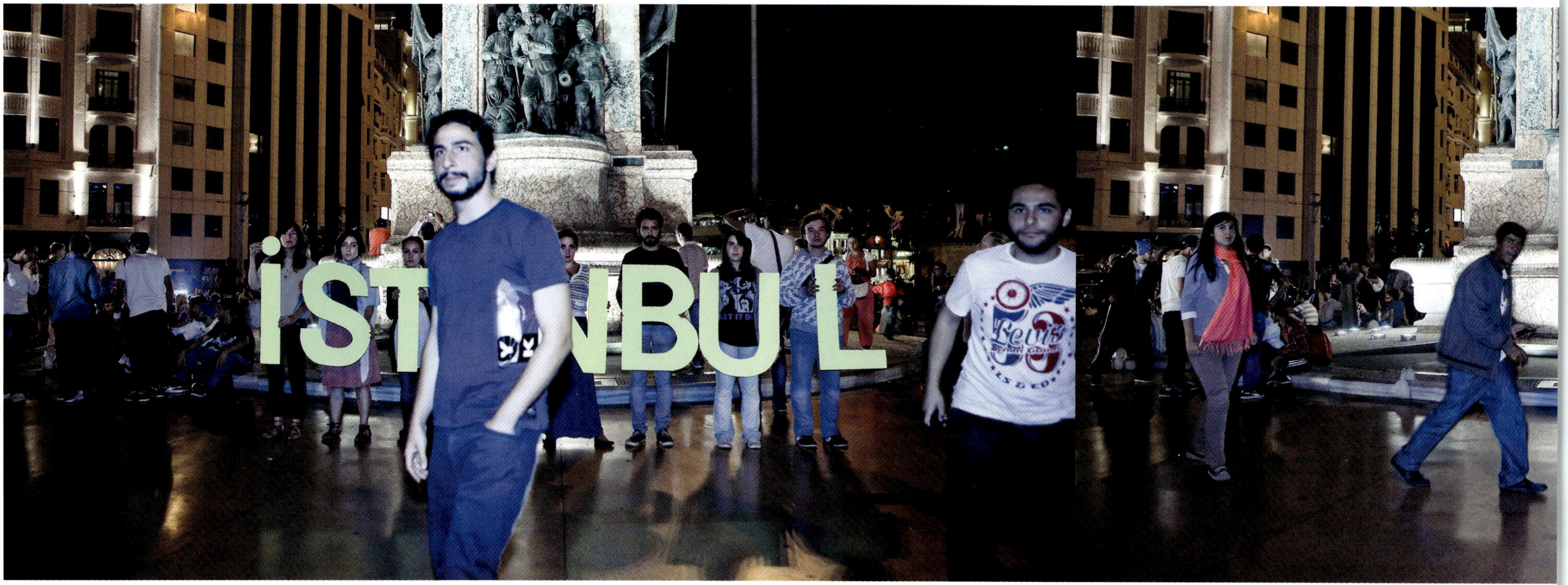


Williamson's group in Istanbul was comprised of members of staff at the 11th Istanbul Biennale, where she was exhibiting. The group decided to illustrate the "relentlessness" of their city by shooting in Taksim Square, the centre of the city, and shortly to become a lot more "relentless" during the protests that would take place there in 2013. The police tried to stop this shoot too, having looked up the word "relentless" on the internet and taking exception to it.

*Istanbul is Relentless: Istanbul*, 2011
*Other Voices, Other Cities* series
Pigment inks on archival cotton rag paper
Dimensions variable

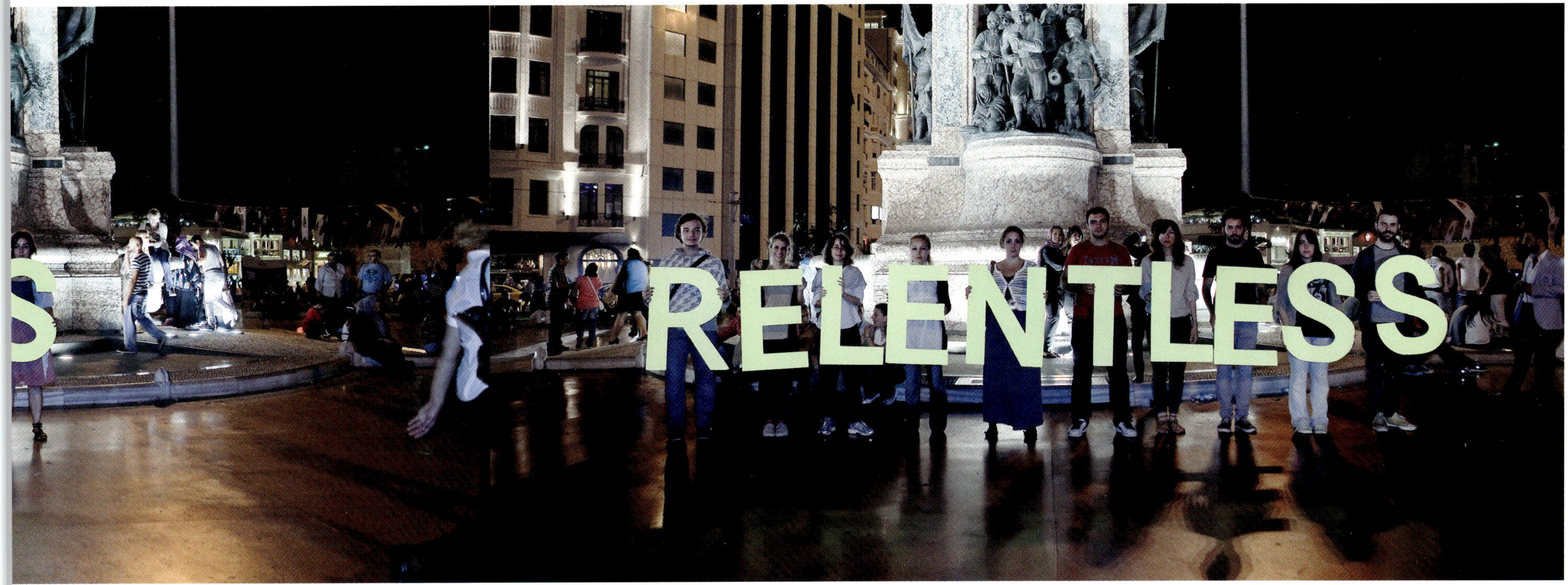
S RELENTLESS

# Three Generations

All Our Mothers

There's something I must tell you

*In* Three Generations, *Sue Williamson looks back over work made decades earlier. In* All Our Mothers, *she reconsiders—and augments—the archive of portraits she had been taking of women since the 1980s. For* There's something I must tell you, *she revisits the generation of remarkable women she first portrayed in* A Few South Africans (1983–7), *and records their conversations with their "grand-daughters". With* A Few South Africans, *early in her career, Williamson had sought to remedy the iconography of the liberation struggle by putting images of strong women into the public domain. Even after South Africa adopted a constitution that entrenches gender equality, Williamson has consciously sought to represent women's subjectivities in the country's narrative of transformation from apartheid to democracy.*

pp. 227-33
pp. 235-43
pp. 10, 31-9

**Mark Gevisser**: You have never, really, stopped taking portraits of women…
**Sue Williamson**: Well, I never really stop taking photographs. But yes, I do find taking portraits of women particularly absorbing, always just using natural light.

In the beginning, I wasn't setting out to take portraits to be printed and exhibited as photographs. I was taking them to be an element in another art work: to be turned into a film positive to expose on to a metal photo etching plate for my *A Few South African* prints, for instance.

Or, in 1990, when I was doing a residency at the National Gallery, I started on a series where I would invite women to collaborate on making collages about their lives on my Canon colour photocopier. I took a few photographs that I really liked at that time, like this one of Cheryl Carolus. She was one of the most committed activists. Here she looks very young and vulnerable. But also full of energy. p. 227

I continued photographing women, when the opportunity arose, and particularly women who had been part of the struggle. I suppose it was a way of keeping a record, in the post-apartheid era, of what these extraordinary women had done, and what had become of them. And so, in recent years, I've gone back to many of the women I photographed in the 1980s, for *A Few South Africans*, and photographed them again.

**MG**: Why did you call this series of photographs *All Our Mothers*?
**SW**: In 2011, *For Thirty Years Next to his Heart* (1990) was part of an exhibition of prints in the collection of the Museum of Modern Art in New York called *Impressions from South Africa: 1965 to Now*. I went to the opening, and a few days later, I was asked to take Kgalema Motlanthe, then South Africa's Deputy President, around the exhibition. When we were introduced Motlanthe said, "Sue Williamson! Honoured to meet you! You're the one who made the portraits of all our mothers!" I was so deeply touched pp. 81-7

that he knew the work. I began thinking again even more about the "mothers" he was talking about—the mothers of the nation, the generation of veteran pp. 10, 31-9 activist women who feature in *A Few South Africans*. I had been thinking a lot about them anyway, but Motlanthe's words strengthened the resolve.

pp. 235-243 **MG**: How did this lead you into *There's something I must tell you*?
**SW**: I was actually in the middle of a Creative Arts fellowship from the Rockefeller Foundation at Bellagio in Italy at the time I met Motlanthe at MoMA. There was a lot of hype, back in South Africa, about "twenty years since the end of apartheid", and I was going through my own process of reflection. Where are we now? And how can we reflect on where we've come from? I did want to interview those women from my *Few South Africans* series again. But at the same time I was wondering what the young people in the country were thinking and feeling. So I came up with the idea of asking my initial subjects to be in dialogue with their grand-daughters, and to make a video work around that.

**MG**: That work has been very well received. You have just returned from Athens where it was part of "Fireflies in the Night", three nights of all night video screenings. What are you doing next?
**SW**: I am beginning to work on another intergenerational piece, part of a project initiated by Pumla Gobodo-Madikizela, who was on the Truth and Reconciliation Commission and is now a research professor of psychology at the University of Free State. I will be interviewing people across the generations—again!—to consider, specifically, how the violence of the apartheid years has impacted on the young people of today. The aftermath of the TRC, twenty years on, as it were. I'll make a video installation—there will also be scholarship, and a theatrical production. I'm particularly interested in Pumla's mission to develop an African way of dealing with the trauma of memory. She talks about the Holocaust, for example, and quotes Hannah Arendt as saying "These are unforgivable sins!" But she maintains that such a moral position is more difficult in countries like Rwanda and South Africa, where perpetrators and victims have to live side-by-side after atrocities. What does this mean, in terms of how people deal with trauma and memory? I'm deeply interested in trying to find out.

I have already started a conversation with Candice Mama, a young woman whose father, Glenack, a driver for the ANC, was shot dead in his vehicle by Vlakplaas commander Eugene de Kock, when Candice was eight months old. Last year, the National Prosecuting Authority approached the Mama family and asked if they would like to meet De Kock in jail. They decided they did want to hear his account of the incident. After listening to his story, the family, each one in turn, told him they forgave him.
The rough storyboard, opposite, shows the opening sequence of the first of the stories planned for the new work, to be projected on to side by side screens. Candice will be filmed in black and white, standing in front of the bridge under which her father drove to his death. She is silent, gazing directly into the camera, but we hear her voice as titles picking up the story scroll down the screen. As the story of the past event ends, we cut to the present, to colour, to close ups of Candice in conversation with others, on the subject of why she has chosen to forgive her father's killer, and how she came to that point.
As this book goes to press, De Kock is out on parole, but it is hoped to include his voice, as the perpetrator, in some way.

Draft storyboard for the opening sequence of a new two channel video currently in preparation

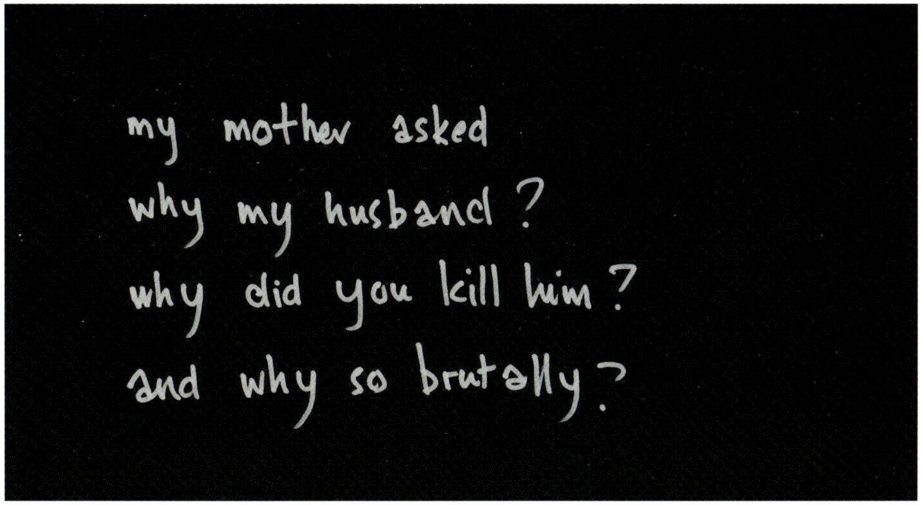
my mother asked
why my husband?
why did you kill him?
and why so brutally?

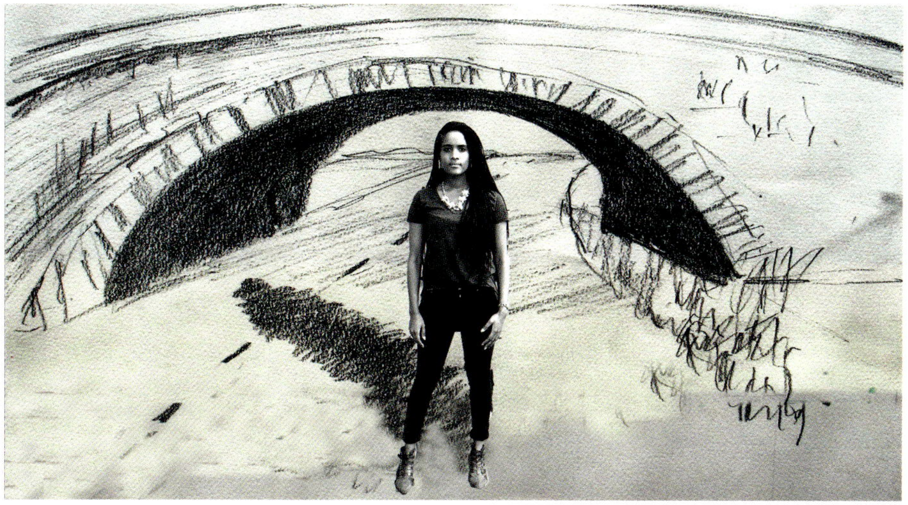

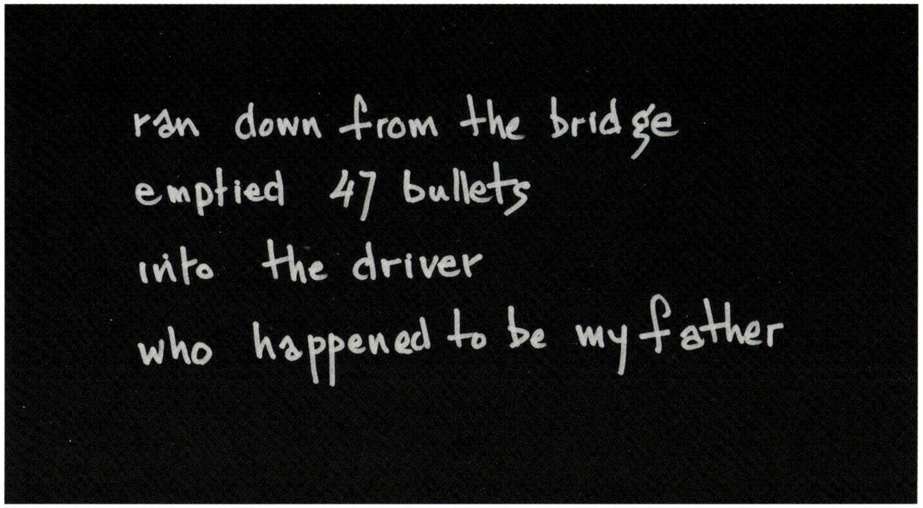
ran down from the bridge
emptied 47 bullets
into the driver
who happened to be my father

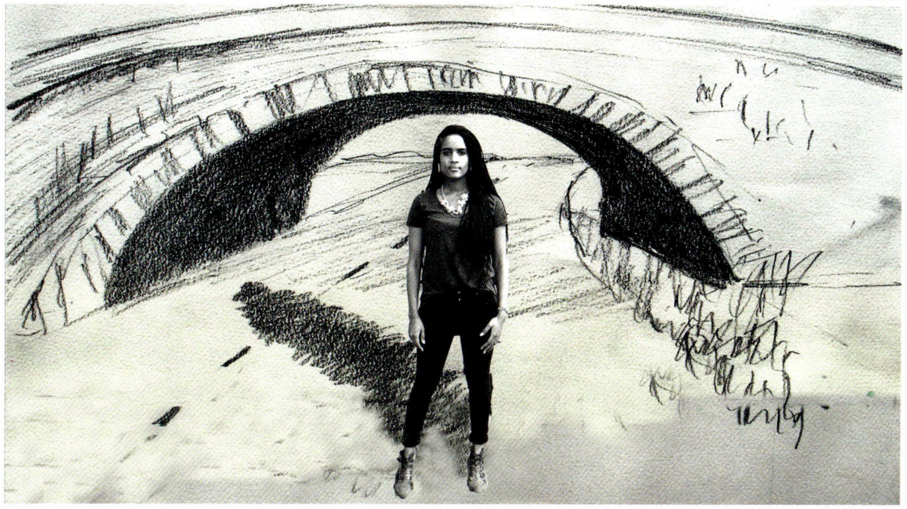

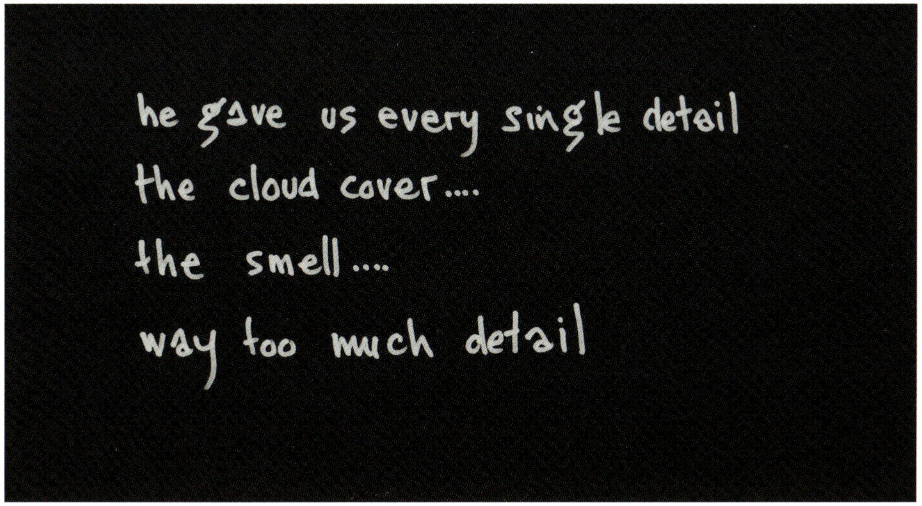
he gave us every single detail
the cloud cover....
the smell....
way too much detail

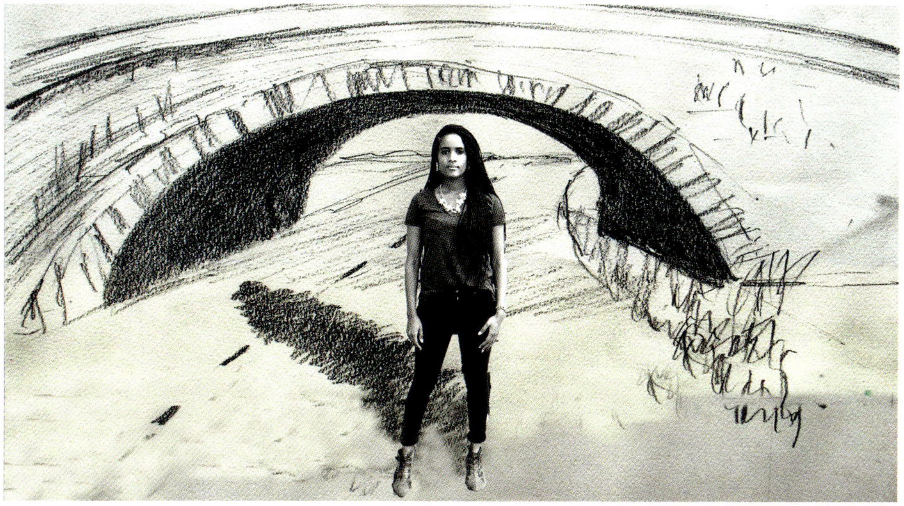

# All Our Mothers

*All Our Mothers* is a survey of the photographs Sue Williamson finds most compelling, out of the many she has taken of women she has met and interacted with—as both an activist and an artist—since the early 1980s. She initially took the photographs to be pp. 10, 31-9 used as the basis for her *A Few South Africans* photo etching series, but when she started paging through all her old black and white contact sheets in 2012, she decided to print selected ones as stand alone images.

p. 231 Here is the Crossroads mother, sitting with her children on her bed, exposed to the elements, first used by the artist with a different background for p. 39 *Case No. 6831/21* (1984). Here we see the photo p. 228 of Ellen Kuzwayo, taken for a book cover design in 1990: the anti-apartheid activist leans forward as she tells the story of the dispossession of her family's p. 228 farm. Here is Fatima Meer, the veteran activist and academic, regal on a chair on the step of a house on the fringes of District Six, where she was visiting. p. 229 And here is Eslina Silinga, turning quizzically as she walks around the Langa graveyard with the artist, who p. 38 will be making a new cradle for the grave for Eslina's mother, Annie.

Two of the women appear twice in the series: Amina p. 230 Cachalia stands outside her Fordsburg house first in 1984, then again outside the same house, though p. 231 she was no longer living there, in 2012. Caroline Motsoaledi appears first in the factory where she worked as a seamstress to support her family with her husband Elias was imprisoned on Robben Island, then thirty years later, in the living room of her Soweto home.

In 1990, Cheryl Carolus, who in 1998 became South African High Commissioner in London, was a dedicated activist member of the United Democratic Front, and is seen in the series in front of a graffiti inscribed wall demanding ONE NATION - ONE EDUCATION.

The 101-year-old Rebecca Kotane is the widow p. 232 of Moses Kotane, who after her husband went into exile in the 1960s, never saw him again. He died in Moscow. Rebecca was photographed in her Soweto home in 2013. Veterans who were in exile in the 1980s were also added to the series: Rica Hodgson, p. 232 who with her husband Jack, once made bombs on her kitchen table to blow up electric pylons with the intention of destabilising the apartheid government is seen in her Johannesburg home. And Ruth Mompati, p. 233 once secretary to the young lawyers Nelson Mandela and Oliver Tambo, was photographed on the occasion of the unveiling of a bust and the naming of a park after her in Vryburg, her home town in North West Province. Two weeks after this celebration in April 2015, she died.

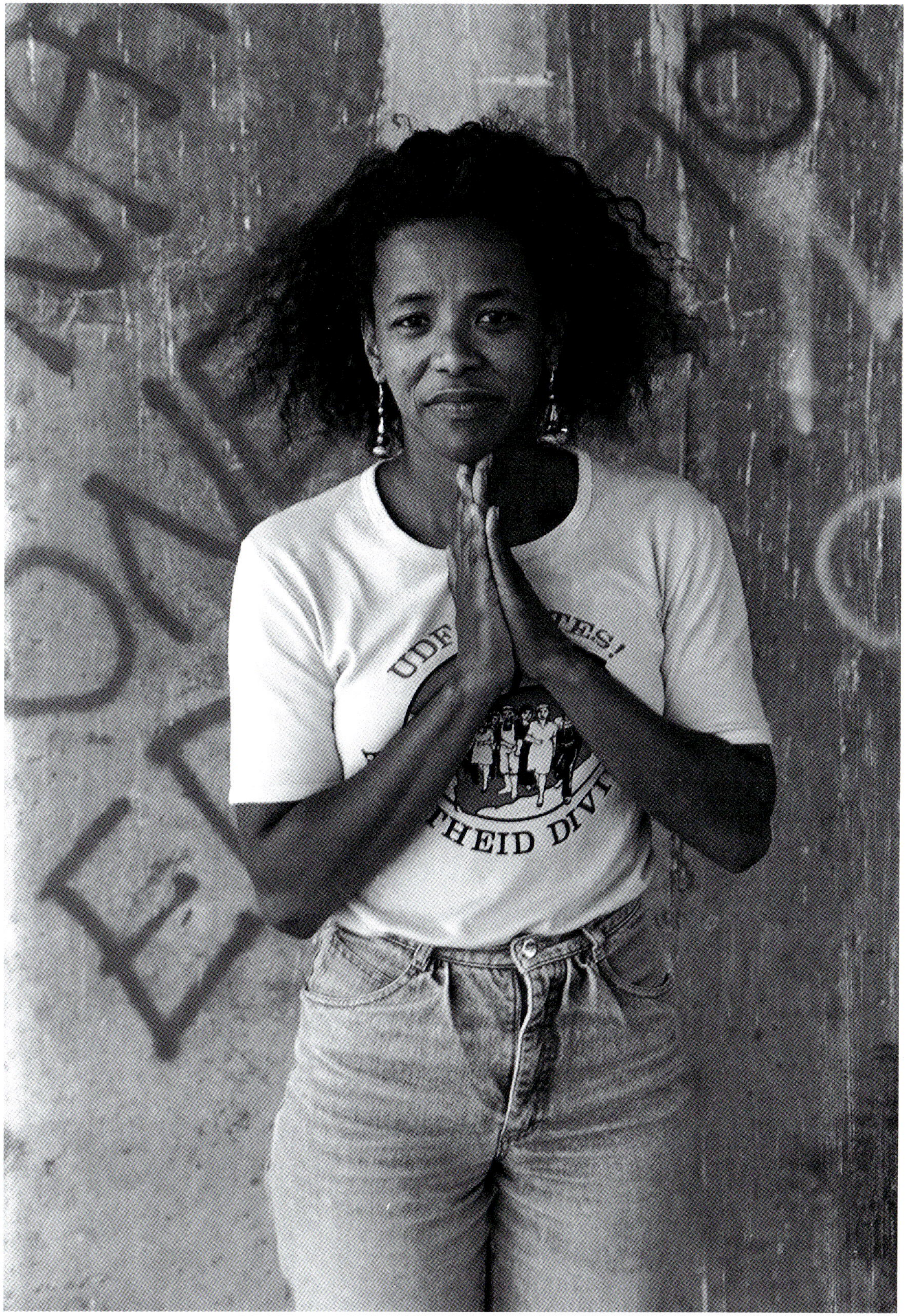

*Cheryl Carolus*
*Cape Town*
1990
*All Our Mothers* series
Pigment inks on archival paper
Image size: 59 x 39 cm

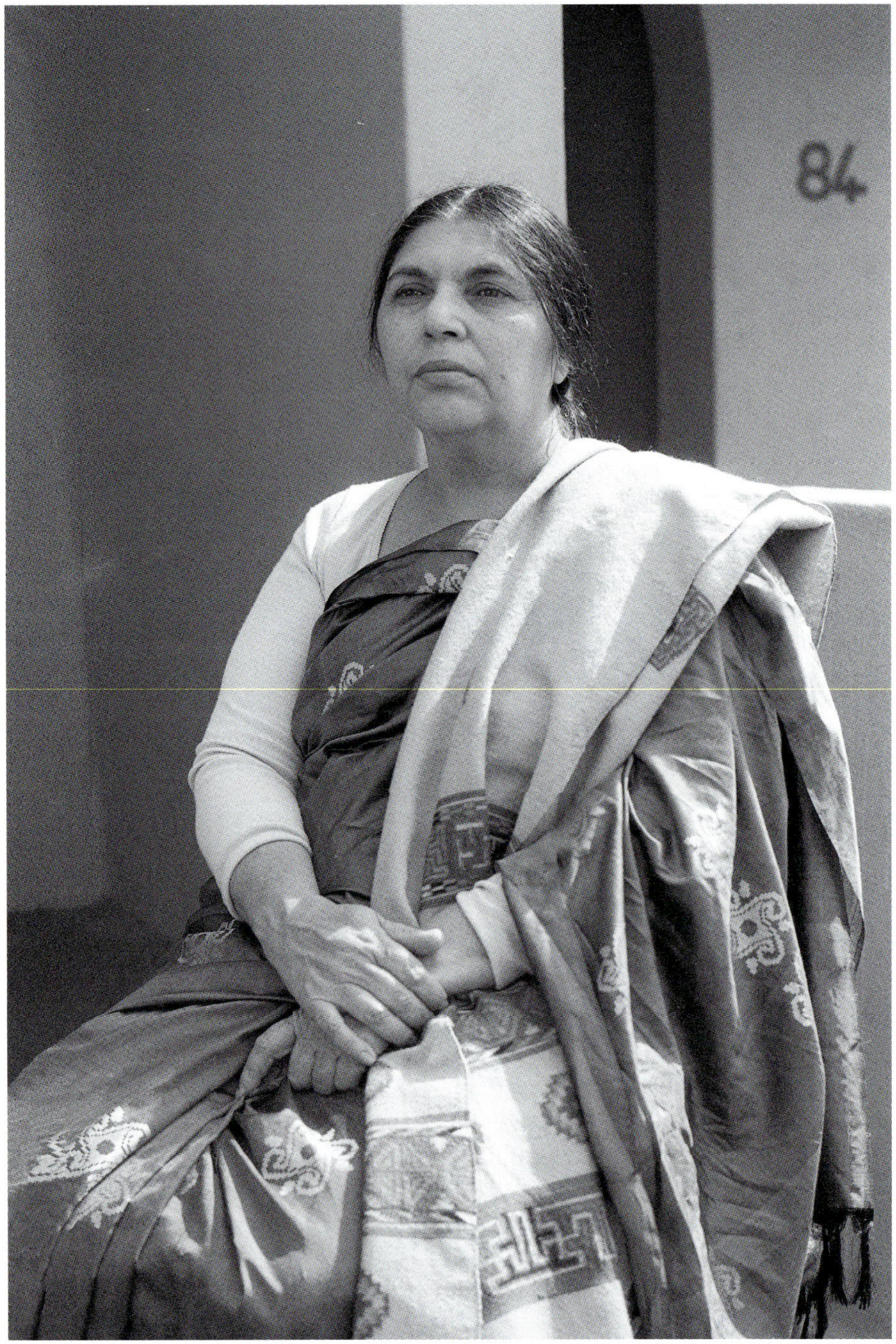


*Fatima Meer*
*Cape Town*
1989
*All Our Mothers* series
Pigment inks on archival paper
Image size: 59 x 39 cm

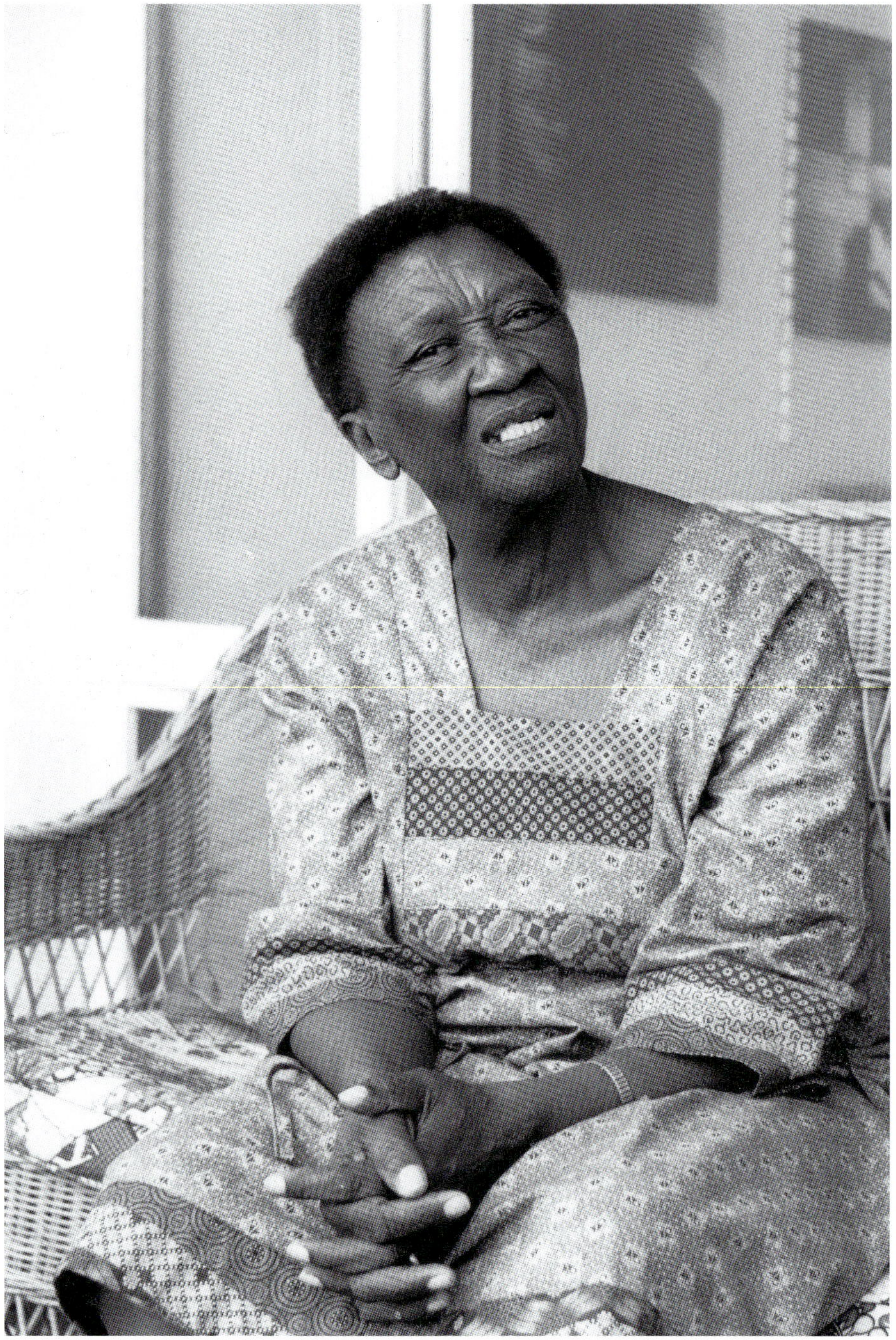

*Ellen Kuzwayo*
*Cape Town*
1983
*All Our Mothers* series
Pigment inks on archival paper
Image size: 59 x 39 cm

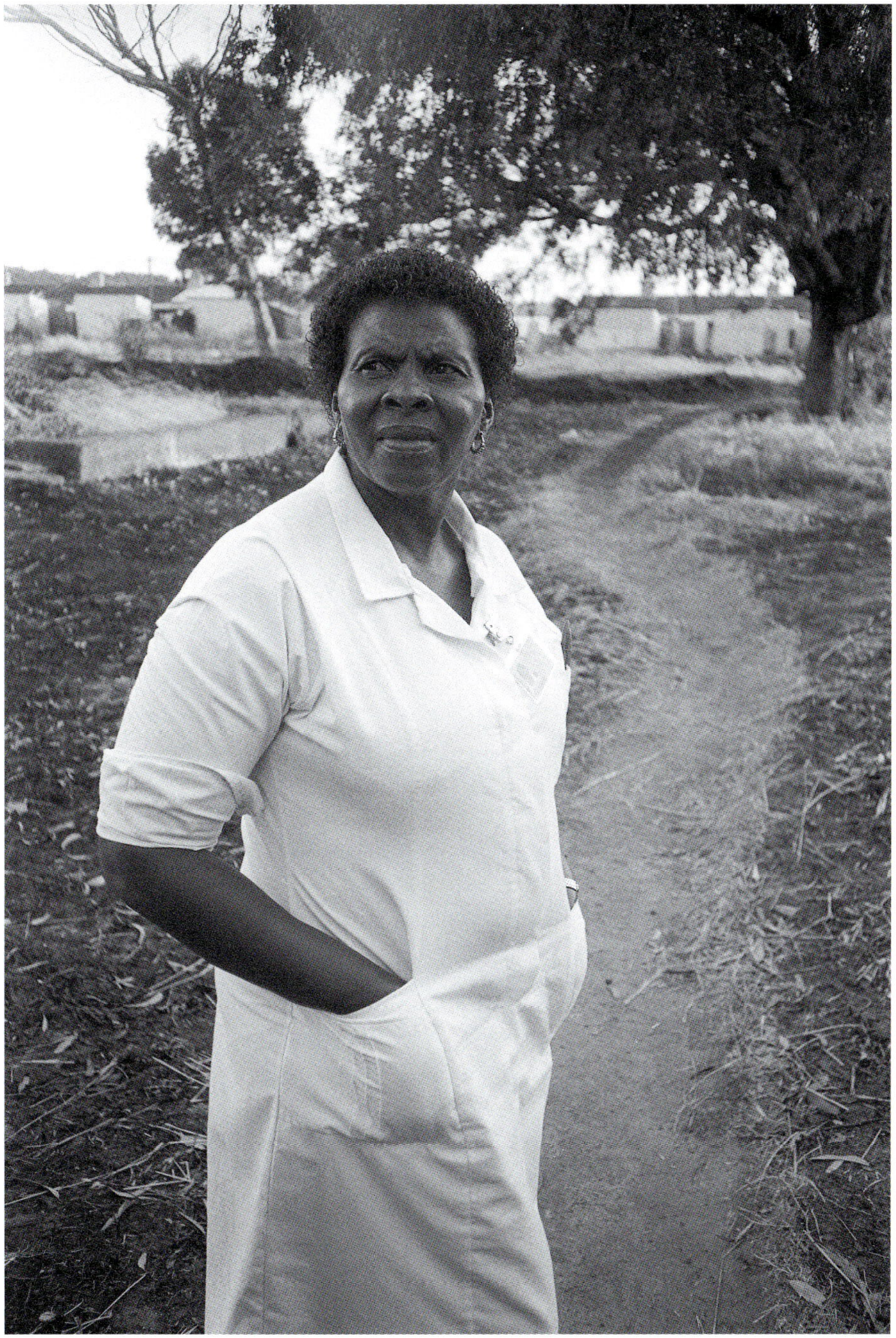

*Eslina Silinga*
*Langa graveyard*
1995
*All Our Mothers* series
Pigment inks on archival paper
Image size: 59 x 39 cm

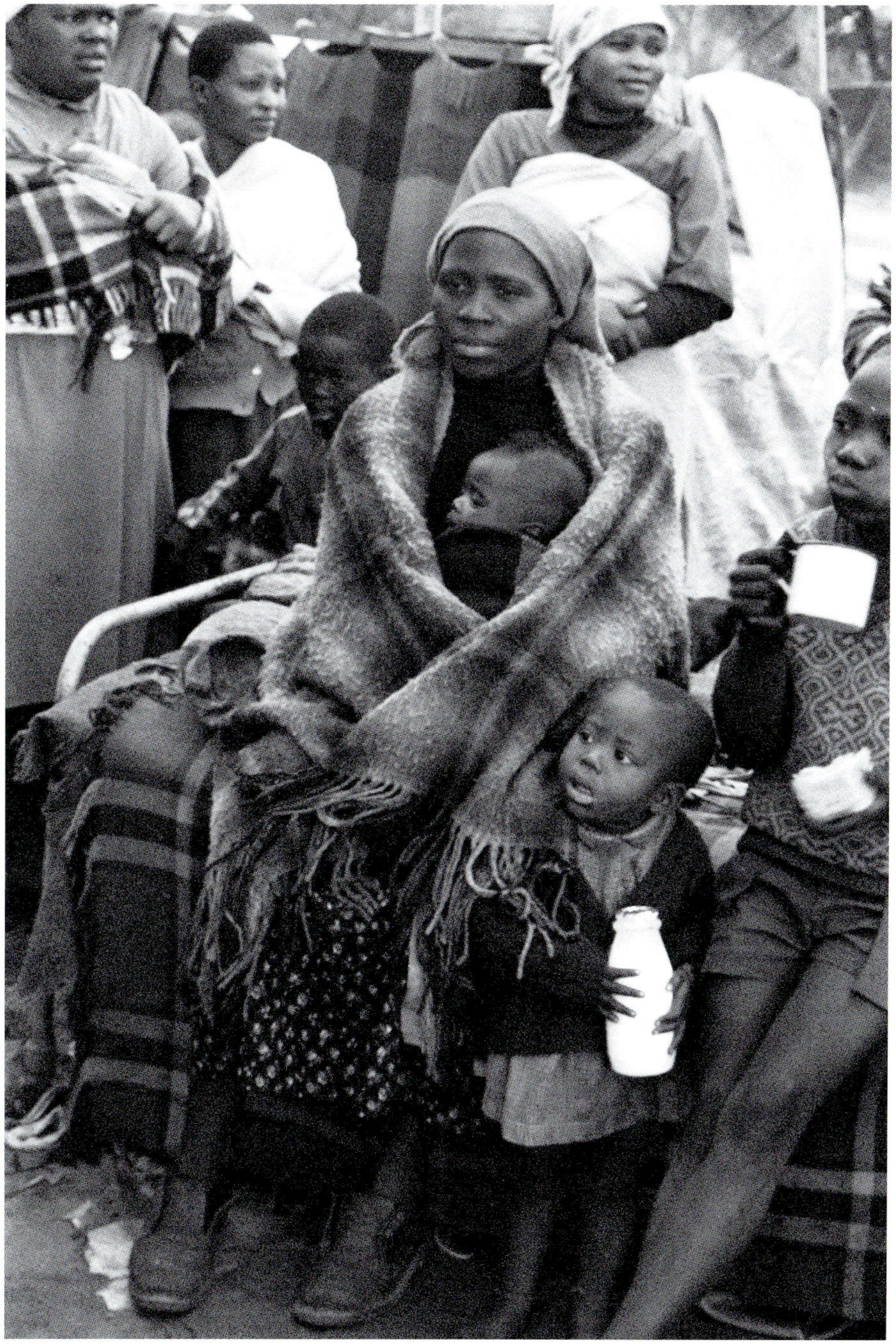

*Anonymous*
*Bed Camp, Crossroads, Cape Town*
1983
*All Our Mothers* series
Pigment inks on archival paper
Image size: 59 x 39 cm

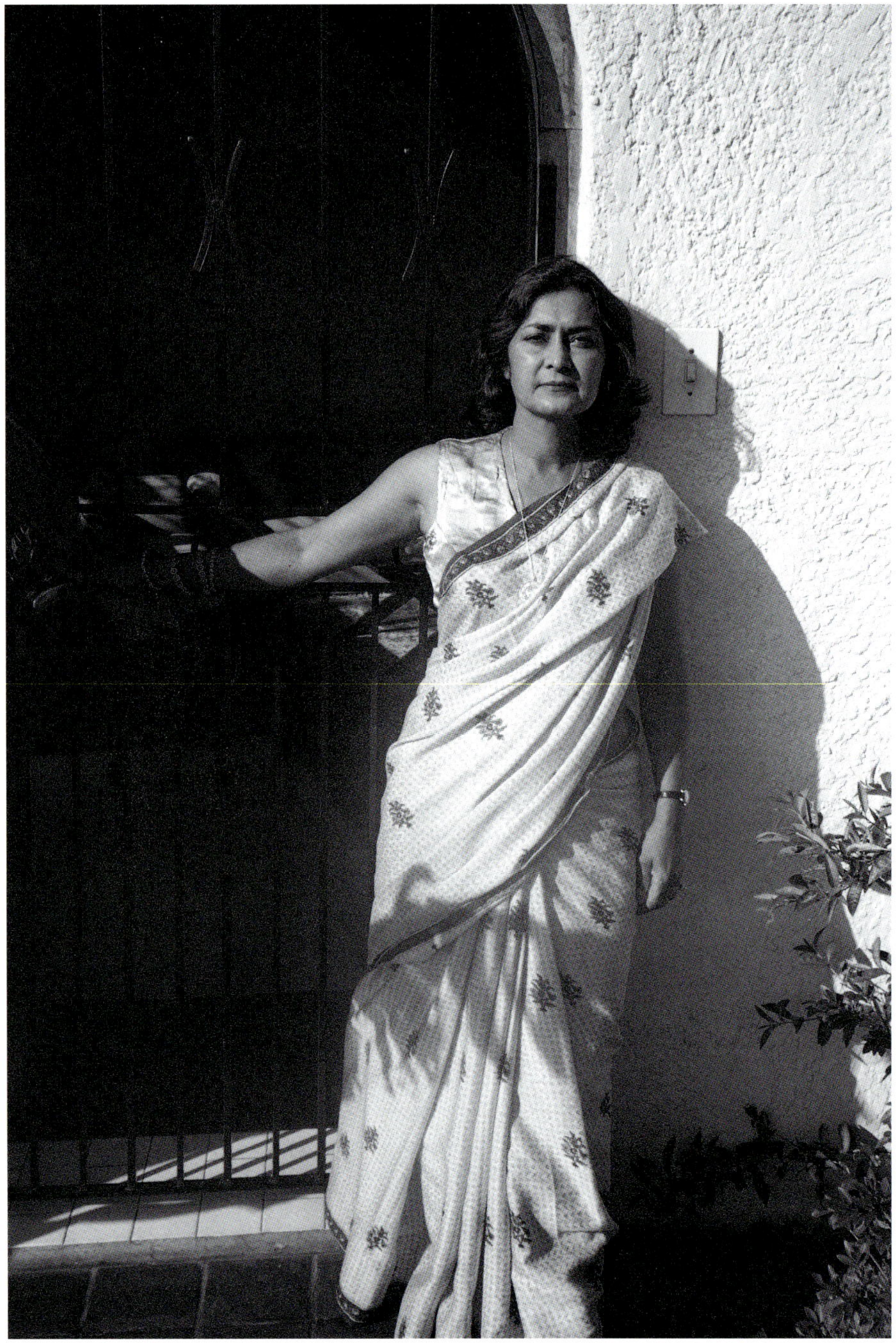

*Amina Cachalia I*
*Fordsburg*
1984
*All Our Mothers* series
Pigment inks on archival paper
Image size: 59 x 39 cm

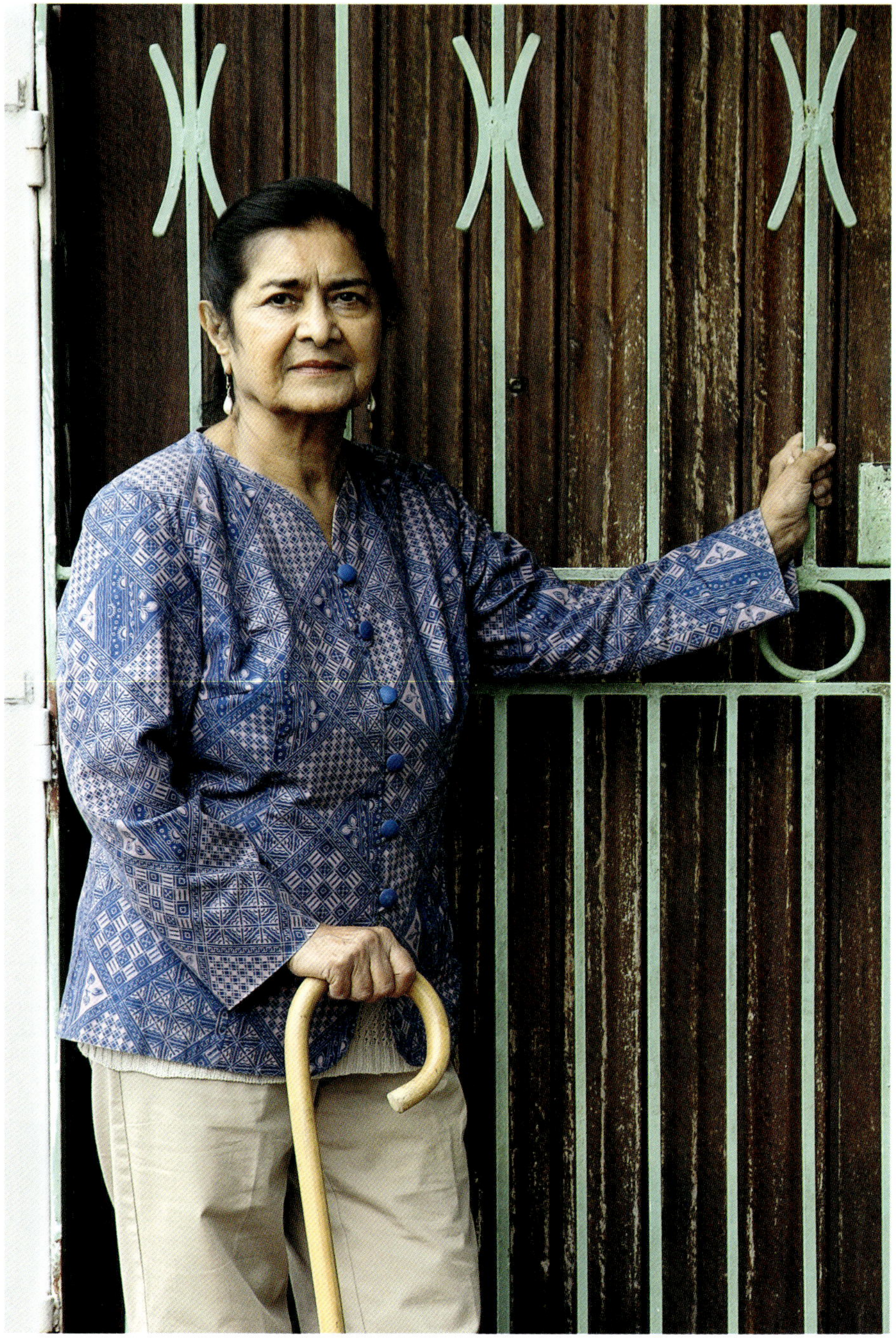

*Amina Cachalia II*
*Fordsburg*
2012
*All Our Mothers* series
Pigment inks on archival paper
Image size: 59 x 39 cm

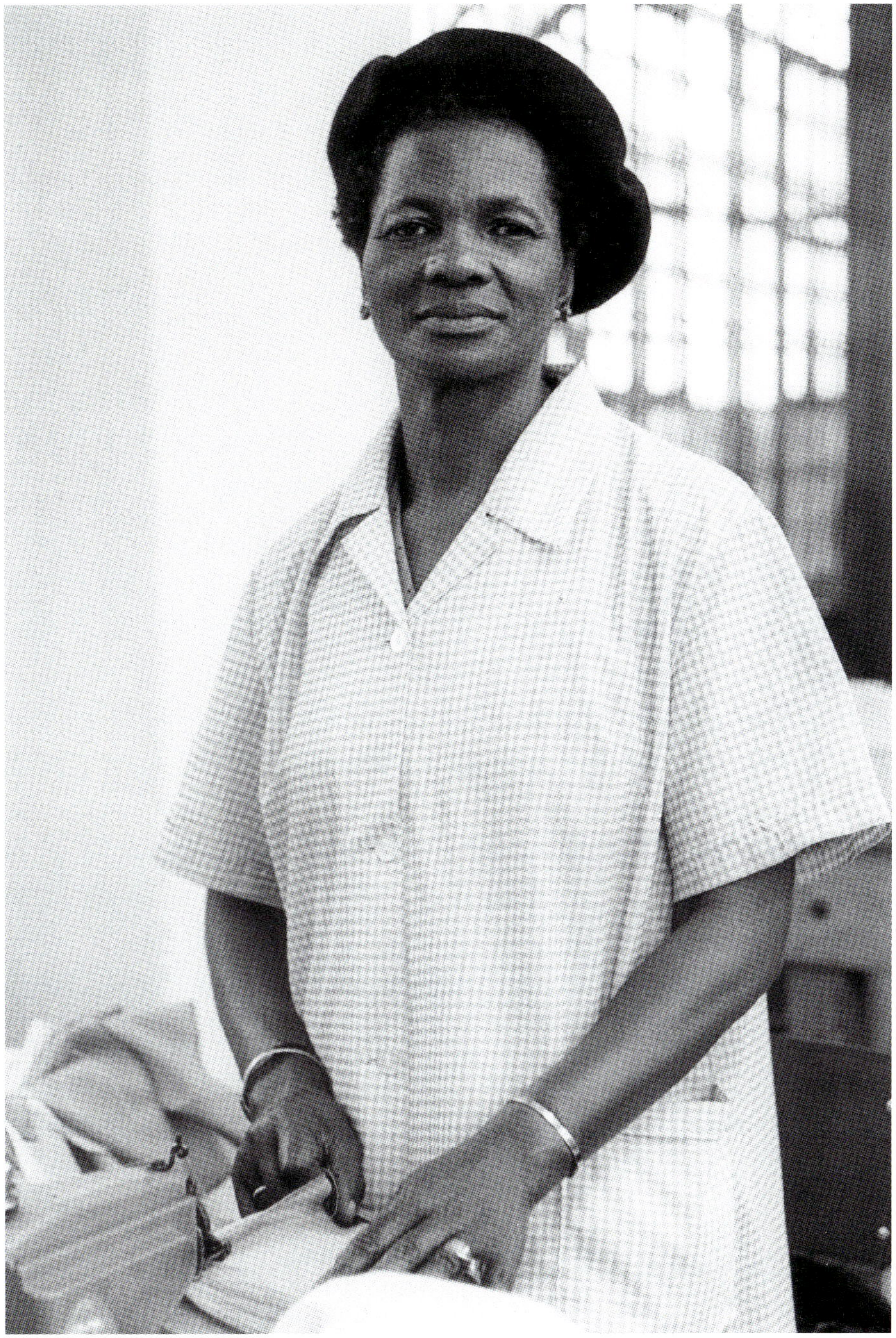

Photograph of Caroline Motsoaledi in the garment factory where she worked. Commissioned for the *A Few South Africans* series

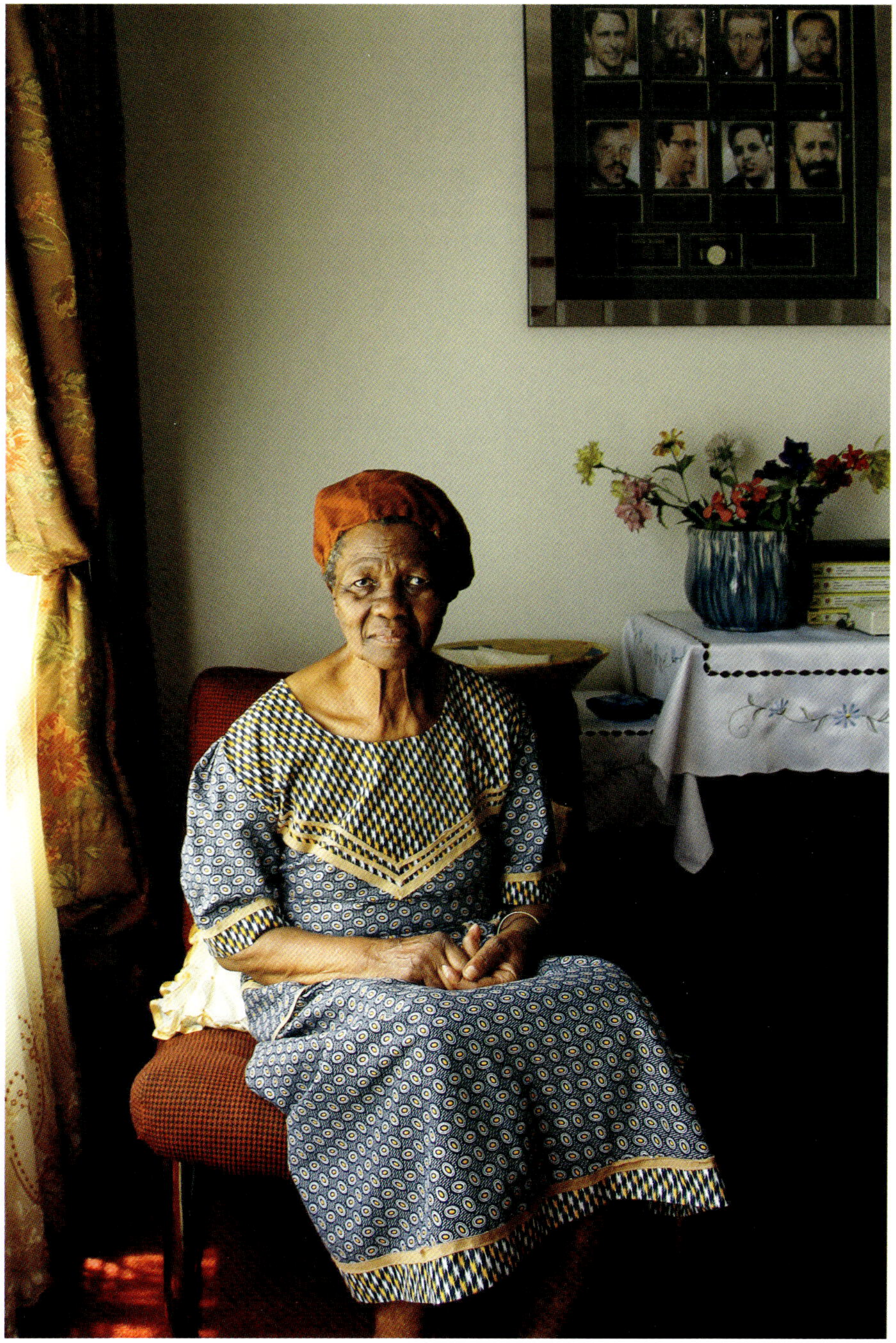

*Caroline Motsoaledi*
*Soweto*
2012
*All Our Mothers* series
Pigment inks on archival paper
Image size: 59 x 39 cm

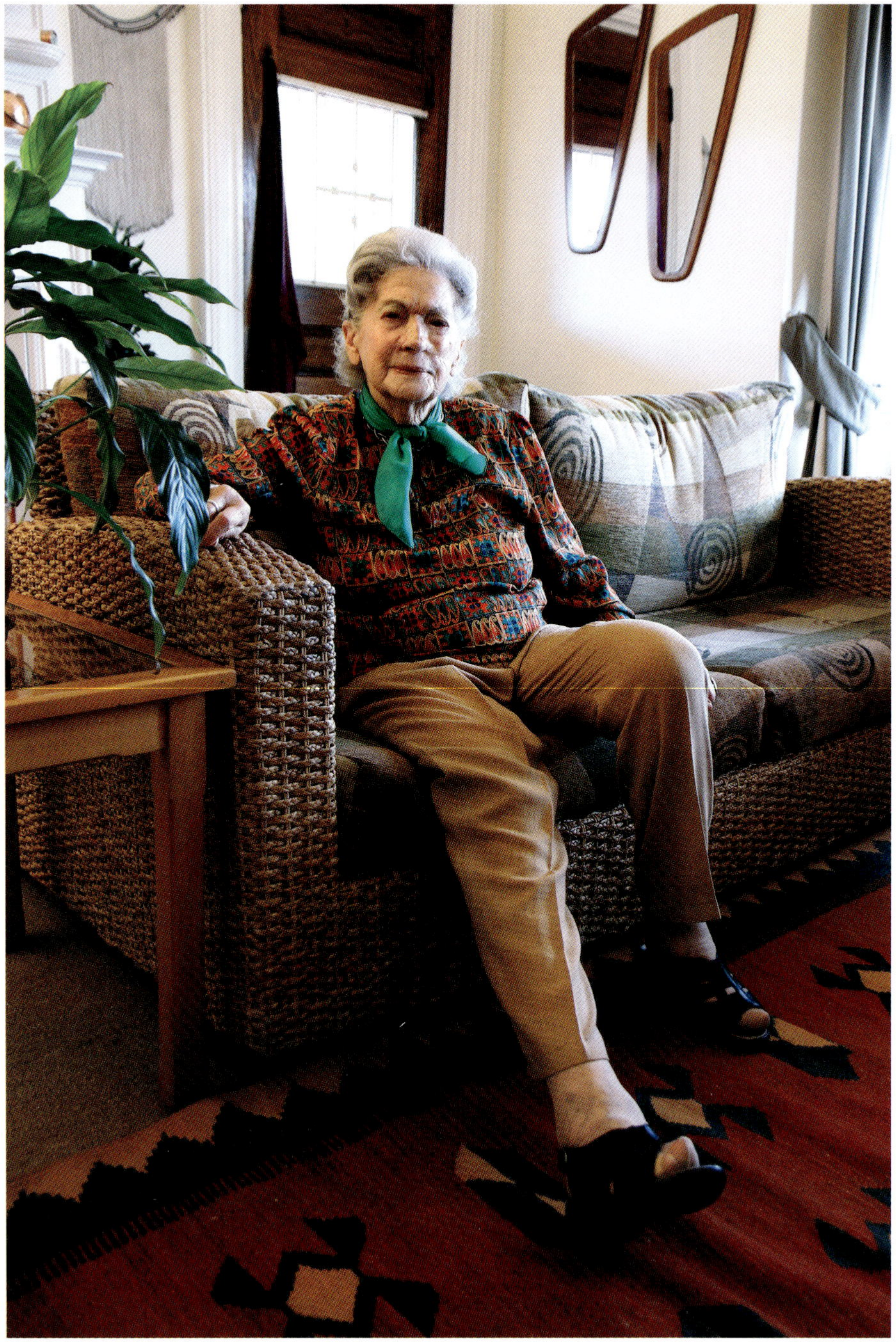

*Rica Hodgson*
*Johannesburg*
2012
*All Our Mothers* series
Pigment inks on archival paper
Image size: 59 x 39 cm

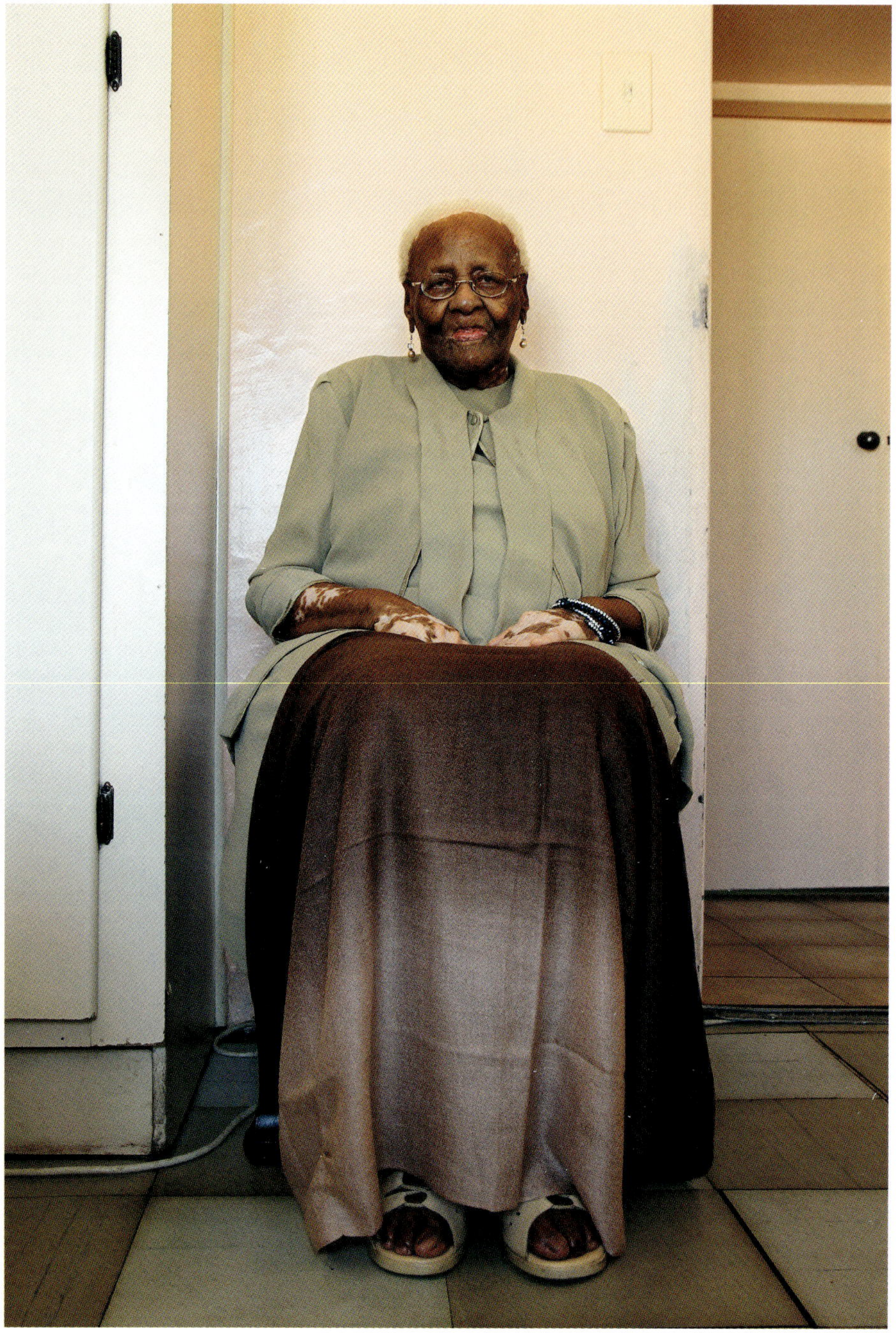

*Rebecca Kotane*
*Soweto*
2013
*All Our Mothers* series
Pigment inks on archival paper
Image size: 59 x 39 cm

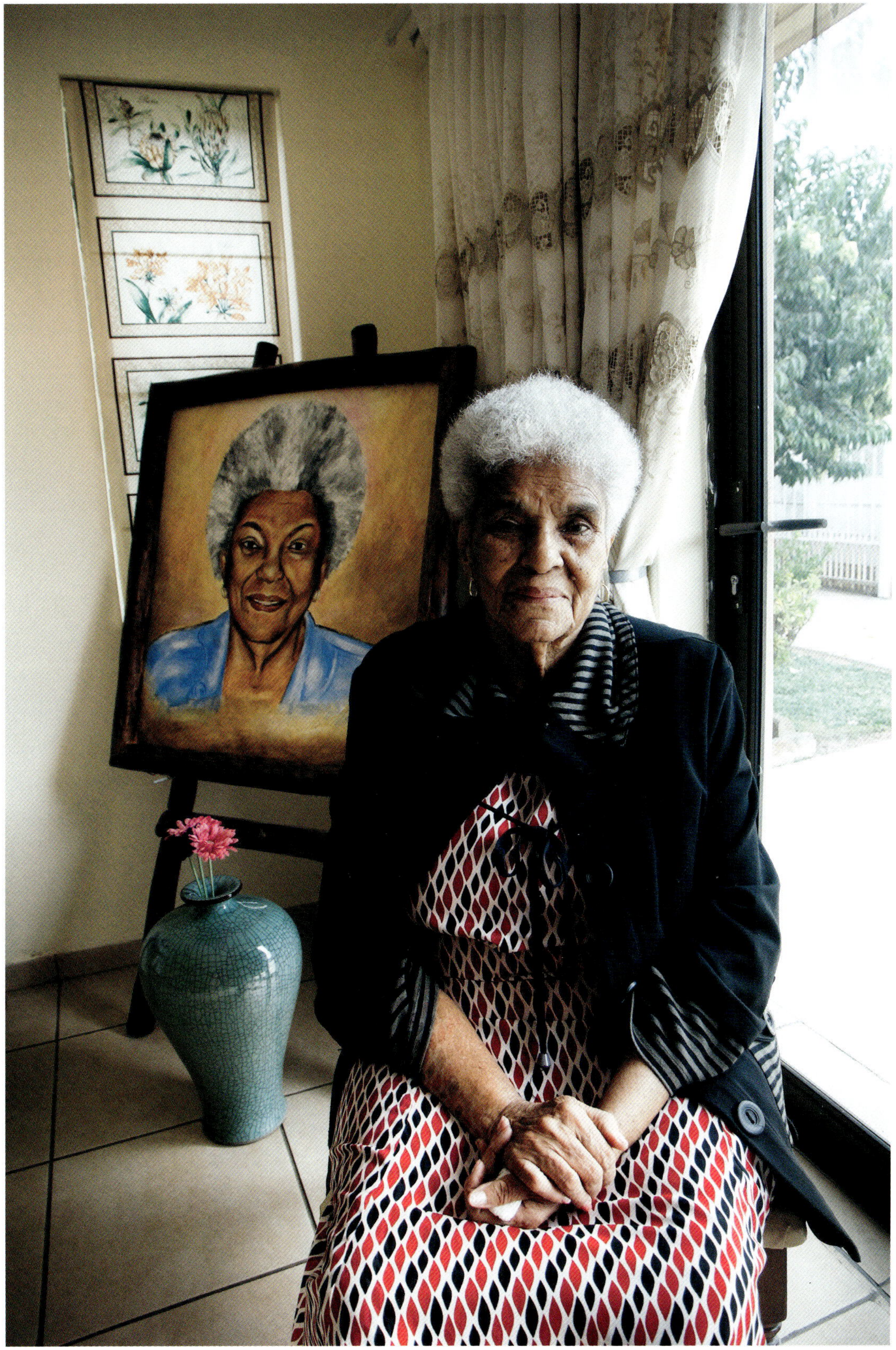

*Ruth Mompati*
*Vryburg*
2015
*All Our Mothers* series
Image size: 59 x 39 cm

# There's something I must tell you

In 2013, Sue Williamson filmed six conversations between "grandmothers" and their "grand-daughters" and titled the result, *There's something I must tell you.* All the older women had played important roles in the struggle for liberation, and the questions Williamson asked were these: Were the sacrifices you made then, worth the country we have today? Do you think the younger generation appreciates the harassment, the jail sentences, the exile you went through to win freedom?

The artist was equally interested in whether the young people were fully aware of the history of their grandmothers, and also in their opinions of the state of the country today. The answers were sometimes surprising.

p. 34 Williamson began with Amina Cachalia, one of the
pp. 10, 31-9 subjects of *A Few South Africans*, in conversation with her grand-daughter Luiza. One of the other
p. 36 grandmothers from the earlier series, Caroline Motsoaledi—the wife of Rivonia trialist Elias Motsoaledi—was filmed with her granddaughter Busisiwe, a business student. Motsoaledi was the wife of Aaron Motsoaledi, jailed for life after being sentenced with Nelson Mandela at the Rivonia trial; she had also spent much time in jail.

The 101-year old Rebecca Kotane was filmed with her grand-daughter Nompumelelo, who works in the music industry. Kotane was the widow of Moses Kotane, the legendary leader of the SA Communist Party, who died in exile in 1978. The veteran activist Vesta Smith was filmed with her grand-daughter Tammy Leigh Lodge. The first head of the Independent Electoral Commission, Brigalia Bam, was filmed with her niece Busiswa.

For her final couple, Williamson paired Ilse Wilson, the daughter of the SA Communist Party leader Bram Fischer, with Thandi Lewin, the daughter of Hugh Lewin, Fischer's cellmate and close confidant.

In installation, the filmed images are rear projected on to frosted Perspex screens suspended from the ceiling. They appear to float in the space. On the far left, images from a "photo album" flip by: the grandmother as a child, a young woman and then an older woman. The next two screens are full-length portraits of the pair, one moving image and one still, and on the right, the two engage in intense conversation.

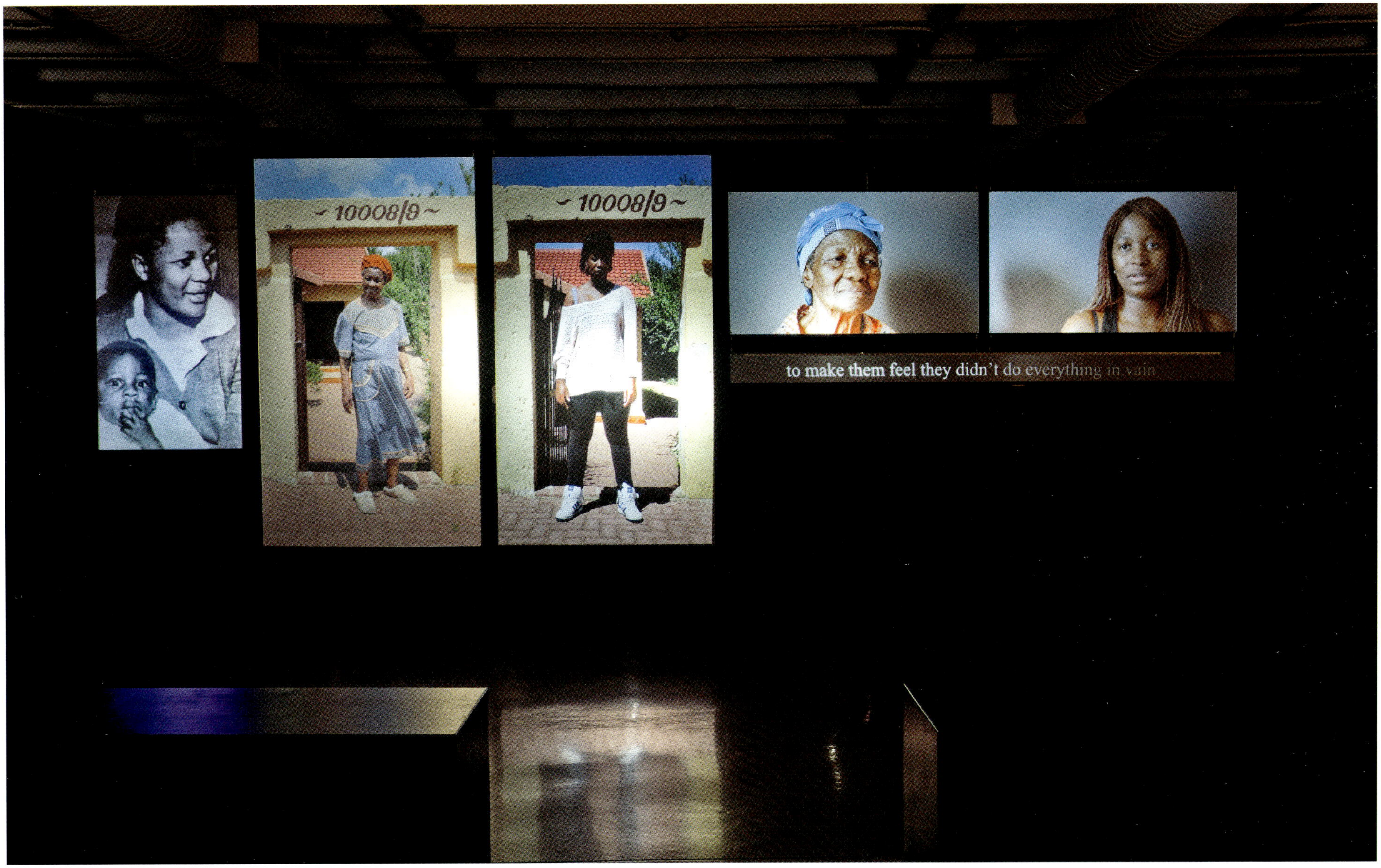


*There's something I must tell you*
2013
Caroline Motsoaledi and Busisiwe Khatibe
Six channel rear projection video
Installation view
Goodman Gallery, Johannesburg

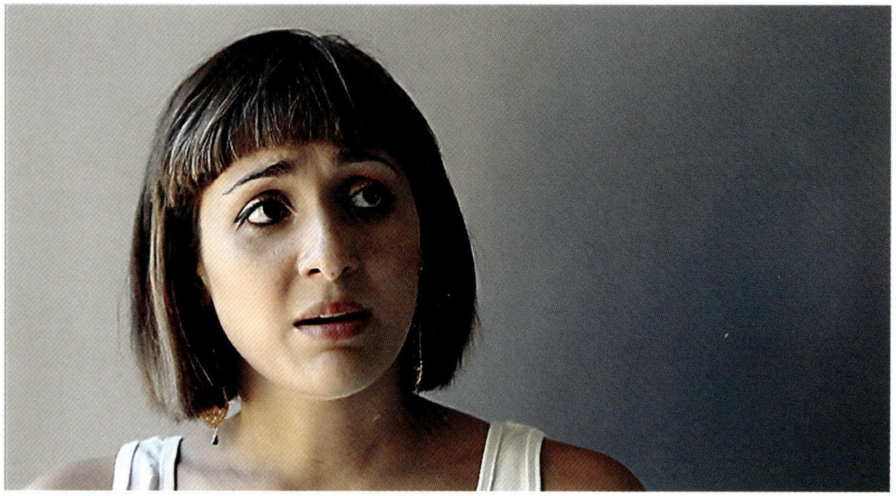

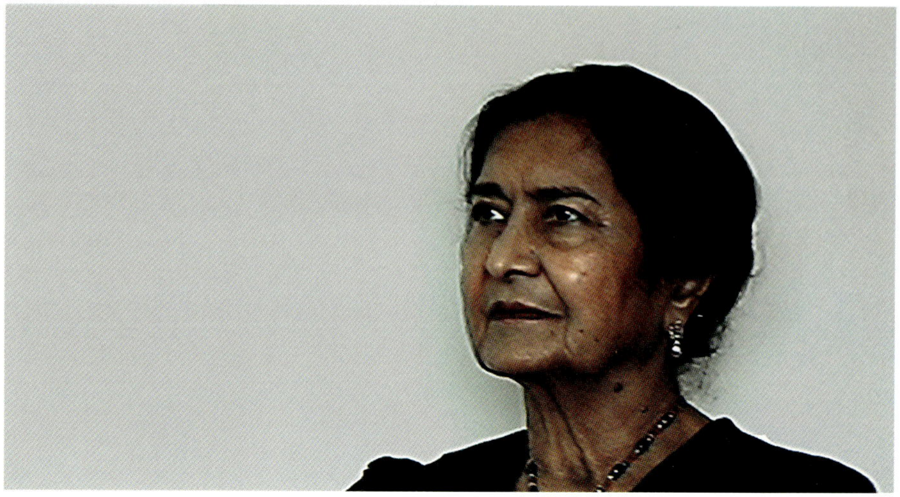

*There's something I must tell you*
2013
Amina and Luiza Cachalia
Video still (detail)

**Amina**: She came up and she rung the bell and I opened the door and for a split second I didn't know who she is, when she said, "Mama!" I realised who Luiza was and she was all blonde! Now, I've got no problem with blondes but I didn't like her being blonde.

**Luiza**: You said blondes are a certain kind of woman.

**Amina**: It didn't suit her. Not one bit!

**Luiza**: You thought I didn't look right, because I mean, that's a type of prejudice, it's a type of "racism" if you like.

**Amina**: Being blonde is no prejudice as far as I am concerned and that is definitely so, but you being blonde was just not on for me.

**Luiza**: That's what you say now.

**Luiza**: You know, it's this reservedness [of your generation] ... I feel suffocated by it. And I think for young people in South Africa, we're very angry and we exhibit that anger… Sometimes when Mama and Nelson [Mandela] get together, sometimes when they talk about apartheid it sounds like they're building it up, you know, building it up like it, kind of like ... I suppose to make yourself feel better…

**Amina**: The past had a very great meaning in my life.

**Luiza**: I know! I want you guys to say, argh ... it was ... arrgggh.

**Amina**: I never cried over apartheid, no, I was fighting apartheid all my life. I didn't want to cry. It wasn't going to beat me, I was going to beat it in the long run.

**Luiza**: I think in many ways we don't understand it. I think we admire it, but I think there's a lot of frustration between two generations and two different situations. There's pacifism and activism, you know. It's not a job. Although I'd like to be like my grandmother, how can I be like my grandmother?

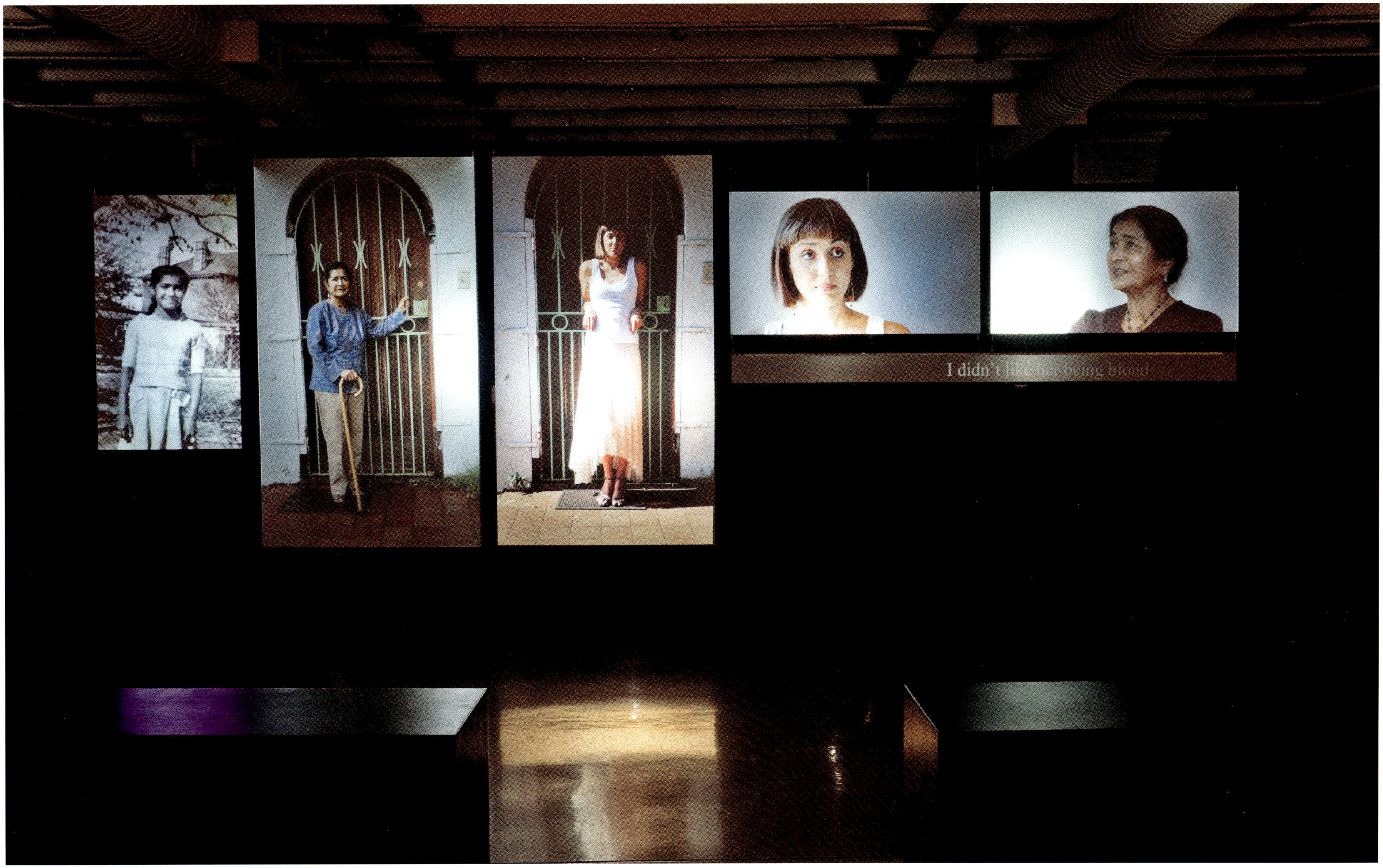


*There's something I must tell you*
2013
Amina and Luiza Cachalia
Six channel rear projection video
Installation view
Goodman Gallery, Johannesburg

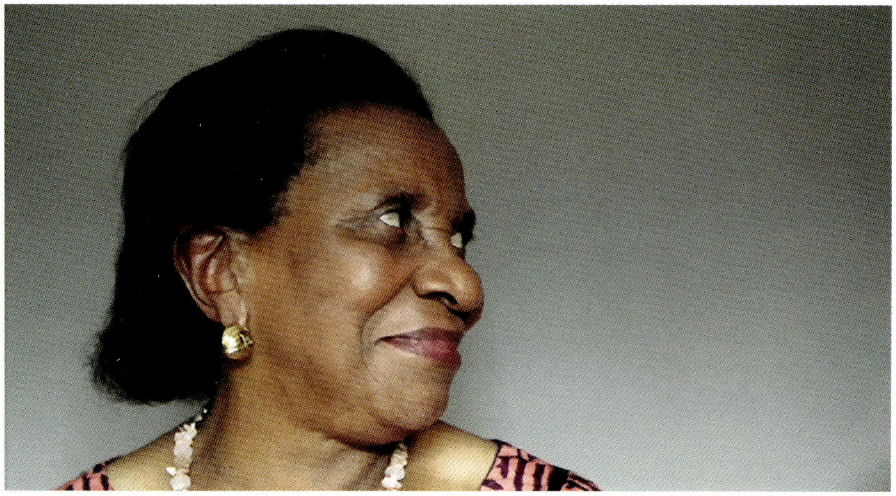

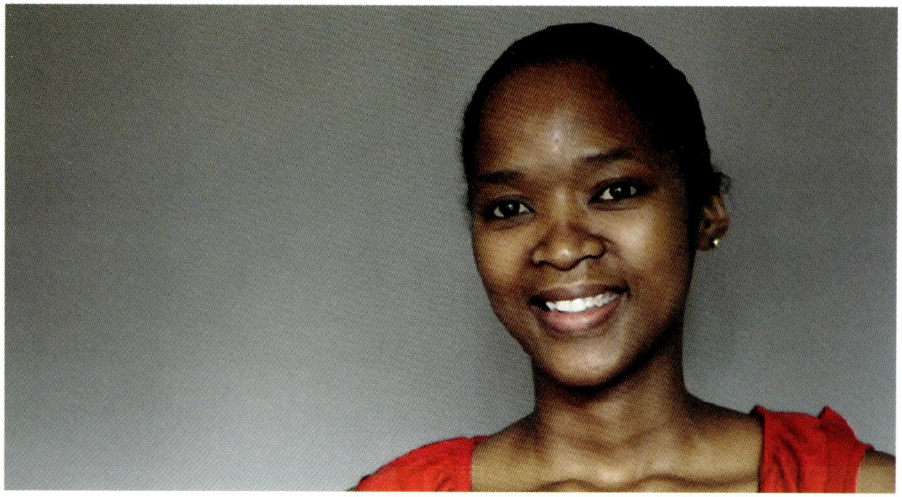

**Busiswa**: I started going to school in 1994. It was an Afrikaans school in the Eastern Cape … we always had this [thing] mentally that if you are black, then your brain's also black. You're dumb. There's no light.

**Brigalia**: The attitude of the teachers was very, very problematic.

**Busiswa**: But then I went to high school in Cape Town and we were mixed [races], that's when I started realising, "No man, I'm not stupid. I'm very smart, actually."

**Brigalia**: Racism acts in some very subtle forms. It also has implications on how we are equal in opportunities.

**Busiswa**: We forget, because we were not part of it and because we did not live in that generation.

*There's something I must tell you*
2013
Brigalia and Busiswa Bam
Video still (detail)

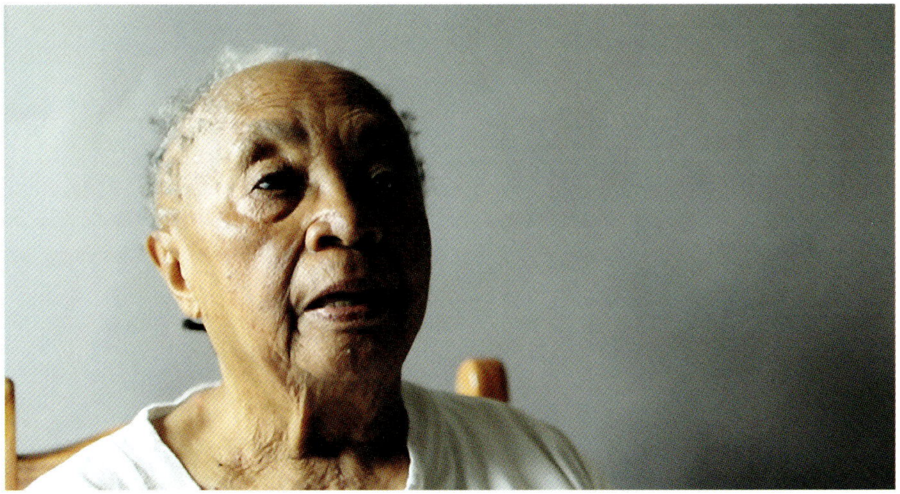

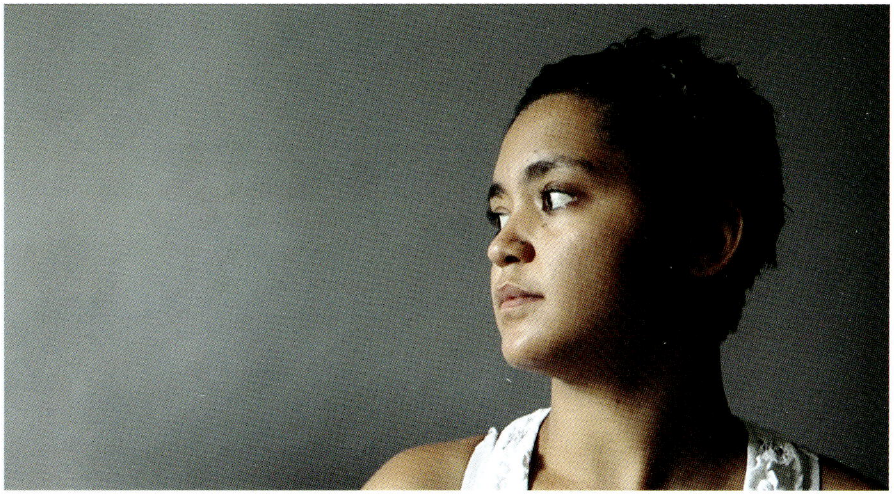

*There's something I must tell you*
2013
Vesta Smith and Tammy Leigh Lodge
Video still (detail)

Tammy: What apartheid means to me was a struggle between black people and white people but only a textbook version. Lungi, my friend at school would call me a bushy and I'd call her darky, but there was no hatred there. It's just names that we call each other, because we have no meaning to put to it.

Vesta: Now, it is just accepted. It's just something that we laugh about.

Tammy: In terms of the freedoms and the struggle and so forth, we as the youth like from the late 1980s onwards, really know nothing about the struggle. We were born into freedom.

Vesta: It was a very bitter thing to go through at the age of fifty-six, to be put into jail and I am not told why I am in jail. And there I sat in jail for six months. My eldest daughter was also put into jail with me. She was expecting a baby then. And then the second time I was put into jail at the Diepkloof jail, this time it was with three of my sons. And there we sat again for six months until we were let out.

Tammy: I knew she was imprisoned but I never knew it was twice and well, I was hoping to hear why today, but clearly she doesn't know why, up until today and neither do I and to a certain extent, bitterness as well, because there's no reason. So it quite bothers me.

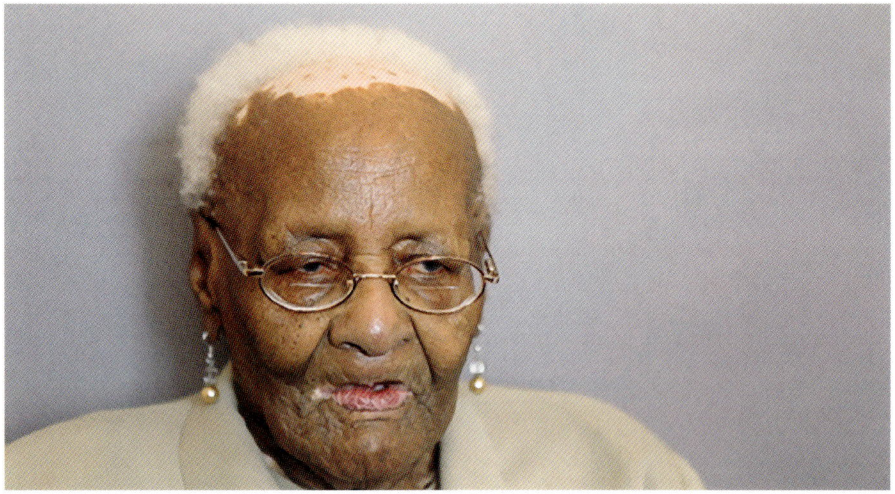

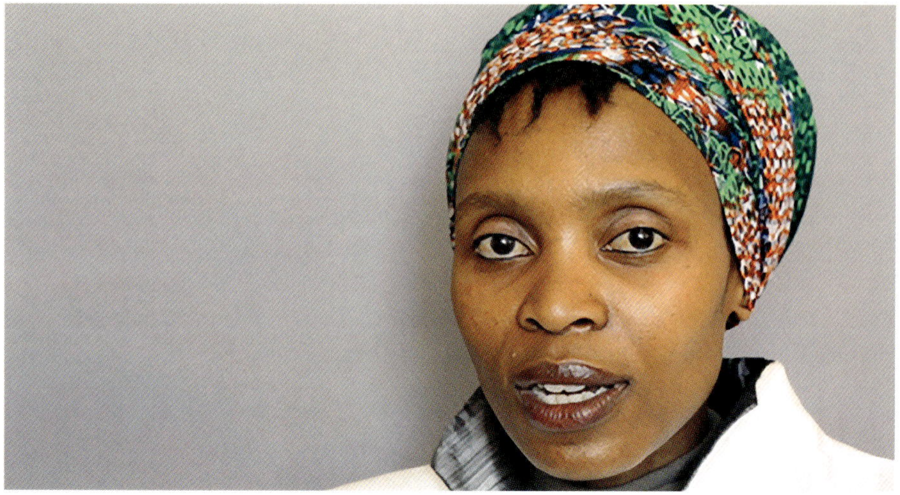

**Rebecca**: It was difficult, but there's nothing I could do. More especially when Moses Kotane was [under] house arrest. The only person who would come and see him was Bram Fischer and he only spoke to him through the window. He couldn't go inside the house.

**Nompumelelo**: It's memories like that, that always replay themselves in her mind, but she's still very happy with the sacrifices that she made, because she knew that it wasn't just for her. It was for the nation. What she loves about my life today is that we have been able to be educated. So, for her to see me growing up like this actually makes her very happy, makes her very proud. And as a young, black, African woman in the context of today, I do believe I'm free. I'm free because I've been able to think for myself. I've been able to make choices for myself.

*There's something I must tell you*
2013
Rebecca and Nompumelelo Kotane
Video still (detail)

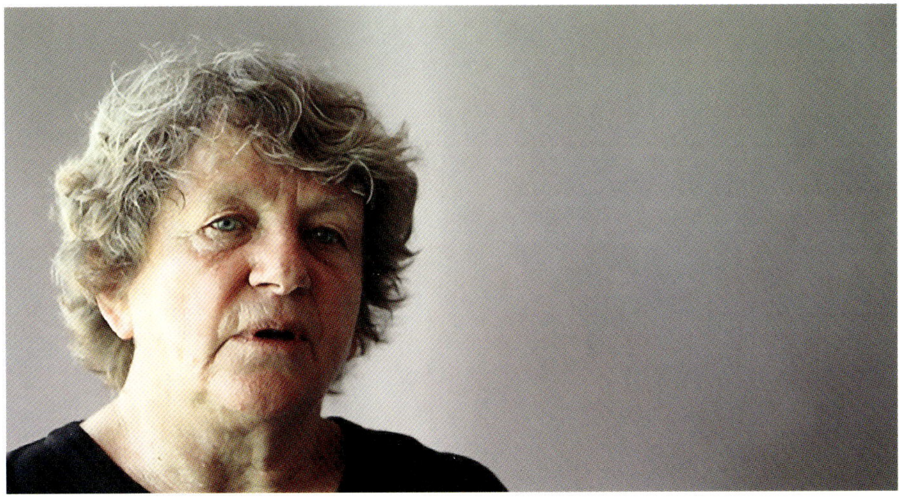

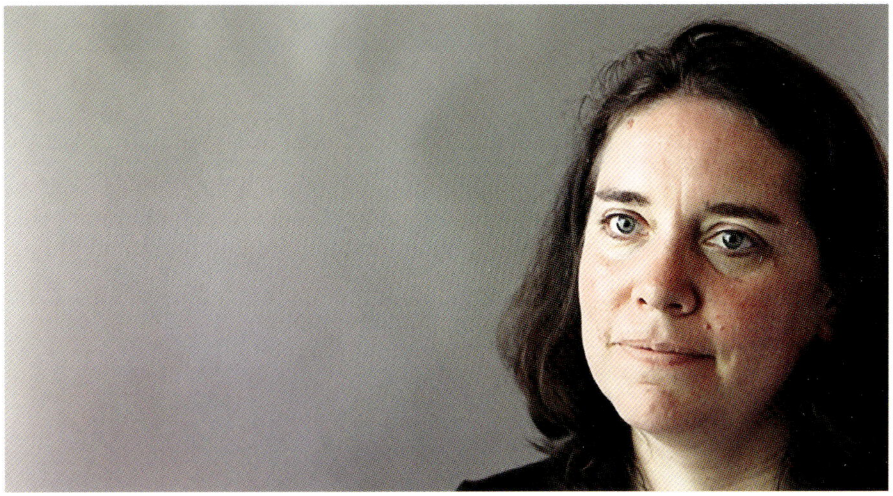

*There's something I must tell you*
2013
Ilse Fischer and Thandi Lewin
Video still (detail)

**Ilse**: Those 1950s when I was a school girl were very exciting years and, you know, whereas some people say that they were ... it was really tough … I mean Walter Sisulu was part of my childhood. Moses Kotane was part of my childhood. One knew that one was part of something much bigger. And really, one felt quite secure. One realised that things were bad in the country but one, one felt very much part of something even as a child. And then of course the 1960s, things were awful. My mother was detained in 1960. Bram was not detained. I was 16 at the time. I was allowed to visit her. I had to run the household. I had to take off time from school to go and visit her in Pretoria. And on my seventeenth birthday I visited her and she pushed violets through the prison grille for me that she'd picked in the prison yard.

**Thandi**: When it came to the Fischers, I mean, I think it says a lot about who they were—the love of the family and it's always fascinated me, you know, how they managed to keep some semblance of family life while being so politically involved and the kinds of stresses and tensions they must have faced. I mean, I experienced none of that.

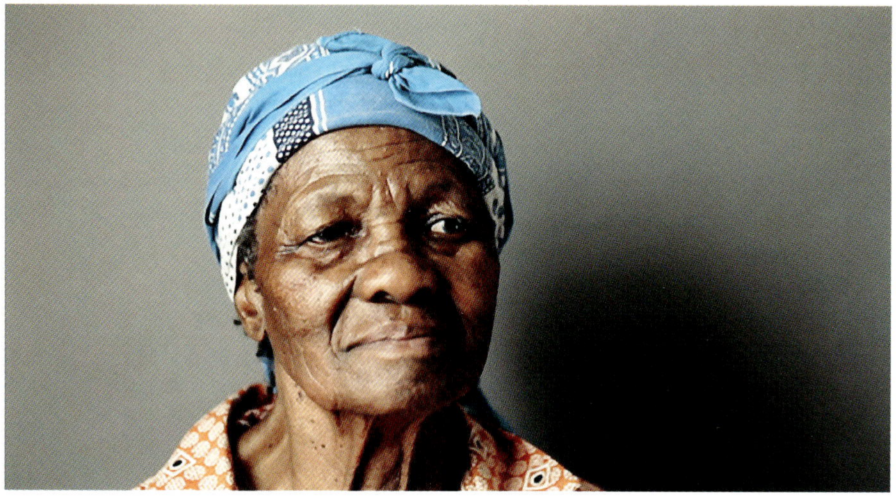

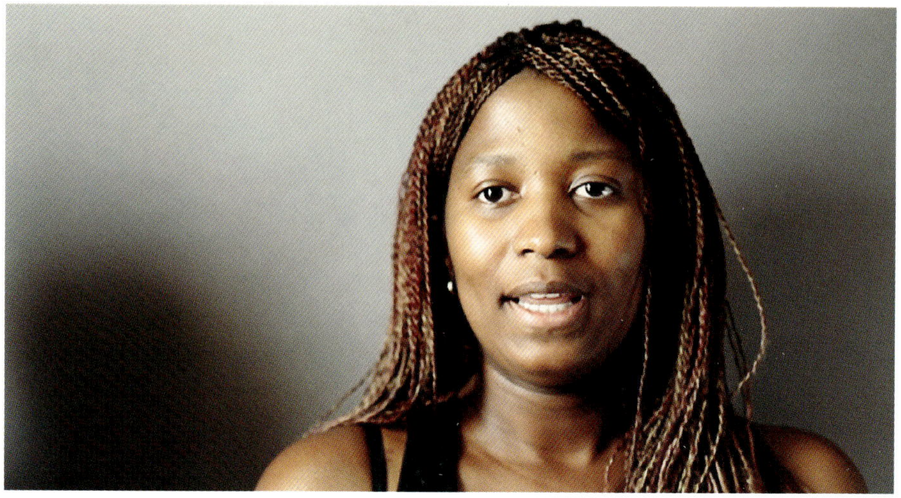

**Caroline**: The young people don't understand what we were fighting for. They just take it, everything for granted. They just want their football club. The only thing they think about—the football club.

**Busisiwe**: I agree with my gran 100%. That is very true. I mean, I was guilty of that when I went to private primary school. You're just some rich kid, and at my school there were some kids that couldn't afford labelled clothes. I would never forget this day. I feel so guilty about it. Some kid came to school and he had, so we all knew that Adidas had three stripes and he had six. And we laughed at that kid and we were like "Why do you have six stripes and Adidas has got three?" My parents sat me down and they were like "This is not right. You shouldn't do this, because not everyone is the same, not everyone can afford Dolce & Gabbana. We're all different, but we're all humans... blood is the same colour. It's red. We have a heart in the same place", and since that day I changed.

*There's something I must tell you*
2013
Caroline Motsoaledi and Busisiwe Khatibe
Video still (detail)

In June 2015, *There's something I must tell you* was screened as part of a three night outdoor video festival entitled *Fireflies in the Night*, curated by Robert Storr, Barbara London and Kalliopi Minioudaki at the Stavros Niarchos Cultural Foundation in Athens

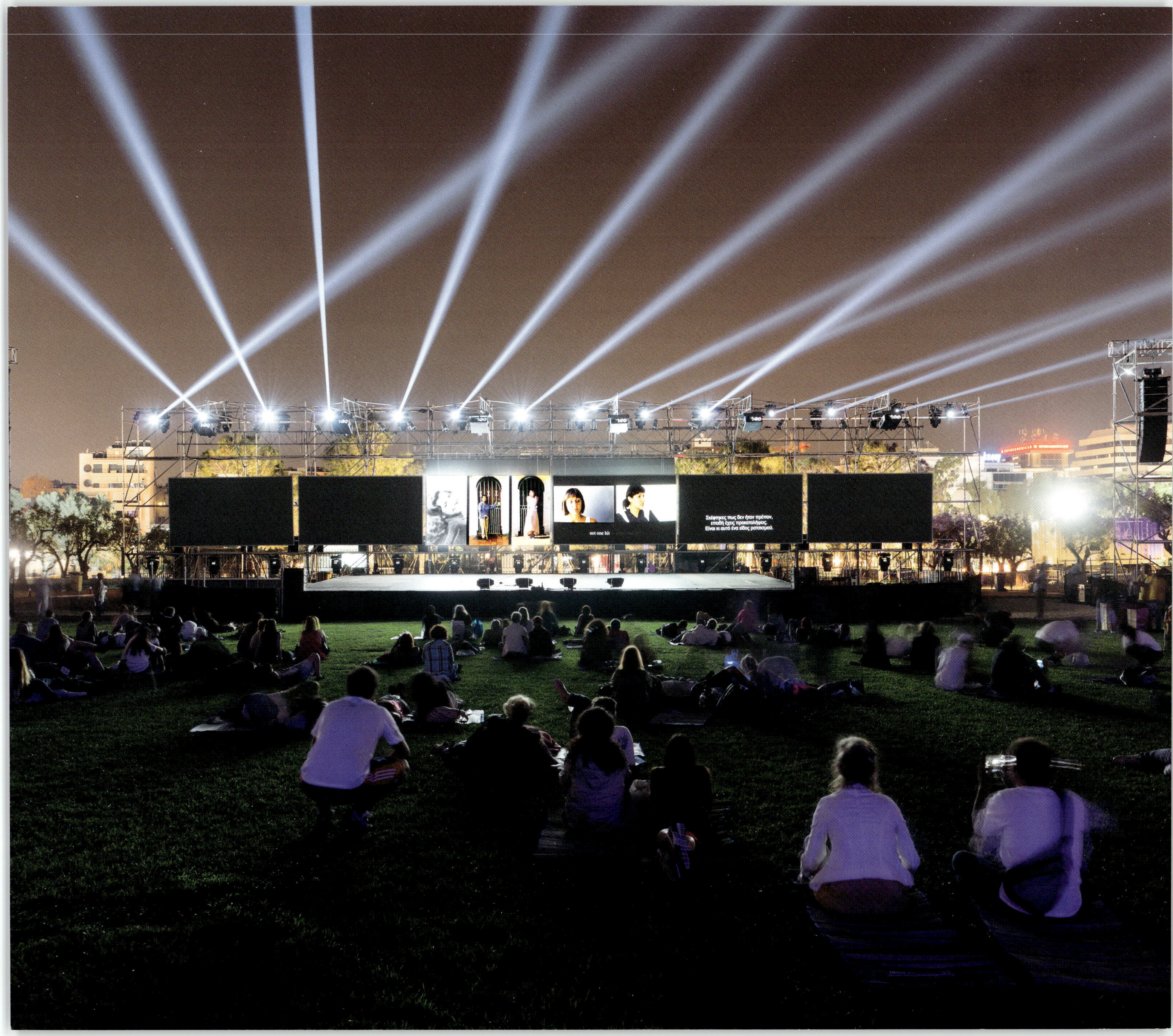
not one bit
Σκέφτηκες πως δεν ήταν πρέπον,
επειδή έχεις προκαταλήψεις.
Είναι κι αυτό ένα είδος ρατσισμού.

# Biography

Sue Williamson lives and works in Cape Town, with a studio in the lively area of Salt River.

She was born in 1941 in Lichfield, England, and her family emigrated to South Africa in 1948, settling just outside Johannesburg. Williamson started her career as a junior assistant and writer in the newsroom of the *Natal Daily News*, studying for a BA at the University of Natal at night, then changed careers to advertising. In 1964 she and her husband moved to New York for five years, where Williamson was a copywriter on Madison Avenue, and began taking life drawing, painting and printmaking classes at the Art Students League of New York. The couple returned to South Africa in 1969 and the artist continued printmaking at The Graphic Workshop in Cape Town.

In 1976, Wiliamson attended the founding meeting of the Women's Movement for Peace in the Cape Town City Hall. This meeting was called to bring together women of all races to plan actions challenging apartheid after the schools' protests which started in Soweto had swept the country. It was the beginning of her involvement with activism.

In 1982 Williamson went to the Michaelis School of Fine Art at the University of Cape Town for a two-year period culminating in an Advanced Diploma in Fine Art. Since then, Williamson has participated in ten international Biennales including Venice, Sydney, Istanbul, Havana and Johannesburg and numerous museum shows. She is represented in such public collections as MoMA, New York and the Tate Modern, London.

Williamson is the recipient of many awards, including a Visual Artist Research Fellowship from the Smithsonian Institution, Washington, a Creative Arts Fellowship at Bellagio, Italy, from the Rockefeller Foundation of New York, and a Lucas Artists Residency Fellowship at Montalvo Art Center, California.
She is also known for her writing, and has authored the seminal work *Resistance Art in South Africa* (1989), *Art in South Africa: the Future Present*, with Ashraf Jamal (1996) and *South African Art Now* (2009). She is the founding editor of the online journal, *ArtThrob*.
Her curatorial activities include the guest curatorship at the Sommerakademie at the Paul Klee Museum in Bern, Switzerland in 2013.
She has three children and three grandchildren.

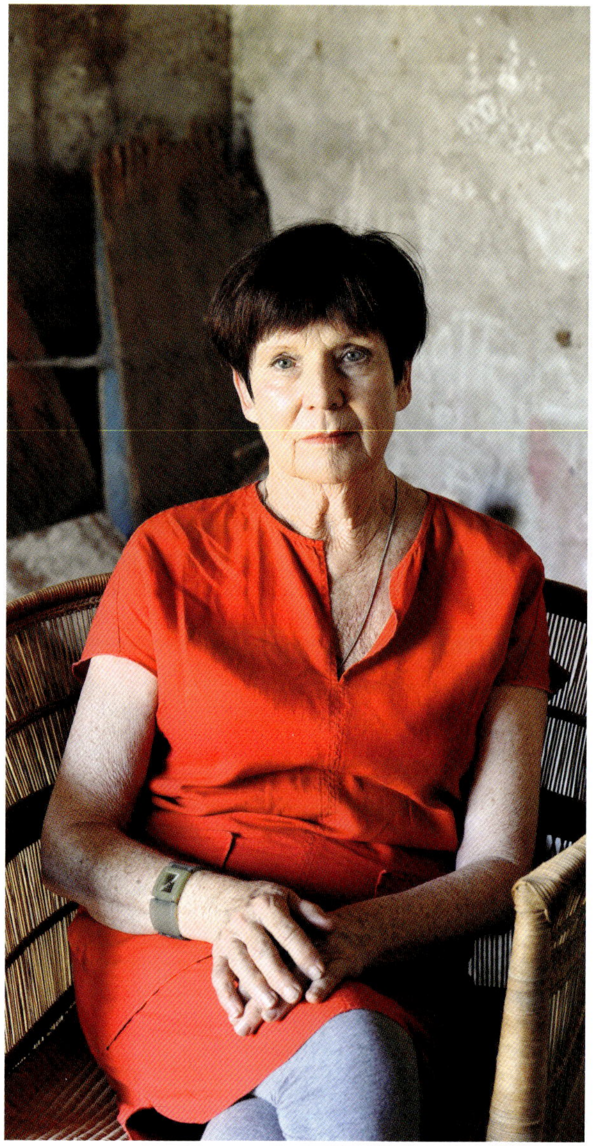

# Contributors

**Mark Gevisser** is one of South Africa's leading journalists, and the award-winning author of the biography, *Thabo Mbeki: A Dream Deferred.* His books include *Portraits of Power: Profiles in a Changing South Africa, Defiant Desire: Gay and Lesbian Lives in South Africa* (co-editor) and, most recently, *Lost and Found in Johannesburg.* His curatorial work has been exhibited at Constitution Hill, the Apartheid Museum and MuseuMAfrica in Johannesburg.

**Pumla Gobodo-Madikizela** is a Senior Research Professor at the University of the Free State. Her books include the award-winning *A Human Being Died That Night*, which has been adapted into a play and produced internationally. She is also the co-author of *Narrating Our Healing: Perspectives on Working through Trauma*, and co-editor of *Memory, Narrative, and Forgiveness: Perspectives on the Unfinished Journeys of the Past.*

**Chika Okeke-Agulu** is an artist, curator and art historian. His books include *Postcolonial Modernism: Art and Decolonization in 20th-Century Nigeria* and *Contemporary African Art Since 1980* with Okwui Enwezor. He is Associate Professor in the Department of Art & Archaeology and the Center for African American Studies, Princeton University.

**Ciraj Rassool** is professor of history at the University of the Western Cape and directs the university's African Programme in Museum and Heritage Studies. He is chairperson of the District Six Museum, a board member of the South African History Archive, and previously chaired the council of Iziko Museums of South Africa. He has published widely on public history, visual history and resistance historiography.

# Exhibitions Bibliography

## Selected Solo Exhibitions

**2015**
*Other Voices, Other Cities*, SCAD Museum, Savannah, Georgia, USA
**2014**
*Sue Williamson*, Goodman Gallery stand, Frieze Masters, London
*There's something I must tell you*, Iziko Slave Lodge, Cape Town
**2013**
*All Our Mothers*, Goodman Gallery, Johannesburg and Cape Town
**2012**
*The Mothers: a 31 Year Chronicle*, Castle of Good Hope, Cape Town
**2011**
*Voices*, Goodman Gallery, Cape Town
**2009**
*Other Voices, Other Cities*, Goodman Gallery, Johannesburg
*The Truth is on the Walls*, Wifredo Lam Centre, 10th Havana Biennale, Havana, Cuba
**2007**
*Hotels and Better Lives*, Wertz Gallery, Atlanta, USA
**2005**
*Hotels and Better Lives*, Goodman Gallery, Johannesburg
**2004**
*Messages from the Moat*, Castle of Good Hope, Cape Town
**2003**
*Sue Williamson: Selected Work*, Centre d'Art Contemporain, Brussels, Belgium
**2002**
*From the Inside*, Goodman Gallery, Johannesburg
*The Last Supper Revisited*, National Museum of African Art, Smithsonian Institute, Washington D.C, USA
**2001**
*Can't forget, can't remember*, Iziko South African National Gallery, Cape Town
**2000**
*Messages from the Moat*, Archive Building, Den Haag, Netherlands
**1998**
*Truth Games*, Goodman Gallery, Johannesburg
**1994**
*Out of the Ashes*, Fortaleza de la Cabana, 5th Havana Biennale, Cuba
**1993**
*The Last Supper Revisited*, Irma Stern Museum, Cape Town
**1985–9**
*A Few South Africans*, University of Oregon, Eugene, Canadian and US tour
**1981**
*The Last Supper*, Gowlett Gallery, Cape Town

## Selected Group Exhibitions

**2015**
*Fireflies in the Night*, Stavros Niarchos Foundation Cultural Centre, Athens, Greece
**2014**
*Artevida (Politica)*, Museu de Arte Moderna, Rio de Janeiro, Brazil
*Imaginary Fact: Contemporary South African Art and the Archive*, South African Pavilion, 55th Venice Biennale
**2013**
*Distance and Desire: Encounters with the African Archive*, Walther Collection, Ulm, Germany
**2012**
*The Rise and Fall of Apartheid: Photography and the Bureaucracy of Everyday Life*, International Center of Photography, New York, USA
**2011**
*Untitled (Passport)*, 12th Istanbul Biennial, Turkey
*Impressions from South Africa: 1965 to Now*, Museum of Modern Art, New York, USA
**2010**
*Darkroom*, Virginia Museum of Fine Art, Richmond, Virginia, USA
**2009**
*Unbounded: New Art for a New Century*, Newark Museum, New Jersey, USA
**2008**
*The Poetics of Cloth*, Grey Art Gallery, New York University, New York, USA
**2007**
*Inscribing Meaning*, National Museum of African Art, Washington D.C. & Fowler Museum, Los Angeles, USA
*Apartheid: The South African Mirror*, Center for Contemporary Culture, Barcelona, Spain
**2006**
Trienal de Luanda, Angola
*Dynamics of Urban Culture*, 9th Havana Biennale, Cuba
**2005**
*Imagining the Book II*, Library of Alexandria, Egypt
**2004**
*Insights*, National Museum of African Art, Washington D.C., USA
Dak'Art, Biennale de Dakar, Senegal
**2003**
*Transferts*, Palais des Beaux Arts, Brussels, Belgium
*Sexuality and Death: Aids in Contemporary African Art*, Rautenstrauch-Joest-Museum, Cologne, Germany
**2002–04**
*History/Now*, Liljevachs Konsthalll, Stockholm
**2002**
*Africa Apart*, New Society for the Visual Arts, Berlin, Germany
**2001–02**
*The Short Century: Independence and Liberation Movements in Africa 1954–1994*, Villa Stuck Museum, Munich, Germany

**2001–03**
*Dis/locations*, Circulo de Bella Artes, PhotoEspana, Madrid, Spain
**2000**
*Mostra Africana de Arte Contemporaneo*; Videobrasil Electronic Art International Festival, SESC, Sao Paulo, Brazil
**2000**
*The New Republics*, Australian Centre for Contemporary Art, Melbourne, Australia
**1997**
*Thirty Minutes*, The Robben Island Visitors Block, Cape Town
*Alternating Currents*, The Electric Workshop, 2nd Johannesburg Biennale, Johannesburg
**1995**
*Ku(n)stlijn*, Hoorn, Netherlands
*Objects of Desire, Spaces of Contemplation*, 1st Johannesburg Biennale, MuseumAfrica, Johannesburg
*Kunst Heimat Kunst*, Kunstlerhaus, Steirischer Herbst Festival of Contemporary Art, Graz, Austria
**1993**
*Incroci del Sud*, Fondazione Levi, Venice, 45th Venice Biennale, Sala Uno, Rome, Italy and Stedelijk Museum, Amsterdam, Netherlands
**1992**
*The Boundary River*, 9th Biennale of Sydney, Gallery of New South Wales, Sydney, Australia
**1991**
*The Challenge of Colonisation*, 4th Havana Biennale, National Museum of Art, Havana, Cuba
**1988**
*Detention Without Trial: 87 Artists Protest*, Market Theatre Gallery, Johannesburg
**1982**
*Art Towards Social Development*, Culture and Resistance Festival, National Museum and Art Gallery, Gaborone, Botswana

## Public Collections

*International*
The Tate Modern, London
Museum of Modern Art, New York, USA
Victoria & Albert Museum, London
Museum of Contemporary Art, San Diego, California, USA
National Museum of African Art, Smithsonian Institution, Washington D.C., USA
The Virginia Museum of Fine Art, Richmond, Virginia, USA
Jochen Zeitz Collection, Germany
Sindika Dokolo African Collection of Contemporary Art, Luanda, Angola
The Museum of the 21st Century, Louisville, Kentucky, USA
Kadist Art Foundation, San Francisco, California, USA
Newark Museum, New Jersey, USA
Birmingham Museum of Art, Alabama, USA
Sir Elton John Photography Collection, Atlanta, Georgia, USA
North Dakota Museum of Art, Grand Forks, Dakota, USA
Wellesley College, Massachusetts, USA
Wifredo Lam Centre, Havana, Cuba
Wheaton College, Norton, Massachusetts, USA
Daimler Collection, Berlin, Germany
Walther Collection, Ulm, Germany

*South Africa*
Iziko South African National Gallery, Cape Town
Houses of Parliament, Cape Town
Constitutional Court of South Africa, Johannesburg
Johannesburg Art Gallery, Johannesburg
BHP Billiton, Johannesburg
Brenthurst Library, Johannesburg
Cape Provincial Library, Cape Town
Durban Art Gallery, Durban
South African Broadcasting Corporation, Johannesburg
United States Embassy, Cape Town
United States Embassy, Johannesburg
Gauteng Legislature, Johannesburg
King George VI Art Gallery, Port Elizabeth
MTN Art Institute, Johannesburg
Standard Bank, Johannesburg
Museum of Art, Pretoria,
MuseuMAfricA, Johannesburg
New Church Art Gallery, Cape Town
Old Mutual, Cape Town
University of Cape Town, Cape Town
University of Stellenbosch, Stellenbosch
University of the Western Cape, Cape Town
University of Witwatersrand, Johannesburg
University of Zululand, KwaDlangezwa
Natal Technicon, Durban
Sasol, Johannesburg
Spier Wine Estate, Cape Town
Tatham Gallery, Pietermaritzburg
District Six Museum, Cape Town

Selected Bibliography


• *Africa Apart – Afrikanische Künstlerinnen und Künstler Konfrontieren AIDS.* Exhibition catalogue. Germany: NGBK, 2002. Pp. 110–1, 139.

• Bedford, E., "Sue Williamson", in Perryer, S. (ed.), *10 Years, 100 Artists: Art in a Democractic South Africa.* Cape Town, South Africa: Bell-Roberts Publishing in association with Struik Publishers, 2004. Pp. 409–13.

• Bester, R., "Spaces to Say". Pp. 26, 28, 30–33; Lamprecht, A., "The Tug of History", pp. 36, 37, in Bedford, E. (ed.), *A Decade of Democracy. Iziko South African Art 1994–2004.* Iziko South African National Gallery in association with Double Storey Publishers, 2004.

• Bester, R., "Sue Williamson" (translated by Sally Latuelle), in *Sue Williamson Plasticienne.* Les Carnets de la Création. France: Editions de l'Oeil, 2005.

• Bilbija, K., Fair, J.E.,Milton, C., Payne, L., *The Art of Truth Telling about Authoritarian Rule.* US: The University of Wisconsin Press, 2005. Pp. 12–3, 24, 26, 28, 88, 99, 107.

• Bond, Anthony, "Sue Williamson", in *The Boundary Rider 9th Biennale of Sydney.* Sydney, Australia: Bloxham & Chambers Pty Ltd, 1992. Pp. 248–9.

• Collet, Anne (ed.), "Truth Games". *Kunapipi Journal of Post-Colonial Writing* 24.1/2. Australia, 2002. Pp. 182–8.

• Coombes, A., "Epilogue: Changing Places" and "Robben Island", in *History after Apartheid Visual Culture and Public Memory in a Democratic South Africa.* Durham, USA and London, UK: Duke University Press, 2003. Pp. 104, 106, 293–4.

• Czekelius, A., "Re-imagining a new nation: An Interview with the South African artist Sue Williamson", in Döring, T. (ed.), *African Cultures, Visual Arts, and the Museum: Sights/Sites of Creativity and Conflict (Matatu 25-26).* Amsterdam, Netherlands, and New York, USA: Editions Rodopi, 2002. Pp. 91–9.

• Enwezor, Okwui, Bester, Rory, eds., *Rise and Fall of Apartheid - Photography and the Bureaucracy of Everyday Life.* New York, USA: International Centre of Photography and DelMonico Books, 2013. Pp. 330–1.

• Enwezor, Okwui, Okeke-Agulu, *Chika, Contemporary African Art Since 1980.* Grafiche Damiani, Bologna, 2009. Pp. 34, 37, 63, 77, 132.

• Garb, Tamar, ed., *African Photography from The Walther Collection: Distance and Desire Encounters with the African Archive.* Neu-Ulm, Germany: Steidl, 2013. Pp. 44, 45, 304, 305, 330.

• Grantham, Tosha, *Darkroom: Photography and New Media in South Africa since 1950.* Richmond, Virginia: Virginia Museum of Fine Arts, USA, 2009. Pp. 5, 92, 114, 123, 143.

• Grünkemeier, Ellen, *Breaking the Silence: South African Representations of HIV/AIDS.* Woodbridge, Suffolk and Rochester, NY, USA: James Currey, 2013. Pp. 58–66.

• Higgins, Jackie, *The World Atlas of Street Photography.* London, United Kingdom: Thames & Hudson, 2014. Pp. 10, 183, 186–7, 244–5.

• Hill, Shannen L., *Biko's Ghost – The Iconography of Black Consciousness.* Minneapolis, USA: University of Minnesota Press, 2015. Pp.154–66, 216, 230–3, 312, 326–7.

• Jantjies, Gavin, "Growing Interest and a New Engagement", p. 35; Sobopha, Mgcineni, "Re-Presenting the Body – In search of a postcolonial moment", p. 97; Richards, Colin, "In Human History – Pasts and prospects in South African art today", p. 47; Smith, Kathryn, "The Experimental Turn in the Visual Arts", p. 131, in Pissara, M., *Visual Century South African Art in Context* 4 (1990–2007). Johannesburg: Wits University Press, 2011. Pp. 35, 48, 97, 131.

• Jason, Stefanie, "Sue Williamson celebrates an enduring female legacy". *Mail & Guardian.* Johannesburg, May 31, 2013. Jouannais, Jean-Yves, "Sue Williamson", in *Un Art Contemporain d'Afrique du Sud.* France: Editions Plume, 1994. Pp. 84–7.

• Kreamer, Christine, "Inscribing Power/ Writing Politics", pp. 142–4; Harney, Elizabeth, "Word Play: Text and Image in Contemporary African Arts", pp. 210–3, 23–4, in National Museum of African Art, *Inscribing Meaning - Writing and Graphic Systems in African Art'.* USA: Smithsonian Institute, 2007.

• La Duke, B., "Sue Williamson and the Struggle for South African Liberation", in *Africa through the Eyes of Women Artists.* New York, USA: Africa World Press, 1991. Pp. 105–14.

• Marlin-Curiel, S., "Re-collecting the Collective: Mediatised Memory and the South African Truth and Reconciliation Commission", in Guerin, F., Hallas, R. (ed.), *The Image and the Witness: Trauma, Memory and Visual Culture.* London, UK, and New York, USA: Wallflower Press, 2007.

• Martin, M., "Post-Apartheid South Africa", in Fall, N., Pivin, J. (eds.), *An Anthology of African Art: the Twentieth Century.* France: Editions Revue Noire in association with D.A.P. USA, 2002. Pp. 371, 375.

• Miller, Kim, "Trauma, Testimony and Truth: Contemporary South African Artists Speak". *African Arts Journal 38.* Autumn, 2005. Pp. 40-51.

• Oguibe, O., "Beyond Visual Pleasures: A brief reflection on the work of contemporary African women artists", in Hassan, S. (ed.), *Gendered Visions: the Art of Contemporary Africana Women Artists.* USA & Eritrea: Africa World Press, 1997. P. 66.

• Okeke, C., "Modern African Art", p. 35; Martin, M., "Independence and Liberation Movements in Africa 1945–1994", pp. 42, 44, in Enwezor, Okwui, *The Short Century: Independence and Liberation Movements in Africa 1945–1994.* Munich, Germany: Prestel, 2001. Pp. 134f, 479.

• Oliphant, Andries Walter, "A Few South Africans – The political image and artistic reproduction in the work of Sue Williamson" in Bitte, John (ed.), *Northwest Review* March 24, 1986. Pp. 51–72.

• Pissarra, Mario, *Recovering Critical Movements*, pp. 3, 7, 9; Simbao, Ruth, "Self-Identification as Resistance: Visual constructions of 'Africaness' and 'blackness' during Apartheid", pp. 55–7, in Pissarra, M., *Visual Century: South African Art in Context 3* (1973–1992). Johannesburg: WITS University Press, 2011. Pp. 3, 7, 9, 55, 57, 56.

• Pollack, Barbara, "Sue Williamson", in *Contemporary magazine* 86 (cover story), 2006. Pp. 34-7.

• Pollak, Lloyd, "There's something I must tell you". *Artthrob.* http://artthrob.co.za/Reviews/Lloyd_Pollak_reviews_Theres_something_I_must_tell_you_by_Sue_Williamson_at_Iziko_Slave_Lodge.aspx (accessed 3 August 2015).

• Powell, Richard J., *Black Art & Culture in the 20th Century.* Singapore: Thames & Hudson, 1997. Pp. 145, 175–6.

• Richards, C., "About face: aspects of art history and identity in SA visual culture", pp. 350–1, 358, 359, in Oguibe, O., Enwezor, O. (eds.), *Reading the Contemporary: African Art from Theory to the Marketplace.* USA: MIT Press, 1999.

• Roper, Chris, "Shock of recognition: Sue Williamson and South African identity", in Peter Anders, Matthew Krouse (eds.). *Positions - Contemporary Artists in South Africa.* Germany: Jacana Media, 2010. Pp. 250-61.

• Smith, Terry, *Contemporary Art: World Currents.* Laurence King Publishing Ltd, 2011. Pp. 221, 230–1.

• Solomon, Andrew, "Separate, and Equal". *The New York Times Magazine.* The Artists of South Africa. 27 March, 1994.

• Subirós, Pep, *Apartheid: The South African Mirror.* Barcelona, Spain: Centre de Cultura Contemporània de Barcelona, 2007. P. 163.

• *Sue Williamson: Selected Work*, Double Storey Publishers Cape Town, South Africa, in association with the Centre d'Art Contemporain, Brussels, Belgium and the Goodman Gallery, Johannesburg, South Africa, 2003.

• Tilkin, Daniela, *Dislocación: Imagen & Identidad, Sudáfrica.* Madrid, Spain: La Fabrica, 2002. Pp. 100–5.

• Valdés, Eugenio, "Sue Williamson", in *Kunstforum Interntional 122.* Afrika – Iwalewa. Berlin, Germany: Martin-Gropius-Bau, 1993. Pp. 323–4.

Works by Sue Williamson

• *Resistance Art in South Africa.* South Africa: David Philip Publishers; USA: St. Martins Press, 1989.

• *Art in South Africa: the Future Present*, with Ashraf Jamal. South Africa: David Philip Publishers, 1996.

• *South African Art in the Nineties: Parts I, II and III* http://www.artthrob.co.za/00jan/news.html#saart3

• *Sue Williamson: Selected Work.* Brussels, Belgium Centre d'Art Contemporain; Johannesburg: Goodman Gallery; Cape Town Double Storey Books, 2003.

• *South African Art Now.* New York, USA: HarperCollins, 2009.

# List of works

*Nokukanya Lutuli*, 1983
*A Few South Africans* series
Photo etching/screenprint collage
100 x 70 cm
Tate Modern, London; Iziko South African National Gallery, Cape Town; Brenthurst Library, Johannesburg; Michaelis School of Art, Cape Town; University of the Western Cape, Cape Town; Tatham Art Gallery, Maritzburg; Parliamentary Art Collection, Cape Town; BHP Billiton, Johannesburg; Durban Art Gallery; Western Cape Provincial Library
p. 10

*Cynthia Gabriel*, 2003
*Better Lives* series
Pigment inks on cotton rag paper
144 x 112 cm
p. 11

*Before and after*, 1978
*The Modderdam Postcard* series
Etching on paper, postage stamp, handwriting
38 x 32 cm
Private collections
p. 16

*Teargas*, 1978
*The Modderdam Postcard* series
Etching on paper, postage stamp, handwriting
38 x 32 cm
Private collections
p. 17

*Rev. Kani*, 1981
Etching, screenprint and embossing on paper
65 x 50 cm
Private collections
p. 18

*Annie Silinga 1*, 1983
*All Our Mothers* series
Pigment inks on archival paper
39 x 59 cm
p. 29

*Virginia Mngoma*, 1984
*A Few South Africans* series
Photo etching/screenprint collage
100 x 70 cm
Tate Modern, London; V&A Museum, London; Newark Museum, New Jersey; Jochen Zeitz Collection, Germany; Iziko South African National Gallery, Cape Town; Brenthurst Library, Johannesburg; Constitutional Court, Johannesburg; Michaelis School of Art, Cape Town; University of the Western Cape, Cape Town; Tatham Art Gallery, Maritzburg; Parliamentary Art Collection, Cape Town; BHP Billiton, Johannesburg; Western Cape Provincial Library
p. 31

*Charlotte Maxeke*, 1984
*A Few South Africans* series
Photo etching/screenprint collage
70 x 100 cm
Tate Modern, London; V&A Museum, London; Newark Museum, New Jersey; Iziko South African National Gallery, Cape Town; Brenthurst Library, Johannesburg, Constitutional Court, Johannesburg; Michaelis School of Art, Cape Town; University of the Western Cape, Cape Town; Tatham Art Gallery, Maritzburg; Parliamentary Art Collection, Cape Town; BHP Billiton, Johannesburg; Western Cape Provincial Library; University of Cape Town
p. 32

*Elizabeth Paul*, 1983
*A Few South Africans* series
Photo etching/screenprint collage
70 x 100 cm
Tate Modern, London; Iziko South African National Gallery, Cape Town; Brenthurst Library, Johannesburg; Michaelis School of Art, Cape Town; University of the Western Cape, Cape Town; Tatham Art Gallery, Maritzburg; Parliamentary Art Collection, Cape Town; BHP Billiton, Johannesburg; MuseumAfrica, Johannesburg; Durban Art Gallery; Western Cape Provincial Library
p. 32

*Winnie Mandela*, 1983
*A Few South Africans* series
Photo etching/screenprint collage
100 x 70 cm
Tate Modern, London; Iziko South African National Gallery, Cape Town; Brenthurst Library, Johannesburg; Michaelis School of Art, Cape Town; University of the Western Cape, Cape Town; Tatham Art Gallery, Maritzburg; Parliamentary Art Collection, Cape Town; BHP Billiton, Johannesburg; Durban Art Gallery; Western Cape Provincial Library
p. 33

*Amina Cachalia*, 1984
*A Few South Africans* series
Photo etching/screenprint collage
100 x 70 cm
Tate Modern, London; V&A Museum, London; Wheaton College, Illinois; Iziko South African National Gallery, Cape Town; Brenthurst Library, Johannesburg; Michaelis School of Art, Cape Town; University of the Western Cape, Cape Town; Tatham Art Gallery, Maritzburg; Parliamentary Art Collection, Cape Town; BHP Billiton, Johannesburg; Western Cape Provincial Library; University of Cape Town
p. 34

*Albertina Sisulu*, 1983
*A Few South Africans* series
Photo etching/screenprint collage
100 x 70 cm
Tate Modern, London; Wheaton College, Illinois; Iziko South African National Gallery, Cape Town; Brenthurst Library, Johannesburg, Michaelis School of Art, Cape Town; University of the Western Cape, Cape Town; Tatham Art Gallery, Maritzburg; Parliamentary Art Collection, Cape Town; BHP Billiton, Johannesburg; Durban Art Gallery, Western Cape Provincial Library, University of Cape Town
p. 35

*Helen Joseph*, 1983
*A Few South Africans* series
Photo etching/screenprint collage
100 x 70 cm
Tate Modern, London; The Walther Collection, Ulm; Iziko South African National Gallery, Cape Town; Brenthurst Library, Johannesburg, Michaelis School of Art, Cape Town; University of the Western Cape, Cape Town; Tatham Art Gallery, Maritzburg; Parliamentary Art Collection, Cape Town; BHP Billiton, Johannesburg; Durban Art Gallery, Western Cape Provincial Library, University of Cape Town
p. 36

*Caroline Motsoaledi*, 1984
*A Few South Africans* series
Photo etching/screenprint collage
100 x 70 cm
Tate Modern, London; Iziko South African National Gallery, Cape Town; Brenthurst Library, Johannesburg, Michaelis School of Art, Cape Town; University of the Western Cape, Cape Town; Tatham Art Gallery, Maritzburg; Parliamentary Art Collection, Cape Town; BHP Billiton, Johannesburg; Western Cape Provincial Library
p. 36

*Miriam Makeba*, 1987
*A Few South Africans* series
Photo etching/screenprint collage
100 x 70 cm
The Walther Collection, Ulm; Iziko South African National Gallery, Cape Town; Tatham Art Gallery, Maritzburg; Parliamentary Art Collection, Cape Town; University of the Western Cape, Cape Town; Western Cape Provincial Library
p. 37

*Jenny Curtis Schoon*, 1985
*A Few South Africans* series
Photo etching/screenprint collage
70 x 100 cm
Iziko South African National Gallery, Cape Town; BHP Billiton, Johannesburg; Parliamentary Art Collection, Cape Town; Tatham Art Gallery, Maritzburg; University of the Western Cape, Cape Town; Western Cape Provincial Library
p. 37

*Annie Silinga*, 1983
*A Few South Africans* series
Photo etching/screenprint collage
70 x 100 cm
Tate Modern, London; Iziko South African National Gallery, Cape Town; MuseumAfrica, Johannesburg; Brenthurst Library, Johannesburg, Michaelis School of Art, Cape Town; University of the Western Cape, Cape Town; Tatham Art Gallery, Maritzburg; Parliamentary Art Collection, Cape Town; BHP Billiton, Johannesburg; Durban Art Gallery, Western Cape Provincial Library
p. 38

*Case no. 6831/21*, 1984
*A Few South Africans* series
Photo etching/screenprint collage
70 x 100 cm
Tate Modern, London; V&A Museum, London; Newark Museum, New Jersey; Iziko South African National Gallery, Cape Town; Brenthurst Library, Johannesburg, Michaelis School of Art, Cape Town; University of the Western Cape, Cape Town; Tatham Art Gallery, Maritzburg; Parliamentary Art Collection, Cape Town; BHP Billiton, Johannesburg; Durban Art Gallery, Western Cape Provincial Library, University of Cape Town
p. 39

*Annie Silinga II*, 1983
*All Our Mothers* series
Pigment inks on archival paper
59 x 39 cm
p. 43

*R.I.P. Annie Silinga*, 1997
Steel, glass, etching, cast resin, plastic domes, laminated colour photocopies, earth
100 x 220 x 120 cm
p. 44

*Last Supper at Manley Villa portfolio*, 1981
Archival print on cotton rag
50 x 67.5 cm
Iziko South African National Gallery, Cape Town, KI Collections, Johannesburg, New Church Museum, Cape Town
pp. 51, 72-3

*The Last Supper*, 1981
Found objects, sound
Dimensions variable
pp. 9, 55-6

*The Last Supper Revisited*, 1993
Glass, steel, found objects in casting resin, digital images, plastic lighting, sound
Dimensions variable
National Museum of African Art Smithsonian Institute Washington DC
pp. 59-61

*Mementoes of District Six*, 1993
Steel, perspex, found objects in casting resin, lighting, sound, earth
Dimensions variable
Birmingham Museum of Art, Alabama
pp. 63-5

*Viewsites District Six: Muir Street*, 1997
Painted steel, found window
250 x 200 x 227 cm
pp. 67-8

*Viewsites District Six: Horstley Street*, 1997
Painted steel, found window
250 x 200 x 227 cm
p. 69

*Naz Ebrahim*
*Last Supper at Manley Villa*,
1981
Archival print on cotton rag
50 x 67.5 cm
p. 71

*Naz Ebrahim at piano*
*Last Supper at Manley Villa*,
1981
Archival print on cotton rag
50 x 67.5 cm
pp. 22, 75

*For Thirty Years Next to his Heart*, 1990
Colour laser prints, hand covered frames
196 x 262 cm
Museum of Modern Art, New York; Virginia Museum of Fine Art, Richmond VA; Sindika Dokolo Contemporary African Art Collection, Luanda, Angola; Iziko South African National Gallery, Cape Town; Gauteng Legislature, Johannesburg; MuseumAfrica, Johannesburg; Ki Collections, Geneva
pp. 21, 81-7

*A Tale of Two Cradocks*, 1994
Colour laser prints, wood, extruded acetate
43 x 500 x 25 cm
Museum of Contemporary Art, San Diego; Ki Collections, Geneva; Tilder Collection, Paris; Old Mutual, Cape Town
pp. 89-93

*Colouring In*, 1992
Colour laser prints, découpage frames, lead, black paint, silver foil, cellophane
148 x 386 cm
Pretoria Art Museum, MTN Art Collection, Johannesburg
pp. 94-9

*Not Unworthy*, 1992
*Pages from a Government Tourist Brochure* series
Steel, extruded acetate, archival digital print, wood, copper
53 x 45 cm
North Dakota Museum of Art
p. 101

*Dinner is ready*, 1992
*Pages from a Government Tourist Brochure* series
Steel, extruded acetate, archival digital print, wood, wire mesh
53 x 45 cm
Private collections
p. 102

*The Hottentot*, 1992
*Pages from a Government Tourist Brochure* series
Steel, extruded acetate, colour laser print, wood, wire
53 x 45 cm
Johannesburg Art Gallery
p. 102

*Contemplation*, 1992
*Pages from a Government Tourist Brochure* series
Steel, extruded acetate, archival digital print, wood, brass-plated chain
53 x 45 cm
Private collections
p. 102

*Ricksha*, 1996
*Pages from a Government Tourist Brochure* series
Steel, extruded acetate, archival digital print, wood, lead, steel ring
53 x 45 cm
Private collections
p. 103

*Zulu Warrior*, 1992
*Pages from a Government Tourist Brochure* series
Steel, extruded acetate, archival digital print, wood
53 x 45 cm
Johannesburg Art Gallery
p. 103

*The band*, 1996
*Pages from a Government Tourist Brochure* series
Steel, extruded acetate, archival digital print, wood, coated wire mesh
53 x 45 cm
Private collections
p. 103

*Messages from the Moat*, 1997
Engraved and stenciled glass, printed canvas, found fishing net, water pump, soundscape
Dimensions variable
Iziko South African National Gallery, Cape Town
pp. 105, 107-9

*Freedom Charter T-Shirt*, 1984–5
Screen printed t-shirt
Dimensions variable
Museum of Modern Art, New York; Iziko Social History Collection, Cape Town
p. 112

*Out of the Ashes*, 1994
Ashes, glass, fabric, lighting, sound and other mixed media
Dimensions variable
pp. 115-7

*Art Home Art*, 1994
Wooden crates, mixed media, sound, lighting
Dimensions variable
pp. 119-121

*Is Anybody ... ?*, 1997
Acoustic tiles, wood, airbrick, monitor, camera, sound
86 x 126 x 94 cm
p. 123

*Nomonde Calata – was everything to me – Harold Snyman*, 1998
*Truth Games* series
Laminated colour laser prints, wood, metal, plastic, perspex
80 x 120 x 6 cm
Sindika Dokolo African Collection of Contemporary Art, Luanda, Angola; Hans Porer Collection, University of Cape Town
p. 129

*De Kock ready to sing*
*Cold Turkey: Stories of Truth and Reconciliation*, 1997
Lightbox, metal, electrostatic prints
63 x 91 x 7 cm
National Museum of African Art, Smithsonian Institute, Washington DC
p. 131

*Poison Victim*
*Cold Turkey: Stories of Truth and Reconciliation*, 1997
Lightbox, metal, electrostatic prints
63 x 91 x 7 cm
National Museum of African Art, Smithsonian Institute, Washington DC
p. 133

*Liezl Ackermann – not a church – Gcinikhaya Makoma*, 1998
*Truth Games* series
Laminated colour laser prints, wood, metal, plastic, perspex
80 x 120 x 6 cm
Hans Porer Collection, University of Cape Town; Stellenbosch University Museum
p. 135

*Nkosinathi Biko – false medical certificate – Dr Benjamin Tucker*, 1998
*Truth Games* series
Laminated colour laser prints, wood, metal, plastic, perspex
80 x 120 x 6 cm
Hans Porer Collection, University of Cape Town Medical School, Durban Art Gallery, Sindika Dokolo African Collection of Contemporary Art, University of Cape Town
p. 137

*Family of Guguletu Seven – why were you smiling – Capt. John Sterrenberg*, 1998
*Truth Games* series
Laminated colour laser prints, wood, metal, plastic, perspex
80 x 120 x 6 cm
Hans Porer Collection, University of Cape Town
p. 139

*Linda Biehl – understand the context – Mongezi Manqina*, 1998
*Truth Games* series
Laminated colour laser prints, wood, metal, plastic, perspex
80 x 120 x 6 cm
Hans Porer Collection, University of Cape Town
p. 141

*Neville Clarence – hold no grudge – Aboobaker Ismael*, 1998
*Truth Games* series
Laminated colour laser prints, wood, metal, plastic, perspex
80 x 120 x 6 cm
Hans Porer Collection, University of Cape Town
p. 143

*Limpho Hani – no remorse – Gaye Derby-Lewis*, 1998
*Truth Games* series
Laminated colour laser prints, wood, metal, plastic, perspex
80 x 120 x 6 cm
Hans Porer Collection, University of Cape Town
p. 144

*Maggie Friedman – senseless murder – Ferdi Barnard*, 1998
*Truth Games* series
Laminated colour laser prints, wood, metal, plastic, perspex
80 x 120 x 6 cm
Sindika Dokolo African Collection of Contemporary Art, Luanda, Angola; Hans Porer Collection, University of Cape Town; Wits Art Museum (WAM), Johannesburg
p. 145

*Winnie Mandela and the Assassination of Dr Asvat*, 1999
Lithograph with printed and collaged gel papers
55.5 x 187 cm
National Museum of African Art, Smithsonian Institute, Washington DC
pp. 146-7

*Can't forget, can't remember*, 1999
Interactive video projection video still
Dimensions variable
National Museum of African Art, Smithsonian Institute, Washington DC; Iziko South African National Gallery, Cape Town; MTN Art Collection, Johannesburg
pp. 149-51

*Peter Busse*, 2002
*From the Inside* series
Pigment inks on archival paper
90 x 200 cm
Hollard Collection, Johannesburg
pp. 155

*Johannes Bukhali, with parents*, 2002
*From the Inside* series
Pigment inks on archival paper
90 x 200 cm
pp. 156-7

*Busi Maqungo*, 2000
*From the Inside* series
Pigment inks on archival paper
90 x 200 cm
Iziko South African National Gallery, Cape Town; Hollard Collection, Johannesburg
pp. 158-9

*Benjamin Borrageiro*, 2000
*From the Inside* series
Pigment inks on archival paper
90 x 200 cm
Iziko South African National Gallery, Cape town; Johannesburg Art Gallery; Wellesley College, MA
p. 160

*Nelson Masombuku*, 2002
*From the Inside* series
Pigment inks on archival paper
90 x 200 cm
Private collections
p. 162

*Nosisa Ndlela*, 2002
*From the Inside* series
Pigment inks on archival paper
90 x 200 cm
Private collections
p. 162

*John Masuku*, 2002
*From the Inside* series
Pigment inks on archival paper
90 x 200 cm
Hollard Collection, Johannesburg
p. 163

*Judy Seidman*, 2002
*From the Inside* series
Pigment inks on archival paper
90 x 200 cm
Hollard Collection, Johannesburg
p. 163

*Pablo Fernandes*, 2004
*From the Inside* series
Pigment inks on archival paper
90 x 200 cm
pp. 164-5

*Albert and Isabelle Ngandu*, 2003
*Better Lives* series
Pigment inks on cotton rag paper
144 x 112 cm
US Consulate Embassy Cape Town US Embassy Johannesburg
p. 167

*Better Lives*, 2003
Video projection
Newark Museum New Jersey
pp. 166, 168-9

*Deka Yusuf Farrh and Nisa*, 2003
*Better Lives* series
Pigment inks on cotton rag paper
144 x 112 cm
Private collection
p. 170

*Francois Bangurambona*, 2003
*Better Lives* series
Pigment inks on cotton rag paper
144 x 112 cm
Kadist Art Foundation, San Francisco
p. 171

*Nelson Manuel*, 2003
*Better Lives* series
Pigment inks on cotton rag paper
144 x 112 cm
Sir Elton John Photography Collection, Atlanta
p. 172

*Richard Belalufu*, 2003
*Better Lives* series
Pigment inks on cotton rag paper
144 x 112 cm
Kadist Art Foundation, San Francisco; Sir Elton John Photography Collection, Atlanta
p. 173

Object for "Off the Record", Shibuya Station, Tokyo, 2006
Archival prints on Tyvek, string, hand stamping, found object
32.5 x 18.5 x 18 cm
p. 175

*Pass the Parcel, Jacob*, 2007
Archival prints on Tyvek, string, hand stamping, found object
189.5 x 385.5 cm
pp. 176-7

*W*A*S*H*, 2007
Single channel video
Playing time: 20 mins
Video stills
p. 183

*Oza's Room*, 2002–3
*What About El Max?* series
Pigment inks on Hahnemühle paper
38.5 x 52 cm
Private collections
p. 184

*Everything fits to our daily needs I*, 2002–3
*What About El Max?* series
Pigment inks on Hahnemühle paper
38.5 x 52 cm
Private collections
p. 185

*We are like fish II*, 2002–3
*What About El Max?* series
Pigment inks on Hahnemühle paper
38.5 x 52 cm
Private collections
p. 186

*We are like fish I*, 2002–3
*What About El Max?* series
Pigment inks on Hahnemühle paper
38.5 x 52 cm
Private collections
pp. 23, 187

*Tell your people this place is perfect II*, 2002–3
*What About El Max?* series
Pigment inks on Hahnemühle paper
38.5 x 52 cm
Private collections
p. 188

*Tell your people this place is perfect I*, 2002–3
*What about El Max?* series
Pigment inks on Hahnemühle paper
38.5 x 52 cm
Private collections
p. 189

*These houses are a part of us II*, 2002–3
*What about El Max?* series
Pigment inks on Hahnemühle paper
38.5 x 52 cm
Spier Art collection
p. 190

*These houses are a part of us I*, 2002–3
*What about El Max?* series
Pigment inks on Hahnemühle paper
38.5 x 52 cm
Spier Art collection
p. 191

*The blockade is also in the mind*, 2009
*The Havana* series
Archival inks on Hahnemühle paper, lasercut letters
60 x 90 cm
p. 192

*We don't see CNN (No vemos CNN)*, 2009
*The Havana* series
Archival inks on Hahnemühle paper, lasercut letters
60 x 90 cm
Private collections
p. 193

*El bloqueo esta también en la mente Fortaleza de la Cabana*, 2009
*The Havana* series
Archival inks on Hahnemühle paper, lasercut letters
60 x 90 cm
Private collections
p. 194

*El Bloqueo esta También en la Mente, The Blockade is Also in the Mind*
2009
*Other Voices, Other Cities* series
Pigment inks on archival cotton rag paper
Dimensions variable
pp. 194-5

*My Son Left*, 2009
*The Havana* series
Archival inks on Hahnemühle paper, lasercut letters
60 x 90 cm
p. 197

*Who is Johannes?: Johannesburg*, 2009
*Other Voices, Other Cities* series
Pigment inks on archival cotton rag paper
Dimensions variable
Private collections
pp. 200-1

*Zuva Rabudirepi? For Whom Has the Sun Risen?: Harare, Zimbabwe*, 2009
*Other Voices, Other Cities* series
Pigment inks on archival cotton rag paper
Dimensions variable
Private collection
pp. 202-3

*Youth Facing History: Krakow*, 2011
*Other Voices, Other Cities* series
Pigment inks on archival cotton rag paper
Dimensions variable
Private collections
pp. 204-5

*I Mean. Where Else Are You Gonna Go?: New York*, 2011
*Other Voices, Other Cities* series
Pigment inks on archival cotton rag paper
Dimensions variable
Museum of the 21st Century, Louisville, KY
pp. 206-7

*You're Free Once You Know The Rules: London*, 2009
*Other Voices, Other Cities* series
Pigment inks on archival cotton rag paper
Dimensions variable
Private collections
pp. 206-7

*It's a Mistake to Ask for Advice: Naples*, 2012
*Other Voices, Other Cities* series
Pigment inks on archival cotton rag paper
Dimensions variable
pp. 208-9

*No Time to Stroll: Hong Kong*, 2013
*Other Voices, Other Cities* series
Pigment inks on archival cotton rag paper
Dimensions variable
SCAD Museum, Savannah, GA
pp. 199, 211-4

*It's a Bit Suspicious if You Have Too Much Money: Berlin*, 2010
*Other Voices, Other Cities* series
Pigment inks on archival cotton rag paper
Dimensions variable
Museum of the 21st Century Louisville, KY;
Daimler Art Collection, Berlin
pp. 216-7

*Even Nothing Works: Bern*, 2009
*Other Voices, Other Cities* series
Pigment inks on archival cotton rag paper
Dimensions variable
Museum of the 21st Century, Louisville, KY
pp. 218-9

*Istanbul is Relentless: Istanbul*, 2011
*Other Voices, Other Cities* series
Pigment inks on archival cotton rag paper
Dimensions variable
Hans Porer Collection, Switzerland
pp. 220-1

*Cheryl Carolus*
*Cape Town*, 1990
*All Our Mothers* series
Pigment inks on archival paper
59 x 39 cm
University of Cape Town
p. 227

*Fatima Meer*, 1989
*All Our Mothers* series
Pigment inks on archival paper
59 x 39 cm
p. 228

*Ellen Kuzwayo*, 1983
*All Our Mothers* series
Pigment inks on archival paper
59 x 39 cm
p. 228

*Eslina Silinga*, 1995
*All Our Mothers* series
Pigment inks on archival paper
59 x 39 cm
p. 229

*Anonymous*, 1995
*All Our Mothers* series
Pigment inks on archival paper
59 x 39 cm
p. 229

*Amina Cachalia I*, 1995
*All Our Mothers* series
Pigment inks on archival paper
59 x 39 cm
p. 230

*Amina Cachalia II*, 1995
*All Our Mothers* series
Pigment inks on archival paper
59 x 39 cm
p. 230

*Caroline Motsoaledi*, 1995
*All Our Mothers* series
Pigment inks on archival paper
59 x 39 cm
p. 231

*Rica Hodgson*, 1995
*All Our Mothers* series
Pigment inks on archival paper
59 x 39 cm
p. 232

*Rebecca Kotane*, 1995
*All Our Mothers* series
Pigment inks on archival paper
59 x 39 cm
p. 232

*Ruth Mompati*, 1995
*All Our Mothers* series
Pigment inks on archival paper
59 x 39 cm
p. 233

*There's something I must tell you*, 2003
Six channel rear projection video
Dimensions variable
Iziko Social History Collections, Cape Town
pp. 24-5, 235-43

*Photo credits*

Digital image © 2015 The Museum of Modern Art, New York / Scala, Florence: p. 81
Colleen Alborough: p. 162 (wall, above)
Africa Media: p. 66
Carina Beyer/Iziko South African National Gallery: pp. 72-3
Michael Buckley: pp. 167, 170, 171, 172, 173
Giile de Vlieg: p. 103
Thys Dullaart: pp. 235, 237
Ozan Eras: pp. 220-1
Husain Essop: pp. 193, 194-5, 197, 198, 202-3
Stefano Fontebasso de Martino: p. 63
Abrie Fourie: pp. 216-7
Anne Gold: p. 115
Duncan Greaves: p. 119
Michael Hall: pp. 90-1, 96-7, 122-3, 176-7
George Hallett: p. 126
John Hodgkiss: pp. 200-1
Mandy Lee Jandrell: pp. 206-7 (bottom)
Michel Kawecki: pp. 204-5
Brenton Maart: p. 155 (wall)
Herschel Mair/Iziko South African National Gallery: p. 105
Werner Maschmann: p. 109
Andrew Meintjes: pp. 82-7
Leslie Montgomery/SCAD Hong Kong: pp. 199, 211-4
National Museum of African Art, Washington D.C.: pp. 60-1
Alain Proust: p. 59
The Argus: p. 55
Matthew Septimus: pp. 206-7 (top)
Dave Southwood: pp. 129, 131, 133, 135, 137, 141, 143-5, 161 (wall)
Rudolf Steiner: pp. 218-9
Ellen van Elmendorp: pp. 127, 244
Olaf Wallgren/Swedish Travelling Exhibitions: p. 149
Eli Weinberg/The Mayibuye Centre: p. 80
Adam Welz: p. 159 (wall)
Neil Williamson: pp. 98, 99, 101-3
Sue Williamson (documentary photos): pp. 28, 30, 44, 45, 46, 47, 52, 54, 56, 62, 64, 65, 67, 68, 69, 89, 104, 107, 108, 112, 114, 116, 117, 118, 119, 120, 121, 122, 142, 156, 157, 160, 166, 175, 182, 196
Roger Wooldridge: pp. 131, 133
YiorgisYerolymbos/Stavros Niarchos Foundation Cultural Center: p. 243